1986

10 Beginning and Ending the Speech
    page 186

11 Outlining the Speech
    page 205

12 Using Language to Communicate
    page 222

13 Using Visual Aids in a Speech
    page 246

14 Using Your Voice and Body to Communicate
    page 264

15 Speeches to Inform
    page 288

16 Public Reasoning and Argumentation
    page 309

17 Speeches to Persuade and Actuate
    page 333

18 Speeches on Special Occasions
    page 357

Speaker's Resource Book
page 376

Tenth Edition

PRINCIPLES AND TYPES OF SPEECH COMMUNICATION

Tenth Edition

PRINCIPLES AND TYPES OF SPEECH COMMUNICATION

Douglas Ehninger

Bruce E. Gronbeck
The University of Iowa

Ray E. McKerrow
University of Maine at Orono

Alan H. Monroe

Scott, Foresman and Company
Glenview, Illinois ▪ London, England

Cover by Jim Deal.

All illustrations in this book are by
Carol Naughton and Associates.

Photo credits are on page 433, which is an extension of this copyright page.

An Instructor's Manual to accompany *Principles and Types of Speech Communication,* Tenth
Edition, is available. It may be obtained through a Scott, Foresman representative or by writing to
Speech Communication Editor, College Division, Scott, Foresman and Company, 1900 East
Lake Avenue, Glenview, Illinois 60025.

Also available is an Instructor's Edition of *Principles and Types of Speech Communication,*
which includes *The Ideabook for Teaching the Basic Speech Communication Course.* Contact a
Scott, Foresman representative or the Speech Communication Editor at Scott, Foresman.

Library of Congress Cataloging in Publication Data

Main entry under title:

Principles and types of speech communication.

   Rev. ed. of: Principles and types of speech
communication / Douglas Ehninger, 9th ed.   c1982.
   Includes bibliographies and index.
   1. Public speaking.   I. Gronbeck, Bruce E.
PN4121.P72   1986   808.5'1   85-10909
ISBN 0-673-18156-1

1 2 3 4 5 6 – RRC – 90 89 88 87 86 85

PREFACE

Principles and Types of Speech Communication has reached a milestone—a mark unparalleled in the modern history of speech communication. No other textbook has reached a tenth edition: over a half-century of continuous use in the United States and, thanks to its Spanish translation, a place in overseas classrooms as well. *Principles and Types of Speech Communication* is truly a "current classic" as it enters a second half-century of service.

As the living authors of this work, we write in the shadows of the two men who made this book what it is. Alan H. Monroe (1903–1975), former Professor of Communication at Purdue University, pioneering social scientist and innovative pedagogue, established the course for this book in the First Edition (1935). Drawing upon his work in sales training processes during the '20s, he originated the famous "Monroe's Motivated Sequence" which forms the conceptual core of so many successful persuasive and actuative speeches. Perhaps even more significant was his conception of the "Monroe Approach to Teaching Speech," a three-step process: Students using this textbook first gain an *overview* of the process of public speaking, then learn the basic *principles* of speech preparation, and finally apply and adapt those principles when preparing various *types* of speeches. That three-step approach to speech pedagogy still is reflected in Parts One, Two, and Four of the Tenth Edition.

As Professor Monroe neared retirement, Douglas Ehninger (1913–1979), Professor of Speech at the University of Florida and then of the University of Iowa, joined the project in the late '50s. His special talents as a rhetorical scholar of international reputation brought a balance between the perspectives of the humanistic rhetorician and the scientific pedagogue. And, as a younger man still active in professional associations, Professor Ehninger was abreast of the field, searching out the latest concerns of speech teachers and incorporating important developments in each new edition of the textbook. Just as Professor Monroe was the person who constructed the book's skeleton and determined its seminal concepts, so was Professor Ehninger the innovator, the man who keep the book fresh and attuned to contemporary currents of instructional thought and practice.

The essential features of the book remain: The motivated sequence is developed in its own chapter (Chapter 8), and it figures prominently in the "types" chapters, especially Chapters 15, 17, and 18. The factors of attention still are laid out in classic Monroe style, in an early chapter (Chapter 3) so they can be taken into account by students from the beginning of the course. Types of imagery still are featured in this edition's chapter

v

on language and style (Chapter 12). And Professor Monroe's concern for tying public speaking principles to group settings is here as well, although in this edition we have given them new status by including them in a new feature, the Speaker's Resource Book.

For a textbook to reach a tenth edition, however, it not only must conserve what is enduring in its formulation, but also must scan the pedagogical and intellectual environment for new ideas, new developments, new practices. As the new authors, we have approached this, the Tenth Edition, with three goals:

1. *Streamlining*. As the two-semester courses of earlier years and even the full sixteen-week semester courses at many other schools disappeared, the need for a shorter, more compact book became apparent. Our first goal over the last three editions has been to shorten the book without sacrificing intellectual integrity and pedagogical utility. User questionnaires are of immeasurable help when authors approach the task of streamlining, because textbook users in the field know what materials work and which don't, what ideas need expansion and which can be eliminated. We thank those committed users who completed questionnaires and provided syllabi (see below). They, together with our formal reviewers, made streamlining an achievable goal.

2. *Flexibility*. With the explosion of graduate programs in communication education in the '60s came greater diversity in the ways the basic public speaking course is taught. Such diversity places demands on a textbook, of course, as it must be able to respond to a variety of classroom styles and atmospheres. In hopes of increasing flexibility, in the Tenth Edition of *Principles and Types of Speech Communication* we have:

   ▪ Added the Speaker's Resource Book, a collection of topics and materials usable in some (but probably not all) classrooms and applicable to some (but not all) speaking situations. This new feature allows both teacher and student to control a series of specific materials on their own.

   ▪ Written most materials so that chapters can be resequenced. Part Three's chapters (voice, body, visual aids, and language) can be taught at any time in a course. The chapters on audience analysis, basic appeals, supporting materials, organizational patterns, and beginnings and endings (Chapters 6–10), as well as the types chapters (15–18), can generally be taught in different orders.

3. *Pedagogical Support Materials*. The modern speech communication classroom teacher is finding more and more support materials and machinery available for expanding instructional resources. *Principles and Types of Speech Communication*, Tenth Edition, as a major classroom resource, is adding the support materials users have asked for. This edition will include:

   ▪ A completely redesigned Instructor's Manual. Thanks to the work of Professor Kathleen German of Miami University, we are able to offer a much more complete instructor's manual—one with more proven classroom exercises, new test questions (both objective and open response), and an updated bibliography.

   ▪ A new instructional videotape. Following the success of our first tape, "Critiquing Student Speeches," we have gone one step further. The new tape includes sample speeches by students from the University of New Mexico who agreed to let their performances be used as models—models of decisions speakers need to make and the results of those decisions.

- A computerized testbank. For the first time, Scott, Foresman and Company has invested in a computerized testbank, allowing classroom teachers the luxury of building objective examinations from pre-tested questions with a minimum of effort. You can have your computer print off the exam, with enough questions so that different versions can be built. Grading, likewise, can be done via machine scoring.

In addition to setting these three primary goals, we also have taken a page from Professor Ehninger's advice on textbook writing by updating all of our chapters. Among the major changes are: *(1)* a new opening section on "rhetorical sensitivity" in Chapter 1; *(2)* a more practical, student-centered chapter on listening; *(3)* a more complete treatment of speech fright or communication apprehension (Chapters 1 and 3 as well as a Speaker's Resource Book section); *(4)* by popular demand, a return to the Speech to Entertain as a general purpose; *(5)* new sections on audience segmentation and audience targeting in the audience analysis chapter; *(6)* inclusion of material on information-seeking interviews in the chapter on supporting materials as well as advice on computerized searches for supporting materials; *(7)* a well-reviewed new section on oral speaking styles in the language chapter; *(8)* a combining of the old chapters on vocal and bodily communication channels to encourage more holistic approaches to delivery; *(9)* reconceptualized treatment of visual aids; *(10)* reworked typologies of types of informative and persuasive speeches, to include speeches of denotation, reinforcement, and attitude change; *(11)* a new section on fallacies in the chapter on argumentation; *(12)* a fuller discussion of the Speech to Entertain in the special occasions chapter, coupled with a module on the use of humor in public speaking in the Speaker's Resource Book; and *(13)* the Speaker's Resource Book itself, including, in addition to materials already mentioned, items dealing with communication models, ethics, freedom of speech, parliamentary procedure, speech criticism, answering questions and objections, and bibliographies.

In all these endeavors, we have been greatly aided in the preparation of this milestone edition by the critical insights and sound advice of a number of speech communication scholars and fellow educators. Among these are: Richard A. Cherwitz, University of Texas; Jean DeWitt, Texas A & M University; James W. Gibson, University of Missouri—Columbia; Wayne E. Hensley, Virginia Polytechnic Institute; Richard A. Katula, University of Rhode Island; William Kushner, Glassboro State College; Linda Moore, University of Akron; John Muchmore, William Rainey Harper College; Richard G. Rea, University of Arkansas; Henry Z. Scheele, Purdue University; and Aileen Sundstrom, Henry Ford Community College.

We are indebted also to the following people who provided feedback on the Ninth Edition: Martha Ann Atkins, Ovid L. Bayless, Robert F. Crowley, Sandra F. Davis, Bobbie Dietrich, Kathleen German, John P. Johnson, Paul O. Johnson, Janice A. Joy, Martin J. Medhurst, James E. Sayer, Eugene Street, Patricia A. Van De Voort, and Barbara P. Washington.

And we wish to thank Scott, Foresman and Company for the extensive resources and talents it invested in this project. The overall shape of the Tenth Edition has been guided

by Communication Editor Barbara Muller. The word-by-word preparation and polishing of the text has been in the able hands of Kathy Lorden who also guided the
material through production. We are grateful for Scott, Foresman's expertise in and
commitment to speech communication.

In the end, of course, we must express our gratitude to you, the students and teachers
of public speaking. Your commitments to excellence in public address, to both the
skills and theories of public talk, have kept this enterprise alive for over fifty years. We
hope your encounters with the materials which follow are productive and satisfying.

Bruce E. Gronbeck

Ray E. McKerrow

CONTENTS

PART ONE
Public Speaking: Communication Process   2

CHAPTER 1
The Public Person and the Speechmaking Process   4

Public Speaking Skills: Public Service and Personal Survival   4
   Public Service: The Roles of Speechmaking • Personal Survival: The
   Roles of Speech Training
Basic Elements of Speechmaking   6
   The Speaker • The Message • The Listeners • The Channels • The
   Communicative Situation
A Model of the Speechmaking Process   12
The Skills and Competencies Needed for Successful Speechmaking   14
   Integrity • Knowledge • Rhetorical Sensitivity • Oral Skills •
   Self-Confidence and Self-Control

CHAPTER 2
Listening: Speaker-Audience Interaction   20

Listening Behavior   20
   Hearing and Listening • Characteristics of Listeners • Purposes of
   Listening
Listeners' Responsibilities   26
   Listener Analysis of Self • Listener Analysis of Speaker • Listener
   Analysis of Message

Speaker's Responsibilities *31*

Preparing the Speech ▪ Capturing and Holding Attention ▪ Presenting the Speech

Listening in the Speech Classroom *34*

CHAPTER 3

Getting Started: Planning and Preparing Speeches *38*

The Essential Steps in Speech Preparation *38*

Selecting and Narrowing the Subject ▪ Determining the General and Specific Purposes ▪ Determining the Central Idea or Claim ▪ Analyzing the Audience ▪ Analyzing the Occasion ▪ Gathering the Speech Material ▪ Arranging Materials into an Outline ▪ Practicing Aloud for Clarity and Fluency

Delivering Your First Speeches *43*

Gaining and Holding Attention ▪ Developing and Communicating Confidence

PART TWO

Public Speaking: Preparation and Adaptation to the Audience *60*

CHAPTER 4

Choosing Speech Subjects and Purposes *62*

Selecting the Subject *62*

Narrowing the Topic *64*

Determining the Purposes *66*

General Purposes ▪ Specific Purposes ▪ Central Ideas or Claims ▪ Wording the Working Title

Selecting Subjects and Purposes: Strategic Choices *74*

Subject Categories: Aids to Choosing Speech Topics *76*

CHAPTER 5

Analyzing the Audience and Occasion   *81*

Analyzing the Audience Demographically   *82*

Analyzing the Audience Psychologically   *84*
Beliefs • Attitudes • Values

Analyzing the Speech Occasion   *89*
The Nature and Purpose of the Occasion • The Prevailing Rules or
Customs • The Physical Conditions • Events Preceding or Following
Your Speech

Using Audience Analysis in Speech Preparation   *92*
Audience Targeting: Setting Purposes Realistically • Audience
Segmentation: Selecting Dominant Ideas and Appeals

A Sample Analysis of an Audience and Occasion   *98*

CHAPTER 6

Determining the Basic Appeals   *105*

Motivation and Motive Needs   *105*
A Classification of Motive Needs

Motivational Appeals   *106*
Some Types and Examples of Motivational Appeals

Using Motivational Appeals in Speech Preparation   *114*
Using Appeals to Extend Audience Analysis • Using Appeals in Your
Speeches: Strategic Choices

CHAPTER 7

Developing Your Ideas: Finding
and Using Supporting Materials   *123*

What to Look For: The Forms of Supporting Materials   *124*
Explanation • Analogy or Comparison • Illustration • Specific
Instance • Statistics • Testimony • Restatement

Where to Look for Information: Sources of Supporting Materials   *136*
Locating Existing Information: Print and Nonprint Resources • Generating
New Information • How to Use What You Locate or Generate •
Integrating Information with Your Ideas

CHAPTER 8

Adapting the Speech Structure to Audiences: The Motivated Sequence   151

Organization from the Perspective of the Listener   151

Five Basic Steps of the Motivated Sequence   153

The Structure and Development of the Steps in the Motivated Sequence   156

The Attention Step · The Need Step · The Satisfaction Step · The Visualization Step · The Action Step

Applying the Motivated Sequence   164

The Motivated Sequence and Speeches to Inform · The Motivated Sequence and Speeches to Entertain · The Motivated Sequence and Speeches to Actuate · The Motivated Sequence and Speeches to Persuade

CHAPTER 9

Adapting the Speech Structure to Audiences: Traditional Patterns of Organization   173

The Motivated Sequence and Traditional Patterns   173

Types of Traditional Patterns · Arranging the Subpoints in the Structure

Selecting an Organizational Pattern: Strategies and Determining Factors   181

CHAPTER 10

Beginning and Ending the Speech   186

Beginning: Initial Considerations   186

Gaining Attention · Stating Qualifications · Satisfying Demands of Audience and Occasion · Creating Good Will · Clarifying the Scope of Your Speech

Types of Speech Introductions   189

Reference to the Subject or Problem · Reference to the Occasion · Personal Reference or Greeting · Rhetorical Question · Startling Statement · Pertinent Quotation · Humorous Anecdote · Real or Hypothetical Illustration · Combining Methods

Ending the Speech: Final Considerations   195

Adapting to Complexity · Answering the "So What?" Question · Creating the Appropriate Mood · Signaling the Ending

Types of Speech Conclusions *197*
  Challenge or Appeal to Listeners • Summary of Major Points or Ideas •
  Pertinent Quotation • Epitomizing Illustration • Additional
  Inducement • Expression of Personal Intention or Endorsement
Selecting Introductions and Conclusions: Strategies and Determining
Factors *201*

CHAPTER 11
Outlining the Speech *205*

Requirements of Good Outline Form *205*
Types of Outlines *208*
  The Full-Sentence Outline • The Phrase Outline
Steps in Preparing a Good Outline *210*
  Selecting the Subject and Determining the Purpose • Developing the
  Rough Draft of the Outline • Developing the Technical Plot • A Sample
  Full-Sentence Outline • Developing a Speaking Outline • Fitting the
  Introduction and the Conclusion to the Speech

PART THREE
Public Speaking:
Modes of Communication *220*

CHAPTER 12
Using Language to Communicate *222*

Essential Features of Effective Speaking Styles *222*
  Accuracy • Simplicity • Coherence • Appropriateness
Selecting the Appropriate Style: Strategic Decisions *225*
  Written *vs.* Oral Language • Serious *vs.* Humorous Atmosphere •
  Person-Centered *vs.* Material-Centered Emphasis • Propositional *vs.*
  Narrative Form
Language Strategies *231*
  Definitions • Restatement • Imagery
Language Intensity *239*
Metaphor *240*

CHAPTER 13

Using Visual Aids in a Speech   246

The Functions of Visual Aids   247
Comprehension and Memory • Persuasiveness
Types of Visual Support   247
Actual Objects • Symbolic Representations
Selecting and Using Visual Aids: Strategies and Determining
Factors   256
Start with Yourself • Consider the Communicative Potential of Various
Visual Materials • Integrate Verbal and Visual Materials Effectively •
Consider the Audience and the Occasion

CHAPTER 14

Using Your Voice and Body
to Communicate   264

Selecting the Method of Presentation   264
The Impromptu Speech • The Memorized Speech • The Manuscript
Speech • The Extemporaneous Speech
Using Your Voice to Communicate   267
The Effective Speaking Voice • Controlling the Emotional Quality •
Practicing Vocal Control
Using Your Body to Communicate   274
Dimensions of Nonverbal Communication
Using Nonverbal Channels: Strategic Choices   279

PART FOUR

Public Speaking:
Types and Occasions   286

CHAPTER 15

Speeches to Inform   288

Types of Informative Speeches   288
Speeches of Denotation • Demonstrations and Instructions • Oral
Reports • Explanations

Essential Features of Informative Speeches   *293*
Clarity · Association of New Ideas with Familiar Ones · Coherence ·
Motivation of the Audience

Structuring Informative Speeches   *296*
Structuring a Speech of Denotation · Structuring a Speech of
Demonstration or Instruction · Structuring an Oral Report · Structuring
a Speech of Explanation

CHAPTER 16

Public Reasoning and Argumentation   *309*

Arguing as a Social Process   *310*
Social Conventions · Technical Rules

Arguments: Elements and Analysis   *312*
Types of Claims · Evidence · Reasoning (Inferences) · Tests for
Reasoning · Detecting Fallacies in Arguments

Structuring Argumentative Speeches   *322*
Constructing Your Case · Anticipating Counterarguments · Rebuilding
Your Case

CHAPTER 17

Speeches to Persuade and Actuate   *333*

Types of Persuasive and Actuative Speeches   *333*
Reinforcement · Psychological Change · Actuation

Essential Features of Persuasive and Actuative Speeches   *339*
Adaptation to Psychological States · Change by Degrees · Saliency and
Its Effect on Strategies · Credibility

Structuring Persuasive and Actuative Speeches   *344*
The Motivated Sequence and Reinforcement Speeches · The Motivated
Sequence and Psychological Change Speeches · The Motivated Sequence
and Actuative Speeches

CHAPTER 18

Speeches on Special Occasions   *357*

Speeches of Introduction   *357*
Purpose and Manner of Speaking · Formulating the Content of the Speech
of Introduction · Organizing the Speech of Introduction

Speeches of Tribute   *359*

Farewells • Dedications • Memorial Services • Purpose and Manner of Speaking for the Tribute Speech • Formulating the Content of Speeches of Tribute • Organizing the Speech of Tribute

Speeches of Nomination   *364*

Speeches to Create Good Will   *365*

Typical Situations Requiring Speeches for Good Will • Manner of Speaking in the Speech for Good Will • Formulating the Content of the Speech for Good Will • Organizing the Speech for Good Will

Speeches to Entertain   *368*

Purposes and Manner of Speaking to Entertain • Formulating the Content of a Speech to Entertain

SPEAKER'S RESOURCE BOOK   *376*

Analyzing and Criticizing the Speeches of Others   *378*

Communication Models   *388*

Ethics and Public Speaking   *393*

Exercises for Voice Improvement   *395*

Finding a Job: The Employment Interview   *399*

Group Discussion: Leadership   *401*

Group Discussion: Participation   *405*

Humor and Public Speaking   *411*

Model for Organizing and Evaluating Arguments (Toulmin)   *413*

Parliamentary Procedure and Speechmaking   *416*

Reducing Communication Apprehension: Systematic Solutions   *419*

Responding to Questions and Objections   *424*

Team Presentations: Panels and Symposiums   *426*

Working Bibliography: Additional Readings   *429*

SAMPLE SPEECHES
for Study and Analysis

A Student Speech
Have You Checked Lately? *Deanna Sellnow*   52

A Student Speech
Ethnocentrism *Chui Lee Yap*   55

A Speech Utilizing the Motivational Appeals
For a Declaration of War Against Japan *Franklin Delano Roosevelt*   119

A Speech Utilizing the Motivated Sequence
Marriage Contracts: For Better or Worse *Linda Hopkins*   155

A Speech of Acceptance
On Accepting the Nobel Prize for Literature *William Faulkner*   242

A Speech to Inform
The Geisha *Joyce Chapman*   304

An Argumentative Speech
A Missing Beat *Timothy L. Sellnow*   329

A Speech to Persuade
The Silent Killer *Todd Ambs*   350

A Speech of Introduction
Introducing a Classmate *Barbara Miller*   359

A Speech of Dedication
The Testimony of Sculpture *Harold Haydon*   360

A Speech to Entertain
Is English a Dying Language? *Dick Cavett*   370

Tenth Edition

PRINCIPLES AND TYPES OF SPEECH COMMUNICATION

PART ONE

PUBLIC SPEAKING:

Communication Process

CHAPTER 1

The Public Person

and the Speechmaking

Process

What we call *public address, public speaking,* or *speech communication* is both a public act and an interrelated set of analytical and motor skills that advance the individual or collective interests of a society. The prefix *com-* (from the Latin *cum,* meaning "with") and *munus* (referring to a service performed for the culture) are combined in our word *communication*—a word that in its broadest sense means sharing experience publicly for the common good. Communicating publicly, therefore, is part of most adults' lives. People frequently are called on to present oral messages of some length and complexity to groups of listeners.

Public Speaking Skills:
Public Service and Personal Survival

Given the historical roots of the idea of "communication," perhaps you can understand why public speaking *skills* are so important to you. Public speaking skills are required of everyone in a society so that *(1)* everyone can serve others, can contribute to the common good, and *(2)* everyone can survive and prosper within that society. Let us examine those two requirements.

Public Service: The Roles of Speechmaking

There are many reasons why your society *needs* your speaking skills. "No Man is an *Island,* intire of it selfe," wrote John Donne; "every man [and woman] is a piece of the *Continent,* a part of the *maine.*"[1] These sentiments, though over 350 years old, still express each individual's social responsibilities. Your society needs your ability to talk well in public. Why? Because it is primarily through skilled public talk that your society shares digested and interpreted information (informative speaking), common delights (entertaining speaking), and attitudes toward and actions in response to common problems (persuasive speaking).

To be sure, many media of communication are available to us in this last quarter of the twentieth century—print, electronic, and film mass media; billboards; even skywriting and signal flags. Nonetheless, face-to-face, speaker-to-audience public speaking has certain advantages over other media in society: *(1)* It is the most humane and human mode of exchange in that the parties to the communciation are present. *(2) Feedback,* the chance to ask for clarification or explanation, is directly available during and after a speech; furthermore, feedback allows speakers to adjust their messages in midstream—even in midsentence—when they see frowns or signs of audience puzzlement. *(3)* Only in oral communication are ideas—information, beliefs, attitudes, and so on—presented to others by a living, breathing human being, by someone with faults, foibles, virtues, vices, wisdom, silliness, and all of the other characteristics shared by all of us.

Ultimately, then, "public service" via speechmaking is a social responsibility. Without such communicative means of sharing information, entertainment, and preferences, our society would be reduced to the impersonalness of written or electronic communication, and to a situation wherein people could not engage in the level of give-and-take, advise-and-consent, which is required for mutually satisfying decisions and contacts.

Personal Survival: The Roles of Speech Training

Lest you think that people talk publicly only for altruistic or humanitarian reasons, remember that public speaking skills are also necessary for personal survival in this world. Unless you have the oral communication talents necessary to engage effectively in committee discussions, employment and appraisal interviews, conferences with clients, and informational meetings with supervisors, you will not be successful on the job.[2] Your public speaking skills also affect your ability to support change in your community at meetings of block and neighborhood associations, city councils, county supervisors, county and district political conventions, state legislative and executive committees, and the innumerable associations, clubs, and pressure groups which affect all of these governmental units. The power of public talk in government is as important as the effectiveness of public talk in the work realm.

You will survive as a fully rounded, thinking, and forceful human being to the degree that you have learned and practiced public speaking and other oral communication skills. Ultimately, then, you speak to serve others, but also to achieve your personal goals on the job and in the public forum. And with the achievement of your personal goals come both a sense of public worth and a sense of self-satisfaction. Knowing you can convey information, entertainments, and important ideas to others effectively gives your ego a tremendous boost. As a matter of fact, talking publicly with others in a skilled manner is just plain fun most of the time. The human being talks with others both to survive and to play.

Before you start improving your public speaking skills, however, it is worth your while to think about the various elements which comprise not just communication in general, but also public speaking in particular. The rest of this chapter will be devoted to an examination of those elements and of the competencies in speechmaking which they demand of you.

Basic Elements of Speechmaking

Individual speeches differ from each other in many ways. Some, such as presidential inaugural addresses, are highly formalized, while others, a few remarks at a city council meeting, for instance, are often very informal. Some are read to an audience, as is frequently the case with a press conference, while others are given in an impromptu manner—for example, when you ask a question of your classroom instructor. After-dinner speeches tend to be humorous, while funeral sermons are dignified and serious.

Despite these and many other differences among speeches given in varied contexts, and despite the individualized communicative skills each of us possesses, there nevertheless exists a fundamental process of oral communication. Every time someone speaks to others, the same set of elements comes into play, the elements interacting with each other to produce a communicative event. Because the event involves several people, each with unique needs and interests, and because a speech extends through time and space, it is useful first to examine each element separately, and then to put them together in an overview of the entire process or event. Because all of the elements interact dynamically—with each element affecting all other elements—we may term the whole process a *speech transaction*. Let us begin, however, by examining the individual elements.

The Speaker

For the speaker, all speech transactions are shaped by four factors: *(1)* communicative purpose; *(2)* knowledge of subject and communication skills; *(3)* attitudes toward self, listeners, and subject; and *(4)* degree of credibility.

Speaker's Purpose.   *Every speaker has a purpose.* Except in the rarest of circumstances, you do not speak to others out of accident or whimsy. You speak to achieve some goal. Your purpose may be as simple as the wish to appear sociable, or as complex as the desire to advocate dangerous courses of public action. You may wish to provide entertainment, call attention to a problem, test an idea, refute an assertion, ward off a threat, establish or maintain status, or gain any number of other ends. The important point is this: Public speaking is a *purposive activity;* that purpose, in large measure, controls what you say and how you say it.

Speaker's Knowledge.   *In every speaking situation the speaker's knowledge of the subject and mastery of communication skills affect the character of the message and the effectiveness with which it is transmitted.* Occasionally, we all like to listen to certain speakers because of their personalities or because they are witty or entertaining; sometimes, we do not especially care what the speaker says. Usually, however, audiences

demand something—something worth thinking about or doing. If you have only surface knowledge of the topic, listeners normally will feel cheated and the communication process will be short-circuited. In other words, your knowledge of the subject in
some ways controls audience response. It also controls the actual shape of the speech—
what is emphasized, what is used as supporting material, and how everything is organized into a coherent message.

Additionally, in order to succeed in the world of oral communication, you must
acquire, refine, and integrate a series of fundamental skills. We will see as we work our
way through this book that the term *communication skills* encompasses a wide variety
of abilities—setting communicative goals, finding and assembling relevant information, organizing messages in coherent and compelling ways, illustrating them visually
when necessary, and delivering them in a manner which clarifies and emphasizes key
notions. You already possess many of the requisite skills; through practice, instruction,
reading, and observation of other speakers, you will improve your command of the
others.

Speaker's Attitudes.   *In every speaking situation the speaker's attitudes toward self,
listeners, and subject significantly affect what is said and how it is said.* All of us carry
with us a picture of ourselves as persons—a self-concept or image of the kinds of
individuals we are and of how others perceive us.[3] That image is complex; it is derived
from numerous experiences in numerous settings, and it controls our self-evaluations
and the ways we interact with others.

Your own *self-image* influences how you will behave in a given speaking situation. If
you have little confidence in your abilities or are unsure of your opinions or knowledge,
you tend to advance ideas hesitatingly. Your voice becomes weak and unsteady, your
body stiffens, and your eyes watch the floor rather than the audience. If you are overly
confident, you may move in the other direction—adopting an overbearing manner,
disregarding the need for facts and logical demonstrations, riding roughshod over the
feelings and needs of listeners. Ideally, you should have enough self-confidence to
believe firmly in your ability to communicate something worthwhile to others, and yet
enough sensitivity to the audience's intelligence, needs, and integrity to keep them
foremost in mind while you speak.

Equally important in speech transactions are your *attitudes toward listeners*. Each
time we speak, we do so from a certain status or role position—as parent or child,
instructor or student, supervisor or employee. These role positions, in turn, affect our
power relationships with audiences, determining whether we are superiors, inferiors, or
equals. And those power relationships often affect the actual ways we talk to others
publicly.

If you perceive someone as intellectually inferior, you tend to use simple vocabulary,
clear structure, and concrete ideas; if someone seems politically inferior, you may talk
condescendingly, self-confidently, assured of your own status. Or, if you view your
auditors as superior, you are likely to talk in a deferential or highly qualified manner,
protecting your ''self'' and sometimes even distrusting your own thoughts. It becomes
important, therefore, to think seriously about your perceptions of your relationships to
your listeners, and to adjust your speaking style and even your speech content according to your attitudes toward those listeners.

Finally, our behavior as speakers inevitably is influenced by how *we feel about the subject* we are discussing. Do you really believe what you are saying? Do you find your subject matter interesting or boring? Is it crucial that your auditors know about it? Is it relevant to someone's needs? Your answers to these questions are reflected in how you use your voice and body, in the intensity of the language you use to communicate your ideas, and even in your selection of ideas.

In summary, as a speaker you convey—verbally and nonverbally—how you feel about yourself, your audience, and your subject matter, and you make many verbal and nonverbal decisions while preparing and delivering a speech based on those attitudes.

Speaker's Credibility.   *In every speaking situation the speaker's success in winning agreement, inspiring confidence, or promoting ideas and action is significantly affected by the listeners' estimate of his or her credibility.* The term *credibility*—and its relatives, *image* or *"ethos"*—refer to the degree to which an audience finds a speaker to be a trustworthy, competent, sincere, attractive, and dynamic human being. Social scientific research has repeatedly demonstrated that if speakers can heighten an audience's estimate of these qualities, they will significantly increase the impact of a message. Although we do not have room to review all of the conclusions reached by researchers, the following generalizations are representative of ways in which the factors of credibility work in communicative interactions. *(1)* References to yourself and your own experience—provided they are not boasting or excessive—tend to increase your perceived trustworthiness and competence, and references to others (authorities) tend to increase your perceived trustworthiness and dynamism. *(2)* Using highly credible authorities increases your perceived fairness. *(3)* If you can demonstrate that you and your audience share common beliefs, attitudes, and values, your credibility will increase. *(4)* Well-organized speeches are more credible than poorly organized speeches. *(5)* The more sincere you appear to be, the better your chances of changing your listeners' attitudes.[4]

An audience's perception of the speaker's credibility, in other words, is affected by a broad range of behaviors and in turn can decisively affect the degree to which the speaker is accepted and successful. Your ability to project yourself as a competent, trustworthy, sincere, attractive, and dynamic person may well determine the fate of your message. The message and the messenger are usually inseparable in the minds of listeners.

The Message

In all speech communication transactions, the message which the speaker transmits is made up of the same three variables: content, structure, and style.

Content.   That the messages we transmit to our listeners have a content—are about something we want them to be aware of—is obvious. What is less obvious, however, are the many different sorts of content which comprise a message. There are, of course, "ideas"—assertions about the state of the world, facts and figures, analogies and examples, generalizations as well as more specific statements. But the content of a speech also includes your feelings about those ideas, interpretations of ideas you wish your audience to accept, courses of action you want the listeners to pursue, beliefs you are attempting to challenge. Many different kinds of "meanings" make up the content of a speech.

Structure.   Any message we transmit is of necessity structured or organized in some way, simply because we say some things first, others second, and still others third, fourth, and so on. Even if you seem to ramble on, auditors will look for a pattern which makes the message seem coherent. It is important, then, for a speaker to provide a pattern in order to guide the audience's search for coherence. That structure may be as simple as numbering points ("First, I will discuss . . . , next I will . . . and finally, I will . . ."), or as complex as a full outline with points and subpoints. One way you control the clarity and force of your message, therefore, is by providing a recognizable pattern for it.

Style.   The third variable in every spoken message is style. Just as you must select and arrange the ideas you wish to convey to audiences, so also must you select words, arrange them in sentences, and decide how to reveal your self-image to that group of hearers. Selecting and arranging words as well as revealing ourselves to be certain sorts of persons are matters of "style." Given the innumerable word-selection choices, the great varieties of sentence structures, and even the many kinds of self-images available to the speaker, a good many styles are possible. Styles can be "personal" or "impersonal," "literal" or "ironic," "plain" or "elevated," even "philosophical" or "poetic"; such labels refer to particular combinations of vocabulary, sentence syntax (arrangement), and images of the speaker. What we call *style,* therefore, really has nothing to do with "prettiness" or "stylishness"; rather, it includes those aspects of language use that convey impressions of speakers, details of the world, and emotional overtones.[5]

The Listeners

In all forms of speech, the listeners—like the speaker—have goals or purposes in mind. Moreover, the way a message is received and responded to varies according to the listener's *(1)* purpose; *(2)* knowledge of and interest in the subject; *(3)* level of listening skill; and *(4)* attitude toward self, speaker, and the ideas presented.

Listeners' Purpose.   *Listeners always have one or more purposes they want to fulfill.* Listeners, no less than speakers, enter into the speech transaction in search of rewards. They may wish to be entertained or informed, advised or guided. These purposes form their expectations—expectations, as we shall see, which control to whom, how, and why they listen. Speakers who violate those expectations—turning an informative talk, say, into a political harangue—risk ineffectiveness or even failure.

Listeners' Knowledge of Subject.   *In speech transactions, the listeners' knowledge of and interest in the subject significantly affect how the message will be received and responded to.* Speakers often are told to address listeners "where they are." "Where they are" is determined by two factors—their knowledge of the topic, and their personal interest in it. A knowledgeable audience is bored by an elementary speech, whereas one with little knowledge is confused by a technical description. Disinterested listeners may even go so far as to walk out on a speaker who has not made the topic relevant to their interests. Audience analysis, therefore, is a matter of *(1)* gauging listeners' prior knowledge so as to achieve an appropriate level of sophistication in the speech, and *(2)* finding ways to make the message relevant to the beliefs, desires, and motivational drives of the auditors.

Listeners' Command of Listening Skills.   *Speakers also must try to estimate the audience's listening skills.* With relatively homogeneous audiences, this may be easy to do. For example, you would expect a group of six-year-olds to have short attention spans, little ability to follow complex chains of reasoning, and a strong need to "see" ideas via visual aids and graphic descriptions. In contrast, you would expect graduate students to be able to sustain attention for long periods of time, to follow multi-stepped logical progressions, and to grasp easily abstract concepts. In other situations, however, it is difficult to predict the auditors' degree of listening sophistication. You then must constantly survey the listeners, looking for signs of understanding or puzzlement, acceptance or rejection. Those signs or cues are termed *feedback*—reactions "fed back" to speakers during the process of communication. Reading feedback is often your only way of determining a listener's skill of comprehension.

Listeners' Attitudes.   *In every speech encounter, the listeners' attitudes toward themselves, the speaker, and the subject significantly affect how they interpret and respond to the message.* Just as the speaker's communicative behavior is influenced by his or her attitude toward self, subject, and listener, so do these same factors affect the listeners' responses. Listeners with low self-esteem tend to be swayed more easily than those whose self-image is stronger. Listeners whose opinions seem to be confirmed by the views of the speaker are also susceptible to great influence. Moreover, as a rule, people seek out speakers whose positions they already agree with, and they retain longer and more vividly ideas of which they strongly approve.[6] In other words, listeners' attitudes—which comprise another extremely important area for audience analysis—can be used (or, conversely, must be overcome) by speakers who wish to maximize their communicative effectiveness.

The Channels

All speech communication is affected by the channels through which the message is transmitted. The transaction between speakers and listeners occurs through several channels. The *verbal channel* carries the words, the culture's agreed-upon symbols for ideas. The *visual channel* transmits the gestures, facial expressions, bodily movements, and posture of the speaker; these tend to clarify, reinforce, or add emotional reactions to the words. At times the visual channel may be supplemented with a *pictorial channel*—so-called "visual aids," such as diagrams, charts, graphs, pictures, objects, and the like. The *aural channel*—also termed the *paralinguistic medium*—carries the tones of voice, variations in pitch and loudness, and other vocal modulations produced by the speaker's stream of sounds. Like the visual channel, the aural channel heightens some meanings and adds others. Because these four channels are heard and seen by listeners simultaneously, the "message" is really a combination of several messages flowing

The visual channel of public communication increases the speaker's ability to relay complex messages to audiences, especially if aural and visual messages are coordinated.

through all of these pathways. You should learn to control or shape the messages flowing through all four channels.

The Communicative Situation
All speech communication is affected by the physical setting and social context in which it occurs.

Physical Setting.   The physical setting of the speech influences listeners' expectancies as well as their readiness to respond. People waiting in the quiet solemnity of a cathedral for the service to begin have quite different expectations than do theatergoers gathered to witness the opening of a new Broadway play. Listeners at an open-air political rally anticipate a different sort of message from those gathered to hear a scholarly lecture on political theory presented in a college classroom.

The furniture and decor of the physical space also make a difference. Comfortable chairs and soft-hued drapes tend to put discussion groups at ease and to promote a more productive exchange. The executive who talks to an employee from behind a large desk set in the middle of an impressively furnished office with the title "President" on the door gains a natural advantage not only because of a superior position but also because of the physical setting.

Social Context.   Even more important than physical setting in determining how a message will be received is the social context in which it is presented. A *social context* is a particular combination of people, purposes, and places interacting communicatively. *People* are distinguished from each other by such factors as age, occupation, power, degree of intimacy, and knowledge. These factors in part determine how one "properly" communicates with others. You are expected to speak deferentially to your elders, your boss, a political leader with "clout," a stranger whose reactions you cannot immediately predict, or a sage. The degree to which people are superior to, equal with, or inferior to each other in part determines each one's communicative style. Certain *purposes* or goals are more or less appropriately communicated in different contexts as well. Thus, a memorial service is not a time for attacking a political opponent—a "meet the candidates" night is. In some contexts it is considered unreasonable to threaten someone before you have tried to find reasonable compromises. Some *places* are more conducive to certain kinds of communicative exchanges than others. Public officials are often more easily influenced in their offices than in public forums, where they tend to be more defensive; sensitive parents scold their children in private, never in front of their friends.

Another way of saying all this is to observe that societies are governed by customs, traditions, or what we now are calling *communication rules*. A "communication rule" is a guide to communicative behavior; it specifies, more or less precisely, what can be said to whom and in what circumstances. While communication rules are guides to communicating, they can, of course, be broken. Occasionally, rule breaking is inconsequential; sometimes, it determines success or failure; and always, it involves a certain amount of risk.[7]

In summary, the social context in which we speak determines an audience's judgment of *appropriateness* and *competency*. We learn to communicate appropriately and competently by learning and, usually, following the communication rules that govern our society. You have spent your lifetime learning those rules; we will cite many of the more explicit ones that govern public speaking throughout this book.

A Model of the Speechmaking Process

All speeches thus entail a complex pattern of interaction among the five primary elements: speaker, message, listeners, channels, and situations. The model of the speechmaking process contained in this chapter is termed a *transactional model* because:

THE SPEECH COMMUNICATION TRANSACTION

Speaker

Influenced by past conditioning, present situation, communicative purpose, level of knowledge, speaking skill, attitudes toward self, subject, and listener

Message

Has content, structure and style

Channel

Limits or shapes messages to one or more

Listener

Influenced by conditioning, purpose, situation, and attitudes toward self, subject, and speaker

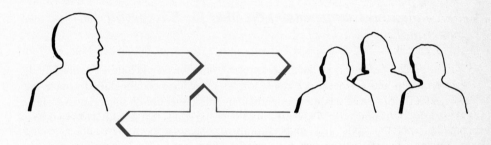

Feedback

Causes speaker to alter his or her verbal or nonverbal behavior

Feedback

Causes speaker to modify message

Response

Feedback to the speaker in the form of visual or verbal signals

- I prepare a speech to "give" to you, and you in turn give me your attention and your reactions (feedback).
- From among all of the things I *could* say about some subject, I *actually* select only a few, and tailor them to your interests, wants, and desires, as well as to limitations of time and space.
- As I assert my right to speak to fellow members of this culture, you also assert your right to listen or not, your right to react as you see fit.
- Public speaking, therefore, is ultimately a kind of communicative exchange we call a transaction, because *(a)* both speakers and listeners have mutual rights and responsibilities; *(b)* both speakers and listeners are generally aware of each others' needs and purposes, and so consciously adapt their messages—speeches and feedback—to the others' presumed conditions and situations; and *(c)* both speakers and listeners are bonded together in a common culture, through what we call *communication rules,* which influences the way they behave in each other's presence.

Indeed, because speeches almost always represent transactions whose appropriateness is determined by cultural rules or expectations, throughout much of this textbook you will find explicit pieces of advice—do's and don'ts—which you will be expected to follow. It's not really "wrong," for example, to skip a summary of your speech as you sit down, but most audience members expect such a summary, and hence may question your *communicative competency* if you fail to offer one. The expectations governing a speech transaction are seldom moral and certainly need not be followed slavishly every time you speak, for conditions do vary from situation to situation and skills do vary from speaker to speaker. But you generally will want to follow the rules of communication most of the time, for only then will you be operating rhetorically within the listeners' general expectations for "proper" communication practices.

The Skills and Competencies Needed for Successful Speechmaking

Because public speaking is an interactive process whereby people transact various kinds of information and business, one must possess or acquire certain skills to make the process work. Six basic qualities, in particular, merit attention in this brief overview: *(1)* integrity, *(2)* knowledge, *(3)* sensitivity to listener needs, *(4)* sensitivity to speaking situations, *(5)* oral skills, and *(6)* self-confidence and control.

Integrity
Your reputation for reliability and high motives is perhaps your single most powerful means of exerting influence as a speaker. Especially in a day of electronic advertising and mass mailings—when every pressure group, cause, and special interest can worm its way into the public mind, often with conflicting analyses and recommendations for action—integrity becomes all important.

How do people sort out good from bad analyses, prudent from imprudent recommendations? Ultimately, most of us make our decisions—especially in areas where we have little firsthand experience—by deciding whom we should trust. If you have a reputation for being truthful, for careful support of your ideas, for fairness in treating opponents, and for a deep-felt commitment to the betterment of your peers, your effectiveness as a speaker will increase markedly.[8]

Knowledge
Expertise, as we noted when discussing credibility, is essential if you want to affect your listeners. As you acquire skills in research and analysis, you will employ your knowledge more and more successfully when speaking.

To broaden your knowledge and enhance your understanding of the world and the ideas and values of people in it, you must read widely and observe carefully. When carefully considered and supplemented by additional study, the background you already have will provide sufficient material for your practice speeches. Selecting and organizing that material will help you marshal and clarify your thinking. Indeed, you

If you speak only from knowledge you now possess, you'll more than likely pass on as much ignorance as insight. Read regularly and widely to help yourself and your listeners.

will do well to begin in just this way—by talking about things that are vivid parts of your personal experience. As you grow in skill and confidence, you will want to reach beyond immediate and familiar topics. You may wish to investigate and speak about ideas and developments relevant to your personal future—your job, your chosen career or profession. Be careful also to acquire knowledge and develop interests *outside* your work, however. To become a well-rounded and interesting speaker, you must know about more than a single subject. Keep abreast of current happenings in your world, your country, your community by reading at least one daily newspaper, listening frequently to news broadcasts, and watching well-documented telecasts.

Rhetorical Sensitivity

Sometimes we talk publicly simply to hear ourselves talk; occasionally we talk for purely *expressive* reasons. Usually, however, we speak for *instrumental* reasons—to give others information or ideas, to influence their thoughts or actions. The most successful public speakers are "other-directed," concerned with meeting their listeners' needs and solving their problems through oral communication. These speakers are rhetorically sensitive to others.

Rhetorical sensitivity[9] refers generally to speakers' attitudes toward the process of speech composition. More particularly, rhetorical sensitivity is the degree to which speakers *(a)* recognize that all people are different and complex and hence must be thought about individually; *(b)* avoid rigid communication practices by adapting messages and themselves to particular audiences; *(c)* consciously seek and react to audience needs and feedback; *(d)* understand the limitations of talk (sometimes even remaining silent rather than trying to express the unexpressible); and *(e)* work at finding just the right set of arguments, linguistic expressions, and the like which will make particular ideas clear and attractive to particular audience members.

Being rhetorically sensitive does not mean that you refuse to adapt messages to listeners; nor does it mean that you must simply say what everyone in the audience wants to hear so that listeners will applaud and think well of you. Rather, rhetorical sensitivity is a matter of careful self-assessment, careful audience analysis, and then careful decision making. What are your purposes? To what degree will they be understandable and acceptable to listeners? To what degree can you, the speaker, adapt your purposes to audience preferences while still maintaining your own integrity and self-respect? These are the sorts of questions—and decisions—faced by rhetorically sensitive speakers. They demand that speakers, when framing purposes and constructing speeches, be sensitive to *listener needs, the demands of speaking situations, and the requirements of self-respect*. Rhetorical sensitivity, then, is not so much a skill as a competency—a way of thinking about and then acting within the world of communication.

Oral Skills

Fluency, poise, control of the voice, and coordinated movements of the body mark the skillful public speaker. Combined with integrity, knowledge, and self-confidence, such skills can significantly increase your effectiveness by enabling you to communicate your ideas forcefully and attractively.

Skill in speaking is gained principally through practice. Practice, however, proceeds best when based on a knowledge of sound principles and carried on under the direction of a competent instructor. Moreover, care must be exercised that in practicing you do not develop distracting habits or acquire an unnatural or artificial manner of delivery. Good public speaking is animated, but it is also natural and conversational. It commands attention not through the use of tricks and techniques, but because of the speaker's earnest desire to communicate. Indeed, many successful public speakers seem merely to be *conversing* with their audiences. In the chapters that follow we shall extend our consideration of these and other communicative skills and suggest how you may develop, refine, and implement their use in practical speaking situations. Also, at the end of the chapters in this textbook we have provided some "Oral Activities" designed to encourage and guide your practice in mastering these necessary skills.

Self-Confidence and Self-Control

The competent speaker has an appropriate measure of self-confidence and self-control. So central are self-confidence and self-control to effective public speaking that, in a sense, much of what we say in this book is aimed toward developing or strengthening those essential qualities. The qualities are attained primarily by overcoming a series of fears.[10]

Self-confidence and self-control are important, for in communicating your own sense of self-assurance to an audience you are improving the effectiveness of public communication. An audience is much more likely to accept ideas and advice from a self-confident person than from a self-doubting person. In Chapter 3 we will discuss some ways in which you can convey to your listeners a sense of your assurance and control.

For now, however, we will continue our general orientation to the speechmaking process by looking at it from the other end—from the vantage of listeners.

REFERENCE NOTES

[1]From "Meditation XXVII" by John Donne, reprinted in *The Complete Poetry and Selected Prose of John Donne & The Complete Poetry of William Blake,* intro. Robert Silliman Hillyer, The Modern Library (New York: Random House, Inc., 1946), p. 332.

[2]Carol H. Pazandak, "Followup Survey of 1973 Graduates, College of Liberal Arts," Minneapolis: University of Minnesota, 1977 (multilith); Jack Landgrebe and Howard Baumgartel, "Results of the Graduation Requirement Questionnaire for College of Liberal Arts and Science Alumni," Lawrence: College of Liberal Arts and Sciences, University of Kansas (typescript); "Instruction in Communication at Colorado State University," Fort Collins: College of Engineering, Colorado State University, July 1979 (multilith); Edward Foster et al., "A Market Study for the College of Business Administration, University of Minnesota, Twin Cities," Minneapolis: University of Minnesota, November 1978 (multilith). These and other studies of communication and employment are reported in Samuel L. Becker and Leah R. V. Ekdom, "That Forgotten Basic Skill: Oral Communication," *Association for Communication Administration Bulletin,* #33 (August 1980).

[3]For a discussion of interrelationships between self-concept and communication, see Gordon I. Zimmerman, James L. Owen, and David R. Seibert, *Speech Communication: A Contemporary Introduction,* 2nd ed. (St. Paul: West Publishing Co., 1977), esp. pp. 32–43; and Gail E. Myers and Michele Tolela Myers, *The Dynamics of Human Communication: A Laboratory Approach,* 3rd ed. (New York: McGraw-Hill Book Co., 1980), Chapter 3, "Self-Concept: Who Am I?", pp. 47–72.

[4]These and other generalizations relative to source credibility are most usefully summarized in Stephen W. Littlejohn, "A Bibliography of Studies Related to Variables of Source Credibility," *Bibliographic Annual in Speech Communication: 1971,* ed. Ned A. Shearer (New York: Speech Communication Assoc., 1972), pp. 1–40; cf. Ronald L. Applebaum et al., *Fundamental Concepts in Human Communication* (San Francisco: Canfield Press, 1973), pp. 123–46.

[5]For a useful discussion of communication stylistic choices, see Gary Cronkhite, *Public Speaking and Critical Listening* (Menlo Park: The Benjamin-Cummings Publishing Co., Inc., 1978), esp. pp. 255–72.

[6]See the personality analysis of receivers in Michael Burgoon, *Approaching Speech Communication* (New York: Holt, Rinehart & Winston, Inc., 1974), pp. 64–69.

[7]Much research on physical setting and social context is summarized in Mark L. Knapp, *Essentials of Nonverbal Communication* (New York: Holt, Rinehart & Winston, 1980), Chapter 4, "The Effects of Territory and Personal Space," pp. 75–96. The determinative aspects of social expectations in human communication generally are discussed in such books as John J. Gumperz and Dell Hymes, eds., *Directions in Sociolinguistics: The Ethnography of Communication* (New York: Holt, Rinehart & Winston, 1972) and Peter Collett, ed., *Social Rules and Social Behavior* (Totowa, NJ: Rowman and Littlefield, 1977). And, more specifically, the current state of our knowledge about "rules" and their importance in communication is documented in Susan B. Shimanoff, *Communication Rules: Theory and Research*, Sage Library of Social Research, No. 97 (Beverly Hills: Sage Publishing, 1980).

[8]A fuller discussion of the role that personal integrity plays in successful public communication may be found in Otis M. Walter, *Speaking to Inform and Persuade* (New York: The Macmillan Co., 1966), Chapter 8, "The *Ethos* of the Speaker."

[9]See Roderick P. Hart and Don M. Burks, "Rhetorical Sensitivity and Social Interaction," *Speech [Communication] Monographs*, 39 (1972), 75–91, and Roderick P. Hart, Robert E. Carlson, and William F. Eadie, "Attitudes Toward Communication and the Assessment of Rhetorical Sensitivity," *Communication Monographs*, 47 (1980), 1–22.

[10]"What Are Americans Afraid Of?", *The Bruskin Report*, 13, #53; "Surveys Reveal Students' Concern Over Jobs, Public-Speaking Anxiety," *Pitt News*, May 1978, p. 4.

PROBLEMS AND PROBES

1. In a notebook set aside for the purpose, start a Personal Speech Journal. The contents will be seen by only you and your instructor, who may call for the journal at intervals during the term. In your first journal entry, write about yourself in relation to the six basic qualities needed for successful speechmaking. Consider your integrity. (If you haven't engaged in an exercise like this before, it should be a fascinating source of enlightenment for you.) In what areas do you feel you have most knowledge? In what areas would you wish to research to gain more knowledge? Look around your classroom at your classmates who will be your listeners this term. What do you know about their needs? What do you know about the speaking situation you are about to face? What do you still need to learn? What oral skills do you already possess and what others do you wish to gain? Finally, consider your own self-confidence and control in light of the task before you.

2. Identify and describe three speech transactions in which you personally participated during the past week. In at least two of these encounters, you should have been the speaker initiating the interaction. Formulate answers to the following questions:

   a. In which of the three situations—person-to-person, small group, or public communication—did each of these three transactions take place?

   b. What channel or channels did you use?

   c. What was your communicative purpose in each case?

d. To what extent do you feel you accomplished your communicative purpose in each transaction? Why?

e. What was the extent of your message-preparation in each of the three instances? If preparation was more mandatory and/or more extensive for one situation than for others, explain why this was so.

f. Show how, in one of these transactions, the physical setting probably influenced what happened. In another, explain how the social context tended to affect the outcome.

ORAL ACTIVITIES

1. To the extent that the physical facilities of the classroom permit, your instructor will arrange for members of the class to seat themselves in a large circle or in smaller groups around two or three separate tables. Informality should be the keynote in this particular activity. After the instructor has completed a brief self-introduction, each class member will provide a self-introduction based generally on the following pattern:

My name is _____

My major (or my major interest) is _____

I am enrolled in this college/university because _____

_____

In addition to a grade credit, what I hope to get from this course in speech communication is _____

2. Working in pairs, present pertinent biographical information about yourself to another member of the class. This person, in turn, will prepare a short speech introducing you to the group. You, of course, will do likewise for the student with whom you are paired. When these speeches have been completed, draw up a composite picture of the audience to whom you will be speaking during the remainder of the term.

3. Prepare a two- to three-minute presentation on the topic, "A speech I shall always remember." In specifying why you consider a particular address notable, focus on one or more of the factors in the speech communication process discussed in this chapter.

4. Participate actively in a general class consideration of the subject "Things That I Like (Dislike) in a Speaker." As you and the other members of the class mention your likes and dislikes, your instructor may want to list them in two columns on a chalkboard. At the conclusion of this oral consideration, help your instructor summarize by formulating a composite picture or list of those speaker traits or qualities to which the majority of the class members would respond favorably and those traits or qualities to which the majority would respond unfavorably. Finally, if you (as a class—collectively) find many traits or qualities which you cannot classify in some absolute manner, ask yourself why. Are there variables within situations, contexts, or our perceptions of "proper" social roles that make absolute categorization impossible? What are some of these variables?

CHAPTER 2

Listening:

Speaker-Audience Interaction

Listening is an activity so common to human experience that you probably think little or nothing of it. When was the last time you listened to someone? It probably was just a few moments ago. Listening accounts for over 40 percent of all your communication time; more time is spent listening than writing, reading, or speaking.[1] Listening serves important functions in our culture because through it we learn the rules and expectations of others, their feelings and needs, and information and ideas we all require to lead productive lives and to make informed decisions. Young children do almost all of their learning aurally; and even adults—via interpersonal interactions, group meetings, and public talks—acquire an amazing amount of information, ideas, and lore by listening to others.

Listening is central to the speechmaking process. It becomes the conduit through which speakers reach their audiences, and, in turn, is a process which allows those audiences in face-to-face situations to send messages back to speakers. Audiences listen to speakers, and, in question-and-answer sessions, speakers listen to the queries of audience members. Thus, listening is not a one-way street; rather, listening is a dynamic process which integrates speakers and auditors in a speech transaction. In this chapter, we will be concerned with listening as an *interactive process*.

We will begin by discussing listening behavior in general. That overview will allow us to characterize more precisely listeners' and speakers' responsibilities. Finally, because your public speaking classroom is a kind of laboratory where you can practice a series of skills—including listening skills—so as to refine them, we will conclude this chapter with some advice on classroom listening.

Listening Behavior

Hearing and Listening

To listen to a message, you first must hear it. Hearing is a *physiological process* whereby sound waves travel through the air and make impact on the tympanic membrane. In this way, hearing is affected by both the laws of physics and the neurophys-

THE PRODUCTION AND RECEPTION OF HUMAN SOUND

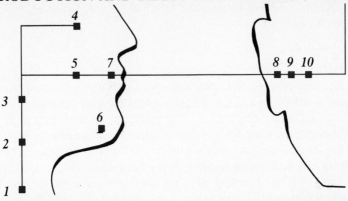

1 ■ A *stream of air* is sent from the lungs through the trachea to

2 ■ the *vocal folds* ("voice box"), which in turn vibrate at various pitches, depending upon tension in the muscles. As the sound proceeds up the throat, it is shaped by

3 ■ the *palate* and given resonance or additional tones by

4 ■ the *nasal and sinus regions.* The sounds or phonemes which make up our language are formed primarily by

5 ■ the *tongue,*

6 ■ *jaw placement* and

7 ■ the *lips.* The formed sound in "waves," travels through the air to an ear.

8 ■ It enters the *outer ear* (concha), moves through

9 ■ the *auditory canal* (external meatus), and strikes

10 ■ the *tympanum* (eardrum). The eardrum "translates" the sound waves once more to physical vibrations, which, through the bones of the middle ear, send the vibrations via nerves to the brain.

---

iology of your body. One's hearing can be impaired in many ways: by distracting noises in the environment, by sources of sound too loud or too soft for the aural mechanism, by illness or other physiological impediments. Generally, hearing, then, is a process out of the speaker's control, except when it comes to the matters of speaking volume and, occasionally, distracting sounds. Listening, on the other hand, is primarily a *psychological process* whereby people attach meanings to aural signals.[2] Once sound waves reach the brain, listening begins. After the waves are translated to nerve impulses by the middle ear and auditory nerve, they are sent to the brain for interpretation. Those processes of interpretation—of registering impulses, assigning them to meaningful contexts, and evaluating them—comprise the heart of listening. The diagram above illustrates the speaking-hearing processes.

All of this becomes complicated by the fact that people who can hear something do not always listen to it. The physiological mechanisms for transmitting and receiving sounds may be working perfectly, yet, for any number of reasons, the receiver may choose not to listen. Getting an audience to actually listen, therefore, is one of the public speaker's primary goals.

Characteristics of Listeners

We have noted that listening is a *joint responsibility*. Both speaker and listener must make reasonable efforts to make sure that intended messages are taken in, comprehended, interpreted, and evaluated fully. Yet problems can arise: Few of us are good listeners. Although researchers vary in their assessments of the average listening comprehension rate, they agree that we do not utilize our listening potential.[3] Some studies indicate that we may be listening at only a 25 percent comprehension rate, that we may be understanding only one-fourth of all of the information received aurally. There are several reasons why people are poor listeners. As a speaker, you must be aware of these so you can adjust and adapt your message. To acquire such awareness, you'll have to imagine yourself as a listener.

One reason we are poor listeners is that our complex minds can comprehend many more words per minute than speakers can produce. As listeners, we can mentally handle more than 400 spoken words per minute, yet the average speaker produces between 125–175 words per minute. Stated in a different way, the listener needs only fifteen seconds of every minute to comprehend what the speaker said. The time lag thus created in the listener's mind presents special problems. In the excess time, the listener begins to think of other things; technically, we can say that thoughts begin to enter the listener's *internal perceptual field,* the listener's intrapersonal thoughts. Recall a situation where you started out listening to a speaker but soon found yourself thinking about lunch or an upcoming test or appointment. As you listened, other priorities gradually took over more of your thinking time. This tendency for listeners to "drop in, drop out" poses many problems for the speaker trying to convey an understandable message, especially if the subject matter is complex.

Furthermore, as listeners, we often bring into the communication setting our past— our feelings, our values, our attitudes. Sometimes the speaker will present a thought or word which triggers a past experience. At that point we start to think about the experience and soon forget the message being presented.

Our attitudes, values, and beliefs can cause us to give personalized interpretations and meanings to spoken messages. When we do not agree with the message, we spend mental time "debating" the ideas of the speaker instead of listening for the full development of those ideas. Much faulty listening can be attributed to the fact that as listeners we do not give the speaker the benefit of a full presentation before drawing conclusions about the "rightness" or "wrongness" of the ideas. At times, our feelings color our reception so much that we attribute ideas to the speaker that were not actually presented. This happens especially when we disagree with the speaker.

A second problem is passive listeners. Listening is an active process. It takes energy, and many of us are lazy listeners. Because it takes energy to focus mentally, we prefer to sit back and assume a passive role. Being passive is much easier than concentrating on the speaker's message, but, unfortunately, it leads to ineffective listening. Think back for a moment to the last time you enjoyed a good movie. When you left the theatre

THE PERCEPTUAL FIELDS OF THE LISTENER

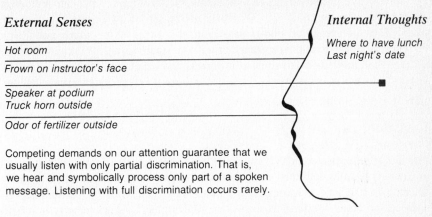

External Senses

Hot room

Frown on instructor's face

Speaker at podium
Truck horn outside

Odor of fertilizer outside

Competing demands on our attention guarantee that we
usually listen with only partial discrimination. That is,
we hear and symbolically process only part of a spoken
message. Listening with full discrimination occurs rarely.

Internal Thoughts

Where to have lunch
Last night's date

you may have felt tired even though you had nothing to do but watch and listen.
Because you empathized with the actors, you were "living" the flow of events with the
characters. This empathic response takes energy, the same type of energy you use when
you are actively listening. It is easier to pretend to listen or to fake attention than it is to
focus on the spoken message.

A third problem is that the physical communication setting can work against listening. Seats are hard; the room is too cold or too hot; the person next to you is coughing;
the heater is making a distracting sound. Just as your other thoughts can invade your
internal perceptual field, so also can distractions outside your body invade your *external perceptual field,* drawing your attention away from the speech. Physical well-being
and comfort often take priority with the listener.[4]

Fourth, the listener's own needs also may compete with the speaker's ideas. Perhaps
you didn't sleep well, have a cold, or are hungry. All of these personal factors compete
for your energy and focus. Again, your physical needs as an individual win out over
your intellectual needs as a listener.

Fifth, because it takes mental and physical energy to deal with words or concepts that
we don't know, it is easier to turn off the listening process when the speaker uses
unfamiliar language. As listeners, we assume that we are unable to understand what the
speaker is talking about if the vocabulary is different or the ideas are new. Unfamiliarity
requires energy that listeners may not be willing to expend. Unless the listener is willing
to take the time to attach meaning to the symbols, true listening is impossible.

And finally, preset ideas about the topic, the speaker, or the occasion also may
interfere with adequate listening comprehension. If you have heard that Professor Smith
is a boring lecturer, you will enter the class with that preset notion. Chances are that you
will find that Professor Smith's lectures are boring, not because they are but because
you allowed the reputation to interfere with the reality of the communication event.
Many speakers are not given a fair hearing because the audience accepts conclusions
about them or their topics beforehand.

What, then, can you as speaker expect from a listening audience? You know they probably will have other things on their minds, things of more concern to them than the information you want to share. They may not be physically or mentally prepared to listen. Their preconceived biases about you, the topic, or the words and ideas you present may interfere with acceptance of your message. Lastly, you know that you, as speaker, will have to make some adjustments and adaptations for your listeners just because they are listeners. We will talk about those speaker responsibilities later in this chapter.

Purposes of Listening

One last set of considerations complicates the speaker-audience relationship in respect to listening. Just as speakers' motivations for talking vary from situation to situation, so, too, do listeners' purposes. Those motivations determine *how* individuals in the audience go about listening to a speaker. Wolvin and Coakley identify five types of listening: listening for appreciation, discrimination, therapeutic value, comprehension, and critical analysis.[5]

Appreciative listening actually encompasses several different purposes. Some listeners simply come to hear and enjoy a "famous" speaker; some enjoy the "arts" of good public speaking, such as pleasing vocal modulation, clever uses of language, impressive phraseology, the powerful use of argumentative materials, and the like; and some members of audiences just like to be in the audience on occasions such as inaugurals, dedications of new city art works, and other special times. Appreciative listening, therefore, is undertaken by people principally concerned with something other than the primary message.

In *discriminative listening,* auditors are attempting to draw inferences about unstated matters—about what speakers "really" think or believe or feel. You often drew conclusions about how angry your parents were with you based not on what they actually said, but how they said it. Often, too, a president's attitudes toward, say, some foreign policy controversy is determined as much by what he did not say as by what he did say: Was his commitment to an invasion absolute or not? How strong was his anticommunist language? Did he dwell on the gory details of atrocities or pass over them? Were there signs of sincerity and deep commitments or only *pro forma* remarks he would be expected to offer? In other words, an important dimension of listening—especially of listeners' judgments regarding emotional impact, speaker credibility, the urgency of some problem—has to do with relatively sophisticated inferences auditors draw from (rather than find in) speeches.

Therapeutic listening actually is more typical of interpersonal than of public communication. In therapeutic listening, the auditor acts as a sounding board for the speaker as that person attempts to talk through a problem, work out a difficult situation, or express deep emotional stress or confusion. Such therapy also can occur in public speaking situations, when a sports star apologizes for unprofessional behavior, when a religious convert talks about a soul-saving experience, or even when a classmate reviews a personal problem and thanks friends for help in solving it. Equally important, therapeutic listening is used in times of joy, as when someone wants to tell others about a new love, a new baby, a promotion at work, or an award at school. People seek out

There is no such thing as "an audience," for speakers face a variety of individuals, not homogeneous masses; audience analysis, therefore, is a key to success in speaking.

others both in times of problems and times of promise. In therapeutic listening, special social bonding between speaker and listener occurs; the speaker-audience relationship itself becomes recognized and even celebrated.

Listening for comprehension is probably the most common auditory activity. It occurs when the listener wants to gain additional information or insights being provided by the speaker. When you listen to radio or TV news programs to find out what's happening, to classroom lectures describing the four principal causes of World War II, or to an orientation official previewing your school's new registration process, you are listening to understand—to comprehend information, ideas, and processes.

The most sophisticated kind of listening is *critical listening*. It demands that auditors become fully engaged with the message in order not simply to understand it, but to interpret it, judge its strengths and weaknesses, and assign some worth to it. You practice this sort of listening when you evaluate commercials, political campaign speeches, advice given you by career counselors, or arguments offered by people for or against some plan of action on the job. When listening critically, auditors decide to accept or reject, to act or delay action on the message.

Such variety in the purposes for listening has serious implications for both listeners and speakers. When you are in an audience, you must decide what your purpose is so that you listen accordingly. Appreciative listeners are highly selective people, watching for metaphors, listening to speaking tones, searching out memorable phrasings; at the other extreme, critical listeners work hard to catch every piece of information relevant

to some proposal, judge the soundness of competing arguments, and consciously decide whether to accept or reject some proposal rationally. Therapeutic listeners must decide when to positively reinforce speakers through applause or other signs of approval; those listening for comprehension must learn to sort out the important from the unimportant ideas. Discriminative listeners must search for clues to unspoken ideas or feelings especially important to themselves. As your skill in listening increases, and as you work to think explicitly about your own purposes *before* attending to a speech, you'll find your experiences with public speeches becoming more pleasurable and complete.

Speakers likewise must consider these purposes for listening before talking. In part, speakers can determine the kinds of listening which occur. For example, you can increase the amount of appreciative listening which occurs by the way you phrase ideas, by the number of humorous anecdotes you offer—by the general tone or atmosphere you set. You sometimes can force more critical listening by emphasizing the rationality of your arguments for or against a proposal. You can even produce some level of therapeutic listening by adopting a confessional tone.

In part, however, speakers *cannot* control listeners' motivations. Many will listen for their own purposes no matter what you do. Some speakers, for example, have reputations which in effect limit the messages they can get across to some audience members. Al Capp, who drew *Li'l Abner* for years, was known to be a humorist, and when he tried to talk seriously about America's political problems in the 1960s, he generally disappointed student audiences; they wanted him to make them laugh, and they *would* laugh, no matter what he said. Similarly, William F. Buckley, Jr., is known for his intellectual sneer and well-turned phrases; his audiences wait for both, and were he not to provide them, people would leave his speeches wondering what was wrong with him. Ultimately, then, understanding something about the range of purposes listeners have helps speakers set goals and expectations.

Listeners' Responsibilities

Having generally reviewed hearing-listening, characteristics of listeners, and the purposes of listening, we can move directly to the heart of public speaking—the responsibilities of both listeners and speakers to make speech communication a rewarding experience. We will begin from the audience side, suggesting ways of improving listening skills through analysis of self, speaker, and message.

Listener Analysis of Self

To become a better listener in public settings, you first must identify your listening patterns and preferences, think about them in terms of their productivity, and then decide which to continue and which to alter. Think about times when you feel you are a good listener, when listening is easy for you and when you remember most of the content of the message. What types of settings are these? What kinds of things do you do to keep your attention focused on the message and the speaker? Think also about those times when it is difficult for you to listen for comprehension and critical analysis.

Why is it difficult to listen? Are you uninterested in the subject? Are you bored or tired? Taking stock of your listening habits will help you recognize your strong and weak listening qualities.

Think also about your listening preferences. Are there people to whom you prefer to listen? Are some classes especially exciting for you even though they are required lecture courses? What features of these people and classes cause you to think and listen with an eager ear? By quickly scanning your habits, patterns, and preferences for listening, you can begin to identify and reinforce positive aspects of your listening behavior.

In addition to reviewing your listening behavior you can begin to correct poor habits by preparing to listen. Before you actually enter the communication event or shortly after the speaker begins the message, ask yourself this series of questions:

1. *What is my purpose in listening?* Do I expect to gain information and understanding or to make a critical decision based on the speaker's presentation? Think about your listening behavior when a teacher announces "This material will be on the next test." You probably pay particular attention to that material, making sure that you understand it. By recognizing why you are listening, you can better analyze the message. If the message has personal importance, you will be more likely to give it your attention.

2. *Am I impartial about the topic being presented?* If you are not willing to let the speaker fully develop ideas before you draw conclusions, you may be wasting the speaker's time and yours. Set aside your prior feelings until the speaker has had a chance to develop a position. That does not mean that you cannot disagree; every listener has the duty to question and evaluate the materials presented. But you should suspend judgment until all of the ideas have been developed.

3. *How much do I know about the topic?* If you still have a great deal to learn, you can better direct your attention to listening. If you know a lot about the topic, be prepared to compare the speaker's information to your knowledge. This may provide additional motivation for listening.

4. *What do I expect from this speech?* Be realistic. If a classmate is giving a speech about the stock market, you will be disappointed if you expect to learn the secret to small investments and quick return. If you expect only to increase your understanding of the way the stock market works, your expectations may be more easily satisfied. Don't burden the speaker with expectations that the person is not prepared to fulfill.

5. *What do I know about the speaking situation?* If you can anticipate the length of and the occasion for the speech, you can better focus your attention. In your class, you will be listening to a variety of speeches. You will know through the description of the assignment how long these speeches will be. Mentally prepare yourself to focus your attention on the speech for the expected period of time. Learning to listen is a skill that develops over time. If you can listen actively for shorter periods of time— for example the five minutes it may take for a classmate to give a speech—you gradually can increase the length of time that you will be able to listen.

6. *What can I expect from the listening environment?* Become aware of the physical environment. Note the temperature and sounds of the room. If you can deal with these and other possible distractions beforehand, you will be less likely to allow your attention to steal away after the speaker begins. Although you may not be able to change the circumstances, by mentally tabulating all of the conditions that could interfere with your skills you can put these concerns into perspective.

7. *What "trigger" words or ideas cause me to stray from the listening situation?* As you listen, don't let past experiences distract you from the current communication event. Take note of special words that seem to pull you away from the speaker's message. After the listening situation is over, try to think why those words caused your attention to be redirected. If they were unfamiliar, look them up in a dictionary. Building vocabulary will also help you prepare for the listening situation. By increasing your vocabulary, you will be less likely to be distracted by unfamiliar words.

Listener Analysis of Speaker

Speaking does not occur in a vacuum. Both speaker and listener bring past experiences to the communication environment. In doing so, the listener attends not only to the message the speaker transmits but also considers the speaker's credibility. The following questions may help you decide how to view the speaker and what impact that perception will have on the message:

1. *What do I know about this speaker?* Rightly or wrongly, the reputation of the speaker will influence how you listen to the message. If your previous experience with the speaker has been favorable, you will be more likely to be receptive to the message. If you have had a disagreement with the person or if the person is someone you do not respect, you may allow that prior knowledge to filter and color the way you understand the message. We tend to do this when listening to political speakers, especially those we do not support. We assume that because we have not agreed with them before, we will not agree now; so instead of listening to the message, we mentally reinforce the reasons why we disagree. Without listening carefully, you may never consider worthwhile ideas which deserve your attention.

2. *How believable is the speaker?* We tend to answer this question based on previous experiences with the speaker or on information about the speaker. If you know that the speaker has misled another audience, you will probably assume that you are being subjected to the same treatment. You may adjust your listening to search out unfounded conclusions, assuming they are untrue. In doing so, you may be listening for detail and not for the main ideas presented. When you listen this way, you do remember the detail but have little reference to what the detail describes or modifies. You need to listen for the main ideas presented; the detail will follow. If you know that the speaker has reported false information, you should weigh that when considering and evaluating the message after it has been fully presented.

3. *Has the speaker prepared for the occasion by conducting adequate research and by considering relationships among ideas?* As listeners, we are more likely to accept messages that we perceive as carefully planned and researched. Yet just because a

source has been cited by the speaker does not mean that careful research and planning have been conducted. You need to listen to the total presentation of ideas, noting the relationships between the message and the supporting materials. Your opinion about the speaker's believability is based partially on his or her knowledge of the subject. Suppose you decided to buy a new car. You enter a showroom eager to find out about fuel efficiency and car durability. A resourceful salesperson volunteers to answer any questions you may have. Upon hearing your concerns, the salesperson begins a prepared speech about the new models, citing commendations from a driving magazine. Your interest will probably slacken because the person skirted the topics you were concerned about. If the salesperson had responded by answering your questions and then offering validation for the response, you would have been a more attentive listener.

4. *What is the speaker's attitude toward this presentation?* As listeners, we use our ears and our eyes to grasp meaning. We assess whether a message is worthy of our time in part by the attitudes the speaker projects. A speaker who appears flippant and uncaring creates an obstacle to productive listening. The speaker's manner of presentation may interfere with your listening skills. Some speakers have annoying habits that draw attention away from the message. Do you recall a speaker who paced back and forth while speaking or one who continually toyed with a paper clip or spoke so slowly that you couldn't follow the train of thought? As listeners, we must be careful that the speaker's mannerisms don't divert our attention from the message.

Listener Analysis of Message

The message is the speaker's product. It gives information about the topic and expresses views. Therefore, the message should be the principal focus of the listener's energy. The receiver can better focus energy on the message by structuring listening behavior to answer three questions:

1. *What are the main ideas of the speech?* Try to discover the speaker's purpose for speaking and the ideas which contribute toward that purpose. Usually these can be found by determining the thesis of the speech and the statements that help the speaker explain the thesis. The main ideas serve as a skeleton on which the speaker builds the speech. The next time you listen to a commercial, listen for the main idea. What types of information does the person give to encourage you to accept the product? Listen the same way to a speech: By focusing on the main idea, we can better recall the message.

2. *How are the main ideas arranged?* By searching for the pattern of organization used by the speaker, the listener can see more easily the relationships between and among the main ideas. If you know that the speaker is using a chronological or spatial pattern of development, it is easier to identify the main ideas and keep them ordered as the speech progresses.

3. *What sorts of supporting materials are used to develop the main ideas?* Consider the timeliness, the quality of the source, and the content of the supporting materials. Supporting materials are used to clarify, amplify, and strengthen the main ideas of

THE PROCESS OF MESSAGE COMPLETION

Person A, listening to the message, completes it by filling in the missing pieces in one way; and Person B, listening to the same message, completes it in quite another way. Neither has received the *actual* message, but at least Person B has picked up the gist, thanks to an acquired habit of listening to the key ideas and of resolving problems of incompleteness in ways consistent with the speaker's intent.

"Today, I want to talk... seriously... about this country... Journalism *(journalism? My gosh! I have an examination next hour in Journalism!)* ... .about political candidates around the country, states in counties and cities, telling us . . . *political lies . . . about good issues and bad issues,* rhetorically clever moves . . . *sophomores (is tonight the sophomore dance? should I ask her?)* than candidates who stand for taxes, social security, jobs, inflation, and morals."

"Today I want to talk with you about a serious problem facing this country: the problem of political journalism. I am disturbed that the journalists who follow political candidates around the country, around the states, around the countries, and around the cities spend more time telling us what the various candidates' statements mean *politically* (was it a good or a bad issue, a rhetorically clever move or a sophomoric tactic, good for your party or good for the opposition?) than what the candidates stand for in terms of taxes, social legislation, jobs, inflation, and public morality."

"Today I want to talk... about a serious problem —political journalism. I am disturbed that journalists...follow political candidates around the country... telling us what...the various candidates mean *politically (what does that mean?)*...than what their stands are on taxes ...legislation for the party of opposition *(what does that mean?),* inflation, publicity, morality."

[Message for Person A: Some candidates tell us lies about anything, while others promise more taxes, inflation, and stuff. Obviously, there are no good politicians.]

[Message for Person B: Political journalists twist what politicians are saying so that we don't really know what they are standing for. I still am not sure what is being said here, but . . .]

the speech. Analyze these materials to help you evaluate the ideas presented. Check to make sure that the supporting materials, as well as the main ideas, make sense to you. If there is a discrepancy between your knowledge and the ideas presented by the speaker, find out why it exists. This should help you clarify the differences and reach a conclusion about the validity of the total message.

To focus your attention on the main ideas of the speech, on the pattern of development, and on the use of supporting materials, you should constantly *review, relate,* and *anticipate*. *Review* what the speaker has said. Take a few seconds to summarize the content of the message, to think about the way the materials have been developed. Mentally add to the summary review each time the speaker initiates a new topic for consideration. *Relate* the message to what you already know. Consider how important the message is to you and how you might use the information at some future time. *Anticipate* what the speaker might say next. Given the development of the materials to that point, what is the speaker likely to say next? Use the anticipation stage as a way of continuing to focus on the content of the message. It's not important if you are right or wrong—the important element is that you have directed your attention to the message. By reviewing, relating, and anticipating you can use up the extra time generated by the speech-thought lag and keep your attention focused on the message.

Speaker's Responsibilities

Even though it is the listener who finally judges the transmitted message, there are several steps that you as speaker can take to help the listener. These efforts are concentrated in three areas: preparing the speech, capturing and holding attention, and presenting the speech.

Preparing the Speech

When preparing the speech, keep in mind that it is often difficult for the listener to follow the structure of your presentation and to keep track of what's been said. Try to use an organizational pattern which is complementary to your purpose and is easy for the listener to follow. You may want to share the means of development with your audience with an initial summary or forecast early in the speech. This will help the listener follow your development.

Careful planning and preparation will help guarantee that your message is clearly presented and is easy to follow. Researching the topic area to select the most appropriate forms of support will help you develop your ideas fully. The supporting materials make it easier for the listener to remember the main ideas of your speech. Poor planning makes the audience lose respect for the speaker; if your topic is worth speaking about, it is worth preparing.

When preparing your speech, anticipate points where your listeners will need special guidance. Forecasts and internal summaries will help the listeners focus on your ideas. Think about concepts that may be especially difficult for the listeners to understand. Try to present those concepts several times using different wording each time so that the listeners can better identify with the materials and ideas. Paraphrasing is a useful tool.

During your planning, remember to keep your listeners in mind. If the audience is expecting a five-minute speech, try to tailor your presentation for that expectation. If you know that the environment is going to be uncomfortable for the audience, try to adapt your topic and length of speech to accommodate the physical situation. Your audience analysis may suggest other ways to adapt your message for easy comprehension.

Preparation also includes practice. While practicing your speech, you can work out awkward phrasing which might confuse the audience. Further, practice helps you feel more comfortable with your ideas. Your presentation will be easier to view, to listen to, and to accept if you are at ease and confident.

Capturing and Holding Attention

Speakers must recognize that listeners' behaviors vary considerably during the course of a speech. Essentially, all members of the audience need to be given reasons for *wanting* to listen. That is a matter of gaining their attention. Even when you have such attention, however, it tends to ebb and flow as the speech unfolds; listeners tune in and also tune out periodically. Speakers must constantly be on the lookout for lapses in attention and take steps to secure it again and again. James Albert Winans, a twentieth-century pioneer in public speaking instruction, expresses this problem succinctly: "Attention determines response." If you cannot gain and hold attention, your speaking effort is likely to be ineffective. The problem of attention is discussed at greater length in Chapter 3.

Even now, as you prepare to give your first speeches, pay this matter some heed and take your first steps toward overcoming the problem of attention. To engage your listeners, be sure that your subject matter, your approach to that topic, your examples or illustrations, and even your choice of words are relevant to your listeners' general beliefs, attitudes, and experiences; people are much more likely to attend to a message if it seems relevant to their lives. And, too, make sure there is variety in your speech; alternate sections of general description and concrete example, statistics and illustrations, (usually) seriousness and humor; variety keeps listeners coming back for more. Overall, *treat listeners the way you yourself wish to be treated when in an audience*. Just as you get tired of overly abstract materials, too many numbers in a row, and dryness, so does everyone else. We will review several other techniques for gaining and renewing attention later. But even now you can start to incorporate attention-gaining and attention-holding strategies in your public talks. That is one of your responsibilities as a speaker, and it helps make every speaking occasion a rewarding one.

Presenting the Speech

The actual presentation of the speech can help the receiver be a better listener. See that your delivery style is appropriate for the audience, topic, and occasion. Be sure also that your nonverbal communication matches your verbalized thoughts and feelings so that you are not sending contradictory messages.

You gain attention simply by rising to speak in front of others. You hold attention, however, only by using the factors of attention throughout your speeches.

Interpreting audience feedback during the presentation will help you modify, adapt, or recast any ideas you see the audience is misunderstanding or doubting. If the listeners notice that you are sincerely making every effort to communicate your thoughts, they will tend to be more receptive and try harder to be good listeners. Your use of feedback is one way the audience assesses your desire to communicate effectively. If you look for nonverbal clues from the audience and determine that they are not understanding your message, quickly think back over what you have said and try to rephrase main points in simpler language. Include a brief internal summary of the points you have covered, and if the situation allows, ask for questions.

THE AUDIENCE PROVIDES BOTH DIRECT AND INDIRECT FEEDBACK TO THE SPEAKER

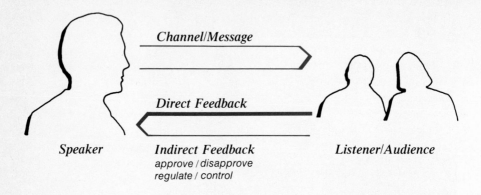

Speaker   *Channel/Message*

Direct Feedback

Indirect Feedback   *Listener/Audience*
approve / disapprove
regulate / control

The speaker should project an appropriate attitude when speaking. If you are talking about a serious topic, make sure your approach and demeanor reflect that. Dealing with life-or-death issues in a humorous manner may be offensive. On the other hand, some topics lend themselves to a lighter approach. The attitude that you project can help your audience better appreciate the ideas you are sharing with them.

Finally, as a speaker, remember how it feels to be a listener. Consider the positive and negative reactions you have to the ways that speakers present ideas. Avoid making some of the same errors that annoy you. Remember that good speakers are also good listeners. Review critiques of your speaking and try to correct any weaknesses before you speak again.

Listening in the Speech Classroom

Critical listening skills can be developed in several ways in this classroom as well as in others. You can *(1)* practice critiquing the speeches of other students, taking part in post-speech discussions; *(2)* listen critically to discussions, lectures, oral presentations, and student-teacher exchanges in your other classes, identifying effective and ineffective communicative techniques employed by a variety of people in several different contexts; *(3)* make an effort to listen to speakers outside of class, in the community, observing carefully their successes and failures and analyzing why they meet with certain reactions; and *(4)* read the sample speeches in this book, taking them apart systematically in order to isolate the communicative cues which might have facilitated comprehension and acceptance.

Undoubtedly you will become a more informed listener after you have studied this book and been part of classroom speaking assignments; but you can now start to become a more proficient listener. First, use the Speech Evaluation Form on pages 35–36 as a checklist of listening concerns. Depending upon the particular assignment, the nature of the audience, and the demands of the occasion, some of the checkpoints on the form will be more significant and applicable than others. For now, use the form as a general guide; later, concentrate upon those aspects of it that are relevant to a specific speech assignment.

And second, participate regularly in post-speech evaluations, even of early classroom speaking assignments. Do not hesitate to provide direct feedback to your classmates, pointing out what was good, what worked and what didn't seem to work so well, what was clear and what remained cloudy. Good, constructive classroom criticism is both positive and negative—but always supportive. Such oral commentary accomplishes two goals: it provides a beginning speaker with much-needed reaction, and it forces you, the listener, to verbalize your thoughts and recognize explicitly your standards and expectations. In this way, both you and the speaker gain: the speaker acquires a sense of the range of reactions being generated in an audience, and you gain a better sense of your own mind.

Listening, then, is a two-way street, a joint responsibility of speaker and listener. Only when both parties are sensitive to its points of breakdown and to techniques which can enhance it will oral communication be a successful transaction. Much of what we will have to say in later chapters will rest directly upon this process.

Speech Evaluation Form

The Speaker

_____ poised?

_____ apparently sincere?

_____ apparently concerned about the topic?

_____ positive self-image?

_____ apparently concerned about the audience?

_____ apparently well prepared?

The Message

_____ suitable topic?

_____ clear general purpose?

_____ sharply focused specific purpose?

_____ well-phrased central idea or claim?

_____ introduced adequately?

_____ concluded effectively?

_____ adequately supported (enough, varied, trustworthy sources)?

_____ supporting materials tailored to the audience?

_____ major subdivisions clear, balanced?

_____ use of notes and lectern unobtrusive?

Transmission

_____ voice varied for emphasis?

_____ voice conversational?

_____ language clear (unambiguous, concrete)?

_____ language forcible (vivid, intense)?

_____ face expressive?

_____ delivery speed controlled?

_____ body alert and nondistracting?

_____ gestures used effectively?

The Audience

_____ all listeners addressed?

_____ their presence recognized and complimented?

_____ their attitudes toward subject and speaker taken into account?

The Speech as a Whole

Audience's expectations met? _____

Short-range effects of the speech? _____

Long-range effects? _____

Possible improvements? _____

REFERENCE NOTES

[1]See studies reviewed by Andrew Wolvin and Carolyn Coakley, _Listening_ (Dubuque, IA: William C. Brown Co., 1982), Chapter 1.

[2]Thomas Lewis and Ralph Nichols, _Speaking and Listening_ (Dubuque, IA: William C. Brown Co., 1965), p. 6.

[3]For a discussion see Carl Weaver, _Human Listening_ (Indianapolis, IN: Bobbs-Merrill Publishers, 1972), Chapter 1, and Larry L. Barker, _Listening Behavior_ (Englewood Cliffs, NJ: Prentice-Hall, Inc., 1971), Chapter 3.

[4]This discussion of internal and external perceptual fields is adapted from Wayne C. Minnick, _The Art of Persuasion_, pp. 38–41. Copyright © 1957 Houghton Mifflin Company. Used by permission.

[5]The materials on purposes are drawn from Wolvin and Coakley, Chapters 4–8.

[6]Richard Heun and Linda Heun, _Public Speaking: A New Speech Book_ (St. Paul, MN: West, 1979), Chapter 3, "Listening to Public Speeches."

[7]Charles R. Petrie, Jr. and Susan D. Carrell, "The Relationship of Motivation, Listening Capability, Initial Information, and Verbal Organizational Ability to Lecture Comprehension and Retention," _Communication Monographs_, 43 (August 1976), 187–94. For other studies of listening skills, see Steven C. Rhodes and Kenneth D. Frandsen, "Some Effects of Instruction in Feedback Utilization on the Fluency of College Students' Speech," _Speech Monographs_, 42 (March 1975), 83–89; and Robert W. Norton and Lloyd S. Pettegrew, "Attentiveness as a Style of Communication: A Structural Analysis," _Communication Monographs_, 46 (March 1979), 13–26.

[8]Mark L. Knapp, _Nonverbal Communication in Human Interaction_, 2nd ed. (New York: Holt, Rinehart & Winston, 1978), Chapter 6, "The Effects of Physical Behavior on Human Communication."

PROBLEMS AND PROBES

1. Think of a course in which you are currently enrolled and having trouble. How are you as a listener in that classroom? Where do you normally sit during class? Do you face any physical barriers to communication? How well can you hear your instructor? Is your seat in the best possible place in the room with the least amount of distractions? Do you sit too close to the door? Are you distracted by conversations or hall movement during classtime? Do you sit near a window? Are you often tempted to look outside? Think about your classmates. Does someone sit near you who captures your attention? What changes could you make to become a better listener in that classroom? Realize that *you* can control your listening environment.

2. What, to your mind, is the importance of physical setting in good listening? How do you react to noises, uncomfortable temperatures in a room, seating which makes a view of the speaker difficult? Does the arrangement of chairs (rows in auditoriums, circles of chairs in classrooms, across-the-desk seating for conferences) affect your listening habits? Do you listen in one manner when seated in front of a lecturer, in another when talking to a friend at a crowded party? Make some useful generalizations regarding the ways in which the speech situation affects the ease or efficiency with which you listen.

ORAL ACTIVITIES

1. Prepare a two- to three-minute oral statement in response to one of the following topics:
    a. Is there anything wrong with tuning out a boring speaker?
    b. "Nature has given to man one tongue, but two ears that we may hear from others twice as much as we speak."   —*Epictetus,* circa 300 B.C.
    c. Can faking attention be harmful?

2. Consider the following question: Can speakers objectively evaluate their own efforts? After a performance assignment, test your self-evaluative skills by completing the Speech Evaluation Form on pages 35–36. When the instructor returns a written critique (and those of any classmates who might also have evaluated the performance), compare these with your responses. Try to account for any differences between your self-evaluation and the evaluations of others.

3. Present a one-minute set of oral instructions for some activity with which the class is not likely to be familiar. Class members should not take notes during presentations, but after each presentation they should try to list the instructions on a notecard. Collect the cards and compare the written versions to the instructions you presented. How do you account for any discrepancies? What could you as a speaker have done to aid your listeners?

4. Challenge your own listening skills. Did you hear what you thought you heard? Approach your instructor after class and say, "I thought I heard you say . . .," or "You listed three main points. Were they . . .?" You will be amazed at how much better you listen if you plan to ask questions about what you heard and you may be pleasantly surprised by your instructor's response. Discuss this activity with other classmates.

CHAPTER 3

Getting Started:

Planning and Preparing Speeches

The preceding chapters provide a foundation for understanding the *process* of communication. In this chapter, we will turn our attention to the *practice* of communication. First, we will consider eight steps that are essential in planning the presentation of a speech. These steps provide a systematic overview of the development of a speech, from selecting the subject to rehearsing the prepared outline. Second, we will discuss the processes involved in gaining and holding attention and in developing and communicating confidence. Advice regarding both attention and confidence-building will assist you in adding interest value to your speeches and in communicating your ideas in a poised, relaxed manner.

The Essential Steps in Speech Preparation

There is no magic formula for planning and preparing speeches. The steps that follow are basic guides to consider as you formulate your speech. While you may not need to follow each in the sequence suggested here, your overall goal of successfully communicating your ideas will be furthered by paying careful attention to each step. A general question to ask yourself is: Have I done what each step suggests I should do in preparing my speech? If you can answer ''yes'' to the question for each step, you will be on your way to presenting an effective speech.

The planning process that will be discussed can be divided into three phases and eight steps:

Phase I: Finding and Fitting the Subject to Self and Situation
1. Selecting and narrowing the subject
2. Determining the general and specific purposes

ESSENTIAL STEPS IN PLANNING, PREPARING, AND PRESENTING THE SPEECH

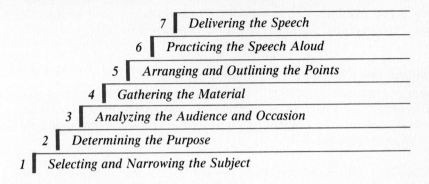

| 7 | *Delivering the Speech* |

| 6 | *Practicing the Speech Aloud* |

| 5 | *Arranging and Outlining the Points* |

| 4 | *Gathering the Material* |

| 3 | *Analyzing the Audience and Occasion* |

| 2 | *Determining the Purpose* |

| 1 | *Selecting and Narrowing the Subject* |

3. Determining the central idea or claim
4. Analyzing the audience
5. Analyzing the occasion

Phase II: Developing the Speech Content
1. Gathering the speech material
2. Arranging the material into an outline

Phase III: Working on Presentational Skills
1. Practicing aloud for clarity and fluency

Selecting and Narrowing the Subject

The most difficult task for many speakers, especially those in a beginning speech class, is to choose a topic. Two important considerations in selecting a subject are "what do you know about?" and "what are you interested in talking about?" You might begin by listing those topics that you feel you have information on, and circling those that you have the most interest in researching further and talking about. Before committing yourself to a firm topic choice, be sure to check your possible subjects against the next two steps in the initial phase of the process.

Once you have selected a suitable topic, the next concern is to narrow the topic so that you can do it justice in the time allowed. How much can you say about your subject in five to seven minutes? If you cannot cover the subject in an adequate manner, you will need to select an aspect of the topic and develop it. For example, if you wish to talk about running road races, will it be possible to say everything that should be said in five minutes? Probably not, in which case you will need to think in terms of a facet of racing: getting ready to run your first five-kilometer race, for example; or avoiding injuries while running a road race; or understanding what happens physiologically and psychologically to runners during a race. Any of these would be easier to cover than the broad topic of running road races. The narrower your subject, the more fully you will be able to explain or prove its essential points. Also, a narrower subject enables you to make your speech more interesting as you will have more time to include a variety of illustrations, statistical data, testimony, and other supportive material.

Determining the General and Specific Purposes

Once you have completed the first step—selecting and narrowing your subject—you can focus more precisely on why you want to talk about this subject. What do you want this speech to accomplish? Answering this question involves consideration of both general and specific purposes.

General Purpose.   What is the general state you wish your listeners to be in when you complete the speech? Are you, for example, simply trying to tell them something they do not—but should—know? Are you seeking to alter the way they feel about some social, economic, or political issue? Or are you interested in having them take some specific action as a result of your speech? Answering one of these questions affirmatively will help focus your general purpose.

Specific Purpose.   Given your topic, specifically what do you want the audience to know, feel, value, do? Within the context of one of the above general purposes, specific purposes focus attention on the particular *substantive* goal of your presentation. Once this is determined, you will be in a position to describe the exact response you want from your listeners: "I want my audience to understand how to prepare for a road race." In this instance, you want to inform your audience (general purpose), but more specifically you want them to know what steps to take in getting in condition to run a race.

Determining the Central Idea or Claim

This step in the initial phase flows directly from the preceding. Can you state your message in a single sentence? If you are seeking to explain an idea or to inform an audience about a process or event, that sentence is called a *central idea* or *claim*. It is a declarative statement which summarizes your speech: "There are five stages in getting ready for a road race." In speeches that aim at persuading an audience to adopt a specific attitude or take a particular action, the claim summarizes the intent of your argument: "As one means of achieving or maintaining a healthy body, you should consider running in road races."

By this point in the planning process, your speech should be narrowed and focused precisely on what you wish to convey to your audience. The central idea, in the context of your general and specific purposes, serves as a constant guide as you move into the next phase of preparation. As you research and outline the substance of your message, the relevance of material to be included will be governed by these prior decisions. Think of each speech you develop as an instrument for winning a particular response from your listeners. Selecting and narrowing your topic, determining the general and specific purposes, and setting forth the central idea or claim will allow you to identify that response with care and precision.

Analyzing the Audience

Listeners are the targets of all speeches. A good public speech, therefore, not only reflects your desires and interests as a speaker, but also is responsive to the interests, preferences, and values of the audience to whom it is presented. As noted in the initial step, your selection of a topic should remain tentative until you have considered the audience: How would they feel about the topic? To do this successfully, you need to analyze the people who compose the group—their age, gender, social-political-economic status, origins, backgrounds, prejudices, and fears. In other words, you need some sense of how they will react to the topic you have chosen. You can help yourself decide on a topic if you are aware of how much the audience already knows about your topic, what their general interest level is in hearing about it, what they may believe in and value, and what their probable attitudes are toward you and your subject. In a public speaking class, you can estimate these factors by listening to comments made during class discussions and by asking some class members what they think about your tentative plans. In other circumstances, gathering this information may be more difficult, requiring you to become more creative in assessing your audience. Regardless of how it is done, audience analysis is a primary determinant of success in speechmaking.

Analyzing the Occasion

The audience is not the only factor that will make a difference in your choice of topics. As noted in Chapter 1, you also will need to consider the setting and circumstances in which you will be speaking. Are there specific rules or customs that will be important to know and to follow? How long will you have to speak? Will you precede or follow other speakers? What impact will events before or after your speech have on topic selection? Will the physical circumstances be amenable to your speaking style? If not, can you alter them prior to the speech? For example, will you need to obtain a microphone in order to be heard, or will you need to rearrange the physical setting in order to be seen by all members of the audience? Analyzing the occasion involves serious issues (the impact of group traditions or customs) and mundane issues (physical setting). Your responses to both sets of issues are important in deciding what to talk about; by having this information in advance you will be more comfortable about the circumstances and about the expectations the audience will have when it is your time to speak.

Gathering the Speech Material

As you move into this second phase of preparation, you will be assembling the materials needed to build your speech. At some point in the initial phase, you undoubtedly assessed your existing pool of information on the subject and made some tentative decisions about personal experiences and other data that could be incorporated into the speech. In most cases, you will find that this knowledge and experience are insuffi-

Gathering materials for your speeches is an easy task when you (1) know what you're looking for, and (2) take time to learn your way around your local library.

cient. You will need to gather additional information with which to develop, expand, or reinforce your major points. You may gather valuable materials from conversations and interviews, from printed resources such as newspapers and periodicals, or from radio or television programs. Thorough research is essential, if only because you never know when a listener will know more than you do. Good speeches are packed with examples, illustrations, stories, figures, and quotations that can be discovered only through systematic and careful research.

Arranging Materials into an Outline

As you assemble the needed material, you can save time by making a preliminary list of the major ideas that you wish to cover in developing your central idea or claim. This list will help guide your selection of specific supportive materials. Your list also can serve as an initial rough outline of the sequence of ideas to be developed. You should wait until you have assembled all of the material to develop a final outline. By keeping the outline flexible, you can adjust the sequence of information as you continue your research.

We will consider outlining in more detail in a later chapter. For the present, follow two rules: *(1)* arrange your ideas in a clear and systematic order, and *(2)* preserve the unity of your speech by making sure that each point is directly related to your specific purpose.

Practicing Aloud for Clarity and Fluency

The final phase of preparation consists of one step: practicing the presentation as you hope to deliver your speech to an audience. You probably will find that the best method is to talk through the outline aloud, following the planned sequence of ideas, facts, and illustrations. Do this until you are comfortable with the sequence and you can express each idea clearly and fluently. The more comfortable you are with the material, the more poise and confidence you will have as you stand before the audience with your notes or brief speaking outline in front of you. The self-assurance each speaker desires comes from knowing what to say next.

When you can go through the speech several times without forgetting major points or without hesitating unduly, you may consider your preparation complete. As you practice speaking from your outline, preserve a mental image of your listeners and project your speech as though you were talking to them. That image will help you transfer your best speaking habits from the rehearsal stage to the actual speaking event.

Delivering Your First Speeches

Two central concerns in delivering your first speech are *gaining and holding attention* and *developing and communicating confidence*. These are interrelated concerns: By communicating in a confident manner, you will make it easier for the audience to concentrate on what you have to say, rather than on any overt nervousness that appears as you express your ideas.

Gaining and Holding Attention

If your ideas are to be heard, they must be attended to by the audience. The fact that you are standing before an audience does not guarantee that they will listen to what you have to say. Thus, gaining and holding their attention becomes your primary goal as you begin to deliver your speech. In essence, attention to your speech requires that a listener concentrate on one facet of his or her environment: your speech. Other facets—the weather, the room temperature, later activities—cease to be a major part of the person's concerns.[1]

Gaining Attention. Ideas can be presented in a variety of ways that will focus the audience's attention on the content of your remarks. Often referred to as *factors of attention,* these include the following:

1. Activity or movement
2. Reality
3. Proximity
4. Familiarity
5. Novelty
6. Suspense
7. Conflict
8. Humor
9. The vital

These various terms overlap, and in practice the qualities they represent often are combined. For purposes of explanation and illustration, we will discuss the factors as separate approaches to gaining attention.

THE FACTORS OF ATTENTION

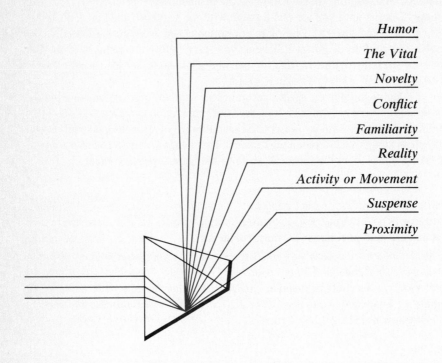

Humor

The Vital

Novelty

Conflict

Familiarity

Reality

Activity or Movement

Suspense

Proximity

Activity.   When we are walking down a street, we naturally attend to the movement of people, animals, and cars. Similarly, we attend best to ideas that appear to ''move''—narratives that suggest action, uncertainty, or moments of crisis add life to the speech. Audiences also will attend to the ''movement'' involved in detailing the steps in a process or in demonstrating how a machine works.

In addition, your speech as a whole should involve the audience in its natural movement from beginning to end. A presentation that seems to be going nowhere in particular may end up without any passengers. For this reason, it is important that the progress of your speech be apparent to the audience. Make sure that your audience understands your ultimate goal or purpose in speaking, and that they are able to follow you as you move toward that goal.

Reality. The earliest words that a child learns are the names of real objects and of tangible acts related to them. This interest in reality—in the immediate, the concrete, the actual—can be a basis for gaining the attention of the audience. Instead of talking in abstractions, mention real-life people, places, and events. Instead of saying "Several people report" or "They say," offer concrete names of persons or groups. Employ pictures, diagrams, or charts to add a sense of realness to complex topics; this is particularly useful when discussing differences in proportion or magnitude, or in offering statistical data. Specific instances are more real to an audience than broad trends or classifications; particular names and places are more interesting than impersonalized, vague allusions.

Proximity. Direct references to the immediate occasion, to a recent event, or to persons sitting in the audience also will focus attention on your comments. A reference to a remark of a preceding speaker can be used to tie your comments to what has already been said. The direct reference to a member of the audience also causes people to focus attention on what is being said. Singling persons out by name and looking directly at them is an effective means of obtaining their immediate attention.

Familiarity. There is an old saying that "familiarity breeds contempt." While this may sometimes be the case, familiarity also generates greater attention. Everyday experiences that are held in common by most people are easy to relate to; when describing unfamiliar concepts, processes, or events, make connections to things the audience already knows. That which is familiar serves a double-duty: It catches our attention and it expands our understanding of what is being explained. A speech which contains only the familiar, however, and does not relate that which we already know or have experienced to new ideas or events will quickly become boring. Familiar stories, such as Washington and the cherry tree or Lincoln as a rail-splitter, will have more impact if they are used in an unusual way or are given an unexpected interpretation.

Novelty. As an old newspaper adage has it, when a dog bites a man, it's an accident; when a man bites a dog, it's news. That which was "news" yesterday is commonplace today. Inventions of such marvels as radio, television, and airplanes were news when first announced. Now, we take these developments for granted. That which is part of our daily routine lacks attention value, unless depicted in some unusual or graphic manner. The student who passed out a plate of chocolate cookies was received in a routine manner until she noted that one or two of the cookies contained just enough arsenic to make you queasy. She was lying, but the point that "the taken for granted may be more important than you think" was clearly made.

The novel can be expressed effectively in terms of *size:* especially large or small objects or amounts attract attention. Reference to a $10,000 automobile or to an $85,000 home would not stand out as unusual; reference to a $40,000 sports car or to a $350,000 home would.

Although attention-getting in themselves, large and small figures become even more compelling when thrown into *contrast* with their opposites. Geraldine Ferraro, in comparing the earnings of men and women, made this observation:

> I wanted to find out how many women in America earn more than $60,000 a year. I picked that number, frankly, because that is what I, as a member of Congress, earn. I learned that there are only 18,000 women in the entire United States, working full-time, who earn

more than $60,000. We represent just one-tenth of one percent of all the women who work full-time in America. By contrast, 885,000 men, 2.1 percent of full-time male workers, are in the $60,000 plus bracket.[2]

Suspense.   The creation of uncertainty in mystery novels or television dramas helps keep the audience focused on the events taking place. Similarly, uncertainty can be created in a speech by noting results which have mysterious unknown causes or by calling attention to forces which have uncertain effects. Recounting the stories of ships and planes lost in the Bermuda Triangle may be an effective means of gaining and holding attention in a speech on that region's mysteries. You can create a mild form of suspense by noting that more valuable information on a point will come later in the speech. In using the factor of suspense, observe two cautions: *(1)* Do not make the information seem so difficult or mysterious that your listeners lose all hope of comprehending it; and *(2)* make sure that the information you finally reveal is important enough to warrant the suspense you have created. Audiences become irritated when a speaker promises ''more about that later'' and then either never gets to the point again or says little of value when he does arrive at the point.

Conflict.   The opposition of forces compels attention—especially if the listeners identify with one side or the other. Constructing a speech in a fashion that reveals the major conflicts between persons or groups is one way of gaining and holding attention. Another way of generating a sense of conflict is to use a narrative approach in retelling the story of a recent controversy. This is especially true if the audience senses they are getting inside information—incidents and events not generally known. In generating a sense of conflict, be certain that your representation of events is as accurate as possible. If you are detailing the sides of a controversy to audience members who belong to one or the other side, you can expect them to be critical of your depiction of their respective positions. Also be wary of using a ''straw man'' approach—setting up a sham conflict and then resolving it. The effectiveness of your message depends on the audience's perception of the sincerity and accuracy of your description.

Humor.   Laughter indicates enjoyment; people pay attention when they are enjoying themselves. Few things, in fact, gain and hold an audience's attention as well as a speaker's judicious use of humor. Humor can defuse a tense situation, and can be an effective antidote to conflict. Whereas an audience is mentally and physically alert in situations of suspense and conflict, humor allows them to relax while still attending to the message. When using humor, remember that its attention-gaining power is likely to be increased if two guidelines are followed: *(1) Be relevant.* Beware of wandering from the point under discussion. Jokes and anecdotes must reinforce rather than divert attention from the central ideas or claims. *(2) Use good taste.* Avoid humor on occasions where it would be out of place, and refrain from using risque and ethnic humor that may offend your listeners and detract from the effectiveness of your presentation.

The vital.   People nearly always pay attention to matters that affect their health, reputation, property, or employment. If you can show your audience that what you are saying concerns them in one or more of these ways, they will likely attend to your message. Pointing out how your subject concerns persons close to them also will command their attention. People identify with family, friends, and associates; what affects members of their social world will affect them as well. Of the factors of attention, appeals to the *vital* are indispensable.

The vital, humor, conflict, suspense, novelty, familiarity, proximity, reality, and activity or movement are attention-attractors that will aid you throughout the presentation of your speech.

Holding Attention.   The preceding factors are useful in gaining attention both at the outset of the speech and at later points in the presentation. Since attention is unstable— audiences will vary in the degree of attention they give at any one moment—recapturing their attention and then attempting to hold it are constant concerns. While the preceding factors can help you accomplish these objectives, there are additional guides that will assist you in holding the attention of your listeners.[3]

Diversity.   Individual members of the audience will vary in their responsiveness to the factors of attention. With this in mind, you should use a variety of factors in your presentation. In addition, audience members are capable of responding to more than one factor; multiple use will increase the chances of their concentration on your message.

Utility.   As the discussion of the vital suggests, audiences will attend to those events that seem to have usefulness for them. By pointing to the utility of the ideas being presented, and being specific about how and why the audience can benefit from your message, you will increase the chances of keeping their attention.

Similarity.   Ideas that appear to be logically related or similar to one another are easier for an audience to attend to. A disjointed, random collection of disparate ideas may soon leave an audience thinking about more useful things. The more an audience can economize by linking thoughts together, the easier it will be for them to maintain their overall attention to your message.

Cueing.   Attention researchers Eleanor Gibson and Nancy Rader point out in their discussion of the advantages of preparedness that "One can be more attentive as he knows what to expect and what to look for."[4] Cueing the audience, or preparing them for what they should expect, can be gained by *forecasting* and by *transitions*.

Forecasting simply tells the audience what the major divisions of the speech will be: "First, I will review the two primary reasons for the increase in the Great White sharks, then I will discuss the major effects of their presence in the area known as the Red Triangle." When used as part of the introduction, forecasting gives the audience an overview of the entire speech and allows them to anticipate major divisions.

Transitions function as verbal "signposts" indicating the next major point in the speech: "With this brief history as a basis, let us next consider the current scene"; "An even more important consideration is . . ."; "Moving on to the second of my three alternatives. . . ."

By using a diversity of attention factors, clearly communicating the utility of the message, and linking similar ideas together, you can maintain the attention of the audience. Cueing, through forecasting and transitions, will give the audience a chance to visualize your entire speech and to follow its development as you speak. These guides, together with the factors of attention, will make your first speech easier to deliver.

Developing and Communicating Confidence

Many beginning speakers feel anxious and nervous about standing before an audience. You may be saying to yourself, "I'm too nervous to stand up there"; "What will I do if I forget a part of my speech?" "My hands are trembling—how can I hold notes when I can't even hold my hands still?" Recognizing that these are common reactions is half the battle. Developing and communicating confidence is the other half.

Developing Confidence.   The anxiety about speaking in public that you feel just before getting up in front of an audience is a part of a general apprehensiveness that people have about any communication encounter. You do not wish to fail; at times, this fear of failure may even overcome the desire to speak. If you have ever been reluctant to raise your hand in class and answer a question, you understand how apprehension can affect your behavior. We can distinguish two broad classes of this communication apprehension you may experience.[5] *State apprehension* refers to the anxiety you feel in particular settings or situations. You may find it easy to talk with friends, but feel very uncomfortable when interviewed for a job. You might not mind speaking within a small group in class or at a rally, but presenting your ideas in a formal setting sends you into a near panic. The phenomenon known as "stage fright" is a common form of state apprehension. In its extreme form, stage fright is experienced physiologically as clammy hands, nervous knees, a dry mouth, and a trembling, cracking voice. Psychologically, stage fright is experienced as mental blocks—forgetting what you were going to say. Recognizing that you will be evaluated by others in a formal setting, whether in a classroom or in a town meeting, can cause some anxious moments.

While some aspects of nervousness derive from the situation, others are a part of your own personality. This class of apprehension, *trait apprehension,* refers to the level of anxiety that you have as you face any communication situation. A high level of anxiety may cause withdrawal from those situations in which interpersonal or public communication with others is required. By attacking these "trait" fears as they manifest themselves in speaking before others, you will be in a better position to reduce your overall level of anxiety. Although there is no foolproof program for developing self-confidence, there are some ways to achieve the confidence necessary to complete the speaking task. For those interested in pursuing the subject of trait apprehension further, see the essay on "Reducing Communication Apprehension" in the Speaker's Resource Book at the end of this textbook.

1. *Realize that tension and nervousness are normal and even, in part, beneficial to speakers.* Fear is a normal part of living; learn how to control it and make it work for you. Remember that the tension you feel can provide you with energy and alertness. As adrenalin pours into your bloodstream, you experience a physical charge, increasing bodily movement and psychological acuity. A baseball pitcher who is not "pumped up" before a big game may find that his fastball has no zip. A speaker who is not similarly charged will undoubtedly come across as dull and lifeless. The time for concern is when you discover that you are not at all worried or tense about speaking in front of a group. Such an attitude leads to a lackluster performance.

2. *Take comfort in the fact that tension is physiologically reduced by the act of speaking.* As you talk and discover that your audience will accept you and some of the things you are saying, your nervousness will tend to dissipate. Physiologically, your

When you take the time to go through the steps of speech preparation and to practice aloud, you gain in personal self-assurance or confidence—and succeed as a speaker.

body is using up the excess adrenalin it generated; psychologically, your ego is getting positive reinforcement. Within moments of your beginning comments, you realize that your prior preparation is working in your favor and that you have the situation under control. The very act of talking aloud thus reduces fear.

3. *Talk about topics that interest you*. Speech anxiety arises in part because of self-centeredness; sometimes you are more concerned with yourself than with your topic. One means of reducing that anxiety, therefore, is to select topics which are of deep, intrinsic interest to you, topics you want to talk about. This makes the situation more topic-centered than self-centered; having a topic of interest focuses your attention on getting across information and ideas rather than on worrying about yourself.

4. *Talk about subjects that you are familiar with*. Confidence born of knowledge increases your perceived credibility and helps control your nervousness. Have you ever wondered why you could talk at length with friends about your favorite hobby, sport, or political interests without feeling anxious, only to find yourself in a nervous state when standing in front of an audience to talk about something you just read in *Smithsonian?* Knowing something about the subject may be part of the answer. Subject mastery is thus closely akin to self-mastery.

5. *Analyze with care both the situation and the audience*. The more you know about the audience and about what is expected of you in a particular situation, the less there is to fear. In the speech classroom, students have indicated that they are far less nervous for their second speech than for their first. They are more comfortable with the audience and are more aware of the demands of the situation. The same is true in other settings as well: careful analysis of the audience and their expectations goes a long way toward reducing a natural fear of the unknown.

6. *Speak in public as often as you can*. Sheer repetition of the public speaking experience will not eliminate your fears, but it will make them more controllable. As noted above, speaking a number of times in front of the same group can help reduce anxiety. Repeated experiences with different audiences and situations also will help increase your self-assurance and your poise; this, in turn, will lessen your apprehension. As a student, force yourself to speak up in class discussions, join in on informal discussions with friends and others, and contribute verbally in meetings of organizations to which you belong. Outside of school, find time to talk with people of all ages; attend public meetings on occasion and make a few comments.

In summary, there are few easy ways to develop self-confidence about speaking in public. For most of us, gaining self-confidence is partly a matter of psyching ourselves up, and partly a matter of experience. The sick feeling in the pit of your stomach probably will always be there, at least momentarily, but it need not paralyze you into inaction or avoidance of the situation. As you become more proficient in meeting the demands of the essential steps—from selecting a subject to practicing the speech—your self-confidence and self-image as a speaker will grow. Certainly you will make mistakes of judgment, but each one is an opportunity to learn something about the complex process of communicating your ideas to others. Overall, your attention and energy will turn to your subject and your audience, and your fears will recede. You will find that you possess the requisite skill to control your anxiety and to succeed in presenting your ideas.

Communicating Confidence. If you are now ready to present your first speech, you may be asking, "How shall I deliver my message? Developing self-confidence is fine, but what can I do that will help to convey that self-confidence to an audience?" The following guidelines should assist you in communicating self-confidence.

1. *Be yourself.* Act as you would if you were having an animated conversation with a friend. Avoid an excessively rigid, oratorical, or aggressive posture. At the same time, don't become so comfortable in front of the group that you are leaning on the wall behind you or sprawling all over the lectern. When you speak, you want the minds of the listeners to be focused on your ideas, not on the manner of their presentation. Anything unnatural or unusual—anything that shifts attention from matter to manner—should be avoided. This attitude will help convey to the audience that you and the situation are a natural fit.

2. *Look at your listeners.* Watch the faces of your listeners for clues to their reactions. Without this essential information, you will be unable to gauge the ongoing effectiveness of your speech. You will be unable to assess what minor, but prompt, adjustments are needed to insure that your message is being heard as you intended. People tend to mistrust anyone who does not look them in the eye. They also may get the impression that you do not care about them, that you are not interested in their reaction to your message. Thus, include them directly by making contact with them. You will find your listeners attentive to you when you are attentive to them.

3. *Communicate with your body as well as your voice.* Realize that as a speaker you are being seen as well as heard. Movements of the body, gestures of the arms and head, changes in facial expression—all can help clarify and reinforce your ideas. Keep your hands at your sides so that when you feel an impulse to gesture, you can easily do so. If you find yourself in a situation without a lectern, don't be afraid to let your notes show. If you are working from a speaking outline, use a hard backing to hold the papers firm (your potential nervousness will be less visible as well). If you have note cards, hold them up so that you can see them clearly, rather than hiding them and then making reference to them both obvious, time consuming, and difficult. Avoid the impulse to curl papers or to fold cards, only to uncrumple them to see your notes. Let other movements of your body respond as your feelings and message dictate. Do not force your actions, but do not hold them back when they seem natural and appropriate to your message. In maintaining your self-confidence, remember that the tremor in your voice or your hand is not nearly as noticeable to your audience as it is to you. Be your natural self and let bodily responses flow from the act of communicating.

In this chapter, we have previewed the essential steps for planning and preparing speeches and have dealt with the tasks of gaining and holding attention and of developing and communicating confidence. The advice we have presented is not foolproof, and we know of none that is; thus, you will need to adapt what is said here to the speaking situation you are preparing for. We recognize that your best efforts may not meet with initial success; it takes time and experience to develop solid, usable skills.

These caveats aside, we are convinced that if you begin working on your speeches—thinking about them, planning how to gain and hold your audience's attention, researching and arranging your materials into a cogent outline—as soon as you know you will be delivering them, you will enjoy successes that will increase your self-confidence and effectiveness.

This chapter has stressed one key to success in speechmaking—the ability to ask and to answer important questions *before* you stand up to speak. By asking pivotal questions about your subject matter, your audience, the occasion, your purposes, your central idea or claim, the material that ought to be included, the effective arrangement of your ideas, and your own delivery habits, you can avoid problems before they appear. A central task in successful speechmaking is to make conscious, strategically sound rhetorical choices. Mastering this task will help build and maintain your self-confidence and will enable you to communicate that sense of sureness and control to an audience.

Sample Speech

The following speech by Deanna Sellnow, a student at North Dakota State University, focuses audience attention on the shortcomings in the methods of determining a person's credit rating. Beginning with an apt illustration, Deanna proceeds to demonstrate that problems do exist, and that they have potentially harmful consequences for unsuspecting consumers seeking credit. The topic is of current concern and has the potential to affect the speaker and the members of her audience. Notice, as you read Deanna's speech, her clear indication of the points to be covered, her careful use of transitions, and her use of varied support materials (statistics, quotations, examples). The claim governing this speech is "The current system of reporting credit ratings fails to adequately protect consumers."

Have You Checked Lately?[6]
Deanna Sellnow

John Pontier, of Boise, Idaho, was turned down for insurance because a reporting agency informed the company that he and his wife were addicted to narcotics, and his Taco Bell franchise had been closed down by the health board when dog food had been found mixed in with the tacos. There was only one small problem. The information was made up. His wife was a practicing Mormon who didn't touch a drink, much less drugs, and the restaurant had never been cited for a health violation.   /1

An isolated case? A little dramatic, maybe, but I'm not so sure it was an isolated case. Few would argue with the contention of lenders that a financial background check is a price consumers must pay for the convenience of credit. But what are they really getting? The issue I would like to explore today is that of the accuracy of credit reporting. In exploring this topic, I think we need to try to identify some of the shortcomings involved in the current practices of credit reporting, identify why these shortcomings come about, and, finally, identify some measures we might take to improve the credit reporting system.   /2

Credit bureaus, private firms that exist by selling credit information, according to a July, 1982, issue of *U.S. News and World Report,* compile more than 25 million reports each year on consumers' dealings. Now stored in their computers are data on more than half the U.S. population, information that may be exchanged among lenders at the push of a button. Oil companies, insurance agencies, department stores, travel and entertainment card companies, as well as banks and finance companies, base their decisions for granting credit on credit reports. The possibility of having a credit request denied awaits each and every one of us; and, thus, it seems that a more crucial question becomes: why do negative credit reports come about? Some are legitimate—but how many? You begin to wonder when you listen to some of the people in the industry.   /3

According to a July, 1982, issue of *U.S. News and World Report,* a former credit bureau employee told the Senate Banking Committee that he had completely invented 25% of his reports, and that he was far from alone in doing so. One investigator even gave a clean bill of health to an applicant who turned out to be dead! Angele Khachadour, chief counsel to the State Insurance Commissioner of California, reported on one of the few studies done on credit reviews. The conclusion of this late 1960's study suggested that "nine out of every ten policy rejections were based on moral grounds, often bearing only tenuous connections to actuality." Despite the 1975 California legislative action to curtail this problem, Khachadour reports in a 1979 issue of *Saturday Review* that it is still common practice. So as you listen to the people in the industry, you really begin to wonder what's going on in the world of credit reporting.   /4

Why do these shortcomings come about? We really can't blame the government for this one. The importance of this issue was recognized by Congress in 1974 when they passed the Equal Credit Opportunity Act prohibiting discriminating in the granting of credit on the basis of sex and marital status. In 1976, it was amended to include race, color, religion, national origin, and age as characteristics. And, in 1977, the Federal Trade Commission decided to devote a significant percentage of its resources to the handling of credit abuse problems.   /5

Why, then, do these shortcomings come about? In part, because of the creativity and unprofessionalism of the investigators, and in part, because of the format the industry uses for credit reporting. I've already mentioned the investigator who testified to the fact that he had invented 25% of the information. That's certainly creative. How about the unprofessional behavior? Why does that occur?   /6

Pressures of completing a quota of reports is one significant factor. Theodore P. Von-Brand, presiding official of the Federal Trade Commission, stated, in his 16,000 page review of the system, that:

> "field representatives staggering beneath an impossible burden of reports—fifteen to twenty per day—often compensate by contacting unqualified sources, fake sources, hurry through interviews, and frequently fail to ask a full range of questions."

A limited time factor also contributes to his unprofessionalism. According to a 1979 issue of *Saturday Review,* the credit investigator is expected to speak to the applicant and two other people who know him, usually neighbors or business associates, when making a report. He is expected to ask each individual up to 30 questions in 20 minutes. A final major problem for these investigators is the unavailability of informants. According to James Traub, in a 1979 issue of *Saturday Review,* the investigators usually work during the day, so it is sometimes difficult to locate people. Also, asking for so much detailed and impressionistic information in such a short time span, the investigation leaves itself open to inaccuracy. Be it pressures, limited time, or unavailable informants, unprofessional behavior does occur. /7

And how about the other part of it—the format used in credit reporting—how does that account for shortcomings? /8

The first format in use today, and the most widely used, is the judgmental method. According to a 1982 issue of the *Journal of Marketing,* its framework consists of the three *c*'s of credit: character, capacity, and capital. The investigator asks questions about the applicant's use of alcohol or narcotics—how much, how often, what kind, when, where— whom he is living with if not his wife, whether there is anything adverse about his reputation, lifestyle, and home environment, and if there are any reports of domestic troubles or dubious business practices. A major inadequacy of this approach is the source of the information. California's Angele Khachadour points out that neighbors simply don't know each other as well as they used to. /9

A second and more modern approach to credit reporting is the credit scoring system. This system proposes to eliminate such problems as credit officer error and irrelevant sources of information. According to Noel Capon, associate professor of Business at Columbia University, in the Spring, 1982, issue of the *Journal of Marketing,* the critical distinction between the credit scoring system and the judgmental method is that the credit scoring system is concerned solely with statistical predictability. Results from an interview with William Fair, chairman of Fair, Isaac, and Company, leading developer of credit scoring systems, indicate that any individual characteristic that can be scored, then, has potential for inclusion in the credit scoring system. Given the concern for creditworthiness, it is difficult to believe that some of the criteria revealed in the interview, such as hair color, zip code, and left- or right-handedness, are accepted components for prediction. According to a 1982 issue of *Credit Card Retailing,* this sole use of statistical prediction may also violate the constitutional guarantees of equal protection and due process clauses of the Fifth and Fourteenth Amendments. /10

While there is probably no way to guarantee that the investigators will do the job in the manner which they should, we can do something to insure that those seeking credit get a fair hearing. /11

We don't need government action this time. We need individual initiative. It is up to us, the consumers, to make use of the rights granted to us under the Equal Credit Opportunity Act and its amendments. If you haven't done so lately, check your credit records for errors and omissions. Tracking down the bureau that has your file—and believe me, if you have ever applied for credit you have a file—is relatively simple. The agencies are usually listed in the Yellow Pages, or you can contact them through your local Better Business Bureau. According to a March, 1979, issue of *Business Week,* most bureaus charge between three and eight dollars per interview. If you have any complaint, the bureau must either investigate it, or you have the right to submit a "Statement of Dispute" which becomes a permanent part of your file. Should the bureau refuse to resolve the dispute, you could also do as John Pontier did, and sue. /12

It is best to check your file for accuracy before you even apply for credit. Even if you have had some credit in the past and/or if you are applying for the first time and find yourself turned down for a loan, mortgage, or some other type of credit, the lender must furnish the name and address of the bureau which supplied the information. And, in that case, you are entitled to a free copy of your file. /13

Within the industry, we need to urge bureaus to rely less on third-party reports, or solely on statistics. The goal of unbiased credit judgments, which the credit scoring system employs, should be adapted to incorporate the relevant credit history which the judgmental method attempts to reveal.   /14

When all is said and done, the major solution rests on our shoulders. We have the right to see our files and verify their validity. There is no reason for us to wait until, like John Pontier, of Boise, Idaho, we are denied the credit we deserve. We can, and should, check our files before we fall victim to inaccurate, irrelevant, and unmerited credit reports.   /15

Sample Speech

The following speech is by Chui Lee Yap, a student at Ohio University. The topic is well chosen—it is one the speaker has personal experience with and cares deeply about. Further, it is relevant to a college audience, most of whose members are "victims" of the ethnocentrism that yields ignorance of languages other than one's own. Notice, as you read the speech, the use of examples—some humorous, others serious—to demonstrate the claim that "Ignorance of foreign languages is harmful to the United States."

Ethnocentrism[7]
Chui Lee Yap

Sociologist Aldous Huxley once said, "Most ignorance is vincible ignorance. We don't know because we don't want to know." Many Americans today are facing a serious problem, a deeply rooted problem of which they are unfortunately ignorant. The problem they choose to ignore is the overwhelming ignorance of foreign cultures and languages. The lack of foreign knowledge on the part of the majority of Americans has caused a severe problem to the United States in both the political and economic worlds. It affects not only America's ability to interact successfully with other nations, but tarnishes the image of the United States in the international arena as well.   /1

In order to understand how harmful language and cultural ignorance can be, we have to first examine its roots in the present educational system, and how it affects the business, political, and foreign attitudes towards Americans.   /2

The educational system is the seed of the problem. It is here that the ignorance is nourished. According to a Presidential Commission Report on Foreign Language and International Studies (1979), a study of American school children's world knowledge revealed that 40% of high school seniors could not locate Egypt on a map, and that 20% could not locate France or China.   /3

Furthermore, in the March 13, 1979, issue of the New York *Times,* it was reported that Americans were ranked next to the last in the comprehension of foreign cultures in a study conducted by UNESCO of 30,000 ten- to fourteen-year-old students. In another assessment of the world knowledge among high school seniors, according to *Change* magazine, October, 1978, 40% of them thought Israel was an Arab nation and that Golda Meir was the president of Egypt.   /4

On the college level, according to Congressman Paul Simon in 1980, the United States remained the only country in the world to allow anyone to graduate without a year of foreign language prior to and including the university years. Today many colleges still do not have any foreign language requirements for graduation.   /5

In a study done at the University of Miami, released in February of this year (1983), 43% of the college students surveyed could not locate London on a map.   /6

The ignorance generated by the educational system has spread to other aspects of daily life. The impact is felt especially when the economy of the country is affected. Foreign trade is very important to the U.S. economy. It directly provides one-sixth of the manufacturing and one-third of the farm jobs in the U.S. The ignorance of its importance is translated in the 1980 Roper Poll which revealed that 49% of the Americans surveyed believed foreign trade "was either irrelevant or harmful to the U.S. economy."   /7

Language and cultural ignorance further worsen the foreign trade situation and have in fact embarrassed Americans in a number of instances. The following examples serve to illustrate this lack of knowledge and its somewhat humiliating consequences. "Body by Fisher," a General Motors product, was translated as "Corpse by Fisher" in Flemish. Schweppes Tonic Water was advertised as "bathroom water" in Italy. A laundry soap ad in Quebec promised its users "clean genitals." Cue Toothpaste, a Colgate Palmolive product, was advertised in France seemingly without errors. But Cue happened to be the name of a widely circulated book on oral sex. "Come alive with Pepsi" was almost advertised in the Chinese version of *Reader's Digest* as "Pepsi brings your ancestors back from the grave."   /8

These may be humorous incidences, but they can become more serious in the political world. The lack of international knowledge can prove to be very embarrassing to the people of the U.S.   /9

This is illustrated in the following rather well-known example. President Carter, as a representative of this country, was in Poland in 1977. His wish to "learn the opinions and understand your desires for the future" came out in translation by his personal translator as "I desire the Poles carnally." This was reported in the September 30, 1977, issue of *The Times* of London and other major newspapers throughout the world.   /10

The seriousness of language ignorance is further aggravated when the security of the country is put into jeopardy. Most area specialist officers in the Executive Branch, including those in the intelligence services, do not and often cannot read the important material in its original form. They also cannot converse in their foreign counterparts' native language besides mere pleasantries.   /11

This embarrassing situation is not aided by the fact that the State Department no longer requires any background in foreign language as a condition of entry into foreign service. In 1980, no one in the U.S. embassy in India spoke Hindi. In the same year, none of the staff in the European division of the Office of the Secretary of Defense, who dealt mainly with base site negotiations, spoke any German or French.   /12

Allen Kassof, Executive Director of the National Council on Foreign Language and International Studies, implied in a 1980 lecture that language ignorance could very well have been the cause of failure to the SALT II treaty. The office of the Secretary of Defense has about 1,500 employees, yet only one job was specially reserved for someone with foreign language capabilities and that job was for a Russian-speaking SALT treaty coordinator. This post was filled by someone who did not speak Russian.   /13

The ignorance of William P. Clark, Deputy Secretary of State, was translated in the following headlines. He was called a "nitwit" in *De Volkstrant,* an Amsterdam daily; "Ask me another" wrote the *Daily Express* of London; and "For all practical purposes, he knows nothing of foreign policy" said the Soviet press agency *Tass*. Mr. Clark had admitted to the Senate Foreign Relations Committee that he did not know the names of the prime ministers of Zimbabwe and South Africa.   /14

From the political and business spheres foreign attitudes towards Americans are formulated. Here is an example: Hsu's postulate of the U.S. culture by Francis Hsu, a native of China who has become one of the world's leading anthropologists as well as one of the most perceptive observers of the culture of the U.S. He postulates (1) An individual's most important concern is his self-interest: self-expression, self-development, and self-gratification. This takes precedence over all group interests. (2) The U.S. has a mission to spread Americanism to all the nations of the world. Obstructions to the spread of Americanisms are intolerable and must be destroyed (by war if necessary) until good prevails.   /15

From this it can be observed that many Americans are being perceived as being uncaring when it comes to the cultures of other countries; a feeling that is resented in most parts of the world.   /16

But Huxley said, "Most ignorance is vincible ignorance"; therefore, there is a solution. My talking to you could be a start. Emphasis on foreign studies and studying abroad could be some of the ways of changing the attitudes of many Americans. You, too, can help by attending as many seminars offered by the International Studies program as possible. Their seminars are usually free; and do encourage your friends to go along. And if such a program does not exist at your university, encourage other campus organizations to hold seminars on international education to promote understanding of foreign cultures and language.   /17

But perhaps the most basic way in which you can help is by looking around you, at your forensics team members. How many of your team members are international students? An academic environment is one of the best in which to meet and interact with students of cultural and language backgrounds. Communication is the essence of the forensics team. We, as communicators, should make the effort to bridge the cultural and language gaps that presently exist.   /18

We live in a revolutionary world, not only in a political, economic, or social sense, but intellectual and cultural as well. To meet the challenges of today's revolutionary world requires the elimination of yesterday's habit of mind which insists that education is only the familiarity of one's own culture and historical heritage. Cure of the problem of ignorance involves the understanding of peoples and cultures that have long been neglected in the American educational system. As Huxley implied, cure of our not knowing is our wanting to know.   /19

REFERENCE NOTES

[1]For a review of current research on attention, see Gordon A. Hale and Michael Lewis, eds., *Attention and Cognitive Development* (New York: Plenum Press, 1979); and Michael R. A. Chance and Ray R. Larsen, ed., *The Social Structure of Attention* (New York: John Wiley, 1976).

[2]From "Women in Leadership Can Make a Difference" by Geraldine Ferraro, *Representative American Speeches,* 1982–1983. Reprinted by permission of Geraldine Ferraro.

[3]For a lucid discussion of the general nature of attention, see Eleanor Gibson and Nancy Rader, "Attention: The Perceiver as Performer," in *Attention and Cognitive Development,* ed. Gordon A. Hale and Michael Lewis (New York: Plenum Press, 1979), pp. 1–22. The guides are adapted from their discussion of attention from the perceiver's perspective.

[4]Gibson and Rader, p. 18.

[5]James McCroskey, "Oral Communication Apprehension: A Summary of Current Theory and Research," *Human Communication Research,* 4 (1977), 78–96.

[6]From "Have You Checked Lately?" by Deanna Sellnow. Reprinted from *Winning Orations,* 1983, by special arrangement with the Interstate Oratorical Association, Larry Schnoor, Executive Secretary, Mankato State University, Mankato, Minnesota.

[7]From "Ethnocentrism" by Chui Lee Yap. Reprinted from *Winning Orations,* 1983, by special arrangement with the Interstate Oratorical Association, Larry Schnoor, Executive Secretary, Mankato State University, Mankato, Minnesota.

PROBLEMS AND PROBES

1. Listed below are three groups of statements about a single topic. Taken as a whole, what does each set of statements claim—what is the central idea expressed in each set? Write what you believe to be the central idea for each set of statements. Meet in small groups in class and compare your phrasing of the central idea with those by others in the group. Prepare a written report with a summary of the best statements of the central idea that your group arrives at.
   a. (1) Many prison facilities are inadequate.
      (2) Low rates of pay result in frequent job turnovers in prisons.
      (3) Prison employees need on-the-job training.
   b. (1) High schools are not demanding enough from students.
      (2) Math skills have declined over several years.
      (3) Verbal skills have declined over several years.
   c. (1) Student fees for athletic events are high.
      (2) Costs for student health services are exorbitant.
      (3) Campus entertainment (films, rock concerts) costs more than it should.

2. Select a general subject area for an in-class speech of three to four minutes. Work through each of the steps in phase one (see pp. 38–41); write a brief essay indicating the process involved in narrowing the subject, determining the general and specific purposes, and determining the central idea or claim. In addition, briefly analyze the audience and occasion: What major concerns need to be considered in developing a speech for this audience and occasion?

3. Attend a lecture on campus or in your community. As you listen to the speaker, concentrate on the manner or method of presentation: Has the speaker thought through the essential steps outlined in this chapter and responded adequately to each? Write a brief report which focuses on what the speaker does well and/or poorly in meeting each of the steps.

ORAL ACTIVITIES

1. Following the principles and guidelines presented in this chapter, prepare a three- to four-minute speech to inform. Narrow the topic carefully so that you can do justice to it in the allotted time. Concentrate on developing ways to gain and hold the audience's attention. Hand in an outline along with a brief analysis of the audience and occasion when you present the speech. In your analysis, indicate why you think your approach to attention will work in this situation.

2. Listen to the first speeches delivered in class. What strategies are employed to gain and hold attention during the speeches? Are these effective strategies? What would be more effective uses of the devices discussed in this chapter? Be prepared to discuss your reactions in class.

3. Listen to the first speeches delivered in class. How confident are the speakers? If they are nervous, how do they control their nervous energy? Are their techniques successful? Be prepared to discuss your reactions in class.

PART TWO

PUBLIC SPEAKING:

Preparation and Adaptation to the Audience

CHAPTER 4

Choosing Speech Subjects
and Purposes

In Chapter 3 we surveyed briefly the steps involved in preparing a speech. In this chapter we will discuss more fully the first two of these steps—selecting a suitable subject and determining the central concerns or purposes of the speech. These two tasks demand that you consider several interrelated questions about yourself and your interests, your audience, and the occasion, because you, your listeners, and the situation are bonded together by what you are speaking about and why you are speaking about it. Although you may decide to adjust your subject matter and your purposes as you proceed through later steps in the speech preparation process, you nevertheless should do some early decision making about these matters.

Selecting the Subject

On many occasions, the subject of your speech will be predetermined, at least in part, by the group you are addressing. If you are speaking at a public hearing on a proposed rezoning of your neighborhood, your topic already is circumscribed by the announced purpose of the meeting. In other circumstances, however, you must exercise choice in subject matters. You must do so, of course, in a speech classroom. Or, if you are to speak to a Rotary Club on some aspect of business economics, you might be faced with several possible topics—should you discuss labor relations or computerized spreadsheets or off-season advertising campaigns? And when addressing a school board meeting devoted to "a nation at risk" in its educational achievements, you may wish to urge the adoption of better elementary textbooks, special reading programs, or high school competency testing.

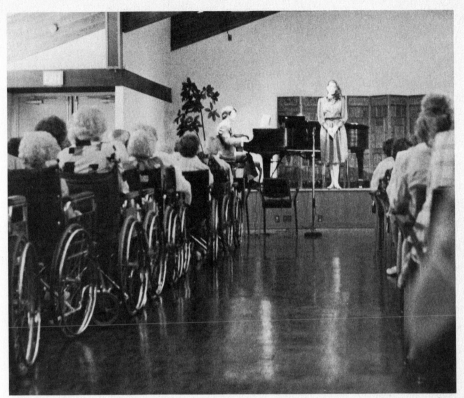

Make a speech subject appropriate to your listeners' situation and attitudes. Draw upon their present circumstances and consider what's relevant to their condition.

When confronted with the task of choosing a subject, observe the following basic guidelines:

Select a subject about which you already know something and can find out more. Knowledge you already possess can guide your efforts to find a suitable focus, to distinguish between good and bad ideas, to assess areas in which your knowledge is thin, to know where to locate additional and updated materials, and to tailor your talk to the specific audience you face. Also, of course, you'll be a more confident—and hence probably more successful—speaker if you talk from personal knowledge rather than second-hand information.

Select a subject that is interesting to you. Some speakers seek a topic to impress an audience, whether or not they are personally interested in it. That way of thinking can lead to disaster. If you are not interested in what you are discussing, you will find preparation dull, and, more important, your presentation probably will reflect your lack of motivation and enthusiasm.

Select a subject that will interest your audience. Another temptation for some speakers is to force a topic on an audience because "it's good for them." That method also is unproductive. Remember that whatever the topic, it is the *speaker's* responsibility to make it interesting to an audience. A topic may be of interest to listeners for one or more of the following reasons:

1. It concerns their health, happiness, or security. For instance, you might talk to a senior citizens group about changes in Medicare regulations.
2. It offers a solution to a recognized problem. You might suggest new ways your citizen action group can raise needed money.
3. It is surrounded by controversy or conflict of opinion.

Select a topic appropriate to the occasion. A demonstration speech on break-dancing might go over very well as an informative speech in your classroom, but it probably would be out of place at a senior citizens' center arts and crafts demonstration.

In sum, remember that even when you are assigned a topic, you still need to approach it in ways that play off your own strengths, reflect interests you and your audience share, and are appropriate to the occasion. If you have difficulty thinking of such a topic, study the list of subject categories at the end of this chapter. Those topics, of course, are very general, but if you think about narrower aspects of each one—our next concern—you will find them helpful.

Narrowing the Topic

A topic is nothing more than a broad area of human endeavor. Before it is suitable for a speech, it must be narrowed down to manageable size. Narrowing involves three primary considerations:

Narrow your subject so that you can discuss it adequately in the time you have. In a ten-minute speech, you cannot cover adequately "The Rise and Fall of Baseball as the Premier American Sport." Instead, you might describe three or four changes baseball has made in response to television coverage. Fit the breadth of your topic to the time available.

Gauge your subject so that it is neither above nor below the comprehension level of your audience. If, for example, you want to talk about laser technology to an audience of beginning students, you might choose to describe only its most basic principles; to a group of physics majors, however, you probably would explain in technical terms its latest applications.

Narrow your subject to meet the specific expectations of your audience. An audience which comes to a meeting expecting to hear about gun safety will probably be distraught if, instead, you lecture on the need for stricter gun-control laws. The announced purpose of the meeting, the demands of particular contexts, and other group traditions can affect an audience's expectations of what it is to hear.

In other words, narrowing a topic involves sorting through all of the things you could say in order to find one, two, or three points you can establish, clarify, and support in the time you have available. For example, suppose you decide to talk informatively about gardening. Within that subject are countless narrower topics, including:

- the growth of personal or hobby gardening over the last decade (facts and figures on clubs, seed sales, the home canning industry, and so on);

- methods for preserving homegrown vegetables (canning vs. freezing vs. drying vs. cold storage);
- soil enrichment (varieties of natural and artificial fertilizers, the strengths and weaknesses of each);
- factors to consider when selecting vegetables to plant (plot size, family eating habits, amount of time available for tending, cost of supermarket vegetables of each type);
- available strains of any given vegetable (selection of seeds based on geography, climate, soil characteristics, regional pests/bacteria, uses to which vegetables will be put, germination and heartiness);
- literature on gardening (library books, television programs, governmental pamphlets, magazines, seed catalogs, fertilizer company brochures);
- varieties of gardening tools (inexpensive hand tools, medium-cost hand tools, expensive power machinery);
- year-round gardening (window-box gardening, "grow" lights, cold frames, hot frames, greenhouses).

Given this list of subtopics, your procedures for narrowing might run something like this:

1. *Subjects I know something about:*
   methods for preserving homegrown food
   soil enrichment
   literature on gardening
   varieties of gardening tools
   year-round gardening

2. *Subjects interesting to me:*
   all except soil enrichment

3. *Subjects interesting to audience* (a 4-H club):
   methods for preserving homegrown food
   literature on gardening
   year-round gardening

4. *Subjects appropriate to occasion* (demonstration speech):
   all three are appropriate

5. *Topics I can talk about in the available time* (note narrowing):
   one or *two* methods of preserving homegrown food
   two or *three* kinds of gardening literature
   one kind of year-round gardening

6. *Topics I can fit to the audience comprehension level:*
   Because 4-H club members are experienced gardeners,
   —don't discuss home food preservation, as most of them already know a lot about this subtopic;
   —don't discuss gardening literature, as few of these kids want to spend more time reading about gardening; in the past they've found it easier to learn from other gardeners than from books;

—they've shown interest before in the topic of year-round gardening (when Henry did a speech on "grow" lights, they followed him easily and enthusiastically)

7. *Topics which will meet their expectations for a 4-H demonstration project:* year-round gardening, specifically, how to build an inexpensive homemade greenhouse

In other words, selecting and narrowing a topic involves: *(1)* probing yourself and your experience for topics about which you are knowledgeable and interested; *(2)* thinking about your audience's interests and abilities; *(3)* considering the demands of the occasion; and *(4)* narrowing the topic according to the decision-criteria which lead you to a particular subtopic you can cover adequately *(a)* in the time available and *(b)* in accordance with audience and situational expectations. All of this may seem like a complicated chore, yet if you attack it systematically, you often can move easily through the rest of your speech preparation.

Determining the Purposes

Once you know what you want to talk about, the next questions you face deal with a series of "whys" already implicit in much that has been said: Why do *you* wish to discuss this subject? Why might an *audience* want to listen to you? Why is what you wish to discuss appropriate to *the occasion*? You should approach these "whys" in three ways: first, think about *general purposes* (the reasons people generally have when they speak in public); next, consider the *specific purposes* (the concrete goals you wish to achieve in a particular speech); and then, focus your thoughts on the *central idea* or *claim* (the statement of the guiding thought you wish to communicate). In addition, you'll probably want to put into words *the working title* of your speech. Selecting a provisional title early in the preparation process helps you keep your primary emphasis in focus and lets you announce it to others ahead of the actual presentation.

General Purposes

In most public speaking situations, you address listeners in order to inform, to entertain, to persuade, or to move them to action:

General Purpose	Audience Response Sought
To inform	Clear understanding
To entertain	Enjoyment and comprehension
To persuade	Acceptance of ideas or
or actuate	recommended behaviors

Usually you talk to others publicly because you possess some knowledge of potential relevance and benefit to them, or because you hope to alter their fundamental beliefs about the world, their attitudes toward life, or the actions they have been or ought to be taking. Hence, to inform and to persuade or actuate are the dominant general purposes of most speeches.

THE GENERAL ENDS OF SPEECH

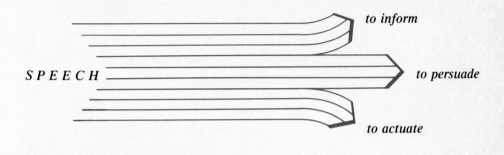

On some occasions, however, either because of the occasion or because of your personal talents, you may seek to entertain an audience, in the process giving them some ideas to think about. Those ideas to think about often are similar to the subject matters of informative and persuasive talks, and so the speech to entertain, in many ways, is a species of the other two general kinds of speeches. Yet, because the techniques and the general strategies you employ in speeches to entertain differ substantially from those used in speeches to inform and to persuade or actuate, we will discuss this general purpose separately. Most of this book, however, will be devoted to informative and persuasive speaking. For now, let's briefly examine each of these three general purposes.

To inform.   When your overall object is to help listeners understand an idea or comprehend a concept or process, or when you seek to widen the range of their knowledge, the general purpose of your speech will be to inform. Such is the goal of scientists who report their research results to colleagues, of public figures who address community groups on subjects on which they are expert, of college lecturers and work supervisors.

To evoke a response of understanding, you must change the level or quality of information possessed by listeners. By providing examples, statistics, illustrations, and other materials offering data and ideas, you seek to expand or alter their reservoir of knowledge. That change alone, however, may not be sufficient to ensure understanding. Not only must an informative speech provide raw data, but its message and supporting materials must be structured and integrated in such a way that listeners perceive the import of the whole. For example, an informative speech on how to build a stereo set must include the necessary information and must present it in an orderly sequence of steps. Understanding in this instance depends not only on learning *what* to do, but also on knowing *when* to do it and *why*. Many of your listeners may already be familiar with

When your general purpose is to inform, consider carefully (1) how much information you can transmit in a single short speech, and (2) how you can use illustrations effectively.

much of your information and yet still lack understanding. They probably have not put the bits of information all together; your job as an informative speaker is to impart both knowledge and overall understanding.

In summary, when your purpose is to clarify a concept or process for your listeners, when you endeavor to explain terms or relationships, and when you strive in other ways to broaden the range of your listeners' knowledge, your objective is to inform. *The response you seek from an informative speech is primarily conceptual or cognitive— some adjustment in an audience's body of knowledge.* Several different types of speeches are considered informative: speeches of definition or denotation, demonstrations, oral instructions, reports from committees or task forces, lectures, and so forth. All have information-sharing as their primary thrust.

To entertain.   To entertain, amuse, or divert is frequently the purpose of an after-dinner speech, but talks of other kinds also may have enjoyment as their principal end. Often a travel lecture, even while presenting a good deal of information, entertains an audience with exciting or amusing tales of adventure. Club meetings, class reunions, and similar gatherings of friends and associates also provide occasions for speeches to entertain. In these situations, speakers often depend chiefly on humor in preparing speeches.

A speech to entertain, however, is *not* simply a comic monologue. The humor characteristic of speeches to entertain, rather, is normally highly purposive. Think of some of the great American humorists: Mark Twain used humor to inform Eastern audiences about life in the Midwest; Will Rogers used his radio talks and commentaries on political realities during the Depression to help create a sense of American unity and common effort; Art Buchwald never tires of showing us our foibles and moral dilemmas; Dick Cavett in the late 1960s used humor to inform audiences about venereal diseases, and, in a speech reprinted elsewhere in this book, talks with college students (humorously) about the importance of preserving the English language.

In short, a speech to entertain is both humorous and yet serious. Evening entertainments, parodies, satires, and most other forms of public-speaking humor are species of speeches to entertain. Because the skills they require of speakers are subtle and often difficult to master, we will discuss them late in this book, after you have basic speech-making competencies.

To persuade or actuate.   The purpose of a speech to persuade or actuate is to influence listeners' minds or actions. While it may be argued that all speeches are persuasive to some degree,[1] there are many situations in which speakers have outright persuasion as their primary purpose. Promoters and public relations experts try to make you believe in the superiority of certain products, persons, or institutions; lawyers seek to convince juries; social action group leaders exhort tenants to believe in the existence of landlord collusion; politicians debate campaign issues and strive to influence voters' thinking.

As a persuasive speaker, you usually seek to influence the beliefs and attitudes of your listeners. Sometimes, however, you will want to go a step further and try to move them to action. You may want them to contribute money, sign a petition, organize into a parade, or participate in a demonstration. The distinguishing feature of an actuative speech is that instead of stopping with an appeal to their beliefs or attitudes, you ask your listeners to alter their behavior in a specified way.

Because the speech to persuade or actuate characteristically is designed to influence or alter beliefs and actions of listeners, you should fill it with well-ordered arguments supported by facts, figures, and examples. Additionally, you will have to go beyond "the facts," for persuasion is a psychological as well as a logical process. You will need to make strong motivational appeals to tap into the needs and desires of listeners. The person able to change minds and move others to action, therefore, must be sensitive to both the rational and nonrational aspects of audience psychology—topics we will develop at some length shortly.

To inform, to entertain, and to persuade or actuate, then, are the general purposes a speech may have. General purposes comprise the basic types of speeches and, as such, are important as overall orientations to your thinking about public talks. But just as subjects have to be narrowed, so do purposes.

Specific Purposes

A second important way to think about speech purposes is to consider them specifically—that is, to think about the challenges related to a particular topic explored before an actual audience on a real occasion by you, a human being. *Specific purposes represent actual goals you want to achieve*. Though concrete, specific purposes can be extremely wide-ranging. Some of them you may verbalize; for example, you may tell

OVERT-COVERT PURPOSE OF SPEECH

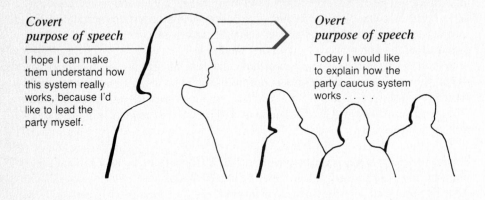

Covert
purpose of speech

I hope I can make them understand how this system really works, because I'd like to lead the party myself.

Overt
purpose of speech

Today I would like to explain how the party caucus system works . . . .

an audience what you want it to understand or do as a consequence of your speech. Some specific purposes are private, known only by you; for example, you probably hope to make a good impression on an audience, although you most likely would not say that aloud. Usually, a speech has short-term specific purposes and, occasionally, long-term specific purposes as well. If you are speaking to members of a local food cooperative on the virtues of baking their own bread, your short-term purpose might be to get people to go home that night and try out your recipe, while your long-term goal could be to have them change their food-buying and food-consuming habits.

Theoretically, you undoubtedly have any number of private and public, short-term and long-term specific purposes whenever you rise to speak. Practically, however, you will want to reduce that mass of goals to a dominant one. We thus may define *the* specific purpose as the precise response desired from the audience by the speaker. Formulated into a clear, concise statement, the specific purpose delineates exactly what you want the audience to understand, enjoy, feel, believe, or do.

Suppose, for example, that you are asked to explain to the Campus Democrats how the party's caucus works, in preparation for their actual participation in the county caucuses during an election year. You might have several purposes: to demonstrate that caucusing allows for full grassroots participation in the electoral process, to review step-by-step the actual procedures for forming "candidate preference groups" the night of the caucus, to explain what happens when a candidate preference group is not viable according to party rules, and even to show that you are a knowledgeable person and hence a potential leader. The first of these specific purposes is a long-range goal, the next two are short-term goals designed to prepare listeners for actual participation in the county caucuses, and the fourth is a private purpose. All of these specific goals can be summarized, however, in a statement of *the* specific purpose: "to show members of the Campus Democrats how they can effectively participate in the county presidential caucuses in an election year."

Central Ideas or Claims

Once you have settled upon the specific purpose, you are ready to translate that goal into concrete subject matter. You are ready to cast into words a central idea or claim (sometimes termed a *thesis statement*) which will form the controlling thought of your speech. A *central idea* is a statement which captures the essence of the information or concept you are attempting to communicate to an audience. A *claim* is a statement which phrases the belief, attitude, or action you wish an audience to adopt. Central ideas are characteristic of informative speeches (and some speeches to entertain), while claims form the core of persuasive, actuative, and some entertaining speeches.

The precise phrasing of central ideas and claims is all-important because your wording captures the essence of your subject matter and purpose, guiding audience expectations. Assume, for example, that you are to give an informative speech on building an inexpensive homemade greenhouse. You might decide to phrase your central idea for that speech in three ways:

> *Wording #1:* "With only a minimum of carpentry skills, even a teenager can build a homemade greenhouse."
>
> *Wording #2:* "With some creative searching around the home and neighborhood, anyone can build a homemade greenhouse for less than $150."
>
> *Wording #3:* "Building an inexpensive homemade greenhouse will allow you to start garden plants early and grow some crops year around."

Note that in the first version the stress is upon audience members' abilities to complete the technical aspects of the task. Presumably, the speech would offer a step-by-step description of the construction process—preparing the bed, pouring cement for the foundation, erecting the superstructure, and covering that structure with transparent materials. The second version suggests quite a different speech, one focused on securing the materials. It might discuss places to find scrapped lumber, ways to get old storm windows to use as the greenhouse's glassed surface, areas in the neighborhood where one can get free sand for the cement. And, in contrast, the third version would discuss the actual construction of the greenhouse only superficially (perhaps with a handout on the construction process), concentrating instead on interior design—which shelves to reserve for seedlings; which shelves to prepare for year-round crops such as tomatoes, herbs, peppers, miniature fruit trees; and the like.

Phrasing a claim or thesis statement is an even more crucial preparatory act than phrasing a central idea, because the wording you select can control several different aspects of your relationship with your audience. Note the following examples:

> Varying the audience's perception of the speaker's intensity:
>
> 1. "Do not eat cured pork because it is *unhealthy*."
> 2. "Do not eat cured pork because it is *carcinogenic*."
> 3. "Do not eat cured pork because it will *kill you*."

As you move from version one to version three, you are phrasing your feelings in progressively more intense language; each successive version expresses your attitude in harsher language.

Varying the reasons for taking some course of action:

1. "Make use of our school's Division of Career Planning because it can help you *plan your curriculum*."
2. "Make use of our school's Division of Career Planning because it will help you *select your major*."
3. "Make use of our school's Division of Career Planning because it will teach you how *to prepare résumés and to interview for jobs*."
4. "Make use of our school's Division of Career Planning because it will put you *in touch with employers*."

In these four examples, you are varying the rationales behind the actions you wish listeners to take. Presumably, one can take some course of action for any number of reasons; your claim should be phrased in a way that captures what you think will be the most compelling reasons for this *particular audience*.

Varying the evaluative criteria for judging something:

1. "The city's new landfill is an *eyesore*." [aesthetic judgment]
2. "The city's new landfill is a *health hazard*." [personal-safety judgment]
3. "The city's new landfill is a *political payoff to the rich companies which supported the council members' campaigns*." [political judgment]

Each of these claims condemns a civic project, but in a different way. The first version judges the landfill negatively on aesthetic grounds, the second, on safety grounds, and the third, on political grounds. Were you to advocate the first version, you would need to demonstrate that (a) aesthetic qualities are important criteria for judging landfills, and (b) the landfill indeed will be visible to a significant number of community members. For the second version, you would need to argue successfully that health hazards are a matter of public concern, then that this particular landfill allows hazardous materials to be deposited. And, in defending the third version you would need to document (a) the campaign contributions and (b) the fact that major users or beneficiaries of the depository are the companies which gave the most money to the successful candidates. In each case, then, the selection of a particular evaluative criterion controls the main features of the speech.

Consider also these examples which put together, overall, what we have been saying about general purposes, specific purposes, and central ideas or claims:

Subject: Cardiopulmonary Resuscitation (CPR).
General purpose: To inform.
Specific purposes:
- to explain the three life-saving steps of CPR.
- to interest the auditors in signing up for a CPR course.
- to impress upon listeners their social responsibilities relevant to CPR.
Central idea: "Cardiopulmonary resuscitation—CPR—is a three-step, life-saving technique for use in emergencies which anyone can learn."

Subject: Accident insurance for students.
General purpose: To actuate.
Specific purposes:
- to get members of the student council to approve the group insurance policy offered by the ABC Insurance Company.

- to provide inexpensive accident insurance for students currently without such protection.
- to demonstrate that the ABC Insurance Company is the best one available for the money.
- to overcome opposition from student council members and to remind the council of its obligations to its constituency.

Claim: "The student council should approve the purchase of the group accident policy offered by the ABC Insurance Company [because many students do not have access to accident insurance, because it is the duty of the student council to serve its constituency, and because ABC's policy is less expensive than others we have examined]."[2]

Carefully explore your general and specific purposes before you begin to construct a public message. A sensitivity to general purposes will guide your thinking about speech materials and their structure. And a realization of your specific purposes will allow you to understand your own hopes and fears, the range of effects you will potentially have upon your audience, and the measures by which you may gauge the effects. Considering thoughtfully both general and specific purposes also enables you to define central ideas or claims and thus capture in your mind the primary thrust or aim of your speech.

Wording the Working Title

To complete your initial thinking about purposes, you often will want to write down a working title. Although it may seem odd or even unnecessary to consider a title during the preliminary stages of speech preparation, think about the advantages of doing so: *(1)* A working title helps you, the speaker, capture the essence of your thoughts and feelings. It can serve as one of the guides you take with you through the rest of your preparatory work, helping you determine what's relevant and irrelevant, central and peripheral, to your upcoming speech. *(2)* Speakers often are required to announce titles ahead of speech delivery. Conventions and conferences always need them ahead of time, and even meetings of organizations you plan to address have agenda which can have titles listed in the call for the meeting.

Three guidelines should be kept in mind as you search for a working title:

1. *A title should be relevant to you, the audience, and the occasion.* If, for example, you are giving a speech on business and political ethics, you might consider a title such as "The Eleventh Commandment," as did the speaker who claimed that the commandment "Thou shalt not steal" has been supplemented in some business and political circles by another: "Thou shalt not get caught." The title had a little cleverness to it, and, as important, it was directly relevant to the speaker's claim and the subject matter.

2. *A title often should be provocative.* Former Speech Communication Association President Marie H. Nichols, during her presidential year (1969), barnstormed the country delivering a speech entitled "The Tyranny of Relevance," an attack on those who felt colleges and universities should be concerned primarily with such relevant courses as those in social action and personal exploration of existential experience. She found those courses potentially university-level courses, but feared

that absorption with "relevance" would cause students to lose sight of the other goals of higher education. Her title captured her spirit, engaged audiences, and helped listeners remember her message. As you think about making your title provocative, however, be sure it is also *productive*. Especially if an audience is hostile to your purpose, do not create irritation through your title; to entitle a speech for a women's political group "The Coddling of Women by Political Parties" is provocative, yes, but unlikely to gain a sympathetic hearing.

3. *The title of a speech should be brief.* Imagine the effect of announcing as a title "The Effects upon High-Track, Mean-Track, and Low-Track High School Juniors of Pretesting of Senior Year Competency Testings." A better choice might be "A Hair of the Dog? Reactions to High School Competency Pretests" or even "A Pretest in Time Saves Nine—Or More." These two may lack some precision, but, in the right context, are generally engaging, certainly more concise, and probably more provocative than the first.

One last comment: Remember that your working title is just that—something to start with. If, in the middle of gathering supporting materials, you become excited about some aspect of your subject matter you weren't going to address, go for it—and change your title. Even if you advertised a title, you almost always can change; further, in explaining the reasons for your change, you might even interest your audience more in your central idea or claim as they get caught up in your enthusiasm.

Selecting Subjects and Purposes: Strategic Choices

If you think of public speaking as eliciting specific mental or behavioral responses from others, and if you think about the selection processes we have reviewed in this chapter as helping you obtain those responses, you will realize that you have many conscious decisions to make even in these early stages of speech preparation. By way of summary, let us review some of the factors that will determine the actual decisions you must make.

Your Private or Ultimate Aim as a Speaker.   You must take into account your own interests and abilities as you select subjects and purposes. Few of us can talk convincingly about something we have no interest in; few of us dare move into specialized areas in which members of the audience are likely to be more expert than we are. Furthermore, at times we must think through carefully how much we are personally willing to risk in front of others. For example, suppose you work for a firm which, you are convinced, is patently sexist in its promotion policies—it seldom promotes women to managerial positions. You find you are given a chance to talk about promotions at an open meeting of the firm. How far do you go? And what do you say? Your *private aim* may be one of ventilation—getting some ideas and feelings off your chest. Your *ultimate aim,* however, is to get some women—perhaps even yourself—into managerial positions. A harangue on the evils of sexism, replete with threats to report the firm to an equal opportunity agency, might satisfy your private aim, but might well frustrate your ultimate aim by hardening others' resistance to change.[3] After thinking through the situation, you might decide on a less risky course—say an informative speech with the specific purpose of presenting a review of numbers of males and females promoted to managerial positions in the firm over the last ten years. You could also point out the number of females potentially ready for promotion within the company and discuss the "head-hunting" agencies which keep records of females interested in mangerial positions in firms such as yours. Casting your speech as an "informative" speech, rather than as an "actuative" speech urging a strong course of action, would allow you to unite your private and ultimate aims.

The Authority of the Listeners or Their Capacity to Act.   For a speaker to demand of a group of students that they "abolish all required courses" would be foolish if the final decision concerning course requirements is in the hands of the faculty. The audience is better advised to take actions within its range of capacities: "Conduct a college-wide survey of student attitudes toward required courses, and present the results of that survey at the next appropriate faculty meeting." As a speaker, limit your specific purposes and claims to behaviors that are clearly within the domain of your listeners' authority. Asking more will only frustrate them.

The Existing Attitudes of the Listeners.   A group of striking workers who believe they are badly underpaid and unfairly treated by their employer probably would be hostile to the suggestion that they return to work under the existing conditions. They might, however, approve submitting the dispute to arbitration by a disinterested person whose fairness and judgment they respect. If you are speaking to an audience whose attitude is hostile to your point of view, you might—by presenting only one speech— convince your listeners that there is something to be said on the other side of the question, but you would probably find it impossible to persuade them to take positive action on it. Your specific purpose, in short, must be adjusted not only to the authority but also to the attitudes of your listeners. Do not ask them for a response you cannot reasonably expect from people holding their particular feelings or beliefs.

The Nature of the Speech Occasion.   To ask for contributions to a political campaign fund might be appropriate at a pre-election rally, but to pursue this specific purpose at a memorial service would be decidedly out of place. An athletic awards ceremony is hardly the occasion on which to seek an understanding of how a catalytic converter works. The members of a little theater association would not want to engage in a discussion of finances between the acts of a play, though they might respond to a brief announcement urging their attendance at a business meeting where the budget will be discussed. Be sure that your specific purpose is adapted to the mood or spirit of the occasion on which you are to speak.

The Time Limits of the Speech.   You may be able in a few minutes to induce an audience that opposes your proposal to postpone action, but you almost certainly will need a much longer time if you hope to change your listeners' feelings and convictions enough to favor your position. Similarly, if your subject is complex, you may be able to inform your hearers, to get them to understand your proposal, in a fifteen-minute speech; but you may need much more time to convince them of its desirability. Do not attempt to get from your audience a response or outcome impossible to attain in the time available.

When you have selected your subject or an aspect of your subject and have determined your general and specific purposes on the basis of the five foregoing factors, your speech preparation will be off to a sound start. You will have a central idea or claim firmly phrased, and hence will be ready to gather your actual materials and to assemble them in ways relevant to yourself, your audience, and the occasion. You will have in hand some yardsticks against which to measure ideas and materials as you research your topic. Finally, you will have increased your self-confidence considerably—you will know better what you are trying to do and how you can go about it. Knowing those ''whats'' and ''hows'' will make you feel more secure in your speech preparation skills.

Subject Categories: Aids to Choosing Speech Topics

When you give speeches, especially in your speech class, we suggest that you study the list of subject categories. These categories are not speech subjects; rather, they are types or classes of material in which speech subjects may be found. To decide on a suitable subject for a public speech, consider them in terms of your own interests and knowledge, the interests of your audience, and the nature of the occasion on which you are to speak. A list of subject categories and possible topics is on pages 78–79.

REFERENCE NOTES

[1]It can be argued that all speeches are persuasive because, presumably, *any* change in a person's stock of knowledge, beliefs, attitudes, or ways of acting, represents a kind of adjustment of the human mechanism we can term the result of ''persuasion,'' as long as symbols were used to produce the change. See, for example, Kenneth E. Andersen, *Persuasion: Theory and Practice*, 2nd ed. (Boston: Allyn and Bacon, Inc., 1978), Chapter 1, ''The Nature of Persuasion.'' Psychologically, it may be impossible to separate ''informative'' and ''persuasive'' messages. Rhetorically, however—that is, in terms of types of speeches, kinds of responses desired, and even kinds of strategies employed—we can separate informative and persuasive speaking. Hence, you will find separate chapters devoted to each later in this book.

[2]Your claim statement may or may not include the reasons—the ''because'' clauses—which justify its acceptance. You may be better able to specify them once you have gone on to the next step, analyzing the audience.

[3]Theoretically, this ''hardening'' process can be explained by any number of psychological models. Within consistency theory (propounded by Percy Tannenbaum and his associates), we would say that any message that is inconsistent or ''discrepant'' with a person's other beliefs will cause that person to react negatively to it. What is called dissonance theory (offered by Leon Festinger and his colleagues) explains the hardening by arguing that when two perceptions clash explicitly, a person goes into a state of dissonance or ''disharmony''; and, because we all prefer to be in a state of consonance or

harmony, we must find some way of reducing the psychological pressure. Thus, we discredit the source of the message or the "facts" undergirding it. Similarly, work done by Muzafer Sherif and others at the University of Oklahoma stresses individuals' "latitudes of acceptance" and "latitudes of rejection." They have shown that each of us can tolerate rather easily certain amounts of information and certain expressions of attitudes counter to our own, but that we all have limits. Appeals to beliefs or attitudes or actions which represent relatively "small" adjustments—that is, fall within our latitudes of acceptance—are likely to be successful; but appeals that fall well outside our acceptable limits—within our latitudes of rejection—are likely to make us stronger than ever in our resistance to those ideas or actions. On topics where we have little information or little direct involvement, our latitudes of acceptance are very "wide," but on other topics where we think we know a lot and where we have strong opinions, those latitudes can be very "narrow." Part of your job as an analyst of an audience, therefore, is to gauge the degree of information and commitment of the auditors.

For reviews of these and other psychological explanations of hardening processes, see R. P. Abelson et al., eds., *Theories of Cognitive Consistency: A Sourcebook* (Chicago: Rand McNally, 1968); G. Lindzey and E. Aronson, eds., *The Handbook of Social Psychology,* 2nd ed., Vol. 1 (Reading, MA: Addison-Wesley, 1968), esp. R. B. Zajonc, "Cognitive Theories in Social Psychology," pp. 320–411. For more applicative discussions, see Herbert W. Simons, *Persuasion; Understanding, Practice, and Analysis* (Reading, MA: Addison-Wesley Pub. Co., 1976), Chapter 5, "Behavioral Theories of Persuasion," and Erwin P. Bettinghaus, *Persuasive Communication,* 3rd ed. (New York: Holt, Rinehart and Winston, 1980), esp. pp. 37–49.

PROBLEMS AND PROBES

1. This chapter makes clear that, for each speech, the speaker must take *occasion* into account. Consider your "classroom occasion"—the room itself, your classmates, and your instructor. How will you decide on your speech topic? You might send around a brief questionnaire asking other students where they stand on several issues that are important to you. Your classmates' answers will give you a composite of their interests. This should help you to decide what your general purpose in speaking might be as well as your specific purpose. (For example, if most of your classmates are already engaged in a daily exercise program, you would probably not want to make a speech to convince them they should begin exercising.)

2. Attend a speech on campus along with several other members of your class. As you listen to the speech, assess the following elements:
    a. the speaker's general purpose, probable specific purposes, and central idea or claim;
    b. the major ideas of the speech; and
    c. the speaker's attempts to use factual and authoritative materials gathered with this particular audience in mind.
Later, discuss your findings with other members attending the session. Compare your judgments and try to explain any differences of opinion.

3. Using the listening skills that you learned from Chapter 2, listen to a radio news magazine such as National Public Radio's "All Things Considered." (Check your local public radio station for time.) Even if you haven't listened much to news radio, you should find such in-depth news reports interesting. Listen to at least one night's news. Take notes during the broadcast. See if you can report to someone else what you heard. In your journal, note your listening problem areas.

SUBJECT CATEGORIES

AIDS TO CHOOSING SPEECH TOPICS

The beginning speaker often has difficulty in selecting a suitable speech subject. If you find yourself in this situation, we suggest that you study the following list of subject categories. These categories are not speech subjects; rather, they are types or classes of materials in which speech subjects may be found. To decide upon a suitable subject for a public speech, consider your own interests and knowledge, the interests of your audience, and the nature of the occasion on which you are to speak.

PERSONAL EXPERIENCE

1. Jobs you have held
2. Places you have been
3. Military service
4. The region you come from
5. Schools you have attended
6. Friends and enemies
7. Relatives you like and dislike
8. Hobbies and pastimes

FOREIGN AFFAIRS

1. Foreign-policy aims
   What they are
   What they should be
2. The implementation of policy aims
3. Ethics of foreign-policy decisions
4. History of the foreign policy of the United States (or of some other nation)
5. Responsibility for our foreign policy
6. How foreign policy affects domestic policy
7. War as an instrument of national policy
8. International peace-keeping machinery

DOMESTIC AFFAIRS

1. Social problems:
   Crime
   The family: marriage, divorce, adjustments
   Problems of cities
   Problems of rural areas
   Problems of races and ethnic groups
   Problems of juveniles or the aged
   Child abuse
   Abortion, adoption
   The drug culture
   Sexual mores
   Pollution
2. Economic problems:
   Federal fiscal policy
   Economically deprived persons and areas
   Fiscal problems of state and local governments
   Taxes and tax policies
   Inflation and price controls
   Unemployment
   International monetary affairs
   Investment opportunities
   Energy
3. Political problems:
   Powers and obligations of the federal government
   Relations between the federal government and the states
   Problems of state and local governments
   Parties, campaigns, and nominating procedures
   The courts
   —Delays in justice
   —The jury system
   —Plea bargaining
   Congress versus the President
   Careers in government

THE ARTS

1. Painting, music, sculpture
2. Literature and criticism
3. Theater, cinema, and dance
4. Government support of the arts
5. The artist as a person
6. History of an art form
7. Censorship of the arts
8. Folk arts
9. Careers in the arts

EDUCATION

1. Proper aims of education
2. Recent advances in methods and teaching materials
3. The federal government and education
4. Courses and requirements
5. Grades and grading
6. Athletics
7. Extracurricular activities
8. Meeting the demand for education
9. Fraternities
10. Student marriages
11. Students' role in educational decision making
12. Parietal rules
13. Alternatives to college

MASS MEDIA

1. Radio, television, and film
2. The press
3. Censorship of mass media
4. Use of mass media for propaganda purposes at home or abroad
5. Employment opportunities
6. The electric church
7. Advances in technology:
   Cable television
   Two-way video
   Home video centers
8. Effects on children

SCIENCE

1. Recent advances in a particular branch of science
2. Science as method
3. Pure versus applied research
4. Government support of science
5. History of science
6. Science and religion
7. Careers in science
8. Ethics of science

BUSINESS AND LABOR

1. Unions:
   Regulation of unions
   "Right-to-work" laws
2. Government regulation of business
3. Ethical standards of business practice
4. Advertising in the modern world
5. Training for business
6. Internships
7. Blue-collar and white-collar status
8. A guaranteed lifetime income
9. Portable pensions
10. Early retirement

PERSISTENT CONCERNS

1. "The good life"—what and how
2. Man and God
3. Beauty
4. The ideal society
5. Life-style—what it is and how to develop it
6. Parents and children
7. The tests of truth
8. Love
9. Discovering one's self
10. Ethical decision making

ORAL ACTIVITIES

1. Deliver a short impromptu speech on a topic that concerns you. Your instructor will allow a question-and-comment period from your listeners so that you may see which areas of your topic are of most interest to your audience.

2. Can you think of topics which might be considered inappropriate subject matter for presentation in this class? Spend a few minutes of class discussion exploring objections to these topics.

3. What topics that interest you are most likely to appeal to your listeners? To be considered controversial by your classmates? List at least five different subjects appropriate for a speech to inform. Do the same for speeches to persuade and to actuate. Meet in small groups with four or five other classmates and share topics. Discuss among yourselves the relevancy and interest level of these subjects. A reporter from each group should report the findings to the entire class. Note in your journal the reactions of your classmates to your list of topics.

CHAPTER 5

Analyzing the Audience

and Occasion

Because public speaking is audience-centered, it is crucial that you understand the people you are addressing. Indeed, audience analysis is pivotal to the whole communication enterprise. Selecting the topic, establishing your purpose, and narrowing the topic require you to consider the audience's interests and levels of knowledge. And the remaining steps in speech preparation—finding and selecting supporting materials, arranging the materials, and casting introductions and conclusions—likewise must be undertaken with a clear sense of who your auditors are. Unless you think about and adapt the elements of your speeches to audience members, clear, relevant, and hence effective communication simply will not take place.

Traditionally, speakers have engaged in essentially two kinds of audience analysis: *demographic analysis* and *psychological profiling*. This is because human beings have been studied both as members of (demographic) groups and as self-contained (psychologically independent) individuals. That is, people exist both in a series of easily identifiable roles—male or female, parent or child, banker or educator, rich or poor, Legionnaire or anarchist—and yet as individual beings who have unique personal experiences, beliefs, feelings, desires, attitudes.

This chapter will help you systematically analyze your audiences and show you how to adapt key portions of your speech to those people. One constant theme will be stressed: *The goal of audience analysis is to discover what facets of listeners' demographical and psychological backgrounds are relevant to your speech purposes and ideas, so that you can adapt your purposes and ideas to those factors.* First, we will examine two ways—demographic analysis and psychological analysis—to approach the goal. Next, we will discuss analysis of speech occasions as they are associated with audience expectations and as they sometimes constrain what a speaker can and should say and do. And then we will explore some ways you can use information you discover through analyses of audience and occasion to adapt your speech purposes, structures, and materials to people and situations.

Analyzing your audiences demographically can help you adapt your purposes, your information, your appeals, your expectations, and your language to your listeners.

Analyzing the Audience Demographically

Especially if an audience is composed of strangers, it may be easiest to begin with a demographic or group-related analysis, because you often can directly observe demographic characteristics. You can identify gender, age, ethnic background (sometimes), group memberships (often), and the like. In doing a comparatively simple demographic analysis, you should ask such questions as:

Age.   Are there primarily young, middle-aged, or older people in the audience?

Gender.   Is the audience predominantly male or female?

Education.   Are many audience members likely to be well informed on my subject? Do they have the educational background which should allow them to learn easily and quickly?

Group membership.   Do these people represent or belong to groups that are known to possess certain kinds of information, particular sets of attitudes, or identifiable values?

Cultural and ethnic background.   Are audience members predominantly from particular cultural groups?

The importance of demographic analysis for the speaker is not simply the asking and answering of these and similar questions. Rather, the key here is to decide how, if at all, any of these demographic factors will affect people's ability or willingness to accept and understand what you want to say. Put more simply, the key is to figure out which, if any, of these factors is *relevant;* if any are, then you will want to adapt your message accordingly.

For example, if you are addressing a group of four-year-olds at a preschool, you obviously must take *age* and *educational level* into consideration, perhaps by *(1)* talking simply, *(2)* using many clarifying examples, and *(3)* being sure you do not present too many ideas at once. Or, if you are addressing a group of *college-age females,* you would be more than foolhardy if you employed sexist language, called them "girls," and assumed they all planned on being "homemakers." *Cultural background* was important to then-President John F. Kennedy when he addressed a German audience gathered at the Berlin wall; he made sure he incorporated references to West Germany's struggle against Communism and used bits of German phraseology (especially "Ich bin ein Berliner") throughout the speech.

Group membership often is a particularly important factor. At least occasionally, you will address homogeneous groups—a local nurses' society, a church congregation, an Asian immigrants' support group. Under these circumstances, you often can assume that members of your audience will share several important beliefs, attitudes, and values, and that many of those tenets will affect their perception of and reaction to your message.

For example, suppose you are speaking for a Tenants' Union that would like financial support from your community's United Way campaign. The United Way Board of Directors is composed of people who, as a group, tend to think that (1) local programs deserve local financial support, (2) human services should be delivered as efficiently as possible, (3) unpaid volunteers help local organizations provide low-cost services, and (4) major support of an organization by prominent members of a community demonstrates that the organization is healthy and valuable. Knowing that the Board of Directors generally is committed to these tenets will help you select and phrase the arguments which comprise your plea for financial support. You will increase your chance for success if you are able to argue convincingly that your Tenants' Union is local and not a puppet of some national organization; that your overhead costs are low; that volunteers provide almost all the counseling and help for tenants in need; and that several well-known law offices in the community are involved in helping your Tenants' Union organization.

Demographic analysis, then, is one important analytical tool for the speaker, because it will help you select appeals or arguments and help you phrase your key ideas. More will be said about using demographic analysis once we examine the other main type of investigation.

Analyzing the Audience Psychologically

Social scientists and communication researchers have found it useful to divide people into psychological groups on the basis of fundamental beliefs, attitudes, and values. Because we will use these three terms throughout this book, we need to define them carefully and discuss ways the concepts can be used by speakers who want to inform and persuade audiences.

Beliefs

A belief is a claim thought by people holding it to accurately represent the state of affairs in the "real" world. A belief asserts something true or false in the world. It has been accepted by people based on their first-hand experience, evidence they have read or heard, authorities who have told them it is true, or even blind faith. So, you might believe that "Eating food hurriedly produces stomachaches" (first-hand experience); that "Iowa never has a killer frost after May 10" (something you read in an Iowa Extension Service pamphlet); that "Tax relief for corporations will create jobs" (something the President of the United States told you); or that "Treating people fairly will cause them to treat you with equal fairness" (something you hope is true).

Beliefs, therefore, are held by people for various reasons. They differ in other important ways as well. Some beliefs we call *facts,* others, *opinions;* some are *fixed,* others, *variable.* Let us examine each of these subclasses.

Facts and Opinions.   We all hold beliefs with varying degrees of certitude. Those beliefs you hold strongly you are likely to call "facts." When you say, "It's a fact that John is six feet tall" or "It's a fact that cuts in government spending will reduce inflation," you are stating that you're very sure of those beliefs (even though the *actual* truth or falsity of those beliefs might be open to question). The beliefs you call "facts" are usually held with certainty because you are convinced that you have hard evidence backing them up. Thus, we may say that a *fact* is a belief held firmly by an individual and undergirded with strong evidence.

"Opinions," however, are a different matter. When you say "It's my opinion that . . . ," normally you are signaling to your listener that your belief is somewhat tentative, that it is held with something less than certainty. Or, when you use *tentative verbs* such as "I think that . . . ," and when you add *qualifiers* ("Perhaps it's true that . . ." or "We probably could say that . . ."), you are letting your listeners know that the belief-statements being offered are opinions. You are "telling" them indirectly that your commitment to the statement is not especially strong and that you don't think you have incontrovertible evidence to support the belief-claim. Hence, we may say that an *opinion* is a belief held with low-to-moderate degrees of certitude and supported with something less than powerful or compelling evidence.[1]

Fixed and Variable Beliefs.   A second way of classifying beliefs is to say that some are fixed and some are variable. "Fixed beliefs" are those which have been reinforced in your life and in your interaction with others over and over again. Obviously, many of your childhood beliefs are fixed (although some of them, such as "Parents are always right," tend to be less well fixed as you grow older). Other sorts of beliefs become

BELIEFS, ATTITUDES, AND VALUES

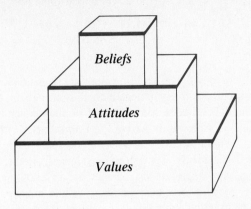

fixed, or *anchored,* as well. Especially as you grow older, many political, economic, social, and religious beliefs harden in your mind. Middle-aged and older people tend to vote political party lines election after election; tend to believe there are proper and improper ways to earn money; tend to believe that certain classes or types of people make better friends and associates than others; tend not to change churches or religions. Fixed beliefs become habituated; they can even be called *stereotypes* because we often generalize our fixed beliefs (as when we say "All Democrats are . . . ," "If you want to get ahead in this world, you must . . . ," "People who go to fundamentalist churches are . . .").

In contrast, "variable beliefs" are less well anchored in our minds and experiences. You might enter college thinking you're very well suited by temperament and talent to be a chemist. Then, after an instructor has praised your abilities in a composition class, you might see yourself as predestined to be a writer. Next, you take a marketing class and find out you're very good at planning advertising campaigns. And on it goes, as you experience one class in college after another, until you somehow come to select a major and degree program. In this case, your beliefs about your talents and ways you can best use them change with your personal experiences and with testimony you heard from various (authoritative) instructors and counselors. Obviously, then, speakers usually need a clear sense about which of their audience's beliefs are fixed and therefore difficult to change, and which are variable and therefore more easily attacked.

Facts and opinions, fixed and variable beliefs—these related distinctions are important to you for two reasons: *(1)* Such assessments should help you outline some of the appeals you can make within your speech. If your investigations show you that the listeners hold some set of beliefs as factual, or accept certain beliefs as true, and if those "facts" and fixed beliefs support your central idea or claim, you will certainly want to incorporate them into your speech. *(2)* These assessments also allow you to set *realistic expectations* as you plan your talk. Do not try to accomplish too much in a single speech if you know you will run into psychological resistance when you try to destroy facts and fixed beliefs; not all audience beliefs are equally amenable to change through speeches. Later in this chapter we will discuss further these questions of selecting belief-claims and setting speech goals.

Attitudes

The second aspect of psychological profiling is attitudes. *Attitudes* may be defined as predispositions to respond positively or negatively to some person, object, or idea; they express our preferences. Attitudes are expressed in such statements as "My dog's *better* than your dog," "Abortion is *wrong*," "I *hate* liars," "The Mona Lisa is a *beautiful* painting," "Public speaking is a *useful* course."

Because attitudinal statements express our preferences, predispositions, reactions, and basic judgments, they represent the core of our psychological life. They often control our behavior, because we tend to do things we like and avoid things we dislike. Most of us avoid even thinking about things we dislike or fear (the suffering of others, death); we prefer instead to contemplate beautiful sights (a summer sunset), positive opinions (a sense of our own innate goodness), and preferred associates (a close friend). A speaker, therefore, should attempt to assess the dominant attitudes of audiences. Especially relevant are the audience's attitudes toward the speaker, the subject, and the speech purpose.

The Audience's Attitude Toward the Speaker.   The attitude of an audience toward you as a speaker will be based partly upon your known reputation and partly upon your behavior during the speech. Two factors about your reputation are especially important: *(1)* the degree of your listeners' *friendliness* toward you, and *(2)* the degree of their *respect* for you and your knowledge of the subject. The potency of these factors may vary widely. A mother's affection for her small son, for instance, may be very strong; but her respect for her son's judgment may not be. On the other hand, the mother may have the greatest respect for the judgment of a neighbor even though she dislikes her as a person. Respect and friendliness are two different attitudes; as a speaker you must attempt to take both into account.

As we noted in Chapter 1, when you begin to speak and throughout the entire time you are talking, the audience consciously or subconsciously assesses your credibility from many points of view. Among other things, they ask: *(1)* Are you a *competent* speaker? Do you give evidence of intelligence and expertise? *(2)* Are you *admirable?* Do you appear to be a morally upright person? *(3)* Are you *trustworthy?* Do you seem honest, just, fair, and sincere? *(4)* Are you *dynamic?* Are you energetic, alert mentally? *(5)* Are you *courageous?* Do you seem to have strength and firmness? Collectively, these factors point up the need to know your subject thoroughly, to respect your audience, and to deliver your speech with sincerity and vigor.

The Audience's Attitude Toward the Subject.   Sometimes people are *interested* in a subject; sometimes they are *apathetic* about it. In either case, the amount of interest they have will influence a great deal their perception of and response to a communication. Some researchers place *prior audience attitude* among the most crucial variables that determine speaking success.[2] If, for instance, the listeners are unfavorably disposed toward the speaker's subject or purpose, they may *(1)* distort the substance of the message, (2) psychologically or physically leave the field, (3) discredit the communicator, or (4) use a host of similar defense mechanisms to avoid accurate perception of the speaker's intent and message-content.

An audience may be apathetic or neutral if its members see no connection between the speaker's subject and their own affairs. When your analysis indicates that your listeners will be apathetic, you need to show them how they are directly concerned with the problem you are discussing, or you need to arouse their curiosity about some novel aspect of the subject. Use all available means for holding and involving their attention. (See page 158.) Even when the members of your audience are already interested, you cannot entirely neglect the problems of commanding and holding attention; but when your listeners are apathetic, you must make a special effort to arouse their interest.

Interest (or the lack of it) is only one aspect of an audience's attitude toward your subject. *Expectancy* is another. For example, as soon as we hear that a speech will be about the Gay Liberation movement, many of us begin to form favorable or unfavorable attitudes toward the speaker and the subject. As a general rule, the more the listeners know about your subject or the stronger the beliefs they hold concerning it, the more likely they are to have well-defined expectations. These expectations may be troublesome, for frequently they operate as listening barriers or as filters which distort the meanings that the audience assigns to your message. The introduction of your speech presents a special opportunity to create or to correct these audience expectations. All the time you are talking, however, you should bear in mind the problem of listener expectation and make adaptations accordingly.

The Audience's Attitude Toward the Speech Purpose.   If, with no preliminaries at all, you told the members of your audience the specific purpose of your speech, what would be their reaction or response? This "attitude toward speech purpose" is not the frame of mind you hope your audience will hold at the end of your speech; it is the one that exists before you begin. Audience predisposition is seldom uniform; many different shades of attitude may be represented. It is best, therefore, to determine—by prior analysis—what attitude is predominant and to adapt your speech to that view while making allowances for variations in the character or intensity of listener belief.

When the general end of your speech is *to inform,* the attitude of your listeners toward the speech purpose will be governed largely by their attitude toward the subject, that is:

(a) interested, or
(b) apathetic.

When your general purpose is *to persuade,* the listeners' attitude toward the speech purpose will be governed also by their attitude toward the specific belief or action which is urged; hence, their attitude will be one of the following:

(a) favorable but not aroused;
(b) apathetic to the situation;
(c) interested in the situation but undecided what to do or think about it;
(d) interested in the situation but hostile to the proposed attitude, belief, or action; or
(e) hostile to any change from the present state of affairs.[3]

Determining the predominant attitude of your audience toward your subject and purpose should guide you in selecting your arguments and developing the structure and content of your message. If your listeners are apathetic, begin your speech on a point of compelling interest or startling vividness. Show them how your subject affects them. If they are hostile to the proposal, you may wish to introduce it more cautiously, emphasizing some basic principle with which you know they agree, and relating your proposal to it. If they are interested but undecided, provide plenty of proof in the form of factual illustrations, testimony, and statistics. If they are favorable but not aroused, try to motivate them by using appeals that directly touch their desires for pleasure, independence, power, creativity, ego-satisfaction, and the like.

No analysis of an audience made prior to a speech is certain to be fully correct, and even if it is, audience attitudes may shift even while you are speaking.[4] Hence, you must watch listeners' reactions closely when your subject is announced and continue to do so throughout your entire speech. The way your hearers sit in their seats, the expressions on their faces, their audible reactions—laughter, applause, shifting about, whispering—all are clues to their attitude toward you, your subject, or your purpose. The conscientious communicator develops a keen awareness of these signs of feedback on the part of the audience and adapts his or her remarks accordingly.[5]

Values

A third important "content" of your mind is composed of values. *Values* may be defined as basic orientations to life—habitual ways of looking at the world or responding to problems. Values, in a sense, are psychologically "larger" than attitudes. Whereas attitudes represent particularized judgments about specific persons, objects, or ideas, values include broad categories into which many specific attitudes are grouped mentally. Thus, for example, a person may hold a specific attitude toward abortion:

> *Attitude:* "Abortion is wrong."

That attitude probably is held, however, because of the way the person conceives of abortion, because of the valuative category into which the person psychologically puts abortion:

> *Values:* Abortion is primarily . . .
>> a medical question (*scientific* value).
>> a moral question (*religious-philosophical* value).
>> a question of a woman's right to control her own mind and body (*psychological* value).
>> a matter of allowing groups in a society to make their own decisions without being dictated to by others (*sociological* value).
>> something to be considered only in life-or-death situations (*pragmatic* value).
>> something to be decided by a nationwide referendum (*political* value).

Thus, a person's attitude, "Abortion is wrong," might be held because the person values scientific evidence which suggests a fetus can survive as a human being; because of religious authority which calls abortion murder; because the person thinks socio-logical, psychological, or pragmatic questions are irrelevant to abortions; or be-cause, politically, most people in this country may be opposed to abortion rights legislation.

Knowing or trying to find out what values members of your audience habitually bring to bear on issues you are discussing, then, is an important part of audience analysis. Knowing, for example, that members of the Board of Directors of United Way are strongly motivated by sociological concerns (concerns for needy groups in the com-munity) and by pragmatic concerns (concerns for fiscal efficiency and responsibility) helped you construct your speech in support of the Tenants' Union.

Values, then, are an individual's habitualized reasons for holding particular atti-tudes. Even more broadly, we can talk about *value orientations*. These represent the positions relatively large groups of people take toward life. Over the last three decades, for example, Americans have read about the Puritan Ethic, the Establishment, the Silent Majority, the Counterculture, Me-ism, Situational Ethics, Freaks, New Politics, the Old Guard, Libbers, Yuppies, Moonies, Rednecks, the Moral Majority, and Neo-Liberals.[6]

Value orientations are the broad, sweeping concepts (sometimes termed *ideologies*) which members of groups apply to basic questions in their lives. They can be thought of as clusters of more specific beliefs and attitudes as well as the judgments groups habit-ually make toward events in the world; they are response tendencies.

As a communicator who wants to understand listeners and to relate harmoniously and productively with them, you need to be highly sensitive to values and value orienta-tions. Unless you recognize the differences that may exist between you and members of your audience and take definite steps to bridge them, you cannot cope effectively with the conflicts and controversies such cultural discrepancies almost certainly will gener-ate. Unless you can discover common ground between you and your audience, you may well be in communicative trouble. A search for common ground represents a crucial step in audience analysis.

Analyzing the Speech Occasion

To this point, we have emphasized the necessity of analyzing the members of the audience. Equally important is the need to analyze the occasion on which you are speaking, for "audience" and "occasion" are usually inseparable for two reasons:

1. The occasion often is what brings audience members together, and hence it can determine their *expectations*. The frame of mind one brings to a funeral is quite different from one's thoughts upon entering the campus fieldhouse to hear a comic monologue. Audience expectations of what will be discussed and how it will be presented differ markedly from one occasion to another.

2. With some occasions there are associated *communication rules*, as we discussed earlier. If, for example, parliamentary procedure is being used at a business or legislative meeting, those rules of procedure will determine who can talk for how long and how often about what. The rules of parliamentary procedure are recorded

Giving a speech at a public meeting demands that you phrase your purpose and select your information in accordance with the demands of the particular occasion you are in.

in books such as *Robert's Rules of Order*.[7] Other communication rules, however, are not recorded. No one tells the President-elect that his inaugural address must contain a greeting, a call for unity, a discussion of domestic policy, a discussion of foreign policy, and a final appeal to the deity. Yet all presidential inaugurals do contain those sections if only because presidents-elect read over the previous inaugural speeches before writing their own. Traditions of these kinds can be forged into unwritten communication rules, attached to particular occasions, and developed into constraints upon speakers every bit as powerful as the written rules of parliamentary procedure.[8]

How, then, can you go about analyzing speech occasions in conjunction with your audience analyses? The key variables you should think about include the nature of the occasion, the prevailing rules, the physical conditions, and the events preceding or following your speech.

The Nature and Purpose of the Occasion

Is yours a voluntary or a captive audience? A voluntary audience attends a speech-making event primarily because of interest in the speaker or the subject. A captive audience is required to attend, perhaps at the explicit instruction of the boss or under threat of a failing grade in a course. In general, the more "captive" your audience, the less initial interest audience members will show and the greater will be their resistance to accepting your information or point of view.

Are people interested in learning more about your subject, in taking some positive action concerning it, or have they perhaps come to heckle or embarrass you? Are your subject and purpose in line with the reason for the meeting, or are you merely seizing the occasion to present some ideas you think important? Are you one in a series of speakers whom the audience has heard over a period of weeks or months? If so, how does your speech subject relate to those subjects which have been previously presented? These are important questions to answer when you are analyzing the nature and purpose of the occasion. In other words, the nature and purpose of the occasion—as well as the interest level you can sense among those attending it—often dictate a series of general decisions you will make in your approach to the speech transactions.

The Prevailing Rules or Customs

Will there be a regular order of business or a fixed program into which your speech must fit? Is it the custom of the group to ask questions of the speaker after the address? Do the listeners expect a formal or informal speaking manner? Will you, as the speaker, be expected to extend complimentary remarks, or to express respect for some tradition or concept? Knowing the answers to these questions will help you avoid feeling out of place and will prevent you from arousing antagonism by some inappropriate word or action.

In addition to probing the general customs prevailing in a group, you may need to go a step further by discovering specific rules for formulating your messages. If you are delivering a report on some research you have undertaken, you will be expected to review the research of others on your topic before you discuss your own study. A member of the U.S. Senate must always refer to an opponent as ''The Honorable Senator from _____'' even if he or she is going to disagree violently with that person. The speaker at the Friars' Club of New York is expected to mercilessly but good-naturedly excoriate the person who is the object of that evening's ''roast.'' One part of your task of understanding communication rules, therefore, is a matter of analyzing the specific customs and traditions governing particular audiences in particular places.

The Physical Conditions

Will your speech be given out-of-doors or in an auditorium? Is the weather likely to be hot or cold? Will the audience be sitting or standing; if sitting, will the members be crowded together or scattered about? In how large a room will the speech be presented? Will an electronic public address system be used? Will facilities be provided for the audiovisual reinforcements you will use, or must you bring your own? Will you be seen and heard easily? Are there likely to be disturbances in the form of noise or interruptions from the outside? These and similar environmental factors affect the temper of the audience, their span of attention, and the style of speaking you will have to employ as you make adjustments to the speech environment or situation.

Events Preceding or Following Your Speech

At what time of day or night will your speech be given? Immediately after a heavy meal or a long program, both of which may induce drowsiness and reduce listener interest? Just before the principal address or event of the evening? By whom and in what manner will you be introduced to the audience? What other items are on the program? What are

When addressing an audience in a large auditorium, you'll have to enlarge your gestures, slow down your speaking rate, improve your articulation, and use a microphone correctly.

their tone and character? All these things will, of course, influence the interest the audience may have in your speech. In some instances, you will be able to use the other events on the program to increase interest or belief in your own remarks; sometimes they will work against you. In any case, you must always consider the effect which the program as a whole may have on your speech.

In summary, "occasions" represent a constellation of audience expectations governed by the fact that all societies set apart certain spaces and certain events for listening to particular kinds of speeches from particular sorts of speakers.[16] That "set-apartness" often takes the form of communication rules—rules you are expected to follow if you are to be judged a competent and appropriate messenger. You may well feel constrained to violate those rules upon occasion, in order to shake a group out of its complacency and lethargy, in order to feel better about yourself by upbraiding a group to whose standards you have too long conformed. When you are moved to violate norms of tradition, civility, or custom, remember you do so at some risk. The risk is yours, and must be taken only after a careful assessment of yourself, your audience, and the occasion.

Using Audience Analysis in Speech Preparation

Neither demographic nor psychological analysis is an end in itself, nor will mere thinking about the speech occasion produce foolproof speech preparation strategies. Rather, you are carrying out such analyses to discover what might affect the reception of you and your ideas. *You are searching for relevant factors which (1) can affect the audi-*

ence's attitudes toward you, your subject, and your purpose, and (2) consequently should guide your rhetorical decisions. What you learn about your listeners and their expectations through systematic investigation can conceivably affect every aspect of your speech—right down to the ways you phrase important ideas and deliver your sentiments. Let's examine ways in which your analytical conclusions or findings ought to help you phrase your purposes and select your dominant appeals.

Audience Targeting: Setting Purposes Realistically

Few of us have difficulty determining our overall or general speech purposes—to inform, to persuade, to actuate. It becomes more difficult, however, to narrow down to specific purposes, and to phrase central ideas and claims for particular speeches. After you have completed your audience analysis, however, you should be better able to target your audience, that is, to determine what you realistically can accomplish with this audience in the time you have available. As you think about targeting an audience, four considerations should arise.

Specificity of Purpose.   Suppose you have a part-time job with your college's Career Planning and Placement Office. You know enough about its operations and have enough personal interest in it to want to speak about career planning and placement to different audiences. What you have discovered about different audiences should help you determine appropriate specific purposes for each audience. If you were to talk to a group of incoming freshmen, for example, you'd know that they probably:

1. know little or nothing about career planning and placement as a college office (that is, have few beliefs, none of which are fixed);
2. are predisposed to look favorably upon career planning and placement (given job anxieties among college graduates);
3. are, at their particular stage of life and of educational development, more concerned with such pragmatic concerns as getting an adviser, getting registered, and learning about basic degree requirements than they are with longer-range matters like post-degree placement (and hence may not value your information without motivation);
4. are likely to see you as an authoritative speaker and hence are willing to listen to you.

Given these audience considerations, you probably should keep your talk fairly general. Feed them basic, not detailed, information about career planning and placement; remind them that the office can relieve many of their later anxieties, as graduation nears; show them how thinking about possible careers will help them select majors and particular courses. You might phrase your specific purpose as follows: "To brief incoming freshmen on the range of services offered by the Career Planning and Placement Office." That orientation would include a basic description of each service and general advice to use the services in making some curricular decisions.

Were you, instead, to talk about this subject to an incoming group of new faculty, you'd assess the audience differently. You probably would discover that they:

1. know quite a bit about career planning and placement offices (having used them themselves and perhaps having worked with them in previous jobs);

2. have mixed feelings about career planning and placement (because some faculty think that too much emphasis upon careers turns colleges and universities into "trade" schools rather than centers of humane learning);
3. tend to value education "for its own sake" (that is, philosophically), rather than as a route to employment (that is, pragmatically);
4. are likely to view you as a mere student or a mere college bureaucrat.

Given these factors, you'd probably have to get a good deal more specific in some areas of your speech. You'd want to describe the particular features of this office's operations rather than only its general duties; your listeners need to know "how" because they already know the "what." You'd have to reassure them that your office is an adjunct to the university's mission, that you realize not all course selections should be based solely on career choices. And, you probably would want to demonstrate your expertise by talking about career possibilities across a variety of fields (especially if you know what fields are represented in the group of incoming faculty). You might phrase your specific purpose like this: "To inform incoming faculty about Langford College's philosophy of career planning and placement, about ways faculty members in all fields can help their students use the Career Planning and Placement Office, and about informational assistance the Office provides faculty members."

Audience analysis, therefore, will help you focus your specific purposes and determine which ones are appropriate to your listeners.

Areas of Audience Interest.   Both demographic and psychological analyses are most useful to you in deciding what ideas will be of interest to your listeners. Suppose you know a good deal about laser technology. A group of industrial managers probably would be most interested in hearing a speech on lasers' manufacturing applications; a group of medical researchers, on its capabilities for improving surgical procedures; a group of physicists, on its theoretical principles; a general "public" audience, on ways lasers will transform their everyday lives.

In other words, you often are able to infer audience interests—at least potential interests—from knowing something about their demographic and psychological characters. This is not to say that you always must cater to them; sometimes, you will want to create a new set of interests in an audience. You might suppose that an audience of doctors is always interested in finding out something about the latest drugs for pain therapy, given their medical-scientific values; but yet, you might want them to know more about the psychological effects of such drugs and to deal professionally with the ethical questions which surround the use of strong drugs with unstable patients. To achieve such a purpose, you'll have to create a new set of interests, especially by tying the new interests to old ones. For this speech, you might phrase your central idea as follows: "Knowing more about the psychological effects of the latest drugs available for pain therapy will make you a more humane as well as a more medically expert physician." Phrasing the central idea in this way explicitly ties the interests you are trying to create to ones the audience already has.

The Audience's Capacity to Act.   As a speaker, *limit your request to an action lying within your listener's range of authority.* Do not ask them to do something they would be unable to do even if they wanted to. As we've already noted, to demand of a group of students that they "abolish all required courses" would be foolish. They do not have the authority to take this action; the final word concerning course requirements belongs to a school's faculty. But students do have the right and the capacity-for-action to bring pressure on the faculty toward this end. A more logical and positively framed claim, therefore, would be "Petition the faculty to make all courses elective."

You determine ranges of authority through analysis of the audience, especially of demographic factors. In the case of comparatively homogeneous audiences (for example, students), this is relatively easy to do. In the case of more heterogeneous groups, however, you may have to take into consideration a broader range of capacities-to-act. For instance, in talking with a local PTA about instituting an after-school program of foreign language and culture instruction, you are addressing an audience comprised of school administrators (who can seek funding from the school board), teachers (who could be asked to volunteer some instructional time), and parents (who could petition the school board, convince their children to enroll, and volunteer their talents to help with the program). You thus would have to include among your specific purposes goals for each of these subgroups of listeners.

Degrees of Change.   Finally, your analyses of audiences, as we suggested earlier, should help you determine how far you can move an audience intellectually, emotionally, and actively. How much new material or new information can you present to an audience in ten minutes? Your answer will depend primarily upon your assessment of your listeners' age, degree of educational development, and previous stocks of knowledge. How intensely positive or negative can you get an audience to feel about some matter? If a group is adamantly opposed to, say, a new parking ramp for downtown, it is unlikely that in a single speech you will be able to make them overwhelmingly in favor of one; an attempt simply to neutralize some of their objections would be better. How much can you expect people to do after your speech? If your pre-speech analyses indicate that this group of listeners strongly favors cycling as an activity, and is valuatively committed to governmental citizens' programs, then you probably can convince many of them to work long hours at mounting a public campaign for new bike paths in town and at convincing city council to commit the money for paths and urban bike lanes. If they are only moderately committed to cycling, however, you might rather appeal to civic pride and to questions of automobile-bicycle problems and of safety, and then ask them to make a small donation to the public campaign others are running.

Audience analysis, in other words, should help you determine how much you can change an audience and what kinds of commitments you can expect from your listeners. You should phrase your specific purposes and central ideas or claims accordingly.

Audience Segmentation: Selecting Dominant Ideas and Appeals

So far, we have been looking at audience analysis as it helps you identify or target your audience, and as it then helps you phrase purposes, central ideas, and claims. Keep in mind, however, that in reality there is no such animal as "an audience." Each person sitting in an auditorium is an individual; no matter how people are crowded together, arranged in rows, or reached electronically by a message, they never completely lose that individuality. As we noted when discussing psychological profiling, your beliefs, attitudes, and values are, ultimately, yours—the products of your experiences, your own mental operations.

Ideally, of course, you would want to approach listeners one at a time. Indeed, often you can; that's called *interpersonal communication*. But, because communicating with individuals is time-consuming and hence inefficient when dealing with matters of large, public concern, speakers try to affect people in groups. There must be a middle ground between thinking of audiences as completely homogeneous masses and as solitary individuals. There is. Among advertisers, the approach is called *audience segmentation*. Audience segmentation is the approaching of a collection of listeners as a series of subgroups, or "differentiated populations." Segmenting your audience into subgroups, or *reference groups,* will help you select your dominant appeals.[9]

Avoiding Unnecessary Irritation.   The first way audience segmentation can help you select speech materials is by making you conscious of appeals to avoid. Were a speaker to say, "Because all you girls are interested in efficient cooking, today I want to talk about four ways a food processor will save you time in the kitchen," he or she probably would alienate two subgroups in the audience: The females probably would be irritated with the stereotyped term *girls,* while the males who cooked would be offended by having been left out. The appeal would be better phrased: "Because everyone who cooks is interested in. . . ." Here, you are aiming the interest-appeal to the proper audience segment—the culinary masters. Similarly, unless you are sure there are no Roman Catholics in your audience, you probably will want to avoid blaming the Catholic religious hierarchy for the anti-abortion movement in this country; because so many people in this country identify with businesses and industries, you probably would not want to blame "the business establishment" alone for inflation; and you probably would be foolhardy to refer to "dumb jocks," "artsy-craftsy theatre majors," and "computer fanatics" in a speech on the goals of college education to your speech class.

This is not to say, of course, that you never confront directly beliefs, attitudes, and values of subgroups represented in your audience—that you always and only say what people "want" to hear. Obviously, in some areas of this country, the Catholic Church was active in the anti-abortion movement; some business practices have been responsible for part of the inflation problem; and it perhaps is possible to distinguish between "essential" and "secondary" goals of education. You can find ways to talk about those sorts of things. Only be sure that you avoid stereotyped references to people and groups, that you avoid blanket condemnation of groups of people, and that, when possible, you work around touchy subjects and cite ample and unbiased evidence when you must attack a group's beliefs, attitudes, and sacred values.

Selecting Relevant Belief- and Attitude-Statements.   More positively, audience analysis and segmentation should help you select belief- and attitude-statements for inclusion in your speech. Suppose you were to give a speech to a local Rotary Club about the establishment of a community hospice—a team of medical personnel, psychologists, social workers, and other volunteers who work with terminally-ill people and their families. Suppose in this speech you are trying to raise money to set up the hospice. As a group, a Rotary Club normally is composed of business people, medical professionals, educators, social service personnel, lawyers, bankers, and the like. By thinking of the Rotary audience as segmented into such subgroups, you should be in a position to offer each subgroup some reasons to support the community hospice. For example:

> *Claim:* A community hospice should be supported by all segments in our town because:
>
> 1. For doctors, nurses, and hospital workers, a hospice provides help for the dying, and therefore is a complement to your work to save the living.
> 2. For those of you working in social services, a hospice uses a social-team concept, and therefore allows you to work with needy people in a way you can't now.
> 3. For those of you in education, a hospice provides unequaled opportunities for on-the-job training for many different kinds of students because it uses volunteers.
> 4. And, for those of you from the banks and businesses of this community, a hospice is a vital local resource, something which can be used by your employees and their families and which sets this community apart from all the others in our area.

Each of these appeals, of course, would be expanded in an actual speech, but you can see how each one of the four is based upon beliefs and attitudes you assume are important to segments of the audence. In our example, there is implicit reference to medical beliefs and attitudes ("Medical personnel provide services for the living," "Our job of providing medical services to the living is good"); to the beliefs and attitudes of social service personnel ("In our work, psychologists treat individuals' problems, social workers treat family problems," "It would be beneficial to provide certain kinds of help to others in a team"); to educators' beliefs and attitudes ("Schools must find all ways possible to educate their students," "On-the-job training is a useful educational tool"); and to business beliefs and attitudes ("Businesses take care of all aspects of their employees' lives," "Our city might grow if we increase our social services and hence make it more attractive," "We will be more competitive if we improve our community"). Thus, audience analysis, in combination with audience segmentation, is an invaluable tool for selecting your main lines of appeal and argument.

Choosing Among Valuative Appeals.   Finally, as you might guess, audience segmentation will help select a valuative vocabulary for your speeches. Even informative speeches, as we will discuss more fully later, need to contain appeals to audience interests; you can use a valuative vocabulary to motivate different segments of the audience to listen to and accept your information. So, for a class demonstration speech, you might say: "Today, I want to teach you three basic techniques of Oriental cooking: cutting meats and vegetables, using spices, and quick-cooking your food in a wok. If you learn these techniques, you'll expand your range of expertise in the kitchen *[personal value]*, you'll save money on your food and energy bills *[economic value]*, you'll prepare satisfying meals for your friends *[social value]*, and you'll prepare nutritious, healthful meals for everyone *[pragmatic value]*." With that statement, you will have given your audience four different reasons for listening, and hence will have a good chance of appealing to everyone in your speech. (If that's not enough, tell them the meals will be beautiful, too, thereby adding an *aesthetic value*.)

Usually, however, valuative appeals are more important to persuasive and actuative speeches. Because these speeches are attempts to alter people's beliefs, attitudes, and behaviors, and because, as we noted, values are a body of beliefs and attitudes, valuative appeals are absolutely crucial for persuasive and actuative communications. For example:

> *Claim:* The United States should take immediate, concrete steps to improve its relationships with the Republic of China. Why?
>
> 1. *Politically,* better relations with China will reduce international tensions and allow us to head off potential conflicts before they explode.
> 2. *Economically,* China represents the world's largest market for U.S. agricultural and industrial goods.
> 3. *Sociologically,* it's desirable for two cultures as different as ours and theirs to better understand each other, for in understanding lies intercultural cooperation.
> 4. *Culturally* (that is, aesthetically), China and the United States have varied artistic traditions, so both worlds will be richer if we can increase cultural exchanges.
> 5. *Psychologically,* the levels of anxiety and distrust existing among citizens of both countries can be reduced through expanded people-to-people exchanges.

We have not used every conceivable value term in this segmentation of appeals, but the procedure is clear: *(1)* Think through possible reasons people might accept your proposition in valuative terms; *(2)* then, use a valuative vocabulary in phrasing your actual appeals for acceptance.

In conclusion, understanding your audience is certainly a crucial step of speech preparation. The competent speaker makes many decisions about topic, specific purposes, phrasings for central ideas and claims, dominant appeals, and phraseology based upon demographical and psychological profiles of audience members. To help yourself with these tasks, you'll want to *(1)* think through your personal experiences with identifiable groups in the audience, *(2)* talk with program chairpersons and others who can tell you "who" is in the audience and something about their interests, *(3)* ask speakers who've addressed these and similar audiences what to expect, and *(4)* interview some people who'll be there, to find out more about their beliefs, attitudes, and values—their range of concerns.

All these are not especially easy tasks, for most of us don't have available the resources of public opinion polling firms and extensive social-psychological target group profiles. You probably will be unable to identify precisely all possible facets of listeners' minds and habits. If you learn all you can about them, however, and if you use that knowledge to help make some key pre-speech decisions by discovering *relevant* considerations, you will significantly improve your chances for communicative success.

A Sample Analysis of an Audience and Occasion

In this chapter we have surveyed an array of choices you must make as you analyze your audience and occasion. Those choices will sort themselves out if you work systematically, trying to make them one step at a time. Observe how one student analyzed her audience as she prepared a speech on behalf of facilities for a women's intercollegiate athletic program.

Prespeech Analysis:
Facilities for Women's Athletics at State University

I. *BASIC SPEECH OCCASION*
    A. *Title:* "A Sound Mind in a Sound Body in a Sound Building: Athletic Facilities for State University's Women"
    B. *Subject:* Training and sports facilities for women athletes
    C. *General Purpose:* To actuate
    D. *Specific Purpose:* To convince the Board in Charge of Athletics to request from the regents and the state legislature money for a women's athletic facility
    E. *Specific Audience:* The Board in Charge of Athletics consists of the Director of Athletics, the Assistant Director of Athletics, the Director of Men's Intramural Sports, the Director of Women's Intramural Sports, six coaches of men's varsity sports, three coaches of women's varsity sports, two elected faculty members, and five elected student representatives. Eight of these people are women. Also in attendance as spectators are approximately two dozen interested women athletes (secondary audience).
    F. *Claim:* "The Board in Charge of Athletics should ask the regents to request from the state legislature money to construct a women's athletic facility."

II. *AUDIENCE ANALYSIS*
    A. *Demographic Analysis*
        1. *Age:* Of the twenty Board members, five are 18–22, and fifteen are between 30 and 55. The spectators are all 18–22. Except for appeals to future growth and school reputation, age will not be an important factor.
        2. *Gender:* On the Board, twelve males and eight females; the spectators are all female. Given the topic and proposition, gender will be a concern for audience members.
        3. *Education:* One-third were physical education majors in college, most with advanced degrees; one-third of the Board members are undergraduates; one-third are Ph.D.s in arts or sciences. Most of the spectators are physical education majors. All audience members know the importance of education for both careers and life in general.
        4. *Group Membership:* All members of the Board also belong to the general academic community. The place of athletics in a learning environment will be on their minds during the speech.
        5. *Cultural and Ethnic Background:* Two Board members are black and two are Hispanic, but ethnic background should not be a factor here.
    B. *Psychological Analysis*
        1. *Beliefs:*
            a. *Accepted Facts and Beliefs:* Most are familiar with federal guidelines for male and female athletics, and were on the Board three years ago when it instituted intercollegiate competition for female athletes. All know the financial straits binding the college, the regents, and the state. Most know that the school recently has had trouble recruiting superior women athletes.
            b. *Fixed Beliefs:* All believe that physical development and talents are as important to life as mental and social development. All but the two intramural directors believe that interscholastic competition is an important college commitment.
            c. *Variable Beliefs:* Most probably believe, though, that male interscholastic competition is more important to the school than female competition; some

may even think that competition in general is more important for males than for females. There may be some subtle sexism which must be addressed gently in this speech. Also, most members of the Board probably think that the regents and legislature will not listen to a proposal for a building program—a belief which will have to be changed by this speech.

2. *Attitudes:*

   a. *Audience Attitude Toward Speaker:* The Board probably is suspicious, even uneasy, about this request to address it; it probably also thinks that "outside" students are naive and idealistic when it comes to money and interaction with the regents and the legislature.

   b. *Audience Attitude Toward Subject:* The Board probably has considerable interest in the subject, although it is uncertain about the exact proposal that will be made.

   c. *Audience Attitude Toward Purpose:* Most Board members probably are undecided; a couple may be hostile, given statements they have made to the campus newspaper; the spectators probably hope the speaker can steamroller the idea through the Board. This is unlikely.

3. *Values:*

   a. *Predominating Values:* Among the spectators especially, the political value of "equality" is paramount, although it may be dangerous in this situation to stress it. Among Board members there is probably valuative commitment to physical achievement in general, to pride in the school's general reputation, and to pride in themselves as overseers of the physical education program. There also, however, is probably a fear of "politics"—of maneuvering through the regents and legislature—as a process which could jeopardize the school's general athletic budget.

   b. *Relevant Value Orientation:* Ideologically, all Board members generally are committed to athletic competition (intramural and intercollegiate) for all students as an ultimate value, even as a hallmark of the American way of life. You should be able to fit your speech purpose within this general outlook nicely.

III. *ADAPTIVE STRATEGIES*

   A. *Audience Targeting*

   1. *Specificity of Purpose:* To defuse one set of suspicions, make it clear that you're not blindly crusading for feminist causes. While you will recognize the importance of women's athletics, put your stress on physical culture—the need for athletic facilities to improve recruitment, training, and competition within the college's general mission.

   2. *Areas of Audience Interests:* Make sure you use Board members' fixed and accepted beliefs and values to advance your own goals; stress the members' commitments—and previous actions—which demonstrate their belief in "a sound mind in a sound body" as a goal of college education. Make them feel pride in an effort to improve the physical education program and the school's general reputation. In other words, show them it is in their self-interest, as well as in the interests of student athletes, to push for the new facility.

   3. *Audience's Capacity to Act:* Stress the desirability of action on this matter, but also work hard to show how it might be done. Suggest ways to approach the regents reasonably; indicate how you and the student athletes in attendance will help mount a lobbying campaign on the legislature. Point out examples of other

schools which have convinced legislatures, even in times of financial trouble, to allow schools to let bonds for such facilities. "Feasibility" and "practicality" should punctuate this speech.

4. *Degrees of Change:* Don't demand a sports complex as large as that available for male athletes. Push instead for a "first phase" building with training rooms and general space.

B. *Audience Segmentation*

1. *Avoiding Irritation:* De-emphasize the feminist aspects of the issue. (That might play nicely with the spectators, but it would only strengthen and energize Board resistance.)

2. *Relevant Belief- and Attitude-Statements:* Do recognize the spectators' commitments to women's athletics and their firm resolve to do what is necessary to see that the college improves its facilities. (They have taken the trouble to come, and their commitments should be recognized.) But aim the bulk of your speech at the Board itself—its commitments, its responsibilities, and its capacities to act. Be sure, too, to undermine some potentially negative beliefs and values: Make them understand you are a reasonable, sensible, understanding advocate; tell them about other schools which have made important strides in recruitment and general reputation by expanding women's athletics, and which even are getting decent gate receipts from women's competitions; stress the importance of competitive athletics to women as well as men, perhaps with examples of females who have moved into professional athletic careers.

3. *Relevant Valuative Appeals:* Underscore the virtues of physical achievement, pride in the school's reputation, pride in the Board itself for courageous action, and the Board's capacity to act positively with the regents and legislature in this situation. Stress, too, the importance of physical environment for both athletes and spectators for athletic competition.

With this much hard pre-speech analysis completed, the student preparing this speech found out what she should do next. The analysis pointed particularly to kinds of *supporting materials* she needed to find:

1. Look up federal guidelines (Government Documents Office in the library) on comparable facilities for men's and women's sports.

2. Read the campus newspaper articles carefully to see if the two Board members really are hostile; also check the paper from three years ago (Newspaper Office) for statements some of the current Board members made in support of women's athletics when the program was instituted.

3. Regarding presumed resistance from the regents and the legislature, find examples from State University's past (Office of Facilities Planning) when those groups went along with school requests for bonding authority to build facilities.

4. Interview the women's athletic coaches (Fieldhouse Offices) concerning the names of specific athletes State University recruited but then lost to schools with superior facilities.

5. Search out quotations (Education Library, with help from Reference Desk) from educational experts regarding the importance of physical training and competition in

college education. Also check the University charter and Athletic Department Mission Statement (Main Library, with help from Reference Desk) for statements requiring physical training and competition.

6. Prepare a list of schools similar to State University which have recently upgraded their women's athletics facilities (from women's athletic coaches). Prepare a brief survey which can be sent to their Women's Athletic Directors; ask on the survey (briefly!) for information on types of facilities, building and equipment costs, methods of financing, role (if any) of student body in the legislative campaign, alumni reactions, and gate receipts for specific sports.

7. Prepare a list of State University and other collegiate women athletes (see coaches of individual sports) who have completed undergraduate degrees here and elsewhere, and then have gone on to professional sporting careers. Also find statements (Main Library) from female athletes regarding the importance of intercollegiate competition for postcollege nonathletic careers.

8. Check (Campus Legal Services) on state laws regarding bonding authority for public buildings.

9. Work out a plan for students, faculty, and alumni cooperation (check with Student Government, Faculty Senate, and Alumni Office) in mounting a facilities campaign to convince the legislature. Also check with the Alumni Office regarding names of legislators who are State University graduates.

In addition to these kinds of guides to necessary supporting materials, the speaker has received a good deal of help in other areas of speech preparation: She knows generally what motive and valuative appeals to focus on, which to avoid; she has a sense for how she should present herself, her role and her ethos, so as to maximize her chances for success; she knows what beliefs she can count on to work in her favor, and what beliefs she has to change if she is to get the Board to take the first important steps. These are valuable kinds of knowledge—knowledge which should make her more confident and more effective.

Analysis of the audience and occasion is hard work, and even involves some guessing. Yet it pays off in later stages of preparation, in the presentation, and in results. You won't regret it.

REFERENCE NOTES

[1]For an enlarged discussion of fixed and variable beliefs, see Milton M. Rokeach, *Beliefs, Attitudes, and Values: A Theory of Organization and Change* (San Francisco: Jossey-Bass, Inc., 1968), and his *Nature of Human Values* (New York: Collier-Macmillan, Free Press, 1973).

[2]See, for example, Muzafer Sherif and Carl L. Hovland, *Social Judgment* (New Haven, CT: Yale University Press, 1961), and Victoria O'Donnell and June Kable, *Persuasion: An Interactive-Dependency Approach* (New York: Random House, 1982), esp. pp. 34–48.

[3]Traditionally, it has been assumed that audiences who are hostile to the speaker's proposal or opposed to any change in the existing state of affairs are most difficult to

persuade. For qualifications of this point of view, see Wayne N. Thompson, *Quantitative Studies in Public Address and Communication* (New York: Random House, Inc., 1967), pp. 38–39.

[4]Such changes during the course of a speech are often dramatic. See Robert D. Brooks and Thomas M. Scheidel, "Speech as Process: A Case Study," *Speech Monographs* 35 (March 1968): 1–7.

[5]On adapting to feedback, see Paul D. Holtzman, *The Psychology of Speakers' Audiences* (Glenview, IL: Scott, Foresman and Company, 1970), pp. 33–36, 117. For a summary of the types of feedback typical of different communication contexts, see Frederick Williams, *The New Communications* (Belmont, CA: Wadsworth Publishing Co., 1984), pp. 33–35.

[6]For discussions of predominant value orientations in American society, see Rokeach (above, n. 1); Robin M. Williams, *American Society: A Sociological Interpretation*, 3rd ed. (New York: Alfred A. Knopf, Inc., 1970), Chapter 11, as well as his "Changing Value Orientations and Beliefs on the American Scene," in *The Character of Americans: A Book of Readings,* rev. ed., ed. Michael McGiffert (Homewood, IL: Dorsey Press, 1970), pp. 212–30; and Frank E. Armbruster, *The Forgotten Americans: A Survey of the Values, Beliefs and Concerns of the Majority* (New Rochelle, NY: Arlington House, Inc., 1972). Also, the Gallup and Harris polling organizations regularly issue reports on attitudes and values in America; check with the reference desk at the library.

[7]*Robert's Rules of Order Newly Revised,* ed. Sara Corbin Robert, Henry M. Robert III, James W. Cleary, and William J. Evans (Glenview, IL: Scott, Foresman and Company, 1970).

[8]Speaking situations—sometimes termed *rhetorical situations*—can contain a broad range of constraints. Group traditions for how people should address others, for topics appropriate to various occasions, even for modes of dress and decorum represent only one class of such constraints. Others include *(a)* the style of speechmaking popular in some particular epic (compare a speech from Queen Elizabeth I's time with one from today); *(b)* the speaker's own resources and abilities; and *(c)* the pool of ideas and values which is capable of being thought about by a culture (for example, until someone "invented" the idea of citizen rights, no one could argue for extending the vote to everyone because of their "rights"). The relationships among rhetorical situations, speech constraints, and the "fittingness" of one's speech in light of those situations and constraints are discussed in Lloyd Bitzer, "The Rhetorical Situation," *Philosophy & Rhetoric* 1 (Fall 1968): 1–14.

[9]The various psychological and sociological variables which bind people together in segments are reviewed in Mary John Smith, *Persuasion and Human Action: A Review and Critique of Social Influence Theories* (Belmont, CA: Wadsworth Publishing Co., 1982), Chapter 7, "Group Interaction and Self-Persuasion," pp. 164–90.

PROBLEMS AND PROBES

1. Using your journal, study the speaking situation that faces you in your classroom. Begin with an audience analysis. What are the most common elements shared by your class members? In what areas are they most different? Develop a questionnaire that will help you discern less readily observable aspects of your classmates' beliefs, attitudes, and values.

2. Study the occasion of your speaking situation with regard to your classroom. Note the nature and purposes of the occasions on which you will speak. What are the pervading rules and customs you will need to follow? What physical conditions are apparent within the classroom? Try to predict the events that will precede and

follow your speech. Make a journal entry of your findings so that you may refer to them during the course of the term.

3. Read or listen to a speech in which the values, beliefs, and attitudes of the listeners are hostile toward the purpose of the speaker. Analyze the speech to ascertain as well as you can how the speaker has endeavored to overcome the hostility or apathy and influence the audience to accept his or her purpose and message.

ORAL ACTIVITIES

1. After your instructor has divided the class into four-person groups, meet with the other members of your group and discuss with them the next round of speeches to be presented: the actual topic you intend to use, your general and specific purpose, development of your idea or proposition, your speech plan or outline, useful kinds of supporting materials. Criticize each other's plans and preparation, offering suggestions for changes and more specific adaptations to this particular classroom audience. After discussing and evaluating the potential of your speech with a portion of your audience, you should be able to develop and present a better and more effectively adapted message to the class as a whole.

2. As a student of speech communication, you can learn something about the principles of audience analysis by observing how such public opinion pollsters as Dr. George Gallup, Jr., analyze "the great American audience" to derive the samples on which they base their predictions. Together with several other members of your class (as your instructor may designate), investigate these methods as described in books, magazine articles, and newspaper surveys, and report on them orally, either in individual presentations or in an informal discussion with the class as a whole.

3. Gather some advertisements (not want ads) and bring them to class. In groups, share your advertisements and see if you can determine the audiences for which they were intended. What needs are the advertisers trying to meet? Are they trying to create needs? What tactics do they use? How effective do you think these tactics are?

CHAPTER 6

Determining the Basic Appeals

In the preceding chapter we emphasized the importance of analyzing your audience and speech occasion in order to discover the listeners' *social characteristics, cognitive structures,* and *expectations and group traditions.* Who people are, what experiences they have had, what they believe, and what they think is appropriate to say on various occasions all determine how they will respond to your speeches. Equally important in governing these responses are their *motives*—their basic needs, wants, or desires. In this chapter we will examine the concept of "motive" as a psychological construct, and will discuss ways in which speakers can tap people's motive (psychological) structures through the use of motivational (linguistic) appeals. Finally, we will offer some advice on how to use knowledge of motives and motivational appeals to extend the analysis of the audience and to construct substantive portions of your speeches.

Motivation and Motive Needs

We may think of a *need* as some desire, want, or uneasiness which individuals sense or think about when considering their own situation. That need may arise from physiological considerations—pain, lack of food, or an uncomfortable room—and it may come about for sociocultural reasons—as when you feel left out of a group or wonder whether your peers judge you to be a "nice" person. If that need is deeply felt, it may impel you to do something about your situation, for example to eat, to adjust the thermostat, to ask to be let into a group. In these situations you have been motivated to act. A *motive need,* then, is a tendency to move or act in a certain direction, an impulse to satisfy a psychological-social want or a biological urge.

A Classification of Motive Needs

The classification of fundamental human needs most often cited today is probably the one developed by psychologist Abraham H. Maslow.[1] Maslow presents the following categories of needs and wants which impel human beings to think, act, and respond as they do:

1. *Physiological Needs* ▪ for food, drink, air, sleep, sex—the basic bodily "tissue" requirements.
2. *Safety Needs* ▪ for security, stability, protection from harm or injury; need for structure, orderliness, law, predictability; freedom from fear and chaos.
3. *Belongingness and Love Needs* ▪ for abiding devotion and warm affection with spouse, children, parents, and close friends; need to feel a part of social groups; need for acceptance and approval.
4. *Esteem Needs* ▪ for self-esteem based on achievement, mastery, competence, confidence, freedom, independence; desire for esteem of others (reputation, prestige, recognition, status).
5. *Self-Actualization Needs* ▪ for self-fulfillment, actually to become what you potentially can be; desire to actualize your capabilities; being true to your essential nature; what you *can* be you *must* be.[2]

These "needs," according to Maslow, function as a *prepotent hierarchy;* that is, lower-level needs must be largely fulfilled before higher-level needs become operative. Persons caught up in the daily struggle to satisfy physiological and safety needs will, for example, have little time and energy left to strive for "esteem" or "self-actualization." Once these basic requirements of living are satisfied, however, higher-level drives take over. We should note, moreover, that as individuals we tend to move upward or downward between one level and another as our life progresses or regresses. Maslow's category of basic human needs and the hierarchical order in which they stand are illustrated in "Maslow's Hierarchy," page 107.

Finally, it should be noted that motives do not always automatically produce certain courses of action. Physiologically, an individual may sense a sharp feeling of pain from not having eaten for two days; yet, because of social-cultural needs or pressures, this person will not gobble down a chocolate cake when presented with one, but will sit politely with fork and napkin. The need for social approval may control the way a person satisfies physiological needs. Nevertheless, the hierarchy of prepotency is useful in conceptualizing human motivation, even if individuals vary in ways they manifest those needs.

Motivational Appeals

Recognizing the power of motive needs to impel human action, you may ask: How can I as a public speaker go about creating, using, and satisfying such needs? How can I translate these basic needs, wants, or desires into verbal acts—into effective public communication? The answer to both of these questions is: with the use of motivational appeals.

MASLOW'S HIERARCHY

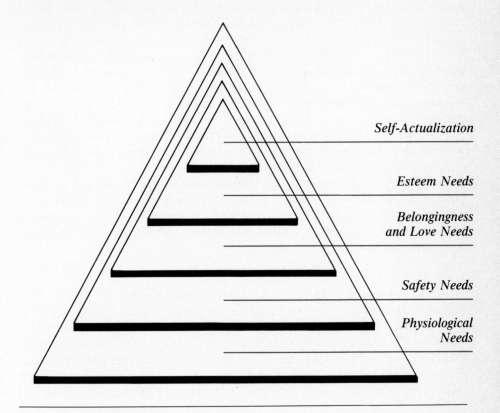

Self-Actualization

Esteem Needs

Belongingness and Love Needs

Safety Needs

Physiological Needs

A *motivational appeal* is either *(1)* a *visualization* of some desire and a method for satisfying it, or *(2)* an *assertion* that some entity, idea, or course of action can be or ought to be linked with an impulse-to-human-action—that is, a motive.

Suppose, for example, that you had been dating a person for some time, and decided one evening that it was time to declare your love. As the evening progressed, you thought about how you were going to talk to your friend. You even created little "movies" in your head—perhaps full pieces of dramatic dialogue—as you rehearsed your speech. Will I be suave, casual, or a stumbling fool? Will I find the words, the looks, the actions to move my beloved? Will the person respond to me with tears or laughter, flippantly or seriously? Here we see the power of visualization. In visualizing various scenarios, you playacted yourself and your speech through a variety of motivational appeals: Is the *fear* of rejection worth the possibility of mutual declarations of *love?* Will *aggressiveness* work better than quiet appeals to *companionship?* By a process of intrapersonal visualization you thus assembled a group of motivational appeals potent enough to move your "audience," your beloved, and you organized those appeals into little stories you could tell.

At other times, instead of visualizing courses of action for yourself or your listener, you may simply try to attach motivational concepts directly to other concepts. Technically, this verbal process is called *attribution*.[3] Suppose, for example, that you had shunned going to church because you thought of churches as *conformist, authoritarian, dominating, repulsive, destructive* institutions. One night, however, you went to a religious meeting, one where the preacher talked about the *adventure* of living a God-based life, the *beauty* of God's creation, the *reverence* one must feel in living a full life, the *endurance* one must have in overcoming doubts. You decided, upon reflection, that you had misconstrued the church's motivation and even misanalyzed yourself. You became a devout churchgoer. What happened? You changed the attributes of "church-ness" in your own mind. Instead of attributing conformity/authority/dominance to that institution and ideal, you began attributing adventure/beauty/reverence to personal religion. Conversion was effected, and your behavior changed.

Motivational appeals, therefore, are verbal attempts to make salient and relevant a series of motives within an audience, within an idea or proposal under discussion, or within a countervailing force which you think is keeping listeners from accepting an idea or proposal. Such appeals work visually (through verbal depiction) or assertively (through verbal association).

Some Types and Examples of Motivational Appeals

Present in every listener and every audience, of course, is a near-infinite number of specific wants and needs to which you could direct your appeals. Any attempt to enumerate them, therefore, must be incomplete and overlapping to some extent. However, we can assemble a representative list of motivational appeals which have been used by many successful speakers, product advertisers, and other persuaders to tap the motives for action possessed by individuals and groups. Once you master the list and understand the uses of each appeal in various situations, you can begin to use them in your analysis of audiences and in your construction of speeches. Following are some typical motivational appeals with brief examples:

Achievement and Display.   "The successful businessperson knows. . . . ," "To make maximum use of your talents, act today to. . . . " These appeals depend upon people's interest in making a mark, in developing or actualizing themselves. Such motivational appeals, therefore, are often found in actuative speeches where the speaker's goal is to produce individualized adoption of some self-help product or course of action.

Acquisition and Saving.   In this era of "me-ism," as seen in the growth of assertiveness training workshops, investment clubs, Individual Retirement Accounts, and the like, the appeal to personal savings and reward is potent. Rewards can be described in materialistic ("Earn money easily"), social ("Become one of the select few who . . . "), spiritual ("Many are called, few are chosen"), or personal ("This is your chance of a lifetime!") terms. Like appeals to achievement and display, motivational appeals to acquisition work on the individual rather than the group, and hence tend to be used in actuative speeches calling for individualized action.

Adventure and Change. "Taste the High Country!" cries the beer commercial. "Join the Army and see the world!" says the local recruiter. The human soul yearns for release; the human body seeks risk as a way of validating human worth. In release and risk, however, are potentials for danger, and not every listener will be willing to put himself or herself in danger. This motivational appeal, therefore, seldom can be the primary appeal for change in people's minds or actions; it tends to work only when individuals are all but ready to commit themselves to some change.

Companionship and Affiliation. We all need others—their presence, their touch, and their recognition of who we are. Indeed, Maslow saw belongingness as the most important human need once physiological and safety needs are fulfilled. Thus, appeals of companionship and affiliation tend to fill persuasive and actuative speeches of con-version—that is, speeches which seek to make individual listeners members of new groups or social movements. Such appeals often are phrased bluntly, as in "We care about you . . . ," "Join our group and find fellowship with kindred souls," or "Thou-sands of people like you have found solutions to their problems by joining. . . ."

Creativity. As Maslow noted, the height of self-actuation is a sense of individualized abilities and talents. The ads that urge you to "Draw Me" so as to get a "scholarship" to a correspondence school art course, and the cookbooks which insist you become a "gourmet" by following step-by-step recipes are appealing to your sense of creativity. Remember, though, that self-actualization is a motive need important to most people only when their more prepotent needs are satisfied. Appeals to creativity cannot stand alone for most listeners; rather, they must be combined with other motivational appeals (often, as in the "Draw Me" ads, with promises of material reward and personal enjoyment).

Curiosity. Children tear open alarm clocks to find out where the tick is, and adults crowd the sidewalks to gaze at a celebrity. Curiosity is sometimes "idle," yet often is the driving force behind such high achievers as experimenters, scholars, and explorers. Indeed, appeals to curiosity probably work best in speeches delivered to educated audiences, to people whose basic survival needs are satisfied and who thus can afford the time and risk to be curious.

Defense. Although the urge to fight and compete (see the discussion of fighting and aggression on page 110) is natural and therefore a source of motive need for many situations, it is an urge we often attempt to submerge. A socially acceptable way to raise a fighting spirit in people publicly, however, is to appeal to common or mutual defense—a motivational appeal so acceptable that it was written into the Declaration of Independence and the Constitution. It may, in most situations, be socially unacceptable to hurt someone to make a personal gain at his or her expense, but it almost always is acceptable to be aggressive "to protect our own interests" or "to save the lives of our children and our children's children." Such appeals tap our fundamental safety needs. Examine their use in the speech by Franklin Delano Roosevelt reprinted later in this chapter.

Deference. When we perceive that others have wisdom, experience, or expertise superior to our own, we defer to their knowledge and judgment. The successful use of testimony as a form of supporting material depends upon listeners' deference to such authority figures. To whom is this audience likely to defer? That is the question you must answer before you select pieces of testimony for your speeches.

Endurance. We all are sensitive to our own relatively short span of earthly existence, and to our place between those who have come before and those who will follow us on this planet. In a word, we are sensitive to *temporality,* to the temporal dimension of existence. Many motivational appeals can be phrased to tap this sensitivity. Appeals to the past (see the discussion of tradition, page 113) are grounded in our debts to ancestors for giving us material, valuative, and spiritual inheritance. Appeals to our present state ("You only go around once, so live life to its fullest now") depend upon our fear of an uncertain future. And appeals to the future ("We shall overcome," as the civil rights workers of the 1960s sang it, or "Let the word go forth from this time and place . . . that . . . a new generation . . . ," as President John Kennedy phrased it in 1961) are especially potent; no matter how happy we are with our current state, we all desire an even brighter future. We all hope, one way or another, to endure.[4]

Fear. Humans have a broad range of fears—of failure, of death, of speechmaking, of inadequacy, of another's triumph. Fear is powerful, and produces both good (as when an individual is driven to achievement and bravery) and evil (as when fear-based prejudice produces bestial behavior toward others). Its power has made the appeal to fear one of the most common motivational appeals in advertising: "Aren't you glad you use Dial? Don't you wish everyone did?" "Ring around the collar! Ring around the collar!" Be careful, however, in your use of fear appeals, making sure that *(1)* you don't transgress the bounds of ethics and good taste, and, more practically, *(2)* you don't make your fear appeals so strong that they actually have an opposite effect (called the "boomerang effect" by social scientists).[5]

Fighting and Aggression. Because human groups and societies tend to be hierarchical, our natural biological urge to fight for our own rights and territory becomes translated into appeals to personal and social competition. Ad after ad tells you how to "get ahead of the crowd" or to "beat your competition to the punch," and many a group leader urges action so "we can win" or so "we can beat them [competing groups or nations] at their own game." The appeal to fighting and aggression is used by speakers when individual action or heroics is called for; when the appeal is phrased collectively, it tends to become an appeal to power (see page 112).

Imitation and Conformity. At times, people's sense of belongingness becomes so strong that they feel psychological pressure to be "one of the crowd." Commercials stressing what "the in-group does," what the "serious jogger runs in," and what "all true Americans believe" contain appeals to conformity. The social scientific research on the power of social comparison and conformity pressures documents the power of this appeal.[6]

BUILDING MOTIVATIONAL APPEALS

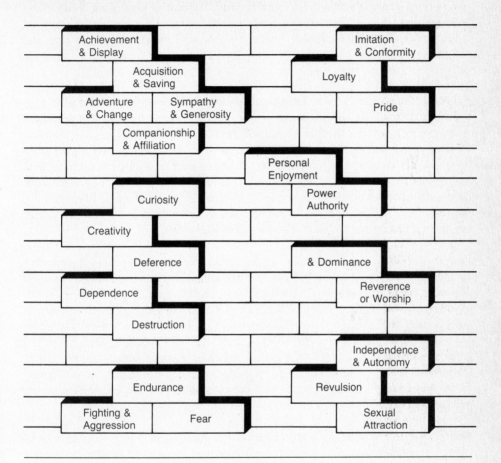

Independence and Autonomy. As often you hear appeals to conformity, you also hear "Be your own person; don't follow the crowd." Appeals to "know yourself," "be yourself," and "stand on your own two feet"—like the appeals to adventure—draw their force from our struggles to stand apart from others. Especially when persuaders are attempting to separate you as an individual from a reference group—from the pressures of conformity—they will make this appeal.

Loyalty. Periodically we all need to celebrate our membership in groups and societies so as to renew our commitments to them and increase our sense of group and social cohesiveness. In times of crisis, speakers often call for "tests of loyalty," for extraordinary actions which visibly demonstrate individuals' adherence to group standards for belief and action. Speakers often ask listeners to be loyal to friends, family, organizations, states, geographical regions, their country. Appeals to loyalty are used little in speeches attempting to change fundamental beliefs, values, or actions; rather, they are typical appeals to the like-minded—that is, to those who already believe or value, and who habitually do act in "correct" ways. Such appeals thus are typical of what are called *reinforcement speeches*.[7]

Personal Enjoyment.   Like appeals to creativity, curiosity, and independence, appeals to personal enjoyment depend on our "selfish" instincts. While we often act as group members, at least as often we will take some course of action because it promises us personal comfort and luxury, aesthetic enjoyment, recreation and rest, relief from home and work constraint, just plain fun, or any number of other personal pleasures. The "pleasure principle" may not be as strong as the "pain principle," and hence more people probably can be driven to action by fear than by its counterpart. But especially when listeners view themselves as individuals—as in demonstration speeches at craft centers, for example—this motivational appeal works well.

Power, Authority, and Dominance.   Like its first cousin, the appeal to fighting and competition, the appeal to power, authority, or dominance depends for its potency upon our sense of aggressiveness. But unlike the appeal to fighting, this appeal moves beyond "mere winning" to *control:* People with power and authority control objects or other prople. Thus, when President Jimmy Carter called his energy policy "the moral equivalent of war," he was urging us to control our energy appetites; when the public service announcement says that "Cancer can be beaten in our lifetime," it is asking you to act from a sense of domination. The appeal to power depends upon your willingness to see yourself as somehow "larger" or more potent than you now are; therein lies its motivational effectiveness.

Pride.   Appeals to pride—a sense of our own or our group's worth—can drive us to collective or individual achievement. Such appeals tighten one's loyalties to groups ("Be proud of America"), and, when coupled with appeals to adventure ("Be all that you can be in the Army"), creativity, and/or independence, they move individuals to great personal exertion. Hence, actuative speeches calling for extra measures of effort from audiences often contain appeals to pride.

Reverence or Worship.   Many times in our lives we must recognize our own inferiority—our inferiority to others of superior qualities, to institutions we admire, to nature and the cosmos, and to deities which humble us in their magnitude and eternity. Beyond deference, a sense of reverence or worship leads to submission. Such reverent submission can take three forms: *hero worship, reverence for institutions,* and *divine worship,* conceived of either religiously or philosophically (as when eighteenth-century philosophers celebrated Nature). As a speaker, you have comparatively limited power to *create* a sense of reverence in your listeners, but, if you know enough about your listeners ahead of time, you can *draw upon* references to objects, people, or institutions they are likely to revere.

Revulsion.   The fragrance of a flower garden attracts people; the odor of a garbage dump repels them. In symbolic terms, you can attract people by depicting verbally the aesthetic pleasures they'll enjoy in acquiring or doing something, or by visualizing in strong images objects of disgust or loathing. (See "imagery" in Chapter 12.) When, for example, you verbally picture the unsanitary conditions of slums or the horrors of war, you often can mobilize people to action. Beware that you don't make such descriptions so gruesome that your appeal to revulsion turns them away in disgust; here, too, watch for the boomerang effect.

Sexual Attraction.   A staple of advertising trying to sell you deodorant, hair rinse and spray, beer and liquor, and a multitude of other sundries is the sex appeal. "Sex sells" is a truism on Madison Avenue. Actually, as you look closely at such appeals, you'll find the core of the appeals lies not so much in bodily functions per se as in a more general idea of personal attractiveness and, in some cases, secret yearning and adventure. Especially over the last decade, as our masculine and feminine consciousness have been raised, we have come to reject most objectionally blatant appeals to libidinous appetites; the days when Noxema could advertise its shaving cream with "Take it off . . . Take it all off . . ." are gone. In most ads these days, the appeal to sexual attraction is approached verbally only in indirect ways ("When you want to look your best, use . . . "; "For the executive who wants to be noticed . . ."). Advertising agencies usually let pictures offer the sexual images directly, reinforcing them with indirect verbal enticements. As a speaker, you, too, are well advised to keep your sex appeals phrased in indirect language so as not to offend some listeners while yet reaching others' concern for personal attractiveness.

Sympathy and Generosity.   Although we often (cynically) assume that most people are basically selfish, we know that, on many occasions, we all can be shamed or drawn to reach out for others. All appeals to giving, to support for others, and to self-sacrifice in the name of the "common good" are based on the assumption that your *social self* (that part of you bonded to others) will overcome your *private self* (that part of you which is self-centered) when the right appeal is made. "Reach out and touch someone," "Give that others might live," "When you care enough to send the very best"— such appeals form the heart of many an actuative speech. Appeals for public generosity depend in part, of course, on our sense of conformity, but also in part on our sense of "There but for the grace of God go I"—our sense that we, too, would want help were we in need or trouble. Sympathy is a powerful appeal, often the heart of fund-raising speeches.

Tradition.   As noted, the appeal to tradition is closely associated with appeals to endurance. It, too, depends upon one's sense of temporality—the past's relationships to the present and future. Tradition also is related to appeals to loyalty—loyalty to one's roots, nurturing institutions, and family. Nevertheless, tradition also can be considered a unique motivational appeal, because it operates psychologically in a different way from its cousins. "Endurance" stretches your mind into the future, while "tradition" draws your thoughts back to the people and the ideas which have formed you, given you strength and a sense of self-identity, and drawn you into a community with other like-minded people. And, while an appeal to loyalty asks you (one being) to attach yourself to another person or institution, thereby in a sense "separating" you from that which demands loyalty, the appeal to tradition psychologically produces a direct identification between you and the institution or person being called up. Appeals to tradition are typical of political speeches: Democrats talk about "Democratic traditions" and Republicans list "Republican principles" which, when you think of yourself as either a Democrat or a Republican, tell you rather precisely what to think, what to do, whom to like, whom to dislike. Leaders of parties, organizations, and various other institutions punctuate almost every speech to their followers with such appeals, in hopes that the followers' sense of public identity and group commitment will keep them identified with the group.

You may have noticed that some appeals in this list seem to contradict each other—for example, fear vs. the drive for adventure, sympathy vs. the appeals to fighting or power, and so on. Remember, however, that the human being is a bundle of contradictory impulses, balancing urges, making decisions between personal gratification and public good; you are a changeable creature who, at various times, may pursue quite different ends or goals. Our discussion of these and other motivational appeals, thus, is not an attempt to organize the human psyche in an orderly manner, but rather an attempt to help speakers comprehend the kinds of motivational weapons at their disposal. Hence, we turn next to questions concerning the rhetorical use of motivational appeals in speechmaking.

Using Motivational Appeals in Speech Preparation

Using Appeals to Extend Audience Analysis

In the previous chapter we presented a step-by-step analysis of a speaking situation in which a speaker proposed to get an athletic board to expand women's competitive sports on her campus (see pp. 99–101). We concluded the speaker's analysis by pointing out some relevant valuative appeals she could make. Now that you have learned in this chapter of more specific motivational appeals, you probably can understand why the speaker's analysis continued with the following:

III. *ADAPTIVE STRATEGIES*
    C. *Motivational Appeals*
        1. *Introduce* speech with thanks for fine intramural program now available to women (appeal to previous *generosity*). Make reference to surrounding facilities and equipment (appeal to current *achievements*).
        2. *Stress* heavily the philosophical values of intercollegiate competition for women (such an appeal to professionals often ridiculed as "jocks" and anti-intellectuals can emphasize *personal worth, adventure, creativity, competition, and pride*). Mention—but with this predominantly male audience, do not overemphasize— the matter of equality between the sexes (allay fears, and only gently move into questions of *dominance*).
        3. *Be prepared* to answer Board's possible questions concerning number of women interested (indirect appeal to *political power*), neighboring schools which could

When your audience is comparatively homogeneous—a labor audience, in this case—you normally can select particular motivational appeals aimed at its beliefs, attitudes, and values.

furnish opponents (appeal to *competition*), estimated cost of the proposed program (appeal to *ease in acquisition*), available locker-room facilities (visualization of proposal's *workability*), and other questions that might be raised.

Overall, this speaker stressed a philosophical plane so as to work in grand motivational appeals to "higher" human achievements, with secondary appeals aimed at political and economic value orientations. As an initial proposal, it maintained a firm, but conciliatory, tone. If the proposal had been rejected unreasonably, the next speech might have made the political and economic values more important, especially if the speaker believed that confrontation was the only route to persuasion.[8]

Reflecting upon this speaker's rhetorical choices raises an extremely important question: How do you decide which motivational appeals to use in your speech? That is a near-impossible question to answer, of course, because so much depends upon the specific group of listeners you face, the occasion, and even your own predilections. But, in general, three factors in the speaking situation ought to guide your consideration of motivational appeals in the speech preparation process:

1. *Type of Speech.* As has been suggested in the descriptions of various motivational appeals, sometimes the type of speech you are delivering helps you select appeals. The various appeals to individuality—adventure, creativity, personal enjoyment, and so on—often appear in attitude-change and even actuative speeches whose goals are to break a person free from previous group associations. For example, if

you are asking fellow classmates to forego a generally accepted B.A. degree in favor of a flexible Bachelor of General Studies (with no major and few requirements, available on some campuses), you could appeal reasonably to creativity (build your own program), adventure (break away from the crowd in all of the courses required for the B.A.), and nonconformity (the feeling of freedom in independently guiding your own fate). In contrast, speeches which reinforce existing beliefs and values tend to work on collective rather than individualized appeals—collective appeals such as those to companionship and affiliation, mutual defense, deference to others, imitation and conformity, loyalty, and power.

2. *Demographic Analysis.* Knowing something about audience members—their ages, walks of life, education, and so on—likewise will help you select potentially powerful motivational appeals. As we noted earlier, for example, educated, upper-middle and upper-class listeners can "afford" to respond to appeals to creativity, independence, the pleasure principle inherent to personal enjoyment, and generosity. Young people are notoriously prone to appeals to sexual attraction and to testimony from cultural celebrities. Appeals to endurance are potent with older listeners, as, in general, are appeals to loyalty and reverence. Appeals to one's ethnic traditions and sense of belongingness within familial circles work well with homogeneous audiences who gather, say, to celebrate "Chicano Pride Week" or "Martin Luther King Day." Concerns for companionship, affiliation, and power typically punctuate speeches given to audiences gathered at a women's political caucus.

3. *Personal Predilections.* Finally, always look to yourself—your beliefs and attitudes, your enduring values—when selecting motivational appeals. Ask yourself such questions as: "Am I willing to ask people to act from fear, or do I think my calls for changes in behavior should be grounded on such 'higher' motives as sympathy and generosity?" "Do I actually believe in the importance of loyalty and reverence?" In other words, assess your own principles before selecting motivational appeals; use only those appeals that *you* think are important motivators of human thought and action.

Using Appeals in Your Speeches: Strategic Choices

It is important, then, to develop skill, tact, and good judgment in your use of motivational appeals. You can gain such attributes by considering your speech purposes, making a technically sound audience analysis, and reflecting on your own habits. Beyond that, certain general communication rules regarding motivational appeals have evolved over the years. Such rules include the following:

1. *Avoid blatant, objectionally obvious, or overly aggressive motivational appeals.* Do not say, as extreme examples, "Mr. Harlow Jones, the successful banker, has just contributed handsomely to our cause. Come on, now. *Imitate* this generous and community-spirited man!" Or, "If you give to this cause we will print your name in the paper so that your *reputation* as a generous person will be known by everyone." Such appeals can produce a boomerang effect. Instead, in making an appeal of this sort, respect the intelligence and—more important—the public sensitivities of your audience. Suggest, through the use of what we earlier described as visualization,

When facing a heterogeneous audience, segment them into identifiable demographic or psychological groups, and then offer arguments and appeals aimed at each group.

that contributors will not only be associated with others in a worthwhile and successful venture, but will also have the appreciation of many who are less fortunate than they. In other words, let listeners "think" about "selfish" motives themselves so they don't feel insulted by your blatancy and aggression. An insulted audience is unlikely to act favorably as a result of your appeal.

2. *Use motivational appeals in combination, especially when some of them are socially suspect.* Appealing to self-centered interests—private fears, monetary gain or acquisition, and self-pride—can represent an excellent persuasive strategy; however, people, especially in groups, are often reluctant to acknowledge that they are acting for selfish reasons. This sometimes creates a dilemma for a speaker: Although person-centered appeals might work well, audience members might not wish to surrender to their own interests in front of others. For example, at the end of the year many people contribute to charitable causes to increase their income tax deductions, but a speaker can hardly tell a group of people that the main reason they should give to a fund drive is to make some personal financial gains. Similarly, many people who are persuaded to join an exercise group because they have deep-seated fears of heart attacks, when asked why they exercise, are likely to say, "Oh, because it makes me feel so good." The response conceals their specific fears. Thus, as a speaker you may need to combine appeals to seemingly self-centered motives with more publicly acceptable motives. Even though people give to some causes for selfish reasons, you must suggest they are doing it for socially valued reasons like sympathy and generosity, loyalty, adventure, or change. The more

self-centered motives can be mentioned, but they probably should not dominate your speech.

3. *Use motivational appeals in combination when you face a heterogeneous audience.* The analysis of social and cognitive structures offered in Chapter 5 can help you select an array of motivational appeals for a particular speech. Think about the range of ages, occupations, ethnic groups, fixed beliefs, valuative orientations, and so on represented in your audience, and then try to select motivational appeals that will be attractive to auditors in each of those categories. Suppose you were speaking to an Optimist Club on the need for a trauma center at the local hospital. In an Optimist Club you are likely to find doctors, storekeepers, old people, young persons, members of social service agencies, minority businesspeople, and the like. This suggests that you will want to appeal to the financial interests of the business community (as more people will be brought to town, the number of consumers will increase); to the self-pride of doctors (who presumably will be able to treat severely injured patients more successfully); to the fears of older citizens (who now will have greatly improved chances of surviving heart attacks); to the innovativeness of younger persons (who usually value progress highly); to the humanitarian orientation of the social service agents (who always approve of ways to increase care for others); and to the medical plight of low-income minorities (who as a group often are denied quick treatment of the type offered by trauma centers). "Something for everyone"—within reason and good taste—should mark the motivational appeal in your speech.

4. *Think through Maslow's hierarchy as you settle on your motivational emphases in speeches.* Suppose you were giving a speech in favor of an urban renewal project to members of a ghetto. Appeals to higher-level needs (esteem needs such as achievement, prestige, or status) are likely to fall on deaf ears, for you would be addressing folks primarily concerned with such basic physiological needs as food and shelter and such safety needs as security, protection, and freedom from harassment. A speech on that topic to that audience probably ought not spend much time discussing beautification; instead it could emphasize increased access to goods and services, improved housing, better streetlighting, controlled traffic, and better opportunities for community-centered law enforcement. The time-honored truism of public speaking, "Hit 'em where they are," deserves your attention when you are selecting motivational appeals.

5. *Think of ways to organize your motivational appeals effectively.* Later, we will discuss organizational patterns and ways of choosing one appropriate to your purpose, your audience, and your materials. For now, we can note that it also is possible to select an organizational pattern appropriate to the motivational appeals you settle upon. Your motivational appeals can control the entire structure; Chapter 8 will offer such a pattern, called the "Motivated Sequence." Read that chapter carefully.

6. *Finally, use motivational appeals in ethically sound ways.* Even in a free and open society, there are ethical bounds which, when crossed by the overzealous speaker,

produce public condemnation or even retribution. Communication ethics are more than a matter of not lying or not misrepresenting yourself to an audience. They also impinge on motives and motivational appeals. Urging an audience to take a course of action because it will make them rich at the expense of others who have less power or knowledge, for example, is an ethically suspect motivational appeal; so is an intense, sustained fear appeal that finds hidden conspiracies to destroy the world under every rock and bush. The demagogue may win a battle now and then, but seldom wins the war. Think carefully about your own ethical limits, and about what kinds of appeals outrage you when *you* are a member of an audience. The social penalties for overstepping moral boundaries in your appeals can be relatively severe, and you must decide to what degree you are willing to risk social censure for what you advocate and how you advocate it.

In summary, think of motives as springs—as wants or desires tightly coiled and waiting for the "right" appeal or verbal depiction to set them off. Those springs, when worked by the skillful speaker, can convert the individuals in an audience into a cohesive group ready to think and act in ways consistent with your purpose. One of your jobs as a speaker is careful preplanning, so that your motivational appeals can release those powerful springs to thought and action. Further information on this vital topic is contained in the Speaker's Resource Book section, "Ethics and Public Speaking," pages 393–95.

Sample Speech

The following speech, delivered to a joint session of Congress on December 8, 1941, was President Franklin Delano Roosevelt's message requesting a declaration of war against Japan. Before that date, the United States had been negotiating around the clock with that nation to keep the peace; and, seemingly, all was going well. Then suddenly, on Sunday morning, December 7, the Japanese launched a massive, surprise attack on Pearl Harbor, Hawaii, sinking eight American battleships and other smaller craft and leveling planes and airfields.

The nation was numbed; Congress was indignant; and the President moved quickly. The joint session was held in the House chamber. The galleries were overflowing, and the speech was broadcast worldwide.

Notice the President's strategies, particularly his use of supporting materials and motivational appeals. Paragraphs 2 and 3 are cast in narrative form so that background information would be easy to comprehend. Paragraph 4 offers the only comparatively detailed illustration; Roosevelt obviously felt that short, quick specific instances—constructed in parallel fashion in Paragraphs 5 through 10—would have greater impact, especially as they could be molded into a reinforcing summary of American beliefs and attitudes in Paragraph 11. The President then was in a position to call for a solution to the problem—the declaration of war—via a series of motivational appeals to power, pride, patriotism, fear, and reverence. Few speeches have ever more efficiently used such a variety of supporting materials and motivational appeals.

For a Declaration of War Against Japan[9]
Franklin Delano Roosevelt

Introduction	TO THE CONGRESS OF THE UNITED STATES: Yesterday, December 7, 1941—a date which will live in infamy—the United States of America was suddenly and deliberately attacked by naval and air forces of the Empire of Japan. /1
Body *Background orientation—Narration of the problem*	The United States was at peace with that nation and, at the solicitation of Japan, was still in conversation with its government and its Emperor, looking toward the maintenance of peace in the Pacific. Indeed, one hour after Japanese air squadrons had commenced bombing in Oahu, the Japanese Ambassador to the United States and his colleague delivered to the Secretary of State a formal reply to a recent American message. While this reply stated that it seemed useless to continue the existing diplomatic negotiations, it contained no threat or hint of war or armed attack. /2
Statement of the problem	It will be recorded that the distance of Hawaii from Japan makes it obvious that the attack was deliberately planned many days or even weeks ago. During the intervening time the Japanese government had deliberately sought to deceive the United States by false statements and expressions of hope for continued peace. /3
Illustration	The attack yesterday on the Hawaiian Islands has caused severe damage to American naval and military forces. Very many American lives have been lost. In addition, American ships have been reported torpedoed on the high seas between San Francisco and Honolulu. /4
Specific instances	Yesterday the Japanese government also launched an attack against Malaya. /5 Last night Japanese forces attacked Hong Kong. /6 Last night Japanese forces attacked Guam. /7 Last night Japanese forces attacked the Philippine Islands. /8 Last night the Japanese attacked Wake Island. /9 This morning the Japanese attacked Midway Island. /10
Reinforcing summary	Japan has, therefore, undertaken a surprise offensive extending throughout the Pacific area. The facts of yesterday speak for themselves. The people of the United States have already formed their opinions and well understand the implications to the very life and safety of our nation. /11
Solution	As Commander-in-Chief of the Army and Navy I have directed that all measures be taken for our defense. /12
Appeal to defense	Always will we remember the character of the onslaught against us. /13
Appeal to power and pride	No matter how long it may take us to overcome this premeditated invasion, the American people in their righteous might will win through to absolute victory. /14

Appeal to patriotism	I believe I interpret the will of the Congress and of the people when I assert that we will not only defend ourselves to the uttermost but will make very certain that this form of treachery shall never endanger us again. /15
Overcoming fear	Hostilities exist. There is no blinking at the fact that our people, our territory, and our interests are in grave danger. /16
Reverence for strength, nation, and God	With confidence in our armed forces—with the unbounded determination of our people—we will gain the inevitable triumph—so help us God. /17
Conclusion *Appeal to aggression*	I ask that the Congress declare that since the unprovoked and dastardly attack by Japan on Sunday, December 7, a state of war has existed between the United States and the Japanese Empire.★ /18

REFERENCE NOTES

[1]Data based on Hierarchy of Needs in "A Theory of Human Motivation" in *Motivation and Personality*, 2nd Edition, by Abraham H. Maslow. Copyright © 1970 by Abraham H. Maslow. Reprinted by permission of Harper & Row, Publishers, Inc.

[2]In the 1970 revision of his book, *Motivation and Personality*, Maslow identified two additional needs—the needs to know and understand and aesthetic needs—as higher need states which frequently operate as part of self-actualization needs.

[3]For a fuller discussion of "attribution," see Philip G. Zimbardo, Ebbe B. Ebbesen, and Christina Maslach, *Influencing Attitudes and Changing Behavior*, 2nd ed. (Reading, MA: Addison-Wesley Publishing Company, 1977), especially pp. 72–80.

[4]*Inaugural Addresses of the Presidents of the United States* . . . (Washington, D. C.: United States Government Printing Office, 1961), p. 267.

[5]For a review of the research on fear appeals, see Erwin P. Bettinghaus, *Persuasive Communication*, 3rd ed. (New York: Holt, Rinehart and Winston, 1980), pp. 145–47. On the boomerang effect, see Thomas M. Scheidel, *Persuasive Speaking* (Glenview, IL: Scott, Foresman and Company, 1967), pp. 81–82.

[6]For discussions of "conformity" and "social comparison theory," see Mary John Smith, *Persuasion and Human Action: A Review and Critique of Social Influence Theories* (Belmont, CA: Wadsworth Publishing Company, 1982), Chapter 7, "Group Interaction and Self-Persuasion," and Chapter 11, "Judgmental Theories of Persuasion," pp. 164–90, 264–83.

[7]For a discussion of reinforcement speeches, see Bruce E. Gronbeck, *The Articulate Person: A Guide to Everyday Public Speaking*, 2nd ed. (Glenview, IL: Scott, Foresman and Company, 1983), Chapter 7, "Reinforcing Old Beliefs and Values," pp. 155–71. See also Chapter 17 of this textbook.

[8]For an interesting attempt to rank-order, in terms of rhetorical sophistication, possible strategies for proposers of significant change, see John Waite Bowers and Donovan J.

★For a fuller analysis of this speech, see Hermann G. Stelzner, " 'War Message,' December 8, 1941: An Approach to Language," *Speech Monographs*, 33 (November 1966), 419–37. Also reprinted in Robert L. Scott and Bernard L. Brock, *Methods of Rhetorical Criticism: A Twentieth-Century Perspective*, 2nd ed. (Detroit: Wayne State University Press, 1980), pp. 298–320.

Ochs, *The Rhetoric of Agitation and Control* (Reading, MA: Addison-Wesley Publishing Company, Inc., 1971), esp. Chapter 2.

[9]Originally printed in the *Congressional Record*, 77th Congress, 1st Session, Volume 87, Part 9, pp. 9504–9505, December 8, 1941.

PROBLEMS AND PROBES

1. Bring to class three examples of speeches which incorporate motivational appeals as discussed in this chapter. Explain what kinds of appeals are used in each and why. Do these motive appeals add to or detract from the speaker's persuasive effort? What other appeals could the speakers have utilized? Combine your examples and analysis in a brief written report and hand it to your instructor.

2. Clip and bring to class ten magazine advertisements which contain one or more motivational appeals. In preparing this assignment, identify each appeal, write a brief statement telling why you think it was selected to sell this particular product, and evaluate its effectiveness. Note that a motivational appeal may be used both in an illustration and in the printed text to reinforce each other and the motivational appeal(s) of the advertisement as a whole. Hand your analyses to your instructor, and be ready to talk about them informally in class.

ORAL ACTIVITIES

1. Present a three- or four-minute speech in which, through the combined use of two or three related motivational appeals, you attempt to persuade your audience to a particular belief or action. (For example, combine appeals to *adventure, companionship,* and *personal enjoyment* to persuade them to take a conducted group tour of Europe; or combine *sympathy* and *pride* to elicit contributions to a charity drive.) At the conclusion of your speech, ask a classmate to identify the motive appeals you used. If other members of the class disagree with that identification, explore with the class the reasons why your appeals did not come through as you intended, and what you might have done to sharpen and strengthen them.

2. In a group discussion with other members of your class, attempt to construct a list of principles which help differentiate ethical from unethical appeals. In the course of discussion, answer the following questions: *(a)* Under what conditions would you consider a motive appeal to the wants or desires of listeners an entirely ethical and legitimate means of persuasion? *(b)* Under what conditions might such an appeal be unethical? *(c)* Where does the ethical responsibility rest: with the speaker? with the audience? or in adherence to a list of external criteria?

3. Assume you have a friend who is considering dropping out of school. What motivational appeal would you use to convince your friend to continue his or her education if you wanted to direct those appeals to your friend's *(a)* physiological needs; *(b)* safety needs; *(c)* belongingness and love needs; *(d)* esteem needs; *(e)* self-actualization needs? What factors help you to distinguish between those appeals? Illustrate your appeals with specific examples or statements. Then get into small groups to discuss your analyses with your classmates.

CHAPTER 7

Developing Your Ideas:

Finding and Using

Supporting Materials

The effective communication of ideas depends on more than the selection of appropriate motivational appeals. If your specific purpose is to provide information on ways to seek summer employment, the central idea "Summer employment opportunities are all around you" may be a good place to start. Now, how do you clarify this statement? What specific materials will you need to dispel possible audience disbelief in your rather optimistic assertion? The central idea calls for examples of employment opportunities and for precise information on how to obtain these jobs. Similarly, if you wish to justify your thesis that nuclear plants should be closed down, you may need to go beyond the assertions "Nuke plants are unsafe" and "Everyone knows that the safe disposal of nuclear waste is impossible." An audience favorably disposed to your claims probably won't require much beyond your simple assertion, as they can expand the statements with information they have in their possession. A neutral or hostile audience, on the other hand, probably will be dissatisfied with your general claims. These listeners will require specific data on the safety question; they also will object to the erroneous assumption that "everyone knows." Your task is to bolster your claims by providing specific information relevant to both issues.

The forms of supporting materials identified in this chapter are the medium of exchange between your personal ideas and audience acceptance. Their function is to amplify, clarify, or justify the beliefs, attitudes, and values you wish to convey to your audience. They are the flesh and blood which bring your leading ideas to life and sustain them once they have been implanted in the minds of others. After identifying the forms and factors influencing their selection, we will consider common sources of such materials and illustrate their use in informative and persuasive contexts.

What to Look For:
The Forms of Supporting Material

There are seven forms of supporting material (see figure, page 125) which you may use to develop or to justify the major ideas in a speech:

1. Explanation,
2. Analogy or comparison,
3. Illustration (detailed example),
4. Specific instances (undeveloped examples),
5. Statistics,
6. Testimony, and
7. Restatement.

Often, two or more of these kinds of materials are combined, as when statistics are used to develop an illustration, or when the testimony of an authority is given to strengthen or to verify an explanation. Whether used singly or in combination, the material you select is governed by your needs. Comparisons and hypothetical illustrations, for example, help make ideas clear and vivid. Specific instances, statistics, and testimony effectively build justifications for your theses. Factual illustrations and restatements serve both purposes. Let us examine each type of supporting material.

Explanation

By definition, an *explanation* is an expository or descriptive passage which seeks *(1)* to make clear the nature of a term, concept, process, or proposal; or *(2)* to offer a supporting rationale for a contestable claim. Three types of explanations are especially useful in making ideas clear and/or forceful: *explanations of what, explanations of how,* and *explanations of why.*[1]

Explanations of What.   Some explanations serve to delineate more specifically what a speaker is discussing; they make ideas clearer and more concrete, giving audiences enough details so that they can get their minds around a concept. For example, Kenda Creasy, Miami University, offered this explanation of a *hospice* in a speech on that subject:

> A hospice is an alternative method of terminal care comprised of a team of doctors, psychologists, clergy, and volunteers who—basically—make housecalls. A hospice's aim is to help people die with as little discomfort and as much serenity as possible, involving family and friends along the way, and usually taking place in the person's home. Hospices do not cure; instead, they make medical, psychological, and spiritual help available to both the patient AND his family, before and after the funeral. As one health analyst put it, "A hospice is really more of an idea than a place."[2]

Kenda's brief definition gives the audience an indication of what a hospice is. Recognizing that this is only a general statement, Kenda goes on in the speech to offer examples of individuals who have benefited from the care provided by a hospice. Through definition and examples, she fully illustrates her thesis that hospices are valuable alternatives to hospital care.

MATERIALS FOR VERBALLY SUPPORTING AN IDEA

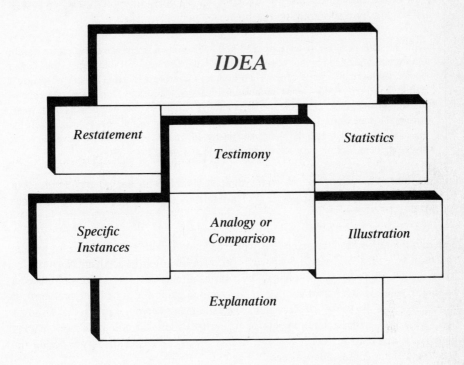

In elaborating on his argument that intelligence tests often are taken as reality, Neil Postman explains what often is meant by *overachiever:*

> It is someone whose score on a standardized IQ test is relatively low—say, a 94—but whose real-life intellectual performance is consistently high. In other words, the test can't be wrong. The student *is* a 94. He merely insists on behaving as if he were not. Perhaps there is even something perverse in him. Certainly, there is an element of perversity in the underachiever—someone whose test score is relatively high but who does not perform well in other respects. The point is that the test score is taken as the reality. The student's behavior in various contexts is to be judged against this standard.[3]

Explanations may ground the entire discussion of a term or concept, or may be an integral part of a larger argument. Where Kenda's explanation of a hospice was central to her entire speech, Neil's explanation of overachievers and underachievers is only a small part of his overall argument.

Explanations of How.   A second class of explanations tells audiences "how"—how something came to be, or how something is done. These explanations are especially appropriate when you are demonstrating a process, such as repairing a rust hole in a car fender or listing the steps in carrying out CPR. P. Dorothy Gilbert introduced a speech on chair-caning by elaborating on the process:

> The intricate patterns of cane or reed you see on chair seats make the process seem mysterious and all too artistic for most of us. On the contrary. As I will demonstrate to you today, anyone can learn to cane a chair in order to restore a valuable antique or to save a family heirloom. Chair-caning involves five easy-to-learn steps. First, soak the cane to make it pliable; then, clean out the holes through which the cane will be stretched. Next, weave the cane or reed through the holes in four to seven operations. Fourth, tie off the pieces of cane underneath the chair. And finally, lace a heavier piece of cane over the holes to cover them. Let me describe each step, one at a time.

Explanations of how things work, with sample items clarifying each step of a process or actual live demonstrations of portions of a total process, can help increase audience attention and interest.

Explanations of Why.   Explanations which account for a thing's existence or present state can be called *explanations of why*. They appear often in academic lectures, as when a chemistry professor explains why a series of chemical interactions produced a particular result. Such explanations can lay the foundation for remedying problems; if we are aware of the causes of a problem, we can move toward a solution that removes the "whys" or at least circumvents or neutralizes their harmful influence. Wendy Fletcher, University of North Dakota, uses a "why" explanation in answering the question "What causes heart disease?":

> Epidemiologists have associated a number of risk factors such as excessive smoking and high concentrations of cholesterol with heart disease. However, not everyone who possesses the risk factor suffers a heart attack, and many people who do have heart attacks are not members of the high-risk groups. While there are many theories concerning heart disease, one of the more widely accepted was developed by Meyer Friedman and Roy Rosenmann of the Mount Zion Hospital and Medical Center in San Francisco. This theory links heart disease to a specific behavior pattern—the Type A or coronary-prone personality. They have characterized the Type A individual as marked by "excessive time-urgency, impatience, competitiveness, aggression and hostility." As a result, the Type A person is often in a state of internal stress that may be largely self-imposed and not necessary for coping with the environment. Persons lacking Type A characteristics are classified as Type B and are at a lower risk level for having heart attacks and other related diseases.[4]

In this instance, Wendy nicely combines an explanation of *why* (Type A) with *what* (the characteristics of Type A). Without the added clarification, the theory offered on the cause of heart disease would be meaningful only to those who already knew the difference between Type A and B personalities.

Explanations of *what, how,* and *why* can assist you in clarifying your meaning or in justifying your position on an issue. In using explanations, keep them brief and to the point, as the above examples illustrate. If you go on at length, adding detail on detail or qualification on qualification, your ideas will become too complex for an audience to follow. In addition, speak in specific, concrete terms. Abstract language or general claims may be necessary in initiating a theme or an issue, but a speech packed with such statements will not draw audiences to your message. Finally, combine explanations with other forms of supporting material to assist in conveying ideas that are clear, interesting, and relevant to your purpose in speaking.

Analogy or Comparison

In an analogy or comparison, similarities are pointed out between something that is already known, understood, or believed by the listeners and something that is not. Thus, you might explain the game of cricket to an American audience by comparing it with baseball, or tell how a thermostat works by comparing it with a simple thermometer. Analogies or comparisons may be either *figurative* or *literal*.

Figurative Analogies.   Figurative analogies involve phenomena which, though basically different, exhibit comparable properties or relationships. They function especially well in making ideas or concepts clear by relating them to ideas or objects already familiar to the audience. Dr. Louis Hadley Evans, minister-at-large for the Presbyterian Church, drew these figurative analogies to distinguish between the terms *deist* and *theist:*

> To you the world is what: a clock or a car? Is it a huge clock, that God once made, that He wound up at the beginning and left it to run of itself? Then you are a *deist.* Do you believe that it is rather a car that God once made, but that does not run without His hand on the wheel, without His ultimate and personal control? Then you are a *theist.*[5]

In this example, the speaker clarifies two terms and an abstract concept (God) by comparing two machines whose operation is familiar to the audience. The notion of independence (clock) versus dependence (car) helps the audience discriminate between two terms whose meaning may be either unknown or unclear.

Literal Analogies.   Although analogies which compare things that are unlike—the world with a clock or a car, for example—may be excellent means of clarifying a point or making it vivid, they generally are of limited value in justifying a thesis. If your purpose is to justify an assertion, it is more effective to employ comparisons of *like* phenomena. Thus, you might argue that a system of one-way traffic on the downtown streets of City X would relieve congestion and promote safety because such a system has had these effects in City Y. In arguing for a needed revision in the way job incentives are viewed, Caroline Bird compares what happened during World War II and what could happen today:

> Most job incentives now assume that we're all living in the 1950s when the top managers who set them up were young men starting out. We need to redesign jobs around the lifestyles of the 1970s. And as F.D.R. said when he asked for the first 50,000 airplanes, "The engineers can do it if they really try."

It's comforting to think back to World War II when we think of this future restructuring, because the engineers did it. They did it by making the jobs fit people. They broke tasks up so that women could do them and blacks could do them, and people could do them part time if needed. They simplified tasks for the newcomers and made them more efficient for everyone.[6]

Caroline suggests that what has been done in a specific time in the past can be done again, and with the same beneficial results. Charlton Heston provides another illustration of a literal analogy, again using past history as a guide to the present:

Less than forty-five years ago, we saw the same phenomenon in Europe we see now. The enemy was Hitler then, but the fear of war was just as real. Then, as now, this fear led many to propose the most irrational compromises, the most cringing accommodations. Winston Churchill, out of office and vilified as a war-monger, fought to stem the tide. A rich lady labourite chided him once at dinner. "Tell me, Mr. Churchill," she said, "Why do you try so hard to persuade us that Hitler is a bad man?" "If I do not succeed, Madam," said Churchill, "I'm afraid you will find out." They did. We may well find out in our time.[7]

Because it attempts to base a conclusion on a parallel instance, an analogy used as proof must meet a rigid test: *The instances compared must be closely similar in all essential respects*. In the examples cited above, how similar are the parallels that are drawn? If jobs could be redefined in order to meet an emergency in 1945, can they today—based on this parallel? Heston's argument is part of a larger attack on the nuclear freeze movement; he implies in the above example that we have replaced Hitler with the Soviet Union, and that Churchill's comments hold true for the present case. The central question is whether the similarity on which the argument is based outweighs any *differences* which could be put forward. This is the question that needs to be asked—and answered—when you try to use an analogy as justification for a contention or claim.

Illustration

An *illustration* is a detailed example in narrative form. It may be used to picture the results of adopting the proposal you advocate, or to describe in detail conditions as they now exist. An illustration has two principal characteristics: *(1)* it uses narrative form—recounting a happening or telling a story; and *(2)* it contains vividly described details. There are two types of illustrations: *hypothetical,* describing an imaginary situation, and *factual,* describing an actual happening.

Hypothetical Illustration.   A hypothetical illustration, although an imaginary narrative, is believable if consistent with known facts. An audience will judge the illustration on the presumed likelihood of its actually occurring. Pam Williams, Ball State University, uses a hypothetical illustration with an unexpected twist:

Suzanne and Jack are going on a trip. They've been preparing for weeks, making sure all their shots, papers, and passports are in order. However, as they board the plane to leave, they are warned repeatedly, "Don't drink the water, it's bad for you." Suzanne and Jack aren't going to Mexico. They don't live in New York City or Chicago. Suzanne and Jack live in France and they are coming to the United States.[8]

In creating a hypothetical illustration, you can manipulate the "facts" at will, so long as your construction remains plausible to an audience. In Pam's illustration, the shock value comes in challenging the normal assumption that people warned about water quality are U.S. citizens who are traveling abroad. This approach creates great attention in her premise that water quality in our own country is deteriorating. Such illustrations can go a long way toward clarifying your ideas or stimulating interest in your thesis. The hypothetical illustration also is useful in explaining how something is done; you can create a person, and then picture that individual going through the steps in the process. If you want to engage the audience even more, select the name of someone from the audience for your imaginary journey. But, while the hypothetical illustration may set up the situation for you, it falls short of justifying your premise. In her speech on water quality, Pam went on to provide concrete evidence of deterioration. Because you can manipulate the details of your illustration, the audience may be understandably reluctant to accept your premise without further support. Be sure to provide that support.

Factual Illustration.   A well-chosen factual illustration is one of the most potent forms of support a speaker can use. The vividness of actual events increases the persuasive impact of the message, drawing the audience into the situation being described. Kathy Weisensel of the University of Wisconsin used her personal knowledge of two retarded persons in removing beliefs that such individuals are ineducable and incapable of leading happy and productive lives. With reference to her brother, David, she noted:

> Under Wisconsin law he was entitled to school until age twenty-one, and he spent all those years in a separate special class. There he learned the basic skills of reading, writing, and mathematics. After graduation he was employed by the Madison Opportunity Center, a sheltered workshop for the retarded. He leaves home each morning on a special bus and returns each evening after eight hours of simple assembly-line work. While he is by no means self-supporting and independent, he loves his work, and he is a happy man and a neat person with whom to share a family.[9]

With this illustration and others, Kathy was able to show that common misconceptions about the retarded can be removed; many such persons can be trained and can lead happy lives.

There are three major questions to consider when using factual illustrations to support or explain an idea:

1. *Is the illustration clearly related to the idea that is to be clarified or justified?* If you stretch the credulity of the listener in making the connection, the illustration will be of little use.

2. *Is it a typical example?* An audience often is quick to notice unusual circumstances in an illustration; if your illustration appears peculiar or odd to the audience (the exception rather than the rule) it will not prove very convincing.

3. *Is it vivid and impressive in detail?* The primary value of an illustration is the sense of reality it creates. If this quality is absent, the advantage of using an illustration is lost.

As you integrate illustrations into your speech, determine whether they meet the tests of relevance, fairness, and vividness of detail.

Specific Instance

A *specific instance* is an *undeveloped* illustration or example. Instead of describing a situation with a detailed narrative, you simply refer to it in passing. Specific instances most often are used to make an idea clear and understandable. The reference may be to an event, person, place, or process that your audience already is familiar with. Jane Scott of the University of Iowa opened a speech on architecture in this way: "You all are familiar with Old Capitol, the beautiful pillared building you pass each day walking from class to class. It's a perfect example of federal period Georgian architecture, the subject of my speech this morning." Her brief reference to a well-known building enabled the audience to orient itself to her topic.

Specific instances also are useful in justifying a claim. In this case, instances may be piled one upon the other until you have firmly established the impression you wish to create. Note, for example, how James K. Wellington demonstrated the serious nature of his claim that "creative and imaginative students often are not recognized by their teachers":

> We should remember that the following persons were all identified as low achievers or misfits:
>
> * Einstein—4 years old before he could speak; 7 before he could read.
> * Isaac Newton—was rated a poor elementary school student.
> * Beethoven—music teacher said, "As a composer, he is hopeless."
> * Thomas Edison—teacher told him he was too stupid to learn anything.
> * F. W. Woolworth—worked in a dry goods store at 21, employers would not let him wait on customers; "didn't have enough sense."
> * Walt Disney—fired by a newspaper editor; "no good ideas."
> * Winston Churchill—failed 6th grade.[10]

With these accumulated data, there could be little doubt that teachers may err in their judgment of a child's ability.

Statistics

Statistics are numbers that show relationships between or among phenomena; the relationships may emphasize size or magnitude, describe subclasses or parts (segments), or establish trends. By reducing large masses of information into generalized categories, statistics are useful in making clear the nature of a situation and in substantiating a potentially disputable claim.[11]

Learning to use a library efficiently is a skill we all need to survive; learning how to record the information thus gathered will save you time and trouble later on.

Magnitudes.   We often use statistics to describe a situation or to sketch briefly the scope or seriousness of a problem. Statistical description of magnitude, especially when complemented by an analogy, helps an audience grasp the dimensions of a problem clearly. U.S. Representative Tom Steed of Oklahoma employed such a combination in a speech on governmental red tape and paperwork:

> Government agencies print about 10 billion sheets of paper to be filled out by U.S. businessmen—enough to fill more than 4 million cubic feet. Paperwork stemming from federal, state, and local governments averages about 10 forms for every man, woman, and child in the United States. Official records stored around the country total 11.6 million cubic feet, or an amount 11 times greater than the volume of the Washington Monument. Paperwork generated by Washington alone in one year would fill Yankee Stadium from the playing field to the top of the stands 51 times.[12]

Each of the comparisons was designed to connect the amount of paper generated with familiar items. In this manner, figures such as 11.6 million cubic feet take on realistic proportions in the minds of listeners.

Not all uses of statistics need to employ analogies. Brenda Theriault of the University of Maine at Orono, arguing that there is "very little nutritional value in a hamburger, chocolate shake and fries," simply noted that "of the 1,123 calories in this meal, there are 15 calories of carbohydrates, 35 calories of protein, and 1,073 calories of fat."[13] The audience did not need an analogy to understand the "nutrition" in a typical fast food meal.

Segments.   Statistics can be used to isolate the parts into which a problem can be subdivided or to show aspects of a problem caused by discrete factors. This descriptive approach is especially helpful when you wish to break a complex topic into its component parts. For example, in a speech before a Public Affairs Council, Federal Elections Commissioner Joan Aiken sought to de-emphasize the importance of political action committees (PACs) in the campaigns of individuals. As support for her position, she segmented PACs' contributions in terms of both dollars and percentages:

> In the 1980 election, there were 2,266 candidates running for the Senate and House. They raised a combined total of $240.1 million, $37.6 million of which came from non-party PAC sources. Corporate-sponsored PACs contributed 4.9 percent of the money received by Democratic candidates and 6.4 percent of the money received by Republican candidates. Organized labor gave 9.62 percent of the money received by Democratic candidates and only 0.65 percent of the money received by Republican candidates. Obviously, the overwhelming majority of the money raised for House and Senate candidates came from individuals.[14]

J. Thomas Cristy presented a breakdown of the financial statement of the American Cancer Society as part of his argument that the society is "a leading force" in the suppression of certain types of cancer research: •

> According to the 1978 financial statements of the American Cancer Society, of the 140 million dollars taken in, less than 30 percent went for research; more than 56 percent went for salaries and office expenditures. . . . The statements also point out that 200 million, of the Society's 228 million dollars of assets, is invested. This makes the ACS a prime banking and investment firm.[15]

In this case, the argument would be made even stronger with a review of several financial statements and a comparison with other charitable organizations that fund medical research. As is, however, Cristy allows the audience to draw the precise conclusion that 30 percent spent on research is insufficient, especially when compared to the total expenses of the society.

Trends.   Statistics often are employed to describe a trend across time. Statistical trends indicate where we have been and where we are going. Pat Schroeder, U.S. Representative from Colorado, noted several trends which suggested social change for women in a speech at Kansas State University. One trend was the increase in women's participation in education and careers:

> *Look at education:* Over the past century, the number of undergraduate degrees awarded to women climbed slowly but inexorably. *In 1870,* 15 percent went to women; by 1930 the number had risen to 40 percent. The GI bill era reversed that trend, but only temporarily.

By 1970, the gap was narrowing again. *In 1980,* women received 49 percent of all undergraduate degrees.

And female students were now majoring in such traditionally male fields as *engineering* (up 830 percent between 1972 and 1982); *agriculture* (up 429 percent); *business* (up 247 percent); *architecture* (up 130 percent); and *computer science* (up 123 percent).

Similar changes were occurring in the professions: between 1972 and 1982, women receiving degrees in *law* quadrupled from 7 percent to 30 percent; *medicine* more than doubled from 9 percent to 23 percent; *dentistry* went up sharply, from 1 percent to 14 percent; and *veterinary science* almost quadrupled, from 9 percent to 33 percent.[16]

Representative Schroeder went on to note other changes, both positive and negative; her use of trends indicated clearly where progress has been made in integrating women into the educational and professional mainstream of the country.

When you use statistics to indicate magnitude, to divide phenomena into segments, or to describe trends, keep these cautions in mind:

1. *Translate difficult-to-comprehend numbers into more immediately understandable terms.* In a speech on the mounting problem of solid waste, Carl Hall pictured the immensity of 130,000,000 tons of garbage by indicating that trucks loaded with that amount would extend from coast to coast.[17]

2. *Don't be afraid to round off complicated numbers.* "Nearly 400,000" is easier for listeners to comprehend than "396,456"; "over 33 percent" is preferable to "33.4 percent," and "over one-third" is even more preferable.

3. *Whenever possible, use visual materials to clarify complicated statistical trends or summaries.* Hand out a mimeographed or photocopied sheet of numbers; draw graphs on the chalkboard; prepare a chart in advance. Such aids will allow you to concentrate on explaining the significance of the numbers, rather than making sure the audience hears and remembers them.

4. *Use statistics fairly.* Arguing that professional women's salaries increased 12.4 percent last year may sound impressive to listeners until they realize that women are still paid almost one-quarter less than men for equivalent work. In other words, provide fair contexts for your numerical data and comparisons.[18]

Testimony

As in the case of other support materials, *testimony*—the opinions or conclusions of others—can be used to clarify or to justify the ideas a speaker advances. In both cases, it heightens the impact of the idea.

Gary Hart used testimony to clarify the sense in which "economic man" does not exist:

In 1967, Robert Kennedy wrote: "The gross national product measures neither our wit nor our courage, neither our wisdom nor our learning, neither our compassion nor our devotion of country. It measures everything, in short, except that which makes life worthwhile; and it can tell us everything about America—except whether we are proud to be Americans."[19]

This well-phrased statement illustrates one use of testimony: the words of others may be far more eloquent than our own. In addition, the statement crystallizes the role of economics in defining who we are.

As public speakers, we often find it necessary to supplement our own experience with that of others by utilizing testimony from *experts*—persons whose background and training qualify them as respected sources of information. Cheri Lindsley of Trevecca Nazarene College sought out such information in buttressing her argument in favor of home childbirth:

> Dr. Robert Bradley, author of *Husband-Coached Childbirth*, tells us that the conditions most conducive for an ideal, peaceful, and undisturbed childbirth atmosphere are ''most nearly met by the environment of a mother's bedroom in her own home and the reassuring nearness of familiar and loved faces rather than those of strangers.''[20]

This student speaker is in agreement with the authority or expert cited. She adds the words of another to broaden the base of support for the idea she is advancing and does not depend solely on her own base of knowledge for support.

There may be occasions when a citation from an expert is useful because you wish to *disagree;* in this case, the testimony summarizes a belief or principle that you wish to attack. Representative Schroeder paraphrased the comments of another and used them as a basis for her response:

> When a nurse or a high school math teacher with a college education is paid less than a liquor store clerk with a high school education, there is something wrong with our wage standards, not to mention our values.
>
> One of the naysayers, Phyllis Schlafly, was in Colorado recently. She said that liquor store clerks should be paid more than nurses because they lift heavy boxes; and tree trimmers should be paid more than teachers because they work outdoors.
>
> Fine, let's pay nurses the same as surgeons, because they both work indoors. And secretaries the same as lawyers because neither lifts heavy boxes. Furthermore, the kids who deliver our newspapers should be paid six-figure salaries because they drag around heavy bundles *and* brave the elements.[21]

Representative Schroeder set up her argument through the words of Schlafly. Testimony need not always follow claims. (Note that the use of paraphrase is an acceptable way to introduce the opinions of others; care must be taken to insure that the paraphrase is an accurate representation of the person's views or statement.)

As you contemplate using specific testimony or consider reacting to the testimony, there are several guidelines which will assist you in appraising the value of the citation:

1. *The person quoted should be qualified by training and experience as an authority*. He or she should be an expert in the field to which the testimony relates.
2. Whenever possible, *the statement of the authority should be based on firsthand knowledge*.
3. *The judgment expressed should not be unduly influenced by personal interest*. An authority with a strong vested interest in the issue is suspect.

4. *The listeners should realize that the person quoted actually is an authority.* They should be aware, or be made aware, of the speaker's status; for the testimony to be effective, they should be disposed to regard the source favorably.

If the persons (or, in some instances, organizations) satisfy these criteria, their opinions should meet the dual requirements of *authoritativeness* and *audience acceptability.* The best testimony comes from those sources whose qualifications or reputation for honesty and objectivity your listeners will recognize and respect.

Restatement

Restatement is the reiteration of an idea in different words. It is distinguishable from *repetition,* in which words remain the same.

Although they provide no real proof, restatement and repetition often have strong persuasive impact. Advertisers realize this, and spend millions of dollars annually repeating the same message in magazines, on billboards, and over radio and television. Slogans such as "Coke is it," "Budweiser—The King of Beers," "Pepsi's got your taste for life," and Wendy's highly popular "Where's the Beef?" have been repeated until they are familiar to everyone.

However, there is a point of diminishing return in using repetition; overused, it may become monotonous and tiresome. This can be avoided by restricting the use of repetition to a single concept or point you are making. Walter F. Mondale, speaking at the 1980 Democratic National Convention, incorporated repetition of a phrase in heightening the impact of his view of the Democratic party and those who speak on its behalf:

> When we speak of peace, the voice is Ed Muskie's. When we speak of workers, the voices are Lane Kirkland's and Doug Fraser's. When we speak of compassion, the fire is Ted Kennedy's. And when we speak of courage, the spirit is Jimmy Carter's. When we in this hall speak for America—it is America that is speaking.[22]

This limited use effectively focuses audience attention on a given point.

Restatement must reflect the intent or meaning of the original expression. Gail Niles of Bethel College uses restatement to advantage in discussing "legalese":

> Please get out a pencil and paper; I have a short quiz for you. Translate the following into English: "We respectfully petition, request and entreat that due and adequate provision be made, this day and the date hereinafter subscribed, for the satisfying of these petitioners' nutritional requirements and the organizing of such methods of allocation and distribution as may be deemed necessary and proper to assure the reception by and for said petitioners of such quantities of baked cereal products as shall, in the judgment of the aforesaid petitioners, constitute a sufficient supply thereof."
>
> Finished? Good. The correct translation is "Give us this day our daily bread," and the passage was in that obscure and difficult language, American legal English.[23]

The seven forms of supporting material—singly or in combination—can be employed to clarify or to justify your claims. Express *your* views, but amplify and develop them further through the judicious use of restatement, testimony, statistics, specific instances, detailed illustrations, analogies, and explanations.

Where to Look for Information: Sources of Supporting Materials

The first place to look for information is within yourself: What do you already know about the subject of your speech? As noted earlier, you will be most comfortable speaking about people, ideas, and events that you have personal knowledge about. These personal experiences contribute to the vividness and clarity of your message. Even when they cannot be cited directly, they are helpful in directing your research, sharpening your perspective on the subject, and providing insights into ways to develop the speech. Whenever possible, make personal experience and observation your first port of call when searching for speech materials.

A speech drawn *solely* on personal experiences may place too great a burden on your credibility, as it involves a narrow base on which to support or justify claims. Hence, you often will find it necessary to broaden your base of support beyond personal experience and add materials such as testimony and statistical data to your speech. When this is the case, several sources of information are open to you. Basically, these can be divided into two broad categories: existing information that you can utilize and information you can create through your own personal efforts. We will consider print and nonprint resources already available and then discuss ways of generating your own data.

Locating Existing Information: Print and Nonprint Resources

The most common source of supporting materials is the printed word—newspapers, magazines, pamphlets, and books. The local library provides abundant information; with the assistance of reference librarians as needed, you can discover more information than you could possibly use.

Newspapers. Daily and weekly newspapers are obvious sources of relevant and timely information. Feature stories and editorials provide a storehouse of illustrations and examples that can enliven your speech. Several papers have national and international reputations as comprehensive, objective sources of information on current and past events. Consult your library to see if they have copies of newspapers such as the *New York Times, Washington Post, Christian Science Monitor,* and *Wall Street Journal.* These papers provide excellent coverage of major political and social events in the United States and throughout the world. If you have access to the *New York Times,* check to see whether the published index (1913 to present) to the paper is available. Another useful and well-indexed source of information on national and international events is the weekly *Facts on File.*

For coverage of state and local events, your library will have major state and community papers available. If your topic deals with state or local issues, do not overlook

RECORDING INFORMATION

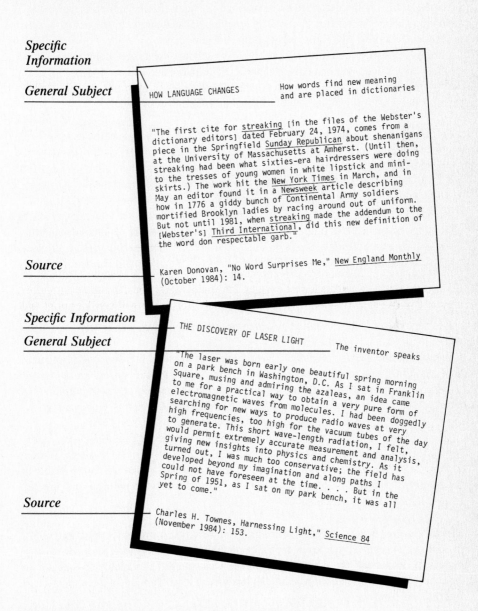

*Specific
Information*

General Subject

HOW LANGUAGE CHANGES

How words find new meaning
and are placed in dictionaries

"The first cite for streaking [in the files of the Webster's
dictionary editors] dated February 24, 1974, comes from a
piece in the Springfield Sunday Republican about shenanigans
at the University of Massachusetts at Amherst. (Until then,
streaking had been what sixties-era hairdressers were doing
to the tresses of young women in white lipstick and mini-
skirts.) The work hit the New York Times in March, and in
May an editor found it in a Newsweek article describing
how in 1776 a giddy bunch of Continental Army soldiers
mortified Brooklyn ladies by racing around out of uniform.
But not until 1981, when streaking made the addendum to the
[Webster's] Third International, did this new definition of
the word don respectable garb."

Source

Karen Donovan, "No Word Surprises Me," New England Monthly
(October 1984): 14.

Specific Information

General Subject

THE DISCOVERY OF LASER LIGHT

The inventor speaks

"The laser was born early one beautiful spring morning
on a park bench in Washington, D.C. As I sat in Franklin
Square, musing and admiring the azaleas, an idea came
to me for a practical way to obtain a very pure form of
electromagnetic waves from molecules. I had been doggedly
searching for new ways to produce radio waves at very
high frequencies, too high for the vacuum tubes of the day
to generate. This short wave-length radiation, I felt,
would permit extremely accurate measurement and analysis,
giving new insights into physics and chemistry. As it
turned out, I was much too conservative; the field has
developed beyond my imagination and along paths I
could not have foreseen at the time. . . . But in the
Spring of 1951, as I sat on my park bench, it was all
yet to come."

Source

Charles H. Townes, Harnessing Light," Science 84
(November 1984): 153.

*From "No Word Surprises Me" by Karen Donovan, NEW ENGLAND
MONTHLY, October 1984, p. 14. Copyright © 1984 by New England
Monthly, Inc. Reprinted by permission.*

the small-town weeklies or the specialty weeklies that may cover important events in your immediate area. In Maine, for example, *Maine Times,* published weekly, covers environmental, social, and political issues in depth. Although its stories often reflect the editorial bias of the writer, the information may be useful in supporting, for example, claims about the hazards of chemical spraying or the disposal of hazardous wastes in area landfill sites, two topics covered by this newspaper.

Finally, your local newspaper probably also publishes syndicated columns. Even if the *New York Times* may be unavailable or difficult to obtain, you can locate commentary by nationally-known columnists on significant issues in most city dailies. Newspapers can be used for more than chronicles of who did what when.

Magazines.   An average-sized community library subscribes annually to scores of magazines and periodicals. If the library is affiliated with a university, the diversity of sources available is even greater. General interest magazines such as *Time, Newsweek,* and *U. S. News & World Report* are best known for their concise summaries of important weekly events. Other general interest magazines such as *New Yorker, Atlantic, Commentary, Nation,* and *New Republic* provide more extensive commentary on a wide range of social, economic, and political topics. Discussions of popular scientific interest appear in *Scientific American* and *Science 85*. Other special interest publications include *Personal Computing, Sports Illustrated, Ms., Working Woman, Psychology Today, Country Journal,* and *Field and Stream*. These are just a few of the literally hundreds of magazines appealing to specific interests. A useful index for such magazines is the *Readers' Guide to Periodical Literature*. This guide indexes most of the magazines you will find useful in researching information for your speech.

Professional and Trade Journals.   Nearly every profession, industry, trade, and academic field has one or more specialized journals. Such publications include *Annals of the American Academy of Political Science, American Economist, Quarterly Journal of Speech, Journal of the American Medical Association, Journal of Communication, Signs, AFL-CIO American Federationist, Trade and Industry,* and *Coal Age*.

In conducting research, you will find the following indexes helpful: *Education Index, Psychological Abstracts, Social Sciences Index, Public Affairs Information Service Bulletin,* and *Humanities Index*. For specific trade or industry journals not available at the library, check area companies; often they will subscribe to publications directed toward their business pursuits.

Special Interest Books.   Check your library card catalog for recently published books in your subject area. If you know the name of a major authority, look for books by that person; if not, check the subject index to see what might be available. Books are an especially useful resource for an in-depth analysis of a problem or for a compilation of information from various sources.

Yearbooks and Encyclopedias.   The most reliable source of comprehensive data is the *Statistical Abstract of the United States,* which covers a wide variety of subjects ranging from weather records and birth rates to steel production and election results. More unusual data on Academy Award winners, world records in various areas, and the "bests" and "worsts" of almost anything can be found in such resources as *World Almanac, The People's Almanac, The Guinness Book of World Records, The Book of Lists,* and *Information Please.* Encyclopedias such as the *Encyclopaedia Britannica* and *Encyclopedia Americana* are chiefly valuable as initial reference sources or for background reading. Refer to these collections of information for important scientific, geographical, literary, or historical facts, and for bibliographies of authoritative books on particular subjects.

Documents and Reports.   Various governmental agencies—state, national, and international—as well as many independent organizations publish reports on special subjects. Among governmental publications, those most frequently consulted are the hearings and recommendations of congressional committees or government agencies such as the Department of Housing and Urban Development, the Department of Transportation, and the Department of Health and Human Services. Reports on issues related to agriculture, business, engineering, and science are published by many state universities. Foundations (Carnegie, Rockefeller, Ford), "think tanks" (American Enterprise Institute, Brookings Institution, Center for the Study of Democracy), and special interest groups (Common Cause, League of Women Voters, U.S. Chamber of Commerce) also publish reports and pamphlets. *The Vertical File Index* is a guide to some of these materials.

In addition, check to see if a library in your area has been designated as a government depository. These libraries regularly receive a variety of government documents: *Congressional Record, Weekly Papers of the President, Congressional Digest,* Congressional Committee Hearings/Reports, and Federal Agency reports.

The following indexes are useful guides to government materials: *Congressional Record Index, Public Affairs Information Service Bulletin,* and *Monthly Catalog of United States Government Publications.* Most state legislatures have a legislative reference bureau or other office which can be contacted for material related to state or local concerns.

Biographies.   Numerous collections contain biographical sketches of well-known individuals you may want to use as authorities in your speech. Examples include: *The Dictionary of National Biography* (deceased Britishers), *The Dictionary of American Biography* (deceased Americans), *Who's Who* (living Britishers), *Who's Who in America, Dictionary of American Scholars,* and *Current Biography.*

Collections of Quotations.   A wide range of quotations useful for illustrating an idea or supporting a point are available. Your library may have one or more of the following: Bartlett's *Familiar Quotations,* H. L. Mencken's *A New Dictionary of Quotations on Historical Principles from Ancient and Modern Sources,* and George Seldes' *The Great Quotations.*

Data Bases.   Your library may subscribe to one or more computerized data bases. These function much like a printed index. To access a data base, you will need to work with a reference librarian in determining what *descriptors* (key words) to enter. An average-sized university library will have access to over 200 data files such as ERIC,

BIOSIS, PsychInfo, AGRICOLA, and MEDLINE. You also might be able to use one or more of the available public data bases. For example, BRS/After Dark is available by subscription to those with personal computers and a modem; CompuServe, The Source, and Dow Jones News/Retrieval are other major consumer-oriented data base services that can be accessed via a modem/computer hook-up. These sources can be valuable time-savers as they will search for and print lists of articles available in your specific research area. Data bases, however, do involve expense. Libraries often charge for computer time spent in searching and printing your information; public data bases charge an initial fee plus per hour charges for on-line time.

Nonprint Resources.   Documentary films, radio and television broadcasts, and public addresses by experts may also be useful sources of information. Television shows such as *20/20, 60 Minutes,* and *Frontline* can provide illustrations and explanations for your speech. If you have the opportunity to view one of these programs or to listen to a major address by an expert talking about your speech subject, take careful notes. Paraphrase the points that are relevant to your address rather than trying to take down quotations verbatim, as you will not readily be able to check your accuracy.

Generating New Information

At times you will find it necessary or useful to generate information on your own. Two common approaches are to conduct interviews with appropriate persons and to construct and distribute a questionnaire.

Informational Interviews.   The goal of an informational interview is rather clear: to obtain answers to specific questions. In conducting the interview, you hope to elicit answers that can be woven into your speech text. Further, the answers can increase your general understanding of a topic so that you avoid misinforming your audience or drawing incorrect inferences from information obtained through other sources. The subject of the interview may be a "content expert" or someone who has had personal experience with the issues you wish to discuss. If you are addressing the topic of black holes, who better to help you than a physicist? If you are explaining the construction of a concrete boat, you might contact a local civil engineer for assistance. If, on the other hand, you wish to discuss anorexia nervosa, it may be helpful to interview a person who has suffered through the disorder. Interviews can provide compelling illustrations of human experiences.

There are three general guidelines to observe in planning an informational interview:

1. *Decide on your specific purpose.* What precise information do you hope to obtain during the interview? One caution: if you are interviewing a controversial figure, you may not be best served by engaging in an argument or by assuming a belligerent or self-righteous manner. Even if you disagree with the answers being given, your role is not that of Perry Mason, seeking to win a jury's vote by the questions asked. This does not mean that your purpose cannot encompass tough questions or questions that seek further clarification of answers that seem "not right." You *can* raise these questions without provoking an argument.

Personal interviews with experts or others in possession of knowledge you want demand self-direction (what do you want?) and preplanning (how can you get it from others?).

2. *Structure the interview in advance.* The beginning of an interview clarifies the purpose and sets limits on what will and will not be covered during the session. You also can use this time to establish rapport with the person being interviewed. The middle of the interview comprises the substantive portion: information being sought is provided. You need to structure your questions in advance so that you have a rough idea of what will be asked when. The actual interview may not follow your list exactly, but you will have a convenient checkpoint to see whether all the information you need has been presented. Finally, you will find the list useful as you summarize your understanding of the major points. This will help you avoid misunderstanding or misinterpreting the meaning given to specific points by the person interviewed. The following format is an example of one you might follow in an informational interview:

Opening
1. Mutual greeting
2. Discussion of purposes
    a. reason information is needed
    b. kind of information wanted

Informational Portion
1. Question #1, with clarifying questions as needed
2. Question #2, with clarifying questions as needed
3. [and so on]

Closing
1. Summary of main points
2. Final courtesies

3. *Remember that interviews are interactive processes.* That is, there is a definite pattern of "turn-taking" in interviews which allows both parties to concentrate on one issue at a time and which assists in making the interview work for the benefit of both parties. The interactive pattern requires that both parties be careful listeners, for one person's comments will affect the next comment of the other. You will need to remain flexible and free to deviate from your interview plan as you listen to the actual answers being given to your questions. You will have to listen to what is said, and almost simultaneously think ahead to the next item on your list of questions. Should you forge ahead or ask intervening questions to clarify or elaborate on a previous response?

Types of interview questions.   Because the communicative basis of interviews is made up of questions and answers, a skilled interviewer must be practiced in phrasing and organizing useful questions. Six types of questions are often asked. *Primary questions* introduce some topic or area of inquiry, while *follow-up questions* probe more deeply or ask for elaboration or clarification. Thus, if you are interviewing a local newspaper editor for a feature article, you might begin with "What background did you have before becoming editor?" and follow up with "Would you elaborate on your experience as a copy editor—what did you do in that position?" You also will develop *direct questions* ("How long have you been the editor?") and *indirect questions* ("What is your goal for the paper five years from now?"). Direct questions allow you to gather information quickly, while indirect probes let you see interviewees "thinking on their feet," structuring materials and responses and exploring their own minds. Interviewers also employ both *open* and *closed* questions. A closed question specifies the direction of the response—"Do your editorials serve to create public concern about local issues?" An open question allows the interviewee to control the categories of response—"How do you perceive your role in the community?" Closed questions require little effort from the interviewee and are easy to "code" or record; open questions allow interviewers to observe the interviewee's habits, to let them feel in control of the interaction. Of course, these various types of questions overlap: You can use a direct or indirect question as your primary question; a closed question can be direct ("Do you function most as editor, reporter, or lay-out specialist?") or indirect ("Of the various jobs you perform—editor, reporter, lay-out specialist—which do you enjoy the most?"). Overall, primary, direct, and closed questions tend to produce a lot of "hard" information quickly; follow-up, indirect, and open questions produce more thought and interpretation—grounds for understanding and analyzing interviewees and their motivations, capacities, and expectations. As you plan interviews, learn to blend questions of all six types—to build an *interview schedule*.

An interview schedule is your effort to organize specific questions so as to elicit systematically the materials and opinions you are seeking. Like any other organizational pattern, an interview schedule should have a rationale, one which *(1)* permits you to acquire systematic information or opinion, and *(2)* seems reasonable to the interviewee, avoiding confusing detours and repetitions. Interview schedules normally are built in one of two forms: the *traditional schedule* and the *branching schedule*.

Traditional Schedule of Questions

I. "What was your background before becoming an editor?" (primary, indirect, open question)
   A. "How many journalism courses did you take in college?" (follow-up, direct, open question)
   B. "What kinds of practical experience did you obtain in your newswriting course?" (follow-up, direct, open question)

II. "How do you perceive your role in the community?" (primary, indirect, open question)
   A. "Several letters to the editor have complained about your bias in favor of the largest employer in the town. How do you respond to these criticisms?" (follow-up, indirect, open question)
      1. "Do you ignore the largest employer when writing editorials, or do you consider its position and then write what you believe in?" (follow-up, direct, closed question)
      2. "Do you find it difficult to take positions counter to those of the largest employer?" (follow-up, direct, open question)

Branching Schedule of Questions

1. "Did you take courses in journalism prior to becoming a journalist?"

   If yes: ⌐   *If no:* ⌐

2. "Did you take courses in newswriting?"   2. "What type of practical experience did you have?"

   If yes: ⌐   *If no:* ⌐

3. "Did you obtain practical experience in the newswriting course?"   3. "Did you do primarily features or general news items?"

   If yes: ⌐   *If no:* ⌐

4. "What specific assignments did you have?"   4. [Note: Go to next area of inquiry.]

Notice that the traditional schedule of questions uses an organizational pattern that first extracts information and then follows with more probing questions. This pattern allows the interviewee to think through his or her experiences concretely before you ask for self-reflection or evaluation. Were that reversed, the interviewee might be asked to evaluate some experience before having recalled it clearly, most likely producing a less-than-complete evaluation. Notice, too, the mixing of types of questions in the traditional schedule, to keep the interaction progressing.

A branching schedule is used in situations where the interviewer knows rather specifically what he or she is looking for. Survey or polling interviewers often use this schedule. In our example, a student employs a branching schedule in order to explore more fully the background of a local newspaper editor. In a complete branching schedule, the *"If no"* questions would likewise have "branches" beneath them; nonetheless, our illustration indicates the essential logic of the pattern.

No matter what type of questions you use and what specific organizational pattern for questions you devise, the important points to remember are these:

1. *Plan your questions* before going into an interview, so that you know your goals and proceed toward them with dispatch.
2. *Organize your questions* in a manner which seems rational and which prepares interviewees adequately before asking them to make abstract, complex evaluations.

Communicative Skills for Successful Interviewers. From this discussion of interviewing and structures for communicating, it becomes clear that adept interviewers must have certain communicative skills:

A good interviewer is a good listener. Unless you take care to understand what someone is saying and to interpret the significance of those comments, you may misunderstand the person. Because questioning and answering are alternated in an interview, there is plenty of opportunity to clarify remarks and opinions. You can achieve clarification only if you are a good listener (see Chapter 2).

A good interviewer is open. Many of us may have become extremely wary of interviewers. We are cynical enough to believe that they have *hidden agenda*—unstated motives or purposes—which they are trying to pursue. Too often interviewers have said they "only want a little information" when actually they were selling magazine subscriptions or a religious ideal. If, as an interviewer, you are "caught" being less than honest, your chances for success are vastly diminished. Frankness and openness should govern all aspects of your interview communication.

A good interviewer builds a sense of mutual respect and trust. Feelings of trust and respect are created by revealing your own motivation, by probing the other party and getting the person to talk, and by expressing sympathy and understanding. Sometimes, of course, your assumptions of integrity and good will can be proved wrong. To start with suspicion and distrust, however, is to condemn the relationship without giving it a fair chance.

Sending Letters and Questionnaires. If you need more data than you can find in the library and do not have access to an expert, you may consider writing away for information. This is always risky, as you may not receive the information in time for the presentation. Thus, be sure to write as soon as you have decided on a topic. If you are requesting general information, be as specific about the purpose of the request as you can; this will assist your respondent in forwarding what you are looking for. A letter to the Department of Housing and Urban Development asking "Do you have any information on housing?" is unlikely to be answered well, if at all. As you ask for information, make clear why you have been unable to locate it on your own. Respondents who think they are being asked to do your work for you will probably be unwilling to help.

On other occasions, you may wish to discover what a group of people knows or thinks about a subject. If, for example, you wanted to give a speech on a proposed halfway house for the mentally ill, you might survey residents in the vicinity. You could send a questionnaire to people chosen randomly from the phone book, or to all living within a three-block radius from the proposed home. If you are seeking information on a new college drinking policy, you could survey dormitory residents or members of several classes. With the results, you could construct your own statistical summaries for presentation as part of your speech.

When developing the questionnaire, there are several guidelines to keep in mind:

1. Be sure the form explains the exact purpose of the questionnaire and the procedures to follow in responding to the questions.
2. Keep the form short and to the specific points you wish to have responses on.
3. For ease of summarizing, use closed questions (For example, ask for "yes/no" responses where appropriate; use categories such as "strongly agree/agree/disagree/ strongly disagree" if you want ranges of opinion).
4. Phrase questions in clear, neutral language. Do not use loaded terms ("Do you wish to see mentally unbalanced, unpredictable people living next to your children?").
5. Pilot-test the form with a few people to see whether the instructions are clear and to determine if any questions need to be rephrased.
6. If mailing the questionnaire, include a stamped, self-addressed envelope to encourage returns.

How to Use What You Locate or Generate

Whether using print or nonprint resources or generating your own information through interviews, letters, and questionnaires, you will need to distill all the materials and make notes on those items that will be of specific help in clarifying or justifying your ideas. When using print resources, you may wish to photocopy the relevant data or take notes on the material. If you are using notes (whether on 4 × 6 note cards or in a notebook), be sure to have an accurate and legible record of the relevant facts and their source. An illegible citation won't be much help days later when you are under the gun and trying to complete the speech. An incomplete source citation may make it impossible to locate the source again later when you recall that it contains just what you need. Note cards are easier to use than a notebook because they allow you to arrange and rearrange the order of your information quickly. If you do use a notebook, record each item on half of each page. You can then cut the sheets in half and sort your data more easily than by shuffling small scraps of paper or full sheets. (An alternative is to develop a classification scheme in advance and record information on appropriate sheets as you discover it. This may prove difficult, however, as some information may simply not fit your predetermined scheme.)

Integrating Information with Your Ideas

Thus far in this chapter we have considered the forms of supporting materials, the influences that guide their selection, and the common sources of information. In this concluding section, we will illustrate how particular types of materials may be packaged to expand or to justify the central idea of your speech. Although a speech normally contains multiple ideas or themes, it is more likely to succeed when it conveys one single overriding idea to the audience. The remaining themes serve to supplement, round out, or otherwise support the central idea. In some cases the central idea may be the *only* point that is being conveyed. As you develop your own speech, you will discover that the units are simply a succession of single points or claims. The examples in the discussions that follow illustrate the process of expanding a single central idea or justifying a thesis or claim.

Expanding a Central Idea.   If the purpose of your speech is to explain an idea, proceed as follows:

1. State the point or idea in a short, simple sentence.
2. Make it clear
   a. by explanations, comparisons, illustrations and/or
   b. by using diagrams, pictures, models, or maps.
3. Restate the idea you have explained.

In making your idea clear, you may present the verbal and nonverbal supporting materials either separately or together. That is, you may tell your listeners and *then* show them, or you may show them *while* you are telling them. The following outline for a central-idea speech illustrates how supporting materials may be assembled to explain an idea and to make it clear to an audience.

The Contributions of Laser Technology Have Changed Our Lives[24]

I. Laser technology has entered almost every facet of our lives.
   A. Lasers have invaded the entertainment field.
      1. At Stone Mountain, Georgia, laser animation creates visual images of famous Civil War heroes.
      2. There is a growing market for laser video discs.
   B. Lasers perform hundreds of manufacturing tasks.
      1. Laser's preciseness cuts fabric for suits.
      2. Laser's heat hardens liners for piston walls.
   C. In medicine, lasers are heralding a new future of "least invasive surgery."
      1. In eye surgery, laser light welds breaks in a retina, seals blood vessels, destroys eye tumors, and makes bloodless incisions.
      2. In other surgery, lasers perform similar functions, destroying cancerous cells in heretofore inoperable regions.

    3. A laser "hole" in a blood cell is 1/2 micron wide; in comparison, a human hair is approximately 8 microns wide.
- D. Law enforcement also is aided by laser technology.
  1. A new laser machine can "lift" fingerprints from a plastic styrofoam cup.
  2. Materials such as leather, which do not yield prints in traditional dusting techniques, do yield prints to laser light.
- E. Military uses for lasers are growing.
  1. Submarines will no longer have to trail a detectable antenna; they can maintain communication through lasers.
  2. Lasers can guide weapons with pinpoint precision to their targets.
- F. Lasers also have varied uses in scientific research, computers, communications, and other fields.
- G. In summary, laser technology will reshape the future in entertainment, manufacturing, medicine, law enforcement, defense, and in other fields.
  1. Laser precision allows for fine, detailed work, and for accuracy.
  2. Laser heat allows for cutting, drilling, welding.

Supporting a Claim.   If your purpose is to obtain audience approval of an idea or claim, follow these steps:

1. State your point.
2. Make it clear by explanation, comparison, or illustration.
3. Justify it by specific instances, testimony, statistics, or additional factual illustrations.
4. Restate your point as an established conclusion.

If your audience is hostile toward your idea, it may be wise to withhold the direct statement of your purpose until you can develop information leading to acceptance of your thesis or claim. This strategy may be more persuasive than allowing the audience to assess your supporting materials as you seek to justify an already announced claim. Because the sample speech in the following outline requires supportive documentation but does not presume a hostile audience, it follows the steps suggested above.

Cable Future Is Bright (for Those with Audiences and Money)[25]

- I. Satellite channels such as ESPN, CBN, and CNN have discovered that "narrowcasting" does not mean "narrow audience appeal."
  - A. Unprofitable systems have folded.
    1. CBS Cable—critical acclaim was not enough to save it.
    2. Telefrance—excellent cultural programming, but cost $3.5 million and only earned $500,000 in revenue.
    3. ABC—only commercial network still in cable, but future is in doubt.
       - a. Lost $25 million in 1983.
       - b. Projects loss of $50 million in 1984.
       - c. Sold unprofitable Satellite News Channel to Turner's CNN.
       - d. Is merging with Cable Health Network and others to remain afloat.
  - B. Satellite channels with "narrow" program focus require wide audience support.
    1. MTV grew from 4.5 million to 15 million homes in last year.
    2. The #1 satellite channel, ESPN, grew from 18 million to 27.5 million homes.

3. The #2 satellite, Christian Broadcast Network (CBN) also grew from 16.2 million to 22.2 million homes.

II. Satellite channels, unlike pay TV, must derive profit from advertising.
    A. Advertising revenue depends on audience size.
        1. Only the top five (ESPN, CBN, CNN, MTV, USA) and the "superstation" WTBS (Atlanta) are covered by Nielsen ratings.
        2. 28 satellite systems depend partially on advertising, but have audiences too small to be covered by Nielsen.
        3. As Allen Gottesman has noted: "The basic thing that advertisers have been seeking for 100 years hasn't suddenly changed with cable. To crack the big time of advertising dollars, you need a big-number audience, because you're always competing with other media on a cost-per-thousand basis."

III. In contrast to satellite television, pay television needs subscribers to survive without advertising.
    A. HBO is the industry leader.
        1. Together with CineMax, it has 15 of 23 million pay TV subscribers.
        2. HBO had a 1982 profit of $100 million.
    B. In contrast is RCA's Entertainment Channel
        1. It survived only 9 months.
        2. It lost $80 million in the search for subscribers.

IV. In sum, the future is bright if cable channels retain audiences and can show a profit.

REFERENCE NOTES

[1]For an informative analysis of explanation, see W. V. Quine and J. S. Ulian, *The Web of Belief* (New York: Random House, Inc., 1970), Chapter 8, "Explanation." These authors also have helpful chapters on "Testimony" (Chapter 4) and "Analogy" (Chapter 6).

[2]From "A Time for Peace," by Kendra Creasy. Reprinted from *Winning Orations,* 1980, by special arrangement with the Interstate Oratorical Association, Larry Schnoor, Executive Secretary, Mankato State University, Mankato, Minnesota.

[3]Neil Postman, "The Technical Thesis," in Wil A. Linkugel, R. R. Allen, and Richard L. Johannesen, *Contemporary American Speeches,* 5th ed. (Dubuque, IA: Kendall/Hunt Publishing Co., 1982), p. 243.

[4]From "Title Unknown," by Wendy Fletcher. Reprinted from *Winning Orations,* 1980, by special arrangement with the Interstate Oratorical Association, Larry Schnoor, Executive Secretary, Mankato State University, Mankato, Minnesota.

[5]Excerpt from "Can You Trust God?" by Dr. Louis Hadley Evans. Reprinted by permission of the author.

[6]Caroline Bird, "Two Paycheck Power," *Contemporary American Speeches,* 5th ed., p. 253.

[7]From "The Peace Movement," by Charlton Heston from *Vital Speeches of the Day,* 49, October 15, 1983. Reprinted by permission of Vital Speeches of the Day.

[8]From "Don't Drink the Water," by Pam Williams. Reprinted from *Winning Orations,* 1980, by special arrangement with the Interstate Oratorical Association, Larry Schnoor, Executive Secretary, Mankato State University, Mankato, Minnesota.

[9]Kathy Weisensal, "David: And a Whole Lot of Other Neat People," in *Contemporary American Speeches,* 5th ed., p. 83.

[10]From "A Look At the Fundamental School Concept" by James K. Wellington from

Vital Speeches of the Day, 46, February 1980. Reprinted by permission of Vital Speeches of the Day.

[11]For a technical yet rewarding introduction to statistical analysis generally, see John Waite Bowers and John A. Courtright, *Communication Research Methods* (Glenview, IL: Scott, Foresman and Company, 1984).

[12]Representative Tom Steed, *Congressional Record,* 95th Congress, 1st Session, Volume 123, Part 8. Washington, D.C.: U. S. Government Printing Office, 1977, H379–H380.

[13]From a speech given at the University of Maine, spring term, 1982. Reprinted with the permission of Ms. Theriault.

[14]From "Working with the Federal Election Commission" by Joan D. Aiken, from *Vital Speeches of the Day,* 47, February, 1981. Reprinted by permission of Vital Speeches of the Day.

[15]From "The Cancer Crusade" by J. Thomas Cristy. Reprinted from *Winning Orations,* 1980, by special arrangement with the Interstate Oratorical Association, Larry Schnoor, Executive Secretary, Mankato State University, Mankato, Minnesota.

[16]From "Great Expectations," by Pat Schroeder from *Vital Speeches of the Day,* 50, May 15, 1984. Reprinted by permission of Vital Speeches of the Day.

[17]From "A Heap of Trouble" by Carl Hall. Reprinted from *Winning Orations.*

[18]To protect yourself from the unscrupulous use of statistics, read Darrell Huff, *How to Lie with Statistics* (New York: W. W. Norton & Company, Inc., 1954).

[19]From "A Time for Economic Reform" by Gary Hart from *Representative American Speeches,* ed. Owen Peterson (New York: H. W. Wilson, 1982), 55:4, p. 58.

[20]From "A Better Way" by Cheri W. Lindsley. Reprinted from *Winning Orations,* 1980, by special arrangement with the Interstate Oratorical Association, Larry Schnoor, Executive Secretary, Mankato State University, Mankato, Minnesota.

[21]From "Great Expectations" by Pat Schroeder from *Vital Speeches of the Day,* 50, May 15, 1984. Reprinted by permission from Vital Speeches of the Day.

[22]Walter F. Mondale, "Vice Presidential Acceptance Address," *Vital Speeches,* 46 (August 15, 1980): 711.

[23]From "Legalese" by Gail Niles. Reprinted from *Winning Orations,* 1980, by special arrangement with the Interstate Oratorical Association, Larry Schnoor, executive secretary, Mankato State University, Mankato, Minnesota.

[24]Information adapted from Allen Boraiko, "The Laser: A Splendid Light," *National Geographic,* 165 (March, 1984): 335–63.

[25]Information adapted from "1984 Field Guide to the Electronic Media," *Channels* (November-December 1983): 5–66.

PROBLEMS AND PROBES

1. Read one of the speeches in this text. Identify the various forms of supporting material employed. How effective are the forms of support material in meeting the purpose of the speech? What else might the speaker have done to improve on the use of support materials?

2. Arrange to meet classmates in the reference room of your college library. Working in groups of four to six, each group member is to locate two of the items on the left-hand column of the following list. First, determine which of the sources listed in the right-hand column contains the material you need. When you locate your items, show your group the source and indicate where it is shelved.

a. Weekly summary of current national news	*Book Review Digest*
	Congressional Record
b. Brief sketch of the accomplishments of Lee Iaccoca	*Encyclopedia Americana*
	Facts on File
c. Description of a specific traffic accident	local newspaper
	New York Times
d. Text of Ronald Reagan's Second Inaugural Address	*Oxford English Dictionary*
	Statistical Abstracts
e. Daily summary of stock prices	*Time*
f. Origin of the word *rhetoric*	*Vital Speeches*
g. Critical commentary on C. Lasch's *The Culture of Narcissism*	*Wall Street Journal*
	Who's Who
h. Current status of national legislation on educational reform	

3. Editorials generally present an abbreviated argument supporting or opposing an issue of current local, national, or international interest. Find a recent editorial in a newspaper or magazine and identify the major premises in the argument. In addition to the supporting materials offered by the author, find three original pieces of support for each point. Consider what kinds of evidence are appropriate to the particular premise and to the argument in general. Does the author provide sufficient and adequate evidence? Using the editorial as the basis for a speech to persuade, construct an outline for the speech that uses your supporting materials.

4. Interview a friend, family member, or classmate regarding some attitude, belief, or value he or she holds strongly. Tape the conversation if possible; if not, simply take notes. Ask the person to state the attitude, belief, or value, to explain why or he she holds it, and to defend the view. Assume the role of a somewhat skeptical observer. Later, analyze the response in terms of the kinds and quality of supporting materials employed. Were they sufficient and adequate? Would the evidence supplied in the interview be sufficient and adequate in a speech? What other supporting materials might strengthen the response?

ORAL ACTIVITIES

1. Present to the class a five-minute central-idea speech, the purpose of which is either to explain or clarify a term, concept, or process, or to verify or prove a point. Use at least three different forms of supporting material in developing your idea. To formulate an evaluation of the effectiveness of your speech, the instructor and the other students will consider the following: *(a)* adequacy of supporting material; *(b)* appropriateness of supporting material, both as to type and to substance; and *(c)* the insight and skill with which the supporting material is developed.

2. Present to the class a five-minute speech in which you support a specific claim, with the purpose of persuading the audience to accept your ideas. Use at least four different forms of supporting material in developing your justification for the acceptance of your ideas. The class will evaluate your presentation along the lines suggested in activity #1 above.

CHAPTER 8

Adapting the Speech Structure to Audiences: The Motivated Sequence

In preceding chapters we considered how to select the basic appeals and support the principal ideas comprising your speeches. It is now time to discuss ways in which those materials should be structured or organized to form the speech as a whole. You cannot simply force ideas down people's throats, nor can you usually get away with stringing them together in a random manner. Ideas must be dissected and then shaped into a sensible, coherent whole, so that people will voluntarily and easily follow them to your conclusions.

Because different organizational patterns serve different audience needs and emphasize different aspects of topics, speakers should have a thorough knowledge of various structures or patterns and the uses to which each can be put on occasion. In this chapter we will examine the psychological bases underlying the need for structure generally, and then discuss in detail a common, highly useful pattern—the Motivated Sequence—so called because it is based on the kind of motivational analysis we reviewed in Chapter 6. Then, in Chapter 9, we will define and exemplify the more traditional patterns which speakers have used for centuries.

Organization from the Perspective of the Listener

Human beings, like all other animals, learn quickly to react to stimuli in their environments; we learn to sort out stimuli (experiences) into various categories of things or events in order to predict consequences. But, unlike most other animals, humans can go beyond sorting, even beyond understanding consequences—they can seek *coherence* in their environments. *(1)* We can *generalize* and *anticipate*. A baby who burns its hand on a hot stove, a match, and a metal sheet sitting in the sun quickly learns that "hot objects produce pain''; the baby can remember past instances of pain and anticipate future pain when it notices even previously unexperienced "hot objects" in its surroundings. *(2)* We search for *coherent structures* in our environments. Young children soon learn to seek relationships between and among items in their environment. They learn early that one set of furniture comprises a bedroom; another set, a kitchen; and another set, a playroom; they soon learn that living and dead objects are treated differently. By early elementary school, children can determine what is "foreground" or "figure" in a picture, and what is "background" or supporting detail. An important part of environmental control is understanding relationships between and among the environmental elements. *(3)* Structures become so important to us psychologically that we learn to *fill in or complete* missing elements. If someone says to you, "One, two, three, four," you almost automatically continue, "five, six, seven, eight." Cartoonists can draw a few features of a famous person, and most readers will be able to identify the person in question. This is because we all have what Gestalt psychologists term the "drive to complete," the need to complete missing elements and thus make sense out of some stimulus.[1]

Speakers and others who work with ideas publicly have an even more important quality of coherence to consider: *(4) People can make ideas coherent in a number of different ways.* Sometimes, people make sense out of their experiences by arranging them chronologically, as when describing the high points in their lives. Occasionally they will discuss something they are looking at by moving from left to right or top to bottom. When they want to understand what events led to what consequences, they may try to relate "causes" to "effects." And sometimes they simply seek "natural" divisions in objects or events—inside vs. outside, the three branches of government, body vs. soul, night vs. day—in order to talk intelligibly about them. All these ways of relating two or more aspects of objects, places, and events to each other form the bases for most of the organizational patterns we will examine in Chapter 9.

Finally, there is one especially important way individuals come to grips with the environment and their own thoughts or actions within it. They systematically examine and then follow up on *their own motivations.* This is a natural tendency, for we all seek not only to rationalize our surroundings but also to find our own place within them. We tend to follow our own motives-to-act in one of two ways:

1. We may tend toward a *world-* or *problem-orientation*. Early in this century the American philosopher John Dewey recognized this tendency when he devised his "psycho-logic"—a pattern for thought he called "reflective thinking." In Dewey's view, individuals tend to (and sometimes do) follow a systematic procedure for solving problems. First, said Dewey, people become aware of a specific lack or disorientation—some situation with which they are, for one reason or another, dissatisfied. Second, they examine this difficulty to determine its nature, scope, causes, and implications. Third, they search for new orientations or operations that will solve the problem or satisfy the need. Fourth, they compare and evaluate the possible solutions that have occurred to them. And, fifth, they select the solution or course of action which, upon the basis of their foregoing reflections, seems most likely to put their minds at rest and to handle the real-world dimensions of the problem.[2] Dewey, in other words, adapted the so-called "scientific method" to individual and group problem-solving.

2. Our other tendency is to be *self-centered, motivation-centered.* Salespersons and advertisers began recognizing this principle in the 1920s. They realized that you and I buy a particular automobile not simply to get from here to there, but also to create a certain image; we buy this or that style of clothes to identify ourselves with others who wear certain sorts of trousers and coats; we buy furniture that is both functional and decorative. In other words, our personal motivations, hopes, fears, and desires often control the ways we act and the goods we consume.

Alan Monroe (1903–1975), the original author of this textbook, knew Dewey's work well and had himself worked in the 1920s training sales personnel. As he thought about Dewey's "psycho-logic" and the various sales techniques he had taught people to employ, Monroe discovered he could unite both sets of procedures—one set based on the personalized scientific method, and the other rooted in an understanding of human motivation—to form a highly useful organizational pattern. Since 1935, that structure has been called "Monroe's Motivated Sequence."[3] We will devote the rest of this chapter to it.

Five Basic Steps of the Motivated Sequence

The motivated sequence derives its name partly because it follows Dewey's problem-solution format for thinking and partly because it makes attractive analyses of those problems and their solutions by tying them to human motives. That is, in terms of our preceding discussion, the motivated sequence is simultaneously problem-oriented and motivation-centered.

There are five basic steps in the motivated sequence: *(1)* To begin with, you must get people to attend to some problem, or to feel disorientation or discomfort strongly enough to want to hear more. *(2)* Then, you can create more specific wants or desires, a personal sense of need. *(3)* Third, when wants or needs are created, you can attempt to satisfy them by showing what can be done to solve the problem or relieve the sense of discomfort. *(4)* Simply describing a course of action, however, may not be enough, so you visualize the world as it would look if the actions were carried out (and often what it might be like if they were not). *(5)* With that, if the speaker has done the preceding four tasks well, audience members should be ready to act, to put into practice the proposed solution to their problems.

Thus, the motivated sequence is composed generally of five basic steps in the presentation of verbal materials (see figure, page 154):

1. *Attention:* the creation of interest and desire
2. *Need:* the development of the problem, through an analysis of things wrong in the world and through a relating of those wrongs to individuals' interests, wants, or desires
3. *Satisfaction:* the proposal of a plan of action which will alleviate the problem and satisfy the individuals' interests, wants, or desires
4. *Visualization:* the verbal depiction of the world as it will look if the plan is put into operation
5. *Action:* the final call for personal commitments and deeds

THE MOTIVATED SEQUENCE

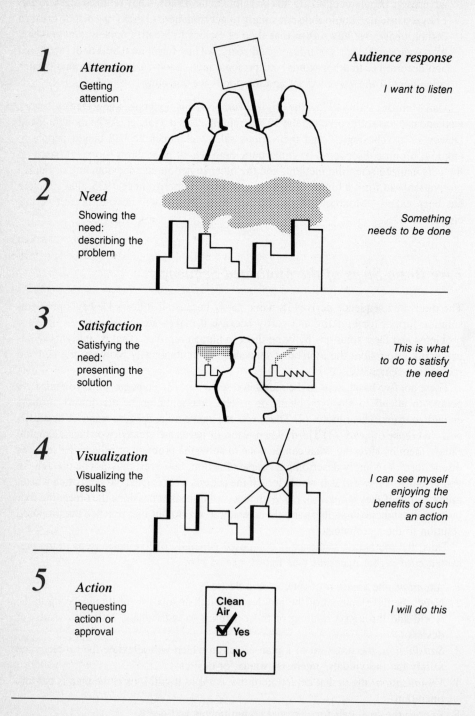

1 *Attention*
Getting attention

Audience response

I want to listen

2 *Need*
Showing the need: describing the problem

Something needs to be done

3 *Satisfaction*
Satisfying the need: presenting the solution

This is what to do to satisfy the need

4 *Visualization*
Visualizing the results

I can see myself enjoying the benefits of such an action

5 *Action*
Requesting action or approval

Clean Air
☑ Yes
☐ No

I will do this

The motivated sequence can be used to structure many different sorts of speeches on many different kinds of topics. It could be used, for example, in a speech urging your classmates to join a blood donors' association: (*Attention*) "If you had needed an emergency blood transfusion in Johnson County on December 17, 1984, you probably would not have gotten it." (*Need*) "Blood drives seldom collect enough blood of all types to meet emergency needs in an area such as this one." (*Satisfaction*) "A blood donors' association guarantees a predictable, steady supply of blood to the medical community." (*Visualization*) "Without a steady supply of blood, our community will face needless deaths; with it, emergencies will be met with prompt treatment." (*Action*) "You can help by filling out the blood donors' cards I am passing out."

Or, you could use the motivated sequence to sell insurance to a friend: (*Attention*) "For pennies a day, you can gain considerable peace of mind and a solid background for future financial security." (*Need*) "Life insurance can protect your family from the impact of an untimely death, guarantee you future security, give you a source of emergency loans, educate your children, and supplement other forms of investment." (*Satisfaction*) "Here's how we can tailor your insurance coverage to meet particular aspects of your own situation." (*Visualization*) "Consider the following situations and what a life insurance program can do to get you out of them." (*Action*) "Get a routine physical examination today, and tomorrow we can start your coverage for as small or as large an investment as you care to make."

The motivated sequence also can be used to talk about larger, more pervasive aspects of social problems. The following speech was prepared by Ms. Linda Hopkins of William Jewell College and was presented in one of the annual contests sponsored by the Interstate Oratorical Association. As you read the speech, note how Ms. Hopkins *(1)* calls *attention* to her subject by piquing curiosity; *(2)* points out—with statistics, specific instances, authoritative testimony, and factual illustrations—the crucial *need* to make marriages work; *(3)* demonstrates, by outlining the elements of a marriage contract, a means of *satisfying* this need; *(4)* briefly *visualizes* the results of carrying out the proposed solution; and *(5)* incorporates into her conclusion an appeal for direct *action* in the form of the willingness to give marriage contracts a try. The purpose of her presentation is to persuade audience members to accept marriage contracts as a useful way of making marriages work.

Marriage Contracts: For Better or Worse[4]
Linda Hopkins

Attention Step

A red rose and a glass of wine. Soft music. A candlelight dinner. Just the two of you. It's the perfect setting for a couple to express their love for each other by getting engaged.   /1

I'm sure those of you who are already engaged or married now can remember the excitement and romance that getting engaged involves. Those of you who are not yet married or engaged—well, you have all that and much, much more to look forward to. I'm certain of it. You see, if there's one thing I have learned about couples who are preparing to wed, partly from being one-half of such a couple and partly from talking with and observing other such couples, it's that when it comes to matrimony we are incredibly starry-eyed and optimistic. We have no desire to become a divorce statistic and, except for a few butterflies before the ceremony, most of us are confident that we won't. Unfortunately, all too many of us don't know exactly how to go about converting our optimistic good intentions into realities so we can actually build successful marriages.   /2

Even though hundreds, perhaps thousands, of approaches to the "perfect" marriage have been publicized in recent years, I would like to talk to you about just one of those today— the personal marriage contract. I hope to convince each of you that marriage contracts, when used as tools of communication, can enhance existing marriages and increase the likelihood that future marriages will be happy marriages. To do this, however, it will be necessary to examine some predominant marital problems and then to take a close look at the contracts themselves to see how they might help alleviate these marital problems.   /3

Need Step
Even though we enter matrimony with good intentions, there is an ever-increasing chance that in 5, 10, or even 20 years we will not be in satisfying relationships and that we may seek a divorce. As Mervyn Cadwallader, a noted sociologist, reported, in 1910 only 87 out of 1,000 marriages ended in divorce. By 1965, the number had risen to 300 out of 1,000. In 1972 the divorce rate hit a staggering 40% and today, in some parts of the country, it has reached an all-time high of 50%. In some areas one out of every two marriages ends in divorce!   /4

But it won't be me who gets that divorce. Or so we tend to think. And maybe it won't be you or me and my fiance who find ourselves in the divorce court. But simply avoiding a divorce does not indicate that a couple is happily married. In fact, the Alameda County study suggests that at any given time there are a significant number of unhappily married couples. The study, which surveyed 4,924 adults on their views about marriage, found that 1,008 or nearly 20% of those surveyed were dissatisfied with their marital relationship and yet had never considered divorce.   /5

Marriage does seem to be a failing institution, but?!   /6

Most experts today agree with Ohio Family Court Judge John R. Milligan when he says that "a lack of communication is the root cause of divorce in this country." Yet, from a very pragmatic standpoint, a lack of communication is far from the only problem couples may face. There may be tension over money, sex, religion, in-laws—the possibilities are countless. All of these problems, however, do share one common denominator. If couples are unwilling or unable to communicate effectively about them, they will never be solved. To illustrate the point, let's examine two common marital problems—money and the division of household labor.   /7

Financial problems of all sorts may plague a married couple but perhaps the primary source of financial conflict is found in our attitude toward money. As David Rice, pro-fessor of psychiatry at the University of Wisconsin, says, "Money is power. How people handle their money gives you a good idea how they handle power." Dr. Rice's comment makes sense. Imagine with me a couple shopping for living room furniture. The husband sees a sofa he likes particularly well and he exclaims, "I love it and I'm buying it. I earn most of the money around here anyway, and I say we buy it." His wife grits her teeth and "suffers in silence." This couple's problem is rooted in a financial situation, true, but it was rendered insolvable by their unwillingness to talk about it.   /8

Another common problem for couples arises when it is time to do the laundry, take out the trash, wash dishes, or mow the lawn. That's right. A division of household chores can be a problem for even the most loving of couples. Believe it or not, one couple had to see a marriage counselor to help them decide who was to clean the shower. You see, Bob was the type of guy who saw no reason to clean the shower before it had mildewed. Terri, on the other hand, saw cleaning the shower as a preventive measure. You did it so the shower wouldn't mildew. So Terri cleaned the shower, as well as the rest of their house, diligently, but alone—and she resented it. But unlike our sofa shoppers, Bob and Terri were all too vocal about their feelings. Harsh words and accusations flew, feelings were hurt, and nothing was really settled because they never really talked about their different attitudes toward cleaning house. /9

I realize that both of these examples I've just discussed seem trivial, even laughable, on the surface. But the point is that the attitudes underlying the behaviors I've just described and the emotions those behaviors arouse are far from trivial. In fact, more often than not, they are significant enough to be a serious detriment to an intimate relationship. /10

Satisfaction Step
Fortunately, none of these marital problems are unsurmountable, provided couples truly communicate about them instead of accusing, arguing, becoming defensive, or refusing to talk altogether. I believe that personal marriage contracts, particularly the process involved in writing and rewriting them, can help alleviate marital problems because it facilitates effective communication. Specifically, this process has six steps. /11

First, couples should discuss potential or actual areas of conflict in their marriages. /12

Second, they should agree on positions or actions that might help alleviate conflict in those areas and write them up in a contract. /13

Third, they should establish a time, usually 3, 6, 9, or even 12 months later, to review their contract. /14

Fourth, at the designated time each spouse should list all positive and all negative points about each contract item and discuss them together. /15

Fifth, if there is any contract item not mutually satisfactory, it should be changed in a way that both believe might be mutually satisfactory. /16

Sixth, another review date needs to be selected so the contract can be rethought and revised as needed. /17

This six-step process instigates communication because it forces couples to talk about their problems and, at the worst, to derive tentative solutions to them. But it is also a flexible process. My parents have always told me that marriage was a series of trials and errors. The marriage contract process is based on that same theory—it's just an organized way to go about it. /18

Visualization Step
Of course, I'm sure by now some of you are chuckling to yourself at my suggestion that we all sit down and write our marriage contracts, and others of you may be sincerely offended. I know when I first heard of personal marriage contracts, I was insulted. How dare anyone who does not know me suggest that I might have trouble making my marriage a success? Or worse yet, how dare anyone suggest that I, a graduating communication major, might have difficulty communicating with someone I love? But then I thought back to fights and disagreements I have had with my fiance and I had to change my mind. I won't tell you that a personal marriage contract is the marital cure-all. If you and your spouse or future spouse write a contract I won't tell you that you'll never have a fight. You will. Neither will I tell

you that you may not someday find yourself in the midst of a divorce proceeding. You may. I *will* tell you that I believe a personal marriage contract, especially the process involved in writing one, will make a positive difference in my marriage and in your marriages or future marriages. /19

Action Step

You see, the responsibility for making marriages that work is yours and mine. Do we care enough to communicate effectively with our mates or future mates? If we find that we have trouble communicating effectively, are we willing to give marriage contracts a try? I hope so. I really hope so. You know, the roses, the wine, the soft music and candlelight are all so nice, but they won't make our marriages last. The problems which confront married couples today can't be countered and solved with romance. They need to be talked about. And personal marriage contracts can help open those communication channels that are so vital in any happy, healthy marriage. /20

The Structure and Development of the Steps in the Motivated Sequence

Now that the entire motivated sequence has been illustrated, we need to examine more closely its individual steps, noting in particular their internal structuring, the methods of their development, and the kinds of materials that may be used effectively in each. The five basic steps in the motivated sequence are illustrated in the diagram on page 154.

The Attention Step

As a speaker, your first task is to gain *attention*. The attributes of attention and the major devices for obtaining attention were covered earlier; as you plan this step in your speech, review the devices and determine which one or ones might best stimulate audience interest in your topic. If the audience is lethargic, tired, or views your appearance with a "ho-hum-here-we-go-again" attitude, you must begin with something more innovative than "Today, I'd like to. . . ." Thus, the nine attention-attractors discussed in Chapter 3 (the vital, humor, conflict, suspense, novelty, familiarity, proximity, reality, and activity or movement) take on special relevance in the opening moments of your presentation.

You will capture listeners' attention, of course, by the way you deliver your speech—the vigor and variety of your gestures and bodily movements, the flexibility and animation of your voice. Your credibility or *ethos* with the audience also will assist you in securing a degree of attention, as will the color and impressiveness of your language and style. Fundamentally, however, you will capture—and hold—attention through the *types of ideas* you present to your listeners. Your ideas must tap their sense of interest and personal motivation to force them to listen.

Although gaining attention is an initial step in bringing your ideas to an audience, remember that *keeping* attention also is vitally important. The same devices can be used as you develop the remaining steps in the motivated sequence; in particular, they may be employed to heighten attention during the need and visualization steps.

Before you can get listeners to do something even as sensible as learning to compute, you have to convince them they need *those skills; you must make your position relevant to them.*

The Need Step

Assuming that the audience is attentive to your message at this point, your next obligation is to lay out the reasons for being concerned about the issue: Why is the information vital to the well-being of the audience and why is the problem an urgent one? In accomplishing this objective, a need step should do the following:

1. *Statement*—Offer a clear, concise statement of the need. This can be in the form of a central idea or claim, depending on your speech purpose. The statement of the need orients the listeners to your specific message; presumably, what you go on to say will be related to this statement.

2. *Illustration*—Present one or more illustrations to give listeners a clear idea of the nature of the problem you are discussing.

3. *Ramification*—Utilize supporting materials to clarify your statement of need, or to justify the urgency of the problem which you wish to have resolved. Additional examples, statistical data, testimony, and other forms of support can supplement the illustrative examples already used.

4. *Pointing*—Impress on the audience the seriousness of the issue, its scope, and its significance to them. Provide, at this stage of the need step, a convincing account of how the issue or problem directly affects the people addressed—their health, happiness, security, or other interests.

This step is one in which *you relate your subject to the vital concerns and interests of your audience*. While all of the outlined stages may not be essential in every speech, the consideration of each is a vital part of your preparation. In some contexts, such as explaining the reasons for supporting a nuclear freeze to an audience of freeze advocates, there may be little reason to fully develop this section of the speech. If the audience is one of freeze opponents, on the other hand, you will find it necessary to flesh out each of these stages and to place particular emphasis on the last one: How does support for a freeze affect each individual in the audience?

The Satisfaction Step

The purpose of the satisfaction step, as we have suggested, is to enable your hearers to understand the information you are presenting or to get them to agree that the belief or action you propose is the correct one. The structure of this step differs somewhat, however, depending on whether your major purpose is primarily informative, entertaining, or persuasive. For this reason, the satisfaction step speeches must be considered separately for these speech purposes.

The Satisfaction Step in Speeches to Inform.   When your purpose is to inform—to give your audience a clear understanding of some subject—the satisfaction step usually will constitute the bulk of your speech and will present the information that was specified as necessary in the need step. The development of the satisfaction step as used in informative speeches customarily includes:

1. *Initial summary*—Briefly state in advance the main ideas or points you intend to cover.
2. *Detailed information*—Discuss in order the facts or explanations pertaining to each of these ideas or points.
3. *Final summary*—Restate the main points or ideas you have presented, together with any important conclusions you have drawn from them.

The Satisfaction Step in Speeches to Entertain.   When your purpose is to entertain—to present some useful thought or sentiment in a light-hearted or humorous manner—the satisfaction step will constitute the major part of your speech. Your goal is to satisfy the audience that the speech is, in fact, entertaining, and that it has conveyed an idea or sentiment worth their time and attention. In developing the satisfaction step, follow these guidelines:

1. *Initial statement of theme*—Briefly indicate the sentiment or idea that you will discuss.
2. *Humorous elaboration*—Develop the theme with particular attention to hypothetical and factual illustrations and specific instances that will convey a light-hearted, yet meaningful, message to the audience.

3. *Final summary*—Restate your main theme by drawing the connection between your illustrations and the point you wish to make.

The Satisfaction Step in Speeches to Persuade.   When the purpose of your speech is to persuade or to actuate, these four elements are usually included in the satisfaction step:

1. *Statement*—Briefly state the attitude, belief, or action you wish the audience to adopt.
2. *Explanation*—Make sure your proposal is understood. Diagrams or charts are often useful here.
3. *Theoretical demonstration*—Show how this belief or action logically meets the problem pointed out in the need step.
4. *Practical experience*—Give actual examples showing that this proposal has worked effectively or that this belief has been proved correct. Use facts, figures, and the testimony of experts to support your claims.

Here again you will probably find that you do not need to include all of these elements or parts in the satisfaction step of every persuasive speech. Nor must they always appear in the same order. For instance, you can sometimes meet objections best by distributing answers strategically throughout the step, at whatever point questions are likely to arise. When developing the satisfaction step in speeches to persuade or to actuate, however, the first four elements—*statement, explanation, theoretical demonstration,* and *practical experience*—offer a convenient and effective sequence: *(a)* Briefly state the attitude, belief, or action you propose. *(b)* Explain it clearly. *(c)* Show how, in theory, it will meet the need. *(d)* Give actual examples of how the proposal or plan is working.

Parallel Development of the Need and Satisfaction Steps.   In some persuasive speeches, the need step may have two or more important aspects. To give each of these aspects sufficient emphasis and to make your discussion clear, you may decide to develop the need and satisfaction steps in a *parallel* order. That is, you first present one aspect of the need and show how your proposal satisfies it; then you follow this same procedure in treating the second aspect, the third aspect, and so on. This method weakens the cumulative effect of the motivated sequence, but the additional clarity often makes up for the loss.

The *normal order* and the *parallel order* for developing the need and satisfaction steps of a speech to actuate are illustrated in the following skeletal outlines:

Outline I: Normal Order

Attention Step

I. While working for the local hospital's emergency ambulance unit this past summer, I responded to several automobile accidents in which the driver was severely injured.
   A. Vivid description of how the accident occurred.
   B. Vivid description of the injuries sustained by the driver.

Need Step

I. In many of these accidents, the primary cause was either drinking or falling asleep at the wheel.
   A. The driver was unable to react properly due to the effect of the alcohol.
   B. The driver awoke too late to take corrective action.

Satisfaction Step

I. In order to combat these two causes of highway accidents, you must do two things above all others.
   A. Do not drive under the influence of alcohol.
   B. Do not drive when you are tired; if you have been driving for a long time, stop and rest.

Visualization Step

I. You will actually enjoy driving more when you have the assurance that these actions will bring.

Action Step

I. Resolve right now to do two things when you drive.
   A. Don't drink and drive.
   B. Don't drive tired.

Outline II: Parallel Order

Attention Step

1. While working for the local hospital's emergency ambulance unit this past summer, I responded to several automobile accidents in which the driver was severely injured.
   A. Vivid description of how the accident occurred.
   B. Vivid description of the injuries sustained by the driver.

Need and Satisfaction Steps (First Phase)

I. In some cases the driver was unable to react properly.
II. To assure yourself that you can react properly, don't mix drinking with driving.

Need and Satisfaction Steps (Second Phase)

I. In some cases the driver awoke too late to take corrective action.
II. To assure yourself that you can take corrective action, do not drive when tired.

Visualization Step

I. You will actually enjoy driving more when you have the assurance that these actions will bring.

Action Step

I. Resolve right now to do two things when you drive.
   A. Don't drink and drive.
   B. Don't drive tired.

Whether using the normal order or the parallel order in the satisfaction step, you will always need to develop support for your statements by supplying an abundance of illustrations, statistics, quotations, and comparisons.

The Visualization Step

The visualization step, as we have said, is commonly used only in the speeches to persuade or to actuate. (See the chart on page 166.) The function of the visualization step is to intensify desire: to help motivate the listeners to believe, feel, or act. In order to do this, it projects them into the future. Indeed, this step might also be called the "projection" step, for its effectiveness depends largely upon the vividness with which it pictures the future or potential benefits of believing or acting as the speaker proposes. Accordingly, the visualization step may be developed in one of three ways: *(1)* by projecting a picture of the future that is positive, *(2)* by projecting a picture that is negative, or *(3)* by projecting first a negative and then a positive picture in order to show contrast.

The Positive Method of Developing the Visualization Step.   When using the positive method, describe conditions as they will be in the future if the belief you advocate is accepted or the action you propose is carried out. Provide vivid, concrete descriptions. Select some situation which you are quite sure will arise in the future, and in that situation picture your audience actually enjoying the safety, pleasure, pride, and so on which the belief or proposal will produce.

The Negative Method of Developing the Visualization Step.   When using the negative method, describe the adverse conditions that will prevail in the future if the belief you advocate is *not* adopted or the solution you propose is *not* carried out. Graphically picture for your audience the danger or unpleasantness which will result. Select the most striking problems or deficiencies you have pointed out in the need step and demonstrate how they will continue unless your recommendations are adopted.

The Contrast Method of Developing the Visualization Step.   The method of contrast combines the positive and negative approaches. Use the negative development first, visualizing the *bad* effects that are likely to occur if your listeners fail to follow your advice; then introduce the positive elements, visualizing the *good* effects of believing or doing as you urge. By means of this contrast, both the bad and the good effects are made more striking and intense.

Whichever method you use, however, remember that the visualization step always must stand the test of *reality*. The conditions you picture must seem probable. In addition, you must to the fullest extent possible *put your listeners into the picture*. Use vivid imagery: make them actually see, hear, feel, taste, or smell the things and benefits you describe. The more real you make the projected situation seem, the stronger will be their reaction.

The following visualization step, in a speech advocating planned and orderly urban growth, illustrates the method of contrast:

Whether we like it or not, then, as these facts show, nearly all of our towns and cities are going to continue to grow and expand in the years ahead. *How* your town grows, however, is going to be entirely up to you.

As new suburbs are developed and annexed, one of two policies can be followed. First, this growth may be haphazard and unplanned, and may occur without strict zoning ordinances to regulate it. In this case, it is likely that paved streets, if they are present at all, will be cheaply constructed without storm sewers or attention to traffic flow. Houses will be crowded together on tiny lots and will vary widely in value and in architectural style. Filling stations, business establishments, and even light industries—with their odors and noises—may appear in the middle of residential neighborhoods. In short, if you were to buy a home in such an area, it is altogether likely that you would soon be faced with huge bills for new streets and sewers, and that your property, instead of appreciating in value, would decline rapidly in the years ahead. As a home buyer you would be a loser all around—a loser not only because of the poor quality of life you and your family would experience, but a loser, and a big loser, in hard dollars and cents.

On the other hand, if additions to your town are properly planned and zoned, as a home owner you will be assured of clean air and adequate living space, will enjoy a house that increases rather than decreases in value, and will be assured that you are not paying for new streets and sewers a few years after you move in. Isn't it worthwhile requiring that your town annex only subdivisions that have been properly planned and zoned—that it insist on orderly responsible growth? Remember, buying a home is very probably the largest single purchase you will make during the course of your entire life. Remember, too, that a healthy, attractive environment is perhaps the greatest gift you can give to your family.

The Action Step

As the chart on page 166 indicates, only the speech to actuate *always* requires an action step. At times, however, as a speaker you may use something resembling an action step to urge further study of the topic dealt with in an informative speech or to strengthen the belief or attitude urged in a persuasive one.

There are many methods for developing the action step, but most commonly these methods employ one or more of the following devices: *(a)* challenge or appeal, *(b)* summary, *(c)* quotation, *(d)* illustration, *(e)* statement of inducement, *(f)* statement of personal intention. These materials are considered in detail in Chapter 10.

Whatever method or material you use, be sure to keep the action step *short*. Someone has given the following rule for effective public speaking: "Stand up, speak up, shut up!" Insofar as the action step is concerned, modify this admonition to read: *Clinch your major ideas, finish your speech briskly—and sit down.*

Applying the Motivated Sequence

As we conclude this chapter, let us see how the motivated sequence can be used to organize your speeches regardless of their general purposes. Because we will discuss it further in later chapters, we here will offer only short outlines, to give you a basic sense of the coherence which can be achieved when you use this organizational pattern.

Perhaps almost all Americans generally believe in the American way of life, in democratic institutions. Yet, you must convince them to act—to actually register to vote.

The Motivated Sequence and Speeches to Inform

Generally, an informative speech concentrates on only three of the five steps. As always, you need to catch your listeners' *attention* and direct it to the substance of your remarks. You must also motivate them by pointing out why they *need* to know what you are about to tell them. And, of course, you have to *satisfy* this need by supplying the information. Here, however, your speech ends, since the purpose for which you are presenting it has been fulfilled. Note how these three steps are applied in an informative speech on how to rescue drowning persons:

Row—Throw—Go

Attention Step

  I. Holiday deaths by drowning are second in number only to automobile accidents.

Need Step

  I. Every person should know what to do when a call for help is heard.
      A. This information may help you save a friend.
      B. This information may help you save a member of your family.

ADAPTATION OF THE MOTIVATED SEQUENCE TO THE GENERAL ENDS OF SPEECH

General End	TO INFORM	TO ENTERTAIN	TO PERSUADE	TO ACTUATE
Reaction Sought	UNDER-STANDING CLARITY	ENJOY-MENT	BELIEF INTERNAL	SPECIFIC ACTION OBSERVABLE
1 *Attention Step*	Draw attention to the subject.	Draw attention to the theme.	Draw attention to the need.	Draw attention to the need.
2 *Need Step*	Show why the listeners need a knowledge of the subject; point out what problems this information will help them meet.	Show why the theme is worthy of consideration.	Present evidence to prove the existence of a situation which requires that something be decided and upon which the audience must take a position.	Present evidence to prove the existence of a situation which requires action.
3 *Satisfaction Step*	Present information to give them a satisfactory knowledge of the subject as an aid in the solution of these problems; begin and end this presentation with a summary of the main points presented. (Normal end of the speech.)	Elaborate on theme through numerous illustrations that will elicit a pleasurable reaction from the audience.	Get the audience to believe that your position on this question is the right one to take, by using evidence and motivational appeals.	Propose the specific action required to meet this situation; get the audience to believe in it by presenting evidence and motivational appeals (as in the speech to persuade).
4 *Visualization Step*	Sometimes: briefly suggest pleasure to be gained from this knowledge.	Sometimes: briefly suggest what is to be gained through humorous examination of the theme.	Briefly stimulate a favorable response by projecting this belief into imaginary operation. (Normal end of the speech.)	Picture the results which such action or the failure to take it will bring; use vivid description (as in the speech to persuade).
5 *Action Step*	Sometimes: urge further study of the subject.	Sometimes: implore audience to consider lighter side of life.	Sometimes: arouse determination to retain this belief (as a guide to future action).	Urge the audience to take definite action proposed.

Satisfaction Step

I. Remember three important words when someone is drowning: *row, throw, go.*
   A. *Row:* Look for a boat.
      1. You can well afford to take a little time to look for a means of rowing to the rescue.
         a. Look for a boat.
         b. Look for a canoe.
         c. Look for a raft.
      2. Rowing to the rescue is always the wisest way.
   B. *Throw:* Look for a life buoy.
      1. See if you can locate something buoyant to throw to the person in distress.
         a. Look for a life buoy.
         b. Look for an inflated inner tube.
         c. Look for a board.
         d. Look for a child's floating toy.
      2. You can throw an object faster than you can swim.
   C. *Go:* As a last resort, swim out to the drowning person.
      1. Approach the victim from the rear.
      2. If you are grabbed, go underwater.
      3. Clutch the person's hair.
      4. Swim for shore.

II. Remember, when you hear the call for help:
   A. Look first for something in which to row.
   B. Look for something buoyant to throw the victim.
   C. Swim out only as a last resort.

The Motivated Sequence and Speeches to Entertain

A Case for Optimism[5]

Attention Step

I. Perhaps you've heard the expression "The optimist sees the doughnut; the pessimist, the hole."

Need Step

I. Is this statement an accurate assessment of people?
   A. To the pessimist, the optimist is a fool: he who looks at an oyster and expects to find pearls is engaging in wishful thinking.
   B. To the optimist, a pessimist is sour on life: he who looks at an oyster and expects to get ptomaine poisoning is missing out on the richer possibilities life can offer.

Satisfaction Step

I. The pessimist responds to every event with an expectation of the worst that could happen.

II. The optimist, on the other hand, looks for the bright side.
   A. The day after a robbery, a friend asked a store owner about the loss. After acknowledging that he had indeed suffered a loss, the store owner quipped: "But I was lucky; I

marked everything down 20 percent the day before. Had I not done that I would have lost even more.''

B. The optimist is one who cleans his glasses before eating the grapefruit.

Visualization Step

I. Cheer up; look for the bright side and you will find things to be happy about.

Action Step

I. Be an optimist: ''Keep your eye upon the doughnut and not upon the hole.''

The Motivated Sequence and Speeches to Actuate

In speeches to actuate, as we have said, the entire sequence is used. Here, in abbreviated outline form, is how a relatively simple speech on fire prevention could utilize the structure:

Fire Prevention in the Home

Attention Step

I. If you like parlor tricks, try this:
    A. Place a blotter soaked in turpentine in a jar of oxygen.
    B. The blotter will burst into flames.

II. If you do not have a jar of oxygen around the house, try this:
    A. Place a well-oiled mop in a storage closet.
    B. In a few days the mop will burst into flames.

Need Step

I. Few homes are free from dangerous fire hazards.
    A. Attics with piles of damp clothing and paper are combustible.
    B. Storage closets containing cleaning mops and brushes are fire hazards.
    C. Basements often are filled with dangerous piles of trash.

Satisfaction Step

I. Protecting your home from fire requires three things:
    A. A thorough cleaning out of all combustible materials.
    B. Careful storage of such hazards as oil mops and paint brushes.
    C. A regular check to see that inflammable trash does not accumulate.

II. Clean-up programs show practical results.
    A. Clean-up campaigns in Evansville kept insurance rates in a ''Class 1'' bracket.
    B. A clean-up campaign in Fort Wayne helped reduce the number of fires.

Visualization Step

I. You will enjoy the results of such a program.
    A. You will have neat and attractive surroundings.
    B. You will be safe from fire.

Action Step

I. Begin your own clean-up campaign now.

Maggie Kuhn, founder of the Gray Panthers, knows you can't simply assume that all older citizens will want to agitate for senior citizens' rights. You have to convince them.

The Motivated Sequence and Speeches to Persuade

Study the following outline for a persuasive speech arguing that students should investigate charities before they contribute. This outline is somewhat longer than the previous ones so that you can see more clearly ways to develop each of the five steps.

Contribute to Charities Wisely[6]

Specific Purpose	To persuade listeners to evaluate carefully the efficiency and effectiveness of the charitable organizations to which they contribute.
Attention Step (Startling statement)	I. In 1975, Americans gave over 11.6 billion dollars to charitable organizations, not counting contributions to religious and educational institutions, but some experts have estimated that 116 million dollars was wasted because it went to fraudulent or poorly managed organizations.
Need Step	II. There are differences in the ways charities distribute their funds.
(Example to describe the problem)	A. Example of a charity which uses 94 percent of its contributions for administration.

           B.   Example of a charity—United Way—which distributes ninety cents out of every dollar collected.

(Call for evalua-tion)   III.   Unless we all simply decide to stop giving to charities, we must come up with criteria for evaluating organizations and procedures for investigating them.

Satisfaction Step (Criteria)   IV.   How, then, can you evaluate charities?

           A.   Fund-raising and administrative costs should total less than 50 percent of the total public contributions.

           B.   An effective charity should be controlled by an active, unsalaried governing board, with no paid employees serving as voting members of that board.

           C.   It should use reputable promotional and fund-raising methods.

           D.   It should publicly disclose a complete and independently audited annual financial report. [Each of these criteria could be justified by appeals to authority and example.]

(Indication of how criteria can be ap-plied)   V.   These criteria can be applied by both governmental units and individuals.

           A.   Both Florida and Pennsylvania have laws governing what percentage of their total contributions charities can spend on fund raising.

           B.   The federal government similarly regulates charities soliciting in more than one state.

           C.   As an individual, you also can check into charities you might wish to support.

              1.   Ask for an annual report before contributing.

              2.   The Council of Better Business Bureaus publishes a rating list.

              3.   The National Information Bureau discloses pertinent information.

Visualization Step   VI.   If both government and individuals do their investigative jobs properly, imagine the benefits which would accrue from the extra money spent on those who need it.

           A.   The number of poor that could be fed and clothed would increase.

           B.   Additional medical and health care facilities could be built.

           C.   Research into killing and crippling diseases could proceed with more vigor.

Action Step   VII.   You have the power to direct your contributions to the most beneficial charities.

(Summary)   A.   Keep the evaluative criteria—efficiency, disinterestedness, fairness, and openness—in mind when you receive a call for help.

(Appeal)   B.   And when you give, open your heart, your pocketbook, and, yes, your mind—give, but give wisely.

The motivated sequence is a time-tested, flexible organizational pattern, one based on a speaker's two fundamental communicative concerns—a concern for creative problem-solving and a concern for the audience's motives. We will return to the motivated sequence at several other points, but, for now, let us examine more specific organizational patterns you will want to consider when it comes time to package your ideas for others.

REFERENCE NOTES

[1]Classical "Gestalt" perception theory, which forms the basis for many of these remarks, is reviewed usefully in Ernest R. Hilgard, *Theories of Learning,* Hawthorn Books (New York: Appleton-Century-Crofts, 1956). There also is an emerging body of literature on "visual literacy"—the ways we learn to process and codify elements in our perceptual fields. See, for example, Doris A. Dondis, *A Primer of Visual Literacy* (Cambridge, MA: The MIT Press, 1973), and Leonard Zusne, *Visual Perception of Form* (New York: Academic Press, Inc., 1976).

[2]John Dewey, "Analysis of Reflective Thinking," *How We Think* (Boston, MA: D. C. Heath & Company, 1910), p. 72.

[3]Anyone interested in how Alan Monroe conceived of and first used the motivated sequence—then a revolutionary idea—should see the first edition, Alan H. Monroe, *Principles and Types of Speech* (Chicago: Scott, Foresman and Company, 1935), esp. pp. vii–x.

[4]"Marriage Contracts," by Linda Hopkins. Reprinted from *Winning Orations,* 1983, by special arrangement with the Interstate Oratorical Association, Larry Schnoor, Executive Secretary, Mankato State University, Mankato, Minnesota.

[5]Based in part on material taken from *Friendly Speeches* (Cleveland: National Reference Library).

[6]This outline is based on a speech given by Steve Favitta, Central Missouri State University, in 1978. We have omitted the supporting materials, but most may be found in "New CT Ratings on 53 Charities," *Changing Times,* November 1976; and "United Way: Are the Criticisms Fair?" *Changing Times,* October 1977. This altered outline is used with the permission of Mr. Favitta. Text supplied courtesy of Professor Roger Conaway and Professor Dan Curtis.

PROBLEMS AND PROBES

1. Choose a social controversy as a topic for a speech and specify two audiences, one opposing the issue and one supporting it (for example, a speech on the nuclear freeze to be given to a group of conservatives and to a group of liberals). Using the motivated sequence as a pattern, specify how you would develop the information for each audience so that your speech serves all five functions. Write a concluding paragraph which compares the approach taken for the two audiences.

2. Using one of the two speeches at the end of Chapter 3, write a brief analysis of its use of the motivated sequence, pointing out where each step begins and noting its method of development. Look in particular at the conclusion of the speech: Does the speaker add to the three basic steps (attention, need, satisfaction) an optional visualization and/or action step? If not, how is the speech terminated?

3. Select two of the following statements (or select your own) and devise a specific purpose for a speech to persuade your classmates. For each specific purpose, develop a five-sentence plan or structure designed to elicit the desired response—

one carefully written sentence for each step in the motivated sequence. Hand in your written statement of specific purpose and the accompanying plan for achieving your purpose.

Strict gun-control laws should be enacted.

Go to church.

Exercise to benefit your heart.

Three years of math should be required for all high school graduates.

We should have a national repertory theatre.

Improve the quality of television programs.

Give American industries protection against imported goods.

We should have free catastrophic illness insurance for all people.

4. The motivated sequence has its own internal logic aimed at satisfying audience questions: attention precedes need; need precedes satisfaction, and so on. What is the utility of this sequence in meeting audience expectations? Would any other ordering have equal or greater utility?

ORAL ACTIVITIES

1. After your instructor has divided the class into small groups of four, five, or six members, meet with your group and discuss your plans for a six-minute persuasive or actuative speech. As a basis for the discussion, each member of the group will read aloud one of the statements selected in Problem 3 of Problems and Probes, the statement of the specific purpose evolved for it, and the five-sentence motivated-sequence plan or structure designed to influence audience belief in and/ or acceptance of the idea or proposal. Other members of the group will then respond to these matters analytically, suggesting clarifications and improvements. Afterward, revise or reconstruct your speech plan, making it as effective as you can.

2. Select a topic for either an informative, a persuasive, or an entertaining speech. Develop a specific purpose and an outline of the steps involved in the motivated sequence that would apply to your topic. Assume that the audience will be your classmates. Working in small groups, present each of your analyses orally to the others in the group. Critique yours and others as appropriate uses of the motivated sequence.

CHAPTER 9

Adapting the Speech Structure

to Audiences: Traditional

Patterns of Organization

The preceding chapter dealt with a holistic approach to the organization of speeches. The motivated sequence is premised on the thought processes that listeners often follow when receiving new information or deciding how a problem may be solved. In this chapter, we will consider the relationship between this holistic approach and other patterns of organization. Each of the patterns will be discussed, and suggestions regarding their use in meeting your specific purpose will be outlined.

The Motivated Sequence and Traditional Patterns

The traditional patterns of organization assume that the initial step in the motivated sequence has been executed—you have achieved the *attention* of the audience. The *need* and *satisfaction* stages are the primary targets for internal organization of the main points you wish to cover. The following outline suggests the relationship between the motivated sequence and the traditional patterns:

Motivated Sequence	Traditional Patterns
Attention	Introduction
Need/Satisfaction	Organized Main Points
Visualization/Action	Conclusion

The application of the traditional patterns to the main points of the speech should satisfy five general criteria for the structure of any speech:

1. *The structure of the speech must be easy for the audience to grasp and remember.* Listeners need to see how your statement of need and your satisfaction of that need fit together into a coherent whole. Otherwise, you will not elicit attention to the

issue because the listeners will be trying to determine what you intend to communicate.

2. *The pattern must provide for a full and balanced coverage of the material under consideration.* You must use a pattern which will complement the ideas and their supporting materials, one which will enhance your ability to clarify your central idea or defend your claim.

3. *The structure of the speech should be appropriate to the occasion.* As we noted in Chapter 1, there are some occasions or settings where speakers are expected to observe group traditions. Presidential inaugural addresses, for example, tend to follow a particular format originally created by our first presidents.[1] Likewise, eulogies[2] and speeches of introduction normally consider themes in an order which members of our culture have come to expect. An occasion, therefore, may dictate the organization of your statement of need and your satisfaction of that need.

4. *The structure of a speech should be adapted to the audience's needs and level of knowledge.* Whereas the motivated sequence focuses broadly on the fundamental thought processes of the audience, particular patterns of organization must consider other aspects of the audience's awareness of the issue. Some of the patterns we will describe are particularly well suited to times when listeners have little background on some subject, while others are useful in situations where the audience is interested and knowledgeable about the subject under discussion. Thus, as you review the patterns which follow, select the pattern that will match your audience's needs and informational background.

5. *The speech must move forward steadily toward a complete and satisfying finish.* As you structure this substantive portion of your speech, give the audience a sense of forward motion—of moving through a series of main points with a clear idea of where your ideas are heading and how you are going to arrive at a termination point. Repeated backtracking to pick up "lost" points will confuse your audience, and you will lose the sense of momentum your structure intended to convey. Throwing out facts in what appears to be a random, thoughtless pattern will not allow you to clarify a point or to amass data that justifies a position you have taken.

These are the major elements which any substantive portion of a speech must satisfy in conveying a coherent, planned message to an audience. Failure to meet any one of the criteria will likewise weaken the impact of the entire speech, regardless of how well planned and executed the other steps in the motivated sequence might be.

Types of Traditional Patterns

There are several ways in which the main points of your speech can be ordered. The four options which are most useful are grouped as follows: (1) *chronological patterns,* (2) *spatial patterns,* (3) *causal patterns,* and (4) *topical patterns.* Following consideration of these organizing patterns, we will examine several ways of arranging subpoints underneath the main points.

ORGANIZATIONAL PATTERNS

Spatial   Geographic Magnitude or Size

Chronological   Narrative Sequence, Temporal Sequence

Causal   Cause - Effect, Effect - Cause

Topical

Chronological Patterns.   The defining characteristic of chronological patterns is their adherence to the order in which events actually occurred. These patterns are useful for informing listeners who know little about the background of a topic, or for showing the audience that they should hold some set of attitudes toward a situation. In the first case, the sequence is called *temporal;* in the second, *narrative.*

Temporal sequence.   When employing a temporal sequence, you begin at a certain period or date and move forward (or backward) in a systematic way, thus offering background on some topic about which the audience knows little. For example, you might describe the methods for refining petroleum by tracing the development of the cracking process from the earliest attempts down to the present time. You might describe the manufacture of an automobile by following the assembly-line process from beginning to end. Your goals are to create an interest in an area you think your audience should know more about and to present basic information in a clear manner. When talking to a group about the history of space flights, you might use the following sequence:

Space Flights

  I.   Pre-NASA planning and development

 II.   The origin of NASA and early space flights

III.   From exploration to payload flights

IV.   Future trends in space flights

In this example, the dates are not precise; instead, the periods overlap one another (for example, there is no precise date separating exploration and payload purposes of space flights). Nevertheless, the general progression is forward-moving.

Narrative sequence. If you want to do more than merely offer background information, you should use a chronological pattern which makes a point. Narratives are stories—stories that allow you to draw some conclusions about a series of events. Aesop's fables are narratives with a moral about human motivation and action; the series of events surrounding a crime usually are reviewed chronologically by lawyers to point toward the innocence or guilt of a defendant. In narrative sequences, therefore, speakers review events or actions to advocate some claim or to clarify the events that have led to the present situation.[3] If, for example, you wanted the audience to understand why the failed Equal Rights Amendment drive is such a complex issue, you could use a narrative format to accomplish that purpose:

The Complexities of the ERA Drive

Central Idea: The Equal Rights Amendment has had a long and complex history.

  I.   The Equal Rights Amendment was first introduced into Congress in 1922, only three years after women received the right to vote.

     A.   It failed to pass either house for many years.

     B.   In 1947, the Senate passed it, although the House did not.

 II.   The main legislative battle over the ERA was waged in the early '70s.

     A.   It had a chance to pass in 1970, but two riders (precluding women from the draft and allowing prayer in schools) met with opposition, and again it died in the Senate.

     B.   The House finally passed it in 1971.

     C.   The Senate then approved the measure in March 1972.

III.   The ratification process began within hours of Senate action.

     A.   Thirty states had ratified it within a year.

     B.   Between 1973 and 1975, only four more states ratified the amendment.

IV.   Countermeasures soon were taken.

     A.   The movement to rescind also began in 1973, with Nebraska and Tennessee rescinding their support in 1973–74.

    B.   Eight states failed to approve the ERA between 1973 and 1975.

    C.   This is when, essentially, the movement came to a halt.

V. Moves to revive the ERA in the early '80s were not successful.

    A.   Congress did extend the timetable for keeping it alive.

    B.   But, supporters were not able to obtain ratification by the deadline.

    C.   Today, ERA is officially dead, although there will be renewed efforts to revive and pass the amendment.

Spatial Patterns.   Generally, spatial patterns for a speech arrange ideas or subtopics in terms of their physical proximity or relationships to each other. Some of these patterns, those normally called *geographical patterns,* organize materials according to well-defined regions or areas so as to visualize physical movement and development. A common presentation of this type is the evening weather forecast: A meteorologist will first discuss today's high pressure dome over your area, then the low pressure area lying over the Midwest which will produce tomorrow's overcast sky, and finally next week's cold snap which will result from the Arctic air mass coming in from northern Canada. The idea of "geography" need not be applied narrowly; the concept also may apply to physical spaces, such as floors in a hospital or library. Such speeches also lend themselves to the use of visual aids, whether finely drawn on poster board or roughly sketched on an available blackboard. The following assumes an accompanying "map" that would help orient listeners:

Alaska's Southeast

  I.   Alaska's Southeast is a long finger-like area known as the Panhandle running between Canada's western border and the Pacific Ocean.

 II.   The major city, Juneau, lies roughly in the center of the Panhandle.

III.   Yakutat Bay and the tiny community of Yakutat lie on the northern edge.

IV.   The communities of Metlakatla and Ketchikan are in the southern tip of the Panhandle.

    Other organizational patterns have some of the qualities of a spatial pattern, but without the sense of geographical movement or development. For instance, a speaker might want to compare *magnitude* or *size*. If, for example, you wanted to talk about the comparative advantages of using a small-town versus a metropolitan bank, or seeking medical treatment at a small rural medical clinic rather than at a large university medical center, you still would be using a spatial pattern but without the physical sense provided by mental or actual maps. Also, a spatial pattern, as is true of a chronological pattern, often can be combined successfully with other patterns. A speech on the effects of nuclear fallout, for example, could be organized spatially by talking about the effects in the inner city, the outlying suburbs, and the rural communities.

    Whether combined with other patterns or used singly, the spatial pattern has the virtue of visualization, allowing you to provide conceptual clarity and to give listeners a sense of growth and development or movement as your speech unfolds.

Causal Patterns.   As their name implies, causal patterns of message organization move either *(1)* from an analysis of present causes to a consideration of future effects, or *(2)* from a description of present conditions to an analysis of the causes which appear to have produced them. When employing the cause-effect arrangement, you might, for instance, first point out that a community's landlord-tenant codes are outdated, and then predict that, as a result of this situation, landlords will take undue advantage of tenants. Or, reasoning in the reverse direction (if the prediction already has come true), you could argue that the effect (tenants are being taken advantage of) is the result of out-dated landlord-tenant codes. Compare the following outlines:

Juvenile Delinquency

I.   There are several factors which, taken together, may account for juvenile delinquency.
   A.   Broken home
   B.   Abusive parent(s)
   C.   Socioeconomic status

II.   The effects of these potential causes are significant.
   A.   Vandalism
   B.   Petty theft
   C.   Court costs
   D.   Lost human potential

The Citrus Crisis

I.   Orange juice lovers know that the price of their favorite drink is skyrocketing, but do they know why?
   A.   Early frosts have damaged fruit headed for market.
   B.   An outbreak of citrus canker has led to the destruction of many large orange groves.

II.   The resulting crop shortage will mean higher prices for oranges and for orange juice.

Note a characteristic of both these outlines: Each starts with the aspect of the situation *better known* to audience members, and then proceeds to develop the *lesser known* facets of the problem. You will find a cause-effect pattern useful if the causes are more familiar to the listeners than the effects; an effect-cause sequence preferable if the opposite is true.

Topical Patterns.   Some speeches on familiar topics are best organized in terms of subject-matter divisions which over a period of time have become standardized. For example, financial reports customarily are divided into assets and liabilities; discussions of government, into legislative, executive, and judicial functions; and comparisons of different kinds of telescopes, into celestial and terrestrial models. Topical patterns are most useful for speeches that *enumerate* aspects of persons, places, things, or processes. Occasionally, a speaker tries to discuss all the aspects of a subject, as in a speech on the three branches of government. More often, however, a partial enumeration of the possible topics or areas is sufficient. For example, a speech on the world of the "new media" might include the following:

The Nature of the New Media

I. Cable technologies distribute information and pictures via telephone and other "hardwired" systems.

II. Microwave technologies distribute information and pictures via comparatively low-powered transmitters over areas roughly fifty to seventy miles in diameter.

III. Satellite technologies distribute information and pictures via high-powered transmission to and from earth-orbiting satellites.

Topical patterns certainly are among the most popular and the easiest of the patterns to employ in organizing your speech. One caution: When doing a partial enumeration of a subject, such as the "new media," you will need to justify your choice of topics covered. If someone should ask "But what about *X?*" it may signal that your choices lacked coherence or that the selection did not include what common sense would suggest.

Arranging the Subpoints in the Structure
After arranging the main points in the speech in one of the patterns discussed above, you need to decide how to arrange the subpoints under each of the major ideas. One approach is to organize the subpoints according to one of the four patterns. Thus, your main heads may be arranged in a spatial pattern, while the subpoints under each may be arranged in chronological order. You can mix and match in almost any fashion needed to convey your ideas in a clear, coherent manner. Whatever pattern is chosen, be sure that you use it consistently, either at the level of main points or as you arrange a set of subpoints under a main head. For instance, do not mix spatial and causal patterns in organizing main heads, and do not mix topical and chronological patterns while arranging subpoints under a single main head.

There are other methods which can be employed in arranging the subpoints of a speech. The following five approaches are useful ways of organizing your information.

Parts of a Whole.   If a major idea concerns an object or a process which consists of a series of component parts, the subpoints may examine these points in order. For example, you might describe the intricacies of a racing bicycle by discussing the wheels, derailleur, and frame. If your subject concerns the number of service organizations in your community, you might list the meetings of the Kiwanis, Lions, and Rotary as subtotals of the aggregate number of clubs in the area.

Lists of Qualities or Functions.   If the main point suggests the purpose of some mechanism, organization, or procedure, the subpoints may list the specific functions it performs. Thus, the nature of sound may be discussed by considering the qualities of

Time spent by speakers in preparation pays off when they deliver their speeches. Taking the time to arrange materials into subpoints produces comprehensible speeches.

timbre, pitch, and loudness; the purpose of a recreation department might be clarified by citing its various responsibilities or functions.

Series of Causes or Results.   If you use the cause-effect sequence to arrange your major ideas, you will often find that neither cause nor effect is single. Each of the several causes or results may then constitute a subpoint. Even when another type of sequence is used for the major ideas, a list of causes or results could form the subpoints under each main head. The causes of highway accidents, for example, could be examined under the subpoints of excessive speed, drinking, poor road conditions, and improperly maintained vehicles. The results of a running program could be discussed under the subpoints of reduced stress, better cardiovascular circulation, and improved fat/muscle ratio.

Items of Logical Proof.   In a speech to persuade or to actuate, the subpoints often provide logical proof for the idea they support. When this is the case, you should be able to connect the major idea and subpoints with the word *because* (acceptance of the main point is justified *because* subpoints a, b, c, and so on are adequate support). Conversely, you should be able to use the word *therefore* when reasoning from the subpoints back to the main point (the subpoints provide adequate support, *therefore* the main point is justified). If you were arguing that "Strikes are wasteful" you might claim as your subpoints: because workers lose their wages, employers lose their profits, and consumers lose the products they might otherwise have had.

Illustrative Examples.   Many times the main point consists of a generalized statement for which the subpoints provide a series of specific illustrative examples. This method may be used both in exposition and in argument, the examples constituting clarification or proof, respectively. Thus, the general statement that fluoride helps reduce tooth decay might have as its subpoints a series of examples citing the experience of those cities which have added fluoride to their drinking water.

Selecting an Organizational Pattern: Strategies and Determining Factors

Selecting the appropriate organizational pattern is not always a matter of chance. Often, the topic itself will suggest the best means of conveying the information. If your subject lends itself naturally to historical treatment, a chronological sequence would be the most useful means of ordering your ideas. If the audience will be confused about the spatial relationships involved in your ideas, a spatial order would be the best means of orienting them to the subject. When the topic implies that an investigation of causes or a listing of effects will be necessary, a causal pattern is the most appropriate. Think in terms of complementing the natural dictates of the topic as you order your main points and subpoints.

The specific purposes also may suggest which of the patterns will be the most useful. If you are attempting to illustrate the effects of long-standing policies, for example, a combination chronological/causal pattern would be the most effective. As you move forward in time, you add cumulative impact to the claim that particular effects are the result of a long-standing policy. If your purpose is to illustrate that the location of an ambulance site will make a difference in response time, a spatial pattern would give you the best means of justifying your claim. As you begin to outline your main points, consider the impact of the topic and your purpose in speaking; your organizational pattern can assist you in dramatizing the claim you are advancing.

Finally, consider the needs and expectations imposed by the audience and the occasion. As noted earlier, the occasion may suggest both the specific themes that should be developed and the particular order in which they are discussed. If the audience already is familiar with the background, or accepts the causes for the current dilemma, you will waste time organizing a speech in a chronological pattern or using a causal pattern to justify the existence of certain effects. Thus, you will need to be sensitive to the demands of the occasion and the status of the audience's knowledge and position on the issues. This is particularly important if you are employing a topical pattern; the audience may have set expectations about what should or should not be covered by any speaker.

The following outline integrates the motivated sequence and the traditional patterns of organizing ideas:

When organizing a speech for a diverse audience, ask yourself: Does the topic itself suggest an appropriate pattern? Is a particular pattern suggested by my specific purpose?

The Plight of the Atlantic Salmon[4]

Attention Step

I.   Are you disgusted by the sight of dead fish floating in the water? Does the smell of polluted water turn your stomach?
   A.   Many of New England's rivers are becoming lifeless wastelands.
   B.   One river hit especially hard by pollution is the Connecticut River.
   C.   Pollution has led to the near elimination of many fish species, notably the Atlantic Salmon.

Need Step

I.   The Atlantic Salmon has been the most severely affected fish in the river.
   A.   At one time fish were plentiful and no laws were necessary to regulate fishing.
   B.   Salmon used to be among the most plentiful.

II.   Pollution by industry has caused the decline in the salmon population.
   A.   Dam construction has severely affected the salmon.
      1.   There are fourteen man-made barriers on the river.
      2.   Eleven of the fourteen barriers are hydroelectric facilities.
         a.   These facilities produce higher water temperatures.
         b.   Estimates of fish loss due to excessive water temperature are as high as 16 percent.
   B.   Chemical and industrial pollution also have harmed the salmon.
      1.   Discharge of chemicals such as PCB has hurt the salmon.
      2.   PCB kills salmon eggs, thus limiting the present and future populations.

    C.   Increased fishing also has limited the population.
        1.   Fishing in the Atlantic has increased markedly.
            a.   In 1960, the Greenland fishery caught an estimated 132,000 pounds of salmon.
            b.   By 1970, this had risen to 5.8 million pounds.
        2.   By thus reducing the number of salmon, there are fewer entering the river to attempt to reach their spawning habitat.

Satisfaction Step
    I.   To restore the salmon, we must eliminate or reduce the detrimental influences.
        A.   First, the hydroelectric facilities must be required to cool water before it is discharged into the river.
        B.   Second, we need to halt the discharge of harmful chemicals into the water supply.
        C.   Third, we need to establish fishing limits in the Atlantic Ocean.

Visualization Step
    I.   If we take all of these steps, we will gain three-fold.
        A.   We will preserve the salmon, thereby enhancing pleasure fishing along the river.
        B.   By cleaning up the river, we will improve the aquatic environment for other species as well.
        C.   Clear, clean water also will enhance the recreational value of the river.

Action Step
    I.   To achieve these goals, we must act now.
        A.   We must pressure state and federal legislatures to take corrective measures.
        B.   We must continually monitor the success of legislation designed to remedy the problem.

Organizing speeches may seem a near-impossible task, especially as you sit at your desk or at the kitchen table surrounded by myriad notes on specific instances, factual illustrations, statistics, and testimony. The possibilities for organizing may seem limitless. As we noted in the beginning of Chapter 8, the task of building a conceptually clear structure for your major ideas is crucial. Listeners need to "see" and comprehend a pattern to the unfolding of your ideas if they are to make sense out of your attempt to convey ideas. When the pattern you select makes sense in terms of the topic, your purpose, and the expectations of the audience and occasion, your message should be received as a logically coherent approach to structuring your ideas.

REFERENCE NOTES

[1]See, for example, Donald L. Wolfarth, "John F. Kennedy in the Tradition of Inaugural Speeches," *Quarterly Journal of Speech*, 47 (April 1961), 124–32.

[2]Kathleen Jamieson, *Critical Anthology of Public Speeches* (Chicago: Science Research Associates, 1978).

[3]For further discussions of narratives and their use in persuasive speeches, see Bruce E. Gronbeck, *The Articulate Person: A Guide to Everyday Public Speaking*, 2nd ed. (Glenview, IL: Scott, Foresman and Company, 1983), and Donovan J. Ochs and Ronald J. Burritt, "Perceptual Theory: Narrative Suasion of Lysias," in *Explorations in Rhetorical*

Criticism, ed. G. P. Mohrmann et al. (University Park, PA: Penn. State Univ. Press, 1973), pp. 51–74.

[4]Adapted from a speech by David Gibbons, University of Maine, Orono.

PROBLEMS AND PROBES

1. Read one of the speeches in this text and examine its organization. Identify the need and satisfaction stages in the development of the speech. What are the major points within each stage and how are they arranged? What are the subpoints supporting each main point and how are they arranged? Write a brief analysis, indicating the organizational patterns used. Comment critically on the overall organization of the speech; give a letter grade *(A–D)* and indicate why it is appropriate. (Note: If you have completed #2 in Chapter 8's Problems and Probes, simply extend the analysis conducted in that assignment.)

2. Study three or four recent presidential inaugural addresses. Note the organization of each. How do the addresses differ? In what ways are they similar? Write a brief paper in which you consider the possible constraints imposed by the occasion on the arrangement of points within inaugural addresses. Evaluate the clarity and appropriateness of each address selected for study as it meets or fails to meet the constraints imposed by the occasion.

ORAL ACTIVITIES

1. Before coming to class, briefly outline a message in two different organizational patterns, noting a general and specific purpose for each organization. Remember that a variety of organizational patterns can be used, depending on what you wish to accomplish. In class, your teacher will divide you into small groups so that group members may share their messages and discuss which organizational pattern best serves their purposes.

2. Prepare a four- to six-minute speech on a controversial topic. Assume that you will be addressing a hostile audience and plan your message accordingly. How would a message directed to a favorable audience differ?

3. Prepare a five- to seven-minute speech on a subject of your choice for presentation in class. After you've delivered it, and without receiving critical comments from your instructor or classmates, write and give to the instructor a short paper titled "If I Had It to Do Over." In this paper, either defend the pattern of organization you employed in arranging the major heads and developing the subpoints; or suggest how, after the experience of actually presenting your material to an audience, you see now where you could make improvements. See if your instructor and the other members of the class agree with your critical perceptions of your own work.

4. With the whole class participating, hold a general discussion in which you consider how each of the following topics might be most effectively arranged for a short speech to be delivered to your speech class:

Why many small businesses fail.

Developments in automotive engineering.

The hot spots of world politics.
Digging for diamonds.
Eat wisely and live long.
How the world looks to your dog.
Bridge for the beginner.
Appreciating contemporary art.
The metric system.
Making out your income tax return.
Computer literacy.

CHAPTER 10

Beginning and

Ending the Speech

Your listeners' receptiveness to your ideas and their understanding of what you are asking of them hinges on an effective beginning and ending to your presentation. Well-thought-out, creative beginnings heighten audience interest in what you are about to say; they provide a reason for listening to the remainder of your speech. Because your audience may not clearly understand your proposal or the importance of your information, you should begin by establishing a context for the substance of your remarks. In closing your speech, an effective ending ties the threads of your talk together into a cohesive unit; it provides your final opportunity to leave the audience with a clear understanding of your central idea or claim, your reasons for presenting it, and your concern for its acceptance.

Beginnings and endings are linked directly to the motivated sequence stages discussed in Chapter 8. Beginnings meet the expectancies of an *attention* step—they increase interest and provide reasons for audiences to attend to the message. Endings satisfy either *visualization* or *action* stages—they bring ideas together and illustrate how the audience will benefit from the information or proposal advanced during the speech. In this chapter, we will consider beginnings and endings as they function in their respective stages of the motivated sequence. We also will present several methods that enable you to accomplish your objectives in beginning and ending your speech.

Beginning: Initial Considerations

Before settling on an opening strategy for your presentation, ask yourself the following questions:

1. Is the audience likely to be interested, or must I arouse interest through some attention-getting approach?
2. Is the audience sufficiently aware of my qualifications or must I establish my expertise?

At the turn of this century, James Albert Winans articulated a core rhetorical truth: "Attention determines response." Gain and sustain it; attentive audiences are accepting audiences.

3. Does my speech fulfill or depart from the expectations of the audience or occasion? If the speech is not consonant with expectations, should I clarify my reasons for the direction I am taking?
4. How important is it to create an atmosphere of good will?
5. Does the audience have prior knowledge of the scope of my speech, or should I forecast the major themes before delving into the substantive portion?

Each of these initial considerations allows you to analyze what functions the beginning of your speech should serve to adapt your message effectively to the audience and the occasion.

Gaining Attention

In most settings your listeners are likely to appreciate an overt effort on your part to focus their attention on you and your subject. Even if they have an initial interest in your talk, various distractions may impede their willingness to attend fully to your ideas. You can use the *factors of attention,* discussed in detail in Chapter 3, to arouse the interest of your listeners. Apply these factors to illustrate why the audience should listen to you—why your topic is important, significant, and deserving of study or action. If the audience is not already convinced that your topic is vital and real, you may help your case by offering reasons for believing—at the very beginning of your speech—that the problem is indeed one of critical importance.

Stating Qualifications

Your listeners are probably unaware of the depth and breadth of your knowledge or of the time you have spent in becoming knowledgeable about your subject. They may not know of your involvement with a local antinuclear or pro-life group, or your attendance at a recent political convention. They may not know that you spent the last ten years working in the family ice-cream shop, or that you spent four hours interviewing environmentalists, scientists, and politicians in preparing a speech on a local controversy over polluted waterways. Although you should not take seven of your allotted ten minutes to extol your experiences as a family helper or an industrious researcher, a brief reference to your qualifications may allay audience concerns over the extent of your expertness.

Satisfying Demands of Audience and Occasion

A third function of the speech beginning is to speak directly to the audience's expectations of what the speech should cover. You may satisfy these expectations at the outset by noting the relationship of your theme to the purpose of the meeting or the ceremonial thrust of the occasion. In some instances, however, a speaker may wish to move in a direction different from that expected by the audience or strongly suggested by the occasion. The keynote speech at a political convention, for instance, usually combines a hard-hitting attack on the opposition with the affirmation of the virtues of the speaker's party.

Creating Good Will

Audiences appreciate speakers who take a few moments to create good will. Recognizing the efforts of the group being addressed, expressing appreciation for being invited, or taking a humorous approach to the beginning of the speech are ways to foster a relaxed atmosphere, one in which your views will be respected because you have recognized and shown your respect for the audience. When you face a hostile audience, you may need to recognize explicitly the differences that exist. Giving credit to your opponents for having thoughtfully considered an issue may go a long way toward creating a more responsive atmosphere for your own address.

Clarifying the Scope of Your Speech

Because the audience is unlikely to know how you plan to develop the topic of your speech, what points you will cover, and whether you will deal briefly with many points or treat a few in depth, you may find it useful to *forecast* the development of the speech. You can accomplish this by enumerating your major ideas or themes—by telling the people in your audience what you will be speaking about—thus helping to guide them through the development of your speech.

Types of Speech Introductions

Not every introduction will require specific development of *all* the functions described in the preceding section. Nevertheless, the speech you are to present is sure to need at least one. To satisfy that function, and any others that may be required or helpful in attaining your purpose, speakers frequently employ one or more of the following methods:

1. Refer to the subject or problem.
2. Refer to the occasion.
3. Extend a personal greeting or make a personal allusion.
4. Ask a rhetorical question.
5. Make a startling statement of fact or opinion.
6. Use an apt quotation.
7. Relate a humorous anecdote relevant to a topical point.
8. Cite a real or hypothetical illustration.

Reference to the Subject or Problem

The approach of referring directly to the subject or problem is most useful when the audience already has a vital interest in hearing your message. Many business conferences invite speakers with a particular topic or theme in mind; the speaker need not go into lengthy detail setting up the importance of the subject. Instead, the speaker can begin by stating the subject and moving immediately to the first major point of the address. When Howard R. Swearer, President of Brown University, spoke to the trustees of the university on the matter of intercollegiate athletics, he used a direct approach:

> The national intercollegiate athletic situation is in considerable flux and, I believe, may have entered a period of rapid transition. Many colleges and universities are facing critical questions which cannot be begged for long.
>
> The driving forces are well known but merit mention anyway, if for no other reason than that many of us in the older generations may tend to view collegiate sports through the now

misty and romantic filter of our own undergraduate days. However, the tug of nostalgia should not inhibit us from making a clear assessment of the contemporary scene.[1]

As we have said, the direct reference to the subject is an appropriate beginning when the audience is familiar with and interested in the message. If, on the other hand, the audience is familiar with the subject but skeptical of your message, you will want to take some time to establish common ground with the audience. By seeking to find themes or values which you and the audience hold in common, or by noting the potentially controversial nature of your remarks, you will establish a basis for the reception of your views.

Reference to the Occasion

Occasions such as commencement addresses, acceptances of awards, major holidays, and keynote addresses at conferences virtually dictate a reference to the reasons you are brought together. Explicit reference to the significance of the occasion helps create a feeling of good will. When the historian Arthur M. Schlesinger, Jr., appeared at the Joint Session of Congress to commemorate the 100th anniversary of Franklin Delano Roosevelt's birth, he opened his remarks in an appropriate manner:

> Mr. Speaker, Mr. President, Members of Congress, friends, it is a high honor for me to share with three such doughty warriors for liberty and justice as Averell Harriman, Claude Pepper, and Jennings Randolph the opportunity to address this most eminent legislative body in the world.
>
> It is, indeed, a most special occasion that brings us together. We have heard all our lives about the first hundred days of Franklin Delano Roosevelt. We gather today to celebrate his first hundred years.[2]

Schlesinger acknowledged the importance of the occasion and, in the process, conveyed a strong feeling of good will toward the audience. If the time, place, or reason for coming together is an important and significant one in the eyes of the audience, be certain that your introductory remarks contain explicit references to the occasion.

Personal Reference or Greeting

Another effective means of establishing common ground or projecting your feelings of good will is to convey a more personal message or a personal greeting to the listeners. Marcie Groover, a student at Stetson University, used her own experience to establish a personal relationship with the audience:

> As I was working my way through the public school system, I, like my peers, believed that I was receiving a fine education. I could read and write, and add and subtract—yes, all of the essentials were there. At least that's what I thought. And then the boom lowered: "Attention class—your next assignment is to present an oral report of your paper in front of the class next week." My heart stopped. Panic began to rise up inside. Me? In front of thirty other fourth-graders giving a speech? For the next five days I lived in dreaded anticipation of the forthcoming event. When the day finally arrived, I stayed home. It

seemed at the time to be the perfect solution to a very scary and very real problem. Up to that time, I had never been asked to say a word in front of anyone, and, more importantly, had never been taught anything about verbal communication skills.[3]

To be effective, your personal reference must be modest and seem sincere. Saying the "right things" may satisfy the conventional expectations of the audience, but they should also sense that you truly mean what you say. At the same time, avoid being overly modest or apologetic; strike a balance between appearing boastful and arrogant and seeming humble and defeatist. If you've not had much time to prepare due to circumstances, forge ahead anyway. Apologizing or blaming others for the circumstances that placed you in this position makes the audience uncomfortable and lessens the respect they may accord you. The last impression you want to create is that neither you nor your message is worthy of the audience's attention. Dan Ramczyk, from the University of New Mexico, successfully balanced modesty and openness in explaining how he came to believe that female sexual harassment in employment was a serious problem:

> To be perfectly honest, I myself never really believed that female sexual harassment was really that significant a problem. My lack of empathy for the woman could be attributed to the differences in our common grounds of identification. However, one Sunday morning several months ago, as I was reading my hometown newspaper, I came across some very disturbing statistics. These statistics made it impossible for me to ignore the problem of female sexual harassment any longer.[4]

In this fashion, he conveyed a sincere interest in a topic and established his qualifications to speak on the issue.

Both of these references—to the subject and to your own experience—share a predominant attribute: They seek to establish common ground with the audience. Your goal in using them is to connect your experience and interests to those of the audience. Establishing common ground is important in all forms of communication, as it provides a foundation for building audience acceptance of your message.

Rhetorical Question

A *rhetorical question* is one which is asked without expecting an immediate verbal response. Although you do not wish the audience to answer you audibly, you do hope that they will consider the question and answer it silently for themselves. If used sparingly, rhetorical questions can focus audience attention on your subject and involve them directly in assessing its significance in their own lives. To be effective, the question should be relevant to your audience. Asking a group of college sophomores, "How would you feel if, at the age of 95, your social security suddenly ran out?" probably would not be very effective. On the other hand, if you began by asking the same group, "How would you feel if the administration changed core requirements in midstream and you would now have to complete four math-science courses before you graduate?" you may succeed in focusing their attention on proposed new requirements. Rhetorical questions, asked in sequence, also can help forecast your main points. Thus, you might ask, "What are the new core requirements? What will their impact be on college sophomores? Is there anything we can do to affect the decision to implement them?'' and thereby structure your speech in advance for the audience: ''I will take up each of these questions in turn.'' Jacqueline Jackson, a student at Regis College, used this approach to focus attention on her topic and at the same time indicate her main themes:

> Johnny can't read. Johnny can't write. Johnny doesn't know how to spell. Johnny's not good with numbers. Johnny has a hard time remembering. Johnny lost the football game. Maybe Johnny's retarded and we're not doing enough for him. Maybe Johnny's gifted and we're holding him back. Johnny can't get along with others; Johnny can't get along with his teachers either. Johnny can't seem to do anything right. But why can't Johnny read, write, spell, play football, or get along with others? Could it be the fault of the schools? That seems to be the answer that the mass media have been promoting for years. Is the American school system responsible for the unbalanced, semi-literate children of today? Should the school system be responsible to educate every unbalanced semiliterate? Are schools being asked to do too much? Are schools being asked to do the right things?[5]

Startling Statement

If your audience is particularly apathetic, if might be appropriate to shock them by beginning with a startling statement. John Knutson, a student at the University of Wisconsin, Stout, began a speech with this statement:

> He told me that ''it would have been better if they would have taken a pistol to his head, and pulled the trigger.'' My friend wasn't talking about someone terribly injured in an automobile accident, nor was he referring to a veteran who never recovered from Vietnam. Fernando was citing the instance of an 18-year-old boy being sentenced to jail for the first time.[6]

A startling fact or opinion, whether used alone or in combination with other methods, can help focus the audience's attention and jar them out of a ''ho-hum'' attitude. But select and phrase such a statement with discretion. If the audience perceives the statement as being in poor taste—shock solely for the sake of shock—they may regard you and the remainder of your presentation with suspicion. The objective is to invite and attract their favorable attention, not to alienate them from you or your message.

Pertinent Quotation

A quotation that conveys the theme or major point of your presentation can provide a good beginning. To be effective, the quotation should be simple and succinct; the audience should not have to ponder its deeper meanings in order to understand its relationships to your message. Observe, for example, how a student at the University of Iowa, Alicia Becker, began a speech on crises in higher education:

> ''It was the best of times, it was the worst of times; it was the age of foolishness, it was the age of reason; it was the epoch of belief, it was the epoch of incredulity; it was the season of light, it was the season of darkness; it was the spring of hope, it was the winter of

A humorous anecdote is a solid introductory strategy if the story is relevant to your purpose and subject matter and is in good taste. It also can relax a speaker and the audience.

despair.'' With those words Charles Dickens described the era of the French Revolution, nearly 200 years ago. But he could just as well have been talking about today and tomorrow. We live in a similar age of contradiction and turbulence, in an atmosphere which threatens to destroy every institution, including this school. Today, I would like to discuss with you some ways in which contradictory forces from the government, the people of this state, the faculty of the university, and the students who attend it are threatening the basic purpose of your education.

Humorous Anecdote

A funny story or a humorous experience may be used to enliven your address. Humorous anecdotes can aptly summarize the main point of your message and relax your audience at the same time. The importance of telling the right story for the situation, and telling it well, make this approach the most risky of all. If you choose a slightly off-color story or one in poor taste, the audience may become uncomfortable; instead of decreasing tension, you will have increased it. Thus, the chosen anecdote must be relevant and appropriate to your subject, your purpose, and your audience. A joke or story unrelated to these critical concerns wastes valuable time and channels the attention and thoughts of your listeners in the wrong direction. Instead of trying to get a good laugh, use a humorous introduction that clearly introduces the subject or conveys your reason for speaking.

Consistent with the requirements we have just described, Hanna Gray introduced the Commencement Address at Duke University in May, 1982:

> There is a famous story, famous at any rate in the Connecticut River Valley, which has to do with a crusty and patriotic old Vermonter who lived on an island in the Connecticut River through which ran the boundary separating New Hampshire and Vermont. One year, a team was sent out to survey that boundary and its members discovered, quite unexpectedly, that the old man lived not as had always been thought in Vermont but on the New Hampshire side of the line. In a state of some anxiety and trepidation, they went to confront him with the news that he lived in New Hampshire, and to their astonishment he replied, "Well, thank the good Lord. I was beginning to think I'd never be able to tolerate another one of them damn Vermont winters." Members of the graduating class: yours is the exact analogue to the old man's position. The boundary that separates you from another Durham winter has been drawn. You have been surveyed, found to be BAs, BSs, MAs, MBAs, MSs, JDs, MDs—I could go on—but in any case, you have been surveyed and found to be all those good things and therefore also citizens of some state which is popularly known as "the real world." Yet, tomorrow your spiritual terrain will be roughly the same as today, and so will you: quite undramatically unchanged, yet perhaps somewhat gratified to have survived into your new citizenship.[7]

One final caution: People who *try* to be funny rarely are. Before using a humorous opening, ask yourself whether you can relate the story in a natural, spontaneous manner. If you pre-plan a joke and then obviously wait for a response, you may be met by thunderous silence. You do not need to be a natural story-teller to relay humorous incidents to the audience. Tell the tale simply and clearly. Let a quiet sense of humor and enthusiasm shine through, and you will convey your intent to the audience.

Real or Hypothetical Illustration

A vivid narrative, whether drawn from real events, fable, or myth, is another way to arouse audience interest in your subject. To be effective, the illustration must be perceived as related to the subject or purpose for speaking. The illustration also should be intrinsically interesting; it should cause the audience to begin thinking about the major idea you wish to communicate. Deanna Sellnow, a student at North Dakota State University, used this technique to introduce a speech on personal credit data banks:

> John Pontier, of Boise, Idaho, was turned down for insurance because a reporting agency informed the company that he, and his wife, were addicted to narcotics, and his Taco Bell franchise had been closed down by the health board when dog food had been found mixed in with the tacos. There was only one small problem. The information was made up. His wife was a practicing Mormon who didn't touch a drink, much less drugs, and the restaurant had never been cited for a health violation.[8]

Combining Methods

The eight methods we have discussed, whether used alone or in combination, serve to arouse interest, gain the good will of your audience, and fulfill other functions of opening remarks. One student combined several methods—quotation, real illustration, and rhetorical question—to orient listeners to the subject:

> "Equality of rights under the law shall not be denied or abridged by the United States or any state on account of sex."
>
> Sounds simple enough—doesn't it? As a matter of fact, 73 percent of all Americans favored the Equal Rights Amendment. It was endorsed by more than 450 national organizations representing 50 million Americans, and it was defeated last summer. The movement for an Equal Rights Amendment and the subsequent support for the amendment reflect a need and desire for change. Yet the defeat of such an amendment illustrates that our attitudes need to be re-evaluated. Today I'd like to examine the issue of equal rights with the objective being a rethinking of our attitudes toward equal rights. First, we must recognize the impact of the discrimination and stereotyping that are occurring right now. Next, we should examine the misconceptions surrounding an attempted solution to the problem—what was known as the Equal Rights Amendment. And finally, we will consider a viable action for all of us.[9]

Note the last four sentences, beginning with "Today I'd like to. . . ." Collectively, they are an example of *forecasting* what the speech will cover. Laying out the main divisions of the speech in this fashion helps the audience conceptualize the total message before the substantive evidence is set forth. Forecasting can also serve as an effective transition between the introduction and the body of the speech.

Finally, the eight approaches to increasing the liveliness and interest value of a speech's beginning can also be used throughout to maintain audience attention. You can relieve an otherwise dry exposition of facts or dramatize a subpoint by using rhetorical questions, humorous anecdotes, and the other methods. Gaining audience attention is not restricted just to the introduction of the speech; maintaining their attention is a goal throughout the substantive portion of the address and on into the concluding remarks.

Ending the Speech: Final Considerations

The principal function of any method used to close a speech is to leave your listeners with a clear understanding of what you want them to know, how you want them to feel, or what you want them to do. As you reflect on the substance of your speech—main ideas and supporting materials—ask yourself the following questions:

1. Is the speech developed in a simple or a complex fashion?
2. Does the content lead naturally to a "so what?" question?
3. What mood do I wish the audience to be in as I conclude?
4. Should I signal the ending of the speech?

BEGINNING AND ENDING THE SPEECH

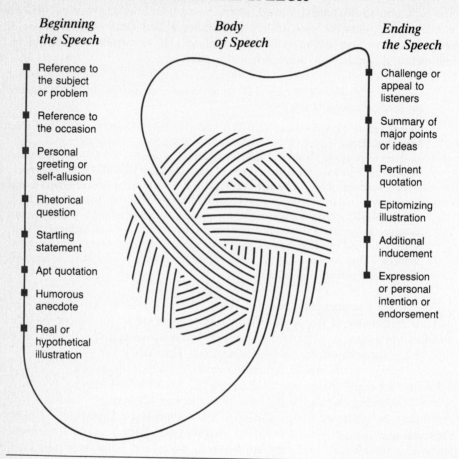

Beginning the Speech	*Body of Speech*	*Ending the Speech*
■ Reference to the subject or problem		■ Challenge or appeal to listeners
■ Reference to the occasion		■ Summary of major points or ideas
■ Personal greeting or self-allusion		■ Pertinent quotation
■ Rhetorical question		■ Epitomizing illustration
■ Startling statement		■ Additional inducement
■ Apt quotation		■ Expression or personal intention or endorsement
■ Humorous anecdote		
■ Real or hypothetical illustration		

Adapting to Complexity

A speech that advances but one idea, fully developed through clear, relevant supporting materials, needs only a simple restatement of the central point to ensure audience understanding. A speech that advances ten claims about the effects of a particular bill or governmental action needs a summary that synthesizes the different ideas into a condensed, unified form. The complexity of your ideas thus affects the choice of an appropriate ending.

Answering the "So What?" Question

Speeches that address the significance of a problem, such as the rising crime rate or the effects of inflation on college-bound students, often leave the members of the audience wondering what they can or should do to alleviate or counteract the indicated condition. Although your purpose may be simply to make people aware of the situation, you may lead them to an action step you did not intend in your more limited purpose. To handle this potential problem, you need to note explicitly that your purpose is to lay the foundation for action through accurate information, and suggest that possible corrective action will be the subject of a later address. Another approach may be to indicate your willingness to discuss ways the audience can help in a question-answer session following the speech, or through individual contacts at a later time. If your presentation is directed toward some type of overt response, your conclusion is the final chance to clarify what you want that response to be.

Creating the Appropriate Mood

The ending of your speech should leave the audience in a mood that is appropriate to your purpose. If you expect your listeners to express vigorous enthusiasm, you must stimulate that feeling by the way you close. If you want them to reflect thoughtfully on what you have said, your conclusion should encourage a calm, judicious attitude. Decide whether the response you seek requires a mood of serious determination or good-humored levity, of warm sympathy or cold anger, of objective deliberation or vigorous action. Then plan to conclude your speech in a way that generates that mood or creates that frame of mind.

Signaling the Ending

A successful speech also conveys a sense of completeness and finality. You can signal the end with transition phrases: "In summary, . . . "; "As I conclude this address, let me reiterate . . . "; "The eminent poet, Robert Frost, best summarizes what I have been saying. . . ." However you signal the final moments of your speech, avoid giving the audience a false sense of when you will finish. Few things annoy an audience as much as thinking a speech is over, only to have the speaker go on, and on, and on.

Types of Speech Conclusions

Thoughtful attention to the initial considerations noted previously will enable you to select an appropriate method of ending your speech. Speakers frequently employ one or more of the following methods in concluding their addresses:

1. Issue a challenge or an appeal to the listeners.
2. Summarize major points or ideas.
3. Provide an appropriate quotation.
4. Epitomize with a thematic illustration.
5. Offer an additional inducement for accepting or acting upon the proposal advocated.
6. Express their own intention or endorsement.

Challenge or Appeal to Listeners

When using this method, the speaker openly appeals for support or action, or reminds the listeners of their responsibilities in furthering a desirable end. Such an appeal must be vivid and compelling and should contain within it a suggestion of the principal ideas

If your goals are serious and your audience includes people who can actualize these goals through their own actions, consider concluding your speech with a personal challenge.

or arguments presented in the speech. Leland Miles, president of the University of Bridgeport, selected this method when urging university presidents to seek peace studies for their campuses:

> Peace is not something that you pick up off the ground and say, oh look, peace! I found peace. Peace you've got to work at, peace you've got to create, peace you've got to make, peace you've got to produce. And the only way I know to produce it is through education, which is our business. Rodrigo Carazo, the president of Costa Rica, has said, "If you want peace, educate for peace." I agree. He has also said, "War begins in the minds of men and women. It is therefore in the minds of men and women that we must construct the defenses of peace." I say let all of us join in building those defenses. Let all of us in our own ways attempt to build on our respective campuses constituencies for peace. We have constituencies for fraternities, constituencies for drugs, constituencies for better jazz concerts, why not constituencies for peace? Let's all transform our institutions into universities for

peace, by requiring some kind of internationalized curriculum for all our students. Let's not leave the critical task of survival to Costa Rica alone.[10]

Summary of Major Points or Ideas

If your speech has raised three or four main points, you may find it helpful to list these briefly in the conclusion of your speech. This summarizing allows the audience to pull together the main strands of your informative address or your argument and evaluate its significance. In the informative address, the summary tells the audience what you want them to remember. In the persuasive speech, the summary provides a final opportunity to present, in brief form, the major points of your argument. Chris Wallace, a student at the University of Nebraska-Lincoln, used a summary to reiterate the problems with current pension plans:

> The idea of Pension Planning is an admirable one which allows people to retire and still enjoy a dependable cash flow. But unless legal loopholes, incongruity in pension plans, inflation erosion, and corporate bankruptcy and dumping are arrested and their crimes made illegal, this idea will continue to be a nightmare for 50% of our work force. They will continue to lose the benefits they have earned, and unless some workable solutions are implemented, such as the ones I have outlined, you could find yourself a statistic, a victim of unsound pension planning.[11]

Pertinent Quotation

At times, someone else's words aptly capture your own message. When quoted material, either in prose or poetic form, is relevant to the central idea of your speech, you might consider using it to end the remarks. Such material often suggests, more strongly than you might, the sentiment or attitude you want the listeners to take. A few lines of poetry, for instance, may provide the essence of your message in climactic, figurative language. Likewise, a brief prose quotation may capture the central idea in a clear, compelling manner, as Leland Miles did before challenging his audience to act with him for peace.

If a quotation is used in the beginning of the speech, you can tie the speech together by a direct reference back to the earlier quotation. Chui Lee Yap began a speech on ethnocentrism by quoting from Aldous Huxley: "Most ignorance is vincible ignorance. We don't know because we don't want to know." After explaining the reasons for American ignorance of other cultures, Chui Lee concluded by noting that "As Huxley implied, cure of our not knowing—is our wanting to know."[12]

Epitomizing Illustration

Just as an illustration which epitomizes your leading ideas may be used to open a speech, so may it be offered at the close of your discourse. A speech-ending illustration should be both *inclusive* and *conclusive:* inclusive of the main focus of your speech, and conclusive in tone and impact. Michael Twitchell used an illustration in both the opening and closing of his speech on the causes and effects of depression:

Opening
Have you ever felt like you were the little Dutch boy who stuck his finger in the leaking dike? You waited and waited but the help never came. The leak became worse and the water rushed around you and swept you away. As you fought the flood, gasping and choking for air, you realized that the flood was inside yourself. You were drowning and dying in your own mind. According to the *American Journal of Psychiatry,* as many as half the people in this room will be carried away by this devastating flood. What is this disaster? Mental depression.

Conclusion
Let's go back to my illustration of the little Dutch boy. He was wise to take action and put his finger in the dike, preventing the flood. In the case of depression, each one of us must be like the little Dutch boy—willing to get involved and control the harmful effects of depression.[13]

Additional Inducement

Sometimes it may be helpful to combine a summary or other means of concluding your remarks with one or two additional reasons for accepting the belief or taking the actions proposed. In his speech, Michael Twitchell elaborated at length on the effects of depression on the family of David Twitchell. Besides tying the introduction and conclusion together with an illustration (see above), Michael added an inducement:

> Why should you really care? Why is it important? The depressed person may be someone you know—it could be you. If you know what is happening, you can always help. I wish I had known what depression was in March of 1978. You see, when I said David Twitchell could be my father, I was making a statement of fact. David is my father. I am his middle son. My family wasn't saved; perhaps now yours can be.[14]

Expression of Personal Intention or Endorsement

When your speech proposes some action or requires taking a stand on an issue, it may be useful to end by stating your own intent. This method is particularly valuable when the audience accepts you as a peer: Your example may encourage their own action. Wanda Coppola, a student at Towson State University, ended her speech on computer anxiety with an endorsement of her own solution to the problem:

> Finally, we who avoid computers because we don't understand them can enroll in a college's or university's introduction to computer course, as I have done. Although it is still sometimes difficult to sit behind the computer terminal without becoming nervous or fidgety, I am convinced it is still worth my while. I believe all of us should become comfortable with computers. Only in that way will we be able to perform in the job market and the educational system, in order to become computer literate and to function effectively in our technological society.[15]

These means of ending speeches can be used alone or in combination. Note, for example, that Twitchell recalled his opening illustration, used rhetorical questions to good advantage, and added a personal reason for being concerned in his conclusion.

Selecting Introductions and Conclusions:
Strategies and Determining Factors

The preceding sections have concentrated on the functions of introductions and conclusions and their means of being fulfilled. In general, each of the means can be an effective way of satsifying one or more of the functions of introductions or conclusions. Thus, a pertinent quotation or a hypothetical illustration may gain attention, create goodwill, or clarify the scope of your speech. Likewise, a challenge or appeal to listeners may signal an ending or answer a "so what?" question. Obviously, some means are better suited than others for fulfilling a particular function. A real illustration will work better than a hypothetical one in stating your qualifications, for instance, while a personal reference may be the most direct means of all. Conclusions which contain pertinent quotations or epitomizing illustrations may be more effective in creating an appropriate mood than would a summary of major points.

As you approach each facet of the total speech, think through what you want to accomplish, and adapt that approach which has the best chance of meeting your goal. As we noted in Chapter 1, creating a text for a speech involves a *rhetorical sensitivity* to the situation in which you find yourself. There are some natural constraints on what you can and should do:

1. *What are your experiences and abilities?* The best source for real illustrations is your own life. Stories of your experiences will come across naturally as you tell them. Stories that you have discovered through research, on the other hand, need to be rehearsed so that they sound "natural." Your experiences also may be the best basis for claiming qualifications in an area; otherwise, you will need to illustrate, through explicit statements or the quality of your research materials, that you know what you are talking about. Your abilities as a speaker also may constrain your choices. If you are not naturally humorous, if you do not tell funny stories in a natural, relaxed manner, perhaps attempting a humorous anecdote would not be wise. On the other hand, if you are known as a clown and want to be taken seriously for a change, you will need to set forth your qualifications explicitly and, in concluding, create a serious mood for the consideration of your views. Humor may not be your best vehicle under these circumstances.

2. *What is the mood and commitment of the audience?* If you are speaking on a subject already announced and known to be controversial, gaining attention through a startling statement or a humorous anecdote may seem highly inappropriate. If, on the other hand, the audience is indifferent or has already heard several presentations on the same subject, a direct reference to the subject may be perceived as dull and unoriginal. Overcoming audience numbness may require originality and creativity. If the audience is in a jolly mood and does not wish to be serious, you have a major problem on your hands. A rhetorical question that forces them to think for a moment, or a startling statement that creates curiosity may be appropriate in this circumstance. Both induce direct participation, rather than passive listening, by the audience.

3. *What knowledge does the audience have about you and your commitment to the subject?* If you are already known as an expert in an area, stating your qualifications

will be repetitious and may even convey conceit. If, on the other hand, your personal experience and depth of feeling is generally unknown, you will want to reveal these through personal reference, or, as done by Michael Twitchell (see p. 200), through an additional inducement at the close of your address. Either approach establishes both your knowledge and personal involvement in the subject. One caution regarding personal experiences: Allow time to pass before you attempt to bring deeply felt experiences before an audience, especially those involving loss of life. If you appear emotionally shaken or teary-eyed, the tension level will increase, as the audience shares your personal discomfort. The effectiveness of your personal revelation will be correspondingly decreased. The use of a challenge or statement of personal intent also are effective means of demonstrating your commitment to the subject.

4. *What constraints are imposed by the situation or setting?* A somber occasion, such as a funeral or a dedication of a war memorial, is hardly the place for gleeful hilarity. On the other hand, some serious occasions, such as commencements, can be enlivened by timely, well-chosen humor. The student speaker who ended his high school address by waving a beer bottle and proclaiming "This Bud's for you" quickly discovered that his attempt at humor was received well by only part of his audience. The faculty and parents did not react as pleasantly as did his peers. Not everything goes, even when *you* see nothing wrong with the story or allusion. A reference to the occasion or personal greeting may be an appropriate reminder to the audience that you, as well as they, appreciate the significance of the occasion. Pertinent quotations and epitomizing illustrations, whether used at the beginning or end, also can convey a sense of the event's meaning for everyone present.

This discussion of the use of appropriate introductions and conclusions is not intended to be exhaustive. Rather, it illustrates the general approach to *thinking through* the reactions you might have as you select various means of introducing and concluding your speech. A "thought-through" speech will be perceived as "thought-out" by an audience, whether they ultimately agree with you or not. If you convey to an audience that you have thought about them and the setting in preparing your remarks, you will enhance your chances of their acceptance of your information and your way of thinking about issues. Though they may not agree with you, they at least have been given reason to respect your attempt to communicate your ideas. That may be the necessary first step in obtaining their eventual approval of your ideas.

REFERENCE NOTES

[1]From "The Separation of Athletics and Academics in Our Universities," by Howard Swearer, *Representative American Speeches, 1982–1983* (Bronx, NY: The H. W. Wilson, 1983). Reprinted by permission of the author.

[2]Arthur M. Schlesinger, Jr., "In Memory of Franklin D. Roosevelt," *Representative American Speeches,* ed. Owen Peterson (New York: H. W. Wilson, 1982), 54:5, p. 161.

[3]From "Learning to Communicate: The Importance of Speech Education in Public Schools" by Marcie Groover. Reprinted from *Winning Orations,* 1984, by special

arrangement with the Interstate Oratorical Association, Larry Schnoor, Executive Secretary, Mankato State College, Mankato, MN.

[4]From "A Harmless Game" by Dan Ramczyk. Reprinted from *Winning Orations*, 1980, by special arrangement with the Interstate Oratorical Association, Larry Schnoor, Executive Secretary, Mankato State College, Mankato, MN.

[5]Jacqueline Jackson, "Why Johnny Can't Read." Reprinted from *Winning Orations* by special arrangement with the Interstate Oratorical Association, Larry Schnoor, Executive Secretary, Mankato State College, Mankato, MN.

[6]From "Community Corrections" by John Knutson. Reprinted from *Winning Orations*, 1983, by special arrangement with the Interstate Oratorical Association, Larry Schnoor, Executive Secretary, Mankato State College, Mankato, MN.

[7]From Commencement Speech by Hanna H. Gray. Given at Duke University, May 9, 1982. Reprinted by permission.

[8]From "Have You Checked Lately?" by Donna Sellnow. Reprinted from *Winning Orations*, 1983, by special arrangement with the Interstate Oratorical Association, Larry Schnoor, Executive Secretary, Mankato State College, Mankato, MN.

[9]From "A Time to Rethink and Respond" by Theresa Krier. Reprinted from *Winning Orations*, 1983, by special arrangement with the Interstate Oratorical Association, Larry Schnoor, Executive Secretary, Mankato State College, Mankato, MN.

[10]From "Universities for Peace" by Leland Miles, from *Vital Speeches of the Day,* 48, March 1982. Reprinted by permission of Vital Speeches of the Day.

[11]From "To Pension Plan or Not to Pension Plan" by Chris Wallace. Reprinted from *Winning Orations*, 1983, by special arrangement with the Interstate Oratorical Association, Larry Schnoor, Executive Secretary, Mankato State College, Mankato, MN.

[12]From "Ethnocentrism" by Chui Lee Yap. Reprinted from *Winning Orations*, 1983, by special arrangement with the Interstate Oratorical Association, Larry Schnoor, Executive Secretary, Mankato State College, Mankato, MN.

[13]From "The Flood Gates of the Mind" by Michael A. Twitchell. Reprinted from *Winning Orations*, 1983, by special arrangement with the Interstate Oratorical Association, Larry Schnoor, Executive Secretary, Mankato State College, Mankato, MN.

[14]Twitchell, p. 6.

[15]From "Technological Society Induces Computer Anxiety" by Wanda Coppola. Reprinted from *Winning Orations*, 1983, by special arrangement with the Interstate Oratorical Association, Larry Schnoor, Executive Secretary, Mankato State College, Mankato, MN.

PROBLEMS AND PROBES

1. Some television stations produce programs wherein speakers discuss items relevant to the particular viewing area. Watch one of these programs, *60 Minutes,* or *Face the Nation,* and then discuss the format. If a speaker is allowed a set time for opening and closing statements (usually separated by questions and responses) evaluate the effectiveness of the introduction and conclusion. If there is no provision for set introductions or conclusions, how does the speaker gain attention, initially secure good will, set the tone for what is to follow; and how does the speaker leave the audience in a specific mood to convey a sense of completeness and finality? How does the moderator introduce and close the program as a whole? How effective is the format overall? What improvements, if any, should be made?

2. After listening to one or more of the following types of speeches, evaluate the introduction and conclusion which the speaker used in *(a)* a classroom lecture; *(b)*

a sermon; *(c)* an open hearing at a meeting of the city council; *(d)* remarks made at a club or dormitory council meeting; and *(e)* a formal address, live or televised, made by a political candidate. In reporting your evaluation, supply sufficient information about the speaker and speaking situation so that someone who was not present could understand why you evaluated a particular beginning or ending as you did.

3. Assume you have been asked to speak on the topic "The Pros and Cons of Television Advertising Aimed at Children" (or some other controversial topic that interests you). Further, you are to present this speech in a variety of settings: as a classroom lecture; before an audience favorable to the pro arguments you will present; before an audience hostile to the pro arguments; as a televised address which exposes you to an audience with a variety of attitudes on the topic. Write a brief report in which you indicate how these different situations would affect your approach in introducing and concluding your remarks. Indicate which techniques in this chapter would be most and least beneficial to use and explain why.

ORAL ACTIVITIES

1. To emphasize the different ways of introducing and concluding a speech, choose a topic and prepare two different one-minute introductions and conclusions to be delivered in an impromptu round of classroom speeches. The class should analyze the varying approaches and compare their benefits and disadvantages.

2. Assume that you have been asked to speak on the topic "The Importance of Self-Confidence." This speech is to be given to the following three audiences:
   a.   the graduating class of a local high school
   b.   a regularly scheduled meeting of the Parent-Teachers Association
   c.   the local Kiwanis Club luncheon
Write a brief introduction for the speech that you think would be appropriate for each audience and identify those factors that would influence the way in which you prepared the three introductions. Be prepared to present your introductions orally in class.

3. Participate in a class discussion concerning introductions and conclusions to public speeches. The discussion might be structured as follows: One student leads off by suggesting a topic for a possible speech to this class. A second student then suggests an appropriate type of introduction and conclusion, justifying those choices. A third student, in turn, challenges that selection, proposing alternative introductions and/or conclusions. Continue this discussion until everyone has proposed and defended the different types of introductions and conclusions that would be appropriate for the speech topics discussed.

CHAPTER 11

Outlining the Speech

An outline for speech serves the same function as a blueprint for a building: When the major structural components of the speech are clear—the main ideas selected and the general pattern identified—you are ready to move to the drawing board. By laying out the structure of your speech in advance, you can determine whether the major sections fit together smoothly, whether each main idea receives its proper emphasis, and whether all the important areas of the subject are covered. Just as a blueprint identifies the building materials that will be essential, so will an outline highlight relationships between main points and supporting material. If you have failed to substantiate any of your leading ideas, your speech blueprint will show this. If information that is obviously needed to support your main idea is missing—statistical data, or specific instances, for example—you will notice this too in a careful review of your completed outline. Finally, just as careful analysis of a finished blueprint fixes the overall structure in the minds of those concerned, so can a thorough study of your outline help you to recall its pattern as you speak. A visual map of your speech can be a valuable aid to remembering what comes next in your presentation.

Requirements of Good Outline Form

The amount of detail and type of arrangement you use in an outline will depend on the simplicity or complexity of your subject. It also will depend on the speaking situation and your prior experience in composing outlines. To be useful as an aid in building your speech, a good outline satisfies four basic requirements:

1. *Each item in the outline should contain only one unit of information.* Outlines that combine a series of phrases or run together several statements under one heading

cannot show relationships between and among ideas. The following examples illustrate incorrect and correct ways to meet this requirement:

Incorrect

I. Athens, Greece, should be the permanent site for the Olympic Games because they have become more and more politicized in recent years.
    A. The U.S. decision to avoid the 1980 Summer Olympics is an example.
    B. The U.S.S.R. decision to avoid the 1984 Summer Olympics is an example.
    C. Also, costs are prohibitive and returning the Games to their homeland would place renewed emphasis on their original purpose.

Correct

I. Athens, Greece, should be the permanent site for the Olympic Games.
    A. The Games have become more and more politicized in recent years.
        1. The U.S. decision to avoid the 1980 Summer Olympics is an example.
        2. The U.S.S.R. decision to avoid the 1984 Summer Olympics is an example.
    B. Costs for building new sites in new locations each four years are becoming prohibitive.
    C. Returning the Games to their homeland would place renewed emphasis on their original purpose.

Note that, in the correct version, the main point has been divided into its respective parts, and the subordinate points (*A* and *B* in the incorrect version) have been placed under their logical heading. Also, *C* in the incorrect version has been divided, creating two new subheadings in the revised outline.

2. *The items in the outline must be properly subordinated.* Subordinate ideas rank below others in both scope and importance. In the preceding correct outline, points *A, B,* and *C* are extensions of the main head; these items explain the reasoning for the major claim *(I).* The following outlines illustrate incorrect and correct ways to place your points in proper subordination:

Incorrect

I. The theft of antiques is a growing problem.
II. Summer homes in resort areas are broken into with increasing frequency.
    A. Year-round residences are not immune from potential losses.
III. Present means of combating this type of crime are ineffective.
    A. Police protection is inadequate.
IV. Home owners fail to provide sufficient protection.
    A. Recovery of stolen antiques is virtually impossible.
V. Antiques are difficult to trace once they have been passed from thieves to dealers.
VI. There is a sizable foreign market for antiques.

Correct

I. The theft of antiques is a growing problem.
    A. Summer homes in resort areas are broken into with increasing frequency.
    B. Year-round residences are not immune from potential losses.

II. Present means of combating this type of crime are ineffective.
    A. Police protection is inadequate.
    B. Home owners fail to provide sufficient protection.

III. Recovery of stolen antiques is virtually impossible.
    A. Antiques are difficult to trace once they have been passed from thieves to dealers.
    B. There is a sizable foreign market for antiques.

The incorrect version makes little logical sense. Main points are treated as subordinate, and subordinate points are elevated to the status of main points. The basic logic governing subordination is whether an item "fits" as a part of a larger whole. In this sense, the main points fit together as part of the total purpose of the speech; the subordinate points are directly related to (as part to whole) the main point that they are placed under.

3. *The logical relation of items in an outline should be shown by proper indentation.* The greater the importance or scope of a statement, the nearer it should be placed to the *left-hand margin*. If a statement takes up more than one line, the second line should be indented the same as the first.

I. Choosing edible wild mushrooms is no job for the uninformed.
    A. Many wild species are highly toxic.
        1. The angel cap *(amanitas verosa)* contains a toxin for which there is no known antidote.
        2. Hallucinogenic mushrooms produce short-lived euphoria, followed by convulsions, paralysis, and possible death.
    B. Myths abound regarding methods for choosing "safe" mushrooms.
        1. Mushrooms with easily peeled skins are not necessarily safe.
        2. Mushrooms eaten by animals are not necessarily safe.
        3. Mushrooms that do not darken a silver coin (placed in a pan of hot water containing mushrooms) are not necessarily safe.
        4. Mushrooms that do not produce a reaction in one person are not necessarily safe for others to consume.[1]

4. *A consistent set of symbols should be used.* One such set is exemplified in the outlines printed in this chapter. But whether you use this set or some other, be consistent; do not change systems in the middle of an outline. Unless items of the same scope or importance have the same type of symbol *throughout,* the mental blueprint you have of your speech will be confused, and the chances of a smooth and orderly presentation impaired. The following example demonstrates the correct usage of this set of symbols.

I. Our penal system should be reformed.
    A. Many of our prisons are inadequate.
        1. They fail to meet basic structural and safety standards.
        2. They lack facilities for effective rehabilitation programs.
    B. The persons who manage our prisons are ill equipped.
        1. All too often they have had little or no formal training for their jobs.
        2. Low rates of pay result in frequent job turnover.

Types of Outlines

The outline can be considered a midpoint in the thought process involved in the construction and presentation of a speech. By this point, you have selected some major ideas, several specific items of support material, and a possible way of arranging these into a coherent structure. The outline will look different as any one of these major components changes. A chronological outline, for example, may have several main points, while a cause-effect outline may be divided into two main headings. As your thoughts about putting all of the pieces together begin to take shape in your mind, the outline begins to "write itself." Problems in the ordering of materials may emerge if your attempt to write it out ends in forcing materials to fit a predetermined shape. Thus, the act of composing an outline is a significant check on the mental map you have drawn in shaping the organization of the speech. The advice presented above will assist you in composing the points and in determining their order. The following suggestions will help you as you write out the entire outline. There are two principal types of outlines, each of which fulfills a different purpose—the *full-sentence* outline and the *phrase* outline. The former helps make the process of speech preparation more systematic and thorough; the latter serves as a memory aid in the early stages of oral practice.

The Full-Sentence Outline

As its name implies, a full-sentence outline represents the factual content of the speech in outline form. Whether you use the traditional divisions of the speech (introduction, body, conclusion) or the steps in the motivated sequence (attention, need, satisfaction, visualization, action), each division or step is set off in a separate section. The principal ideas are stated as main heads, and subordinate ideas—properly indented and marked with correct symbols—are entered in their appropriate places. *Each major idea and all of the subordinate ones are written down in complete sentences.* In this manner, their full meaning and their relation to other points within the speech are clearly established. Sources for supporting material may be placed in parentheses at the end of each piece of evidence, or combined in a bibliography at the end of the outline. Once the outline has been completed, you or any other person can derive a clear, comprehensive picture of the speech as a whole. The only features missing are the specific wording you will use in presenting your speech, and the visible and audible aspects of your delivery. By bringing together all the material you have gathered and by phrasing it in complete sentences and in detail, you ensure thoroughness in the preparation of your speech. The outline that follows, which forecasts material in the next section of this chapter, is an example of a full-sentence outline:

Steps in Preparing a Good Outline

I.   The first step in preparing a good outline is to determine the general purpose of the speech for the subject you have selected.
  A.   You will need to limit the subject in two ways.
    1.   First, limit the subject to fit the available time.

      2. Second, limit the subject to ensure unity and coherence.

  B. You also will need to phrase the specific purpose in terms of the exact response you seek from your listeners.

II. The second step is to develop a rough outline of your speech.

  A. First, list the main ideas you wish to cover.

  B. Second, arrange these main ideas according to the methods discussed in Chapters 8 and 9.

  C. Third, arrange subordinate ideas under their appropriate main heads.

  D. Fourth, fill in the supporting materials to be used in amplifying or justifying your ideas.

  E. Finally, review your rough draft.

      1. Does it cover your subject adequately?

      2. Does it carry out your specific purpose?

III. The third step is to put the outline into final form.

  A. Begin this process by writing out the main ideas as complete sentences or as key phrases.

      1. State the main ideas concisely, vividly, and—insofar as possible—in parallel terms.

      2. State the major heads so that they address directly the needs and interests of your listeners.

  B. Write out the subordinate ideas in complete sentences or in key phrases.

      1. Are they subordinate to the main idea they are intended to develop?

      2. Are they coordinate with other items at the same level (that is, are all *A–B–C* series roughly equal in importance; are all *1–2–3* series roughly equal in importance)?

  C. You now are ready to fill in the supporting materials.

      1. Are they pertinent?

      2. Are they adequate?

      3. Are there a variety of types of support?

  D. Finally, recheck the completed outline.

      1. Is it written in proper outline form?

      2. Does the speech, as outlined, adequately cover the subject?

      3. Does the speech, as outlined, carry out your general and specific purposes?

The Phrase Outline

The phrase outline and the full-sentence outline use the same indentation and symbol structure. The major difference between the two is that each item of a phrase outline is referred to by a phrase—key words (on occasion, a single word will suffice) that may be more easily remembered. This outline can be used as a basis for your *speaking outline* as the key words are easy to see as you stand at a lectern. You are not distracted as you might be if you used a full-sentence outline. But be sure that when you look down and see a key word or phrase, you know what to say. Another advantage of the phrase outline is that it can be used to practice the speech. By reading a phrase outline through several times, you will fix the sequence of ideas in your mind. Then, as you speak, you will be able to recall the structure of your presentation.

    If you use a phrase outline and want to insure accuracy when citing statistics or when quoting authorities, you might place these on separate note cards and key them to the appropriate place in the speaking outline. Or, if this seems cumbersome, you might insert each item into the appropriate place in your phrase outline. This will lengthen your phrase outline, but will insure that you don't misplace items that you want to cite.

The preceding sample outline, if developed as a phrase outline, would look like this:

I. Determine general purpose.
   A. Limit subject.
      1. Fit available time.
      2. Assure unity and coherence.
   B. Phrase in terms of listener response.

II. Develop rough draft.
   A. List main ideas.
   B. Arrange main ideas.
      1. Motivated sequence.
      2. Traditional pattern.
   C. Arrange subordinate ideas.
   D. Add support materials.
   E. Review rough draft.
      1. Adequacy?
      2. Meet specific purpose?

III. Final outline form.
   A. Complete sentences or key phrases.
      1. Concise, vivid, parallel phrasing.
      2. Address needs and interests of listeners.
   B. Subordinate ideas—complete sentence or key word.
      1. Under appropriate main head.
      2. Coordinate with subordinate ideas of equal weight.
   C. Add support materials.
      1. Pertinent.
      2. Adequate.
      3. Variety.
   D. Review outline.
      1. Good form.
      2. Adequate coverage.
      3. Meets purpose.

Steps in Preparing a Good Outline

Three major steps—selecting and limiting the speech subject, developing a rough outline, and preparing the outline in final form—are essential in outlining your speech.

Selecting the Subject and Determining the Purpose

Suppose your instructor asks you to prepare a persuasive speech on a subject in which you are interested. You decide to talk about the dangers of suntanning because you know that many think a good tan is essential to looking healthy. You also know that

Developing a rough draft, for many, is a matter of sketching, throwing away, sketching again and again—until you find just the right combination of ideas and patterns.

tanning can be dangerous. Your broad topic, therefore, is "The Effects of the Sun on Your Health." In the five to seven minutes that you have to speak, you will not be able to cover all aspects of this subject. Therefore, recalling what you learned in Chapter 4 about adapting your material to your listeners and to the time-limit, you decide to focus your discussion on some of the results of overexposure, spending proportionately more time on sun-related skin cancers, and on some preventive solutions to those results. You are now prepared to limit the broad topic to this: "Suntanning: Not as Healthy as You Might Think" (a description of the results of overexposure, and the preventive steps that might be taken).

Developing the Rough Draft of the Outline

In determining the limits of your subject, you already have made a preliminary selection of some of the principal ideas to be dealt with in your speech. By listing these points, you can see how they might be modified and fitted into a suitable sequence. Your list may look something like this:

1. Prematurely aged skin
2. Keratoses
3. Minor skin cancers—basal and squamous cell cancers
4. Major skin cancer—melanomas
5. Who is at risk
6. Some drugs promote sunburning
7. Preventive drugs
8. Clothing helps prevent sunburn

This list covers most of the points you want to include, but in random order. As you think further about the order of these items, you might review the various patterns discussed in Chapter 9. Within the need stage, a topical pattern may be the best approach. The satisfaction stage can be organized in a similar manner. In both cases, the topical pattern allows you a certain flexibility in ordering the items you want to cover. You can determine, for example, which of the various topics seems the most or least crucial, or which should be covered in more rather than less detail. As you work with the major themes you want to cover, you rearrange and modify your ideas until the following general pattern emerges:

> *Effects of Suntanning:*
> sunburn, aging skin, keratoses, types of skin cancer
>
> *Preventive Measures:*
> sunscreens, sunblocks, timing exposure, light clothing

As you think about this general pattern, you note that the individual items can be arranged as subpoints. In enumerating effects, you can order the ideas from least to most severe consequences. In discussing preventive measures, you can discuss the items in terms of the amount of protection they provide. The resulting outline looks like this:

I. The effects of suntanning
   A. Sunburn
   B. Prematurely aging skin
   C. Keratoses
   D. Skin cancers

II. Protective measures
   A. Timing exposure
   B. Sunscreens
   C. Sunblocks
   D. Light clothing

You now have prepared a *rough outline*. You have identified your topic, clarified your purpose, considered various subtopics and settled on a reasonable number of them, and decided on a coherent, cohesive method for organizing your speech. The main points have been arranged in a "need-satisfaction" or "problem-solution" arrangement, and the subpoints, although presented in a topical pattern, also have an internal logic to their order of appearance. You would not, for example, talk about skin cancer before keratoses, since the latter is often a precancerous stage of skin reaction. When you have chosen your major and subordinate points and have arranged them in a suitable fashion, you are prepared to develop the remainder of the outline. The attention, visualization, and action stages also need to be filled in.

Developing the Technical Plot

As you work on the full-sentence outline, it often is helpful to work out a *technical plot* of the speech. What this amounts to is noting, in the left margin of your outline, the types of introduction and conclusion, supporting materials, visual aids, and other devices you are employing. You also can note the function of certain points in the speech ("beginning of main point"; "details of early warning signs"). Used as a testing device, a technical plot can help you determine whether your speech is structurally sound. It also can pinpoint whether there are weaknesses in support material, whether one or more forms are overused or should be used, and whether your appeals are clearly formed.

The advantage of the technical plot is that it highlights what you are doing and why you think you are doing it. By forcing your attention on the functions of your ideas and supporting materials, the technical plot becomes an early warning system for flaws in the planned presentation. As you gain more experience, you may be able to check these items visually, without writing out the technical plot; once the checklist approach becomes second nature, you will find yourself asking such questions as you write the full-sentence outline.

A Sample Full-Sentence Outline

You are now ready to assemble the full-sentence outline. The sample below shows both the form for the outline and the technical plot. Since you might not use a full-sentence outline in presenting a speech, we also will consider the development of a phrase outline for the speaking situation.

Suntanning: Not as Healthy as You Might Think[2]

Technical Plot	Attention Step
	I. "Gee, your suntan looks great!" "He must live in a darkroom; his
Rhetorical question	arms and legs are so pale!" Have you ever heard, or used, these or similar expressions?
	A. Many people think that a suntan makes them look more attractive.

B.   Some people think that getting a good suntan makes them healthy.

C.   The actual truth is that too much sun can be harmful to your health.

Forecast   II.   In convincing you of the truth of this thesis, I will concentrate on two main tasks:

A.   I will discuss the major effects of suntanning.

B.   I will explain some preventive measures that you can take to avoid these ill effects.

Need Step

Cause-effect arguments   I.   Three of the main effects range from the uncomfortable to the potentially health-damaging.

A.   First, you can receive a severe sunburn.

1.   Many of us have already experienced this discomforting condition.

2.   In its more severe forms, sunburn must be treated just as a burn received from being scalded with hot water or from burning your hand on a hot stove.

B.   Another result of too much sun is prematurely aged skin.

(Descriptive materials)

1.   The skin looks leathery.

2.   The skin loses its elasticity.

C.   A third result of too much sun might be a condition known as *keratoses*.

1.   These are dark patches or scaly, grey growths.

2.   They often are precancerous.

(Statistics)   II.   The fourth effect is the most severe: Skin cancer strikes 300,000 Americans annually.

A.   There are several early warning signs.

1.   A sore may not heal.

2.   A wart or mole may change size or color.

3.   An unusual pigmented (colored) growth may appear.

(Descriptive materials)

B.   Basal and squamous cell skin cancers often appear as waxlike, pearly nodules.

1.   They may also appear as a red, scaly, sharply outlined patch.

2.   If detected and treated early, these forms are almost always curable.

C.   Melanoma is the most serious form of skin cancer.

1.   These begin as small mole-like growths that increase in size, and change color.

2.   If malignant, these can cause death within five years.

D.   Melanoma can be treated through several means.

1.   A patient can undergo surgery.

2.   Radiation therapy can be prescribed.

3.   A heat process can destroy the affected tissue.

4.   The tissue can be destroyed by freezing.

Satisfaction Step

I.   If you still must have sun, at least take the following precautions:

Attack on the causes so as to eliminate the need

A. Control the amount of time you absorb the sun's rays, especially at the beginning of the sunning season.
   1. Sun before 10 a.m. and after 3 p.m. when the sun's rays are at their weakest.
   2. Sun only fifteen minutes the first day during high radiation hours.
   3. Sun only five minutes each day thereafter during high radiation hours until you have a good base tan.
B. Use a sunscreen that contains PABA (para-aminobenzoic acid)
   1. Sunscreens work best when applied forty-five minutes before exposure.
   2. Sunscreens come in varying strengths.
C. A sunblock may be an effective supplement to sunscreens.
   1. Sunblocks do not absorb any ultraviolet rays from the sun.
   2. The sunblock is helpful in shielding lips, nose, or previously burned areas.
   3. Lifeguards and others constantly exposed to the sun use zinc oxide as a blocking agent.
D. Light, cool clothing also is an effective preventive measure.
   1. Loose-fitting robes for beachwear can help.
   2. Hats can help shield you from the sun.

Visualization Step

Negative and positive visualization

I. Is carefree and careless pursuit of the sun worth tomorrow's damaged skin or next month's keratoses or skin cancer?

II. Careful, consistent use of the preventive measures will leave you with a good suntan and less chance of skin damage.

Action Step

Short action step

I. Plan your time in the sun with care—the skin you save is your own!

Developing a Speaking Outline

As noted earlier, you probably would not use the above full-sentence outline in an actual speech because it is too dense to manage effectively from a lectern. One danger a full-sentence outline poses is that is can be simply read aloud to an audience. After all, it contains virtually everything you want to say. To preserve the naturalness and sense of spontaneity that enables you to maintain contact with the audience, you can compress the full outline into a phrase outline. This involves rewording the main heads into phrase form on a sheet or series of note cards. Whether you use sheets of paper or cards, be comfortable with your choice of notes. Your speaking outline should serve two functions:

1. It should provide you with reminders of the overall structure of your speech as well as the subpoints you want to cover.

2. It should record verbatim material that you wish to express precisely.

There are four characteristics of the speaking outline:

1. Most points are expressed in phrases or, in some cases, single words. If you have practiced the speech using the full-sentence outline, a word or phrase should be enough to trigger your memory at critical points during the actual delivery.

2. A full sentence is used when you want to say something in a precise way or you want to be sure that you are quoting accurately.

3. Directions to yourself, such as "Show visual," may be included at the appropriate point in your outline.

4. Emphases can be indicated by underlining words, using all capital letters, or any other means that will convey to you what is expected.

The following speaking outline is a sample for the speech on suntanning.

Suntanning: Not as Healthy as You Think

Attention Step

I. "Gee, your suntan looks great!" "He must live in a darkroom; his arms and legs are so pale!"
   A. Suntan—attractive
   B. Suntan—healthy
   C. Truth—harmful

II. Convincing—two themes
   A. Effects
   B. Preventive measures

Need Step

I. Three effects—uncomfortable to potential harm
   A. Severe sunburn
      1. Familiar
      2. Severe—treat like other burns
   B. Aging
      1. Leathery
      2. Lose elasticity
   C. Keratosis
      1. Dark patches, scaly growths
      2. Often precancerous

II. Fourth—300,000 Americans annually contract skin cancer
   A. Early warning signs
      1. Sore—not healing
      2. Wart or mole—change
      3. Unusual growth
   B. Basal and squamous cell cancers
      1. Red scaly patches
      2. Detection and treatment—cure

   C. Melanoma—worst
       1. Small mole-like growth—increase in size, change color
       2. Malignant—causes death in 5 years
   D. Melanoma treatment
       1. Surgery
       2. Radiation therapy
       3. Heat tissue
       4. Freeze tissue

Satisfaction Step

I. Precautions
   A. Time
       1. 10 to 3 worst
       2. Day one—15 min.
       3. Days after—5 min. till base tan
   B. Sunscreen—PABA (para-aminobenzoic acid)
       1. 45 min. prior
       2. Varying strengths
   C. Sunblock
       1. No rays
       2. Shield lips, nose
   D. Light, cool clothes
       1. Loose robes for beach
       2. Hats

Visualization Step

I. Today carefree, tomorrow damages: worth it?

II. Careful attention—good tan, less damage

Action Step

I. Plan your time in the sun with care—the skin you save is your own!

Fitting the Introduction and the Conclusion to the Speech

The motivated sequence and more precise patterns of organization have been incorporated in the full-sentence and speaking outlines presented above. By including the introduction and conclusion (attention and action steps), we have illustrated the integration of these elements into the total speech structure. In essence, the relationships between the motivated sequence, the terms *introduction, body,* and *conclusion,* and the integration of these into an outline can be schematized as follows:

Traditional Divisions	*Motivated Sequence*	*Outline*
Introduction	*Attention Step*	*I.* _____
		A. _____
		B. _____

Body	*Need Step*	*I.* _____
		A. _____
		B. _____
		1. _____
		2. _____
		II. _____
		A. _____
		B. _____
	Satisfaction Step	*I.* _____
		A. _____
		B. _____
		C. _____
		D. _____
Conclusion	*Visualization Step*	*I.* _____
		II. _____
	Action Step	*I.* _____

Of course, the arrangement of your own main and subpoints may not follow the exact pattern on the right column, but the major divisions will remain the same.

In summary, arranging and outlining do appear to require a lot of effort; in fact, they may even strike you as "busy work." In some situations, you might find such careful preparation inappropriate. If you are given only a few moments to collect your thoughts and present a coherent response to a question, for instance, your impromptu preparation may consist solely of scratching out a few ideas on a piece of paper. However, in the case of longer, more important speeches, careful arrangement of ideas can be helped immensely by taking the time to outline the speech. Arranging and outlining, therefore, helps you check on your speech's *form,* its *coverage* of the subject, and its *suitability* to your purpose and to the needs of the audience.

REFERENCE NOTES

[1]Information taken from Vincent Marteka, "Words of Praise—and Caution—About Fungus Among Us," *Smithsonian,* May 1980, pp. 96–104.

[2]Information adapted from student outline by Sandra Ginn, University of Maine-Orono. Sources used include pamphlets from the American Cancer Society ("Sense in the Sun"; "Cancer Facts and Figures"); Kushio Michio, *Cancer and Heart Disease,* Japan Publishing Co., 1982, pp. 41, 46; Mark Renneker, *Understanding Cancer,* Bull Publishing Co., 1979, pp. 4, 28.

PROBLEMS AND PROBES

1. Revise both *a* and *b* below, following the guidelines for correct outline form.
   a. The nuclear freeze concept is a good idea because it allows us to stop nuclear proliferation and it will help make us feel more secure.
   b.   I.   We should wear seatbelts to protect our lives.
        II.   Studies indicate seatbelts protect children from serious injury.
       III.   Studies indicate seatbelts reduce risk of head injury.

2. Select a speech from this text or from a speech anthology available in the library. Develop a full-sentence outline for the speech, then an abbreviated phrase outline. Add to these outlines a technical plot in which you indicate the forms of support, attention factors, and motivational appeals used by the speaker. Hand in your written outlines and technical plot. Your instructor may have you meet in small groups to compare your analyses of a single assigned speech.

3. For a speech entitled "The Investigator as Resource," discussing why a lawyer may want to hire a private detective on a case-by-case basis, rearrange the following points and subpoints in proper outline form:
   a. Investigative services can save the lawyer time.
   b. Investigative reports indicate areas where the lawyer should concentrate in building a case.
   c. It's advantageous for a lawyer to employ an investigator on a case-by-case basis.
   d. The investigator performs two basic services.
   e. Known witnesses must be interviewed and other witnesses sought out.
   f. The detective examines reports from the FBI or other governmental and private agencies and evaluates them for reliability and to determine what has to be done.
   g. The investigator examines, collects, preserves, and analyzes physical evidence.
   h. The investigator compiles information in an effort to reconstruct an incident.
   i. Lawyers may need only occasional detective assistance on especially critical cases.
   j. Investigative reports can be used in out-of-court settlements.

ORAL ACTIVITIES

1. For a speech assigned by the instructor, draw up a full-sentence outline and a technical plot in accordance with the sample forms provided in this chapter. Hand in your speech outline in time to obtain feedback before presenting your speech.

2. Working in small groups, select a controversial topic for potential presentation in class. Brainstorm possible arguments that could be offered on the pro and con sides. With these as a basis, develop a phrase outline of the main points to be presented on both sides.

3. For the next round of classroom speeches, your instructor will divide the class into groups and ask each student in the group to outline the presentations of their respective group members. Working in groups, the students will compare and contrast their outlines of what was heard with the speaker's own outline.

PART THREE

PUBLIC SPEAKING:

Modes of Communication

CHAPTER 12

Using Language

to Communicate

In Part Two we focused on the process of creating speeches: preparing, organizing, and adapting messages to their intended audiences. Here in Part Three, we shall turn our attention to the modes of creating (encoding) and interpreting (decoding) messages. These modes—language, bodily and vocal behaviors, and visual reinforcement—are the means by which public speakers communicate ideas, beliefs, attitudes, and values to listeners.

We begin the discussion of modes by examining language, the word choices that you as a speaker must make when you encode your ideas and feelings. First, we will suggest the essential features of effective speaking styles—that is, oral language styles—which improve listeners' chances for understanding what you want to say. Then, we will look at some aspects of those language styles that can create differing impressions within the audience of you, your message, and your goals in oral communication. Once we have considered these larger features of a speaking style, we then will move to more particular aspects of language strategies—the use of definitions, restatements, imagery, varying degrees of intensity, and metaphor. Overall, therefore, our goals are to get you to think about both large, or global, aspects of oral communication styles and small, or more microscopic, aspects of word choice.

Essential Features of Effective Speaking Styles

Communicating with precision and clarity is not always easy. Yet, rhetorical and communication theorists for centuries have known that speakers increase listener comprehension and retention if certain virtues of oral style are kept in mind. The virtues of *accuracy*, *simplicity*, *coherence*, and *appropriateness* are widely recognized as the primary features of effective speaking styles.

Accuracy

Careful word choice is an essential ingredient in transmitting your meaning to an audience. The man who tells a hardware store clerk that he has "broken the hickey on my hootenanny and needs a thingamajig to fix it" had better have the hootenanny in his hand to procure the right thingamajig. The ambiguity of his message is no greater, however, than that of the orator who proclaims that "we must follow along the path of true Americanism." The sentiment being expressed may be a noble one, but it is cast in lofty generalities which not only are trite but have different meanings for different people.

When you speak, your goal should be precision. Leave no doubt as to your meaning. Words are symbols that stand for the concepts or objects they represent; thus, your listener may attach to a symbol a meaning quite different from the one you intend to convey. *Democracy,* for example, does not mean the same thing to a citizen of the United States as it does to a citizen of the Soviet Union, or, in fact, to one American citizen and another. The term *democracy* will elicit different meanings in those belonging to the Moral Majority and those belonging to the American Communist Party.

It is also imprecise to discuss people or objects in a particular class as though they were no different from other members of the same class. Asian-American *A* differs from Asian-Americans *B* and *C;* one Oldsmobile may be an excellent car and another may be a lemon. Students of General Semantics continually warn us that many errors in thinking and communication arise from treating words as if they were the actual conditions, processes, or objects and, as such, were fixed and timeless in meaning. From their perspective, the phrase "once a thief, always a thief" is an imprecise and inaccurate reference to apply to all persons convicted of theft; a person is more than a label.[1]

To avoid vagueness in definition and elsewhere, choose words that express the exact shade of meaning you wish to communicate. Although dictionary definitions are not infallible guides, they do represent commonly accepted usages stated as precisely as possible. Observe, for example, the distinctions a good dictionary makes among related words, such as *languor, lassitude, lethargy, stupor,* and *torpor*. In a synonym dictionary or a thesaurus the words listed for the verb *shine* are *glow, glitter, glisten, gleam, flare, blaze, glare, shimmer, glimmer, flicker, sparkle, flash, beam*. The English language is rich in subtle variations. To increase the precision of your expression, make use of this range of meaning in your choice of words.

Simplicity

"Speak," said Lincoln, "so that the most lowly can understand you, and the rest will have no difficulty." This advice is as valid today as when Lincoln offered it; and because modern audiences as created by the electronic media are vaster and more varied than any Lincoln dreamed of, there is even more reason for contemporary speakers to follow it. Say "learn" rather than "ascertain," "try" rather than "endeavor," "use" rather than "utilize," "help" rather than "facilitate." Never use a longer or less familiar word when a simpler one is just as clear and accurate. Billy Sunday, the famous evangelist, gave this example:

If a man were to take a piece of meat and smell it and look disgusted, and his little boy were to say, "What's the matter with it, Pop?" and he were to say, "It is undergoing a process of decomposition in the formation of new chemical compounds," the boy would be all in. But if the father were to say, "It's rotten," then the boy would understand and hold his nose. "Rotten" is a good Anglo-Saxon word, and you do not have to go to the dictionary to find out what it means.[2]

Simplicity does not mean that your language must be simplistic or that you should "talk down" to your audience; it does suggest that you consider the advantages of short, easily understandable words that convey precise, concrete, specific meanings. The able speaker, regardless of experience, pays close attention to these qualities because they contribute vividness and interest to the speech.

Coherence

Transmitting ideas orally requires attention to the perceived coherence of your message. Audiences do not have the luxury of going back over your points as they do in reading an essay; nor do they have punctuation marks to help them distinguish one idea from another. Hence, speakers use *signposts,* in the form of carefully worded phrases and sentences, that enable listeners to follow the movement of ideas within a speech and to perceive the overall message structure.

Summaries are useful signposts in ensuring that your audience is able to see the overall structure; *preliminary* and *final summaries* are especially helpful in laying out or pulling together the major divisions or points of the speech:

Preliminary Summaries	Final Summaries
Today I am going to talk about three aspects of . . .	I have talked about three aspects of . . .
There are four major points to be covered in . . .	These four major points—[restate them]—are the . . .
The history of the issue can be divided into two periods . . .	The two periods just covered—[restate them]—represent the significant . . .

In addition to these summarizing strategies, signposts may be connectives which move an audience from one idea to another within the speech. The following are typical *transition* statements you might employ:

In the first place . . . The second point is . . .
In addition to . . . notice that . . .
Now look at it from a different angle . . .
You must keep these three things in mind in order to understand the importance of the fourth . . .
What was the result? . . .
Turning now . . .

The preceding signposts are *neutral*—they tell the audience that another idea is coming, but do not indicate the more subtle relationships that exist between the points being made. You can improve the clarity and coherence of your message by being precise about such relationships as parallel/hierarchical, similar/different, and coordinate/subordinate. Expressing these relationships requires *connectives* or *transitions* such as:

> Not only . . . but also . . . [*parallel*]
> More important than these . . . [*hierarchical*]
> In contrast . . . [*different*]
> Similar to this . . . [*similar*]
> One must consider X, Y, and Z . . . [*coordinated*]
> On the next level is . . . [*subordinated*]

By using preliminary or final summarizing statements to capture the holistic structure of your speech and more specific signposts to distinguish ideas and indicate their relationship to each other, you will help your audience perceive your message as a coherent whole.

Appropriateness

Besides being accurate and clear, your language should be appropriate to the topic and the situation. Serious or solemn occasions call for diction that is restrained and dignified; light or joyful occasions, for diction that is informal and lively. Just as you would never use slang in a speech dedicating a memorial, so you should never phrase a humorous after-dinner speech in a heavy or elevated style. Suit your language to the spirit and tone of the occasion; be dignified and formal when formality is expected, and light and casual when informality is called for. Be sure, also, that your language is appropriate to the audience you are addressing—that the terms you employ and the allusions you make are within the realm of the listeners' understanding.

Selecting the Appropriate Style: Strategic Decisions

Thus far, we have discussed the general qualities of an effective style, such as accuracy, simplicity, coherence, and appropriateness. Those qualities are absolutely necessary for communicating *clearly* and *understandably* with others in oral modes. Next we will consider the aspects of speaking styles which more particularly control an audience's impression of you as a person and of your message as a compelling vehicle for feelings, attitudes, and even impressions of the situation or context in which you are speaking. These aspects of oral discourse are generally called *tone*. *Tone* refers, basically, to how people feel about you and your speech: Are you a person sensitive to the demands of the situation? Are you basically an informal, happy-go-lucky person, or someone talking seriously and formally about matters of importance? Are you arguing with audience members or telling them stories? Are you principally concerned with yourself and the audience's impressions of you, or are you trying to force attention to be given primarily to your ideas?

While tone is an elusive quality of oral speech, it nevertheless is possible to identify

Selecting an appropriate speaking style is difficult but important. Your stylistic choices should reflect your own self-concept, purpose, audience's expectations—and physical location.

some of its primary dimensions or aspects. Four dimensions—discussed here as variables of language—deserve special attention: *written vs. oral language, serious vs. humorous atmosphere, person-centered vs. material-centered emphasis,* and *propositional vs. narrative form.*

Written vs. Oral Language

Oral speech developed in humans long before written language. That may seem like a harmless fact, yet its implications are far-reaching. Oral speech, we presume, sprang directly from early humanity's harsh contact with its environment, and it still retains features of its origin. Generally, spoken language, in both its words and its vocal characteristics, is expressive of inner emotion; spoken language, because it (unlike written language) springs immediately from the human mechanism in the presence of another, is deeply personal; spoken language, because we use it more in informal settings—grocery stores, backyard fences, the supper table, the street—than we do written language, is looser, less complicated, simpler. So, you might write someone a note "requesting that they please leave the area," while you would say orally "Get outta town!" Words such as *honey, sweetie, lover, dear* look absolutely terrible on the printed page, yet when actually spoken by intimates can elicit highly positive reactions. And, of course, the stereotyped waitress' "Whutkinahgitcha?" makes no sense in this book, yet it certainly does the job at 7:25 a.m. in the local greasy spoon.

Thanks to your general cultural education, you probably are well aware of the differences between oral and written language. You probably already know that you'd likely *say* "Thanks for the quick service" after a breakfast uptown, and *write* "I very much appreciated the sumptuous dinner you served last evening" to a Snob Hill hostess. Where most speakers get in trouble is in more or less well-defined speeches, because "speeches" seem to be neither strictly oral (informal) communications nor strictly written (formal) pieces of address. And that is confusing.

As a result—and especially because we're usually tense about speaking in public—we often err in the direction of formality. We may even go so far as to write out the whole speech. Because we are used to composing on paper for the eye (for a reader) rather than for the ear (for a listener), most of us compose speeches in a written rather than oral style. The speeches sound stilted, stiff. They're likely to have sentences such as these:

> I am most pleased that you could come this morning. I would like to use this opportunity to discuss with you a subject of inestimable importance to us all—the impact of inflationary spirals upon students enrolled in institutions of higher education.

Translated into the kind of oral style preferred in most speaking situations, those sentences would run something like this:

> Thanks for coming. I'd like to talk today about something which everyone here has had experience with—the rising costs of going to college.

Notice the differences in the two versions: the first is wordy, filled with prepositional phrases, larded with complex words, formal in its address of the audience. The second contains shorter sentences, a more direct address of the audience, and a simpler vocabulary. The first is in a written style; the second, in an oral style.

On most occasions, you'll want to cultivate an oral style. To be sure, there are some highly ceremonious occasions and situations such as news conferences where you'll read from a prepared text, but even at those times, you'll want to aim at oral style.[3]

Serious vs. Humorous Atmosphere

Related to the matter of written vs. oral style is another variable: the seriousness with which a speaker expects an audience to take a speech and a speaking situation. You convey your impressions of the atmosphere of the occasion—and even the degree to which you yourself expect to be taken seriously—largely by your speaking style.

Sometimes the speaking occasion dictates an appropriate atmosphere. We do not expect a light, humorous speaking style to be used, for example, during funerals or presidential inaugural addresses. This is not to say that jokes are never told during a funeral; often a minister, priest, or rabbi will tell a heart-warming, even humorous, little story about the deceased. Yet, the overall tone of a funeral speech or sermon is somber, meditative, serious. In contrast, a speech after a football victory, election win, or successful fund drive is seldom heavy, philosophical, or penetrating in its analysis of the human condition. Victory speeches are times for celebration, humor, warmth, joy, applause, and a feeling of unity with others who've worked on the cause. Humor, laughter, and mutual enjoyment characterize these situations, and hence speeches delivered at such events tend to be drawn from the "humor" end of the serious-humorous continuum.

Again, this is not to say that *humorous* means there are no audience-centered, non-frivolous purposes for speaking involved here. As we'll note in Chapter 18, even speeches to entertain have worthy purposes; they can be persuasive in their goals, and they can be given in grave earnestness. The political satirist who throws humorous but barbed comments at pompous, silly, or corrupt politicians is very concerned about political reform.

Here we're not talking about serious or humorous speaking *purposes,* but, rather, serious or humorous linguistic *atmospheres*—the mind-set or mental attitude a speaker attempts to create in audiences. A speech urging individuals to be and think for themselves, cast in a serious atmosphere, might contain a section such as: "Be yourself. Trust in your own decision-making powers. Whenever you turn over your decision-making powers to a group, you become a dependent human being." That same section of a speech offered within a humorous atmosphere might look like this: "Remember that a camel is a horse built by a committee. And when God put the universe together, she didn't consult with the angels and the archangels, the cherubim, seraphim, and the other folks hanging around heaven. If God had done that, they'd all still be arguing to this day, trying to figure out who should be in charge of stars, and of planets, and of moons—and you and I would still be dustballs in the back pocket of God. Socrates said, 'Know thyself,' and he could have added, 'Get off your duff and do something with that knowledge!'"

Sometimes, you'll want to create a serious, sober atmosphere, a time for personal reflection and commitment on the part of your listeners. At other times, you'll wish to loosen them up, to penetrate their defenses, to share humor and joy with them. Make sure that the atmosphere you attempt to create is appropriate to the speaking situation and your purposes.

Person-Centered vs. Material-Centered Emphasis

Another important variable in one's speaking style centers on the degree to which the speaker—or an impression of the speaker we often call a *persona*—is the object of attention. Generally, a speech is primarily person-centered or primarily material-centered. That is, it can feature the personality, talents, experience, and wisdom of the speaker as its central engines of persuasion, or it can feature facts, figures, other sorts of evidence, social values, and the like in its emphasis upon the world and society. Indeed, since Aristotle wrote his *Rhetoric* in the fourth century B.C., rhetoricians have wondered whether the strategically conscious speaker should stress self (*ethos* in Greek) or material (*logos*).

Of course, a speaker always is mixing the two, making both self references and material references. Yet one or the other often dominates sections of speeches or even entire discourses. Consider, for example, the following two passages from speeches by the same man, Revolutionary War hero Patrick Henry. The first is the opening of his famous "Give Me Liberty or Give Me Death" speech in 1775, to the Virginia Convention:

> No man thinks more highly than I do of the patriotism, as well as the abilities of the very worthy gentlemen who have just addressed the house. But different men see the same subject in different lights; and therefore, I hope it will not be thought disrespectful to those gentlemen, if, entertaining as I do opinions of a character very opposite to theirs, I shall speak forth my sentiments freely and without reserve. This is no time for ceremony. The question before the house is one of awful moment to this century. The question of freedom or slavery; and in proportion to the magnitude of the subject ought to be the freedom of the debate. It is only in this way that we can hope to arrive at truth, and fulfill the great responsibility which we hold to God and our country. Should I keep back my opinions at such a time, through fear of giving offense, I should consider myself as guilty of treason toward my country, and of an act of disloyalty toward the Majesty of Heaven, which I revere above all earthly kings.[4]

Note Henry's use of the first-person singular "I," as well as his use of personal verbs ("I do," "I shall speak," "I consider," "I should consider," "I revere"). Attention is directed to Patrick Henry, to his rights, his obligations, his thinking. The *persona* of Henry as a clear-thinking, morally indignant, freely speaking citizen dominates the language and style of this paragraph.

In contrast, notice how Patrick Henry talks thirteen years later, when he is opposing in 1788 the proposed Constitution for the United States:

> This proposal altering our Federal Government is of a most alarming nature; make the best of this new Government—say it is composed of anything but inspiration—you ought to be extremely cautious, watchful, jealous of your liberty; for, instead of securing your rights, you may lose them forever. If a wrong step be now made, the Republic may be lost forever. If this new government will not come up to the expectation of the people, and they should be disappointed, their liberty will be lost, and tyranny must and will arise.[5]

Here, Henry is again speaking of governmental tyranny and freedom, but notice his emphasis upon the ideas of republicanism and liberty in relation to the audience rather than, as earlier, his emphasis upon his own person and persona. The style shifts markedly.

Fundamentally, therefore, the person-centered emphasis arises from a focus, in a speech's language, upon relationships between the speaker and the subject matter or the speaking process, while the material-centered emphasis stresses relationships between the audience and ideas. As a speaker, sometimes you'll want to offer a person-centered emphasis, especially in situations where you're an expert on some subject or when you're dealing with your own reactions to things around you. At other times—as in most kinds of informative speeches and on occasions for persuasion when you and the audience have little direct experience with problems—you probably will employ a material-centered emphasis.

Propositional vs. Narrative Form

Finally, speaking styles can differ greatly in another important way: Some styles are highly *propositional*—that is, they are dominated by an argumentative method of composition; while other styles are highly *narrative*—that is, they are dominated by storytelling. When using a propositional form of speaking, the speaker offers a series of claims or assertions and supports each one with evidence the audience should consider important. When using a narrative form, the speaker offers a story which contains a message or "moral" the audience should consider compelling.

Suppose, for example, that you wished to convince your classmates to make appointments to see their academic advisers regularly. Such a speech, in propositional form, might run something like this:

I. You ought to see your adviser regularly because he or she can check on your graduation requirements.
    A. Advisers have been trained at this school to understand the college's requirements.
    B. They also probably helped write the departmental requirements for your major, and so know them, too.

II. You ought to see your adviser regularly because that person usually can tell you something about careers in your field.
    A. Most faculty members at this school regularly attend professional meetings and find out what kinds of schools and companies are hiring in your field.
    B. Most faculty here have been around a long time, and thus have seen what kinds of academic backgrounds get their advisees good jobs after school.

III. You ought to see your adviser regularly so that you can check out your own hopes and fears with someone.
    A. Good advisers help you decide whether you want to continue with a major.
    B. And, if you do decide to change majors, they often will help you find another adviser, in another department, who can work with a person like you.

This same speech, cast into narrative form, would come out as a story about someone's successes and difficulties:

I. I thought I could handle my own advising around this school, and that attitude got me into trouble.
    A. I could read, and I thought I knew what I wanted to take.
    B. I decided to steer my own course, and here's what happened.

II. At first, I was happy, taking any old course I wanted to.
    A. I skipped the regular laboratory sciences (chemistry, biology, physics) and took "Science and Society" instead.
    B. I didn't take statistics to meet my math requirement, but instead slipped into remedial algebra.
    C. I piled up the hours in physical education so I could have a nice grade-point average to show my parents.

III. When I was about half done with my program, however, I realized that:
    A. I hadn't met almost half of the general educational graduation requirements.
    B. I wanted to go into nursing.

IV. Therefore, I had to go back to freshman- and sophomore-level courses even though I was technically a junior.
  A. I was back taking the basic science and math courses.
  B. I was still trying to complete the social science and humanities requirements.

V. In all, I'm now in my fifth year of college, with at least one more to go.
  A. My classmates who used advisers have graduated.
  B. I suggest you follow their examples rather than mine if you want to save time and money.

Most of the time, speakers rely upon propositional forms of speaking—most audiences expect them. But, in situations where a story or a personal illustration will allow you to make all of the points you want to, you may wish to employ a narrative form; it naturally catches up an audience in a situation—if, of course, you're a good storyteller—and usually is easier for people to remember than a bundle of arguments. (See the discussion in Chapter 16 of narrative persuasion.)

Ultimately, selecting an appropriate style is a matter of assessing yourself, your audience, the situation or context, and your purposes as a speaker. Thinking through those aspects of the communication model will help you select an appropriate style and decide whether to be formal or informal, serious or humorous, person-centered or material-centered, and propositional or narrative in form.

Language Strategies

By knowing the essential features of effective speaking styles and selecting appropriate styles of speaking, you can not only help listeners comprehend and retain what you are saying, but also control the general atmosphere while talking publicly. Now it is time to get a good deal more specific about "language strategies"—about the particular words you choose to use when you talk and about how you can use different sorts of words and phrases to increase the comprehensibility and impact of your speeches.

There are countless language strategies available to speakers. We will review five of the most common and discuss ways they are used by effective speakers. These categories are: *definitions, restatements, imagery, language intensity,* and *metaphor.*

Definitions

In most speaking situations, audience members need fundamental definitions of concepts. You cannot expect them to understand ideas if the words are unfamiliar or if you're using words in a manner different from their generally accepted definition. Eight sorts of definitions are useful to speakers:

Defining from Dictionaries.   A dictionary definition is a *reportive definition,* one which indicates how people in general use a word. Dictionary definitions put an object or concept in a category and specify its characteristics: "An orange is a *fruit* [category] which is *round, orange* in color, and a member of the *citrus family* [characteristics]." Dictionary definitions sometimes help you learn an unfamiliar or technical word, but they are seldom helpful to speakers because they only use large categories and the most general characteristics in the defining clauses. So, dictionary definitions can provide you and your audience with a general orientation to an idea and its dimensions, but normally must be followed by other kinds of definitions that more precisely clarify a concept.

Defining in Your Own Words.   Occasionally, a word has so many meanings that speakers have to indicate which one they wish to use. In that case, you must use a *stipulative definition*—one that stipulates the way you will use a word: "By *speech* I mean the act of offering a series of ideas and arguments to a group of hearers in a face-to-face situation." Such a definition orients the audience to your subject matter. Furthermore, if you think an audience respects an authority or expert, you can use that person's stipulative definition (an *authoritative definition*): "Hyman Smith, president of this school, defines a *liberal arts education* as one in which students are taught not merely technical operations and job-related skills, but rather ways of thinking and reasoning. Today, I want to explore that definition and what it means to you in your four years here."

Defining Negatively.   Further clarity can be added by telling an audience how you are *not* going to use a term or concept—by using a *negative definition*. Along with the stipulative definition of speech, for example, we could have said: "By *speech* I do not mean to refer to the production of the 'correct' sounds and words of the English language, even though that is a common meaning of the word; rather, I will mean. . . ." Defining negatively can clear away possible misconceptions. Using a negative definition along with a stipulative definition is a technique that is especially useful when you are trying to treat a familiar concept in a novel or different way.

Defining from Original Sources.   Sometimes you can reinforce a series of feelings or attitudes you wish an audience to have about a concept by telling them where the word came from: "*Sincere* comes from two Latin words: *sine,* meaning 'without,' and *ceres,* meaning 'wax.' In early Rome, a superior statue was one in which the artisan did not have to cover his mistakes by putting wax into flaws. That statue was said to be *sine ceres*—'without wax.' Today, the term *a sincere person* carries some of that same meaning. . . ." This is called an *etymological definition* when you trace a word's meaning back into its original language. It's termed a *genetic definition* when you explain where the idea rather than the word comes from. You could, for instance, explain the American concept of freedom of speech by looking at important discussions of that idea in eighteenth-century England, and then showing how the American doctrine took its shape from our ancestors' British experiences. Defining from original sources, either of the word or of the idea, gives an audience a sense of continuity and at times explains certain nuances of meaning we cannot explain in any other way.

Defining by Examples.   Particularly if a notion is unfamiliar or technical, one of the best ways to define is an *exemplar definition*—one that simply points to a familiar example: "Each day, most of you stroll past Old Capitol on your way to classes. That building is a perfect example of what I want to talk about today—Georgian architecture.'' Be careful to pick only defining examples that your audience members will be familiar with.

Defining by Context.   You also can define a word or concept by putting it in its usual context—through a *contextual definition*. This can be done verbally, as when a speaker says, ''The difference between the words *imply* and *infer* is best understood in this way: The person generating a message *implies* a meaning; an observer *infers* an interpretation. Thus, *you* imply some idea or feeling in what you say, while *I* draw inferences about what you meant.'' A contextual definition also can go beyond such verbal descriptions, and, like a definition which uses examples, can point to a ''real'' context: ''While there are many possible meanings to the word *revolution,* today I want to use it to describe the events which produced the American Revolution.'' You then would go on to specify those events. Defining by context gives an audience a sense of meaningfulness, and is a good tactic for making certain kinds of concepts concrete.

Defining by Analogy.   Still another means for making technical or abstract notions easier to understand is the *analogical definition*. An analogy compares a process or event that is unfamiliar or unknown with something that is familiar or known: ''Perhaps you can better understand this school's registration procedure if you think of it as an assembly line. First, raw materials (student identification cards, registration forms, lists of available classes and times) are brought into the plant (our fieldhouse). Then, those materials are shaped by skilled craftsmen (advisers, departmental representatives, and you). Next the needed adjustments are put together to make the product (your schedule). And finally, the completed product is checked by quality control people (representatives of the dean's office). Let's go through these steps one at a time.'' By relying upon a familiar concept or process, the analogical definition can make the unfamiliar idea much easier to grasp. Be sure, however, that the essential features of the two compared objects or processes are more similar than different. Don't confuse an audience with an analogy that doesn't fit.

Defining by Describing Operations.   Some words or concepts are best defined by reviewing the operations or procedures used in making or measuring something—by offering an *operational definition*. For example, we have no good way of defining *intelligence* with words. Rather, we usually define it in terms of how it is measured: ''*Intelligence quotient* is a person's score on the Wechsler-Bellevue Intelligence Test compared with the scores of other members of the population.'' Along with exemplar and analogical definitions, operational definitions are especially good for making an audience ''see'' an idea or process.

Restatement

Were accuracy and simplicity your only criteria as an oral communicator wishing to convey meanings clearly, messages might resemble the famous bulletin of World War II: ''Sighted sub, sank same.'' But because you are working with your listeners face-to-face, in oral and not written language, another criterion becomes important. *Restatement,* as we use the term, is intentional repetition of two kinds: (1) *rephrasing* of ideas or concepts in more than one set of words or sentences, and (2) *reiteration* of ideas or concepts from more than one point of view. Because words literally disappear into the atmosphere as soon as you speak them, as an oral communicator you do not have the writer's advantage when transmitting ideas to others. Instead, you must rely heavily upon rephrasing and reexamination.

Rephrasing.   The effect of skillful rephrasing to clarify a message and make it more specific can be seen in the following passage from John F. Kennedy's inaugural address:

> Let the word go forth from this time and place, to friend and foe alike, that the torch has been passed to a new generation of Americans—born in this century, tempered by war, disciplined by a hard and bitter peace, proud of our ancient heritage—and unwilling to witness or permit the slow undoing of those human rights to which this nation has always been committed, and to which we are committed today at home and around the world.
>
> Let every nation know, whether it wishes us well or ill, that we shall pay any price, bear any burden, meet any hardship, support any friend, oppose any foe to assure the survival and the success of liberty.[6]

Reiteration.   Reiterating an idea from a number of perspectives usually can be done by reformulating the elements that make it up or by redefining the basic concept. You can see this principle of reiteration at work in the following excerpt from a student speech. Note how the speaker defines and redefines *political image* in a variety of ways, thereby providing metaphorical, psychological, and sociological perspectives:

> A "politician's image" is really a set of characteristics attributed to that politician by an electorate [*formal perspective*]. A political image, like any image which comes off a mirror, is made up of attributes which reflect the audience's concerns [*metaphorical perspective*]. An image is composed of bits and pieces of information and feelings which an audience brings to a politician [*psychological perspective*], and therefore it represents judgments made by the electorate on the bases of a great many different verbal and nonverbal acts a politician has engaged in [*sociological perspective*]. Therefore, if you think of a political image only in terms of manipulation, you are looking only at the mirror. Step back and examine the beholder, too, and you will find ways of discovering what a "good" image is for a politician.

If carefully handled, restatement in the form of rephrasing or reiteration can help you clarify ideas and help your listeners remember these ideas more readily. Be careful, however, of mindless repetition; too many restatements, especially restatements of ideas already clear to any alert member of your audience, are sure to be boring.

Imagery

We receive our impressions of the world around us through sensations of sight, smell, hearing, taste, and touch. If your listeners are to experience the object or state of affairs you are describing, you must, therefore, appeal to their senses. But you cannot punch them in the nose, scatter exotic perfume for them to smell, or let them taste foods which

TYPES OF IMAGERY

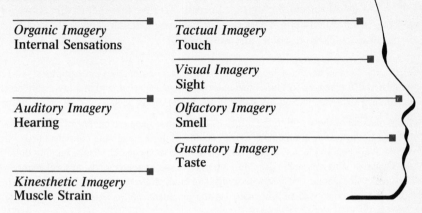

Organic Imagery
Internal Sensations

Tactual Imagery
Touch

Visual Imagery
Sight

Auditory Imagery
Hearing

Olfactory Imagery
Smell

Gustatory Imagery
Taste

Kinesthetic Imagery
Muscle Strain

are not present. The primary senses through which you as a speaker can reach your listeners *directly* are the visual and the auditory: they can see you, your movements, your facial expressions, and objects you use as "visual aids"; and they can hear what you say.

Despite this limitation, however, you can *indirectly* stimulate all of the senses of your listeners by using language that has the power to produce imagined sensations or which causes them to recall images they have previously experienced. Through image-evoking language, you can help your hearers create many of the sensory pictures and events that you yourself have experienced or encountered. Through vivid words, you can project the desired image swiftly into the mind's eye of your listeners. The language of imagery is divided into seven classes, or types, each related to the particular sensation that it seeks to evoke. They are:

1. Visual *(sight)*
2. Auditory *(hearing)*
3. Gustatory *(taste)*
4. Olfactory *(smell)*
5. Tactual *(touch)*
   a. Texture and shape
   b. Pressure
   c. Heat and cold
6. Kinesthetic *(muscle strain)*
7. Organic *(internal sensations)*

Visual Imagery.   Try to make your audience "see" the objects or situations you are describing. Mention *size, shape, color,* and *movement.* Recount events in vivid visual language. For example, in a time of cold war between the United States and Russia, General of the Army Douglas MacArthur knew he had to steel the cadets of the United

States Military Academy for their uncertain future. His central theme—"duty, honor, and country"—was a refrain through the speech. To give that theme life, however, General MacArthur relied upon a variety of visual images in his view of the dedicated soldier stressing size, shape, color, and movement:

> In twenty campaigns, on a hundred battlefields, around a thousand campfires, I have witnessed that enduring fortitude, that patriotic self-abnegation, and that invincible determination which have carved his statue in the hearts of his people.
>
> From one end of the world to the other, he has drained deep the chalice of courage. As I listened to those songs in memory's eye I could see those staggering columns of the First World War, bending under soggy packs on many a weary march, from dripping dusk to drizzly dawn, slogging ankle deep through mire of shell-pocked roads; to form grimly for the attack, blue-lipped, covered with sludge and mud, chilled by the wind and rain, driving home to their objective, and for many, to the judgment seat of God.
>
> . . . Always for them: Duty, honor, country. Always their blood, and sweat and tears, as they saw the way and the light. And twenty years after, on the other side of the globe, again the filth of dirty foxholes, the stench of ghostly trenches, the slime of dripping dugouts, those boiling suns of relentless heat, those torrential rains of devastating storms, the loneliness and utter desolation of jungle trails, the bitterness of long separation of those they loved and cherished, the deadly pestilence of tropical disease, the horror of stricken areas of war.
>
> Their resolute and determined defense, their swift and sure attack, their indomitable purpose, their complete and decisive victory, always through the bloody haze of their last reverberating shot, the vision of gaunt, ghastly men, reverently following your password of duty, honor, country.[7]

Auditory Imagery.   Through auditory imagery, speakers use words which help their listeners "hear" what they are describing. Auditory imagery may be used to project an audience into a scene, as Tom Wolfe does in the following example, where he is describing the opening of a demolition derby:

> Then the entire crowd, about 4,000, started chanting a countdown, "Ten, nine, eight, seven, six, five, four, three, two," but it was impossible to hear the rest, because right after "two" half the crowd went into a strange whinnying wail. The starter's flag went up, and the 25 cars took off, roaring into second gear with no mufflers, all headed toward that same point in the center of the infield, converging nose on nose.
>
> The effect was exactly what one expects that many simultaneous crashes to produce: the unmistakable tympany of automobiles colliding and cheap-gauge sheet metal buckling.[8]

Gustatory Imagery.   Sometimes you may even be able to help your audience "taste" what you are describing. Mention its saltiness, sweetness, sourness, or its spicy flavor. Observe how Jane Bochman, a student at the University of Iowa, describes the taste of granola not only to stimulate the imagination of her listeners, but also to appeal to their aesthetic values:

Few people forget their first taste of homemade granola. Unlike the commercial varieties, which are so heavily sugar-coated that they are almost indistinguishable from the usual Kellogg's products, homemade granola provides you with confusing sensations. The sweetness of honey is mixed with the saltiness of nuts. The rolled oats have a mealiness which contrasts sharply with the firmness of whole grain wheat. Your tongue bravely battles both stringy coconut and small, firm flax seeds. Overall, the first impression of sweet treats is followed by a lingering sourness. Your system as well as your taste buds are pleasantly awakened as you do early morning encounter with nature's best. If you have not had these experiences, then you obviously have not been making use of the health food store down the street.

Olfactory Imagery.   Help your audience smell the odors connected with the situation you describe. Do this not only by mentioning the odor itself, but also by describing the object that has the odor or by comparing it with more familiar ones, as shown in this example:

> As he opened the door of the old apothecary's shop, he breathed the odor of medicines, musty, perhaps, and pungent from too close confinement in so small a place, but free from the sickening smell of stale candy and cheap perfume.

Such associations also allow your audience to make positive or negative judgments about the experience.

Tactual Imagery.   Tactual imagery is based upon the various types of sensation that we get through physical contact with an object. Particularly it gives us sensations of texture and shape, pressure, and heat and cold.

Texture and shape.   Enable your audience to feel how rough or smooth, dry or wet, or sharp, slimy, or sticky a thing is.

Pressure.   Phrase appropriate portions of your speech in such a way that your auditors sense the pressure of physical force upon their bodies: the weight of a heavy trunk borne upon their backs, the pinching of shoes that are too tight, the incessant drive of the high wind on their faces.

Heat and cold.   These sensations are aroused by what is sometimes called *thermal imagery*.

Review the excerpt from Douglas MacArthur's speech on page 236 for some vivid examples of tactual imagery.

Kinesthetic Imagery.   Kinesthetic imagery describes the sensations associated with muscle strain and neuromuscular movement. Phrase suitable portions of your speech in such a way that your listeners may feel for themselves the stretching, tightening, and jerking of muscles and tendons, the creaking of their joints.

Jason Elliot, a student at the University of Iowa, makes skillful use of kinesthetic imagery to describe the experience of jogging:

> Even if you've gone through a brief warmup, early morning jogging can be a jolt to both mind and body. As you start, you first notice tiny cramps in your lower legs. Then, small,

shooting pains begin to work their way upward, and you soon realize your knee sockets are literally pounding with each step. The muscles in your thighs complain bitterly about having to bear the brunt of the effort. Just when you think you're starting to get your legs under control, you notice that your chest is not happy about the whole affair, either. You feel like you have two cement blocks resting squarely on it; the arteries leading from your heart threaten to burst; your lungs seem to search in vain for a little more oxygen. Your breathing comes in gulps and gasps. But then almost magically, something happens: your legs feel like they could keep going forever, and your breathing becomes regular and painless. Serenity and tranquility set in, and you finally can occupy your mind with the landscape, the sunrise, the day's activities. You remember why you started jogging in the first place.

Organic Imagery.   Hunger, dizziness, nausea—these are a few of the feelings organic imagery calls forth. There are times when an image is not complete without the inclusion of specific details likely to evoke these inner feelings in listeners. Be careful, however, not to offend your audience by making the picture too revolting. Develop the sensitivity required to measure the detail necessary for creating vividness without making the resultant image so gruesome that it becomes either disgusting or grotesque. Observe how H. G. Wells has made use of organic imagery to create a desired effect:

> That climb seemed interminable to me. With the last twenty or thirty feet of it a deadly nausea came upon me. I had the greatest difficulty in keeping my hold. The last few yards was a frightful struggle against this faintness. Several times my head swam, and I felt all the sensations of falling. At last, however, I got over the well-mouth somehow and staggered out of the ruin into the blinding sunlight.[9]

The seven types of imagery we have considered—*visual, auditory, gustatory, olfactory, tactual, kinesthetic,* and *organic*—may be referred to as "doorways to the mind."[10] They open the audience to new levels of awareness in understanding and believing speakers and acting on their messages. Because people differ in their degrees of sensitivity to different types of imagery, you should try to build into your messages as many appeals to their senses of these perceptual "doorways" as possible.

In the following example, note how the speaker has combined various sensory appeals to arouse listener interest and reaction:

> The strangler struck in Donora, Pennsylvania, in October of 1948. A thick fog billowed through the streets enveloping everything in thick sheets of dirty moisture and a greasy black coating. As Tuesday faded into Saturday, the fumes from the big steel mills shrouded the outlines of the landscape. One could barely see across the narrow streets. Traffic stopped. Men lost their way returning from the mills. Walking through the streets, even for a few moments, caused eyes to water and burn. The thick fumes grabbed at the throat and created a choking sensation. The air acquired a sickening bittersweet smell, nearly a taste. Death was in the air.[11]

In this example, college student Charles Schaillol uses vivid, descriptive phrases to affect the senses of his listeners: *visual*—"thick sheets of dirty moisture"; *organic*—"eyes to water and burn"; *olfactory, gustatory*—"sickening bittersweet smell, nearly a taste."

LANGUAGE INTENSITY CHART

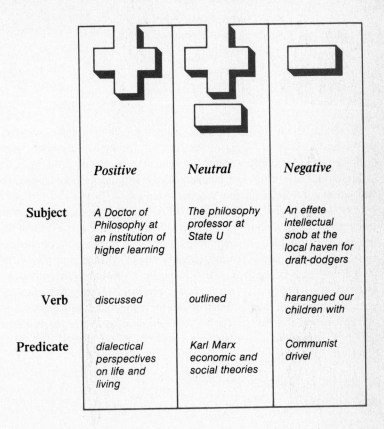

	Positive	**Neutral**	**Negative**
Subject	A Doctor of Philosophy at an institution of higher learning	The philosophy professor at State U	An effete intellectual snob at the local haven for draft-dodgers
Verb	discussed	outlined	harangued our children with
Predicate	dialectical perspectives on life and living	Karl Marx economic and social theories	Communist drivel

To be effective, such illustrations must appear plausible: The language must convey an impression that what is being described did or could happen in the way the speaker chooses to relate it. The "strangler" that struck Donora offers a plausible account of the event. More importantly, it does so in a fashion that arouses feelings. Audiences would not be as likely to share the experience if the speaker had simply said, "Air pollution was the cause of death in Donora."

Language Intensity

As a speaker, your word choice is determined partially by the way you feel about the object you are describing and the strength or intensity of that feeling. That is, by word or phrase you often communicate your *attitude* toward it. Consider, for example, the following "attitudinally weighted" terms:

Highly Positive
$\left\{\begin{array}{l}\text{``officers of the law''}\\ \text{``safety officials''}\\ \text{``men in blue''}\end{array}\right.$

Relatively Neutral
$\left\{\begin{array}{l}\text{``traffic officials''}\\ \text{``police personnel''}\\ \text{``cops''}\end{array}\right.$

Highly Negative
$\left\{\begin{array}{l}\text{``the brass''}\\ \text{``the fuzz''}\\ \text{``pigs''}\end{array}\right.$

These nine terms are roughly rank-ordered according to their intensity, ranging from the highly positive "officers of the law" to the highly negative "pigs." These are examples of attitudinally weighted statements with highly positive, relatively neutral, or highly negative language intensity. Such language choices signal the intensity of your attitude toward a subject to your listeners.

How intense should your language be? This will depend on the issue position of your listeners. Professor John Waite Bowers has suggested a useful rule of thumb: Let your language be, roughly, one step more intense than the position or attitude of your audience.[12] If your audience seems generally neutral toward your idea or proposal, make your key pieces of language slightly positive or slightly negative in the degree of intensity you employ. If your audience already is committed, say, to your positive position on reform, then you can afford to make your language quite intense. In general, audiences that are hostile to your proposal will reject highly intense language; audiences sympathetic to your views will not be negatively affected by your use of "loaded" language.

Metaphor

The images created by appealing to the various senses often use *metaphors*—words which suggest a comparison between two dissimilar things. Charles Schaillol's "fog . . . thick sheets" is one example of a metaphor used to illuminate the image he wished to create of the fog's effect. To be successful, as Michael Osborn notes, the metaphor should "result in an intuitive flash of recognition that surprises or fascinates the hearer."[13] Furthermore, good metaphors should extend our knowledge or increase our awareness of a person, object, or event. A reference to a table's "legs" may illuminate the object, but it lacks any fascination. When they are fresh or vivid, metaphors can be powerful aids to the evoking of feelings in listeners (for example, "balanced on four obese toothpicks, the antique table swayed under the heavy load"). Their potency cannot be discounted, nor can their prevalence as descriptive labels for people or events be ignored.

While vividness and freshness can make metaphors highly appealing to audiences, on other occasions you will want to employ metaphors drawn from everyday or common experiences. In almost every public speech he delivered, for example, Martin Luther King, Jr., appealed to our experiences of lightness and darkness, as he did in the following quotation:

When discussing highly abstract or theoretical material, speakers often find metaphors to be among their best friends. When drawn from the audience's experiences, they bring ideas to life.

> With this faith in the future, with this determined struggle, we will be able to emerge from the bleak and desolate midnight of man's inhumanity to man, into the bright and glittering daybreak of freedom and justice.[14]

This simple light-dark metaphor was important to King's thinking and speechmaking because it allowed him to suggest *(1)* sharp contrasts between inhumanity and freedom, and *(2)* the inevitability of social progress (as "daybreak" always follows "midnight"). In other words, the metaphor worked—it worked in communicating King's beliefs about justice and injustice, and in urging his followers to act.

In summary, words are not neutral conduits for thought. Words not only reflect the "real" world outside your mind, but they also, as rhetorical critic Kenneth Burke suggests, help to *shape* our perceptions of people, events, and social contexts. It is clear that language has a potent effect on people's willingness to believe, to feel, and to act. Wording the speech, therefore, for you becomes matters of *(1)* adopting a speaking style which increases comprehensibility via accuracy, simplicity, coherence, and appropriateness of language; *(2)* selecting an overall speaking style which is sensitive to your decisions about written vs. oral language, serious vs. humorous atmosphere, person-centered vs. material-centered emphasis, and propositional vs. narrative form; and *(3)* employing such language strategies as definitions, restatements, imagery, varied language intensity, and metaphors to re-create within audiences the understandings and feelings you yourself have.

Sample Speech

William Faulkner (1897–1962) presented the following speech on December 10, 1950, in accepting the Nobel Prize for Literature. As he had no reputation as a lecturer, the public might well have expected a lesser speech filled with the kind of pessimism so characteristic of his novels. Instead, he greeted his listeners with a stirring challenge to improve humankind.

Notice in particular Mr. Faulkner's use of language. Though known for the tortured sentences of his novels, he here offered ideas expressed clearly and simply. His tone was closer to a written rather than an oral language, yet his use of organic imagery and powerful metaphors kept the speech alive. The atmosphere generally was serious, befitting the occasion. While one might expect a Nobel Prize winner to offer a person-centered emphasis, Mr. Faulkner did just the opposite, stressing his craft—writing—and what audience members must be committed to in order to practice that craft; this material emphasis led naturally to an essentially propositional rather than narrative form. Overall, William Faulkner offered in 1950 a speech which meets even today's oral language requirements and challenges.

On Accepting the Nobel Prize for Literature[15]
William Faulkner

I feel that this award was not made to me as a man, but to my work—a life's work in the agony and sweat of the human spirit, not for glory and least of all for profit, but to create out of the materials of the human spirit something which did not exist before. So this award is only mine in trust. It will not be difficult to find a dedication for the money part of it commensurate with the purpose and significance of its origin. But I would like to do the same with the acclaim too, by using this moment as a pinnacle from which I might be listened to by the young men and women already dedicated to the same anguish and travail, among whom is already that one who will some day stand here where I am standing.   /1

Our tragedy today is a general and universal physical fear so long sustained by now that we can even bear it. There are no longer problems of the spirit. There is only the question: When will I be blown up? Because of this, the young man or woman writing today has forgotten the problems of the human heart in conflict with itself which alone can make good writing because only that is worth writing about, worth the agony and the sweat.   /2

He must learn them again. He must teach himself that the basest of all things is to be afraid; and, teaching himself that, forget it forever, leaving no room in his workshop for anything but the old verities and truths of the heart, the old universal truths lacking which any story is ephemeral and doomed—love and honor and pity and pride and compassion and sacrifice. Until he does so, he labors under a curse. He writes not of love but of lust, of defeats in which nobody loses anything of value, of victories without hope and, worst of all, without pity or compassion. His griefs grieve on no universal bones, leaving no scars. He writes not of the heart but of the glands.   /3

Until he relearns these things, he will write as though he stood among and watched the end of man. I decline to accept the end of man. It is easy enough to say that man is immortal simply because he will endure: that when the last ding-dong of doom has clanged and faded from the last worthless rock hanging tideless in the last red and dying evening, that even then there will still be one more sound: that of his puny inexhaustible voice, still talking. I refuse to accept this. I believe that man will not merely endure: he will prevail. He is immortal, not because he alone among creatures has an inexhaustible voice, but because he has a soul, a spirit capable of compassion and sacrifice and endurance. The poet's, the writer's, duty is to write about these things. It is his privilege to help man endure by lifting his heart, by reminding him of the courage and honor and hope and pride and compassion and pity and sacrifice which have been the glory of his past. The poet's voice need not merely be the record of man, it can be one of the props, the pillars to help him endure and prevail.   /4

REFERENCE NOTES

[1]For more extended treatments of this subject, see Doris B. Garey, *Putting Words in Their Places* (Glenview, IL: Scott, Foresman and Company, 1957), and Roger Brown, *Words and Things* (Glenview, IL: Scott, Foresman and Company, 1968).

[2]Quoted in John R. Pelsma, *Essentials of Speech* (New York: Crowell, Collier, and Macmillan, Inc., 1934), p. 193.

[3]For a summary of several technical studies distinguishing between oral and written styles and for a discussion of sixteen characteristics of oral style, see John F. Wilson and Carroll C. Arnold, *Public Speaking as a Liberal Art,* 5th ed. (Boston: Allyn and Bacon, Inc., 1983), pp. 227–29.

[4]Excerpt from "Give Me Liberty Or Give Me Death" by Patrick Henry, March 23, 1775, as reprinted in *The World's Best Orations: From the Earliest Period to the Present Time,* ed. David J. Brewer (St. Louis: Ferd. P. Kaiser, 1899), VII, 2475.

[5]Excerpt from " 'We the People' or 'We the States' " by Patrick Henry, June 4, 1788, as reprinted in Brewer, VII, 2479.

[6]From *Public Papers of the Presidents of the United States: John F. Kennedy.* Washington, D.C.: U.S. Government Printing Office, 1961.

[7]Excerpts from "Duty, Honor and Country" by Douglas MacArthur in *The Dolphin Book of Speeches,* edited by George W. Hibbitt. Copyright © 1965 by George W. Hibbitt. Reprinted by permission of Doubleday & Company, Inc.

[8]A selection from *The Kandy-Kolored Tangerine-Flake Streamline Baby* by Tom Wolfe. Copyright © 1963, 1965 by Thomas K. Wolfe, Jr. Copyright © 1963 by New York Herald Tribune, Inc. Reprinted with the permission of Farrar, Straus & Giroux, Inc. and International Creative Management.

[9]H. G. Wells, "The Time Machine," *The Complete Short Stories of H. G. Wells* (London: Ernest Benn, Ltd., 1927), p. 59.

[10]Victor Alvin Ketcham, "The Seven Doorways to the Mind," in *Business Speeches by Business Men,* ed. William P. Sandford and W. Hayes Yeager (New York: McGraw-Hill Book Company, 1930).

[11]From "The Strangler" by Charles Schaillol. Reprinted from *Winning Orations* by special arrangement with the Interstate Oratorical Association, Larry Schnoor, Executive Secretary, Mankato State College, Mankato, MN.

[12]John Waite Bowers, "Language and Argument," in *Perspectives on Argumentation,* ed. G. R. Miller and T. R. Nilsen (Glenview, IL: Scott, Foresman and Company, 1966), esp. pp. 168–172.

[13]Michael Osborn, *Orientations to Rhetorical Style* (Chicago: Science Research Associates, 1976), p. 10.

[14]From "Love, Law and Civil Disobedience" by Martin Luther King, Jr. Copyright © 1961, 1963 by Martin Luther King, Jr. Reprinted by permission of Joan Daves.

[15]"On Accepting the Nobel Prize for Literature" by William Faulkner. Reprinted from *The Faulkner Reader.* Copyright 1954 by William Faulkner, Random House, Inc.

PROBLEMS AND PROBES

1. Make a list of ten neutral words or expressions. Then for each word in this list find *(a)* an attitudinally weighted synonym which would cause listeners to react favorably toward the object or idea mentioned, and *(b)* an evaluative synonym which would cause them to react unfavorably toward the same object or idea. (Example: neutral word—*old;* complimentary synonym—*mellow;* uncomplimentary synonym—*senile.*)

2. What connective phrase might you use to join *(a)* a major idea with a subordinate one, *(b)* a less important idea with a more important one, *(c)* two ideas of equal importance, *(d)* ideas comparable in meaning, and *(e)* ideas that stand in contrast or opposition?

3. Using varied and vivid imagery, prepare a written description of one of the following:

Sailboats on a lake at sunset
Goldfish swimming about in a bowl
Traffic at a busy intersection
Sitting in the bleachers at a football game in 15° weather
The hors d'oeuvre table at an expensive restaurant
The city dump
A symphony concert

ORAL ACTIVITIES

1. Describe orally to your class a mundane object, such as a paper clip, brick, or pen, and the purposes to which it might be put. Employ vivid imagery in describing this object to help your audience visualize it.

2. Write a three- to four-minute speech narrating your feelings about a particular location. For instance, you might describe the town in which you grew up, a building you always dreamed of seeing, or a place made famous by one of your favorite

authors. Present the speech from manuscript. Carefully revise your manuscript to take advantage of the suggestions made in this chapter. In particular, make generous use of varied and vivid imagery, appropriate words with connotative effect, and clear and graceful connective phrases.

3. Prepare a description of some process with which you are familiar, such as how to ride a bicycle, how to operate a machine, how to prepare a meal, or some other process of your choosing. Prepare and deliver a speech for each of the following audiences: *(a)* a group of first-graders, *(b)* your peers, *(c)* a group of college graduates. How does your choice of language differ for each group? How did your word choice, sentence structure, and overall approach differ? For example, do you need to repeat more for younger audiences? Does your language need to be more vivid?

CHAPTER 13

Using Visual Aids in a Speech

From ancient cave drawings by Neanderthals to the most recent sci-fi film, humankind has sought to communicate through visual symbols. Visual art, in fact, preceded attempts to communicate through the arbitrary system of signs that we call "language." Visual communication has become an important area of study and practice in its own right. Research on the perception and integration of discrete visual experiences informs us about how we process stimuli. Interactions between visual media, learning, and attitude change have attracted particular attention in the academic and business communities.[1] Such on-going research is vitally important in a world in which computers can generate slides and graphic representations and copying machines can put realistic duplicates in the hands of others, a world in which we are bombarded daily by visual messages through printed T-shirts, buttons, signs, mass-mailed circulars, and a myriad of other forms.

The importance of visual communication to the act of presenting a speech cannot be overestimated. First, as a speaker, you are a virtual "visual message": audiences literally read your expressions and movements in order to understand your mood or intent as you speak. Second, as a speaker you need to make decisions about how to supplement your oral message and physical or vocal behavior. How can visual aids complement your message? What kinds will maximize audience understanding of the point you are making? If you are employing pictures or graphs, when and how should they be introduced into the speech? These practical questions will be addressed in this chapter. We will begin by discussing the general functions of visual aids. Then, we will discuss specific types and indicate practical ways of using each. Finally, we will suggest to you some general considerations to help refine your effective use of visual materials.

The Functions of Visual Aids

Visual materials enhance your presentation in two important ways: *(1)* they aid listener comprehension and memory; and *(2)* they add persuasive impact to your message.

Comprehension and Memory

The truth of the old saying "A picture is worth a thousand words" depends on whether the picture adds information that is more easily understood visually than aurally. Visual research has demonstrated that bar graphs, especially, make statistical information more accessible to an audience. Similarly, simple drawings enhance recall, and charts and human interest visuals such as photographs help listeners process and retain data.[2] Pictures which accompany a story being read aloud to children have significant effects on listener recall and comprehension.[3] Thus, visuals can be of immense value if your purpose is to inform or teach an audience.

Persuasiveness

In the process of enhancing comprehension and memory, visuals also will save you precious time in persuasive situations. Visuals can heighten the persuasive impact of your ideas. Lawyers, for example, have taken advantage of the dramatic effects which accompany the visual evidence of injuries or crimes in eliciting a favorable response from juries. Some lawyers are experimenting with the use of video technology to create dramatic portrayals of events—the condition of a road in an involuntary manslaughter case, the person's evident sense of caring and loving in a custody battle—in order to influence jury decisions. Undeniably, your credibility as a speaker, as well as the credibility of the message, is positively affected by the effective use of appropriate visuals.[4]

While we normally think of supporting materials as expressed in verbal form, they can also be expressed visually. With care, visual aids can be integrated into a public presentation and play a major role in oral instruction and in persuasion. Visual materials satisfy the "show-me" attitude that is prevalent within many audiences; in this sense, they provide one more crucial means of meeting listener expectations.[5]

Types of Visual Support

Visual materials can be divided into two broad classes: real objects, and symbolic representations of actual objects. As we discuss both broad groupings, specific tips will be provided on how you can use them to supplement your oral presentation of ideas.

Actual Objects

The objects you bring to a presentation, including your own body, can be discussed under two headings: animate objects and inanimate objects.

This sequence depicts the process of bringing a building down within a predetermined space.

Animate Objects.   Live animals or plants can, with appropriate discretion, be brought into a speaking situation. If you are demonstrating the "care and feeding of laboratory mice," bringing one or two in a cage may be useful in clarifying points of your speech. Acknowledging the differences between two varieties of plants may be possible with real plants. However, you might be stretching your luck a bit by bringing a real horse into class and showing how one is saddled (it happened), although it is a useful way of making the procedure clear. Discretion and common sense about what is possible and in good taste will help make such visuals work for you rather than against you.

As is true of other visuals, you will want to maximize audience attention on your commentary *about* the actual object, rather than allowing the audience to become absorbed *by* the object. A registered Persian cat may be perfect for a speech illustrating what judges look for in cat shows, but if it gets loose or is passed around the class, your message may be lost in the process. Keeping the animal restrained and firmly in your possession will help. Where appropriate, you may be able to "hide" the animal or plant so that it is not the focus of audience attention before and after you want to make use of the object.

Speeches on yoga positions, various ways of stretching out prior to running, ballet steps, or tennis strokes gain concreteness and vitality from speakers who illustrate such subjects personally. The entire speech need not be devoted to a "physical" subject in order to effectively use your own body in illustrating action. A yoga position may be well executed, but it won't help if you are on the floor and the members in the back rows can't see you (use the top of a sturdy table). Slow down the tempo so that the audience can see discrete movements; fast tennis swings won't help the audience understand what is being done. One advantage to such visual action is that you *can* control the audience's attention to the demonstration.

Inanimate Objects.   Demonstrations often are enhanced by the presence of the actual object being discussed. Telling an audience how to string a tennis racket will be aided by bringing one in to illustrate the process. Showing the best means of repairing rust holes in a car is made easier if you have samples of the work required in the separate

The pictures enhance the speaker's verbal description of the process.

stages. As in television cooking shows, you do not have the time to do the actual work. By preparing samples before the presentation, you save valuable time and illustrate what must be done.

As noted above, you will want to keep audience attention focused on the message, and not solely or completely on the object. Moving objects to "center stage" and then removing them will help you control the flow of attention from the object to your narrative. Keeping the object between you and the audience, to the extent possible, also will allow greater visual contact. If you stand in front of the object or to the side, you run the risk of blocking the audience's perceptual field.

Symbolic Representations

When you cannot actually bring the object in or use your own movement to clarify your meaning, you may resort to symbolic representations of the objects or the concepts being discussed. These representations may be relatively *concrete,* as in the use of pictures, slides, films, or videotapes. They also may be *abstract* drawings, graphs, charts, or models which depict the object or concept.

Concrete Representations.   *Photographs* can give the audience a visual sense of what you are talking about. You can illustrate flood damage by using photos of ravaged homes and land, for instance, or depict the beauty of an area threatened by a new dam. One problem with photographs is that audiences may not be able to see what is being shown as you hold a picture in front of them. If you need to pass pictures around, try to keep the number limited, and hand out each one after discussing the point that the photo helps you make. This will help minimize audience distraction as photos are passed from one person to another. If you can enlarge a small photograph so that people can see it more easily, this too would help control audience attention on your message.

Slides also allow you to depict color, shape, texture, and relationships. If you are doing a travelog, slides are virtually a necessity in discussing buildings and landscape. A speech on the days of the steam engines can be more interesting and informative if you can obtain appropriate slides of various machines in operation. The persuasive impact of a speech against the construction of a dam can be enhanced by slides depicting the white water that will be destroyed. Slides of the work of famous artists will enable you to illustrate differences in their work.

Slides do require some familiarity with projection equipment and some forethought about how to set up the presentation so that people can see. Attention to small, seemingly inconsequential details will make a major difference in how smoothly the presentation goes. Do you know how to change the projection lamp (and did you bring a spare bulb along just in case)? Will you need an extension cord, or will the projector's cord reach the outlet? Do you know how to remove a jammed slide? If you operate on the assumption "Whatever can go wrong, will," you will be prepared for most circumstances. One final suggestion: Limit the number of slides shown and vary the content. By keeping the presentation brief and by showing a variety of slides, you can make the issue both interesting and meaningful to the audience.

Videotapes and *films* also can be useful in illustrating the point you want to make. Segments from several current sitcoms can dramatically illustrate your claim that child stars are forced into adult roles. Taping two or three political ads can help you illustrate the packaging of a candidate. Lawyers are finding depovisions—videotaped testimony from doctors or others who find it difficult to attend the trial in person—a convenient way to obtain needed information on behalf of their clients. Again, familiarity with the operation of a videocassette recorder and monitor will help ensure a smooth presentation.

If you are using films, be sure that you can thread the machine. Too often, speakers bring films with them, assuming that a projector and a skilled technician will be provided, only to find that no one can get the machine running properly. Such delays increase your nervousness, and make it more difficult to get the audience to concentrate on your presentation once the equipment problems have been solved. Again, knowing how to change a projection lamp will help you avoid a crisis.

Abstract Representations.   If you need to illustrate the growth or decline of inflation or show how revenue will be spent in the next six months, you will find yourself resorting to more abstract representations than those discussed above. The form and style of the representation—drawings, charts, graphs—will depend on the formality of the situation. If you are discussing a building plan for a prospective client, a quick sketch may suffice. However, if you are meeting with the client's board of directors, the same rough drawing will be inadequate. The board will expect a polished presentation, complete with a professionally prepared prospectus. Similarly, a chalkboard drawing may be sufficient in explaining the process of cell division to a group of classmates. But when presenting the same information as part of a formal project, you will want to refine the visual support materials. The care with which you prepare these visuals will convey to the audience an attitude of indifference or concern.

Chalkboard drawings are especially valuable when you want to unfold an idea step by step. By drawing each stage as you come to it, you can control the audience's attention to your major points. Coaches often use this approach in showing players how a particular play will work. Time lines and size differences also can be depicted with

CHALKBOARD DRAWING

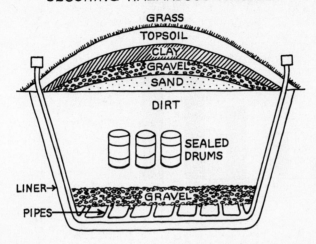

SECURING HAZARDOUS WASTES

Source: Adaptation of the drawing "Anatomy of an insecure landfill" by Richard Farrell from "Securing Hazardous Wastes" by Diana Morgan, *Science 83*, September 1983, pp. 78–79. Reprinted by permission of Richard Farrell.

The speaker wishes to illustrate, in general outline, the features of a landfill for the disposal of hazardous waste. Using the chalkboard drawing, the speaker quickly sketches the overall outline, then proceeds to fill in details. Since accuracy is not critical, the rough sketch gives listeners an adequate visual image.

---

rough sketches on a chalkboard. The size of a micro dot might be indicated by comparison to a known object: "If a micro dot were the size of a small pea, the small pea would be the size of. . . ." The relatively short history of life forms can be shown visually by a quick time line, showing approximations of when life began, when recorded history began, and the time elapsed since the fall of the Roman Empire.

When using the chalkboard, draw objects large enough for the audience to see them. You can continue to talk to the audience as you draw, as long as you are brief; the audience will lose attention if you talk to the board for 3 or 4 minutes while drawing. Consider the visual field when drawing—where should you stand to avoid blocking the audience's vision? Once you have finished explaining the drawing, you may want to take a second to erase it. This will give you a clean surface for a new drawing, and will remove a possible distraction as you continue with the remainder of your message.

Graphs require more attention than quick drawings as they normally are used to compare or show relationships between various parts of a whole, or between two

BAR GRAPHS

**Companies Filing for Chapter 11 Protection
Since Liberalization of Bankruptcy Law
in October 1979**

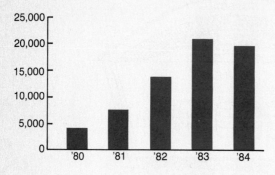

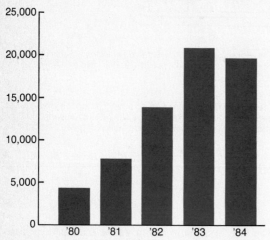

*Bar graphs, like line graphs,
visually illustrate relationships.
Changing spacings and size
of bars can affect the visual
message, though the effect
is not as dramatic as in the
case of line graphs.*

Source: *USA TODAY*, January 28, 1985. Copyright © 1985 *USA TODAY*. Reprinted by permission.

variables across time. In these cases, accuracy may be critical in visually illustrating the degree or extent of difference. Graphs can take several forms:

1. *Bar graphs* show the relationships between two or more sets of figures. If you are indicating the discrepancy between income earned by various groups of professionals, or between men and women in the same occupations, bar graphs will be an appropriate visual support for your oral presentation.

2. *Line graphs* show relations between two or more variables. If you are trying to explain a complex economic relationship involving supply and demand, a line graph will be a useful tool.

LINE GRAPHS

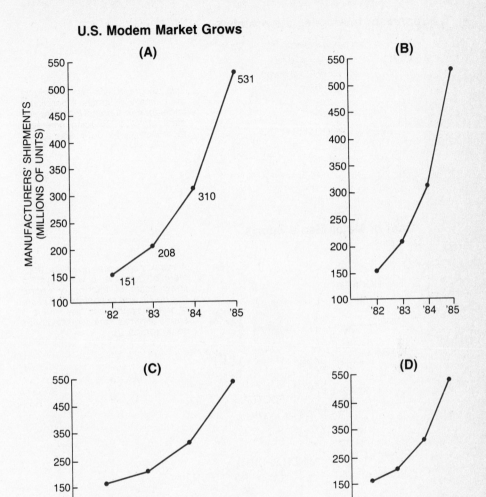

U.S. Modem Market Grows

Source: *USA TODAY*, January 28, 1985. Copyright © 1985 *USA TODAY*. Reprinted by permission.

Line graphs can reveal relationships; they also can deceive the unwary. The above graphs show the same data, but use different spacing along one or both axes to change the visual image. Graphs B and C are very different: Which would provide a more compelling rationale for investing in the modem market?

3. *Pie graphs* show percentages by dividing a circle into the proportions being represented. A charity may use a pie graph to show how much of its income is spent on administration, research, and fund-raising campaigns. Town governments use pie graphs to show citizens what proportion of their tax dollars went to municipal services, administration, education, recreation, and so on.

PIE GRAPHS

$ Support for Intercollegiate Athletics

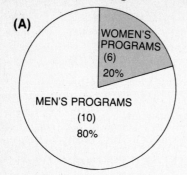

(A)

This pie graph, with two segments, dramatically illustrates a perceived imbalance in funding for intercollegiate athletics. Shading one segment also helps draw attention to the difference.

Cost of Major Men's Sports

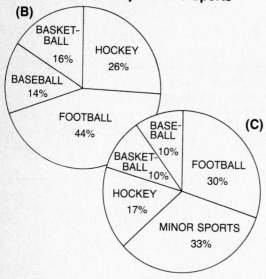

(B)

(C)

A speaker can break down one segment of graph A in two ways: to show costs of four major sports (graph B), and to contrast the costs of major sports and the "minor" sports of tennis, golf, wrestling, and so on (graph C).

Male-Female Athletics

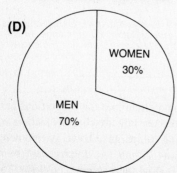

(D)

Having illustrated what appears to be an imbalance in the funding of intercollegiate athletics, a speaker may offset some of that argument by discussing the male/female ratio of total players funded.

When used in conjunction with graph A, the disparity is lessened: 80% of the money supports 70% of the participants. Taken alone or together, the data in these graphs do not provide compelling evidence that women's sports are treated fairly or unfairly. Nevertheless, using such visual aids heightens interest and dramatizes points made orally.

4. *Pictographs* signify size or number through the use of symbols. A representation of the U.S. and Soviet missile strength would use drawings of missiles (one symbol equals 1,000 actual missiles), allowing a viewer to see at a glance the disparity between the two countries.

Your choice of bar, line, pie, or pictorial graphs will depend on the subject and the nature of the relationship you wish to convey. A pie graph, for example, will not illustrate discrepancies between two groups nor will it show effects of change over time. To visually represent these relations, a bar graph or a line graph might be employed. As you think about using graphs, your first consideration is to select the form which will most easily and clearly convey the relations you want to talk about. As with chalk drawings, graphs must be large enough to be seen. Speakers sometimes transfer a graph onto a transparency and, using an overhead projector, display it on a screen. The writing of numbers and the designation of bars, lines, or segments of a pie also need to be done neatly and clearly. In rendering your various graphs, be sure to check the accuracy of the representation. A bar graph can create a misleading impression of the difference between two items if one bar is short and wide while the other is long and narrow. Line graphs can distort time if the units of measurement are not the same for each time period. These problems can be avoided by using consistent measurements in the creation of the graphs.

Charts and *tables* also lend support and clarity to your ideas. If you are trying to indicate the channels of communication or lines of authority in a large company, your presentation will be much easier to follow if each listener has an organizational chart to refer to. If the organization is large and complex, you may want to develop a series of charts, each one focusing on a smaller subset of the original. A dense chart showing all the major and minor offices may simply overwhelm the listeners as they try to follow you through the maze.

Unveiling successive charts (through the use of a *flipchart*) also will focus audience attention on specific parts of the speech. If you hand an audience a complete chart, they will tend to stray from your order of explanation as they read parts of the chart. A *flow chart* can assist in indicating the actions that might be taken across time; planners can indicate what will be done by whom and in what order. If you are explaining a fundraising campaign, a flow chart can keep all of the various relations in view as you talk through the stages of the campaign. As long as the information is not too complex or lengthy, *tables* can indicate changes in inventory over time. They also can be used to rank lists of items and their cost, frequency of use, or relative importance. As with charts, tables should be designed so that they can be seen and so that they convey data in a simple, clear form; too much information will force the audience to concentrate more on the visual support than on the explanation.

Models of real objects that cannot be brought into a room or cannot be seen because of their small size can assist in dramatizing your explanation. Architects construct models of new projects to show to clients. Developers of shopping malls, condominiums, and business offices use models when persuading zoning boards to grant needed right-of-ways or variances. An explanation of the complexity of the DNA molecule would be aided by a model; chemical changes in the molecule also can be shown by physically altering the model. Explanations of machines, such as engines, and of parts of the body, such as the heart and the eye, can be enhanced by using models of the

PICTOGRAPH

Cabling the Nation

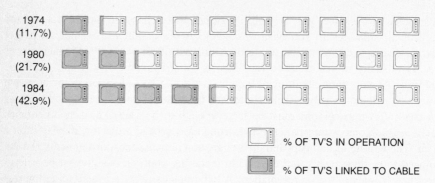

1974
(11.7%)

1980
(21.7%)

1984
(42.9%)

% OF TV'S IN OPERATION

% OF TV'S LINKED TO CABLE

Source: *USA TODAY*, January 28, 1985.

The speaker uses artistic skill to depict the number of houses (represented by television sets) being accessed by cable systems. The artistry draws attention to the information.

objects. Models need to be manageable and clearly visible to the audience. If you are using a model that will come apart so that different pieces can be explained, practice removing and replacing the parts beforehand.

Selecting and Using Visual Aids: Strategies and Determining Factors

Your decisions of which visual material to employ and how to best utilize the material will be based on three factors: (1) your own personality and purposes, (2) the communicative potential of each type of visual material, and (3) the nature of the audience and the occasion.

Start with Yourself

Visual materials may contribute in important ways to your audience's perception of you as a person—your concerns, your values, your feelings, and your ideas. A speech on scrimshawing, with examples of objects that you have carved from whalebones, not only tells an audience that you have certain skills and hobbies, but also indicates your attitudes toward the preservation of folk culture. The bar graphs you utilize in a speech on inflation not only demonstrate support for your claim, but also represent your attitudes toward concrete, summary data. Visual aids, especially those you prepare in color and detail, communicate both your forethought (you cared enough for your audience to make something for them) and, perhaps, a measure of your ingenuity and flair for the artistic.

TABLE

Basic World Economic Indicators at Three Oil Price Levels, 1950-82

Period	Oil Price Per Barrel (dollars)	Oil Production	Grain Production	Automobile Production	Gross World Product
			annual change (percent)		
1950-73	2	7.6	3.1	5.8	5.0
1973-79	12	2.0	2.1	1.1	3.5
1979-82	34	−5.7	1.8	−5.3	1.6

Source: American Petroleum Institute, U.S. Department of Agriculture, Motor Vehicle Manufacturers Association, U.S. Department of State and Worldwatch Institute.

This table makes the speaker's argument about the impact of changes in the price of oil abundantly clear. The rate of increase in three basic areas fell as oil prices went up.

Consider the Communicative Potential of Various Visual Materials

Keep in mind that each type of visual material has certain potentials for communicating particular kinds of information, and that each type interacts with your spoken presentation as well as your audience's state of mind. In preparing speech materials of this kind, remember that visuals primarily pictorial or photographic in nature have the potential for making an audience *feel* the way you do. Aids such as slides, movies, sketches, and photographs often may be used effectively to accompany travelogs or reports of personal experiences because they illustrate or reproduce in others the kinds of feelings you experienced in another place, situation, or time.

Visuals containing descriptive or verbal materials, on the other hand, can help an audience to *think* the way you do. In contrast to pictorial materials, such aids as models, diagrams, charts, and graphs frequently add rational support to claims you are attempting to defend. Your topic and your communicative purpose, therefore, play large roles in determining the kinds of visuals you ought to employ in a given circumstance. A speech informing listeners of your experiences in Indonesia should probably be accompanied by slides or films and even some household artifacts. A speech to persuade your listeners that the United States ought to sever all association with the Southeast Asia Treaty Organization probably should be supported by maps, charts, and chalkboard drawings.

Integrate Verbal and Visual Materials Effectively

To be effective, visual aids should be relevant to your topic and your communicative purpose. Your goal is to employ visuals to save time, to enhance the impact of your message, to clarify complex relations, and to generally enliven your presentation. The following suggestions build on, and in some cases reinforce, those already presented in

FLIPCHARTS

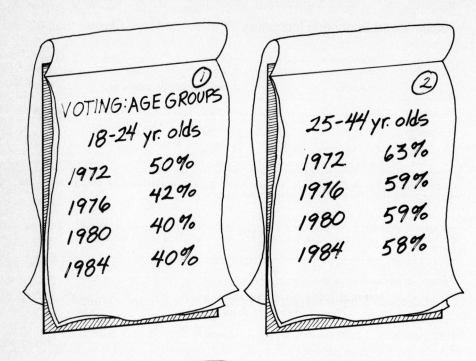

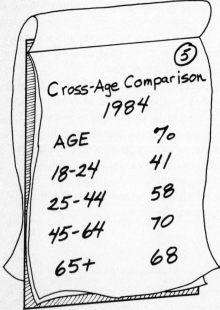

Chart 1:
VOTING: AGE GROUPS
18-24 yr. olds

1972	50%
1976	42%
1980	40%
1984	40%

Chart 2:
25-44 yr. olds

1972	63%
1976	59%
1980	59%
1984	58%

Chart 5:
Cross-Age Comparison
1984

AGE	%
18-24	41
25-44	58
45-64	70
65+	68

In preparing this speech, the speaker breaks down statistical data into units that can be shown easily on a flipchart. By moving from one chart to the next, the speaker controls the pacing and sequencing of information. Transparencies projected onto a screen also could be used for the same effect.

Source: U.S. Census Bureau.

the discussion of specific aids. Attention to each suggestion will enable the visual material to work for rather than against you.

1. *Design abstract symbolic representations with care.* Use contrasting colors (red on white, black on yellow) to highlight the information in an organizational chart or table. Segments of a pie graph can be differentiated by using contrasting colors. A bar graph can use the same color for two or more bars, or it can be designed so that the difference between each bar is highlighted by using a new color.

2. *Keep charts and other graphic aids clear and simple.* Research has demonstrated that plain bar graphs—probably because they offer not only numbers but also a visualization of numbers through the use of "bars"—are the single most effective method for displaying statistical comparisons.[6] Make sure that the essential information you want your audience to focus on stands out clearly from the background of your chart or other visual depiction. Let simplicity be your watchword in the preparation of all visual aids. Cut away extraneous information, however interesting, and display your material in a clear simple form—bars, pies, and pictures.

3. *Make your visuals—especially those with materials which must be read or scrutinized closely—large enough to be seen clearly and easily.* Listeners get frustrated when, in the middle of the speech, they suddenly notice that they are having to lean forward and squint in order to see a detail on a sketch or graph. Make your figures and lettering large enough so that, as John Hancock noted in connection with the Declaration of Independence in 1776, they "can be seen by the King of England without his glasses."

4. *In preparing to present visually the details of an object, device, or process, decide well in advance whether or not to bring in the object or device itself or a model of it.* This is especially pertinent to the so-called "demonstration" speech. For instance, if you have practiced a particular craft or mastered a certain skill and wish to communicate the details or steps in the creative process, you probably will want to show a working sample or product of that process. This can be effective; but when you elect to do it, keep in mind throughout the demonstration speech that the object or process model is communicating at the same time and very possibly as much as you are. It is telling the audience: "Here's what it is; here's why it's worth your while." Take pains to ensure, therefore, that everyone in your audience can clearly see the object or device—perhaps even to handle it. This latter possibility gives rise to a fifth precaution.

5. *Be prepared to compensate orally for any distraction your visual aid may inadvertently create among your audience.* If you do pass around a sample of your work—a leather purse you have made or a silver ring you have handcrafted—remember that an actual object or a detailed model is a complex, potent visual stimulus. This makes it a "message-maker" in its own right, and you must compete with it for the listeners' attention. Very carefully tell your audience what aspects of it to examine closely, and which ones they may ignore. If, despite your precautions, the actual object or full-scale model is likely to prove unavoidably distracting, build enough reiteration into your speech to make reasonably certain your hearers can follow your

train of thought even while they are studying the object and passing it around. As added insurance, you might also provide a rough sketch of it on the chalkboard, visually reinforcing the verbal message you are trying to communicate.

6. *When using slides, films, overhead projectors, or videotapes, be prepared to make the verbal and physical adjustments necessary to coordinate the visual materials with the spoken materials.* With these aids, you often darken the room, thereby compelling your audience to concentrate upon a source of light: the "silver screen" in the case of slides and films, the 19-inch screen in the case of a TV set. At such times, you—the *oral* communicator—must compete with the *machine* or *electronic* communicator. If, as often happens, your audience begins to concentrate harder on the flow of light than on the flow of words, you defeat your own purpose. Therefore, when using projected materials as visual support, either *(a)* talk more loudly and move more vigorously when communicating simultaneously with the machine, or *(b)* refuse to compete with it at all. That is, show the film or the slides either *before* or *after* you comment on their contents. Whatever strategy you use, however, make sure that the projected visual materials are well integrated into the rest of your presentation.

7. *Hand to your listeners a copy of those materials you wish them to think back on or carry away from your speech.* If, for example, you are making recommendations to a student council, you may provide copies of a proposal for the council's subsequent action. Or, if you are reporting in a speech the results of a survey, the most pertinent statistics will be more easily comprehended (and remembered later) if you give each listener a duplicate copy. Few people can recall the seven warning signs for cancer, but they could keep a list of them in a handy place if you presented each member of your audience with a note card on which such a list appears. Remember that we are referring here only to speech material that is legitimately a *visual aid*. Obviously, you will not put everything you have to say on a photocopied page. Select only those elements or items bearing upon the information you have introduced in your speech, especially those having future or lasting value.

Although more could be said about choosing and using the various types of visual media to which we have referred, the foregoing suggestions should enable you—with some prespeech thought and planning—to take good advantage of their communicative potential. In any event, it should be apparent that by judicious selection, preparation, and handling of charts, models, slides, and similar graphic aids, the conscientious speaker can increase listeners' comprehension. In sum, good visual material is not distracting. It "fits," it is essential to the verbal messages, and it leaves an audience with a feeling of completeness.

Consider the Audience and the Occasion

In choosing the types and contents of the visual supporting materials you will use, your common sense will tell you that you must also take into consideration the *status* of the subject in the minds of your audience. Ask yourself: Do I need to bring a map of the United States to an audience of American college students when discussing the westward movement of population in this country? Or, if I'm going to discuss offensive and defensive formations employed by a football team, should I or should I not bring in a play book showing such formations? And, can I really expect an audience to understand the administrative structure of the federal bureaucracy without an organizational chart?

How much an audience *already knows, needs to know,* and *expects to find out* about you and your subject are clearly determinants which must weigh heavily when you choose the types and numbers of visual supports you will use in a speech. How readily that audience can comprehend *aurally* what you have to say is another. Granted, it is not always easy to assess any of these conditions or capabilities. It may be exceedingly difficult, in fact, to decide how much an audience of college freshmen and sophomores knows about college or governmental structures; and, certainly, you cannot judge easily how well acquainted a Rotary Club audience is with football plays. That being the case, probably the best thing you can do is to check out your speculations by asking around among your probable listeners well ahead of the time you are scheduled to deliver your speech. In other words, before making any final decisions about visual supporting materials, do as much audience research and analysis as you possibly can.

As a part of your advance planning for the use of visuals, also take into account the nature of the occasion or the uniqueness of the circumstances in which you will be speaking. You will find that certain kinds of occasions seemingly cry out for certain types of graphic supporting materials. The corporate executive who presents a projective report to the board of directors without a printed handout and without diagrams and pictures probably would be drummed out of the firm. The military adviser who calls for governmental expenditure for new weapons without offering pictures or drawings of the proposed weapons and printed technical data on their operations is not likely to be viewed as a convincing advocate. At halftime, an athletic coach without a chalkboard may succeed only in confusing team members, not helping them. In classroom settings, students who give demonstration speeches without visuals frequently feel inadequate, even helpless—especially when they realize that most of the other speakers are well fortified with such support. In short, if you are to speak in a situation which demands certain kinds of visual media, plan ahead and adapt your message to take full advantage of them. If the speech occasion does not appear to require visual supports, analyze it further for possibilities anyway. Use your imagination. Be innovative. Do not overlook opportunities to make your speech more meaningful, more exciting, and more attention-holding in the eyes of your listeners.

REFERENCE NOTES

[1]The general theories of Gestalt psychology are reviewed understandably in Ernest R. Hilgard, *Theories of Learning* (New York: Appleton-Century-Crofts, 1956). Their applications in areas of visual communication can be found, among many other places, in Rudolph Arnheim, *Visual Thinking* (Berkeley: University of California Press, 1969); John M. Kennedy, *A Psychology of Picture Perception* (San Francisco: Jossey-Bass, Inc., Publishers, 1974); Sol Worth, "Pictures Can't Say Ain't," *Versus,* 12 (December 1975): 85–108; and Leonard Zusne, *Visual Perception of Form* (New York: Academic Press, Inc., 1976). For a discussion of research on media and learning, see Gavriel Salomon,

Interaction of Media, Cognition, and Learning (San Francisco: Jossey-Bass, 1979); E. Heidt, *Instructional Media and the Individual Learner* (New York: Nichols, 1976).

[2]William J. Seiler, "The Effects of Visual Materials on Attitudes, Credibility, and Retention," *Speech Monographs,* 38 (November 1971): 331–34.

[3]Joel R. Levin and Alan M. Lesgold, "On Pictures in Prose," *Educational Communication and Technology Journal,* 26 (1978): 233–44. See Marilyn J. Haring and Maurine A. Fry, "Effect of Pictures on Children's Comprehension of Written Text," *Educational Communication and Technology Journal,* 27 (1979): 185–90.

[4]For more specific conclusions regarding the effects of various sorts of visual materials, see F. M. Dwyer, "Exploratory Studies in the Effectiveness of Visual Illustrations," *AV Communication Review,* 18 (1970): 235–40; G. D. Feliciano, R. D. Powers, and B. E. Kearle, "The Presentation of Statistical Information," *AV Communication Review,* 11 (1963): 32–39; William J. Seiler, "The Effects of Visual Materials on Attitudes, Credibility, and Retention," *Speech Monographs,* 38 (November 1971): 331–34; M. D. Vernon, "Presenting Information in Diagrams," *AV Communication Review,* 1 (1953): 147–58; and L. V. Peterson and Wilbur Schramm, "How Accurately Are Different Kinds of Graphs Read?" *AV Communication Review,* 2 (1955): 178–89.

[5]For a clear exploration of the relationships between ideas and visuals, see Edgar B. Wycoff, "Why Visuals?" *AV Communications,* 11 (1977): 39, 59.

[6]See Feliciano et al., Vernon, and Peterson and Schramm (note 4).

PROBLEMS AND PROBES

1. Think of several courses you have taken in high school and/or college. How did the instructors use visual aids in presenting the subject matter of these courses? Were such materials effectively used? Was there a relationship between the subject matter of the course and the type of visual aid used? Give special consideration to proper and improper uses of the chalkboard by the instructors. What communicative functions are best served by the chalkboard? least served? Are there special problems with the use of visuals when audience members are taking notes while listening? Prepare a brief written analysis of these questions which includes several illustrations from the classes. How might your instructors have expanded or improved the visual presentation of information?

2. Visual supporting materials capture appropriate moods, clarify potentially complex subjects, and sometimes even carry the thrust of a persuasive message. Examine magazine advertisements and "how-to-do-it" articles in periodicals; look at store windows and special displays in museums and libraries; and observe slide-projection lectures in some of your other college classes. Then *(a)* using the types considered in this chapter, classify the nonverbal supporting materials you have encountered; *(b)* assess the purposes these materials serve—clarification, persuasion, attention-focusing, mood-setting, and others you may wish to cite; *(c)* evaluate the effectiveness with which each of the materials you have examined is doing its job; and, finally, *(d)* prepare a report, a paper, or an entry in your journal on the results of your experiences and observations.

3. Prepare an outline for a descriptive or a "how-to" speech (such as "What My Paradise Island Looks Like," or "How to Use a Typewriter") assuming you may use visual aids. Now rewrite the outline assuming you may *not* use any visual aids. What new pressures are on you as a speaker? How can you handle them? Is it still possible to give an effective speech?

ORAL ACTIVITIES

1. Present a short oral report in which you describe a speech you will give and the ways you will incorporate visual materials and coordinate them with the verbal materials. Specify the characteristics you might try to build into each visual aid to maximize clarity. If you can, bring in some rough-draft examples of the visuals for the purpose of illustrating your intentions.

2. Prepare a short speech explaining or demonstrating a complex process. Use two different types of visual aids. Ask the class to evaluate which of these aids was more effective. Try this same speech without the use of any visual materials. What new pressures do you feel as a speaker? How can you deal with them? Can you still give an effective presentation?

3. Repeat exercise #2 with a classmate. Working together, develop two different visual aids to enhance your joint presentation. Plan a performance in which the two of you share the delivery responsibilities. When one speaker talks, the other may be in charge of displaying visual aids. How effective are these duet performances? How does having a thoroughly initiated partner increase the speaking options?

CHAPTER 14

Using Your Voice and

Body to Communicate

Thus far in Part Three, we have discussed two modes of oral communication: linguistic and visual. While these channels usually carry the substances of your ideas and, in part, your feelings and attitudes, listeners normally get a much stronger sense of your emotions—your feelings toward yourself, your subject matter, and your listeners—from aural and visual messages.

In fact, you can think of the sounds of your voice and the sight of your body and face as messages in their own right. Many of the impressions formed in a listener's mind about the strength of your commitments—the degree to which you care about your audience and about what you're saying—come from the sound of your voice. And many of the impressions which are made upon that listener regarding your attitudes toward the person (Do you feel superior or inferior to the person? Are you angry or happy about talking to him or her? Are you holding back or reaching out for others?) are derived from reading your body language.

To help you better understand this final set of oral communication channels—how to use them, what to avoid doing—we will discuss three important aspects of oral presentation: selecting the overall method of presentation, using your voice to communicate, and using your body to communicate. These discussions will be followed by some time-tested general advice on using both voice and body when talking with audiences.

Selecting the Method of Presentation

What method should you use when presenting your speech? The method selected should be based on at least four criteria: the type of speaking occasion, the seriousness and purpose of your speech, audience analysis, and your own strengths and weaknesses as a speaker. Attention to these considerations will help you decide whether your method of presentation should be *(1)* impromptu, *(2)* memorized, *(3)* read from a manuscript, or *(4)* extemporized.

The Impromptu Speech

An impromptu speech is one delivered on the spur of the moment. No specific preparation is made; the speaker relies entirely on previous knowledge and skill. The ability to speak impromptu is useful in an emergency, but you should limit your use of this method to situations in which you are unable to anticipate the need to speak. Too often the "moment" arrives without the "spur." When using this method, try to focus on the central idea, carefully relating all significant detail to it. This strategy will help you avoid the rambling, incoherent "remarks" that the impromptu method often produces.

The Memorized Speech

As its name implies, this type of speech is written out word for word and committed to memory. Although a few speakers are able to use this method effectively, it presents certain problems. Usually memorization results in a stilted, inflexible presentation; the speaker may be either excessively formal and oratorical, or may tend to hurry through the speech—pouring out words with no thought as to their meaning. Using the memorized speech makes it difficult for the speaker to take advantage of audience feedback to adapt and adjust ideas as the speech progresses. If you memorize your speech, you first should write it out to help with recall. Remember that you tend to use more formal language when writing than you do when speaking. Be sure that your speech doesn't sound like a written essay.

The Manuscript Speech

Like the memorized speech, the manuscript speech is written out, but in this method the speaker reads from a text. If extremely careful wording is required—as in the President's messages to Congress, where a slip of the tongue could undermine domestic or foreign policies, or in the presentation of scholarly reports, where exact, concise exposition is required—the manuscript speech is appropriate. Many radio and television speeches also are read from manuscript because of the strict time limits imposed by broadcasting schedules. The ability to read a speech effectively is valuable in certain situations. But this method should not be employed when it is neither useful nor necessary. No matter how experienced you may be, when you read your message, you will inevitably sacrifice some of the freshness and spontaneity necessary for authentic communication. As with the memorized speech, it is difficult to react to audience feedback. Also, the speech may sound somewhat stilted because you used more formal written language. If you use this method, talk through the speech as you are writing it to ensure a sense of oral style.

Many beginning speakers believe a manuscript speech is easy to deliver. That's not true, for you must compensate for your loss of directness with added vigor and vocal variety.

The Extemporaneous Speech

Representing a middle course between the memorized or manuscript speech and the speech that is delivered impromptu, the extemporaneous speech requires careful planning and a detailed outline. Working from an outline, practice the speech aloud, expressing the ideas somewhat differently each time you go through it. Use the outline to fix the order of ideas in your mind, and practice various wordings to develop accuracy, conciseness, and flexibility of expression. If the extemporaneous method is used carelessly, the result will resemble an impromptu speech—a fact which sometimes leads to a confusion of these two terms. A proper use of the method, however, will produce a speech which is nearly as polished as a memorized one and certainly more vigorous, flexible, and spontaneous. With few exceptions the speeches you deliver will probably be extemporaneous. For that reason, most of the advice in this textbook is geared to that method.

Using Your Voice to Communicate

Regardless of your method of presentation, the effectiveness of your speech will depend in large measure on your voice. Your voice is the instrument that helps convey the meaning of your message. The way your voice transfers language can affect how the listener perceives and interprets the meaning of that language.[1] A good voice enables a speaker to make a message clearer and more interesting. Listen to a child at a church or school program rattle off a poem or speak lines in a play. Even though every word may be clearly audible, the child's vocal expression often is so drab and monotonous that the author's ideas are imperfectly conveyed. On the other hand, recall a play-by-play account of a football or baseball game broadcast by skilled sports announcers. Didn't the vividness of their descriptions depend greatly on how they used their voices?

Currently our culture seems to prize one essential vocal quality above all others—a sense of "conversationality." The most successful speakers of our time have cultivated the ability to make the members of an audience feel they are being directly, even intimately, addressed. There is no trick for learning the art of conversationality. It comes primarily from the realization that you are speaking "with," not "at," an audience, that you are addressing a group of living, breathing human beings who want to be talked to as such. Your principal concern, then, as you consider the vocal channel of public speaking, should be mental rather than physical.

However, there are some physical aspects of voice worth thinking about. Because voice is so important in conveying impressions of yourself, in getting clear concepts across to an audience, and in emotionally coloring your thoughts, we will review some general characteristics of an effective voice, and consider ways it can be adapted to particular speaking situations.

A flexible speaking voice has intelligibility, variety, and understandable stress patterns. These vocal attributes comprise the "meanings" public speakers convey to audiences via their use of the vocal fundamentals of communication. Furthermore, the successful speaker is able to employ the voice to emotionally color the ideas captured in the words.

The Effective Speaking Voice
Intelligibility.   "Speak clearly!" "Speak up!" "Slow down!" Each of us has been subjected to such commands throughout most of our lives. People who make these remarks are essentially asking that our speech be more intelligible, more understandable. In normal person-to-person conversation, we all tend to articulate sloppily and to speak more rapidly and softly than we would in public speaking situations. We can

VOCAL CHARACTERISTICS

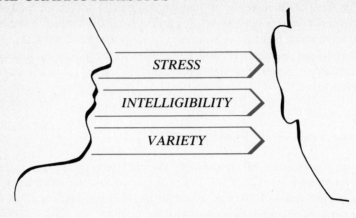

usually do so with no ill effects because we know the people we are talking to and because we are probably only three to five feet apart. But in public speaking, you often are addressing people you do not know and are twenty-five feet or more away from your auditors. In such situations, it is more difficult for you to be understood. To ensure maximum intelligibility while speaking publicly, you must consider four independent but related factors: *(1)* the overall level of loudness at which you speak; *(2)* the rate at which you speak; *(3)* the care with which you enunciate important words; and *(4)* the standard of pronunciation you observe.

Adjusting the loudness level.   Probably the most important single factor in intelligibility is the loudness level at which you speak as related to the *distance* between you and your listeners and the amount of *noise* that is present.[2] Obviously, the farther away your listeners are, the louder you must talk for them to hear you well. Most of us make this loudness-level adjustment unconsciously when projecting our voices over extended distances. What we often forget is that a corresponding adjustment is required when the listeners are only a few feet away. You must realize also that your own voice will always sound louder to you than to your listeners because your own ears are closer to your mouth than theirs are.

In addition to distance, the amount of surrounding noise with which you must compete has an effect on the required loudness level. Even in normal circumstances some noise always is present. For example, the noise level of rustling leaves in the quiet solitude of a country lane (10 decibels) is louder than a whisper six feet away. The noise in empty theaters averages 25 decibels, but with a "quiet" audience it rises to 42. In the average factory, a constant noise of about 80 decibels is characteristic. This is just about the same level as very loud speaking at a close range.

How can you determine the proper strength of voice to use in order to achieve sufficient loudness for the distance and noise conditions of a particular speech situation? You can always use your eyes to see if your auditors appear to be hearing you; even better, you can *ask* them. Get your instructor's advice on this point. Ask your friends to report on the loudness of your voice as you talk in rooms of various sizes and under varying noise conditions. Listen to the sound of your voice so that you can begin to correlate your own vocal production with their reports. You will soon learn to gauge the volume you must use in order to be heard.

Controlling the rate.   In animated conversation, you may well jabber along at 200–250 words per minute. This rate is especially characteristic of people raised in the North, Midwest, Southwest, or West. As words tumble out of your mouth in informal conversational situations, they usually are intelligible because the distance they must travel is short. In large auditoriums or outdoors, however, rapid delivery can impede intelligibility. Echoes can often distort or destroy sounds in rooms, and in outdoor situations words often seem to drift and vanish into the open air.

When addressing larger audiences, then, most of us must slow down to an average of 120–150 words per minute. Obviously, you do not go around timing your speaking rate, but you can remind yourself of potential rate problems as you rise to speak, and, again, you certainly can get feedback from your instructors and your classmates regarding their perceptions of your speaking rate.

All of this is not to say, of course, that you never should speak rapidly. Undoubtedly, there are temperamentally excitable persons who tend to talk rapidly most of the time, and there certainly are situations when a quickened delivery will help you stir and intensify the emotions of your auditors. If you are such a person and if you talk in emotion-charged situations, you will have to learn to compensate. As your rate increases, for example, you must often adjust your volume. And you should almost always take more care in your enunciation of sounds and words.

Enunciating clearly.   *Enunciation* refers to the crispness and precision with which we form words vocally. Most of us are "lip lazy" in normal conversation: we tend to slur sounds, drop out syllables from words, skip over beginnings and endings of words. Careless enunciation may not inhibit communication between intimate friends, but it can seriously undermine a speaker's intelligibility in front of an audience.

When speaking publicly, you may have to force yourself to say "go*ing*" for "go-*in*," "j*u*st" instead of "j*i*st" (which can aurally be mistaken for *gist*), gov*ern*-ment instead of "*guv*-ment." Physiologically, this means opening your mouth a bit more widely than usual, forcing your tongue to move around your mouth, and forming the consonants of English firmly with your lips and tongue. If you are having trouble making your vocal mechanism enunciate well, ask your instructor for some exercises to improve your performance.

Meeting standards of pronunciation.   Related to questions of enunciation or articulation are those of pronunciation and dialect. To be intelligible, not only must you form sounds carefully, but you also must meet audience expectations regarding acceptable pronunciation. If you fail to pronounce words acceptably, your listeners will not be able to grasp easily and quickly the meaning or significance of what you say. And, even if your words are recognized, any peculiarity of pronunciation is almost sure to be noticed by some of the people who hear you. Such a mistake not only may distract their attention from your line of thought, but may also discredit your knowledge and authority as a speaker.

Standards of pronunciation, of course, differ from region to region. These differences we term *dialects*. A dialect is "a variety of language that is used by one group of persons and has features of vocabulary, grammar, and pronunciation distinguishing it from other varieties used by other groups."[3] Thus, your pronunciation of words, together with the ways in which you arrange them grammatically or syntactically, determines your dialect: a British or German "accent," a white Southern or black Northern dialect, a Detroit vernacular, a New England "twang," and so on. Any given dialect has its own rules for pronunciation which may be quite different from the rules of another dialect. When a Midwestern American ear tries to interpret the sounds emitted by a cockney English mouth, noncommunicative confusion may result.

Unfortunately, dialects may produce not only misunderstandings between speakers and listeners, but often they may also produce *negative judgments*—judgments which may seriously affect some auditors' perceptions of the speaker's credibility, education, reliability, responsibility, and capabilities for leadership.[4] This happens because dialects and even professional jargon contribute heavily to what paralinguists call "vocal stereotypes."[5] As a speaker, then, you have to make some serious decisions regarding your accent: Should you learn to talk in the grammar, vocabulary, and vocal patterns of "middle America" when addressing such audiences? Many speakers of dialects are forced to become "bilingual," using the vocal patterns of their own background when talking with local audiences, and patterns we call Midwestern American when facing more varied audiences.

Variety.   As you move from intimate conversation to the enlarged context of public speaking, you may find that you tend to lull an audience with the sameness of your vocal style. You may also discover that many listeners will accuse you of monotony— especially a monotonous pitch or rate. When speaking in a large public setting, you should compensate for the greater distance sounds travel by varying characteristics of your voice. You must learn to vary *rate, pitch, force, and pauses*.

Varying the rate.   Earlier we discussed the overall rate at which one normally speaks. Your speaking rate can also be altered in accordance with the ideas you are expressing and the emotional character of your subject. Consider slowing down to add emphasis to a particular point, or to indicate your own thoughtfulness. And you probably will want to quicken the pace when you are offering general background material or when your ideas are emotionally charged. Observe, for example, how a sports announcer varies speaking rate from play to play, or how an evangelist changes pace regularly. A variable rate helps keep an audience's attention riveted on the speech.

Changing the pitch.   As a public speaker you should concern yourself with three aspects of pitch (the musical "notes" in your speaking voice): *(1) pitch level*—whether your pitch is habitually in the soprano, alto, tenor, baritone, or bass range; *(2) pitch range*—the number of "notes" you actually use while speaking; and *(3) pitch variety*—how often you change the pitch level of your voice. Let's examine each of these aspects separately.

We all have a *habitual pitch level,* which would be charted on a musical score. This you can consider your normal speaking level, and it forms the heart of your vocal communication. Unless you are doing impressions or seeking a job as a low-voiced FM radio announcer, you probably should not tamper with it. You need to think about your habitual pitch level only when you practice to extend your pitch range.

People unaccustomed to speaking publicly often employ too limited a *pitch range*. In normal conversation, you may use only a few notes—even less than an octave—and get away with it. If you talk in a limited range from a podium, however, you may seem monotonous. Given the distances sounds must travel between speaker and audience and the length of time speakers talk, you have to exaggerate, to employ a larger than normal range. Your pitch "highs" must become higher and your "lows" must become lower. Only in this way will you be employing an effective variety and using vocal tones appropriate to the emotional content of your speech. Obviously, you can get carried away. Just as a narrow pitch range communicates boredom or a lack of involvement, an extremely wide pitch range can communicate overenthusiasm, artificiality, or uncontrolled excitement or fear.

The key to successful control of pitch ultimately depends on understanding the importance of *pitch variation*. Pitch variations should be conditioned by two considerations: *(1)* As a general rule, employ higher pitches to communicate excitement, and lower pitches to create a sense of control or solemnity. Use different parts of your range, in other words, for different kinds of emotions. *(2)* Second, let the sense of any particular sentence control pitch variations. Move your voice up at the end of a question; change to higher or lower notes to add emphasis within a particular sentence.

Stress.   A third significant aspect of vocal behavior is stress—the ways in which sounds, syllables, and words are accented. Without vocal stress, everything in a speech would sound the same, and the resulting message would be both incomprehensible and emotionless. Without vocal stress, you would sound like a computer. Vocal stress is achieved in two ways: through vocal emphasis and through the judicious use of pauses.

Adding emphasis.   *Emphasis* refers to the points in a sentence where, principally through increased vocal energy (loudness), changes in intonation (pitch), or variations in speed (rate), one vocally makes certain words or phrases stand out. By emphasis, we mean the way you accent or "attack" words. Emphasis is most often achieved through changes in loudness or energy; variations in loudness can affect the meanings of the sentences you utter. Consider a simple sentence, "Our friends are in the living room." Notice how the meaning varies with the word being emphasized:

1. OUR friends are in the living room. (not *their* friends)
2. Our FRIENDS are in the living room. (not our enemies)
3. Our friends ARE in the living room. (even though you do not think so)
4. Our friends are in THE living room. (the one you and I agree is a special place)
5. Our friends are in the LIVING ROOM. (and not the bedroom)

Without careful control of vocal force, a speaker is liable to utter messages subject to a great many possible meanings. A lack of vocal stress, therefore, not only creates an impression of boredom, but also can cause needless misunderstandings.

Emphasis also is fostered through changes in pitch and rate. Relatively simple changes in pitch, for example, can be used to "tell" an audience where you are in an outline, as when a speaker says,

"My ⌒second point⌒ is ⌒ We must not forget⌒temporary⌒ this: ⌒ workers."

In this sentence, the audience can hear that the speaker has completed one idea and moved on to the next, and that temporary workers will be the principal concern of that section. Variations in rate can operate in the same way. Consider the following sentence:

> "We are a country faced with . . . [moderate rate] balance of payments deficits, racial tensions, an energy crunch, a crisis of morality, unemployment, government waste . . . [fast rate] and-a-stif-ling-na-tion-al-debt." [slow rate]

This speaker has built a vocal freight train. The ideas pick up speed through the accelerating list of problems, and then come to an emphatic halt when the speaker's main concern—the national debt—is mentioned. Such variations in rate essentially communicate to an audience what is and what is not especially important to the speech. Emphasis has been achieved through the control of speaking rate.

Emphasis is an important characteristic of the flexible speaking voice. When talking informally to a friend on the street, we all emphasize "naturally," the way our culture has taught us to communicate. Many people, however, become so stiff when talking from a podium that they retreat to vocal patterns characterized by little force, a single pitch, and a steady rate. They become monotonous, especially when they try to read from a manuscript. Remember that conversationality is your goal when standing before an audience.

Employing helpful pauses.   Pauses are intervals of silence between or within words, phrases, or sentences. Pauses punctuate thought by separating groups of spoken words into meaningful units. When placed immediately before a key idea or the climax of a story, they can create suspense; when placed immediately after a major point or central idea, they add emphasis. Introduced at the proper moment, a dramatic pause may express your feeling more forcefully than words. Clearly, silence can be a highly effective communicative tool if used intelligently and sparingly, and if not embarrassingly prolonged.

Not all pauses, of course, are silent. Sometimes, speakers fill gaps in their discourse with sounds—"umms," "ahs," "ers," "well-uhs," "you knows." No doubt you have heard speakers say, "Today, ah, er, I would like, you know, to speak to you, umm, about a pressing, well-uh, like, a pressing problem facing this, uh, campus." Such vocal intrusions destroy any chance the speaker has of getting a firm, convincing message through to an audience.

Don't be afraid of a little silence. Pauses allow you to achieve stress for important ideas, as the audience awaits the outcome of a story, the key concept toward which you have been building, or the poignant identification of the person you have been describing. Too many pauses, of course, can make you appear manipulative. But strategic silence is an important weapon in the effective oral communicator's arsenal.

Controlling the Emotional Quality

A listener's judgment of a speaker's personality and emotional commitment often centers on that person's vocal quality—the fullness or thinness of the tones, whether or not it is harsh, husky, mellow, nasal, breathy, resonant, and so on. Depending upon your vocal quality, an audience may judge you as being angry, happy, confident, fearful, sincere, sad.

Fundamental to an audience's reaction to your vocal quality are what G. L. Trager calls *emotional characterizers*—a sense of laughing, crying, whispering, inhaling or exhaling, and the like.[6] Physiologically, such characterizers are produced by highly complex adjustments of your vocal mechanism—lips, jaw, tongue, hard and soft palates, throat, and vocal folds. Psychologically, they combine in various ways with the words you speak to communicate different shades of meanings to a listener. Consider, for a moment, a few of the many ways you can say the following sentence:

"Tom's going for pizza tonight with Jane."

First, say it as though you were only *reporting* the fact to a mutual friend. Now say it as though *you cannot believe* Tom is going with Jane. Or, again, as though it is *impossible* Jane would go with Tom. Then indicate that you wish *you were going* instead of Tom or Jane. Next, say it as though you cannot believe Tom is *actually spending money* on pizza when he could be purchasing something less expensive. Finally, say it as though you are *expressing doubts* about Tom's motive—indicate that you think he is after more than pizza on this trip.

As you said that sentence over and over, you not only varied your pitch and loudness, but probably also made some strange and complicated changes in your emotional characterizers. Such changes are important determiners of how a message should be taken or interpreted by listeners, who want to know how you feel (angry, sad) and how they should "take" the message (literally, ironically, satirically, honestly). In brief, the characterizing aspects of voice, or what David Crystal defines as "a single impression of a voice existing throughout the whole of a normal utterance,"[7] are of prime importance in determining the overall or general impression you make on an audience.

While, of course, you cannot completely control such vocal qualities, you can be alert to the effects they are likely to produce in listeners and make adjustments in your voice consistent with the demands of your spoken messages—as you have just done in repeating the simple statement about Tom, Jane, and pizza. We are not urging that you experiment over and over again with every sentence in a speech so as to achieve the desired emotional overtone. We are saying, however, that key ideas and, especially, key evaluations and expressions of your attitudes will be interpreted more accurately by your audience if you consider such characterizers. Keep your repertoire of vocal qualities in the forefront of your mind as you decide whether to yell at, cry with, sneer at, plead with, harp upon, or humble yourself before an audience.

Practicing Vocal Control

Do not assume that you will be able to master in a day or a week all of the vocal skills that have been described. Take time to review and digest the ideas presented. And above all, *practice*. Ask your instructor to provide exercises designed to make your vocal apparatus more flexible—breathing, phonation, resonance, articulation, and control of rate, pause, and inflection. When you are able to control your vocal mechanism, to make it respond to your desires, then you will be able to achieve vocal intelligibility, variety, and stress. You will be able to add the emotional coloring the well-tuned vocal instrument is capable of generating. Remember that any vocal skill, before it can be natural and effective with listeners, must be so much a habit that it will work for you with little conscious effort throughout your oral message. (If advisable, practice the vocal exercises in the Speaker's Resource Book.)

Once your voice can respond as you want it to in the enlarged context of public speaking, you will be able to achieve the sense of *conversationality* so highly valued in our society.

Using Your Body to Communicate

Just as your voice gives meaning to your message through the aural channel, your physical behavior carries meaning through the visual channel. While the audience is using the aural channel to grasp your ideas, it is simultaneously using the visual message you send to add clarity. You can use the two complementary channels to create a better understanding of your presentation.[8] To help you explore ways of enhancing the use of the visual channel, we will examine the speaker's physical behavior on the platform.

Dimensions of Nonverbal Communication

In recent years a growing body of research has emphasized the important roles that physical or nonverbal behaviors play in effective oral communication.[9] Basically, those roles can be reduced to three generalizations: *(1)* Speakers reveal and reflect their emotional states by their nonverbal behaviors in front of audiences. Your listeners read your feelings toward yourself, your topic, and your audience from your facial expressions, from the way you stand and walk, from what you do with your head, arms, shoulders, and hands. Summarizing a good deal of research into nonverbal communication processes, communications scholar Dale G. Leathers has noted: "Feelings and emotions are more accurately exchanged by nonverbal than verbal means. . . . The nonverbal portion of communication conveys meanings and intentions that are relatively free of deception, distortion, and confusion."[10] *(2)* The nonverbal cues which emanate from a speaker can enrich or elaborate the message which comes through words. A solemn face can reinforce the dignity of a funeral eulogy. The words, "Either you can do this or you can do that," can be illustrated with appropriate arm-and-hand gestures. Taking a few steps to the left or right "tells" an audience that you are moving from one argument to another. *(3)* As we noted in Chapter 2, nonverbal messages can be sent from the audience back to the speaker, providing useful feedback in the form of frowns, smiles, nervous shifting, and the like.

In other words, nonverbal communication is a two-way street, with messages sent both from speaker to listener and from listener back to speaker. Because we already have discussed feedback, we will concentrate here upon the speaker's control of "body language." Such language can usefully be discussed under four heads: *(1)* proxemics (the use of space), *(2)* movement and stance, *(3)* facial expressions, and *(4)* gestures.

COMMON STANCES OF THE PUBLIC SPEAKER

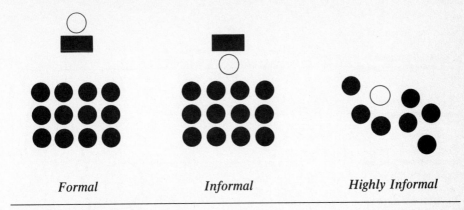

| Formal | Informal | Highly Informal |

Proxemics.   One of the most important but perhaps least recognized aspects of non-verbal communication is *proxemics,* or the use of space. Two components of proxemics are especially relevant to public speakers:

1. *Physical Arrangements*—the layout of the room in which you are speaking, including the presence or absence of a lectern, the seating plan, location of chalkboards and similar aids, and physical barriers between you and your audience.

2. *Distance*—the degree of separation between you and your audience.[11]

Each of these components influences how well you can communicate publicly. Most public speaking situations include an audience seated or standing, a lectern or table, and a speaker facing the audience. Objects in the physical space—the lectern, table, flags—tend to set the speaker apart from the listeners. This "setting apart" is both physical and psychological. Literally as well as figuratively, objects can stand in the way of open and free communicative exchange. As a result, especially if you are trying to create a relatively informal and direct atmosphere, you will want to reduce those barriers. Some speakers talk from beside a lectern instead of behind it. Others stand in front of it, or even sit on the front edge of a table while talking. There is no single rule for using space. Rather, consider the formality of the occasion (working from behind a lectern is more formal and therefore is better suited to lectures, presentations, prepared reports, and the like); the nature of the material you are offering (you may need a lectern to read from if you are dealing with statistics or extensively quoted material); and your personal characteristics (some speakers need the "protection" provided by a lectern, while others feel much more comfortable speaking beside or in front of it). Your instructor can give you further advice.

The distance component of proxemics adds a second set of considerations. Speakers in most situations are talking over what Edward T. Hall has termed a "public distance"—twelve feet or more away from their listeners.[12] To communicate with people at that distance, you obviously cannot rely on your normal speaking voice, minute changes in posture or muscle tone, and so forth. Instead, you must compensate for the

CLASSIFICATION OF INTERHUMAN DISTANCE

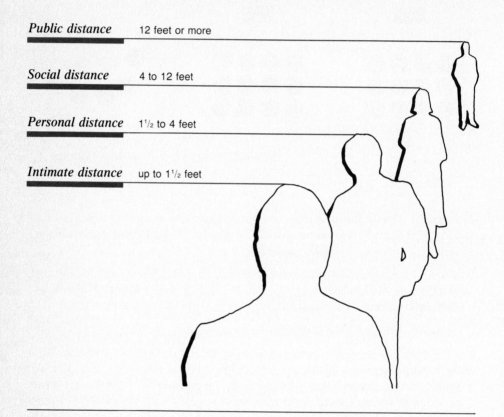

Public distance   12 feet or more

Social distance   4 to 12 feet

Personal distance   1¹/₂ to 4 feet

Intimate distance   up to 1¹/₂ feet

distance by employing larger gestures, broader shifts of your body from place to place, and increased vocal energy. Perhaps the necessity to communicate in larger terms, with bigger-than-usual movements, is one of the qualities which makes public speaking such a new and strange experience to some people. With practice, however, you can acquire and refine the techniques of effective nonverbal delivery, and can overcome these fears and feelings of strangeness.

Movement and Stance.   How you move and stand provides a second set of nonverbal cues for your audience. *Movement* includes shifts you make from one spot to another during the delivery of a speech; *posture* refers to the relative relaxation or rigidity of your body, as well as to your overall stance (erect, slightly bent forward or backward, or slumping).

Purposive movements can communicate ideas about yourself to an audience. The speaker who stands stiffly and erectly may, without uttering a word, be saying either "This is a formal occasion" or "I am tense, even afraid, of this audience." The speaker who leans forward, physically reaching out to the audience, is saying silently but eloquently "I am interested in you. I want you to understand and accept my ideas." Sitting casually on the front edge of a table and assuming a relaxed posture communicate informality and a readiness to engage in a dialogue with your listeners.

Movements and postural adjustments *regulate* communication. As a public speaker, you may, for instance, move from one end of a table to the other to indicate a change in topic; or you may accomplish the same purpose simply by changing your posture. At other times, you may move toward your audience when making an especially important point. In each case, you are using your body to signal to your audience that you are making a change or transition in the subject matter of the speech, or are dealing with a matter of special concern.

An equally important point to remember is that your posture and movements can also work against you. Aimless and continuous pacing back and forth is distracting. A nervous bouncing up and down or swaying from side to side will make the audience tense and uneasy. If you adopt an excessively erect stance, you may lose rapport with your listeners. Your movements, in other words, should be purposive. Only then will stance and movement help your communicative effort and produce the sense of self-assurance and control you want to exhibit. [13]

Facial Expressions.   Your face is another important nonverbal message channel. When you speak, your facial expressions function in a number of ways. First, they communicate much about yourself and your feelings. What Paul Ekman and Wallace V. Friesen call *affect displays* are given to an audience via your face. That is, an audience scans your face to see how you feel about yourself and how you feel about them. [14] Second, facial details provide listeners with cues that help them *interpret the contents* of your message: Are you being ironic or satirical? How sure are you of some conclusion you have stated? Is this a harsh or a pleasant message? Psychologist Albert Mehrabian has devised a formula to account for the emotional impact of a speaker's message. Words, he says, contribute 7 percent, vocal elements 38 percent, and facial expressions 55 percent. [15] And third, the "display" elements of your face—your eyes especially—establish a *visual bonding* between you and your hearers. The speaker who looks down at the floor instead of at listeners, who reads excessively from notes or a manuscript, or who delivers a speech to the back wall has severed visual bonding. Our culture has come to expect eye-to-eye contact from speakers who are deemed "earnest," "sincere," "forthright," "self-assured." In other words, it is in part through regular eye contact with individuals in your audience that you establish your *credibility*, that you convince your audience that you are a trustworthy, sincere, dynamic human being. [16]

Of course, you cannot control your face completely, which is probably why listeners search it so carefully for clues to your feelings, but you can make sure that your facial messages do not belie your verbal ones. In practical terms this means that when you are uttering angry words, your face should be communicating anger; when you are sincerely pleading with your listeners, your eyes should be looking at them intently. In short, use your face to maximum communicative advantage.

Gestures.   Gestures include purposeful movements of the head, shoulders, arms, hands, or some other part of the body. Fidgeting with your clothing or aimlessly rearranging note cards on the lectern are not gestures because they are not purposeful, and they distract from, rather than support or illustrate, the ideas you are expressing. The public speaker commonly employs three kinds of gestures:

1. *Conventional Gestures*—signs or symbols which have had specific meanings assigned to them by custom or convention. The raised-hand "stop" gesture of the policeman directing traffic, the hand-and-finger language of deaf persons, and the arm signals of football referees are examples of conventional gestures.

2. *Descriptive Gestures*—signs or symbols which depict or describe more or less directly the idea to be communicated. Speakers, for example, often describe the size, shape, or location of an object by movements of hands and arms. They may extend an upraised arm to indicate the height of a stranger. They may make hand-and-finger motions to help describe what a punch press looks like or to demonstrate the successive steps in its use.

3. *Indicators*—movements of the hands, arms, or other parts of the body which represent feelings. Thus, speakers may throw up their arms when disgusted, pound the lectern when angry, shrug their shoulders when puzzled, or point a threatening finger when issuing a warning. In using such indicators or signs, speakers are in a sense trying to transmit their own feelings directly to their listeners.[17]

In sum, gestures aid the speaker in three important ways: *(1) Pictorialization.* Gestures can be used to "draw pictures" for the audience, especially to indicate sizes, shapes, and relationships between objects. Such pictures depend primarily upon what we have called descriptive gestures. *(2) Condensation.* Gestures, particularly conventional gestures, may take the place of words in many instances. They can be shorthand movements for things it would take many words to describe fully. *(3) Arousal.* Gestures often work with facial expressions to communicate your state of mind to the audience. Indicators are especially important in this regard because an audience usually reads not only your face but also the rest of your body for cues concerning how your message is to be interpreted.

Characteristics of effective gestures.   Although you can perfect your gestures only through practice, you will obtain better results if, as you practice, you keep in mind three characteristics of effective gestures: *(1) relaxation, (2) vigor and definiteness,* and *(3) proper timing.*

When your muscles are strained or tense, you have difficulty expressing yourself naturally, and awkward gestures result. One of the best ways to relax is to move about. "Warm up" by taking a few easy steps or by unobtrusively arranging your notes or papers. To avoid stiffness and awkwardness, make a conscious effort to relax your muscles before you start to speak.

Good gestures are lively, vigorous, and definite. Put enough force in them to make them convincing; a limp shaking of your fist is a poor way to make an impression upon an audience. Make them big enough to be seen and accurately interpreted by your listeners. A tiny hand movement behind the lectern can be seen by no one but yourself, and hence is not "telling" the audience anything. And make them carefully: a badly executed conventional gesture or sloppy descriptive gesture looks like confused, random arm movements to your listeners. Liveliness and definiteness are important; listeners then will sense your enthusiasm and conviction.

Timing likewise is crucial to effective gestures. Try making a gesture after the word or phrase it was intended to reinforce has already been spoken, and observe the ridiculous result. The stroke of a gesture—that is, the shake of a fist, the movement of a finger, or the downward movement of an arm—should fall exactly on or slightly precede the point the gesture is supposed to be emphasizing. If you practice making gestures until they become habitual and then use them spontaneously as the impulse arises, you will have no trouble on this score.

Overall, remember one major point about bodily communication with audiences: Speakers can and should practice bodily movement, facial expressions, and gestures, *but* they should never try to reproduce exactly the movements they've practiced when speaking to live audiences. This may sound odd, especially to people who are anxious about how they'll sound and look to an audience. Yet, speech teacher after speech teacher, student after student has had to learn that lesson. If you try to reproduce at the lectern everything you practiced back in your room, you'll almost inevitably run into trouble. You'll be so busy talking to yourself in your head—"How did I show this relationship yesterday? Am I supposed to look angry or just concerned in this part of my speech? Should I move to the left or the right?"—that you'll likely fall apart right there in front of everybody.

Rather, practice movements, facial expressions, and gestures, but do so to get a "feel" for them. Your goal is to practice so that particular kinds of movements, expressions, and gestures don't seem odd or foreign to you; so that you're used to moving a bit more, making facial expressions broader and gestures more widely when speaking publicly than you do when talking quietly with friends at intimate distances. Once you're used to moving, expressing feelings, and gesturing, then the visual channels of oral communication will be working for you, not against you.

Using Nonverbal Channels: Strategic Choices

Although you never can control completely your vocal and bodily behavior, you can gain skills in orchestrating your movements and voice. Although we have talked in Part Three about language, visual aids, voice, and body as separate channels—and they are—nevertheless you must remember that they work together while you are speaking to others. You should not attempt to control your messages in each channel separately and continuously; however, you should make fundamental choices about how to present your oral messages to audiences. As we conclude this chapter and section, let us review some of those choices.

1. *Start with your "self."* You must always begin, of course, with your "self"— with self-directed questions about whether you are basically quiet and reticent or excitable and extroverted; whether you enjoy vigorous physical activity or avoid exertion; whether you talk easily on your feet or prefer to sit while talking; whether you're comfortable with broad movements or not; whether you feel silly shouting at an audience or not. The point is, you should *(1)* not try to copy some speaker

you've heard and admire if your personality is very different from that person's, and *(2)* not reach for delivery techniques which are unnatural to your self-image. In our culture, there is a rather broad range of acceptable modes of public speaking— from the wild, excitable, rhythmic delivery patterns of a Jesse Jackson or a Joan Rivers to the soothing, calm, contemplative delivery patterns of a Charles Kuralt or a Barbara Walters. Don't model yourself on someone else; learn to work publicly as the person you really are.

2. *Plan a proxemic relationship with your audience which reflects your own needs and attitudes toward your subject and listeners.* If you feel more at home behind the lectern, plan to have it placed accordingly. If you want your whole body visible to the audience, yet feel the need to have notes at eye level, stand beside the lectern and arrange your cards on it. If you want to relax your body—and are sure you can compensate for the resulting loss of action by increasing your vocal volume—sit behind a table or desk. If you feel physically free and want to be wholly "open" to your audience, stand in front of a table or desk. As far as possible, make the physical arrangements work for you.

3. *The farther you are from your listeners, the more important it is for them to have a clear view of you.* The speaker who crouches behind a lectern in an auditorium of three hundred people soon loses contact with them. The farther away your audience is, the harder you must work to project your words and the broader your physical movements must be. Think about large lecture classes you have attended, sermons you have heard in large churches, or political rallies you have attended. Recall delivery patterns of speakers who worked well in such situations, and choose and modify those that might also work for you.

4. *Insofar as practical, adapt the physical setting to the visual aids you plan to use.* If you are going to use such visual aids as a chalkboard, flipchart, working model, or process diagram, remove the tables, chairs, and other objects which would obstruct the listeners' view and therefore impair their understanding of your messages.

5. *Adapt the size of your gestures, the amount of your movement, and the volume of your voice to the size of audience.* Keeping in mind what Edward Hall noted about public distance in communication, you should realize that subtle changes of facial expressions, small movements of your fingers, and small changes of vocal characteristics cannot be detected when you are twenty-five feet or more from your listeners. Although many auditoriums have a raised platform and a slanted floor to allow a speaker to be seen and heard more clearly, you should, nonetheless, adjust to the physical conditions.

6. *Regularly scan your audience from side to side and from front to back, establishing eye contact with specific individuals.* This does not mean, of course, that your head is to be in constant motion. *Regularly* does not imply rhythmical, nonstop bobbing. Rather, it implies that you must be aware—and must let an audience know you are aware—of the entire group of human beings in front of you. Take them all into your field of vision periodically; establish firm visual bonds with them. Such bonds enhance your credibility and keep listeners' attention from wandering.

7. *Use your body to communicate your feelings about what you are saying.* When you are angry, don't be afraid to gesture vigorously. When you're expressing tenderness, let that message come across a relaxed face. In other words, when you are communicating publicly, employ the same emotional indicators you do when you are talking on a one-to-one basis.

8. *Use your body to regulate the pace of your presentation and to control transitions.* Shift your weight as you move from one idea to another. Move more when you are speaking rapidly. When you are slowing down to emphasize particular ideas, decrease bodily and gestural action accordingly. What these changes in movement and action do, as we've noted before, is allow your listeners to get the same message across multiple communication channels. Your words, your vocal characteristics, and your physical movements, when orchestrated, mutually reinforce each other and hence emphatically drive home your ideas.

9. *Adjust both vocal characteristics and head movements when you must use a microphone.* If you're ever interviewed or if you have occasion to speak to a large audience in a room with a public address system, you'll be confronted with a threatening device: a microphone. Mikes can create terror in some speakers in two ways: *(1)* If you're being interviewed or are broadcasting a talk or interview, you have to watch your pronunciation, as the mike tends to "explode" certain sounds; and you must keep an optimal distance—not too close and not too far away—from the mike, which freezes your body in one position. *(2)* When using a public address system in a large auditorium, you can easily become disoriented because your voice seems to come back to you; about the time you're trying to form the third word in an important sentence, your first two words have bounced off the back wall and come running for your ears.

There's not much you can do about either set of problems, outside of avoiding microphones altogether. You can, however, minimize the terror and disorientation produced by mikes:

- Practice with mikes before you go on live. Especially if you're doing an interview, you can practice in your own room, with any object playing the part of the microphone. If you're going to talk over a public address system, see if you can get into the room ahead of time, to practice maintaining the right distance away from the mike.
- Slow down a bit when talking to others via a public address system. If you slow down, those first two words already will have reverberated before you say the third and fourth words. And soon, you'll not even notice your own voice coming back to your ears.
- Remember to decrease your volume and to minimize variations in volume. Think of speaking into a microphone as speaking at an intimate distance—the equivalent of five or six inches from someone's ear. At the intimate distance, you talk more softly than in normal conversation, and you usually don't vary your volume (from quiet whispers to overpowering shouts) so much. Cut the shouting especially.
- Likewise, pay special attention to articulation. If you're normally a bit "lip lazy," you'll have to form words more carefully into a mike. And if you nor-

When using a microphone (especially outdoors), articulate carefully, reduce your speed if you are getting electronic feedback, and keep a steady distance from the mike.

mally "pop your plosives"—vocally hit your *p*'s and *b*'s—hold back. Keep the build-up of air behind those sounds under conscious control for a bit. Soon, you'll "naturally" keep them controlled. (Don't worry: If you aren't under control, you'll hear the mike "explosions" yourself and remember to adjust.)

10. *Finally, use your full repertoire of descriptive and regulative gestures while talking publicly.* You probably do this in everyday conversation without even thinking about it; re-create that same attitude when addressing an audience. Physical readiness is the key. Keep your hands and arms free and loose so that you can call them into action easily, quickly, naturally. Let your hands rest comfortably at your sides, relaxed but in readiness. Occasionally, rest them on the lectern. Then, as you unfold the ideas of your speech, use descriptive gestures to indicate size,

shape, or relationship, making sure the movements are large enough to be seen in the back row. Use conventional gestures also to give visual dimension to your spoken ideas. Keep in mind that there are no "right" number of gestures that you ought to use. However, during the preparation of your talk, think of the kinds of bodily and gestural actions that will complement your personality, ideas, language, and speaking purposes.

Selecting the appropriate method of presentation and using your voice and body productively to communicate will enhance your chances of gaining support for your ideas. The key to the effective use of these elements is *practice*. Through practice, both by yourself and in speech classrooms, you can better select a method of presentation. You also will have more opportunities to see how your voice and body reinforce or detract from your ideas. The more confident you feel about presenting your speech, the more comfortable you will be, and confidence is built through careful preparation and practice.

REFERENCE NOTES

[1]For examples of how the listener uses voice to judge the speaker, see David W. Addington, "The Relationship of Selected Vocal Characteristics to Personality Perception," *Speech Monographs* 35 (November 1968): 492–503; L. S. Harms, "Listener Judgments of Status Cues in Speech," *Quarterly Journal of Speech* 47 (April 1961): 164–68; Robert Hopper and Frederick Williams, "Speech Characteristics and Employability," *Speech Monographs* 40 (November 1973): 296–302; James D. Moe, "Listener Judgments of Status Cues in Speech: A Replication and Extension," *Speech Monographs* 39 (November 1972): 144–47.

[2]The term *loudness* is here used synonymously with *intensity* because the former term is clearer to most people. Technically, of course, *loudness*—a distinct function in the science of acoustics—is not strictly synonymous with *intensity*. To explain the exact relationships between the two terms is beyond the scope of this book because the explanation involves many complicated psychophysical relationships. For a full discussion of these relationships, see Stanley S. Stevens and Hallowell Davis, *Hearing: Its Psychology and Physiology* (New York: John Wiley & Sons, Inc., 1938), pp. 110ff.

[3]By permission. From *Webster's Third New International Dictionary* © 1981 by Merriam-Webster® Inc., Publishers of the Merriam-Webster Dictionaries.

[4]In support of these ideas see Mark L. Knapp, *Essentials of Nonverbal Communication* (New York: Holt, Rinehart & Winston, 1980).

[5]Studies of vocal stereotyping may be found in W. E. Lambert, H. Frankel, and G. R. Tucker, "Judging Personality Through Speech: A French-Canadian Example," *Journal of Communication* 16 (1966): 312–13; David W. Addington, "The Relationship of Selected Vocal Characteristics to Personality Perception," *Speech Monographs* 35 (1968): 492–503; W. J. Weaver and R. J. Anderson, "Voice and Personality Interrelationships," *Southern Speech Communication Journal* 38 (1973): 275–78; and B. L. Brown, W. J. Strong, and A. C. Rencher, "The Effects of Simultaneous Manipulations of Rate, Mean Fundamental Frequency, and Variance of Fundamental Frequency on Ratings of Personality From Speech," *Journal of the Acoustical Society of America* 55 (1974): 313–18. (The last study is particularly interesting because it offers advice on ways of altering vocal stereotypes.)

[6]For an analysis of emotional or vocal characterizers, see George L. Trager, "Paralanguage: A First Approximation," *Studies in Linguistics* 13 (1958): 1–13.

[7]David Crystal, *Prosodic Systems and Intonation in English* (Cambridge: University Press, 1959), p. 123.

[8]See, for example, Haig Bosmajian, ed., *The Rhetoric of Nonverbal Communication* (Glenview, IL: Scott, Foresman and Company, 1971); Paul Ekman, "Differential Communication of Affect by Head and Body Cues," *Journal of Personality and Social Psychology* 2 (November 1965): 726–35; Julius Fast, *Body Language* (New York: M. Evans & Co., Inc., 1970); Edward T. Hall, *The Silent Language* (New York: Doubleday & Company, Inc., 1973); Mark L. Knapp, *Nonverbal Communication in Human Interaction,* 2nd ed. (New York: Holt, Rinehart & Winston, Inc., 1978); Albert Mehrabian, "Communication Without Words," *Psychology Today* 2 (September 1968): 52–55; B. G. Rosenberg and Jonas Langer, "A Study of Postural-Gestural Communication," *Journal of Personality and Social Psychology* 2 (October 1965): 593–97.

[9]Most of this research is summarized in three books: Randall P. Harrison, *Beyond Words: An Introduction to Nonverbal Communication* (Englewood Cliffs, N.J.: Prentice-Hall, Inc., 1974); Mark L. Knapp, *Nonverbal Communication in Human Interaction,* 2nd ed. (New York: Holt, Rinehart & Winston, Inc., 1978); and Dale G. Leathers, *Nonverbal Communication Systems* (Boston: Allyn & Bacon, Inc., 1976).

[10]Dale G. Leathers, *Nonverbal Communication Systems* (Boston: Allyn & Bacon, Inc., 1976), pp. 4–5.

[11]For a fuller discussion of each of these components, see Leathers, pp. 52–59.

[12]Hall divides interhuman communication distances into four segments: *intimate distance*—up to 1½ feet apart; *personal distance*—1½ to 4 feet; *social distance*—4 to 12 feet; and *public distance*—12 feet or more. On the basis of these distinctions he has carefully noted how people's eye contact, tone of voice, and ability to touch and observe change from one distance to another. See Edward T. Hall, *The Hidden Dimension* (New York: Doubleday & Company, Inc., 1969), Chapter X, "Distances in Man."

[13]See F. Deutsch, "Analysis of Postural Behavior," *Psychoanalytic Quarterly* 16 (1947): 195–213; W. James, "A Study of the Expression of Bodily Posture," *Journal of General Psychology* 7 (1932): 405–36; Albert Mehrabian, "Significance of Posture and Position in the Communication of Attitude and Status Relationships," *Psychological Bulletin* 71 (1969): 359–72.

[14]An excellent review of research on facial communication can be found in Leathers, Chapter 2. Those wishing a larger treatment should see Paul Ekman, Wallace V. Friesen, and P. Ellsworth, *Emotion in the Human Face: Guidelines for Research and an Integration of Findings* (New York: Pergamon Press, Inc., 1972).

[15]"How to Read Body Language," by Flora Davis. *Glamour Magazine,* September 1969.

[16]For a difficult but rewarding essay on the management of demeanor, see Erving Goffman, *Interaction Ritual: Essays on Face-to-Face Behavior* (New York: Doubleday & Company, Inc., 1967), "On Face-Work," pp. 5–46.

[17]For a more complete system for classifying gestures, see Paul Ekman and Wallace V. Friesen, "Hand Movements," *Journal of Communication* 22 (December 1972): 360.

PROBLEMS AND PROBES

1. Divide the class into teams and play charades. (Those needing rules for classroom games should read David Jauner, "Charades as a Teaching Device," *Speech Teacher* 20 [November 1971]: 302). A game of charades not only will loosen you up psychologically but will help sensitize you to the variety of small but perceptible cues you "read" when interpreting messages.

2. Meet briefly in task groups to determine which of the four methods of speaking would be most appropriate in each of the following situations. Choose a reporter to convey the group's justification for selections to the class.

a. A college president addressing her faculty on the goals of the college for the school year.

b. A student's response to his speech professor when asked what he hoped to learn in the course.

c. A president of a large company reporting to all administrative personnel on the success/failure of the company for the past year.

d. A student participating in the National Oratorical contest.

e. An alumna of a local high school attending a reunion and being asked to comment on the adequacy of her high-school training for college.

f. A sales representative attempting to get the board of directors of a business chain to use his advertising agency.

ORAL ACTIVITIES

1. Can your speaking voice be easily understood? As a test of your intelligibility, the instructor may ask you to deliver a short speech with your back to the audience. Stand in approximately the same position where you normally do when speaking to the class.

2. Your instructor will provide the class with a list of emotions. Each student is to choose one emotion and to decide on a number. Using only vocal cues and speaking only that number, each student is to try to express that emotion. The class should try to guess what emotion is being expressed. After each attempt, the class should suggest additional cues that will help the speaker express the emotion.

3. Present a two- or three-minute speech explaining to the class how to do something: drive a golf ball, bowl, perform a sleight-of-hand trick, cut out a shirt, tie some difficult knots, or play a musical instrument. Use movement and gestures to help make your ideas clear. Do not use the chalkboard or previously prepared diagrams.

4. Prepare and present a short speech describing some exciting event you have witnessed—an automobile accident, a political or campus rally, a sporting event. Use movement and gestures to render the details clear and vivid. That is, the audience should be able to "see" and "feel" the event as you integrate words/ideas and movements/actions for maximum impact. Successful completion of this assignment should demonstrate your ability to employ all of the available message systems.

PART FOUR

PUBLIC SPEAKING:

Types and Occasions

CHAPTER 15

Speeches to Inform

Ours is a society which almost worships "the facts." Particularly because of such technological developments as electronic media, photostatic printing, computerized data storage and retrieval systems, and miniaturized circuits, a staggering amount of information is available to us. Mere information, however, makes no decisions by itself; information is all but useless until it is shaped and interpreted by human beings, who then can employ it for the betterment of themselves and their society. As a speaker, you often will be called upon to assemble, package, and present information to others.

In this chapter we will discuss various types of informative speeches, outlining their essential features and reviewing some of their structural characteristics.

Types of Informative Speeches

Fundamentally, as we have noted previously, the main purpose of a speech to inform is to secure understanding among listeners. Creating understanding is not a matter of parading knowledge or endless facts and figures before an audience. People, after all, seek information and understanding from speakers only to meet their perceived needs. Like all other oral transactions, informative speeches depend on the speaker's sensitivity to listeners' purposes, knowledge, and attitudes.

Because these needs, purposes, level of knowledge, and attitudes vary from situation to situation, informative speeches take many different forms. Some forms are no more complicated than the set of oral instructions you receive as you are about to begin a midterm examination; others—such as those used in scientific reports offered at academic conventions—can be understood only by specialists in a field of endeavor. Although the range of these forms is great, four types of informative speeches—*speeches of denotation, demonstrations and instructions, oral reports,* and *explanations*—are given so frequently that they merit special attention.[1]

Speeches of Denotation

Speeches of denotation offer an audience a vocabulary for dealing with concepts it already knows, or present a vocabulary that identifies some aspect of the world about which the listeners know little. Almost everyone gives and listens to these sorts of speeches regularly. When you start college, someone tells you what an Associate of Arts degree or a core requirement is. When you take your first astronomy course, you are introduced to black holes in the universe. When you buy your first house, the realtor explains what earnest money is. These messages give you words for dealing with concepts unfamiliar to you.

In a junior high school science class, a teacher discusses weather changes by referring to the jet stream, high and low pressure domes, and humidity. A television talk show guest urges that you think of children not as private possessions, but as pre-adults having the same basic human rights and responsibilities as older people. Politicians insist that we stop piecemeal attacks on the social services system in this country and find more fundamental ways to break the welfare syndrome. These are messages delivered by speakers trying to get you to look at familiar objects, people, and processes in a new light.

Notice that most of these examples of speeches have two characteristics: *(1)* You are offered a *vocabulary*—"core requirements," "black holes," "earnest money"—for dealing with the objects, people, and processes under consideration, and *(2)* you are given an *orientation,* a way of thinking about some phenomenon. The idea of "core requirements," for example, forces you to think about intellectual breadth—the liberal arts—as a goal for your college education; previously you may have thought about higher education as only preparation for a career. The notion of "the welfare syndrome" forces you to look beyond food stamps, unemployment compensation, and Social Security checks in order to visualize what is essentially a separate subculture in this country, one with its own ways of thinking and acting. A good denotative speech, therefore, provides listeners with symbols to which they can attach ideas, and with conceptualizations that organize bits and pieces of information into coherent wholes.

Demonstrations and Instructions

Instructions and demonstrations are the kinds of informative speeches with which you have been familiar since childhood. In a complex culture, classroom instructions, job instructions, and instructions for the performance of special tasks play a vital role. Teachers instruct students in ways of preparing assignments. Supervisors tell their subordinates how a task should be performed. Leaders explain to volunteer workers their duties in a fund-raising drive or a cleanup campaign. For convenience, such

Ours is a "show-and-tell" culture. Successful communicators are able to coordinate their ideas and their speaking habits with a number of visual aids to demonstrate concepts and processes.

instructions usually are given to a group of persons rather than to individuals, and, even when written, often are accompanied by oral explanations that amplify and clarify the written material. The feedback mechanisms provided in public speaking are especially important and valuable when instructions are offered.

Frequently, however, we have to do more than "tell." We also have to "show" people how to carry out the desired actions. A demonstration speech is one in which a speaker describes to an audience the steps involved and the physical and mental skills required to carry out a certain task. A supervisor may need to walk through new office procedures even while telling employees about them. An instructor in an art class usually gives careful, step-by-step instructions in how to prepare a canvas while actually doing it.

Speeches of demonstration and of instruction have two essential features: *(1)* Both involve the *serial presentation* of information, usually in clearly defined steps or phases. They normally are organized, therefore, in chronological and/or spatial patterns. *(2)* Both demand *utter clarity,* simply because your listeners are expected to be able to repeat or reproduce the steps through which you have instructed them.

Oral Reports

An *oral report* is a speech in which one assembles, arranges, and interprets information gathered in response to a request made by some group. A business firm may ask one of its members to assemble statistics relative to employment, sales, or cost overruns; a congressional committee may call in outside experts to offer testimony; a club may ask its treasurer to report on patterns or trends in its finances over a specified period; or a college might wish its registrar to report to the faculty on steps the school can take to recruit more students with particular backgrounds or interests. As these examples indicate, we may usefully think of two basic types of reportive speeches: the *factual report* concentrates upon assembling, arranging, and interpreting raw information; and the *advisory report* makes a set of recommendations relative to information which has been prepared.

As a reporter, you should be aware of certain restrictions. Above all, bear constantly in mind your role as an *expert*—the *source* of predigested information for an assemblage of people who, in turn, will act upon it. That role carries with it tremendous responsibilities. It demands that you prepare with special care and that you present your material with clarity and balance. The success of a business firm, the government's legislative program, or your club's future—all may depend upon your reporting abilities. Therefore, keep the following guidelines in mind as you prepare and deliver your report:

1. *The information you present must be researched with great care.* Although you may be asked only to present a series of statistical generalizations in a short, five-minute report, your research must be extensive and solid. You must assemble your material cleanly, free of bias or major deficiency. The quarterly report for a business which relies upon material gathered from only one of the territories in which it operates may not only be partial, but also skewed. Furthermore, even though you may be asked only to report the bare facts of your information, in a question-and-answer session you could be asked to expand upon what you say—to supply the figures on which you based your statistical conclusions. Have all of your information available even if you are allotted only a short time for your actual presentation.

2. *When making recommendations rather than merely reporting information, be sure to include a complete rationale for the advice you present.* Suppose, for example, that you have been called upon by your student-government council to recommend how certain developmental monies should be spent. First, you will need to gather information on specific needs: Does this campus require additional buses (and should you, therefore, recommend further subsidy for public transportation)? Could it use more student-sponsored scholarships? Might it profit from a "careers week" during which recruiters from various businesses, industries, and other endeavors hold special seminars for interested students? To make recommendations on these needs, you must have financial information on the costs incurred in filling each demand. Second, you will need to assemble data on student interest, based upon interviews and patterns of usage observed in the past. Third, in order to make sound recommendations, you will have to rank the options open to the group. Fourth, you will need to build a rationale for your ranking, including answers to such questions as: What student needs will each course of action meet? Why do you consider one need more pressing than the other? Why should student government, and not some other college or university agency, act to meet that need? Were student government to act on a specific need, what other kinds of university, community, and/or governmental supports would be forthcoming over the short and long term?

Answers to such questions in each case provide the rationale for decision. This is important for two reasons: *(1)* Such a rationale enhances your image or credibility because it demonstrates your ability to think through and rationally solve problems. Unless your credibility is strong, your recommendations have little chance for action. *(2)* More importantly, if your rationale is a good one, it probably will be adopted by the audience as a whole; for the audience, in turn, has constituencies—the student body, specific organizations represented on the government council, and so on—to which it must answer when it takes action. In other words, by making recommendations and also offering reasons, you allow your auditors to meet objections, to urge the action, and so on in the important second step of persuasion—the appeal to secondary audiences.

3. *Make full use of visual aids when giving reports.* Because reports often have to be short and to the point and yet contain a great amount of information, the reporter must decide how to present a maximum amount of useful material in the shortest period of time. The advice on the employment of visual aids presented in Chapter 13 (pages 257–60) is germane.

4. *Whatever you do, stay within the boundaries of your report-making charge.* As a reporter, you are a conduit—a pipeline between the audience and some subject of interest. You therefore must be highly sensitive to the audience's expectations: Were you charged with gathering information only? Or were you told what kind of information to bring in? Did your instructions say to assemble recommendations for action? Were you to include financial and impact analyses along with those recommendations? Most reporters are given a charge, a duty to perform. If you depart too far from that charge—if you make recommendations when you are expected only to gather information, *or* if you only gather information when you have been asked to make recommendations—you are likely to create ill will among your listeners. When this occurs, your work often will be for naught; you will have failed as a reporter. So clarify the boundaries within which you are operating; when given a task, ask for relevant instructions. In that way, as you discharge your duties, you probably will satisfy the group and, consequently, will also increase (or at least not decrease) your own credibility and status.

Explanations

An explanatory speech is one in which the speaker either *(1)* makes clear the nature of a concept, process, thing, or proposal, or *(2)* offers a supporting rationale for a contestable claim. The notion of "making clear" means that speeches of explanation have much in common with denotative messages, because one function of a denotation is to clarify. Normally, though, an explanatory speech is less concerned with the word or vocabulary than it is with connecting one concept with a series of others. For example, a denotative speech on political corruption would concentrate on the term, telling us what sorts of acts committed by politicians are comprehended by the term. An explanatory speech on corruption, however, would go into more depth, indicating perhaps the social-political conditions likely to produce corruption or the methods that are available for eliminating it. The "making clear" involved in an explanatory speech, therefore, is considerably broader and more complex than that demanded of a denotative speech.

However, the key to most explanatory speeches lies in the second notion—"offering a rationale." Most explanations do their explaining from a particular point of view. Suppose, for example, you wanted to tell an audience how the American Revolution came to be. You could offer, potentially, a great number of explanations, depending on your point of view. One explanation might be economic, stressing the idea that the Revolution was the result of disagreements between Americans and Britons over trade and taxation policies. Another might be political, noting that the Americans felt a strong need for self-government. A third might be social or cultural, for surely the Revolution could not occur until the colonists had a strong sense of their own social identity as separate from the mother country. Similarly, you could offer several different explanations of how contagious diseases spread: You could talk about the biochemical processes of contagion, the physiological processes of debilitation, the environmental means by which diseases spread, or even the sociological relationships between subgroups of people which allow viruses to spread through some parts of a population but not others.

The point is, each of these explanations of the American Revolution and of the spread of communicable diseases is "correct": each explains satisfactorily how war or pestilence spread through a country. There are probably as many different explanations of phenomena as there are vantage points. By now you have probably heard economic, sociological, and political explanations of urban decay; moral, educational, and sociological ramifications of the country's high divorce rate; and every explanation possible of the effects of excessive TV viewing.

Explanations, therefore, represent some of the most sophisticated and complicated kinds of informative speeches you will ever give. They are needed whenever an audience is in *confusion* or *ignorance*. An explanation is called for any time concepts are fuzzy, information is only partial, effects cannot easily be attributed to their causes, or competing claims are at loggerheads. Explanatory speeches arise whenever people ask the questions "What?", "How?", or "Why?" when trying to understand ideas and physical processes.[2]

Essential Features of Informative Speeches

Four qualities should characterize any speech to inform: *(1)* clarity, *(2)* the association of new ideas with familiar ones, *(3)* coherence, and *(4)* the motivation of the audience.

Clarity

The quality of clarity is largely the result of effective organization and the careful selection of words. Informative speeches achieve maximum clarity when your listeners can follow you and understand what you are saying.

In organizing your speech, observe the following rules: *(a)* Do not have too many points. Confine your speech to three or four principal ideas, grouping whatever facts or ideas you wish considered under these headings. Even if you know a tremendous amount about your subject matter, remember that you cannot make everyone an expert in a single speech. *(b)* Clarify the relationship between your main points by observing the principles of coordination. Word your transitions carefully—"*Second,* you must prepare the chair for caning by cleaning out the groove and cane holes"; "The Stamp Act Crisis was *followed by* an *even more important* event—The Townshend Duties"; "To test *these* hypotheses, we set up the *following* experiment." Such transitions allow auditors to follow you from point to point. *(c)* Keep your speech moving forward according to a well-developed plan. Do not jump back and forth between ideas, charging ahead and then backtracking; that creates more smoke than light.

In selecting your words, follow the advice we offered in Chapter 12: *(a)* Use a precise, accurate vocabulary without getting too technical. In telling someone how to finish off a basement room, you might say, "Next, take one of these long sticks and cut it off in this funny-looking gizmo with a saw in it, and try to make the corners match." An accurate vocabulary would help your listeners remember what supplies and tools to get when they approach the same project: "This is a ceiling molding; it goes around the room between the wall and the ceiling to cover the seams between the paneling and the ceiling tiles. You make the corners of the molding match by using a mitre box, which has grooves that allow you to cut 45 degree angles. Here's how you do it." *(b)* Simplify when possible, including only as much technical vocabulary as you need. Don't make a speech on the operation of a two-cycle internal combustion engine sound as if it came out of a lawnmower mechanic's operational manual. An audience bogged down in unnecessary detail and vocabulary can become confused and bored. *(c)* Use reiteration when it clarifies complex ideas, but don't simply repeat the same words. Seek rephrasings that will help solidify ideas for those who had trouble getting them the first time: "Unlike a terrestrial telescope, a celestial telescope is used for looking at moons, planets, and stars; that is, its mirrors and its lens are ground and arranged in such a way that it focuses on objects thousands of miles, not hundreds of feet, away from the observer."

Association of New Ideas with Familiar Ones

Audiences grasp new facts and ideas more readily when they can associate them with what they already know. Therefore, in a speech to inform, try to connect the new with the old. To connect the new with the old, of course, you need to have done enough solid audience analysis so that you know what experiences, images, analogies, and metaphors to call upon in your speech.

Sometimes the associations you ought to make are obvious. A college dean talking to an audience of manufacturers on the problems of higher education presented his ideas under the headings of raw material, casting, machining, polishing, and assembling. He thus translated his central ideas into an analogy his audience, given their vocations, would be sure to understand and appreciate. At other times, if you cannot think of any obvious associations, you may have to rely upon commonplace experiences or images. For instance, you might explain the operation of the human eye pupil by comparing it to the operation of a camera lens aperture.

ASSOCIATION OF NEW IDEAS WITH FAMILIAR ONES

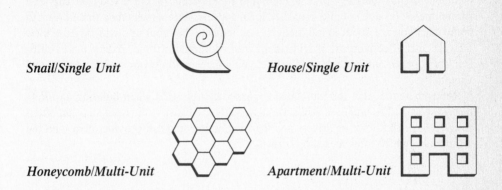

Snail/Single Unit

House/Single Unit

Honeycomb/Multi-Unit

Apartment/Multi-Unit

Coherence

Coherence is in part a matter of organization—of finding a pattern which fits your subtopics together in a meaningful manner. Sometimes it is relatively easy to create a sense of coherence, as when giving a speech on the executive, legislative, and judicial branches of government, for there are only these three branches. At other times, especially when you are not covering all components of a subject, you have to manufacture coherence.

Occasionally, you may have to do a little forcing. Suppose you decided to give a speech on the Nielsen television program rating system. You might decide to discuss only three aspects of the system—what it is, how it works, and how it is used by network executives to determine what programs to continue and which shows to drop. To give the speech coherence, you could use a question-answer organizational pattern and move into the body of your speech in this fashion: "People who worry about the effect of the Nielsen ratings on what they watch usually ask three questions: 'What *is* a Nielsen rating, anyhow?' 'How is the rating done?' 'Why do the networks rely on it for making decisions on shows?' To answer these common questions, and to explain the 'what,' 'how,' and 'why' of television ratings, today I first will. . . .'" Notice that the speaker has taken a common trio of words—*what, how, why*—and used them as an organizing principle to give coherence to this explanatory speech.

Motivation of the Audience

Finally, and perhaps most important, you must be able to motivate the audience to listen. Unfortunately, many people ignore this essential feature of good informative speeches. Many of us blithely assume that because *we* are interested in something, our audience also will want to hear about it. To you, stamp-collecting may be an interesting, relaxing, and profitable hobby, but until your listeners are likewise convinced that it is, they will yawn through your speech on American commemoratives.

Keep in mind, therefore, what we have said about attention and motivation even when preparing informative speeches: *(a)* Use the factors of attention to engage the members of your audience, to draw them into your speech. *(b)* Once you have captured them initially, be sure to build in motivational appeals, reasons why they should want to know what you are about to tell them. If you indicate that your talk will increase their interpersonal effectiveness, provide them with additional income, reduce their confusion about important matters, and the like, you will be making your speech relevant and compelling.

Remember, too, that the motivated sequence can be used when building an informative speech. The attention step should pique their curiosity, the need step can effectively engage their motive drives, and the satisfaction step can provide them with the information which alleviates those drives.

Structuring Informative Speeches

Now that we have described the various types of informative speeches and treated their essential features, it is time to examine ways to structure each of those types. Of course, potentially any of the organizational patterns we have described earlier can be used, but traditionally some of these patterns are better suited to particular types than others.

Structuring Speeches of Denotation

Introduction. Because denotative speeches treat either unfamiliar concepts or familiar concepts in a new light, their introductions must create *curiosity* and *need* in listeners. Curiosity is a special challenge in speeches on unfamiliar concepts, for we are all tempted to say, ''Well, if I've made it this far through life without knowing anything about black holes or carcinogens or trap blocking, why should I bother with learning more about these ideas now?'' The answer, to a large extent, depends upon your ability to make people wonder about the unknown. You may want to concentrate part of your introduction to a denotative speech, therefore, on making listeners desire to know more about unknown aspects of their everyday environment or of far-away segments of life.

Speeches on both unfamiliar and familiar concepts must be attentive to the needs or wants of the listeners. This means that the introductions should include motivational materials—explicit statements which indicate how the information can affect the audience members. Thus, one often hears statements such as the following: ''Understanding the dynamics of trap blocking will allow you to better appreciate line play in football, and therefore increase your enjoyment of the game every Saturday afternoon in our stadium.'' ''Most students fill out the short form of their U.S. income tax return each April without giving it much thought. If you understand some of the deductions and educational expenses you as a student are allowed to write off, however, and if you take the few extra minutes you'll need to use the long form, you may save a significant amount of money each year.''

In presenting new information to audiences, do what you can to relate new ideas to old ones and to make that information relevant to the audience's background, interests, and experiences.

Body.   Most denotative speeches use a topical pattern or one of the task-related patterns (discussed earlier in the book) because such speeches usually describe various aspects of some thing or idea. It seems natural, for example, to use a topical pattern when giving a speech on a career in computer programming and to organize the body of the speech around such topics as "the duties of a computer programmer," "skills needed by a computer programmer," and "training you will need to acquire to become a computer programmer."

There are occasions, too, when other patterns may serve your specific purpose well. You might use an effect-cause pattern, for example, when preparing an informative speech on the laws of supply and demand. You could enumerate a series of effects with which people are already familiar—soaring prices coupled with seemingly fantastic sales, interest rates which apparently change every other week—and then discuss the laws of supply and demand which contain the causes for such confusing fiscal patterns in society.

A speech on cancer could be outlined as follows:

What Does Cancer Mean?[3]

I. "You have cancer" is a phrase that can strike fear into the hardiest among us. Fear of the unknown is the most difficult to accept. Thus, if we are to understand *cancer,* we must know more about what the term means.
    A. My intent is to acquaint you with several terms that, together, will give us a better understanding of cancer.
    B. By knowing more about what is involved in cancer, hopefully we will have less fear.

II. There are several terms used in the scientific discussion of cancer. Not all are clearly understood.
    A. *Carcinogen:* Chemicals from various products (for example, cigarette smoke) may lead to cancer.
    B. *Activation:* The carcinogen must be chemically changed in order to start the cancer process.
    C. *Detoxification enzymes:* These are naturally occurring chemicals in the body which detoxify—take the poison out of substances ingested into the body.
        1. Most carcinogens entering the body are detoxified, and can cause no harm.
        2. In some cases, the detoxification process goes wrong, and the carcinogen is rendered capable of entering a cell's nucleus and attaching itself to DNA.
    D. *DNA attachment:* The DNA is the central "code" which determines the function of the cell, the central operating system of the human computer.
        1. The "second line of defense" occurs when "scavenger molecules" attack the activated carcinogen and render it harmless.
        2. Unfortunately, this line of defense sometimes fails.
        3. DNA has a third line of defense, as invading activated carcinogens can be isolated by DNA "repair molecules."
        4. Unfortunately, this line of defense also can fail.
    E. *Cell mutation and division:* Remember your junior high biology? Cells divide and create exact replicas.
        1. If the defenses have failed, an active carcinogen is attached to DNA inside a cell.
        2. Cell division will produce two new cells with the carcinogen-affected DNA.
        3. Mutation is not an automatic sign of cancer, for the alteration may only cripple one cell.
    F. *Promoter chemicals:* These are chemicals near the mutated cell that foster its multiplication, to the detriment of other non-mutants nearby.
        1. The mutant cell also may be attacked by a second carcinogen.
        2. If all of the defenses again fail, a second mutation occurs.
        3. After several cycles of mutation and promotion, a group of cells may begin to form a tumor.

III. I hope this review of the major terms and their meanings gives you a better understanding of the term *cancer*.

Conclusion. Conclusions for denotative speeches frequently have two characteristics: *(1)* They usually include a summary, especially if a good many facts, figures, and ideas have been covered, and *(2)* they often stress the kinds of applications people can make of the ideas they have been given. For example, a speech on Transcendental Meditation could conclude with a review of the main features of TM and with a list of some situations in which one might want to meditate. As with all good conclusions, the ending of a denotative speech should not come abruptly, as a dictionary definition does; rather, round it off for your listeners, tying it up in a useful way.

Structuring a Speech of Demonstration or Instruction

Introduction.   In most situations where you will be called on to give instructions or offer a demonstration, you will need to spend little time piquing curiosity or motivating people to listen. After all, if you are instructing your listeners in a new office procedure or giving a workshop on how to build an ice boat, you already have the prerequisite interest and motivation; otherwise, they would not have come. If your listeners' attendance is not voluntary (as can be the case in speech communication classrooms!), then you will have to pay attention to motivational matters. Normally, however, you must concentrate your introduction on two other tasks: *(1) Preview* your speech. If, say, you are going to take the members of your audience through the seven steps involved in making a good tombstone rubbing, give them an overall picture of the process before you start describing each operation in detail. *(2) Encourage* them to follow along, even through some of the more difficult steps. A process like tombstone rubbing, for example, looks easier than it is; many are tempted to quit listening and trying along the way. If, however, they are forewarned and are promised special help with the difficult techniques, they are more likely to bear with you.

Body.   As we suggested earlier, most speeches of demonstration and instruction are packaged in a chronological and/or spatial pattern, simply because you are teaching people a serial process you want them to be able to carry out on their own. A nonsequential organizational pattern would be very confusing. Even when the truncated motivated sequence is used, one normally arranges the material for the satisfaction step in this type of speech in a sequential pattern.

In other words, speakers usually have little trouble organizing the body of a speech of demonstration or instruction. Their problems are more likely technical ones: *(a) The problem of rate*. If the glue on a project needs to set before you can go on to the next step, what do you do? You cannot just stand there and wait for it to dry. You need to have preplanned some material for filling the time—perhaps additional background, perhaps a brief discussion of what problems one can run into at this stage. Preplan your remarks carefully for those junctures; otherwise, you are likely to lose your audience. *(b) The problem of scale*. How can you show various embroidery stitches to an audience of twenty-five? When dealing with minute operations, you often must increase the scale of operation. In this example, you might use a large piece of poster board or even a 3' by 4' piece of cloth stretched over a wood frame. By using an oversized needle, yarn instead of thread, and stitches measured in inches instead of millimeters, you could easily make your techniques visible to all audience members. At the other extreme, in a speech on how to make a homemade solar heat collector, you probably would want to work with a scaled-down model. *(c) The coordination of verbal and visual materials*. Both instructions and demonstrations usually demand that speakers "show" while "telling." To keep yourself from becoming flustered or confused, be sure to practice talking while doing—offering demonstrations while explaining to others what you are doing. Decide where you will stand when showing a slide so that the audience can see both you and the image; practice talking about your aerobic exercise positions while you are actually doing them; work a dough press in practice sessions as you tell your mythical audience how to form professional-looking cookies. If you do not, you will inevitably get yourself into trouble before your real audience.

Thinking through such procedural and technical problems you can face might lead to a speaking outline like the following one on planting tomatoes:

How to Plant Tomatoes

Coordinate verbal and visual materials

I. First, you must select a variety of tomato seed which is suited to various geographical, climatological, agricultural, and personal factors. [*display chart, showing varieties in columns along with their characteristics*]
  A. Some tomatoes grow better in hard soils; some, in loose soils.
  B. Some varieties handle shade well; some, direct sunlight.
  C. Some are well suited to short growing seasons; others, to long seasons.
  D. Each variety tends to resist certain diseases such as blight better than others.

II. Once you have selected a variety (or maybe even two, so that they mature at different times), next you must start the seeds.

Coordinate verbal and visual materials

  A. Prepare a mixture of black dirt, peat moss, and vermiculite as I am doing. [*do it, indicating proportions*]
  B. Fill germination trays, pots, or cut-off milk cartons with the germination soil, and insert seeds. [*do it*]

Reduce time delay (rate)

  C. With watering, sunlight, and patience, your plants will grow. I can't show you that growth here today, but I can use these seedlings to illustrate their care along the way. [*bring out half-grown and fully-grown seedlings*]

Coordinate verbal and behavioral actions

   1. When the seedlings are about an inch or two tall, thin them. [*demonstrate*]
   2. At about six inches [*show them*], you can transplant them safely.
   3. But, you'll know more about which plants are strong if you wait until they are ten to twelve inches tall. [*show them plants of different strengths*]
  D. Now you are ready to transplant the seedlings to your garden.
   1. Carefully unpot the seedlings, being sure not to damage the root network. [*demonstrate*]

Coordinate visual and verbal materials; enlarge materials

   2. Put each seedling in a hole already prepared in your plot; this diagram shows you how to do that. [*show an enlarged drawing which illustrates hole size and depth, a mixture of peat moss and vermiculite in the bottom, and spacing of plants*]
   3. Pack the garden soil firmly, but not so hard as to crush the roots.

4. Water it almost every day for the first week.

Coordinate verbal and visual materials; reduce size of materials

5. Put some sort of mulching material—grass clippings, hay, black sheets of plastic—between the rows if weeds are a problem. [*another drawing or picture*]

E. Once you know your plants are growing, cage or stake each plant. [*show sketches of various styles of cages or stakes, discussing the advantages of each*]

Conclusion. Conclusions for demonstration speeches usually have three parts: *(1)* First, *summaries* are offered. Most audiences need this review, which reminds them to ask questions about procedures or ideas they do not understand fully. *(2)* Second, some *bolstering* has to take place. People trying their hands at new processes or procedures usually get into trouble the first few times, and need to be reassured that this is natural and can be overcome. *(3)* Finally, *future help* should be offered. What sounded so simple in your talk can be much more complicated in execution. If possible, make yourself available for later assistance: "As you fill out your registration form, just raise your hand if you're unsure of anything and I'll be happy to help you." Or point to other sources of further information and assistance: "Here's the address of the U.S. Government Printing Office, whose pamphlet X1234 is available for only a dollar; it will give you more details"; "If you run into a filing problem I haven't covered in this short orientation to your job, just go over to Mary McFerson's desk, right over here. Mary's experienced in these matters and is always willing to help." These sorts of statements not only offer help, but assure your audience members that they won't be labeled as dull-witted if they actually have to ask for it.

Structuring an Oral Report

Introduction. Oral reports are called for by some group, committee, or class; the audience, therefore, generally knows what it expects and why. In introducing oral reports, then, you need not spend much time motivating your listeners—they already are motivated. Rather, you should concentrate upon *(1)* reminding them of what they asked for, should their memories be short; *(2)* describing carefully the procedures you used in gathering the information; *(3)* forecasting the development of various subtopics so the audience can follow you easily; and *(4)* pointing ahead to any action they are expected to take in light of your information. The key to a good introduction for an oral report, thus, is *orientation*—reviewing the past (their expectations and your preparations), the present (your goal now), and the future (their responsibilities once you are done). A report is given to an audience for some purpose, and neither you nor they should ever forget that.

Body. The principle for organizing the body of an oral report can be stated clearly: *Select an organizational pattern which best reflects the audience's needs.* Have you been asked to provide them with a history of some group or problem? Use a chronological pattern. Do they want to know how some state-of-affairs came to be? Try a cause-effect format. Have you been asked to discuss an organizational structure for the group? A topical pattern would allow you to review the constitutional responsibilities of each officer. If you were asked to examine the pros and cons of various proposals and to recommend one to the group, the elimination pattern is the way to go, as in the following example:

Report from the Final Examination Committee

I. My committee was asked to compare and contrast various ways of structuring a final examination in this speech class, and to recommend a procedure to you. [*the reporter's "charge"*]
   A. First, we interviewed each one of you.
   B. Then, we discussed the pedagogical virtues of various exam procedures with our instructor.
   C. And next, we deliberated as a group, coming to the following conclusions. [*orientation completed*]

II. Like many students, we first thought we should recommend a take-home essay examination as the "easiest" way out.
   A. But, we decided our wonderful textbook is filled with so much detailed and scattered advice that it would be almost impossible for any of us to answer essay-type questions without many, many hours of worry, work, and sweat.
   B. We also wondered why a course which stresses oral performance should test our abilities to write essays.

III. So, we next reviewed a standard, short-answer, in-class final.
   A. Although such a test would allow us to concentrate upon the main ideas and central vocabulary which has been developed in lectures, readings, and discussion, it would require a fair amount of memorization.
   B. And, we came back to the notion that merely understanding communication concepts will not be enough when we start giving speeches outside this classroom.

IV. Thus, we recommend that you urge our instructor to give us an oral examination this term.
   A. We each could be given an impromptu speech topic, some resource material, and ten minutes to prepare a speech.
   B. We could be graded, in this way, on both substantive and communicative decisions we make in putting together and delivering the speech.
   C. Most important, such a test would be consistent with this course's primary goal—and could be completed quickly, almost painlessly.

   Conclusion.   Most oral reports end with conclusions which mirror the introduction. A mention often is made again of the report's purpose, a review of the main points is presented, committee members (if there are any) are thanked publicly, and then either a motion to accept the committee recommendations (if there are any) is offered or, in the case of more straightforwardly informative reports, questions from the audience are called for. Conclusions to reports—when done well—are quick, firm, efficient, and pointed.

Structuring a Speech of Explanation

   Introduction.   Introductions to explanatory speeches can employ many of the techniques we have described thus far. You may have to raise curiosity in some instances (how many of your classmates wonder about the causes of the American Revolution at ten o'clock in the morning?). You might also have to generate a need or desire to listen, especially if your topic seems distant or irrelevant. And, too, if the explanation will be somewhat complex, a forecast of coming ideas is almost mandatory. Finally, you may need to encourage your listeners to follow along, telling them you will go into greater detail especially in the sections of greatest difficulty.

Body.   Most explanations fit well into causal and topical organizational patterns. If you are trying to explain how or why something operates the way it does, either cause-effect or effect-cause order works very well. Or, if you are trying to explain how some problem can be or should be solved, you might find a straightforward problem-solution format advantageous, especially if your listeners are unsure what the solution might be. These organizational patterns are well suited to explanatory speeches because, as we noted earlier, explanations seek to interrelate phenomena and/or ideas.

Conclusion.   Typically, conclusions of good explanations develop additional implications or call for particular actions. If, for example, you have explained how contagious diseases spread through a geographical area, you probably will want to conclude that speech by discussing a series of actions which could be taken to halt the process of contagion. Or, in explaining what courts are starting to mean by the idea of "children's rights," you might close by asking your listeners to consider what the idea *should* mean to them—how they should change their thinking and their behaviors toward six-year-olds. Do not simply sit down when you have completed the explanation; reinforce its importance to your listeners by treating its implications. In that way, it will gain considerably more meaning for them and will more likely be remembered.

Overall, you should visualize the structure of an explanatory lecture in the following terms:

Introduction

I.   Introduction of topic, using one of the beginnings described in Chapter 10.

II.   Reasons the audience should be motivated to listen:
A.   First reason,
B.   Second reason, etc.

III. Forecast of the development of the body of the speech.

Body

I.   First cause or problem, with developmental material;

II.   Second cause or problem, with developmental material, etc.

III. First effect or aspect of solution;

IV.   Second effect or aspect of solution, etc.

Conclusion

I.   Summary.

II.   Treatment of implications (in the case of speeches in the causal pattern) or indication of desired actions (in the case of problem-solution patterns).

III. Formal closing, using one of the ending tactics described in Chapter 10.

A Sample Speech to Inform

The following text is Joyce Chapman's speech, "The Geisha," which she delivered when she was a freshman at Loop College, Chicago. It illustrates well most virtues of a good informative speech: *(1)* It provides enough detail and explanations to be clear. *(2)* The speech works from familiar images of geishas, adding new ideas and information in a way that enlarges audience members' conceptions. *(3)* Its organizational pattern—a topical pattern—makes it both easy to follow and coherent. *(4)* It includes the sorts of motivational appeals to make an audience want to listen.

The Geisha[4]
Joyce Chapman

Introduction *Personal reference*	As you may have already noticed from my facial features, I have Oriental blood in me and, as such, I am greatly interested in my Japanese heritage. One aspect of my heritage that fascinates me the most is the beautiful and adoring Geisha. /1
Specific instances	I recently asked some of my friends what they thought a Geisha was, and the comments I received were quite astonishing. For example, one friend said, "She is a woman who walks around in a hut." A second friend was certain that a Geisha was "A woman who massages men for money and it involves her in other physical activities." Finally, I received this response: "She gives baths to men and walks on their backs." Well, needless to say, I was rather surprised and offended by their comments. I soon discovered that the majority of my friends perceived the Geisha with similar attitudes. One of them argued, "It's not my fault, because that is the way I've seen them on TV." In many ways my friend was correct. His misconception of the Geisha was not his fault, for she is often portrayed by American film producers and directors as a prostitute, as in the movie, *The Barbarian and the Geisha;* a streetwalker, as seen in the TV series, "Kung Fu"; or as a showgirl with a gimmick, as performed in the play, *Flower Drum Song.* /2
Central idea *Denotation*	A Geisha is neither a prostitute, streetwalker, or showgirl with a gimmick. She is a lovely Japanese woman who is a professional entertainer and hostess. She is cultivated with exquisite manners, truly a bird of a very different plumage. /3
Partition: *Forecasts speech* *development*	I would like to provide you with some insight to the Geisha, and, in the process, perhaps correct any misconception you may have. I will do this by discussing her history, training, and development. /4
Body *First point: history*	The Geisha has been in existence since 600 A.D., during the archaic time of the Yakamoto period. At that time the Japanese ruling class was very powerful and economically rich. The impoverished majority, however, had to struggle to survive. Starving fathers and their families had to sell

their young daughters to teahouses in order to get a few yen. The families hoped that the girls would have a better life in the teahouse than they would have had in their own miserable homes.   /5

Example

During ancient times only high society could utilize the Geisha's talents because she was regarded as a status symbol, exclusively for the elite. As the Geisha became more popular, the common people developed their own imitations. These imitations were often crude and base, lacking sophistication and taste. When American GIs came home from World War II, they related descriptive accounts of their wild escapades with the Japanese Geisha. In essence, the GIs were only soliciting with common prostitutes. These bizarre stories helped create the wrong image of the Geisha.   /6

Second point: training

Today, it is extremely difficult to become a Geisha. A Japanese woman couldn't wake up one morning and decide, ''I think I'll become a Geisha today.'' It's not that simple. It takes sixteen years to qualify.   /7

Chronological development

Description

At the age of six a young girl would enter the Geisha training school and become a Jo-chu, which means housekeeper. The Jo-chu does not have any specific type of clothing, hairstyle, or make-up. Her duties basically consist of keeping the teahouse immaculately clean (for cleanliness is like a religion to the Japanese). She would also be responsible for making certain that the more advanced women would have everything available at their fingertips. It is not until the girl is sixteen and enters the Maiko stage that she concentrates less on domestic duties and channels more of her energies on creative and artistic endeavors.   /8

Example

The Maiko girl, for example, is taught the classical Japanese dance, Kabuki. At first, the dance consists of tiny, timid steps to the left, to the right, backward and forward. As the years progress, she is taught the more difficult steps requiring syncopated movements to a fan.   /9

Illustration

The Maiko is also introduced to the highly regarded art of floral arrangement. The Japanese take full advantage of the simplicity and gracefulness that can be achieved with a few flowers in a vase, or with a single flowering twig. There are three main styles: Seika, Moribana, and Nagerie. It takes at least three years to master this beautiful art.   /10

Illustration

During the same three years, the Maiko is taught the ceremonious art of serving tea. The roots of these rituals go back to the thirteenth century, when Zen Buddhist monks in China drank tea during their devotions. These rituals were raised to a fine art by the Japanese tea masters, who set the standards for patterns of behavior throughout Japanese society. The tea ceremony is so intricate that if often takes four hours to perform and requires the use of over seventeen different utensils. The tea ceremony is far more than the social occasion it appears to be. To the Japanese, it serves as an island of serenity where one can refresh the senses and nourish the soul.   /11

Illustration

One of the most important arts taught to the Geisha is that of conversation. She must master an elegant circuitous vocabulary flavored in Karyuki, the world of flowers and willows, of which she will be a part.

Consequently, she must be capable of stimulating her client's mind as well as his esthetic pleasures. /12

Third point: development

Illustration

Comparison/ contrast

Having completed her sixteen years of thorough training, at the age of twenty-two, she becomes a full-fledged Geisha. She can now serve her clients with duty, loyalty, and most important, a sense of dignity. /13
The Geisha would be dressed in the ceremonial kimono, made of brocade and silk thread. It would be fastened with an obi, which is a sash around the waist and hung down the back. The length of the obi would indicate the girl's degree of development. For instance, in the Maiko stage the obi is longer and is shortened when she becomes a Geisha. Unlike the Maiko, who wears a gay, bright, and cheerful kimono, the Geisha is dressed in more subdued colors. Her make-up is the traditional white base, which gives her the look of white porcelain. The hair is shortened and adorned with beautiful, delicate ornaments. /14

As a full-fledged Geisha, she would probably acquire a rich patron who would assume her sizable debt to the Okiya, or training residence. This patron would help pay for her wardrobe, for each kimono can cost up to $12,000. The patron would generally provide her with financial security. /15

The Geisha serves as a combination entertainer and companion. She may dance, sing, recite poetry, play musical instruments, or draw pictures for her guest. She might converse with them or listen sympathetically to their troubles. Amorous advances, however, are against the rules. /16

Conclusion

So, as you can see, the Geisha is a far cry from the back-rubbing, street-walking, slick entertainer that was described by my friends. She is a beautiful, cultivated, sensitive, and refined woman. /17

REFERENCE NOTES

[1]Should you wish for more detail on each of these types of informative speeches, read Bruce E. Gronbeck, *The Articulate Person; A Guide to Everyday Public Speaking*, 2nd ed. (Glenview, IL: Scott, Foresman and Company, 1983), Chapters 5 and 6.

[2]For a difficult but highly interesting discussion of the what/how/why aspects of explanation, see W. V. Quine and J. S. Ullian, *The Web of Belief* (New York: Random House, Inc., 1970), Chapter 7, "Explanation."

[3]Boyce Rensberger, "Cancer—The New Synthesis: Cause ," *Science 84*, 5 (September 1984), pp. 28–33.

[4]"The Geisha" by Joyce Chapman, *Communication Strategy: A Guide to Speech Preparation* by Roselyn L. Schiff et al. Copyright © 1981 by Scott, Foresman and Company.

PROBLEMS AND PROBES

1. Attend an informative speech such as an expository sermon, oral report, guest lecture, or informative television or radio address. Write a short paper analyzing the content of the speech. Consider the following questions as you write: Did the

speaker keep the leading ideas few in number? Were the terms used by the speaker concrete and unambiguous? Was the organization of the speech appropriate and effective?

2. In a concise written report, indicate and defend the type of arrangement (chronological sequence, spatial sequence, and so on) you think would be most suitable for an informative speech on at least five of the subjects listed below.

The campus parking situation
Recent developments in the women's rights movement
Indian jewelry of the Southwest
Saving our environment
How the stock market works
Censorship of the arts
Wonder drugs of the 1980s
The fraternity tradition
Space stations: Living in a weightless world
What life will be like in 2000

3. Select a principle of physics, chemistry, biology, or a similar science and describe how you might explain this principle to: *(a)* a farmer, *(b)* an automobile mechanic, *(c)* a twelve-year-old newsboy, *(d)* a blind person, *(e)* a well-educated adult who is just learning to speak English. See how inventive you can be in making the principle clear without resorting to highly technical language.

4. Listed below are possible subjects for a speech. Select three of these subjects for a speech to inform (general purpose), and list what you think would be appropriate specific purposes. Using the same subjects for a speech to persuade (general purpose), list what you think would be appropriate specific purposes. What are the differences between the specific purposes for the two types of speeches? Are there any similarities?

The Electoral College   Use and abuse of drugs
Coeducational housing on campus   American cities
Health food   The political process in America

For each of the subjects you selected above, write an appropriate central idea and claim statement. How do your central idea statements differ from your claims? Compare your specific purposes and central ideas and claims with those of members of a small task group. Do the central ideas seem strictly informative, or could some kind of ultimately persuasive goal be hidden in the central ideas?

ORAL ACTIVITIES

1. Plan a two- to four-minute speech in which you will give instructions. For instance, you might explain how to calculate your life-insurance needs, how to "door knock" for a political candidate, or how to make a charter or group flight reservation. This exercise is basically descriptive in nature, so limit yourself to use of a single visual aid.

2. Prepare a speech to inform for delivery in class. Using one of the topics suggested below or a similar one approved by your instructor, select and narrow the area of the subject to be covered, develop whatever visual aids may be appropriate, and settle on the order or pattern you will follow in setting forth the information.

Take special pains to make clear why the audience needs to know the material you are presenting. Suggested topics:

Contemporary American writers (artists, musicians)
How to become a better listener
A first lesson in aircraft-recognition
Changing perspectives in American foreign policy
How to read lips
The romance of archaeology
Exercising to lose weight
How television programs are rated

3. Since history courses have a way of getting rushed at the ends of terms, you may not have spent much time studying events since World War II. To get a better idea of the historical factors that have influenced your parents' and your own lives, prepare a six- to eight-minute report on an important historical event since World War II.

4. Describe a unique place you have visited on a vacation, for example, a church in a foreign city, or a historical site. Deliver a four- or five-minute speech to the class in which you describe this place as accurately and vividly as possible. Then ask the class to take a moment to envision this place. If possible, show them a picture of what you've described. How accurately were they able to picture this place? How might you have insured a more accurate description? What restrictions did you feel without the use of visual aids?

CHAPTER 16

Public Reasoning and

Argumentation

The idea of arguing with someone is not always socially acceptable in this society. Marriage counselors sometimes speak of "family difficulties" or "spats" rather than husband-wife "arguments." Employees say "I want to discuss this with you, not argue about it" when differing with their employers. And those evenings when presidential candidates clash in face-to-face verbal confrontation are officially called "joint appearances," not "arguments." All in all, many associate *argument* with attacks, fighting, nastiness, and any number of other socially rude acts.

Yet *argumentation*—the communication process whereby speakers offer specific, identifiable reasons in support of particular claims in the face of opposing claims—is essential. Decision making by means other than executive fiat or brute power requires communication processes that stress the freedom to advance and appraise arguments for and against specific claims. Because there seldom are certain, completely untainted answers to most questions of public belief, value, and policy, democratic groups and countries depend upon public debate to make the best decisions they can.

Fighting and nastiness, then, are not really what argumentation is all about. To be sure, in some situations, arguers fight unfairly and go for the jugular. We'll discuss some of the techniques such pseudo-arguers use later in this chapter. The bulk of our attention, however, will be paid to the more positive aspects of arguments (the units of discourse) and argumentation (the process of exchanging ideas). First, we will define *arguing* as a social process, and then break down *argument* into its elements (claims, evidence, and reasoning). Further, we will review fallacies which can short-circuit constructive argumentation. Finally, we'll discuss ways of structuring various kinds of argumentative speeches.

Arguing as a Social Process

Arguing is differentiated from other forms of verbal conflict because it adheres to a set of communication rules. Instead of verbally assaulting someone, the act of arguing commits you to communicating according to certain rules, especially social conventions and technical regulations.

Social Conventions

In our society, there are tacit yet potent *conventions* or habitual *expectations* which govern argument. That is, when you decide to argue with another person, you are making, generally, commitments to four standards of judgment:

Convention of Bilaterality.   Argument is explicitly bilateral: it requires at least two people or two competing messages. The arguer, implicitly or explicitly, is saying that he or she is presenting a message which can be examined and evaluated by others. The seller of toothpaste seldom invites this kind of critical examination of the product; Procter and Gamble is in the business of persuasion, not argumentation. A U.S. senator, in contrast, assumes a party label and pits a proposed solution to some social problem against solutions proposed by others, thus specifically calling for counter-analysis or counterargument. The arguer invites reasoned inquiry in return.

Convention of Self-Risk.   By at least implicitly calling for a critique of your ideas and claims from others, you assume certain risks, of course. There is the risk of failure, naturally; but you face that risk any time you open your mouth. More importantly, in argument there is the risk of being proven wrong. For example, when you argue that a federal system of welfare is preferable to a state- or local-based system of relief, you face the possibility that your opponent will convince *you* that local control creates fewer problems and more benefits than does federal control. The bright light of public scrutiny often can expose your own as well as your opponent's weaknesses and shortcomings. That risk is strong enough to make many people afraid of arguing publicly.

The Fairness Doctrine.   Arguers also commit themselves to some version of what the radio and television industry calls the "fairness doctrine." The fairness doctrine of the Federal Communications Commission maintains that all competing voices ought to be given equal access to the airways to express their viewpoints. Similarly, arguers say, in effect, "You may use as much time as I have (or as much time as you need) to criticize my claims and reasons." This is why, for example, most legislative bodies are reluctant to cut off debate by invoking cloture rules even in the face of political filibustering. Our legislative bodies are committed to the fairness doctrine: the idea that debate (argument) ought to be as extended and as complete as possible in order to guarantee that all viewpoints be aired, considered, and defended.

Commitment to Rationality.   Arguers commit themselves to a willingness to proceed logically. That is, when you argue, you are at least implicitly saying, "Not only do I believe X, but I have *reasons* for doing so." When you argue, for instance, that non-

In a democracy, argumentation often is the communicative core of decision-making processes, as contrasting ideas can be rubbed against each other in productive ways.

returnable bottles should be banned by state law, someone else has the right to say "No" (the convention of bilaterality) and the right to assert a contrary proposition (the fairness doctrine). In addition, all parties to the argument have a right to ask, "*Why* do you believe that?" (the convention of rationality). As an arguer, you are committed to giving reasons, reasons that you think support your claim and ought to be accepted by unsure or doubtful listeners. Argument, therefore, is a rational form of communication, not in the sense that speakers often use syllogisms or other strictly logical structures, but in the sense that all arguers believe they have good reasons for the acceptance of their claims. They are obligated to provide those reasons; they cannot get away with saying, "Oh, I don't know—I just feel that is true." If the reasons given are relevant to the claim being advanced and if they are acceptable to the audience hearing the claim defended, then the arguer will have met the commitment to rationality.

Technical Rules

Arguers also should pay close attention to the soundness of their arguments and to any procedural rules that are relevant to the situation. The *soundness* of an argument differs from its *validity*. An argument is considered valid if its structure adheres to rules of reasoning. An argument is sound if its content offers good reasons for the adoption of the claim being advanced. Applying the tests of reasoning to your own arguments and avoiding common fallacies will help you meet these technical rules for the conduct of argument.

Procedural rules also can play a part in determining the conduct of an argument. At a monthly meeting of a computer club, for example, you may be expected to offer motions and amendments according to *Robert's Rules of Order*.[1] *Robert's Rules* or other sets of parliamentary procedures function as technical rules: They limit *what* you can say (some motions are out of order), *how* you can say it (you may not be allowed to defend an idea unless your motion is seconded), and even *when* you can say it (everything you say must be relevant to the motion under consideration). Argumentation in many formal situations—legislatures, courtrooms, clubs, service groups—is governed by such specifically defined procedural rules. (See the Speaker's Resource Book for more on parliamentary procedure.)

In other settings and contexts, arguers are expected to follow somewhat different, but analogous, technical rules. The social scientist who has made a study, say, of the effect of source credibility upon the persuasiveness of messages must report the results in a specific way. The "scientific method" is, in effect, a set of rules—rules of procedure; rules for proper statistical measurement; and rules of inference: what we can infer about the whole society as the result of a limited experiment carried out on a small portion of that society. The social scientists who, in writing reports of their findings, do not carefully define, scrupulously measure, and statistically compare data, and who then draw broad conclusions about the universe from a limited study, will not be published. The argument would not be "proper," and the report would be rejected. Various academic and business disciplines thus lay out their own rules for arguing, rules which must be followed if you are going to engage in argument in a given profession or field.[2]

Arguments: Elements and Analysis

In this section we will examine the anatomy of argument at the cellular level, concerning ourselves with how a unit of argument is built and evaluated. Basically, an argument consists of the *claim* to be defended, the relevant *evidence* you can accumulate in support of that claim, and the *reasoning pattern* you use to connect the evidence to the claim. The evaluation of an argument includes satisfying the *tests of reasoning* and avoiding common *fallacies* of evidence, language, and reasoning.

Types of Claims

Most argumentative speeches assert that in the opinion of the speaker *(1)* something is or is not the case; *(2)* something is desirable or undesirable; or *(3)* something should or should not be done. Such judgments or recommendations, when formally addressed to others, are called the speaker's *claims*. The first step in constructing a successful argument is to clearly determine the nature of the claim you wish to establish.

Claims of Fact.   If you were trying to convince your listeners that "price controls on raw agricultural products result in food shortages," you would be presenting a factual claim—asserting that a given state of affairs exists or that something is indeed the case. When confronted with a claim of this sort, two questions are likely to arise in the mind of a thoughtful listener:

1. *By what criteria or standards of judgment should the truth or accuracy of this claim be measured?* If you were asked to determine a person's height, you would immediately look for a yardstick or other measuring instrument. Listeners likewise look for a standard when judging the appropriateness of a factual claim. In the example given above, before agreeing that price controls result in shortages, the members of your audience would almost certainly want to know what you as a speaker mean by "shortages." Does it mean "the disappearance, for all practical purposes, of a given kind of food" or merely "less of that food than everyone might perhaps desire"? Against what standard, precisely, is the accuracy of the claim to be judged?

2. *Do the facts of the situation fit the criteria as set forth?* Does the amount of produce and other raw agricultural products presently on supermarket shelves fall within the limits set by your definition of "shortages"? First, get your listeners to agree to certain standards or measurements for judgment and then present evidence to show that a given state of affairs meets these standards. Then you will, in most instances, be well on your way toward winning their belief.

Claims of Value.   When, instead of asserting that something is or is not so, you assert that something is good or bad, desirable or undesirable, justified or unjustified, you are advancing a claim of value—a claim concerning the intrinsic *worth* of the belief or action in question. Here, as in the case of claims of fact, it is always appropriate to ask: (1) *By what standards or criteria is something of this nature to be judged?* (2) *How well does the item in question measure up to the standards specified?* We may, for example, assert that the quality of a college is to be measured by the distinction of its faculty, the excellence of its physical plant, the success of its graduates in securing positions, and the reputation it enjoys among the general public; and then proceed to argue that because the college we are concerned with meets each of these tests, it is indeed a good one.

Claims of Policy.   A claim of policy recommends a course of action you want the audience to approve. Typical examples are: "Federal expenditures for pollution control *should be* substantially increased"; "The student senate *should have* the authority to expel students who cheat." In both instances, you are asking your audience to endorse a proposed "policy" or course of action. When analyzing a policy claim, four subsidiary questions are relevant:

1. *Is there a need for such a policy or course of action?* If your listeners do not believe that a change is called for, they are not likely to approve your proposal.

2. *Is the proposal practicable?* Can we afford the expenses it would entail? Would it really solve the problem or remove the evil it is designed to correct? Does such a policy stand a reasonable chance of being adopted? If you cannot show that your proposal meets these and similar tests, you can hardly expect it to be endorsed.

3. *Are the benefits your proposal will bring greater than the disadvantages it will entail?* People are reluctant to approve a proposal that promises to create conditions worse than the ones it is designed to correct. Burning a barn to the ground may be a highly efficient way to get rid of rats, but it is hardly a desirable one. The benefits and disadvantages that will accrue from a plan of action always must be carefully weighed along with considerations of its basic workability.

4. *Is the offered proposal superior to any other plan or policy?* Listeners are hesitant to approve a policy if they have reason to believe that an alternative course of action is more practicable or more beneficial.

From what has been said about the three types of claims, you should now be able to see the importance of knowing exactly the kind of claim you are seeking to establish. Is it a claim of policy, fact, or value? If it is a claim of policy, do you need to answer all four of the basic questions listed above, or is your audience likely to accept one or more of them without proof? If yours is a claim of fact or value, what criteria should you use as bases for judgment, and how well are they met by the evidence?

Finally, unless there are sound reasons for delay, you should announce early in your speech the claim you are going to support or oppose. If your listeners do not see the precise point on which they will be asked to judge, your strongest arguments and appeals probably will prove useless.[3]

Evidence

By *evidence* we are referring to nothing more complicated than kinds of supporting materials. Thus, explanations, comparisons and contrasts, illustrations, specific instances, statistics, and testimony represent types of evidence as well as, more generally, types of supporting materials.

For the arguer, the question of *kinds* of evidence should cause no problem; you simply must go out and find it, as you have been doing throughout this course. But, the *selection of relevant evidence* is another matter. Evidence is supporting material which must be relevant to some claim in both logical and psychological terms. It must seem relevant *rationally* to the type of claim being advanced; yet it also must be relevant *motivationally* to members of the audience.

Rationally Relevant Evidence.   As our analysis of types of claims suggests, the rational requirements for evidence are related to the types of claim being defended. For example, testimony and definitions are kinds of evidence useful in defending your selection of standards of judgment of fact- and value-based claims; statistics, examples, and illustrations are useful when you must urge that the situations being discussed "fit" the criteria or standards you set out. Or, when defending policy claims, you often must document the need for a change with statistics, examples, and testimony; the proposal's benefits can be supported with explanations and illustrations; the practicality and supe-

The foundation of any compelling argument is evidence: What kind of evidence do you need for particular kinds of claims? What kind will your audience accept as valid and forceful?

riority of your proposal may be defended with comparisons and contrasts. As you consider the questions we have asked about each type of claim, you should be asking yourself, "What type of evidence is logically relevant in support of this claim?"

Motivationally Relevant Evidence.   Your evidence must be more than rationally relevant. You also must answer a perhaps tougher question: "What sort of evidence will this audience accept as relevant to its decision making?" Buried within that question are two subquestions:

1. *What type of evidence will this audience demand?* The social scientists we referred to earlier will demand, from a fellow scientist reporting on an experimental study, operational definitions of key concepts, expert testimony from other researchers who have investigated the same phenomena, examples of ways in which the experiment was carefully controlled, statistical tests and inferences, and perhaps comparisons between this study and the others which have been done in the same area. Mere examples or illustrations or even figurative analogies will not be accepted as proof. In contrast, were you evaluating a novel for an audience of literary buffs, examples, illustrations, figurative analogies, and the like would be much more

forceful as "proof" than statistical counts of words or even the testimony of other literary critics. Careful audience analysis will help you determine what type of evidence is needed psychologically to move your particular group of listeners.

2. *Which actual pieces of evidence of a given type will this audience prefer?* This is an even harder question to answer. Whom should you quote if you decide to use testimony? What comparisons and contrasts will make sense to this audience? Should you use big city or small town, classical or contemporary, nearby or faraway examples? In dealing, say, with the problem of a federal farm program, should you use a highly personalized or a general illustration?

To answer these and similar questions about evidence, you need to analyze your audience. A homogeneous, hometown audience probably would prefer local experts, everyday comparisons, nearby examples, and an illustration about a farmer who lives outside of town. A heterogeneous audience (such as the people making up your class audience) probably would prefer more generally recognized authorities, more college-oriented comparisons, geographically varied examples, and illustrations dealing with farmers from several parts of the country. Democrats will want Democratic experts; Republicans, GOP authorities; a Chamber of Commerce audience will like business illustrations; a Future Farmers of America audience, agricultural illustrations; and so on. You cannot always wholly tailor your evidence to your audience's demographical or psychological characteristics; but always, at least, attempt to take them into account.

In sum, it is one thing to discover evidence, another to select it. Select evidence with both your claim and your audience in mind.

Reasoning (Inferences)

The third element of a unit of argument is that element which "connects" the evidence with the claim. This is called *reasoning* or *inference*. *Reasoning* is a process of connecting something which is known or believed (the evidence) to some concept or idea (the claim) you wish others to accept. Patterns of reasoning, therefore, are habitual ways in which a culture or society uses inferences to connect that which is accepted to that which is being urged upon them. There are five basic reasoning patterns.

Reasoning from Examples.   Reasoning from instances or examples involves examining a series of particular examples or known occurrences (evidence) and drawing a general conclusion (claim). The inference in this reasoning pattern can be stated, "What's true of particular cases is true of the whole class." This represents a kind of mental inductive leap from specifics to generalities. For example, the Food and Drug Administration will study the effects of cyclamates on a few people and discover a larger than normal incidence of cases of visceral cancer (the examples or evidence). With an inductive leap they'll move to the factual claim, "Cyclamates can cause visceral cancer in the general population," and hence ban the sweetener. You use a similar pattern of reasoning every time you drive home during rush hour. After trial and error, you decide that Street A is the best one to take home between 5:00 and 5:30 p.m., and

Street B, between 5:30 and 6:00 p.m. After enough instances, in other words, you arrive at a generalization and act upon it.

Reasoning by Parallel Case. Another common reasoning pattern involves thinking not in terms of generalizations, but solely in terms of closely similar events. Your city, for example, probably designed its transit system or its parking lots by examining the transit systems or parking arrangements in cities very much like it. The evidence was the occurrences in a *parallel* town; the claim was that certain policies ought to be implemented in your city; the inference ran something like, "What worked in City A will work here because of similarities." As a parent, you employ reasoning by parallel case every time you say, "Don't run into the street. Remember what happened to Jamie Johns when she did?" Obviously, you're not generalizing (for not everyone who goes into a street will be struck down). Instead you are asserting that Jamie and your child are parallel cases—that they have enough features in common to increase the likelihood of another accident in the neighborhood.

Reasoning from Sign. A third reasoning pattern uses an observable mark or symptom as proof for the existence of a state of affairs. You reason from sign when you note the rash or spots on your skin (the evidence) and decide you have measles (the claim). The rash doesn't "cause" measles; rather, it's a sign of the disease. Detectives are notorious reasoners from sign. When they discover someone had motive, had access, and had a weapon in his or her possession (the signs), they move to the claim that the person might be the murderer. Your doctor works the same way every time she asks you to stick out your tongue, looking for signs of trouble. These signs, of course, are circumstantial evidence—and could be wrong. Just ask detectives and doctors. The inference, "This evidence is a sign of a particular conclusion," is one you have to be careful with. Reasoning from sign works pretty well with natural occurrences (ice on the pond is always a sign that the temperature has been below 32 degrees Fahrenheit). But this sort of reasoning can be troublesome in the world of human beings (as when we take people's skin color as a sign that they are lazy/dishonest/rhythmical). Yet we often have to use signs as indicators; otherwise we could not project our economy, predict our weather, and forecast the rise and fall of political candidates.

Reasoning from Causal Relation. Reasoning from causal relation involves associating known antecedents (that which comes before or "pushes") with certain consequents (that which comes after as a result of the "push"). Such cause-effect reasoning is so important, you'll remember, that it is frequently used as a basic pattern for organizing speeches. Its power derives from our hope that the world is regularized and predictable, one in which every occurrence has a cause. Hence, if crime rises in your community, there's an immediate scramble to find the causes—drugs, economic deterioration, inept law enforcement, or bad street lighting. We also can reverse the process by reasoning from causes to possible effects. When the Great Plains are threatened with drought, the government moves immediately to head off bad effects by stockpiling grain, by arranging for airlifts of hay for animals, by raising beef import quotas, and by planning for emergency loans to build irrigation projects. The evidence and the claim, therefore, are the identified causes and effects, while the inference is the simple but important generalization, "Every cause has an effect."

Reasoning from Generalization or Axiom.   A final kind of reasoning pattern, often called *deduction,* is essentially the reverse of reasoning from instances (induction). Even as a child you probably were taught that buying goods in large quantities saves money (the generalization or evidence). Therefore, because discount stores purchase goods in quantity, you will be able to save money shopping there (the claim deduced from the evidence). Or, to take the classic example, because all people are mortal (generalization or axiom), and because Socrates is a person, therefore Socrates is mortal (the claim). Note that the inference can garner its power from one of two sources: in the first case, it is justifiable because of *experience* (by shopping around a lot we arrived at the generalization); and in the second, the generalization really is a *definition* (that is, one innate characteristic of human beings is mortality). In other words, we accept the first inference because of uniformities in the world, and the second because of ways we use words such as *human* and *mortal.*

These five forms of reasoning are judged logical or rational in this culture, and hence are the primary means for connecting evidence with a claim.

Tests for Reasoning

Because argumentative speaking is preeminently a reason-giving communicative activity, and because the reasoning process is really the fulcrum on which the entire argument turns, it is essential that you test your reasoning. This testing is a quasi-logical activity; you engage it not to discover your logicalness, but simply to protect yourself as both a generator and a consumer of arguments. Each form of reasoning has its own tests or questions to which it must respond if an argument is to be found sound. Consider the following questions as you construct your own arguments and listen to those of others:

Reasoning from Examples

1. *Have you looked at enough instances to warrant generalizing?* (You don't assume spring is here because of one warm day in February.)

2. *Are the instances fairly chosen?* (You certainly hope your neighbors don't think you've got a rotten kid just because he picked one of their flowers; you want them to judge your son only after seeing him in many different situations.)

3. *Are there important exceptions to the generalization or claim which must be accounted for?* (While it is generally true, from presidential election studies, that "As Maine goes, so goes the nation," there have been enough exceptions to that rule to keep losers in Maine campaigning hard even after that primary.)

Reasoning from Parallel Case

1. *Are there more similarities than differences between the two cases?* (City A and City B may have many features in common—size, location, and so on; yet they probably

also have many features in which they differ—perhaps in the subgroups that make up their populations, the degree of industrial development, and the like. Too many differences between the two cases will rationally destroy the parallel.)

2. *Are the similarities pointed out the relevant and important ones?* (So there are two tads in your neighborhood who are the same age, live on the same block, and wear the same kinds of clothes; but are you therefore able to assume that one is a saint simply because the other is? Probably not, because more relevant similarities would include their home lives, their school backgrounds, their relationships with siblings, and so forth. Comparisons must be made on relevant and important similarities.)

Reasoning from Sign

1. *Is the sign fallible?* (As we noted already, many signs are merely circumstantial, as in the case of the murderer and racial examples above. Be extremely careful not to confuse sign reasoning with causal reasoning. If sign reasoning were infallible, your weather forecaster would never be wrong!)

Reasoning from Causal Relation

1. *Can you separate causes and effects?* (We often have a difficult time doing this. Do higher wages cause higher prices, or is the reverse true? Does a strained home life make a child misbehave, or is it the other way around?)

2. *Are the causes strong enough to have produced the effect?* (Did Ronald Reagan's boyish grin really give him the election, or was that an insufficient cause? There probably were much stronger and more important causes.)

3. *Did intervening events or persons prevent a cause from having its normal effect?* (If the gun's not loaded, no matter how hard you pull the trigger you won't shoot anything. Even if droughts normally drive up food prices, that might not happen if food has been stockpiled, if spring rains left enough moisture in the soil, or if plenty of cheap imported foods are available this year.)

4. *Could any other cause have produced the effect?* (Although crime often increases when neighborhoods deteriorate, increased crime rates can be caused by any number of other changes—alterations in crime-reporting methods, increased reporting of crimes which have been going on for years, or closings of major industries. We rationally must sort through all the possible causes before championing one.)

Reasoning from Generalization or Axiom

1. *Is the generalization true?* (Remember how long sailors set certain courses on the assumption that the world was flat, or the number of years parents in this country accepted as gospel Benjamin Spock's generalizations about childrearing.)

2. *Does the generalization apply to this particular case?* (If a small neighborhood store has a sale, it may well offer better prices than discount houses. Or the old saw "Birds of a feather flock together" certainly applies to birds, but perhaps not to human beings.)

Detecting Fallacies in Arguments

One of your jobs as a listener and as a person who often will be called upon to answer to arguments of others is to evaluate the claims, evidence, and reasoning of other speakers. Whether you are evaluating speakers' claims as a "mere" listener or whether you are judging those claims so you can respond publicly, you must be able to think sensibly through what has been said. In part you are looking for ways in which others' ideas and reasons are relevant to your own situation and world view. And in part you are trying to examine the soundness—the logical foundations—of their thought. A *fallacy* is a flaw in the rational properties of an argument or other inference. Although we cannot present a complete course in logical fallacies in this textbook, we will review some basic errors in reasoning that often are presented, and urge you to attack them in your own mind or in your refutative speeches. Such fallacies can be placed into three categories: *fallacies in evidence, fallacies in reasoning,* and *fallacies in language.*

Fallacies in Evidence.   Fallacies in evidence occur in the management of ideas or supporting materials. Three of them stand out:

Hasty generalization (faulty inductive leap).   A hasty generalization is one made on the basis of too little evidence. Has the arguer really examined enough typical cases to make a claim? Urging the closing of a hospital because two people have successfully brought malpractice suits against it is an example of a hasty generalization.

False division.   A false division is an attempt to argue that some process or idea can be subdivided in only one particular way, when in fact numerous alternative divisions or additional properties or ideas are being ignored. When someone argues there are only three ways to rejuvenate your community's uptown district, be on the lookout. *Only* often signals a false division; there well may be other plans worth considering.

Genetic fallacy.   Many people argue for an idea by discussing its origins. They may suggest that it is "rooted in sacred traditions" and trace its ancestry back to respected sources. Many people defended the ideas of slavery in the nineteenth century by talking about the Founding Fathers and the seemingly racist ideas in the Bible; such arguments suggest that an idea "must" be true because it's been around in respected circles for a long time. But times change; new values arise to replace old ones. Genetic definitions may help us understand some concept, but they hardly are "proof" of correctness or justice.

In addition, the other tests of reasoning we reviewed earlier can be applied to other categories of evidence. Be on your guard against what are called "the material fallacies."

Fallacies in Reasoning.   We already have reviewed some of the sources of fallacious reasoning. Five additional *logical fallacies* are:

Appeal to ignorance (**argumentum ad ignoratiam**).   People often argue with double-negatives ("You *can't* prove that it *won't* work"), or may even attack an idea because of gaps in human knowledge ("We can't write laws about euthanasia because we know so little about death"). Both of these strategies are appeals to ignorance. Sometimes we simply must act on the basis of knowledge we have, despite our ignorance. To overcome this appeal, you often can cite parallel cases and carefully constructed arguments from example.

Appeal to popular opinion (**argumentum ad populum**).   Many an argument begins "Everyone knows . . . "; "Everyone knows the world is flat"; "Everyone knows that blacks are inferior to whites." These appeals to popular opinion may be useful in setting out valuative claims, but, when used as the basis for factual claims especially, they are fallacious. (To make them "legal," the word *knows* must be changed to *thinks, believes,* or *values.* If you *know* that, you won't advance the claims we just did!)

Sequential fallacy (**post hoc, ergo propter hoc**).   Literally translated "after this, therefore because of this," the sequential fallacy is one to look for in arguments from causal relations; it's based on the assumption that because one event occurred after another, the first must have caused the second. Given that intervening causes often intercede between two events, one must watch for this fallacy in asserting a cause-effect relationship.

Begging the question (**petitio principii**).   "Begging the question" is simply re-phrasing an idea and then offering it as its own reason. If someone argues, "Marijuana smoking is immoral because it just isn't right," that person has begged the question—simply rephrasing the claim (it is immoral) to form a reason (it just isn't right). Especially in the case of claims of value, watch for *petitio principii.*

Either-or (two-valued) logic.   We often hear, "Either it is or it isn't," "Either it's good or it's bad," "Either you're for us or against us." All these statements are examples of two-valued logic or either-or reasoning. Sometimes such reasoning applies, as when you say, "Either that's a dog or it isn't." A so-called "*A* or non-*A*" ("dog or non-dog") argument is perfectly acceptable. But, that is different from an "*A* or *B*" argument: "Either you're for Proposition 12 *(A)* or you're against it *(B)*"; "Either you must fight *(A)* or surrender *(B)*." Either-or reasoning of this type ignores compromises, additional alternatives, or even combinations of both *A* and *B*—Proposition 13, perhaps, or negotiation rather than fighting or surrender.

Fallacies in Language.   Certain fallacies creep into people's speeches simply because of the ways words are used. Because word meanings are so slippery, language can be used sloppily or manipulatively. Five *linguistic fallacies* appear often:

Ambiguity.   *Ambiguity* is the fallacy of using one word with two or more meanings in the same context. Suppose you heard, "The end of a thing is its perfection; death is the end of life; therefore, death is the perfection of life." Here, the word *end* has been used ambiguously; in the first statement, *end* means "goal," but in the second, it means "final state." Watch out for shifting meanings.

Nonqualification.   It is all too easy to drop out some important qualifications as an argument progresses. Words such as *maybe, might,* and *probably* tend to fall by the wayside. An expert may have said "*Perhaps* this is the best answer," or "Plan A will work *if* Committees X, Y, and Z get behind it." If arguers use such pieces of expert testimony but drop out the qualifications, the argument is verbally distorted.

Is-faults.   One of the trickiest verbs in English is *is.* "John is a man" and "John is a radical" are grammatically equivalent sentences, but in the first case we are identi-fying an essential characteristic of John, and in the second we are specifying a change-able attribute of his thinking. Learn to distinguish between the *is* of classification and the *is* of attribution, especially in condemnatory speeches (and advertisements).

Persuasive definition.   In the heat of a dispute, many advocates try to win by persuading you to accept their definition of an idea, especially a value or an abstract concept. Two clear signals of a persuasive definition are *true* and *really.* "True liberty consists of freedom from governmental regulation"; "A real university education is one which leads to a post-college job." In both cases, you are being asked to accept someone's arbitrary definition; if they get you to accept the definition, the argument is over.[4]

Name-calling.   *Name-calling* is a general label for several kinds of attacks on people instead of on their arguments. *Argumentum ad hominem* is an attack on the special interests of a person: "You can't offer a fair analysis of 'right to work' questions because you are a union member." *Argumentum ad personam* is an attack upon a personal characteristic of someone: "You are a sniveling liar (or Irishman or male)." Even liars, Irishmen, and males occasionally offer solid argumentative analyses. *Ideological appeals* give some idea or person a political evaluative label: "The Kaiser medical plan is really communistic socialized medicine and thus un-American." This appeal attaches a value label to an idea rather than examining its merits and operational faults; arguments, whomever their source, ought to be judged on their own features, not personalities and ideologies.

These are only some of the material, logical, and linguistic fallacies which creep into argument. Armed with knowledge of only these thirteen fallacies, however, you should be able to construct some ideas for refutative speeches and to protect yourself against unscrupulous demagogues, sales personnel, and advertisers.

Structuring Argumentative Speeches

Arguing with others usually involves more than a single presentation of your ideas. If you are going to be faced with an opponent's presentation, there is more pressure to orchestrate the materials that will be used to defend your position. When you have the opportunity to respond formally to an opponent—either in the same setting or at a later time—you need to think in terms of *multiple messages.* More specifically, you will need to plan your argumentative approach with respect to *(1)* constructing your case, *(2)* anticipating counterarguments, and *(3)* rebuilding your case.

Constructing Your Case

Your first concern is finding suitable materials for the development of your argument. Assume, for example, that your community is considering the use of its present landfill dump as a site for the disposal of hazardous wastes. In presenting an argument against this proposal at a city council hearing called to review the merits of the plan, you know that in attacking this policy claim you must *(1)* gain attention, *(2)* develop the specific criteria for allowing hazardous waste disposal at the dump, *(3)* demonstrate the failure of the dump to meet the established criteria, *(4)* note the advantages to be gained by the acceptance of your analysis, and *(5)* appeal for a "no" vote on the proposal.[6] As you think about this skeletal outline in terms of your argument, notice that you have several major problems to overcome in constructing your case:

THE PROCESS OF ARGUMENTATION

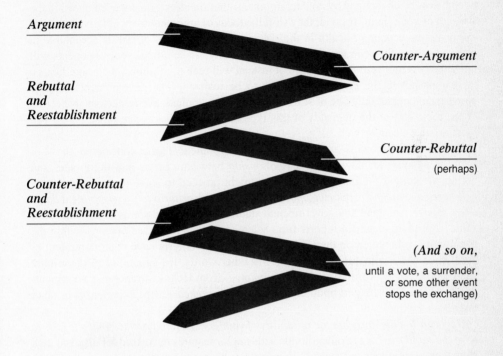

Argument

Counter-Argument

Rebuttal
and
Reestablishment

Counter-Rebuttal

(perhaps)

Counter-Rebuttal
and
Reestablishment

(And so on,

until a vote, a surrender,
or some other event
stops the exchange)

A. You must demonstrate that the *criteria* for allowing hazardous waste disposal provide a relevant, comprehensive, and significant set of standards for judging any proposed dump site. If you cannot do this, your opponents can argue that the criteria you propose are irrelevant or insignificant. And if your set of criteria is incomplete, your opponent can counter by arguing that you have unfairly "stacked the deck" by your selection of "convenient" standards.

B. Even if your criteria are acceptable, you must address the *relationship* between the criteria and the dump site in question. Does the site meet the standards considered acceptable? If this is not answered in direct, explicit fashion, you leave yourself open to the accusation of having failed to discharge your major burden. However, dealing with this issue does not mean that your opponents will quit the fight; they can still object to the relationship you seek to establish.

C. The *advantages* that would flow from acceptance of your position may appear obvious and important to you, but they often must be weighed against other advantages to be gained by your opponent's position. You may be faced with issues that have little to do with the case you are building: for example, a chemical company employing 2,000 workers has threatened to close its plant if it cannot use the existing site; the town stands to profit from dump fees charged for disposal and claims a reduction in property tax as a side benefit.

Thus, your carefully constructed case may meet the problems cited in *A* and *B*, but will nonetheless be challenged by counterarguments that, in effect, do not even question the strength of your claim. Instead, they shift the focus of argument to the relative merits of safety versus economic health in the community: What level of risk is acceptable in order to sustain the economic life of the community? In so doing, your opponents will not directly refute your allegations, but instead will seek to minimize their significance in relationship to the economic benefits to be realized. The developmental outline above is, of course, only one of several that might be applied; even a cursory inspection of the topic and of the demands of this type of speech will indicate those points you must argue especially well.

Returning to problems associated with the hypothetical case considered above—establishing *criteria,* developing a *relationship* between criteria and dump site, and noting *advantages*—think about how you might proceed to solve them.

Where can you find supporting materials to establish criteria for determining a dump site's safety? Are there any governmental studies or agency standards that would be of value? Are there technical reports from scientists? Have respected persons within the community commented on the issue of criteria? What criteria have other communities used when faced with similar questions? In other words, the suitability of the criteria can be obtained by various kinds of *testimony*—from technical reports, government-approved standards, expert opinion—and from *parallel cases* (the experiences of other towns).

How can you demonstrate the reliability of your conclusion that the dump site fails to meet the standards? Have other dumps with similar features been used for disposal, and have they been judged successful? Have studies been done to determine the characteristics of the landfill (for example, proximity to underground water sources)? Have scientists or others already commented on the suitability of the site? Once you have specific information on the characteristics of the dump site, the relationship to criteria can be accomplished in a fairly straightforward manner, by citing the relevant features of the dump and drawing conclusions that the site will not meet the necessary conditions adequately. You also can argue from *parallel cases,* using past experiences at similar dump sites as a basis for comparison to the potential experience with this dump site. You also could develop, in more dramatic style, a *hypothetical illustration* of what would happen in a "worst-case" scenario if the dump site were utilized.

How do you deal with issues that challenge the advantages you cite? To begin with, the advantages you might stress would center on the health of citizens in the area surrounding the dump site or those affected by its use. Although this general advantage may seem obvious, it may be useful to underline its significance with *testimony* from medical experts or from respected town leaders on the problems that dumping hazardous waste products would cause. Without anticipating, at this stage of the analysis, other issues that may be brought forward (for example, unemployment, increased revenue), the best approach is to build the strongest case you can for the health issue. When and if the argument shifts to a comparison of advantages, you will have made it more difficult for the opposition to undermine the significance of your advantage. Leaving it as "obvious" may only serve to quicken its dismissal by the opponents.

With the preceding analysis as a guide, it does appear possible to construct a reasonable case for your position. The foregoing has, in a general fashion, identified the potential sources and kinds of information that may prove helpful and has revealed several possible points on which you can be attacked. Of course, you still have to assemble the actual *materials*—the technical data, expert opinion, relevant parallel cases—that will allow you to present your case. As you put this together, the next element of the process will assist you in carrying your argument forward.

Anticipating Counterarguments

As you construct your case and outline your argument, you will be sensitized to potential attacks. We already have mentioned possible strategies for dealing with counterattacks; in this section we flesh them out in more detail. For instance, if you are opposing the use of the local community dump as a hazardous waste disposal site, your opponents may counter your arguments by maintaining that your parallel instances are insufficient or irrelevant as evidence of the unsuitability of the present site. They also may attack your evidence concerning the composition of the soil, its likelihood of leaching substances into the local water supply, and so on. Other opponents will no doubt bring up the threatened closure of the town's major employer if the site application is not approved, or will concentrate their responses on the projected revenue loss to the city. Thus, even before you actually present what might be called your "constructive case," you will need to be aware of some potential objections and vulnerabilities.

Do not, however, build defensive reactions into your initial argument. If you are a speaker who attempts to anticipate and answer all possible objections before they are lodged, you are in double danger: *(1)* You may appear paranoid and thereby cause listeners to say, "Boy, if she is this unsure, then maybe the proposal isn't any good." *(2)* Worse, you may actually suggest negative aspects of your proposal others had not thought of. You may, in other words, actually fuel discontent by proposing counterarguments.

As a rule, therefore, you should set forth your initial case directly and simply, and then sit back and await the counterarguments presented by others. You may even want to work from a flowchart—a sheet of paper which enumerates your principal arguments down the left-hand side, with space along the right-hand side for recording objections. In that way, you can identify where you are being questioned, note carefully how the attacks affect your overall analysis, and think specifically in terms of answers.

In sum, reacting critically to attacks on your arguments involves *(a)* a careful recording of counterarguments so as to be fair, and *(b)* a decision on how to answer germane objections. You have to be cool and dispassionate enough to do both.

Rebuilding Your Case

Having isolated and considered possible counterarguments, your next task is to answer those arguments so as to rebuild your initial case. This rebuilding requires *rebuttal* and *reestablishment*.

Rebuttal.   Your first rebuilding task is to rebut counterarguments. In our example this would mean answering to the satisfaction of your audience objections based on revenue loss to the city or potential unemployment if the plant closes because the application fails. To refute the revenue loss argument, you might indicate that the loss is projected rather than actual; you also may be able to demonstrate insignificance if the amount of revenue lost would not appreciably affect local tax rates. The objection regarding projected unemployment is much harder to meet as there will be members in the audience who are dependent on the plant for their own jobs. You might be able to argue that closure is likely on other grounds, hence negative action on the dump site is a moot point. This is, however, a weak counter, as your opponents may quickly point out that approving the application is precisely the gesture the company needs to be convinced that it should remain. You also may be able to rebut the argument by examining the potential impact of such unemployment and by noting the probability of new industry absorbing much of the loss without the same risk to the health and safety of the community. Finally, you may have no other choice but to rebut by facing the possibility straight on and arguing that the risk to health and safety outweighs any possible economic considerations.

In this extended illustration, we see most of the principal communicative techniques used by successful respondents:

Be both constructive and destructive when responding to objections.   Do not simply tear down the other person's counterarguments; constructively bolster your original statements as well. Reestablishment not only rationally shores up your position, but it psychologically demonstrates your control of the ideas and materials, thereby increasing your credibility.

Answer objections in an orderly fashion.   If two or three objections are raised, sort them out carefully and answer them one at a time. Such a procedure helps guarantee that you respond to each objection, and aids listeners in sorting out the issues being raised.

Attack each objection systematically.   A speech which rebuts the counterarguments of another ought to be shaped into a series of steps, to maximize its clarity and acceptability. A *unit of rebuttal* proceeds in four steps:

1. State the opponent's claim which you seek to rebut. ("Joe has said that a management-by-objectives system won't work because supervisors don't want input from their underlings.")

2. State your objection to it. ("I'm not sure what evidence Joe has for that statement, but I do know of three studies done at businesses much like ours, and these studies indicate that. . . .")

3. Offer evidence for your objection. ("The first study was done at the XYZ Insurance Company in 1976; the researchers discovered that. . . . The second. . . . And the third. . . .")

4. Indicate the significance of your rebuttal. ("If our company is pretty much like the three I've mentioned—and I think it is—then I believe our supervisors will likewise appreciate specific commitments from their subordinates, quarter by quarter. Until Joe can provide us with more hard data to support his objection, I think we will have to agree. . . .")

Merely constructing and presenting an argumentative speech is not enough. You usually, as well, have to take an extra step, refuting opposing arguments and rebuilding your own.

Keep the exchange on an impersonal (intellectual) level.   All too often counterarguments and rebuttals degenerate into name-calling exchanges. We all are tempted to strike out at objectors. When you become overly sensitive to attacks upon your pet notions and other people feel similarly threatened, a communicative free-for-all can ensue. Little is settled in such verbal fights. Reasoned decision making can occur only when the integrity of ideas is paramount. And the calm voice of reasonableness is more likely to be listened to than is emotionally charged ranting.

In sum, answering questions and responding to objections can be a frightening experience. Many of us feel threatened when we are made accountable for what we say by questioners and counterarguers. Yet, we must overcome our natural reticence in such situations if we are to weed out illogic, insufficient evidence, prejudices, and infeasible plans of action from our group deliberations.

Reestablishment.   In most instances you cannot be content merely to answer opponents' objections. You also should take the extra step of reestablishing your case as a whole. That is, you should first point out what portions of your argument have *not* been attacked and indicate their importance. Then you should introduce more evidence in support of your reconstructed case—further testimony, additional parallel cases—to bolster your argument as a whole. To return to our earlier example, you might indicate that no one has questioned your evidence on the site's unsuitability or the parallel cases you have presented. Underscoring these points once again with new material (perhaps held in reserve for just this situation) that paints a more dramatic picture of the safety risks may cause the audience to heed the issue, in spite of the counterarguments.

In conclusion, argumentative speaking demands many talents. To argue well, you must be able to determine rationally the evidence and inferences needed to support your claim; to distinguish between solid and fallacious reasoning; and to build both constructive and refutative speeches to meet the demands of give-and-take in public decision making. These are not easy tasks. Yet, they are worth attempting to accomplish. In times when people don't or can't argue well, despotism and chicanery tend to triumph, whether in the political arena of legislation or the business arena of marketing and sales policy. In learning to argue well, ultimately, you are learning to make yourself and your world more informed and enlightened.

A Sample Argumentative Speech (Claim of Policy)

Often it is not enough simply to argue in favor of some policy. Especially if you are challenging a generally valued institution with your policy claim, you have to be careful to (1) undermine (refute) the current policy of that institution, and yet (2) not destroy the overall credibility of the valued institution. This sort of problem was faced by Timothy L. Sellnow of St. Cloud State University when he proposed changes in the federal Food and Drug Administration's policy on artificial hearts.

Note his responses to his challengers: Paragraphs 1–3 introduce the subject matter and forecast the speech's developmental pattern; paragraph 4 finishes the orientation by describing an artificial heart. Then, Mr. Sellnow devotes paragraphs 6–11 to a refutation of the FDA's refusal to allow the University of Utah to do an artificial heart transplant. Furthermore, in offering and defending an alternative policy in paragraphs 12–16, he is very careful to protect the FDA's general reputation even while asking for changes. All that remains, then, is a quick call for action in paragraphs 14, 15, 18, and 19. As you read this speech, also be sensitive to the valuative premises Mr. Sellnow uses as foundations for his policy claim.

Arguments like those offered here apparently worked; the University of Utah surgical team was allowed to transplant an artificial heart into Dr. Barney Clark in December 1982. Since then, the team at St. Louis' Humana Hospital has performed several more artificial heart transplants.

A Missing Beat[7]
Timothy L. Sellnow

Attention step: *Use of startling* *statement*	"It's a miracle! The greatest single development in the battle against our nation's number one killer." These were the words chosen by doctors and journalists across the country to describe one of history's greatest developments in medical technology. The world watched in disbelief as the amazing function of the Artificial Heart was displayed through the mass media. The artificial heart's creators watched in disbelief as the American Food and Drug Administration refused to allow the use of this device.

/1

Need step: *Develops signifi-* *cance of issue*	The impact of this FDA decision can easily be seen through the current studies of the National Heart, Blood and Lung Institute which claims that 50,000 Americans per year could be given artificial hearts. This figure may seem inflated until one considers the fact that heart diseases will kill over a million Americans this year alone. /2
Statement of claim *Partition:* *Forecasting*	My goal today is to prove to you that the FDA is making a grave mistake by holding up the therapeutic application of the artificial heart. To do so, first I'll explain the artificial heart's function. Second, I'll present the FDA's arguments against the artificial heart along with upholding arguments by the heart's backers. Finally, I'll offer a practical solution to this problem. /3
Description	What is this new weapon in the arsenal of heart therapy? Experimentation with the artificial heart has continued over the past two decades. The particular heart in question is the Jarvik-7, developed by American Dr. Robert Jarvik. This mechanical heart is composed of plastic and aluminum and fits in the space left by a person's original heart. It is powered by a small air compressor connected by narrow tubes outside the body. This compressor is designed to be easily wheeled or placed in a wheel chair. It is keeping dogs, goats, and calves alive and active indefinitely, and its two temporary trials with humans were both highly successful. /4
Rhetorical *question* *Listing of major* *opposing argu-* *ments*	Why then if this device is safe and in such demand has the FDA banned its use? The FDA offers several basic reasons. First is a concern over when and how doctors would decide to implant the device. The FDA also wondered whether the proposed patient consent forms accurately describe the kind of life the implant recipient should expect. Finally, the FDA believes the proposal does not go into enough detail on what information will be gathered after the implant. /5
Factual claim *Testimony* *Value appeal*	If you're thinking that much of this reasoning sounds more technical than medical, you're right. Wayne Pines, a spokesman for the FDA, told a *New York Times* reporter that, "The main problem is with the study plan, not with the actual heart." It's sad to think that doctors helplessly watch 3,000 Americans a day die of heart disease while our FDA worries about study plans. /6
Refutation of op- *posing arguments* *(1) = (A)* *Testimony*	Dr. Jarvik and the rest of the University of Utah's research team have some powerful arguments to counter the FDA's concerns. They first address the issue of when and how the artificial heart would be used. Dr. Willem Kolff, overall director of the research team, stated that the decision to use the heart would come only in the operating room when the heart of a patient who has undergone conventional surgery cannot be revived. Only when all known means for reviving the natural heart fail, and the doctors would ordinarily give up, will they turn to artificial hearts. /7
(2) = (B) *Testimony*	Next, the team turns to the FDA's concern about the consent form. First, Dr. William DeVries, the team's chief surgeon, is careful to point out that no heart will be forced on anyone. All patients must give approval before undergoing serious heart surgery of any kind. DeVries says the patient and his spouse or family would be counseled before surgery, letting them know all risks and limitations involving the artificial heart. He says, ". . .

only families deemed likely to cope well with such circumstances will be considered.''   /8

(3) = (C)

Example

The research team's response to the FDA's challenge of observing their patients closely after the implant is, in their opinion, obvious. The Utah researchers feel they are very close to such developments as an electrically powered heart which could allow a patient full mobility and eliminate any outside equipment. Developments such as these are absolutely impossible without the close monitoring and analysis of all artificial heart recipients.   /9

Transition
Rhetorical
questions—
anticipate/answer
objections

Comparison/
contrast

At this point, two other questions arise. Could enough artificial hearts be produced to meet the tremendous demand, and how will recipients pay for it? Will enough artificial hearts be produced? With FDA approval, mass production of the artificial heart could begin immediately. In fact, Dr. DeVries maintains that up to 5,000 successful operations could be performed within approximately a year of the heart's approval. This is a sharp contrast to the 30 annual organic transplants performed today.   /10

Causal argument

Cost will certainly be an obstacle in the beginning, but because the artificial heart can be produced in mass production, and requires no continuous hospitalization, the Utah medical crew believes the cost will steadily drop after its approval. With FDA approval, further financial support would be given by such insurance agencies as Blue Cross and Blue Shield, and the artificial heart's research and use would receive extensive government financial assistance.   /11

Now that you are aware of the evidence that the artificial heart can work, and that it is in great need, the only question remaining is how to solve this controversy. I would like to offer a solution aimed at the immediate problem, as well as future benefits.   /12

Solution to current
problem

Benefit

Value appeal

The most immediate compromise that can be reached with the FDA is to use the artificial heart as a temporary substitute for patients awaiting an organic heart for transplant. Though the Utah experts are ready for its permanent use, they are willing, and anxious to begin the implant process with even this short-term measure. Thus they can continue perfecting the artificial heart while saving human lives. The heart's creators are ready to save lives, now we must urge the FDA to do the same.   /13

Appeal for assistance

Rhetorical question—anticipates objection

Benefits

It is up to each one of us to stay informed, and speak out to friends and family about the artificial heart, and the immediate necessity for its acceptance. Ask your doctor about it and urge him to actively support the artificial heart as well. The way is open for us to take a direct part in this issue. Call or write your local chapter of the FDA and urge others to do so. Sounds like the first step to nearly every solution, right? That may be so, but in this case it bears special weight. Already the organized opposition to this FDA ruling has become so great, that the FDA is publicly considering allowing the artificial heart's use in a closely monitored experiment involving seven hopeless heart patients. With our support and pressure, that number can grow from 7 to the 5,000 the artificial heart can reach now, and the 50,000 the device can reach annually in the near future.   /14

You can individually aid the cause by continuing your financial support of such research organizations as the American Heart Association, one of the many organizations which gives its full fledged support for the immediate use of the artificial heart.   /15

Solution to future
problems

In the long run, some changes need to be made in the FDA's methods. I'm not denouncing the FDA as an administration. I'm not even asking them to stop anything. Instead, the FDA needs to add a clause to their current policy for dealing with therapeutic devices. Today, the FDA is forced to say yes or no to the regular use of a medical device. What is needed is an intermediate clause that would allow the FDA to say no to a device they feel needs more work, yet allow its use in people who oth-

Benefits

erwise stand no chance for survival. This step would at least lessen the blow of such FDA decisions as with the artificial heart.   /16

Finally, for your own benefit, make sure your health insurance includes coverage of such therapeutic operations, and take care of your own heart.   /17

These actions and changes will not only aid in the development of the artificial heart, they will benefit whatever medical breakthroughs lie ahead.   /18

Closing

Please join in this effort. So many people stand to benefit, maybe even you. I'll leave you with the words of Dr. Steven Fredman: "In matters of

Testimony

the heart, procrastination is hardly the best policy."   /19

REFERENCE NOTES

[1]See Henry M. Robert, *Robert's Rules of Order Newly Revised,* ed. Sarah Corbin Robert, Henry M. Robert III, William J. Evans, and James W. Cleary (Glenview, IL: Scott, Foresman and Company, 1981).

[2]See Richard Rieke and Malcolm O. Sillars, *Argumentation and the Decision Making Process,* 2nd ed (Glenview, IL: Scott, Foresman and Company, 1983); Stephen Toulmin, Richard Rieke, and Allan Janik, *An Introduction to Reasoning* (New York: Macmillan, 1979), Chapters 13–17.

[3]A full discussion of the logical grounding of claims in evidence and reasoning is presented in Douglas Ehninger and Wayne Brockriede, *Decision by Debate,* 2nd ed. (New York: Harper & Row, Publishers, 1978).

[4]For a fuller discussion of persuasive definitions, see Charles L. Stevenson, *Ethics and Language* (New Haven: Yale University Press, 1944), Chapter 9, "Second Pattern of Analysis: Persuasive Definitions."

[5]For further information and discussion, see a good introductory logic textbook such as Irving M. Copi, *Introduction to Logic,* 5th ed. (New York: Macmillan Pub. Co., Inc., 1978), especially Chapters 2 and 3.

[6]See Charles S. Mudd and Malcolm O. Sillars, *Speech: Content and Communication,* 4th ed. (New York: Harper and Row, 1979), Chapter 7, "Analysis of Issues." Also, see the discussion of a criteria case in George Ziegelmueller and Charles S. Dause, *Argumentation: Inquiry and Advocacy* (Englewood Cliffs, NJ: Prentice-Hall, 1975), pp. 168–70.

[7]"A Missing Beat" by Timothy L. Sellnow. Reprinted from *Winning Orations,* 1982, by special arrangement with the Interstate Oratorical Association, Larry Schnoor, Executive Secretary, Mankato State College, Mankato, Minnesota.

PROBLEMS AND PROBES

1. How influential are political debates in campaign years? In researching this question, consult such sources as S. Kraus, ed., *The Great Debates, 1976,* and L. Bitzer and T. Reuter, *Carter vs. Ford.* Present your critical summary in written form or as part of a class discussion on the role of argument in decision making.

2. Think through two or three of the informal arguments you have engaged in during the last few days: in the student union; in classroom discussions; in exchanges with an instructor, a close friend, or your roommate. *(a)* In any of them, did you present a relatively sustained speech? *(b)* What kinds of arguments and reasons for accepting those arguments did you offer as the disagreement progressed? *(c)* Did you or any of the other arguers become angry? If so, who handled it—and how? *(d)* Looking back, recall whether you or any others invoked conventions of self-risk ("How can you stubbornly hold that view?"), the fairness doctrine ("Come on! Give me a chance to explain!"), or a commitment to rationality ("That's the dumbest reason I ever heard! Don't you have any better reasons than that?"). Prepare a short paper summarizing the foregoing analysis and, in addition, clearly distinguishing informal arguments of this type from the more formal ones we have considered in this chapter. Hand your written analysis to the instructor and be prepared to discuss your ideas.

3. Assume you are going to give a speech favoring the draft to an audience of fellow students who are hostile to your proposal. Outline your speech by utilizing Toulmin's model of argument as it is discussed in the Speaker's Resource Book. What factors do you consider as you construct and frame your argument? Assume several counterarguments are made from audience members. Rebuild your case utilizing the Toulmin model. What new factors must you now consider?

ORAL ACTIVITIES

1. Prepare a ten-minute argumentative exchange on a topic involving you and one other member of the class. Dividing the available time equally, one of you will advocate a claim, the other will oppose it. Adopt any format you both feel comfortable with. You may choose: *(a)* a Lincoln/Douglas format—the first person speaks four minutes, the second, five, and then the first person returns for a one-minute rejoinder; *(b)* an issue format—you both agree on, say, two key issues, and then each one of you speaks for two and a half minutes on each issue; *(c)* a debate format—each speaker talks twice alternatively, three minutes in a constructive speech, two minutes in rebuttal; and *(d)* a heckling format—each of you has five minutes, but during the middle of each speech, the audience or your opponent may ask you questions.

2. Turn the class into a parliamentary assembly; decide on a motion or resolution to be argued; and then schedule a day or two for a full debate. This format should utilize particular argumentative roles: advocate, witness, direct examiner, cross-examiner, summarizer. It allows each speaker to be part of a team; what you do affects not only yourself but also other speakers on your side of the argument. (For guidance in the use of this format, see John D. May, ed., *American Problems: What Should Be Done? Debates from "The Advocates"* [Palo Alto, CA: National Press Books, 1973]).

CHAPTER 17

Speeches to Persuade and Actuate

We live in a complex society, one guaranteeing that no one can accomplish any sizable task without help. Others must be convinced that the task is worthwhile and offer time, effort, and money to see that it's completed. Today's advocate has to be able to persuade people to change their beliefs, attitudes, and sometimes their basic values, and to move them to act upon those changes. Speeches to persuade and actuate fill evening newscasts and talk shows, political rallies and conventions, neighborhood meetings, public hearings, and church basements. They come in many forms—ads, radio and television interviews, street corner and front porch solicitations, auditorium-filled rallies, city council hearings, and garden party conversations. Persuasive talk keeps our society moving forward. Informative speeches assemble and package important data and ideas, while persuasive and actuative messages bring about subsequent alterations in thought and action.

In this chapter, we will examine some of the skills especially important to persuasive and actuative speakers; drawing upon some of the psychologically and structurally oriented chapters from Part Two of this book, we'll extend and apply those ideas within a distinctively persuasive frame of reference. First, types of persuasive and actuative speeches will be discussed. Next, we will review four essential features of all persuasive messages, regardless of type. Finally, we'll illustrate the typical structures or outlines of persuasive speeches of each kind.

Types of Persuasive and Actuative Speeches

Although there are many ways to classify persuasive and actuative speeches, we will discuss them here by reference to their essentially human elements—their psychological and behavioral force. That is, in classifying these speech types, we are interested in the demands each type makes upon the audience's mental state and level of activity.

Such a focus will allow us to identify three principal types of persuasive and actuative speeches and also to examine some subtypes. We will examine *speeches of reinforcement, psychological change,* and *actuation,* together with three kinds of psychological change.

Reinforcement

Americans are joiners. Since childhood, you have been urged to join something—the Boy Scouts, the Campfire Girls, the church choir, the school band, the volleyball team. To get our political, economic, social, and personal work done, we constantly organize ourselves into groups and associations. Such groups provide each of us with part of our identity, as when you tell people, "I'm a Sierra Club member" or "I'm a Chicano Studies major." They also serve you by gathering and packaging the latest information, keeping on top of problems and proposals for solutions, dispensing funds and other resources to needy people, playing the watchdog, sponsoring retreats and conferences, and on and on.

Even the most dynamic group or association, however, discovers along the way that its membership declines, that its joiners get tired, that its cause gets lost among all of the other causes in society. Periodically, people have to be reminded of why they joined the group, what the services are, and how the group helps them meet their personal goals. Those reminders are matters of reinforcement. *Reinforcement,* in public speaking, is a process of calling up the original beliefs and values which caused people to join a group in the first place, and of reinvigorating audiences so that they once more contribute their time, energy, and finances to the tasks needing to be done.

Psychologically, reinforcement speeches are built around beliefs, attitudes, and values already possessed by audience members; the appeal is to "old" commitments. The dominant state of mind of listeners in situations calling for reinforcement is *apathy,* with lethargy being the state of their physical activity. Every fall the United Way asks you to contribute; such public lobbies as Common Cause or the American Rifle Association periodically send out an SOS to their members when an important bill is up for consideration and when they need public pressure to ensure its defeat or passage; labor and other group conventions are keynoted by fiery orators who point out the work to be done by the organizations. These are times for reinforcement speaking.

The key to reinforcement speaking is *motivation.* While people may say, "Sure, I support the Republican Party," or "Yeah, I believe in People for the American Way and their efforts to stop censorship in public school libraries," they often seem unmotivated. They need to have their original commitments resurrected; they need to be stirred to action. Those tasks are accomplished by reinforcement speakers principally through motivational appeals.

Psychological Change

Although the study of rhetoric is nearly three thousand years old, over the last half-century persuasion has been increasingly considered more than the art of rhetoric; it has become a science based on audience psychology. Also, professional persuasion has become big business. Universities and colleges spew forth hordes of trained "practi-

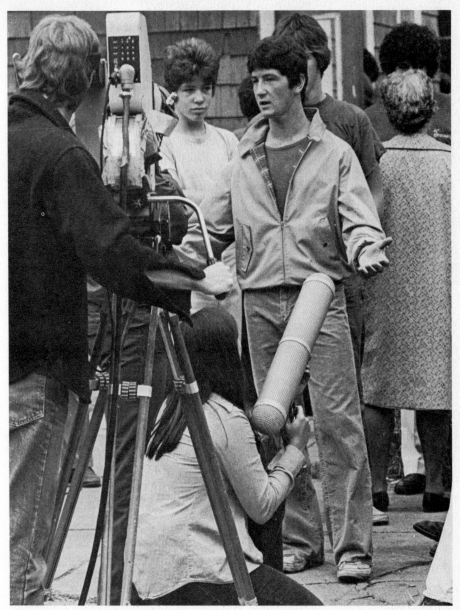

Societies overcome shortcomings, conquer new collective problems, and get their members involved with others through persuasion. Persuasion processes provide social bonds.

cal'' researchers who fill jobs with television networks, religious establishments, public relations departments in corporations, governmental bureaus, and public utilities. The business of changing people's minds is everywhere.

Persuasion, in general, therefore, is an idea encompassing a tremendously broad range of communication activities. Because we are focusing on speechmaking in this book, however, we will narrow the concept somewhat: *Persuasive speaking is the process of producing oral messages which alter some set of beliefs, attitudes, or values of an audience.* Persuasive speeches, within this technical definition, are aimed at changing the mental contents of listeners' heads. Using the vocabulary of "beliefs-attitudes-values" as it was developed earlier, we can identify three subtypes of speeches aiming at the psychological change:

Changing Beliefs.   The psychological basis for most speeches attempting to change someone's beliefs about the world is *differentiation*. That is, one can get you to change your beliefs about everything from eating seaweed to the balance of power between the U.S. and the U.S.S.R. by getting you to perceive those matters in different ways. Such persuaders who are attempting to get you to differentiate between your old way of looking at something and a new way of seeing it may use one or more of three basic strategies:

1. *Selective description.* The persuader may accentuate the positive and ignore the negative. You may be persuaded to accept seaweed as an edible food by someone who assures you that its vitamin and mineral content is superior to that of land-raised greens and that its taste is enhanced in processing, while ignoring questions you might have about other health-related questions or about cost of processing.

2. *Narrative.* A persuader may use narrative forms as we discussed them earlier, telling you a story about England in the 1930s, a country which ignored the arms buildup in Germany and its own lack of military preparedness before the beginning of World War II, with the moral of the story being that the U.S. likewise has to be ready for militaristic advances from Russia.

3. *Appeals to uniqueness.* Someone attempting to get you to change your beliefs about a politician may convince you that Candidate X is "not like all the others," pointing to unique aspects of the candidate's background, experience, public service, honesty, and commitments.

In all three examples, differentiation is being attempted. You as an audience member are asked to perceive some thing, relationship, or person in a new way so that you will change a belief you held before.

Changing Attitudes.   Attitude-change is probably the most heavily researched psychological change in this century.[1] Given our definition of *attitudes* earlier, you already know that attitude-change is a process of changing someone's evaluative predispositions—of convincing them that something previously thought to be good, beautiful, or right really should be thought of as bad, ugly, or wrong. Because attitudes, as we noted, are attached to beliefs ("The U.S. is militarily superior to Russia [the belief] and that is good [the attitude]"), sometimes persuaders attempt to change an attitude by attacking the underlying belief (in this case, showing you the U.S. is militarily inferior to Russia, and hence that's bad). And, because attitudes are organized into groups under some value in one's head, attitudes also can be changed occasionally by getting people to think in different valuative terms. For instance, proponents of a freeze on nuclear weapons have attempted to get members of the western and eastern blocs to think of their weaponry not in terms of power (a political value), but in terms of sheer human survival (a sociological value).

Attitudes can be changed not only by attacking underlying beliefs or overarching values, but also by direct assault. Parents often attempt to instill any number of attitudes in their young children—"Spinach is good for you"; "Children should be seen and not heard"; "Don't do something simply because your friends do it"—by repeatedly offering short lectures on those subjects. The attitude is expressed over and over and over again, and, sooner or later, the children accept it as their own. Such direct assaults on attitudes are called *brainwashing* when "they" (enemies or malicious people) use this technique and *education* when "we" (friends or "right-thinking" people) use it.

Because attitude-change is central to the persuasion process, we will examine more attitude-changing techniques in the next section of this chapter.

Changing Values.   Perhaps the most difficult challenge for any persuader is changing people's orienting values. As we noted in earlier chapters, a person's values are fundamental anchors, basic ways of organizing one's view of the world and one's actions in it. Attitudes are difficult to change in many circumstances. Yet, talented persuaders can meet these challenges. Three techniques often are used:

1. *Valuative shifts*. One technique parallels differentiation, asking you to look at something differently, but, in this case, from a different valuative vantage point. The person asking you to buy insurance, for example, tells you to look at it not simply as financial protection (a pragmatic value), but as family protection and a source of peace of mind (sociological and psychological values). Such appeals can get people to shift their valuative orientation.

2. *Appeals to consistency*. When you hear such appeals as "All members of the American Legion favor . . . ," you as a member of that organization are being asked to favor some measure in order to be in a way consistent with your positive evaluation of that group. Or, when someone says, "If you liked *Jaws II* you'll love *Jaws III,*" they're again appealing to cognitive consistency.

3. *Transcendence*. A sophisticated method for getting you to change your values attempts to get you to see some object or action from a "higher" value. Such appeals were used on both sides of the Watergate issue in the early 1970s. President Richard Nixon appealed to "national security" (which was why he wouldn't release White House records) and "the integrity of the presidency" (which is why he wouldn't answer every little question asked of him). And, his detractors constantly told us that more was at stake than the 1972 election, as they in grandiloquent words implored us to see as their "mission" the destruction of "political corruption" and the return of America to a course of "public morality." Both sides sought to change evaluations of their activities by appealing to higher values.

Psychological change, therefore, takes at least three different forms—changing beliefs, attitudes, and values. Speeches seeking these kinds of mental adjustments from listeners demand a level of communicative competence which exceeds the skills needed for most other kinds of speeches. Yet, as you know from your own experience, these competencies can be acquired by speakers willing to think through situations calling for such kinds of persuasion and willing to work hard at speech preparation.[2]

Actuation

Moving the uncommitted or apathetic members in society to action is a chore many people would as soon avoid: "I don't like to ask people to contribute money to a cause, even if it's worthy"; "Don't ask *me* to take that petition out for signatures—I feel like I'm intruding on others' privacy"; "I'm just not persuasive enough to get people to volunteer to work at the Senior Citizens' Care Center—ask Joe." But the world would never improve, causes would not attain their goals, and lots of us would not make much of a living if we didn't learn how to move people to action. Sooner or later, the buck will stop at *your* front door, and you'll have to give an actuative speech.

An actuative speech seeks as its final outcome a set of specifiable actions from its audience. "Moving an audience to action" includes several different kinds of behaviors—the giving of one's time to some activity (writing letters to state legislators for or against a bill), contributing of money for some product or cause (purchasing a brand of computer or sending in a donation to Ducks Unlimited), or altering one's general lifestyle (stopping smoking or taking up a fitness program). "Moving to action" is a phrase normally applied to two kinds of communication situations. The first is characterized by apathetic believers—the situation we discussed in part already. The second is characterized by doubting, uninformed, or uninvolved audiences—the situation we're concerned with here.

Actuative speeches of this sort, then, are those which demand significant behavioral change from listeners. They demand *action* as we defined that concept in Chapter 8. (As noted in that chapter, the motivated sequence was designed primarily to bring about overt changes in human behavior.) That action might be as short-range as making a profit the next quarter of the fiscal year, or as long-range as the sociopolitical revolution of one's society.

Whatever the extent or loftiness of the goal, all actuative speeches depend, psychologically, upon making salient a body of needs within an audience, and then showing the audience that some course of action will satisfy those needs. Structurally, almost all actuative speeches fit into the motivated sequence, although some will use one of the other organizational patterns discussed in Chapter 9. And, as in all the kinds of speeches discussed in this chapter, the key to effectiveness is *motivation*. No matter how wonderful the new product, no matter how exciting you think a political candidate is, no matter how worthy the cause, unless a listener is personally convinced that the product, the candidate, or the cause will make a significant change in his or her life, your speech is likely to fail.

Overall, then, it is useful to think of persuasive and actuative speeches as coming in three varieties—centering on reinforcement, psychological change, and actuation—with "psychological change" subdivided into speeches which attempt to change beliefs, attitudes, and values. Now that we have introduced these types of speeches and a few of their basic techniques, let's look more closely at some essential features of the persuasion and actuative processes that operate in oral communication situations.

Essential Features of Persuasive and Actuative Speeches

Regardless of the specific type of speech you are giving, persuasive and actuative speeches include a series of challenges that speakers must meet. These challenges comprise their essential features: *(1)* adaptation to psychological states; *(2)* change by degrees; *(3)* saliency and its effect upon strategies; and *(4)* credibility.

Adaptation to Psychological States

By *psychological states* we refer to audience members' general predisposition to respond to certain messages even before they are delivered. The general psychological states of audiences tend to vary a good deal from situation to situation, from group to group; you must try to assess that state, therefore, before constructing any persuasive or actuative speech. While the social-scientific communication research on psychological states of listeners increases with each new issue of journals such as *Human Communication Research* and *Communication Monographs,* there are some indisputable truisms which follow from research already done. We can discuss these conclusions conveniently under three headings: audiences' general predispositions toward the topic, their cognitive complexity or sophistication, and their dependence upon reference groups.

General Predisposition Toward Topics.   As we have said earlier, generally speaking an audience may have any one of five attitudes toward your topic and purpose. It may be *(a)* favorable but not aroused to act; *(b)* apathetic toward the situation; *(c)* interested in it but undecided what to do or think about it; *(d)* interested in the situation but hostile to the proposed attitude, belief, or action; or *(e)* hostile to any change from the present state of affairs. Furthermore, when talking about beliefs and attitudes, we noted that, for all of us, our specific beliefs about some thing or our specific attitudes toward it may be well fixed or very infirm, depending upon their importance to us and our view of the world. All of this means that you must pre-gauge these dispositions toward your purpose and topic, and be able to adjust your communicative strategies accordingly.

More specifically: *(1)* When an audience is hostile toward your claim, be sure that you present a *two-sided message*. A one-sided speech offers only arguments for your claim, while a two-sided speech takes into account opposing ideas and proposals and then answers them. If you expect resistance, do not simply ignore it. *(2)* If the hostility is extreme, deal with it *early* in the speech; if it is moderate or if the audience is nearly neutral, deal with opposing arguments *late* in the speech. In other words, the skilled persuasive or actuative speaker always tries to deal with the main thrust of the audience's predispositions toward the purpose and topic near the beginning.

Regarding specific beliefs and attitudes: *(3)* The more *fixed* and *important* the beliefs and attitudes you are trying to change, the more resistant individuals will be. Conversely, the more a person's beliefs and attitudes depend upon peripheral authorities and experiences, the easier they are to change. *(4)* The more *central* some set of beliefs, attitudes, and values are to a person, the more likely it is that you will run into a *network* of interconnected concepts. A study by Prescott demonstrated clearly, for example, people who are against abortion are likely to be in favor of physical punishment of children, capital punishment for criminals, and domineering fathers, and against pros-titution, nudity, premarital sex, and drugs.[3] You as a persuader, therefore, must attempt to assess the degree to which you are invading cognitive or emotional networks when you advocate change. If you are, you should either attempt to deal with the whole complex (which is extremely difficult to do) or work hard at separating one issue from the interconnected ones.

Cognitive Complexity.   The term *cognitive complexity* refers to the conceptual sophis-tication of people—not simply the number of things they know, but rather their abilities to deal mentally with a wide range of causes, implications, and associated notions when thinking about some idea or event. A person's cognitive complexity is in part intelli-gence, in part maturity, and in part experience. Although not all the evidence on the effects of cognitive complexity is in as yet, this much we know: *(1)* cognitively com-plex audiences demand and can follow relatively *sophisticated arguments; (2)* they respond better to *two-sided* rather than one-sided presentations; *(3)* they require a com-paratively large amount of *evidence* before they will change beliefs and attitudes. We also know that *(4)* cognitively complex speakers generate more *strategically sound tactics* and hence are (and are perceived as) more *effective communicators.*[4]

Demagogues for years have assumed that they can hoodwink any audience, but as our population as a whole has gained experience in group dynamics and decision-making, and as our country's general educational level has risen markedly, we are undermining that assumption. Unless you are dealing with a group of fledgling five-year-olds, you had better be prepared to offer well-developed analyses of problems and their solutions, replete with authoritative supporting materials, with answers to counterarguments, and with logical structures. You may not need all of those materials once you are perceived as a true expert, but few of us have achieved or will attain that level.

Reference Groups.   *Reference groups* are collections of people and organizations which affect individuals' beliefs, attitudes, and values. You may or may not hold an actual membership in such groups; you may belong, say, to the Young Republicans Club and not belong to a sorority, yet each group can influence your beliefs. Some groups you may join voluntarily, as in the examples just noted, while others are invol-untary, as for instance your membership in a male or female gender group or your cultural-ethnic heritage. Some groups may affect you positively, as do those which believe what you do, while others can produce negative reactions, as is the case for people who say, "If the communists are for it, I'm against it." We may think of reference groups, then, as *membership* and *nonmembership groups, voluntary* and *involuntary groups,* and *positive* and *negative groups.*

Individuals vary in the degree to which they rely upon reference groups when they are making a decision on what to think or do; yet all of us, to some extent, have beliefs, attitudes, and values rooted in our group experiences. As a speaker, you should use this aspect of people's general psychological state when constructing all persuasive and actuative messages: *(1)* Citing the opinions of voluntary, positive membership groups which *coincide* with positions you are taking is likely to increase your effectiveness. This is a matter, as the Greeks noted 2500 years ago, of "praising Athens to the

Athenians,'' of using the positive characteristics of the group to influence the individual member of that group. *(2)* Citing the opinions of voluntary, negative nonmembership groups which *oppose* positions you are taking is likely to increase your effectiveness. Such groups can be thought of as ''devils'' to which people react; if the claims you are defending go counter to the thinking and actions of devil-groups, your audience will tend to agree with your proposals. *(3)* The greater people's *roles* are in any group, the more that group's norms and beliefs will influence their thought and behavior. Corporate executives, for example, tend to have more important roles in business than do new, relatively powerless workers; hence, it is more difficult to produce radical business-oriented changes in executives than in front-line workers.[5]

In summary, audiences' predisposing psychological states—their attitudes toward the purpose and topic, their cognitive complexity, and their group memberships—can affect, even decisively, their reactions to your persuasive and actuative messages, and hence should help you determine your overall strategies.

Change by Degrees

A second essential feature of all persuasive and actuative speeches is that people will change only so much when they hear a speech. It is almost literally impossible, except in the rarest of circumstances (for example, radical religious experiences), to make wholesale changes in people's beliefs, attitudes, and values. Ordinarily, you should attempt to make *incremental changes*—moving people toward some goal step by step. The distance you can move an audience is determined by two principal psychological factors: *(a)* their *initial attitudinal predisposition,* and *(b)* the *latitude of change* they as individuals can tolerate.

Initial Attitudinal Predisposition.   Imagine a line which represents someone's attitude toward, say, abortion; imagine, too, that it is divided into ten segments, with *1* representing ''extremely favorable toward abortion laws''; *3*, ''moderately favorable''; *4,* ''mildly favorable''; *5,* ''neutral''; *6,* ''mildly unfavorable''; *8,* ''moderately unfavorable''; and *10,* ''strongly unfavorable toward abortion laws.'' If you attempted to convince someone who was strongly unfavorable (''*10*'') that federal abortion laws should be fervently supported (a *1* position), you undoubtedly would fail miserably in most circumstances. Even in the face of credible speakers and well-thought out arguments, most radical ''anti's'' could be moved only a short way toward the ''pro'' position—say, to a *6* or a *5,* or maybe a *4* position. Trying to change them too much in a single speech can produce what we earlier termed a *boomerang effect;* such people, in the face of the strong *1* speech, will become even more committed to their *10* position.[6]

Obviously, it is impossible for a speaker to interview all audience members, writing down their attitudinal predispositions numerically. Good audience analysis, however, allows you at least to guess shrewdly and to adjust your appeals and plans of action accordingly.

Latitudes of Change.   A second question of degree can be phrased: How much change does an individual tolerate? The answer to this question varies from individual to

INCREMENTAL APPROACH TO ATTITUDE CHANGE

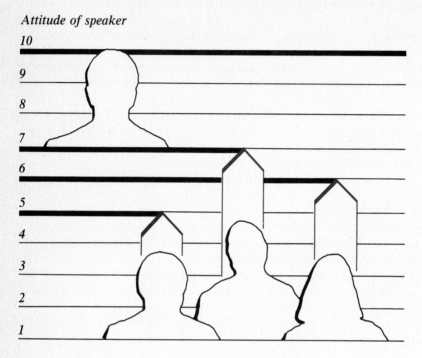

Incremental attitude change of audience

individual as well as from topic to topic. Some people—often termed *authoritarian* or *dogmatic personalities* in the research literature—tolerate little change. These people have a narrow "latitude of acceptance"; in terms of our numerical scale, we can say that their attitudes are anchored firmly on, say, the 6 or the 5 and 6 positions. Other people, however, are more nonauthoritarian or non-dogmatic; they may accept proposals across the entire 3–6 range without trouble. In other words, they are what we normally call "open-minded" personalities, and are more easy to persuade or to move to action.[7]

Again, the rhetorically sensitive speaker should attempt to assess the authoritarianism or dogmatism of listeners. Deeply committed groups—especially those on the right or left ends of the social-political spectrum—are extremely difficult to persuade in a single speech; they may demand a sustained campaign in which you move them toward your desired end only by small steps. You must try, in your audience analysis, to estimate the latitudes of acceptance operative in that group and adjust your appeals and proposals accordingly, just as you did when you assessed its initial attitudinal predisposition.

Saliency and Its Effect on Strategies

Saliency refers to the relevance and interest level of some belief, attitude, or topic. For example, topics making front-page news are highly salient to people, as are beliefs and attitudes we think about regularly, experiences we often have, and people we are close to. Two aspects of saliency are especially important as you consider persuasive and actuative speeches: *(1)* The more salient a particular topic, the more likely members of your audience will have *preknowledge* of it and perhaps even specific beliefs about and attitudes toward it. *(2)* And, the more salient a particular topic, the more likely listeners will *resist changes* in their beliefs and attitudes. Topics in the news or those dealing with everyday occurrences probably need little development of their attention step, for example, while those with low saliency may demand considerable background. Again, if you are attacking a highly salient belief or attitude, you can expect listeners to oppose your positions; as we suggested earlier, you probably ought to deal explicitly with their opposition early in the need step, and work hard in the satisfaction step to demonstrate that new beliefs and reformed attitudes are necessary if the problem is to be solved. Finally, a third facet of saliency should be noted: *(3)* Quote salient *authorities* in your persuasive and actuative speeches. George Washington, for example, was indeed President of the United States and hence an authority, but he perhaps is not nearly so salient an authority as a President from recent years.[8]

Credibility

This last point brings us to another essential feature of all persuasive and actuative speeches: A good deal of your potential effectiveness will depend upon your perceived credibility or *ethos*. In Chapter 1 we outlined several factors which can determine an audience's sense of your credibility—their sense of your expertise, trustworthiness, competency, sincerity or honesty, friendliness and concern for others, and personal dynamism. While you should work to maximize all these factors whenever you speak, some of these factors are especially important in persuasive and actuative speeches:

1. Try to maximize an audience's sense of your *competency* and *sincerity* when seeking to *persuade*. People are unlikely to change their beliefs and attitudes if they think you have incompetently reviewed alternatives and evaluated the current attitudes toward some proposal. And, if they find you pig-headed and insincere, they will be convinced you have ulterior motives in mind as you talk to them. You can increase their confidence in your competency by: *(a)* carefully sorting through all of the competing positions, ideas, and proposals relevant to some topic before you come to your judgment; *(b)* reviewing various criteria for judgment (see above) to show that your recommendations or positions flow from accepted and generally held criteria; and *(c)* showing that recommendations you offer will actually solve problems you have identified in the need step. And, you can increase their sense of your sincerity by: *(a)* showing yourself to be open to correction and criticism should any listener wish to question you; *(b)* exuding personal warmth in your relations with them; *(c)* maintaining direct eye contact with listeners; and *(d)* recognizing anyone who has helped you understand and work on this problem. These simple but important pieces of advice, if followed, should bolster your credibility when persuading others.

2. Heighten the audience's sense of your *expertise, friendliness,* and *dynamism,* especially when seeking to move them to *action.* People are unlikely to change their
routines and behaviors on your recommendation unless they feel you know what you
are talking about, have their best interests in mind, and get excited by your commitment and enthusiasm. A perception of expertise can be created by: *(a)* docu-
menting your sources of information; *(b)* using varied sources of information as
cross-checks on each other; *(c)* carefully presenting your information and need
analyses in well-organized ways; *(d)* building easy-to-understand visual aids when
you use them; *(e)* providing enough background information on controversial issues
so that your listeners can understand why you are proposing what you are; *(f)*
separating causes from effects, short-term from long-term effects, hard facts from
soft wishes or dreams, and one proposal from others in a competent manner; and *(g)*
delivering your speeches in a forthright and calm manner. A sense of friendliness
and concern for others can be generated by: *(a)* treating yourself and others as
human beings no matter what the topic and no matter how much you disagree with
others; and *(b)* depersonalizing issues, talking in terms of the "real world" and its
problems rather than in terms of personalities and ideologies. And an audience's
perception of your dynamism can be fostered by *(a)* a use of vivid examples, sharp
and fresh metaphors, active rather than passive verbs, and short, hard-hitting oral
sentences rather than long, cumbersome written sentences; and *(b)* a use of varied,
conversational vocal patterns, an animated body, direct eye contact with freedom
from your notes, and a firm upright stance.[9]

In summary, remember that a public speaker's principal communicative virtue is the
presence of a living, active human being behind the lectern—a person *embodying* a
message. People command more attention and interest than written words; and, people,
unlike films and videotapes, can feel, can react to audience members, can create a sense
of urgency and directness. Hence, personal presence and credibility are extremely
valuable assets for the would-be persuader and actuator.

Structuring Persuasive and Actuative Speeches

Presumably, any of the organizational patterns could be used for structuring persuasive
and actuative speeches; consider each one carefully when thinking about ordering your
speech materials. For the sake of convenience and for comparative purposes, however,
we will illustrate utilitarian structures for persuasive and actuative speeches here by
employing the motivated sequence. The sequence represents a time- and experience-
tested formula for meeting the demands of most speaking situations.

The Motivated Sequence and Reinforcement Speeches
Generally, for reinforcement speeches, the visualization and action steps are the crucial
segments. This is because the listeners usually have been attending to the problem for
some time, certainly have been aware of the problem, and even have accepted various
plans of action as satisfactory in the past. The most important goal in a reinforcement

A SAMPLE OUTLINE OF A SPEECH ON A CLAIM OF FACT

Safe At Home

Specific Purpose:
To convince listeners to take steps
to prevent home accidents.

*Attention
Step*

I. Everyone has heard the expression "safe at home."
II. But is your home really a safe place to live?

*Need
Step*

I. This is a question of importance to each of us.
A. Our own well-being is at stake.
B. The well-being of our families is at stake.

*Satisfaction
Step*

I. In answering the question of home safety, we must consider two *additional* questions.
A. How many accidents occur in the home?
B. How serious are these accidents?
II. In neither case are the facts encouraging.
A. Statistics gathered by the National Safety Council show that, in the year 1979, accidents in the home were responsible for 4,200,000 disabling injuries.
B. In the same year, home accidents were the cause of 27,500 deaths.

*Visualization
Step*

I. Unless we are aware of these dangers and guard against them, we, too, may be numbered among the victims of home accidents.
A. We may be "laid up" for long periods of time.
B. Our children and loved ones may be killed or permanently injured.

*Action
Step*

I. Take steps today to avoid such tragedies.
A. Put firm railings and good lights on all staircases.
B. Keep matches and combustible materials out of the reach of children.
C. Dispose of all plastic bags as soon as they are emptied.
D. Keep all poisonous substances under lock and key.
II. Remember, your home will be a safe place only if you yourself make it so.

speech is to get listeners to renew their previous commitments and to once more charge into the public arena to get something done.

Thus, a typical reinforcement speech following the motivated sequence usually has a short attention step, a need step which documents recent gains and losses (especially losses which illustrate the desirability of reattacking the problem), little or no satisfaction step, a more fully developed visualization step (which lets listeners "see" themselves back at work), and an action step which focuses on particular steps to take now (as audiences for these speeches usually are ready to go). Following is an outline for a speech aimed at members of Common Cause, a citizens' lobby concerned with governance procedures at the national and state levels of government. Little time is spent telling listeners what Common Cause is all about, because they already know that; most of the time is devoted to reminding them of problems they pledged to fight, visualizing the fights left to be waged, and calling them into specific action in the near future.

In Common We Can Win[10]

Specific Purpose: To reinforce the listeners' previous commitments to Common Cause so that they once more become actively involved in the organization's programs.

Attention Step

I. First off, let me thank the hundreds of you who sent letters and telegrams to our congressional delegation in support of changing laws on financing federal congressional campaigns.
   A. Five out of six of our congressional representatives voted for the recent bill.
   B. Even though it did not pass, your efforts did not go unnoticed; and your messages are being passed on to the House Committee on Elections for further consideration.

II. Even though we have had some successes in this state, there is more to be done.
   A. Although corporations, banks, and unions by law cannot contribute directly to candidates for federal office, they can set up voluntary political action committees (PACs) to channel contributions.
   B. Today, I want to review the operations of some PACs aligned against us, and suggest steps we can take to blunt their power.

Need Step

I. As Fred Wertheimer, Senior Vice-President of Common Cause, has noted, "interest group political giving is a growth industry," and figures from the Federal Election Commission bear him out.
   A. Between 1974 and 1976, 650 new PACs were born.
   B. In 1977, another 230 new PACs appeared.
   C. In just the first two months of 1978, 132 more registered with the federal government.
   D. Another 350 new PACs were organized in 1979.
   E. In all, by 1980, there were more than 2000 PACs ready to spend between $50 million and $60 million.

II. The problem those of us in state Common Cause organizations face is this: The 1974 Presidential Election Financing Act allows little of this money to be channeled into presidential campaigns. Therefore, most of this money must go to congressional and state elections.

A. As the *Wall Street Journal*'s Washington Bureau chief, Norman C. Miller, has written: "The bulk of special interest contributions represents a sort of investment in the careers of incumbent Congressmen and Senators, with the aim of enhancing the influence of the financing groups."

B. The examples supporting Mr. Miller's view of special interest conspiracies are numerous.

   1. In 1974, the Senate passed no-fault legislation by a vote of 53–42; but after the American Trial Lawyers Association (which generates income from automobile negligence suits) organized a campaign fund, the bill failed in the Senate, 49–45.

   2. Common Cause researchers have discovered that the American Medical Association and Federation of American Hospitals PACs have contributed $73,462 to the campaigns of members of the House Ways and Means Health Subcommittee.

   3. Among top PAC recipients were Democratic Senator Alan Cranston of California, who received nearly $439,000, and Democratic House Majority leader James C. Wright, Jr., of Texas, who got more than $293,000.

D. All of this means that those of you who faithfully contribute $5 here, $10 there in support of reform-minded political candidates are facing financial powers who can swamp your efforts to bring about the demise of special interests, because you can't match their money when reelections come up.

Satisfaction and Visualization Steps
(combined, as the general plan already is accepted)

I. It is time to renew your commitment to the efforts of Common Cause and other concerned citizens' groups.

A. You must rededicate yourself to the goals which got you to join Common Cause in the first place.

B. Such a commitment pays off with an increased sense of self-satisfaction and with the knowledge that your children will participate in a government characterized by open decision making.

C. Though PACs are organized against us in all states, we can win.

   1. Our Washington lawyers were in large part responsible for writing the 1974 Presidential Campaign Financing Act, over the objection of big corporations.

   2. State Common Cause organizations led the fights in New Jersey and Wisconsin to pass laws which provide for public financing of gubernatorial, state senate, and state house races. They came within an eyelash (one vote) of getting the California Assembly committee on financing to recommend a similar measure.

Action Step

I. Most of you have been in this organization long enough to know what has to be done.

A. As our membership continues to grow, we add more and stronger voices to our efforts.

B. And, we face a crucial test in our own state, where a bill to publicly finance statewide campaigns and congressional races comes up for consideration in one or two months.

   1. On the sheet of paper which you have been handed are the names and addresses of our state legislators and those of the members of the Subcommittee on Elections. Write them tomorrow.

2. And when your local state house or senate representatives hold office hours in town—and these are published in the paper—drop by for a little chat on these bills.

II. Our state organization's motto is a simple one: "In Common We Can Win."
   A. Just as the federal government has reduced the power and influence of PACs on elections, so can our state government.
   B. We can once again have government "of the people, by the people, and for the people" if you'll do your part to make governmental officials unequivocally accountable to individuals rather than groups.
   C. Let's work as hard as we have in the past to keep government open!

The Motivated Sequence and Psychological Change Speeches

No matter what psychological change you are asking of your listeners, you can profitably follow the motivated sequence in structuring this speech. When asking people to accept your judgments about some person, practice, institution, or theory, you can seek to: *(1)* Capture the attention and interest of the audience. *(2)* Make clear that a judgment concerning the worth of the person, practice, or institution is needed. Do this by showing *(a)* why a judgment is important to your listeners personally, and *(b)* why it is important to their community, state, nation, or world. *(3)* To satisfy the need, *(a)* set the criteria upon which an intelligent judgment may be based, and *(b)* advance what you believe to be the correct judgment, showing how it meets the criteria. *(4)* Picture the advantages that will accrue from agreeing with the judgment you advance or the evils that will result from failing to endorse it. *(5)* Finally, appeal for the acceptance of the proposed judgment, if appropriate.

Adapting the motivated sequence to the demands of a claim of value should produce a speech outline much like the following:

Contribute to Charities Wisely[11]

Specific Purpose: To persuade listeners to evaluate carefully the efficiency and effectiveness of the charitable organizations to which they contribute.

Attention Step

I. In 1975, Americans gave over 11.6 billion dollars to charitable organizations, not counting contributions to religious and educational institutions, but some experts have estimated that 116 million dollars was wasted because it went to fraudulent or poorly-managed organizations.

Need Step

I. There are differences in the ways charities distribute their funds.
   A. Example of a charity which uses 94 percent of its contributions for administration.
   B. Example of a charity—United Way—which distributes ninety cents out of every dollar collected.

II. Unless we all simply decide to stop giving to charities, we must come up with criteria for evaluating organizations and procedures for investigating them.

The psychological center of the Motivated Sequence is the need step—using motivational appeals together with solid evidence to stir the minds and feelings of listeners.

Satisfaction Step

I. How, then, can you evaluate charities?
   A. Fund-raising and administrative costs should total less than 50 percent of the total public contributions.
   B. An effective charity should be controlled by an active, unsalaried governing board, with no paid employees serving as voting members of that board.
   C. It should use reputable promotional and fund-raising methods.
   D. It should publicly disclose a complete and independently audited annual financial report. (Each of these criteria could be justified by appeals to authority and example.)

II. These criteria can be applied by both governmental units and individuals.
   A. Both Florida and Pennsylvania have laws governing what percentage of their total contributions charities can spend on fund-raising.
   B. The federal government similarly regulates charities soliciting in more than one state.

C. As an individual, you also can check into charities you might wish to support.
   1. Ask for an annual report before contributing.
   2. The Council of Better Business Bureaus publishes a rating list.
   3. The National Information Bureau discloses pertinent information.

Visualization Step

I. If both government and individuals do their investigative jobs properly, imagine the benefits which would accrue from the extra money spent on those who need it.
   A. The number of poor that could be fed and clothed would increase.
   B. Additional medical and health care facilities could be built.
   C. Research into killing and crippling diseases could proceed with more vigor.

Action Step

I. You have the power to direct your contributions to the most beneficial charities.
   A. Keep the evaluative criteria—efficiency, disinterestedness, fairness, and openness— in mind when you receive a call for help.
   B. And when you give, open your heart, your pocketbook, and, yes, your mind—give, but give wisely.

The Motivated Sequences and Actuative Speeches

Demands for action can be issued and defended very efficiently by using the motivated sequence; after all, it was designed originally for precisely this sort of oral message. Rather than offer another outline, therefore, let's conclude this chapter with a sample student speech. The following speech, prepared by Todd Ambs of Eastern Michigan University, was presented in one of the annual contests sponsored by the Interstate Oratorical Association. Mr. Ambs faced two particular problems in presenting this speech on hypertension and heart disease: *(1)* The majority of his audience were college students, who undoubtedly felt they were too young to worry about heart disease; *(2)* the setting was a speech contest, where audience members probably were more concerned about their own speeches than about Mr. Ambs' call for action. As you read the speech, notice how he attempted to break down the attitudes of apathy and complacency through a combination of fear appeals, statistics, specific instances, and authoritative testimony; pay particular attention to his call for action both from governmental agencies and individuals "hardened" to persuasive messages.

The Silent Killer[12]
Todd Ambs

Attention Step

For many Americans, life can seem to be a maze of numbers. We use many numbers so often that to be without them seems almost impossible.

Rhetorical questions How long could college students survive without their student numbers?

Startling statement

How many businesses could operate without a phone number? How many of you have never had use for your social security number? The answers to these quetions are easy. But there is one other set of numbers that could set us on the road to preventing an estimated 300,000 deaths and over two million serious illnesses each year, if we would only pay attention to them. For no student number, phone number, or social security number will ever be as vital to you as your blood pressure reading.   /1

The human blood pressure is a veritable measuring stick of good health. Normal blood pressure (that is, anything between 90/70 to 140/90) is generally a good indication of normal health. Unfortunately, over 25 million Americans do not have a blood pressure within this range. They suffer from high blood pressure, or hypertension.   /2

Testimony
(Appeals to fear
and authority)

Indeed, according to the Department of Health, Education, and Welfare, this year, 310,000 Americans will perish from illnesses whose major contributing factor is hypertension. Two million will suffer strokes, heart attacks, and kidney failure as a direct result of hypertension. Even more startling is the realization that of that 25 million, 11 million aren't even aware of their condition. According to Dr. Theodore Cooper, Director of the Heart and Lung Institute, "Hypertension can be brought under control through proven treatment which is neither unduly hazardous, complicated or expensive."   /3

Definition and
explanation

Need Step
Before we can fully understand the magnitude of the problem, though, we need to know what high blood pressure does to the body. When the pressure of the blood becomes too great for the arterial walls, high blood pressure results. This is somewhat like giving your circulatory system a headache. Fatty tissues, salts and fluids build up and the heart must be made to work harder than it should to keep the blood flowing properly. In this case, however, one tiny time pill won't relieve the pressure, or the irreparable damage that follows.   /4

That information may sound familiar to many of you. But then, why is hypertension still responsible for one out of every eight deaths in this country!   /5

Testimony

The National High Blood Pressure Council attempted to answer that question when they said: "Half of those who have high blood pressure don't even know that they do. Of those who do, only half are being treated, only half again of those have their blood pressure under control. Patients and physicians alike just don't seem to take this condition very seriously."   /6

Such carefree attitudes leave many people's lives just hanging in the balance because high blood pressure has no symptoms. Contrary to popular belief, high blood pressure is not confined to trapeze artists, overactive children, or the Annie Hall's of the world. There is, in fact, no direct correlation between tension and nervousness and high blood pressure. The only way you can tell if you have high blood pressure is to get it checked. As Dr. Frank Finnerty, author of the book, *High Blood Pres-*

Illustrations

sure—The Silent Killer, put it: "You can look great and feel healthy and have been living for years with the hidden time bomb of high blood pressure doing internal damage to your body." For Bill, a 49-year-old account executive, the time bomb was about to explode. One minute he was walking along seemingly in the best of health. The next he was on the ground clutching his chest. The heart attack would be the last event in Bill's life. He would never know the anguish that his family would suffer when they discovered that high blood pressure, a totally preventable condition, had caused his death. The silent killer had quietly destroyed life again.   /7

A routine physical could have saved Bill's life. And it could save yours. But unfortunately, our hectic, fast-paced lifestyles often provide easy excuses for not getting that needed physical. Lack of time, money, and the ever-popular lack of awareness can all be easy rationalizations for our failure to diagnose and treat hypertension. And our health care systems have failed to adjust to this reality at home, or especially on the job. A recent major manufacturing study found that on the average, businesses

Statistics

spend over $300 per employee per year for illnesses caused by hypertension. Dr. Andrea Foote and Dr. John Erfurt, the country's leading specialists in hypertensive care, painted the picture in this light: "The current inadequacy of treatment suggests that the problem is a matter of social organization and lies primarily in the inability of the health care delivery system to provide health care for this disease."   /8

And here we reach the apex of the problem. Simple diagnosis must be followed by constant treatment if hypertension is to be controlled. Unfortunately, many people do not continue this vital treatment. Mike Gorman, Executive Director of the Citizens for the Treatment of High Blood Pressure, estimates that at least 50% of those diagnosed drop out of treatment

Illustration

after a few months. One man who had a severe attack of high blood pressure on his vacation came home, followed a steady treatment plan, and brought his pressure down. After a while, he foolishly decided to try foregoing the medication. Within a month, he had a stroke which left him with irreversible brain damage. This man should have known better. He was a doctor, who was about to be nominated to the A.M.A. presidency. Unbelievably, a man who had frequently prescribed treatment for hypertension, and ignored his own warnings! The precautions must be heeded; anyone can be a victim.   /9

Satisfaction Step

Obviously then, the public needs to be made aware of the dangers of hypertension, health care systems should be improved to provide adequate health care for the disease, and finally, hypertensives must realize that constant treatment is essential to effective control.   /10

Thankfully, the goals I have mentioned are not just mere ideals proposed by a few specialists in hypertensive care. In 1972, the National Heart, Lung and Blood Institute organized the National High Blood Pressure Education Program, a program that all of us can get involved in. Their goal is to alert people to the dangers of hypertension through location,

Statistics

diagnosis, and treatment. The results have been astounding. According to the National Center for Health Statistics, 290,000 people leading normal lives today would have died, were it not for the Hypertensive Education Program. Over eight million people now have their blood pressure under control, a 100% increase since 1972.   /11

And it touches all sectors of society, for the Hypertensive Education Program is nationwide. Here in Michigan, for instance, you can contact Steve Renke at the University of Michigan's hypertensive care unit in Ann Arbor if you want to help.   /12

Visualization Step

Statistics

But we cannot rest on the laurels of this program. A disease which claims the lives of over 300,000 people annually is hardly under control. Doctors Foote and Erfurt have found that blood pressure control, for employed people, can best be carried out in the work setting. Their Worker Health Program was tested at four different job sites. As a result, 92% of the hypertensives at these jobs have their blood pressure under control, and the cost to the businesses involved has been cut from $300 per employee to $6.21. The program has been so successful that Blue Cross/Blue Shield of Michigan and Connecticut are now undergoing pilot programs of their own, based on the Worker Health Program.   /13

Illustration

On the local level there are things you can do as well. In 1970, Savannah, Georgia, had the infamous title of Stroke Capital of the World. Today, Savannah has 14 permanent blood pressure reading stations and the stroke toll in that city has been cut in half. A program like one of these can work in your community.   /14

Action Step

So often, those of us in forensics use persuasive ploys instead of getting right to the heart of the problem. As a result, we tend to perform instead of persuade. And you in turn as an audience listen, but don't hear. *Please,* if you do nothing else today, hear what I'm saying. There are people in this country who are dying because they have high blood pressure and there is

(Appeals to fear and belongingness)

not enough being done about it. You could be one of the 11 million Americans who has high blood pressure and does not even know it. If you are lucky enough to not be inflicted with the malady of hypertension, certainly someone that you know is. Don't let yourself or someone you know become a number on a fatality sheet. Get your blood pressure checked and save a life—your own.   /15

The arts of persuasion and actuation are fundamental to any democratic society. Unless enough citizens are skilled both in preparing and listening to appeals for changes of mind and action, a country is likely to fall victim to unscrupulous, self-serving advocates. As we have noted in this chapter, it is by no means easy to deliver or to react to effective persuasive communications. Yet, if you as a speaker systematically analyze your audiences and as a listener analyze the persuasive appeals aimed at you personally and work your way through situations demanding such speeches a step at a time, you, too, can make a real contribution as an informed and enlightened citizen.

REFERENCE NOTES

[1]For the most complete summary of attitude-change research currently available, see Gerald R. Miller, Michael Burgoon, and Judee K. Burgoon, "The Functions of Human Communication in Changing Attitudes and Gaining Compliance," in *Handbook of Rhetorical and Communication Theory*, ed. Carroll C. Arnold and John Waite Bowers (Boston: Allyn and Bacon, Inc., 1984), pp. 400–474.

[2]Fuller discussions of the strategies involved in changing people's beliefs, attitudes, and values are offered in Chapters 7 and 8 of Bruce E. Gronbeck, *The Articulate Person: A Guide to Everyday Public Speaking*, 2nd ed. (Glenview, IL: Scott, Foresman and Company, 1983).

[3]The classic research on audience predispositions and order of ideas in the face of those predispositions is summarized in Carl I. Hovland et al., *The Order of Presentation in Persuasion* (New Haven, CT: Yale University Press, 1961). Additional studies on one-sided vs. two-sided presentations are capsulized in Erwin P. Bettinghaus, *Persuasive Communication*, 3rd ed. (New York: Holt, Rinehart and Winston, 1980), esp. pp. 141–43. The main source of research on central and peripheral beliefs and attitudes is Milton Rokeach, *Beliefs, Attitudes, and Values* (San Francisco: Jossey-Bass, 1968); Rokeach's main findings are also summarized in Bettinghaus, pp. 23–26. A similar discussion in highly readable form can be found in Daryl Bem, *Beliefs, Attitudes and Human Affairs* (Belmont, CA: Brooks/Cole Publishing Co., 1970). The study of attitudinal networks referred to in this chapter is J. W. Prescott, "Body Pleasure and the Origins of Violence," *The Futurist*, 1975, pp. 64–74.

[4]The great research studies on intellectual sophistication and persuasion were done originally by the Yale group, and are summarized in Carl I. Hovland, Irving Janis, and H. H. Kelley, *Communication and Persuasion* (New Haven, CT: Yale University Press, 1953). More modern research, on the topic of cognitive complexity, is being done principally at the University of Illinois, under the leadership of Jesse Delia and Ruth Ann Clark. Those studies are too numerous to review here, although a good number of them (with useful footnotes to other pieces) can be found in the November 1979 issue of *Communication Monographs* (Vol. 46). And, as evidence of our fourth point here, see Claudia L. Hale, "Cognitive Complexity-Simplicity as a Determinant of Communication Effectiveness," *Communication Monographs*, 47 (November 1980), 304–311.

[5]The general notions standing behind reference group theory are developed in H. H. Kelley, "Two Functions of Reference Groups," in H. Prohansky and B. Seidenberg, eds., *Basic Studies in Social Psychology* (New York: Holt, Rinehart & Winston, 1965), pp. 210–14. The idea of positive and negative groups is developed in Theodore M. Newcomb's article, "Attitude Development as a Function of Reference Groups," in the same book, pp. 215–25. The conclusions about the effects of reference groups on beliefs and attitudes we offer here, as well as other propositions, are defended in Bettinghaus' fine chapter, "Successful Persuasion: Predicting Group Response," in his book (n. 1), pp. 70–88.

[6]The view that attitudes, in part, are cognitions which can be thought of as existing on a continuum is central to most "balance theories" of attitudes. A must for starting any investigation of these theories is R. P. Abelson et al., *Theories of Cognitive Consistency: A Sourcebook* (Chicago: Rand McNally, 1968). And, periodically, new anthologies appear, summarizing the continuing research programs. Among the best are J. P. Robinson and P. R. Shaver, eds., *Measures of Social Psychological Attitudes* (Ann Arbor, MI: Institute for Social Research, 1973); H. Triandis, *Attitude and Attitude Change* (New York: John Wiley and Sons, 1971); and Martin Fishbein, ed., *Readings in Attitude Theory and Measurement* (New York: John Wiley and Sons, 1967). For a condensed treatment of balance theories, see Herbert W. Simons, *Persuasion: Understanding, Practice and Analysis* (Reading, MA: Addison-Wesley Pub. Co., 1976), esp. pp. 119–28.

[7]The basic research on latitudes of acceptance and rejection is covered in Muzafer Sherif, Carolyn Sherif, and Roger Nebergall, *Attitude and Attitude Change* (Philadelphia: Saunders, 1965).

[8]A more expanded discussion of saliency and its effects can be found in Kenneth E. Andersen, *Persuasion: Theory and Practice,* 2nd ed. (Boston: Allyn and Bacon, Inc., 1978), esp. pp. 95–96, 110–11, 250–53.

[9]A complete summary of research on credibility supporting these and other conclusions is found in Stephen Littlejohn, ''A Bibliography of Studies Related to Variables of Source Credibility,'' in *Bibliographical Annual in Speech Communication: 1971,* ed. Ned A. Shearer (New York: Speech Communication Association, 1972), pp. 1–40. New research on credibility, showing that it tends to vary from situation to situation and topic to topic, is represented by such studies as Jo Liska, ''Situational and Topical Variations in Credibility Criteria,'' *Communication Monographs,* 45 (March 1978), 85–92.

[10]The supporting material in this outline is taken from *In Common: The Common Cause Report from Washington* (Spring 1978). Reprinted by permission of Common Cause. Additional updating materials come from ''Campaign 80: How Special Interest Groups Use Their Power,'' *Nation's Business,* June 1980, pp. 38–41, and ''Election Tab: A Billion Dollars, and Rising,'' *U. S. News and World Report,* 15 December 1980, p. 33.

[11]This outline is based on a speech given by Steve Favitta, Central Missouri State University, in 1978. We have omitted the supporting materials, but most may be found in ''New CT Ratings on 53 Charities,'' *Changing Times,* November 1976; and ''United Way: Are the Criticisms Fair?'' *Changing Times,* October 1977. This altered outline is used with the permission of Mr. Favitta. Text supplied courtesy of Professor Roger Conaway and Professor Dan Curtis.

[12]''The Silent Killer'' by Todd Ambs. Reprinted from *Winning Orations,* 1980, by special arrangement with the Interstate Oratorical Association, Larry Schnoor, Executive Secretary, Mankato State University, Mankato, Minnesota.

PROBLEMS AND PROBES

1. Analyze the differences between an appeal to persuade and an appeal to actuate in relation to the essential features of these appeals (that is, adaptation to psychological states, change by degrees, saliency, credibility) for each of the following situations: *(a)* you want your parents to stop smoking; *(b)* you try to convince your best friend not to drop out of school; *(c)* you want a stranger to donate money to the American Cancer Society. Why do your appeals differ among the above situations? Which factors are the most difficult to analyze in each of the above situations and why?

2. Comment on this statement: "Most people act out of desire rather than reason; they only use reason to justify to themselves what they want to do anyway." Use the remark to formulate at least three useful principles for speeches to actuate.

ORAL ACTIVITIES

1. Build and present to the class a five- to seven-minute persuasive speech. Follow carefully the steps in the motivated sequence appropriate to the type of speech chosen. Make sure that you have an abundance of appropriate facts and data, that

your reasoning is sound, and that your major ideas are cast in a form that will motivate your listeners. In developing your remarks, keep in mind the probable attitude of the audience toward your claim or proposal, and make such adaptations as may be necessary.

2. Present a five- to eight-minute speech, the purpose of which is to persuade members of your speech class to take a recommended action. Show that a problem or situation needing remedy actually exists. Show your listeners why they (and not someone else) should be concerned, and why you think a specific action on their part will be a concrete, influential move toward a remedy. On a future "checkup" day, see how many members of the audience have taken the recommended action. For example, you may urge an audience to sign a petition proposing that graduating seniors should be excused from their final examinations or that the college should establish a cooperative bookstore. Or, you may ask members of your class to write letters or send mailgrams to their congressional representatives urging that all election campaigns should be financed publicly or that Bill X should be passed. (Be sure to tell them who their representatives are and where they can be reached.) Or, you can ask members to attend a meeting of a newly organized campus group to participate in an activity such as giving blood during the next visit of the Red Cross Bloodmobile.

CHAPTER 18

Speeches on Special Occasions

Speeches to inform and persuade represent the two kinds of presentations you will be called upon to make most often. Many occasions, however, require special types of speeches. These occasions call in part for information, and sometimes in part for persuasive efforts, yet they also require more: They require demonstrating and even celebrating group solidarity or membership. You are familiar with many such occasions—funeral speeches for friends and fallen heroes; tributes to outstanding humanitarians, artists, and professionals; speeches of good will offered by representatives of business and government to visitors; even after-dinner and other entertaining speeches.

These occasions can stretch the rhetorical skills of speakers to their fullest because of the pomp and ceremony associated with some of them, and because of special expectations audiences have in others. Indeed, audience expectations are especially important in these special-occasion speeches: The audience expects something profound in retirement speeches; something probing in funeral speeches; something honorary in introductions for famous people; something humorous yet relevant in after-dinner speeches.[1]

Such expectations put extraordinary social and psychological pressures on speakers at special occasions. Yet, if you know something about those expectations, you can reduce much of that pressure; and if you prepare well, you'll deflate the rest. The purpose of this chapter is to review the particular expectations you face when presenting five types of special-occasion speeches—speeches of introduction, tribute, courtesy, and nomination, and speeches to entertain. We will include examples that demonstrate how those expectations can be met.

Speeches of Introduction

Speeches of introduction usually are given by the person who arranged the program or by the chairperson or president of the group to be addressed. Sometimes, however, they are presented by another person who, because of personal association or professional interests, is especially well acquainted with the featured speaker.

Purpose and Manner of Speaking

The purpose of a speech of introduction is, of course, to create in the audience a desire to hear the speaker you are introducing. Everything else must be subordinated to this aim. You are not being called upon to make a speech yourself or air your own views on the subject. You are only the speaker's advance agent; your job is to sell him or her to the audience. This task carries a two-fold responsibility: *(1)* You must arouse the listeners' curiosity about the speaker and/or subject, thus making it easier for the speaker to get the attention of the audience. *(2)* You must do all that you reasonably can to generate audience respect for the speaker, thereby increasing the likelihood that listeners will respond favorably to the message that is presented.

When giving a speech of introduction, your manner of speaking should be suited to the nature of the occasion, your familiarity with the speaker, and the speaker's prestige. If you were introducing a justice of the United States Supreme Court, for instance, it would hardly be appropriate to tell a joke about him. Nor would this approach be tactful if the speaker were a stranger to you, or the occasion serious and dignified. On the other hand, if you are presenting an old friend to a group of associates on an informal occasion, a solemn and dignified manner would be equally out of place.

Formulating the Content of the Speech of Introduction

The better known and more respected a speaker is, the shorter your introduction can be. The less well known he or she is, the more you will need to arouse interest in the subject or build up the speaker's prestige. In general, however, observe these principles:

1. *Talk about the speaker*. Who is he? What is her position in business, education, sports, or government? What experiences has he had that qualify him to speak on the announced subject? Build up the speaker's identity, tell what he knows or what she has done, but do not praise his or her ability as a speaker. Let speakers *demonstrate* their skills.

2. *Emphasize the importance of the speaker's subject*. For example, in introducing a speaker who is to talk about the oil industry, you might say: "All of us drive automobiles in which we use the products made from petroleum. A knowledge of the way these products are manufactured and marketed is, therefore, certain to be valuable to our understanding and perhaps to our pocketbooks."

3. *Stress the appropriateness of the subject or of the speaker*. If your town is considering a program of renewal and revitalization, a speech by a city planner is likely to be timely and well received. If an organization is marking an anniversary, the founder may be one of the speakers. Reference to the positions these persons hold is obviously in order and serves to relate the speaker more closely to the audience.

Organizing the Speech of Introduction

The necessity of a carefully planned introduction depends on the amount of time available and the need to elaborate on the topic's importance or the speaker's qualifications. A simple introductory statement, "Ladies and Gentlemen, the President of the United States," obviously requires little in the way of organization. For longer, more involved introductions, consider how much attention should be devoted to the background and expertise of the speaker and to the interest, importance, or urgency of the topic. A good way to start is to make an observation or expression designed to capture the attention of the audience and proceed to develop one or both of the above topics as the circumstances warrant. Remember that your introduction should not be longer than the speech it introduces—keep biographical details, personal allusions to your involvement with the speaker or topic, and details of the topic itself to a minimum. In other words, be brief. The virtues of an excellent introduction, displaying tact, brevity, sincerity, and enthusiasm, are evident in the following introduction prepared by Barbara Miller.

Introducing a Classmate
Barbara Miller

We all have come to know Greg Latham in this class. When we introduced ourselves during the first week of class, you learned that Greg was raised on an Illinois farm, later moving to Chicago when farming became a losing proposition for the five members of his family. Greg's dual background—rural and urban—has obviously affected him strongly, as you can tell from various topics he's addressed in speeches to us. The farmer in him emerged when he delivered his first speech, the one classifying various types of pesticides. He changed into a city slicker, however, in his visual-aids speech—the clever battleplan for making your way through and around Chicago's expressway and tollway systems. Three weeks ago, in the group discussion on health care, he once again put on his straw hat and bib overalls, speaking out strongly for the need to increase health care facilities in rural areas.   /1

Today, we will see Greg combine his double background. If you followed the state legislature's recent public hearings, if you read the front page of *The State Journal* last week, or if you saw ABC's special report on foreign investments in American land two nights ago, the term "agribusiness" became a part of your vocabulary. Agribusiness, which involves the consolidation of farming operations within corporate structures, may well profoundly affect each of us within a decade. Greg this morning will trace those direct effects upon your daily life in his speech, "Agribusiness: Panacea or Pandora's Box?" /2

Speeches of Tribute

As a speaker you may be called upon to pay tribute to another person's qualities or achievements. Such occasions range from the awarding of a trophy after an athletic contest to delivering a eulogy at a memorial service. Sometimes tributes are paid to an entire group or class of people—for example, teachers, soldiers, or mothers—rather than to an individual. Frequently, awards are presented to groups or to individuals for outstanding or meritorious service. In such cases, public tribute often is paid, and the presentation calls for appropriate remarks from a speaker. The following typically require a speech of tribute:

Farewells

In general, speeches of farewell fall into one of three subcategories: *(1)* When people retire or leave one organization to join another or when persons who are admired leave the community where they have lived, the enterprise in which they have worked, or the office they have held, public appreciation of their fellowship and accomplishments may be expressed by associates or colleagues in speeches befitting the circumstances. *(2)* Or the individual who is departing may use the occasion to present a farewell address in which she voices her gratitude for the opportunities, consideration, and warmth given her by coworkers and, perhaps, calls upon them to carry on the traditions and long-range goals which characterize the office or the enterprise. In both of these situations, verbal tributes are being paid. What distinguishes them, basically, is whether the retiree or departing one is *speaking* or is being *spoken about*. *(3)* More rarely, when individuals—because of disagreements, policy-differences, or organizational stresses, for example—decide to resign or sever important or long-standing associations with a business or governmental unit, they may elect to use their farewell messages to present publicly the basis of the disagreement and the factors prompting the resignation and departure.

Dedications

Buildings, monuments, or parks may be constructed or set aside to honor a worthy cause or to commemorate a person, a group, a significant movement, a historic event, or the like. At such dedications, the speaker says something appropriate about the purpose to be served by whatever it is that is being set aside and about the personage(s), event, or occasion thus commemorated.

The following remarks were made by Mr. Harold Haydon at the unveiling of *Nuclear Energy,* a bronze sculpture created by Henry Moore and placed on the campus of the University of Chicago to commemorate the achievement of Enrico Fermi and his associates in releasing the first self-sustaining nuclear chain reaction at Stagg Field on December 2, 1942. The unveiling took place during the commemoration of the twenty-fifth anniversary of that event. Mr. Haydon was Associate Professor of Art at the University and is presently art critic for the *Chicago Sun-Times*. By combining specific references to the sculptor and his work with more general observations concerning the function of art and humankind's hopes and fears in a nuclear age, Mr. Haydon produced a dignified and thoughtful address, well suited to the demands of the occasion.

The Testimony of Sculpture[2]
Harold Haydon

Since very ancient times men have set up a marker, or designated some stone or tree, to hold the memory of a deed or happening far longer than any man's lifetime. Some of these memorial objects have lived longer than man's collective memory, so that we now ponder the meaning of a monument, or wonder whether some great stone is a record of human action, or whether instead it is only a natural object. /1

Speeches of dedication allow a culture to look back at its past so as to remember enduring social values, values which can support that culture as well in the future.

There is something that makes us want a solid presence, a substantial form, to be the tangible touchstone of the mind, designed and made to endure as witness or record, as if we mistrusted that seemingly frail yet amazingly tough skein of words and symbols that serves memory and which, despite being mere ink blots and punch-holes, nonetheless succeeds in preserving the long human tradition, firmer than any stone, tougher than any metal.   /2

We still choose stone or metal to be our tangible reminders, and for these solid, enduring forms we turn to the men who are carvers of stone and moulders of metal, for it is they who have given lasting form to our myths through the centuries.   /3

One of these men is here today, a great one, and he has given his skill and the sure touch of his mind and eye to create for this nation, this city, and this university a marker that may stand here for centuries, even for a millennium, as a mute yet eloquent testament to a turning point in time when man took charge of a new material world hitherto beyond his capability.   /4

As this bronze monument remembers an event and commemorates an achievement, it has something unique to say about the spiritual meaning of the achievement, for it is the special power of art to convey feeling and stir profound emotion, to touch us in ways that are beyond the reach of reason.   /5

Nuclear energy, for which the sculpture is named, is a magnet for conflicting emotions, some of which inevitably will attach to the bronze form; it will harbor or repel emotion according to the states of mind of those who view the sculpture. In its brooding presence some will feel the joy and sorrow of recollection, some may dread the uncertain future, and yet others will thrill to the thought of magnificent achievements that lie ahead. The test of the sculpture's greatness as a human document, the test of any work of art, will be its capacity to evoke a response and the quality of that response.   /6

One thing most certain is that this sculpture by Henry Moore is not an inert object. It is a live thing, and somewhat strange like every excellent beauty, to be known to us only in time and never completely. Its whole meaning can be known only to the ever-receding future, as each succeeding generation reinterprets according to its own vision and experience.   /7

By being here in a public place the sculpture *Nuclear Energy* becomes a part of Chicago, and the sculptor an honored citizen, known not just to artists and collectors of art, but to everyone who pauses here in the presence of the monument, because the artist is inextricably part of what he has created, immortal through his art.   /8

With this happy conjunction today of art and science, of great artist and great occasion, we may hope to reach across the generations, across the centuries, speaking through enduring sculpture of our time, our hopes, and fears, perhaps more eloquently than we know. Some works of art have meaning for all mankind and so defy time, persisting through all hazards; the monument to the atomic age should be one of these.   /9

Memorial Services

Services to pay public honor to the dead usually include a speech of tribute or *eulogy*. Ceremonies of this kind may honor a famous person (or persons) and be held years after his or her death. For example, many speeches have paid tribute to Abraham Lincoln. More often, however, a eulogy honors someone personally known to the audience and only recently deceased.

At other times, a memorial—particularly to a famous person—honors certain qualities that person stands for. In such a situation, the speaker uses the memorial to renew and reinforce the audience's adherence to certain ideals, ideals possessed by the deceased and worthy of emulation by the audience.

Purpose and Manner of Speaking for the Tribute Speech

The *purpose* of a speech of tribute is, of course, to create in those who hear it a sense of appreciation for the traits or accomplishments of the person or group to whom tribute is paid. If you cause your audience to realize the essential worth or importance of that person or group, you will have succeeded. But you may go further than this. You may, by honoring a person, arouse deeper devotion to the cause he or she represents. Did he give distinguished service to his community? Then strive to enhance the audience's civic pride and sense of service. Was she a friend to youth? Then try to arouse the feeling that working to provide opportunities for young people deserves the audience's support. Create a desire in your listeners to emulate the person or persons honored.

When delivering a speech of tribute, suit the manner of speaking to the circumstances. A farewell banquet usually blends an atmosphere of merriment with a spirit of sincere regret. Dignity and formality are, on the whole, characteristic of memorial services, the unveiling of monuments, and similar dedicatory ceremonies. Regardless of the general tone of the occasion, however, in a speech of tribute avoid high-sounding phrases, bombastic oratory, and obvious "oiliness." A simple, honest expression of admiration presented in clear and unadorned language is best.

Formulating the Content of Speeches of Tribute

Frequently, in a speech of tribute a speaker attempts to itemize all the accomplishments of the honored person or group. This weakens the impact because, in trying to cover everything, it emphasizes nothing. Plan, instead, to focus your remarks, as follows:

1. *Stress dominant traits.* If you are paying tribute to a person, select a few aspects of her personality which are especially likeable or praiseworthy, and relate incidents from her life or work to illustrate these distinguishing qualities.

2. *Mention only outstanding achievements.* Pick out only a few of the person's or group's most notable accomplishments. Tell about them in detail to show how important they were. Let your speech say, "Here is what this person (or group) has done; see how such actions have contributed to the well-being of our business or community."

3. *Give special emphasis to the influence of the person or group.* Show the effect that the behavior of the person or group has had on others. Many times, the importance of people's lives can be demonstrated not so much by any traits or material accomplishments as by the influence they exerted on associates.

Organizing the Speech of Tribute

Ordinarily you will have little difficulty in getting people to listen to a speech of tribute. The audience probably already knows and admires the person or group about whom you are to speak, and listeners are curious to learn what you are going to say concerning the individual or individuals being honored. Consider the following steps in preparing your speech:

1. Direct the attention of the audience toward those characteristics or accomplishments which you consider most important. There are three commonly used ways to do this: (*a*) Make a straightforward, sincere statement of these commendable traits or achievements or of the influence they have had upon others. (*b*) Relate one or more instances which vividly illustrate your point. (*c*) Relate an incident which shows the problems faced by your subject.

2. Were there obstacles or difficulties that the person or group being honored had to overcome? If so, dramatize the impact of the accomplishment by noting these problems and their successful resolution. Thus, you might describe the extent of the air

pollution problem in a large city before paying tribute to the individuals who developed and enforced an effective pollution-control plan.

3. Develop the substance of the tribute itself—relate a few incidents to show how the personal or public problems you have outlined were met and surmounted. In doing this, be sure to demonstrate at least one of the following: (*a*) how certain admirable traits—vision, courage, and tenacity, for example—made it possible to deal successfully with these problems; (*b*) how remarkable the achievements were in the face of the obstacles encountered; (*c*) how great the influence of the achievement was on others.

4. Synthesize the attributes of the person or group in a vivid, composite picture which summarizes the accomplishment and its significance. It will help you to achieve this if you: *(a) Introduce an apt quotation.* Try to find a bit of poetry or a literary passage which fits the person or group to whom you are paying tribute, and introduce it here. *(b) Draw a word picture of a world (community, business, or profession) inhabited by such persons.* Suggest how much better things would be if more people had similar qualities. *(c) Suggest the loss which the absence of the individual or group will bring.* Show vividly how much he, she, or they will be missed. Be specific: "It's going to seem mighty strange to walk into Barbara's office and not find her there ready to listen, ready to advise, ready to help." In closing, connect the theme of the speech with the occasion on which it is presented. Thus, in a *eulogy,* suggest that the best tribute the audience can pay the person being honored is to live as that person did or to carry on what he or she has begun. In a *dedication* speech, suggest the appropriateness of dedicating this monument, building, or plaque, to such a person or group, and express the hope that it will inspire others to emulate their accomplishments. At the close of a *farewell* speech, extend to the departing person or persons the best wishes of those you represent, and express a determination to carry on what they have begun. Or, if you yourself are saying farewell, call upon those who remain to carry on what you and your associates have started.

By adapting the foregoing principles and procedures to the particular situation in which you find yourself, you should be able to devise a useful framework upon which to build a speech of tribute. To complete your speech, however, you will need to fill out this plan with vivid illustrative materials and appropriate motivational appeals.

Speeches of Nomination

The speech to nominate contains elements found in both speeches of introduction and speeches of tribute. Here, too, your main purpose is to review the accomplishments of some person whom you admire. This review, however, instead of standing as an end in itself (tribute) or of creating a desire to hear the person (introduction), is made to contribute to an actuative goal—obtaining the listeners' endorsement of the person as a nominee for an elective office.

In a speech of nomination, your manner of speaking generally will be less formal and dignified than when you are giving a speech of tribute. It should, however, be businesslike and energetic. In general, the content of the speech will follow the pattern of a speech of tribute; but the illustrations and supporting materials should be chosen with the intent of showing the nominee's qualifications for the office in question. Although the speech to nominate has certain special requirements, fundamentally it is a speech to actuate. Organize it, therefore, as follows: Begin with a statement of your intent—to rise to place a name in nomination. Second, describe the qualifications required by the job, the problems to be dealt with, and the personal qualities needed in the individual to be selected. Next, name your candidate and state this person's qualifications for the position—describe the individual's training, experience, success in similar positions, and personal qualities. Your objective is to show why you believe your nominee will be an excellent choice for the position. Finally, urge audience endorsement as you formally place the person's name in nomination.

An alternative to this pattern is to begin with the name of the nominee. This is an acceptable practice if the audience is already favorably disposed toward the nominee. However, if your choice is likely to stir opposition, it may be wiser to establish first the qualities needed for the position and then, in naming your candidate, indicate how this nominee's qualifications will satisfy the requirements.

Not all nominations, of course, need to be supported by a long speech. Frequently, especially in small groups and clubs, the person nominated is well known to the audience, and his or her qualifications are already appreciated. Under such circumstances, all that is required is the simple statement: "Mr. Chairman, given her obvious and well-known services to our club in the past, I nominate Marilyn Cannell for the office of treasurer."

Speeches to Create Good Will

The fourth type of special-occasion speech we will discuss is the speech to create good will. While ostensibly the purpose of this special type of speech is to inform an audience about a product, service, operation, or procedure, actually it is to enhance the listeners' appreciation of a particular institution, practice, or profession—to make the audience more favorably disposed toward it. Thus, the good-will speech is also a mixed or hybrid type. Basically, it is informative, but with a strong, underlying persuasive purpose.

Typical Situations Requiring Speeches for Good Will
There are numerous situations in which good-will speeches are appropriate; the three which follow may be considered typical:

Luncheon meetings of civic and service clubs.   Gatherings of this kind, being semisocial in nature and having a built-in atmosphere of congeniality, offer excellent opportunities for presenting speeches of good will. Members of such groups—prominent men and women from many walks of life—are interested in civic affairs and in the workings of other people's businesses or professions.

Educational programs.   School authorities, as well as leaders of clubs and religious organizations, often arrange educational programs for their patrons and members.

After receiving awards or tributes, speakers must come up with appropriate acceptance speeches, as did Mary Tyler Moore upon receiving an award from Harvard University.

At such meetings, speakers are asked to talk about the occupations in which they are engaged and to explain the opportunities offered and the training required in their respective fields. By use of illustrations and tactful references, a speaker may—while providing the desired information—also create good will for his or her company or profession.

Special demonstration programs.   Special programs are frequently presented by government agencies, university extension departments, and business organizations. For example, a wholesale food company may send a representative to a nutritionists' meeting to explain the food values present in various kinds of canned meat or fish products, and to demonstrate new ways of preparing or serving them. Although such a speech would be primarily informative, the speaker could win good will indirectly by showing that his or her company desires to increase customer satisfaction with its products and services.

Manner of Speaking in the Speech for Good Will

Three qualities—modesty, tolerance, and good humor—characterize the manner of speaking appropriate for good-will speeches. Although you will be talking about your business or vocation and trying to make it seem important to the audience, you should never boast or brag. In giving a speech of this type, let the facts speak for themselves. Moreover, show a tolerant attitude toward others, especially competitors. The airline representative, for instance, who violently attacks trucking companies and bus lines is likely to gain ill will rather than good. Finally, exercise good humor. The good-will speech is not for the zealot or the crusader. Take the task more genially. Don't try to force acceptance of your ideas; instead, show so much enthusiasm and good feeling that your listeners will respond spontaneously and favorably to the information you are providing.

Formulating the Content of the Speech for Good Will

In selecting materials for a good-will speech, keep these suggestions in mind: (1) *Present novel and interesting facts about your subject*. Make your listeners feel that you are giving them an inside look into your company or organization. Avoid talking about what they already know; concentrate on new developments and on facts or services that are not generally known. (2) *Show a relationship between your subject and the lives of the members of your audience*. Make your listeners see the importance of your organization or profession to their personal safety, success, or happiness. (3) *Offer a definite service*. This offer may take the form of an invitation to the audience to visit your office or shop, to help them with their problems, or to answer questions or send brochures.

Organizing the Speech for Good Will

Because of its close relationship to speeches to inform and to persuade, the organization of the materials we have just described can be discussed in terms of the motivated sequence:

Attention step.   The purpose of the beginning of your speech will be to establish a friendly feeling and to arouse the audience's curiosity about your profession or the institution you represent. You may gain the first of these objectives by a tactful compliment to the group or a reference to the occasion that has brought you together. Follow this with one or two unusual facts or illustrations concerning the enterprise you represent. For instance: "Before we began manufacturing television parts, the Lash Electric Company confined its business to the making of clock radios that would never wear out. We succeeded so well that we almost went bankrupt! That was only fifteen years ago. Today our export trade alone is over one hundred times as large as our total annual domestic business was in those earlier days. It may interest you to know how this change took place." In brief, you must find some way to arouse your listeners' curiosity about your organization.

Need step.   Point out certain problems facing your audience—problems with which the institution, profession, or agency you represent is vitally concerned. For example, if you represent a radio or television station, show the relationship of good communications to the social and economic health of the community. By so doing, you will establish common ground with your audience. Ordinarily the need step will be brief and will consist largely of suggestions developed with only an occasional illustration. However, if you intend to propose that your listeners join in acting to meet a common problem, the need step will require fuller development.

Satisfaction step. The meat of a good-will speech will be in the satisfaction step. Here is the place to tell your audience about your institution, profession, or business and to explain what it is or what it does. You can do this in at least three ways: (1) *Relate interesting events in its history.* Pick events which will demonstrate its humanity, its reliability, and its importance to the community, to the country, or to the world of nations. (2) *Explain how your organization or profession operates.* Pick out those things that are unusual or that may contain beneficial suggestions for your audience. This method often helps impress upon your listeners the size and efficiency of your operation or enterprise. (3) *Describe the services your organization renders.* Explain its products; point out how widely they are used; discuss the policies by which management is guided—especially those which you think your audience will agree with or admire. Tell what your firm or profession has done for the community: people employed, purchases made locally, assistance with community projects, improvements in health, education, or public safety. Do not boast, but make sure that your listeners realize the value of your work *to them.*

Visualization step. Your object here is to crystallize the good will that the presentation of information in the satisfaction step initially has created. Do this by looking to the future. Make a rapid survey of the points you have covered or combine them in a single story or illustration. Or, to approach this step from the opposite direction, picture for your listeners the loss that would result if the organization or profession you represent should leave the community or cease to exist. Be careful, however, not to leave the impression that there is any real danger that this will occur.

Action step. Here, you make your offer of service to the audience. For example, invite the group to visit your office or plant, or point out the willingness of your organization to assist in some common enterprise. As is true of every type of speech, the content and organization of the speech for good will sometimes need to be especially adapted to meet the demands of the subject or occasion. You should, however, never lose sight of the central purpose for which you speak: to show your audience that the work which you do or the service which you perform is of value to them—that in some way it makes their lives happier, more productive, interesting, or secure.

Speeches to Entertain

To entertain an audience presents special challenges to speakers. As you may recall, we identified "to entertain" as an independent type of speech in Chapter 3 because of the peculiar force of humor in speechmaking. Discounting slapstick humor (of the slipping-on-a-banana-peel genre), most humor depends primarily upon a listener's sensitivities to the routines and mores of one's society. If you have ever listened to someone from a foreign country tell a series of jokes, you already know that; much humor cannot really be translated, in part because of language differences (puns, for example, don't translate well), and in even larger measure because of cultural differences.

Purposes and Manner of Speaking to Entertain

Like most humor in general, speeches to entertain usually work within the cultural frameworks of a particular group or society. Such speeches may be "merely funny," as in certain types of comic monologues, but most are serious in their force or demand upon audiences. After-dinner speeches, for example, usually are more than dessert; their topics are relevant to the group at hand, and the anecdotes they often contain usually are offered to make some point. That point may be one as simple as deflecting an audience's antipathy toward the speaker, as group-centered as making the people in the audience feel more like a group, or as serious as offering a critique of one's society. (See the Speaker's Resource Book for a fuller discussion of these purposes.)

Speakers seeking to deflect an audience's antipathy often use humor to ingratiate themselves. For example, Henry W. Grady, editor of the *Atlanta Constitution*, expected a good deal of distrust and hostility when, after the Civil War, he journeyed to New York City to tell the New England Society about "The New South" in 1886. He opened the speech not only by thanking them for the invitation, but also by telling stories about farmers, husbands and wives, and preachers; he praised Abraham Lincoln, a Northerner, as "the first typical American" of the new age; told another humorous story about shopkeepers and their advertising; poked fun at the great Union General Sherman, "who is considered an able man in our hearts, though some people think he is a kind of careless man about fire"; and assured his audience that a New South, one very much like the Old North, was arising from those ashes.[3] Through the use of humor, Mr. Grady had his audience cheering every point he made that evening about the New South.

Group cohesiveness also can be created through humor. Politicians, especially when campaigning, spend much time telling humorous stories about their opponents, hitting them with stinging remarks. In part, of course, biting political humor degrades the oppositional candidates and party; however, such humor also can make one's own party feel more cohesive, more unified. So, Democrats took a slogan from Barry Goldwater's 1964 presidential campaign ("In your heart you know he's right") and added a phrase—"yes, *far* right"; and they collected Nixon's 1972 bumperstickers which said "Nixon Now," so they could cut off the *w* and put them on their own autos. Republicans likewise were not above calling the 1984 Democratic presidential candidate "Walter *Mono-dull*" during that campaign. Such zingers allow political party members to laugh at the others and to celebrate their membership in a "better" party.

Finally, speeches to entertain can be used to critique one's society. Humor can be used to urge general changes, to urge reform of social practices. This purpose is evident in Dick Cavett's graduation address on pages 370–74.

Formulating the Content of a Speech to Entertain

When arranging speech materials for these sorts of speeches, you should develop a series of illustrations, short quotations or quips, and stories, each following the other in fairly rapid succession. Most important, *make sure that each touches upon a central theme or point*. An entertaining speech is more than a comic monologue; it must be cohesive and pointed. Speeches to entertain can be put together in the following steps:

1. Relate a story or anecdote, present an illustration, or quote an appropriate passage.

2. State the essential idea or point of view implied by your opening remarks.

3. Follow with a series of additional stories, anecdotes, quips, or illustrations that amplify or illuminate your central idea. Arrange those supporting materials so that they are thematically or tonally coherent.

4. Close with a striking restatement of the central point you have developed. As in Step 1, you may use another quotation or one final story which clinches and epitomizes your speech as a whole.

The following speech by public television's Dick Cavett illustrates many of the ideas we have been discussing. Though Mr. Cavett was concerned with the ceremonial demands of a commencement speech (see his comments in paragraphs 1–4), he obviously also knew that, given his usual speaking style and reputation, the audience expected him to be funny. These, to some speakers, would have seemed like contradictory audience expectations. Not to Mr. Cavett. He chose to use an entertaining speech to make a serious point about the personal and social uses of the English language in American society. The resulting speech was appropriate for the special occasion, for the speaker's reputation, and for the audience of college students.

Is English a Dying Language?[4]
Dick Cavett

Mrs. Villard, President Smith, members of the faculty, students of Vassar, and friends: /1

The last college commencement I attended was my own. That, as President Smith mentioned, was at Yale in 1958. So if I get rattled here this morning, don't be surprised if I suddenly take out my handkerchief and launch into a chorus of "Bright College Years."   /2

Actually, that was not only the last commencement I attended, but the only other one I've ever attended; so my whole sense of these affairs comes from that single experience. I gather that the speaker in my position is expected to address himself to some vaguely uplifting topic that has a bearing on the academic career you graduates are leaving behind you, but also looks ahead to some problem that awaits you, some challenge that will be put to you to try to make the world a better place. In 1958 I seem to remember being urged to go out and do something about the Cold War. And, as you can see, the results speak for themselves.   /3

Anyway, those are the requirements as I understand them. And I'm sorry to tell you I have a topic that meets them perfectly. But don't worry—I don't think I'll use it. After all, the world would little note nor long remember what I might say here about "Ethical Dilemmas in Ecology During a Nuclear Age."   /4

Instead, let me begin on what, for me, is firmer ground: humor, or at least a humorist. James Thurber was talking at a party with an actress he knew. She was telling him about the troubles of a mutual friend. The friend, she said, had had her apartment broken into so many times that she finally had to have it "burglarized." Thurber thought about that for a moment and said, "Wouldn't it have been simpler for her just to have it alarmed?"   /5

Now, there's more than a joke here, as Thurber was quick to point out when he told this story in one of his essays. "Ours is a precarious language," he said, " in which the merest shadow line often separates affirmation from negation, sense from nonsense, and one sex from another." In his later years, when he was blind, Thurber took in the world mostly through his hearing, and what he heard, acutely, was how our language was being mangled. He wrote often about "The Spreading You-Know" and other blights that he wished would pass "from the lingo into limbo." Even the sound and the fury, he said, had become the unsound and the fuzzy.   /6

Thurber was one of a long line of people who have confirmed what George Orwell wrote nearly 35 years ago—that "most people who bother about the matter at all would admit that the English language is in a bad way." We can confirm it ourselves, every day.   /7

We can confirm it when we take an airplane, and the pilot doesn't tell us he expects a bumpy ride; he says he anticipates experiencing considerable turbulence. Or we open a newspaper and read that a government office isn't going broke; it's undergoing a budget shortfall situation. Or we hear a policeman who doesn't say the suspect got out of the car; he relates that the alleged perpetrator exited the vehicle.   /8

We can confirm it when we encounter viable, meaningful, beautiful, "in" buzz-words; for example, "input," "interface," and "thrust," which, as somebody said, shouldn't be used in public but might be all right in private among consenting adults.   /9

We can confirm it when we hear people using "disinterested" as if it meant the same thing as "uninterested"; or "infer" as if it meant the same thing as "imply." To confuse any such pair is to take two distinct, useful words and blur them into a single, useless smudge. Every time it happens the language shrinks a little.   /10

Of course, I work in television, which is one of the designated disaster areas of language. In the past 11 years I've conducted thousands of hours of interviews, during which I've probably been an accessory to, or committed myself, all the known violations. I shouldn't even talk about this subject unless I'm granted complete immunity. Television is, among other things, a machine for turning nouns into verbs. I "host" a show. It's "funded" by the Chubb Corporation and "aired" by PBS. And naturally I always hope it will be "successed."   /11

I could go on and on. The phrase "between you and I" appears, like an upraised pinkie, whenever people who should know better try for refinement. We seem to be stuck with that barbarous abbreviation "Ms.," which doesn't abbreviate anything, except common sense. The "you-know" is still spreading.   /12

Worst of all is the fact that the very authorities we might expect to shore up these collapsing standards—the experts in linguistics, the dictionary makers, the teachers of English—are in many cases leading the onslaught. It's as if, in the middle of a coup, we turned to the palace guard for help and saw them coming at us with bayonets.   /13

I had several linguistics professors on a series of shows about language earlier this season. They assured me that things like grammar, syntax and spelling were mere superficial details that shouldn't be allowed to interfere with the deeper importance of self-expression.

In fact they suggested that, in matters of language, rules and standards of any kind were snobbish, authoritarian and downright undemocratic. Most of them were apostles of a group called the Council on College Composition and Communication, which a few years ago put out a policy statement advocating "the student's right to his own language," no matter what dialect, patois, slang or gibberish it might be. This idea could revolutionize education. I keep waiting for other departments to pick it up: the student's right to his own math, the student's right to his own history, and so on.   /14

In Browning's poem "The Grammarian's Funeral," the grammarian himself was dead, obviously. Today the grammarian is underground in a different sense. A man named Richard Mitchell, who teaches English at Glassboro State College in New Jersey, publishes a monthly broadside called *The Underground Grammarian,* which is his one-man guerrilla war on jargon, cliches and fuzziness. The point is, his chief target is not the Philistine outside the ivied wall, but his own colleague, the English teacher sitting in the library—excuse me, I mean the language skills instructor sitting in the learning resources center.   /15

Yes, the English language *is* in a bad way. In my business there's a famous phrase characterizing the Broadway theater as a "fabulous invalid." To me, that's exactly what the language has become. My late friend, the writer Jean Stafford, once described its symptoms in the following clinical terms: /16

"Besides the neologisms that are splashed all over the body . . . like the daubings of a chimpanzee turned loose with finger paints, the poor thing has had its parts of speech broken to smithereens . . . and upon its stooped and aching back it carries an astounding burden of lumber piled on by the sociologists and the psychologists, the Pentagon, the admen, and, lately, the alleged robbers and bug planters of Watergate. The prognosis for the ailing language is not good. I predict that it will not die in my lifetime, but I fear that it will be assailed by countless cerebral accidents and massive strokes and gross insults to the brain and finally will no longer be able to sit up in bed and take nourishment by mouth."   /17

Members of the class of 1979, I can imagine you saying to yourself, "I'm sorry the language is ailing, but there's nothing I can do. It doesn't affect me anyway, since that's not my field. I can still get through the day. I can always get my meaning across."   /18

At this point the sharper students among you will recognize that I have come around the back way and snuck up on my subject. For I am here this morning to say it *does* affect you, and there *is* something you can do. No matter what you majored in, you're still English majors. We're all English majors, willy-nilly, until the day we join Browning's grammarian. The breakdown of language isn't just something that happens to language. It's something that happens to us, and to our lives   /19

Let's go back for a moment to Thurber and the actress at the party. They were, as Thurber put it, on the shadow line, close to losing rational touch with each other. Of course, it wouldn't have mattered all that much if they had. There are many occasions when it doesn't matter all that much if words and meaning part company—if an undertaker advertises coffins with a "lifetime guarantee," for example; or if the *New York Times* prints this sentence about Nelson Rockefeller: "He was chairman of the Museum of Modern Art, which he entered in a fireman's raincoat during a recent fire, and founded the Museum of Primitive Art."   /20

But E. B. White, who found that sentence in the *Times,* reminds us that muddiness of meaning isn't always such harmless fun. "Muddiness," White says, "is not merely a disturber of prose, it is a destroyer of life, of hope: death on the highway caused by a badly worded roadsign, heartbreak among lovers caused by a misplaced phrase in a well-intentioned letter, anguish of a traveler not being met at a railroad station because of a slipshod telegram.''   /21

You will live a lot of your lives on this mundane, practical level, exchanging gossip at a party, giving and taking directions, making and breaking plans. If your language is faulty, then these transactions will be faulty. Each of you literally will be in danger of not knowing what the other is talking about. Reconsider for a minute: can you really get through the day? Can you really always get your meaning across? When the gravedigger catches Hamlet out in a bit of muddiness, Hamlet says to his friend Horatio, ''We must speak by the card, or equivocation will undo us.'' E. B. White believes it, and so do I. /22

Beyond this practical level, there are two other levels on which the breakdown of language affects you. One is moral and esthetic. Language is ''the defining mystery of man,'' in George Steiner's phrase. It is the index to our civilization, the history of our race, the living web of our shared values and emotions. But it doesn't only define man generally and culturally. Specifically and personally it defines *men,* or rather, persons. The cardinal virtues of language are: clarity; simplicity; precision; vigor, if possible; and, on good days, gracefulness. What you ask of yourselves in each or those categories will define the terms by which you perceive things, by which you think, by which you register on the world around you. It will also define the terms by which other people judge you.   /23

I'm not talking about language as an ornament, or about having a good prose style the way you might have a good backhand. I don't mean something external like Gucci stripes. I mean some outward sign of an inner dimension. Come to think of it, Gucci stripes probably are an outward sign of an inner dimension. But anyway, consider the phrase, ''I could care less.'' It means exactly the opposite of what it's intended to mean. If you could care less, then you *do* care. But people use the phrase as a corruption of ''I *couldn't* care less,'' which apparently is now too much trouble to say. And I judge their inner dimensions accordingly. The woman who says to me, '' I could care less,'' is numb to logic and meaning. She simply isn't thinking about what she's saying, and I don't want to have anything to do with her—even if she *is* my wife.   /24

Finally, the breakdown of language affects you politically, and I'm using the word in the broad sense that George Orwell used it in the essay I quoted at the beginning, ''Politics and the English Language.'' By politics I think Orwell meant that whole way we order our public life and common welfare. When politics in this sense is decayed, language tends to be decayed too. This was true in Nazi Germany. It's true today in Soviet Russia. Part of what Solzhenitsyn and other Russian dissidents are protesting is the repression of the mother tongue, the debasement of words like ''truth'' and ''freedom'' into Newspeak, the twisting of a term like ''insane'' until it means any thought that departs from the Party line.   /25

Alas, we have more of that kind of decay in the West, specifically here in America, than we like to think. Vietnam taught us that, if nothing else. When soldiers bombard a village, drive the peasants into the countryside, burn their huts, machine-gun their cattle and then call it ''pacification,'' how different is that from Newspeak?   /26

Orwell wasn't sure whether politics debased the language, or vice versa, or whether it was a cycle. Our language ''becomes ugly and inaccurate because our thoughts are foolish,'' he said, ''but the slovenliness of our language makes it easier for us to have foolish thoughts.'' What Orwell *was* sure of was that the condition was curable, that we could shake off dead verbiage and mindless orthodoxy.   /27

If one simplifies one's English, he said, ''one can think more clearly, and to think clearly is a necessary first step towards political regeneration. . . . When you make a stupid remark its stupidity will be obvious, even to yourself. Political language . . . is designed to make lies sound truthful and murder respectable, and to give an appearance of solidity to pure wind. One cannot change this all in a moment, but one can at least change one's own habits, and from time to time one can even, if one jeers loudly enough, send some worn-out and useless phrase . . . into the dustbin where it belongs.''   /28

''If one jeers loudly enough . . .'' That takes me back, again, to Thurber. What appeals to me about that moment at the party is that Thurber not only skewered the actress's verbal absurdity, but he did it with humor. If I've raised any laughter here this morning, it hasn't been to reconcile you to the follies and abuses I've been talking about. It's been to hold them up to ridicule, to shame the people who commit them, and to render them so silly and contemptible that you won't commit them yourselves.   /29

There are other ways to achieve the same ends. There are a thousand ways. Humor is mine. The important thing is for you to find yours.   /30

Thank you.   /31

REFERENCE NOTES

[1]On the importance of people's expectations within various situations, see Lloyd Bitzer, ''The Rhetorical Situation,'' *Philosophy & Rhetoric*, 1 (Winter 1968), 1–14.

[2]''The Testimony of Sculpture,'' by Harold Haydon. Copyright © 1968, *The University of Chicago Magazine*. Reprinted with permission from *The University of Chicago Magazine*.

[3]Henry W. Grady, ''The New South,'' reprinted in *American Public Addresses; 1740–1952*, ed. A. Craig Baird (New York: McGraw-Hill Book Co., 1956), esp. pp. 181–85.

[4]''Is English a Dying Language?'' by Dick Cavett. Given at Vassar College Commencement, May 27, 1979. Reprinted by permission of Dick Cavett.

PROBLEMS AND PROBES

1. This chapter has argued that good-will speeches usually are informative speeches with underlying persuasive purposes. Describe various circumstances under which you think the informative elements should predominate in this type of speech, and then describe other circumstances in which the persuasive elements should be emphasized. In the second case, at what point would you say that the speech becomes openly persuasive in purpose? Or, if you prefer to work with advertisements, scan magazines to find public service ads—ones which emphasize what a company is doing to help society with its problems or to promote social-cultural-aesthetic values. Then ask yourself similar questions about these advertisements.

2. In this chapter we have discussed speeches of introduction and tribute, but we have ignored the *responses* which speakers make to them. After you have been

introduced, given an award, and received a tribute, what should you say? Knowing what you do about speeches of introduction and tribute, what kinds of materials might you include as attention, satisfaction, and visualization steps?

ORAL ACTIVITIES

1. Assume that you are to act as chairperson on one of the following occasions (or on some other similar occasion):
   a. A student government awards banquet.
   b. A special program for a meeting of an organization to which you belong.
   c. A kickoff banquet for a schoolwide charity fund-raising program.
   d. A student-faculty mass meeting called to protest a regulation issued by the dean's office.

In your role as chairperson, *(a)* plan a suitable program of speeches or entertainment; *(b)* allocate the amount of time to be devoted to each item on the program; *(c)* outline a suitable speech of introduction for the featured speaker or speakers; *(d)* prepare publicity releases for the local media; *(e)* arrange for press coverage; etc. Work out a complete plan—one that you might show to a steering committee or a faculty adviser.

2. Giving speeches to entertain is quite difficult because humor is a delicate art that only few can master. However, many audiences, as well as speakers, have come to expect the inclusion of jokes and funny stories in even the most serious of presentations. Make a collection of jokes, anecdotes, and cartoons which fit a certain genre such as ethnic, religious, or sex-role related. Analyze your collection with audience adaptation in mind. How might these jokes be offensive to some groups? How might they be modified so they are no longer offensive? How useful is material which is offensive even though it may seem funny to you? Also collect jokes, anecdotes, and cartoons which are not offensive to anyone and suggest how they might be useful in speaking situations. Be prepared to share your observations with your classmates.

3. Your instructor will give you a list of special-occasion, impromptu speech topics, such as:
   a. Student *X* is a visitor from a neighboring school; introduce him/her to the class.
   b. You are Student *X;* respond to this introduction.
   c. Dedicate your speech-critique forms to the state historical archives.
   d. You have just been named Outstanding Classroom Speaker for this term; accept the award.
   e. You are a representative for a Speechwriters-for-Hire firm; sell your services to other members of the class.

You will have between five and ten minutes in which to prepare, and then will present a speech on a topic assigned or drawn from the list. Be ready also to discuss the techniques you employed in putting the speech together.

SPEAKER'S RESOURCE BOOK

Analyzing and Criticizing the Speeches of Others 378

Communication Models 388

Ethics and Public Speaking 393

Exercises for Voice Improvement 395

Finding a Job: The Employment Interview 399

Group Discussion: Leadership 401

Group Discussion: Participation 405

Humor and Public Speaking 411

Model for Organizing and Evaluating Arguments (Toulmin) 413

Parliamentary Procedure and Speechmaking 416

Reducing Communication Apprehension: Systematic Solutions 419

Responding to Questions and Objections 424

Team Presentations: Panels and Symposiums 426

Working Bibliography: Additional Readings 429

Principles and Types of Speech Communication, *Tenth Edition,*
introduces an important new feature, the Speaker's Resource
Book. This is a collection of generally short presentations of
materials especially relevant to some speaking situations or to
particular speakers facing special problems. Some of these
materials were included within the regular chapters in earlier
editions of this book. Some materials are new to this edition and
have been requested by users of the book. All are relevant in some
degree to the public speaker's task—to share information,
experience, or ideas publicly for the common good. Use them as
directed by your instructor or independently to refine your public
speaking skills.

Analyzing and Criticizing the Speeches of Others

The bulk of this book has been concerned with making you a more skillful producer of oral messages. Except for some comments on listening in Chapter 2, we've not discussed explicitly the matter of analyzing and evaluating the messages of others. Because during your lifetime you'll spend more hours listening than talking, however, you certainly should know something about speech analysis and criticism. In a short space, we can only introduce the subject; hopefully you will learn enough here to want to study and practice speech analysis and criticism later.

What Is Speech Analysis and Criticism?

For most people, the word *criticism* calls up images of parents lecturing their kids, of politicians shouting at each other in a "Did not! Did too!" sort of way, or of teachers telling you about your shortcomings. Those kinds of negative or corrective judgments are part of what criticism *can* be about, but they're only that—negative judgments. There's much more to a complete act of criticism.

Suppose you come out of a classroom lecture and say to a friend, "That was the worst lecture I've heard all term." Your friend replies, "How so?" You answer, "The professor was disorganized, he turned his back on us most of the time and talked to the chalkboard, and the point he made about audience analysis as the single most important part of public speaking was just plain dumb." Your friend responds, "Oh, I don't know about that. He did outline the lecture pretty well, I thought, and of course he turned his back—he had a lot to write down. And what do you mean, audience analysis is 'just plain dumb'?" "Well," you counter, "he didn't really follow the outline—remember when . . . ?" And on it goes, until you both agree or get tired of discussing the topic.

In dialogues like this one—and you may have many of them each day—you're engaging in analysis and criticism. *Criticism is an argumentative process of analytical description and reasoned evaluation aimed at producing interpretations and judgments.* It is argumentative in that it is based on a disputable claim ("That was the worst . . ."). It is a process in that it is aimed at another party, either someone who responds or someone who simply reads what you've written. Analytical description provides the "evidence" one uses to support the claim. The evaluative aspects of criticism aren't simply self-reports of likes and dislikes, but are based on accepted criteria for judgment (in the example, on the positive values of good organization, eye contact with audiences, and audience analysis).

The goals of criticism—what someone else should get from your efforts to criticize well—are twofold: *Interpretation.* Critics are in the business of getting others to view something in a particular way, from a particular vantage point. In our example, you tried to get your friend to examine the professor's effort from three perspectives—organizational skills, delivery skills, and assertions about audience analysis. All three of these points of view fit under a general category one could call "technical speaker competencies"; technical speaker competencies is a kind of vantage point for evaluating that teacher's lecturing on that day. (Other vantage points, each with its own vocabulary, could have been used, as we'll note shortly.)

Judgment. Also, criticism as a kind of argumentative discourse usually ends in judgment. A critic normally ends up asserting that someone or something is beautiful/ugly, useful/useless, ethical/unethical, good/bad. In a fully rounded piece of criticism, those judgments are reasoned, are argued for in the ways we talked about argumentation earlier in this book.

All criticism, therefore, includes three elements: *(1)* an interpretive-judgmental assertion, *(2)* evidence in support of that assertion, and *(3)* a perspective or way of looking at something which makes the assertion in some way important or worthy of consideration. More specifically, then, rhetorical criticism or speech criticism focuses on informative and persuasive messages (often, but not only, speeches, for persuasion also can be sought via newspapers, magazines, radio and television programs, propagandistic art, and so on). The rhetorical critic or analyst seeks to interpret and judge those rhetorical messages in particular ways and from certain perspectives.

Speech Criticism vs. Speech Evaluation

As you'll recall from Chapter 2, you evaluate classroom speeches and others you hear from your personal perspective and from the speaker's as well. From your personal perspective you ask, "What's in this speech for me? What can I learn? What should I be wary of? What does this person think of me?" Or, from the speaker's perspective—as when you're giving someone feedback about his or her oral performance—you ask, "How did this person come across? Was the claim or central idea clearly stated? Was the speech well organized and easy to follow? Were the supporting materials adequate? Was the language clear and appropriate?" *Speech evaluation,* then, is aimed at oneself and at the speaker—for the listener's and the speaker's personal benefit.

Speech criticism usually is quite different. It is an *independent* message aimed at *a public*. Speech analyses and criticisms are messages about other messages. A speech seeks to accomplish an informative, persuasive, or entertaining purpose, while criticism of that speech interprets and judges that performance or transaction *with some other, usually larger, purpose in mind*. That larger purpose is determined in part by what you, the analyst-critic, want other people to understand about the performance or transaction, and in part by what your readers (your public) want to learn.

Types of Speech Analysis and Criticism

That last statement leads us to consider the range of purposes critics and readers can have, which in turn produces a list of types of rhetorical criticism. Actually, there are almost as many purposes and types of criticism as there are individual critics, especially when you think about specific purposes as we discussed them in Chapter 3. However, most of the specific purposes can be placed under one of the three following categories:

1. *To Account for the Effects of Communication.* Perhaps the most common end of rhetorical analysis is to account for the effects of a message or speaker upon an audience. Almost anyone, with sense and a bit of energy, can describe many of these effects. When assessing the effects of a presidential speech, for example, you can:
   - note the amount of applause and its timing;
   - read newspaper accounts and commentary on it the next day;
   - check public opinion polls, especially those assessing the President's performance thus far in his term and those dealing with the particular subject of the speech;
   - notice how much it is quoted and referred to weeks, months, or even years after it was delivered;
   - examine votes in Congress and election results potentially affected by the speech;
   - read memoirs, diaries, and books treating the event, the speaker, and the speech;
   - read the President's own accounts of the speech.[1]

   But mere description of effects is not criticism; after all, you can do that without even reading the speech. The important phrase in this purpose, therefore, is "accounting for." Rhetorical analysts discussing the effects of a speech take that extra step, delving into the speaking process to see if they can discover what in the message, the situation, the speaker, and other elements of the speech produced those results. That is no easy task, yet it's central to improving our knowledge of speechmaking and its effects on society. Following are examples of where you might look in the communication process to find elements which can account for a message's reception by the audience:

   a. *The situation.* Did the situation make certain demands which the speaker had to meet? A series of events, the traditions of discourse surrounding the occasion (that is, the expectations we have about inaugurals, sermons, and the like), or even the date of the speech (it is one thing for a presidential aspirant to make promises in October, but quite another for the elected person to make them in January)—all these can provide critics with clues to situational demands.
   b. *The speaker.* Did the speaker have the authority or credibility to affect the audience, almost regardless of what he or she said? Some speakers have such reputations or carry so much charisma that they can influence an audience with the sheer power and dynamism of their words and presence. The rhetorical critic is interested in such phenomena and seeks to find specific word patterns and speech behaviors which account for listeners' reactions to these factors.[2]
   c. *The arguments.* Did the speaker's message strike responsive chords in the audience? Were the motivational appeals those to which this audience was susceptible? Why? Were the beliefs, attitudes, values, and ideological orientations advanced by the speaker likely to have made impressions on this audience?

Why? Were the supporting materials—and specific combinations of the various types—useful in helping an audience comprehend and accept the overall message? Why? (These "whys" usually have to be answered by assessing the temperament of the times, the dominant ideologies in the culture, and the facts of the situation, as well as the internal and external characteristics of audiences discussed in Chapter 5.)

d. *Uses of modes of communication.* Were the linguistic, paralinguistic, bodily, and visual modes of communication used effectively? In other words, as a critic you must look at more than the words on a printed page. Oral communication always needs to be explained as completely as possible, either from videotapes, films, or—if necessary—newspaper descriptions of the speaker and the occasion.

e. *Audience susceptibility.* In general, why was *this* audience susceptible to *this* message delivered by *this* speaker in *this* setting at *this* time? The critic seeking to explain the effects of a speech ultimately has to answer that single, all-important question.

A solid analysis of communication effects, therefore, demands a careful integration of "who did what to whom, when, and to what effect."[3] It demands thoughtful assessment—the hard work of deciding which among all of the elements of the speaking process were responsible for particular aspects of audience reaction. Ultimately, your quest for "why" will lead you to look at more than the speech itself. For example, determining why the audience was particularly receptive to President Johnson's call for a "blank check" during the 1964 Gulf of Tonkin crisis will require a historical examination of public attitudes at the time. To determine the effect of President Carter's debates on his 1976 victory and 1980 defeat will require more than an analysis of his arguments or his use of the media in both campaigns.

At times, it may be necessary to combine scientific research with historical explanation.[4] An example will illustrate this point. Two teams of rhetorical analysts—Andrew A. King and Floyd D. Anderson, and Richard D. Raum and James S. Measell—were interested in techniques presumably used by Richard Nixon, Spiro Agnew, and George Wallace to polarize public opinion and divide voting groups in order to win elections in the '60s. King and Anderson examined with considerable care the speeches of Nixon and Agnew between 1968 and 1970, while Raum and Measell looked at Wallace's speeches between 1964 and 1972. Neither team felt that a mere listing of argumentative and linguistic techniques was enough, for the listing did not provide them with answers to the question, "Why did these techniques work?" Both teams, therefore, read the social-psychological literature on the concept of *polarization.* King and Anderson then used this research to shed light on ways words can be used to affirm a group's identity (in this case, that of the silent majority), and on methods for isolating or negating the voting power of an opponent. The concept of polarization seemed to them to explain why those tactics supposedly created two different political power blocs or "societies" in the late 1960s.

Raum and Measell, however, went further. They not only examined the tactics and psychological dimensions of polarization, but also looked at the concept as they deemed it to occur in specific situations. George Wallace's effectiveness, they concluded, lay in the kinds of people he appealed to, in his vocabulary which charged his audiences emotionally, and in the ways in which Wallace made himself a social redeemer who could save the country from the "enemy."[5] You may not find it necessary to resort to such sophisticated strategies to explicate a message's effects. Nevertheless, your analysis of a contemporary speech may be based on information you possess about how people behave in crowds, what their attitudes are, or what a particular psychological theory would predict given certain speech strategies. This information becomes a central part of your critical evaluation. The difference is one of degree, not of kind, as you proceed to offer your interpretation of why a speaker succeeded or failed. The rigor of analysis may separate you from the professional rhetorical analyst, but the process is the same. The critical judgment in both cases is not based just on a "gut reaction" to the speech or on an uninformed response of liking or disliking.

2. *To Explore the Critical Dimensions of Communication.* So far, we have been discussing a focus on criticism which examines the effects of speeches—changes in attitudes or behavior, voting shifts, and acknowledgment of a speaker's rhetorical expertise are potential items mentioned or examined in the process of arriving at a critical judgment. This is not, however, the only way of looking at a speech. A speech, after all, is many things on many different levels; hence it is possible to talk about a number of different critical perspectives. A *critical perspective* is, in language we already have used, a human design or purpose. It is the reason-for-being of a piece of criticism, the particular viewpoint a critic is interested in bringing to bear on a discourse. Just as you can be looked at in a number of different ways—as a student, as a son or daughter, as an employee, as a lover—so, too, can a speech be examined from different vantages, depending upon the observer's purposes or designs. For example, speeches have been viewed critically in the following ways:

   a. *Pedagogically.* You can use the speech as a model, as a way of examining public communicators who have made judicious rhetorical choices. You can learn how to speak well, in part, by looking at and listening to other speakers.
   b. *Culturally.* You can examine a discourse to acquire a better understanding of the times. For example, you may look at speeches from the Revolutionary War period or from the nineteenth century to better understand *how* our ancestors thought, *how* the great American values were spread through the society, and *how* we as a nation came to be what we are.
   c. *Linguistically.* Because human beings are symbol-using animals—because we are distinguished from other animals by the complexity of our symbol systems— it makes sense to be particularly interested in the language used in public discourses. Some critics look at oral language to better comprehend the communicative *force* of words—how some words plead, others persuade, still others threaten, and so on. Some critics are concerned with *condensation symbols*—the process by which certain words (for example, *communist* in the '50s, *hippie* in the '60s, *polluter* in the '70s, *vigilante* in the '80s) acquire a broad range of

ideologically positive or negative connotations. Other critics are especially interested in *metaphors*—in ways we describe experiences vicariously with words ("He's an absolute *pig*") or, in the case of *archetypal metaphors*, ways by which we can capture the essence of humanity by appealing figuratively to the great common human experiences (light and dark metaphors, birth and death metaphors, sexual metaphors, and so on). Whatever approach linguistic critics take, however, they ultimately seek to illuminate what it means to communicate as a symbol-using human being.

   d. *Generically.* In this decade especially, we have seen a great number of critics addressing the problem of classifying speeches into types or genres. For example, in this book we generally have classified speeches into three basic types—speeches to inform, to persuade, and to actuate—and we have done this because we think you are most interested in grouping communicative techniques by the ways in which they help you accomplish certain *purposes*. Other critics classify speeches by *situation* or *location*—for instance, the rhetoric of international conflict, the rhetoric of the used-car lot, the political-convention keynote address—in order to uncover the ways in which the location or expectations created by the occasion determine what must be said. Others argue that speeches are best categorized by *topic* because certain recurrent themes congregate around recurrent human problems. Hence, they write about the rhetoric of war and peace, the rhetoric of women's issues, of reform or revolution. Whatever approach critics employ in the process of classification, however, they all generally have a singular goal: to categorize speeches in order to find *families of discourses* which have enough in common to help us understand dominant modes of thought or modes of expression typical of an age, a problem, or a set of speakers.[6]

Pedagogical, cultural, linguistic, and generic critics, therefore, all examine specific aspects of discourses, features they think deserve special attention. They make this examination in order to learn what these aspects tell us about communication practice *(pedagogy)*, the condition of humanity *(culture)*, the potentials of language codes *(linguistics)*, or the dominant species of discourse *(genres)*.

3. *To Evaluate the Ethics of Communication.* In an age of governmental credibility gaps, charges of corporate irresponsibility, situational ethics, and the rise of minorities who challenge the prevailing social and ethical systems of the United States, a host of ethical questions have come to concern speech analysts: Can we still speak of the democratic ideal as *the* ethical standard for speakers in this country? What are the communicative responsibilities which attend the exercise of corporate, governmental, and personal power? For example, President Nixon's speech on November 3, 1969, in which he talked about the "silent majority," his quest for peace, and three alternatives for ending the war in Vietnam—escalation, withdrawal, or gradual de-escalation –naturally aroused considerable controversy. One critic, Forbes Hill, found no special ethical problems in the speech because the President's appeals to the majority of Americans were consistent with the country's values at that time. Another, Robert P. Newman, assuming the "democratic ideal" as his standard, decried the speech because he claimed that it violated the individual's right to know

fully all that a government plans and does. A third critic, Karlyn K. Campbell, argued that the standards initially set for evaluating the alternatives were violated later in the speech. And Philip Wander and Steven Jenkins accused the President of lying.[7] Thus, each critic assumed a particular ethical posture, and from that posture proceeded to evaluate the speech in accordance with his or her own views and biases.

Essential Critical Activities

Rhetorical analysis, no matter what its specific purpose, always demands certain activities of the critic. No matter what goal you're attempting to accomplish, as a critic you need a way of talking about the speech event, a plan for observing or reconstructing it, and a method for writing up your critical thoughts.

A Coherent Vocabulary for Rhetorical Evaluation.   Perhaps the most difficult task a beginning critic faces is that of settling on a rhetorical vocabulary, a way of talking. The "who? what? when? where? why? how?" questions of the journalist may provide a starting point for analysis, but they won't get a critic very far in examining the speech. Unlike the journalist, the critic is engaged in a systematic, coherent pursuit of specialized knowledge *about* communication. The description of the event itself is only a part of that process, therefore; the actual analysis demands a language that "talks about" talk. There are many such critical vocabularies. Let us look at one as an example.

In an article referred to earlier in this book, Lloyd Bitzer discusses the "rhetorical situation."[8] In this essay, he argues that the *rhetorical situation* almost literally dictates what kinds of things ought to be said, to whom they ought to be said, and in what forms the messages should be presented. More specifically, he maintains that situations are marked by *exigencies* (events, peoples, or happenings which call forth discourse from someone because they are important, serious, demanding, and so on), by *audience expectations* (thoughts of who should say what to whom, when, and where), and by *constraints* (the limits of choices speakers can make—for instance, the rules governing congressional debate, the boundaries of social propriety, the availability or not of certain audiences). If a speaker in a rhetorical situation satisfies the reasons calling forth talk, meets the audiences' expectations, and abides by the constraints, the speech will be considered a *fitting response* to the situation.[9] Thus, in Bitzer's model, the main emphases are upon *the primacy of situation and the importance of speech competencies*.

Bitzer's approach to rhetorical analysis and the vocabulary he uses are especially useful when, as a critic, you are studying the speeches of those who act as representatives for particular groups. The behaviors of heads of state, congressional politicians, leaders of churches, labor unions, and the like are in part dictated by the groups they represent. They are not speaking for themselves as individuals, but rather for groups or institutions. Hence, no matter what they believe personally, their public utterances always must be consistent with the organization's goals, reinforce its viewpoints, and voice its concerns. They may even be pressured by the forces inherent in certain occasions—by what custom dictates *must* by said in inaugurals, in Labor Day speeches, in

Easter sermons, and the like. In short, when speakers are constrained by situationally imposed roles, Bitzer's approach and vocabulary help us examine how these constraints affect the way people talk publicly and upon what bases we judge them competent speakers.

Careful Observation.   The second task you must grapple with as a critic is that of deciding *what* to look at and *how*. In part, of course, this problem is solved by your selection of a vocabulary. If, for example, you employ a textbook vocabulary, you know you will have to isolate motivational appeals, look for an arrangement pattern, and see if you can find out how the speaker delivered the message. Yet, the vocabulary does not, as a rule, exhaust your task of looking. You may need to expand it to include searches for information both inside and outside the speech text itself.

Outside observation.   Often you have to look for relevant information about the speech, the speaker, the audience, and the situation *outside* the actual text of what was said. As we have already suggested, if you are interested in the effects of a presidential speech, you probably will want to check public opinion polls, memoirs, diaries, the results of subsequent voting on the issue or issues, and newspaper and magazine reactions. If you are working from the textbook vocabulary, you probably will need to see what the audience knew about the speaker beforehand (prior reputation), what kind of people made up the audience present, and what ratings were given to radio or television broadcasts of the speech. Or, if you are doing a cultural analysis of the speech, you will have to read whatever you can find on the cultural values and mores of the era in which the speech was delivered. You cannot, for example, do a study of Daniel Webster as a typical ceremonial orator of the 1830s or 1840s without having a solid grasp of what Americans were doing and thinking about during that early national period. Webster's political generalizations, metaphors, and sweeping vision of the Republic make little sense unless you are acquainted with political-economic expansion, the settling of the Midwest and West, the growing fight between states' righters and nationalists, the problem of slavery, and other key cultural battles which characterized the period. Many kinds of critical studies of speeches, therefore, require you to spend time in the library with newspapers, magazines, history books, and biographies.

Inside observation.   As a critic, you also will have to live with the speech for a while. Often, an initial reading of it produces either a "So what?" or a "What can I say?" reaction. You should read it time and again, each time subjectively projecting yourself into the situation, into the frame of mind of the speaker and the audience. You probably should even read the speech aloud (if you do not have a recording or videotape of it), trying to capture emphases, rhythms, and sounds. Part of inside observation, then, is a process of "getting the feel" of the speech.

The other part is discovering the key points on which it turns. Certain statements or phrases in great speeches became memorable because they were pivotal. They summarized or encapsulated an important idea, attitude, or sentiment. As you read over, say, Cicero's "First Oration Against Cataline," you are impressed by the initial series of eight rhetorical questions, which immediately put the Roman audience into an abusive frame of mind. You may be similarly impressed by the way Queen Elizabeth I used *I* and *we* in her speeches in order to make her dominance over Parliament eminently clear, or by British Prime Minister David Lloyd George's preoccupation with light-dark archetypal metaphors which elevate his discourse. Contemporary speeches, too—those published in *Vital Speeches of the Day,* for example—have certain elements in common: a heavy reliance upon particular forms of support, especially statistics, quotations from authorities, and explanations.

In other words, looking inside speeches intently forces your critical apparatus to operate. Your mind begins to catch points of dominance and memorability—aspects of discourse which you find noteworthy and even fascinating. When those insights are coupled with research you have done on the outside—in newspapers, magazines, books, and the like—you soon find that you have something critical to say about a particular speech or group of speeches.

Composing Your Critical Evaluation. Acts of criticism are arguments: Your critical evaluation functions as a *claim* that must be supported with specific reasons justifying its soundness. Your process of observation and the vocabulary you employ come together into a cogent explanation of why the speech was effective, how certain identification strategies functioned, or why cultural symbols in a speech were ignored by the audience. The plan for writing your critical evaluation outlined below is not the only way in which your argument may be organized. Nevertheless, it may be helpful as a general guide to the organization of your critical response. The plan also may be useful for term papers or research papers you will be asked to write.

A Plan for Writing Speech Criticism

I. Introduction
- A.   As a "starter" for your paper, introduce a quotation, a description of events, a statement of communication principles, or whatever will indicate your approach to the speech or your point of view about it.
- B.   Make *a statement of questions or claims*—the point or points you wish to develop or establish in the paper.
- C.   Make *a statement of procedures*—how you propose to go about answering the questions or proving the claims.

II. Body
- A.   After you have thus described the basic speech material or the situation with which you are dealing, take the steps of your critical analysis one point at a time, looking, for example, at *exigencies/audience expectations/constraints/fittingness* if you are using Bitzer's critical techniques, making sure in this approach that you have carefully described the situation around which you are building your analysis.
- B.   As you offer the subpoints or claims, liberally illustrate them with quotations from the speech or speeches you are analyzing, quotations which serve as evidence for your point of view or argument. Also quote from other critical observers to further support your position if you wish.

III. Conclusions
- A   In your *summary,* pull the argument of your paper together by indicating how the subpoints combine to present a valid picture of public communication.
- B.   Draw *implications,* commenting briefly upon what can be learned from your analysis and this speech (or set of speeches) about communication generally. That is, you say in effect that this is a case study of something having larger implications.

With a coherent vocabulary for thinking about public communication, with patient and thoughtful observation, and with a plan for reporting your reactions, you should be able to produce useful and stimulating evaluations and analyses of speeches. Ultimately, your practice in communication criticism will help you better understand the ways by which public discourse affects the beliefs, attitudes, values, and behaviors of yourself and your society.

In this short appendix, we have been able to describe only *briefly* a few critical frameworks or approaches and to allude to a limited number of actual speeches and speaking events. A good general introduction to rhetorical criticism suitable for undergraduate students can be found in James R. Andrews' *The Practice of Rhetorical Criticism* (New York: Macmillan Publishing Co., 1983).

REFERENCE NOTES

[1]For an example of how skilled critics search out the effects of a controversial speech of this kind, see Paul Arntson and Craig R. Smith, "The Seventh of March Address [Daniel Webster]: A Mediating Influence," *Southern Speech Communication*, 40 (Spring 1975): 288–301.

[2]For a discussion of ways to talk critically about *charisma*, see George P. Boss, "Essential Attributes of the Concept of Charisma," *Southern Speech Communication Journal*, 41 (Spring 1976): 300–313.

[3]For a detailed discussion of the kinds of information which can be produced by "effects studies" (also called historical studies), see Bruce E. Gronbeck, "Rhetorical History and Rhetorical Criticism: A Distinction," *The Speech Teacher*, 24 (November 1975): 309–320.

[4]On the relationships between rhetorical criticism and the social sciences, see John W. Bowers, "The Pre-Scientific Function of Rhetorical Criticism," in *Essays on Rhetorical Criticism*, ed. Thomas R. Nilsen (New York: Random House, Inc., 1968), pp. 126–45.

[5]Andrew A. King and Floyd D. Anderson, "Nixon, Agnew, and the 'Silent Majority': A Case Study in the Rhetoric of Polarization," *Western Speech*, 35 (Fall 1971): 243–55; Richard D. Raum and James S. Measell, "Wallace and His Ways: A Study of the Rhetorical Genre of Polarization," *Central States Speech Journal*, 25 (Spring 1974): 28–35.

[6]Literature for these "families of discourse" abounds. For samples of cultural studies, for instance, see Ernest Wrage, "The Little World of Barry Goldwater," *Western Speech*, 27 (Fall 1963): 207–215; and Theodore Balgooyen, "A Study of Conflicting Values: American Plains Indian Orators vs. the U.S. Commissioners of Indian Affairs," *Western Speech*, 24 (Spring 1962): 76–83. For an example of linguistic analysis—especially as it involves condensation symbols—look at Doris Graber, *Verbal Behavior and Politics* (Urbana: University of Illinois Press, 1976), especially Chapter 7. Additional examples of families of discourse are included in the "Checklist."

[7]Forbes I. Hill, "Conventional Wisdom—Traditional Form: The President's Message of November 3, 1969," *Quarterly Journal of Speech*, 58 (December 1972): 373–86; Robert P. Newman, "Under the Veneer: Nixon's Vietnam Speech of November 3, 1969," *Quarterly Journal of Speech*, 56 (December 1970): 432–34; Karlyn Kohrs Campbell, "Richard M. Nixon," *Critiques of Contemporary Rhetoric* (Belmont, CA: Wadsworth Publishing Co., 1972), pp. 50–57; and Philip Wander and Steven Jenkins, "Rhetoric, Society, and the Critical Response," *Quarterly Journal of Speech*, 58 (December 1972): 373–86.

[8]From "The Rhetorical Situation," by Lloyd F. Bitzer, *Philosophy and Rhetoric*, 1 (Winter 1968): 1–14.

[9]For a study clearly illustrating Bitzer's method of analysis, see Allen M. Rubin and Rebecca R. Rubin, "An Examination of the Constituent Elements in Presenting an Occurring Rhetorical Situation," *Central States Speech Journal*, 26 (Summer 1975): 133–41.

Communication Models

A model is a picture or representation of a thing or a process which identifies the key parts or elements and indicates how each element affects the operations of all of the other elements. A communication system can be reduced to such a model—in fact, to many models, depending upon what aspects of communication are of primary interest.

Before examining some communication models, however, we might legitimately ask, "Who cares?" "Of what importance or use are models?" While it undoubtedly is true that some speakers create and deliver extraordinarily powerful speeches without having seen—much less drawn up—a communication model, the fact is that most of us need help in conceptualizing the oral communication process; its primary features are not always clear. Further, armed with models that direct our attention to particular aspects or features of oral communication, we're more likely to create strategically sound and situationally sensitive speeches than if we're unaware of the importance of particular elements or aspects of communication.[1] Models can control our perception of the communication process; in turn, the way we perceive communication can govern our practice.

For example, one of the earliest definitions of communication came from the Greek philosopher-teacher Aristotle (384–322 B.C.). He defined communication, then called "rhetoric," as "the faculty of observing in any given case the available means of persuasion" (*Rhetoric* 1335b). With his stress upon "observing in any given case the available means" and with his long lists of things a speaker might want to say when talking in the Greek law courts and assemblies, his was a *speaker-centered* model of communication. Translating some of his Greek concepts into more contemporary language, his model looked essentially like this:

ARISTOTLE'S MODEL[2]

A SPEAKER discovers logical, emotional, and ethical proofs,

　　　　arranges those materials strategically,

　　　　　　clothes the ideas in clear and compelling words, and

　　　　　　　　delivers the resulting speech appropriately.

As time passed, rhetoricians or communication theorists became less concerned with the speaker or writer and more concerned with types and contents of actual messages. For example, in the late eighteenth and nineteenth centuries the "belletristic" approach to communication education developed in the schools. After learning as much as they could about language—its origins, its main elements, and its eloquent use—students were put through a series of exercises. These began with the construction of relatively simple descriptive passages, then moved on to more complicated historical narratives, and culminated in the writing of argumentative, persuasive, and literary works.

All of this emphasis upon preparing various kinds of messages led to *message-centered* theories of communication, theories which could be used to describe both oral and written discourse. The simplest and most influential message-centered model of our time came from David Berlo:

BERLO'S MODEL[3]

A **Source** encodes a **MESSAGE** for a **Receiver** who decodes it, or, the S-M-R model.

This model was useful for the post World War II world of communication study for several reasons: *(1)* The idea of "source" was flexible enough to include oral, written, electronic, or any other kind of "symbolic" generator-of-messages. *(2)* "Message" was made the central element, stressing the transmission of *ideas*. *(3)* The model recognized that receivers were important to communication, for they were the targets. *(4)* The notions of "encoding" and "decoding" emphasized the problems we all have (psycholinguistically) in translating our own thoughts into words or other symbols and in deciphering the words or symbols of others into terms we ourselves can understand.

The model was (and still is) popular. It does, however, tend to stress the manipulation of the message—the encoding and decoding processes; it implies that human communication is like machine communication, like signal-sending in telephone, television, computer, and radar systems. It even seems to stress that most problems in human communication can be solved by technical accuracy—by choosing the "right" symbols, preventing interference, and sending efficient messages.

But the problems of human communication are not as simple as that. Even when we know what words mean and choose the right ones, we still can misunderstand each other, because we all have different experiences and interests in life. Even when a message is completely clear and understandable, we often don't like it. Problems in "meaning" or "meaningfulness" often aren't a matter of comprehension, but of reaction, of agreement, of shared concepts, beliefs, attitudes, values. To put the *com-* back into communication, we need a *meaning-centered* theory of communication. While there are many such theories, perhaps one of the simplest was that offered by theorist Wilbur Schramm in 1954:

SCHRAMM'S MODEL[4]

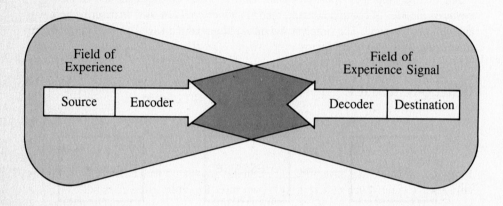

This model is elegant, picturing as it does the meaning-sharing process simply and graphically. It essentially argues that, in any given signal (message), you and I will comprehend and understand each other to the degree that our "fields of experiences" (interests, feelings, values, goals, purposes, information, ideas) overlap. That is, we can communicate in any given situation only to the degree that our *prior* experiences are similar.

Now we're getting somewhere. But before we assume we have frozen interhuman communication in a simple process, we must take into account three other aspects of people-talk: feedback, context, and culture.

Feedback

First, we must remember that communication is usually a two-way path. Most communication systems these days allow receivers to feed back or return messages to sources.

We all have been taught a multitude of ways for sending messages back to communicators. Some of these methods are very *direct,* as when you talk in direct response to someone. Others are only *moderately direct;* you might squirm when a speaker drones on and on, wrinkle your nose and scratch your head when a message is too abstract, or shift your body position when you think it's your turn to talk. Still other kinds of feedback are completely *indirect.* For example, politicians discover if they're getting their message across by the number of votes cast on the first Tuesday in November;

commercial sponsors examine sales figures to gauge their communicative effectiveness in ads; teachers measure their abilities to get the material across in a particular course by seeing how many students sign up for it the next term. Direct, moderately direct, and indirect feedback all offer opportunities to make a communication system work in both directions.

Context

A message may have different meanings, depending upon the specific context or setting. The message "Let's get out of here" has one meaning when cooed by a member of the opposite sex at a dull party, but quite another when snarled angrily in front of a waiter who has been providing bad service. Shouting "Fire!" on a rifle range produces one set of reactions—reactions quite different from those produced in a crowded theater. Meaning depends in part on context or situation.[5]

Culture

Finally, a message may have different meanings associated with it depending upon the culture or society. Each culture has its own rules for interpreting communicative signals. A hearty belch after a dinner in Skokie, Illinois, is a sign of impoliteness; but it is a supreme compliment to the host or hostess in other cultures. Negotiating the price of a T-shirt at Macy's is unheard of; yet it is a sign of active interest in an Istanbul bazaar or a neighborhood garage sale. Communication systems, thus, operate within the confines of cultural rules and expectations to which we all have been educated.

When we add the ideas of feedback, context, and culture to some of the other elements of communication we have been discussing, we come up with a model which looks like the one on page 392.

Our model now includes all the elements of a communication system that we need. To understand how systems operate, though, you also must keep in mind some of the characteristics of the elements we have alluded to:

1. *Sources* and *receivers* hold differing bundles of beliefs, attitudes, values, expectations, skills.
2. *Messages* are encoded into a variety of symbol systems (words, gestures, tones of voice, pictures, bodily postures).
3. *Contexts* provide almost innumerable cues that help receivers interpret what is being said or done.
4. *Cultures* provide even more complex rules for offering and interpreting messages.[5]

If you look at the following model carefully and then examine the one offered in Chapter 1, you'll note some important similarities. That is because this *general* model of human communication formed the basis for the *specific* model of public speaking— one kind of human communication—we've been operating from in this textbook. As a matter of fact, were you to go through the entire book with this model in hand, you'd

A CONTEXTUAL-CULTURAL MODEL

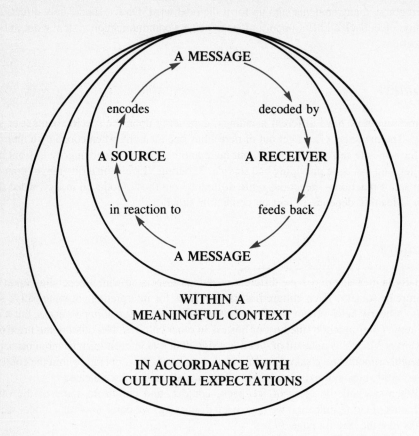

discover that the language, general advice, and even lists of specific "do's" and "don'ts" we have presented throughout the preceding chapters are grounded in this model. Our stress upon making rhetorical choices based on your assessments of situation, audience, and purpose; the references to communication rules and roles; the expressed hope that you'll develop a broad range of oral communication skills—all of these concerns are rooted in this model.

Communication models *are* merely pictures; they're even distorting pictures, because they stop or freeze an essentially dynamic interactive or transactive process into a static picture. Nevertheless, a well drawn model—and certainly you are able, if you think about it, to draw a model which reflects your own view of communication practices—can direct your attention to key aspects of human communication and hence affect your oral communication performance. A picture may well be worth a thousand words—especially if it helps you shape those words into a coherent, powerful speech.

REFERENCE NOTES

[1]For a helpful and more sophisticated introduction to communication models, see C. David Mortensen, *Communication: The Study of Human Communication* (New York: McGraw-Hill Book Co., 1972), Chapter 2, "Communication Models."

[2]Aristotle's speaker-centered model received perhaps its fullest development in the hands of Roman educator Quintilian (ca. 35–95 A.D.), whose *Institutio Oratoria* was filled with advice on the full training of a "good" speaker-statesman.

[3]Simplified from David K. Berlo, *The Process of Communication* (New York: Holt, Rinehart, and Winston, 1960).

[4]From Wilbur Schramm, "How Communication Works," in *The Process and Effects of Communication,* ed. Wilbur Schramm (Urbana: University of Illinois Press, 1954), pp. 3–26.

[5]For an expanded discussion of this model, see Bruce E. Gronbeck, *The Articulate Person: A Guide to Everyday Public Speaking,* 2nd ed. (Glenview, IL: Scott, Foresman and Company, 1983), Chapter 1.

Ethics and Public Speaking

Four main demands are made upon the responsible speaker: the demands you make on yourself, the demands imposed on you by the situation, the particular audience's sense of what will be ethically proper, and constraints imposed by societal standards of conduct.

1. *Self.* You are the best judge of your personal standards of conduct. Not everyone is able to sell encyclopedias to young, struggling couples and feel good after closing the sale. Not all people are willing to sell a car they know is a lemon without mentioning the possibility of problems. While there may be a sucker born every minute, every speaker is not inclined to exploit that possibility in selling his or her ideas to an audience. Each of us has limits beyond which we are uncomfortable in advancing ideas or selling products. First and foremost, then, you need to be consistent with your own standards for the ideas you advocate, the information you dispense, and the techniques you use to convey it to others.

2. *Situation.* Some people will attempt to take advantage of a situation in order to sell an idea or a product. News stories about elderly persons who have been swindled are all too common. For this reason, there are laws that restrict conduct in particular situations. "Truth in advertising" legislation, disclosure of information by used car dealers, provisions for ensuring that estimates are given and agreed to before work is performed on your car or home, and "truth in lending" statutes all work to limit the range of unethical practices that people might otherwise be prone to commit. While they do not guarantee that frauds will not occur, they do provide recourse in the event of irresponsible behavior. Adhering to legal statutes or to situational standards dictated by custom also will help prevent irresponsible speech.

3. *Audience.* Some audiences are more gullible than others. One audience's level of knowledge, interest, or even comprehension may make it possible to capture that audience without their realizing that you have been less than candid or honest. Another audience, in contrast, will appraise your ideas critically. What does this mean for you as a public speaker? Should you take advantage of the less critical audience and hope to slide your ideas past them without their noticing that the reasoning and support are weak? Your own standards and those implicit in the situation should prevent you from taking this route.

4. *Society.* If your standards and those of the specific situation are not sufficient to prevent unethical practices, the standards of the society often prove potent enough to prevent abuses. Where there are no formal laws or rules to follow, communities nonetheless have established general standards which a speaker violates at his or her peril. One question you might ask before embarking on a questionable practice is, "What happens if I get caught?" You will recognize this as the familiar "means-ends" dilemma: Is the practice justified because the end being sought is "noble" or "good"? Unfortunately, this issue cannot be answered in a simple absolute: ends do not justify means. Again, we are forced to rely on a speaker's own code of conduct, as well as on the conduct expected or required by the situation and the audience.

None of the above standards operates in isolation. Taken together, they form a whole and act as a check on the excesses of ethical abuse.

Guides to Practice

Thinking about being ethical in your presentation and actually being ethical are quite different. Knowing what should be done does not guarantee against mistakes. The following guidelines will help you translate the above cautions into actual practice.

Advocate Ethically-Based Proposals.   Audiences can challenge your techniques of presentation as unethical, or they can challenge the ideas themselves. Topics that evoke heightened emotional feelings (for example, abortion) may be rejected on the basis of the position you take. If the audience feels that your proposal is questionable, how far will you get with it, regardless of the techniques you use? You have an obligation to be sensitive to community standards regarding the ideas and proposals you submit for approval and action. You are not being asked to say whatever the audience wants to hear or to refrain from advocating controversial proposals. Rather, you will need to gauge audience reaction to the viability of your ideas, and offer the best possible arguments you can for their adoption. You may be convinced that the proposal is an ethical one, but you may still need to persuade your audience that it does not violate community standards.

Protect the Rights of Others.   The language you use and the claims you advance should not be so abusive as to libel or slander others. You need to defend claims about the wrongdoing of others and state your case in clear, precise terms without resorting to loaded language or name calling. When in doubt, be very careful in your accusations regarding the behavior of other people.

Subordinate Techniques to Ideas. You want the audience to focus on your message, not on the artistry of your approach, style, or delivery. Whatever techniques you use should be in the service of the message, rather than so transparent that they assume a significance of their own. Techniques perceived as "too smooth" may cause the audience to question the sincerity of your motives in persuading them. Going beyond what an audience feels is reasonable for the topic under discussion or the situation will bring attention to the techniques and damage your effectiveness.

Responsible speech, in essence, requires a sensitivity to the total communicative situation. Speaking with knowledge and skill, drawing on your knowledge of yourself, the situation, the audience, and the broader community standards, and limiting the potential for abuse by following the above guidelines will help you practice ethically responsible communication.

Exercises for Voice Improvement

In Chapter 14, as you will recall, our emphasis was primarily on the psychological aspects and implications of vocal communication. Here, our concerns center on the *physiological* nature of the human voice as an instrument of communication and on some of the practical means by which you may improve its effectiveness.

Good vocal behavior is *habitual*. Any vocal skill, before it can seem natural and effective with listeners, must become so much a habit that it will work for you without conscious effort when you begin to speak, and will continue to do so throughout the course of your message. Second, however, effective vocal behavior is *responsive*. There are times, for example, when you will want to stretch your voice—to shout, to reach listeners with almost a whisper, to put purposively a sense of irony or disbelief into your vocal tones. In these instances, you need to have confidence in yourself and your vocal mechanism as you reach for non-ordinary vocal effects.

To improve your normal, habitual vocal patterns and to provide yourself with a vocal instrument capable of reaching for special effects, you may well need to practice using it; simple vocal exercises, especially when monitored by a speech teacher with some training in voice and articulation, can be employed in practice sessions. (Comparatively severe voice problems, of course, should be taken to your school's speech correction clinic, where certified clinicians will work patiently and personally with you. Most of us, however, do not need the services of a clinic; we need, rather, to reform a few of our vocal habits.)

Exercises for Voice Practice[1]

Breath Control

Before you can learn to control the voice, you must control the breathing processes. Before you can control the breath, you must develop a sensitivity to the physical processes involved in breathing. Try these exercises.

1. Get down on hands and knees. Breathe through your mouth. Take three or four deep breaths. You will notice that when you inhale, the diaphragm (or stomach, it will seem) drops down. When you exhale, the diaphragm rises as it contracts to expel the air from the lungs. Keeping your arms and shoulders stiff, breathe as rapidly as you can without becoming dizzy. This will help you develop a sensitivity to the respiratory mechanism while developing control over the basic muscles of respiration.

2. Humans don't usually breathe while on "all fours," however. Standing upright, take ten deep breaths, very slowly. Feel how the rib cage expands on inhalation and contracts when you exhale. Notice that if you slump forward (relax the shoulders) and drop your chin onto your chest, you can feel the interaction of the lungs and rib cage. Take five deep breaths while in that posture. Now stand as straight as you can, shoulders back, chin up. Take five deep breaths. You should notice that the air enters the lungs more quickly, with less effort.

3. Say "hep, hop, hope, hoop." Now repeat, putting a one-second pause between each word. Repeat the exercise using only one breath for all four words. Now try it again, saying each word as loudly as you can—remember, all in one breath. You are developing control of all the muscles of respiration as you do this repeatedly.

4. Say the entire alphabet, using only one breath. Can you do it? Many people can do it but they slur the pronunciation of the letters. Using distinct pronunciation, try it again. When you have mastered one "run-through" of the alphabet, try to get through all twenty-six letters again on one breath. The more you practice, the better you will control the flow of air. It is possible to articulate the alphabet clearly in five, six, or even seven repetitions in one breath.

Control of Phonation

Phonation is the process by which the sound which we call "voice" is produced. Since the voice is actually a vibration of the muscles of the larynx called the "vocal folds," these muscles must be cared for and their control developed by practice.

5. Try to relax the throat; give a deep sigh, then a low, broken whisper, then count to ten as softly as you can without whispering.

6. Sing "low, low, low, low," dropping one note of the musical scale each time you sing the word until you reach the lowest tone you can possibly produce. Then sing your way back up the scale until you reach the tone you find most comfortable. Now sing "high, high, high," going up the scale until you reach the highest tone you can produce. Now, come back down to the tone you feel most comfortable with. This tone will be your optimum pitch—the one from which and around which most of your speech should be executed.

7. From your optimum pitch, drop two or three notes and then—very softly—sing "do-re-mi-fa-sol-la-ti-do." Repeat this process, increasing your volume each time until your voice is so loud that it is uncomfortable. This done, you will have

examined your volume range. You should try to speak comfortably, but loud enough so that you are audible to all.

Control of Resonance

Resonance gives the voice the desirable quality that we seek. Always try to keep the throat relaxed, the mouth as open as possible, and nasal resonance restricted to nasal sounds (*n, m,* and *ng*) alone.

8. Sing "ah" with the mouth open; gradually bring the teeth together; notice the different quality of resonance as you reduce the resonating cavity.

9. Say "hung-ah-ng-eh-ng-ah-ng-eh-ng" and feel the resonance move from mouth to nose and vice versa.

10. Speak clearly the following paragraph which contains no nasal sounds. Your speech mechanisms are not used to speaking for so long without nasal sounds, so you might find this difficult. Check yourself for improper nasal resonance.

   > He was a rare fellow. At first sight, people quickly perceived that he was hardly of the average sort. His hearty laugh, his quick, catlike posture shifts, his clear, careful gaze—all helped folks to appreciate his special qualities. Yet, he was always quiet. He saw beauty where others failed to detect it. He loved art as well as every object, every creature that had life. He was a rare fellow.

Articulatory Control

11. Each word in the following groups is to be pronounced differently, but careless speakers often blur the articulatory differences. Pronounce each word group, making sure that each word can be distinguished from the others. Get a friend or classmate to check your accuracy.

jest—gist—just	pan—pin—pen—pun—peen
thin—think—thing	wish—which—witch
roost—roosts—ghost—ghosts	character—caricature
hold—hole—holder—holer—holler	conquerer—horror—mirror
allusion—illusion—elude	affect—effect
began—begun—begin	twin—twain—twine

12. Control of articulation can best be gained by becoming proficient in the articulation of tongue-twisters. You may have your favorites. Practice these for starters.
   - Barry, the baby bunny's born by the blue box bearing rubber baby buggy bumpers.
   - The little lowland lubber was a lively lad, lucky, liberal, and likeable.
   - He mangled his ankle as he bungled a shot out of the bunker.
   - The sixth sheik's sixth sheep's sick.
   - Oil from the cod's liver annoys the boy.
   - While we waited for the whistle on the wharf, we whittled the white weatherboards on a whim.

- Sid said to tell him that Benny hid the penny many years ago.
- Three gray geese in the green grass grazing; gray were the geese and green was the grazing.
- The seething sea ceaseth and thus the seething sea sufficeth us.
- Polly played prettily on the Peterson's piano preparing for Plato Peterson's pleasant party.
- Charles Cherry Mitchell, the rich bachelor merchant, had wretched speech as a child.
- Zeb, the boys zinged the zithers and zonged the xylophones busily and brazenly on the plains of Zion.
- How, now, do brown cows and browner sows take their bows while they carouse around their houses in their blouses?
- Clear around the rugged rocks the cunning ragged rascal climbed and ran, raging and ranting, cursing and cajoling.

Control of Rate, Pause, and Inflection

The way in which words are spoken influences meaning as much as the words themselves. Practice using the voice as a tool for creating meaning.

13. Speak the following paragraph so that the meaning is clear to a listener who has not heard it before.

> Bill Bell builds bells. The bells Bill
> Bell builds bang and bong on Beele
> Boulevard. Bill builds bells with brass
> bell balls. Bell's bell balls build big
> bells. Bill Bell built brass ball-built
> bells for the Beal's bull, Buell. Buell's
> Bell-built brass bell banged when Buell
> bellowed on Beele and bore Bell's bells
> bong abroad. Bill Bell's bells, brass-
> ball-built for Beal's Beele-based bull
> Buell biased brass bell builders toward
> Bell brass ball-built bells. Boy!

14. In the manner suggested, vary the *force* for the following:

   a. "I hate you! I hate you! I hate you!"
      (1) Increase the degree of force with each repetition, making the last almost a shout.
      (2) Say the second "hate" louder than the first, and the last one *sotto voce*.
      (3) Shout the first statement; then let the force diminish as if echoing the mood.
   b. "What kind of thing is this?"
      Repeat the question, stressing a different word each time. Try not to raise the pitch, but to emphasize by force alone.

c. "I have told you a hundred times, and the answer is still the same."
   (1) Make the statement a straightforward assertion, using sustained force.
   (2) Speak the sentence with a sudden explosion of force, as though you were uncontrollably angry.
   (3) Speak the sentence with deep but controlled emotion, applying force gradually and firmly.

Should you or your instructor wish to pursue further vocal training in a good deal more depth, we would suggest the following textbooks:

Joseph A. DeVito, Jill Gianttino, and T. D. Schon, *Articulation and Voice: Effective Communication* (Indianapolis: The Bobbs-Merrill Company, Inc., 1975).

Donald H. Ecroyd, Murray M. Halfond, and Carol C. Towne, *Voice and Articulation: A Handbook* (Glenview, IL: Scott, Foresman and Company, 1966), especially Chapters 3–7 and 9.

Robert G. King and Eleanor M. DiMichael, *Improving Articulation and Voice* (New York: The Macmillan Company, 1966), especially Chapters 2, 5, 6, and 8.

REFERENCE NOTES

[1] Exercises for Voice Practice were prepared by Professors James L. Booth, Vernon Gantt, Jerry Mayes, and Robert Valentine, of Murray State University.

Finding a Job: The Employment Interview

The employment interview can be a crucial communicative experience. The outcome may enhance your career aspirations or simply ensure that the rent will be paid on time. Either way, you often have a lot at stake in an interview situation. Seldom will you enter an interview with no real concern over whether the interviewer responds positively to you, or whether you actually get the job. The suggestions offered regarding building self-confidence (see Chapter 3) apply to the interview situation as well. By being prepared in advance, you will be able to respond appropriately to the questions you are asked. The following guidelines may be helpful in preparing for and participating in an interview.

Preparing for an Interview

As you prepare for an interview, consider the following questions:

1. *Why do you want this job?* Aside from the fact that jobs mean money, what is your reason for seeking this particular job?

2. *What knowledge or skills does the job require?* What skills, talents, abilities can you contribute? List the major skills that you possess; which ones are most relevant to

this particular job? What courses or work experiences would be especially mean-ingful in this position? What should you stress in explaining your qualifications? Keep in mind that some courses provide you with necessary technical knowledge (a course in finance, for example), while others may be relevant because they helped refine skills (a course in contemporary American literature, for example, which stressed research and writing skills).

3. *What information can you gather about the company before the interview?* What homework should you do to indicate that you are seriously interested in this com-pany and what it offers? Check with a campus placement office or with a local employment agency; they may have useful information available. If the company is a large national firm, check business publications for relevant information. Call the company's public relations office and request an annual report or other informative materials.

4. *What working conditions* (location, extent of travel, benefits, salary) *are you willing to accept?* How much of this information is available in the job description? If not mentioned there or by the interviewer, what issues are important enough to be raised by you during the interview? Make a short list of your key concerns; refer to the list as the interview progresses to see what important concerns still need to be raised.

5. *What is the most appropriate apparel for the interview?* How will the interviewer expect you to dress? How do you want to present yourself?

By thinking through these and similar questions, you can go into an interview with a clear idea of what you want to accomplish.

Participating in an Interview

An interviewer seldom gets down to business in the initial moments of the interview. There is a brief time for exchanging social talk about the day, last night's game, and so on. This period of time allows you to relax and to establish a communicative relation-ship with the interviewer. Does the interviewer seem to be friendly, outgoing, and relatively informal in conducting the interview? Or is the interviewer likely to be all-business once the obligatory social niceties are out of the way? You will need to adapt to the social atmosphere that the interviewer seeks to establish. During this brief time, both of you are gaining first impressions of the other. If the interviewer responds positively to you in the first minutes, the interview will probably proceed smoothly.

Follow the lead of the interviewer: When he or she is ready to move to more formal questions, you should be able to shift gears and begin answering and asking questions regarding the position for which you are applying. The interviewer generally will begin with background information about the position, and will ask general questions about your academic and work experience. As you respond to general questions, be wary of "overtalking" a question—going on and on without end. Give precise answers, devel-oped in sufficient detail to respond fully to the question. You can tell stories that will make a point, so long as the stories remain relatively brief and are clearly relevant to the question.

You will be expected to ask questions as well as respond to them. Appropriate questions may include asking the interviewer what he or she likes about the company, what the opportunities for advancement are, how much travel would be involved, and what kind of equipment you will be working with. Asking questions about salary and benefits can be a delicate matter. If you probe too much or spend an inordinate amount of time on details, the interviewer may get the impression that you are only interested in making a buck. If the interviewer does not offer the information, you can ask what the expected salary range will be and what benefits, in general terms, the company has for its employees. You want to appear interested in how supportive the company is; at the same time, you want to demonstrate your willingness to earn a salary.

Be sensitive to the interviewer's cues that the interview session is coming to an end. This might be an appropriate time to review your notes and ask if you could get some information on one or two brief points that were not covered. Asking a dozen specific questions of no clear importance, however, will not create a positive impression. As the interview closes, you can pull together your earlier statements regarding your qualifications and briefly restate them for the interviewer. This gives you a chance to express your perception of what you can contribute to, and why you are interested in working for, the interviewer's company.

Sending a follow-up note thanking the interviewer for his or her time and reiterating your interest in the position is a helpful touch. Besides being a social nicety, it gives you a chance to clarify any points made, to add information you felt was not adequately covered in the interview, or simply to say ''thanks'' for an enjoyable experience.[1]

REFERENCE NOTES

[1]For further information on employment interviewing, consult Lois Einhorn, Patricia Hayes Bradley, and John E. Baird, Jr., *Effective Employment Interviewing* (Glenview, IL: Scott, Foresman and Company, 1982).

Group Discussion: Leadership

Our culture has a particularly ironic way of cooling down zealots and go-getters. If you're the person in your organization, business, or classroom with ideas, enthusiasm, and commitments, you're immediately made the group's leader. Suddenly, where you once were a strong advocate and a hard worker in the trenches, you now are expected to be impartial, organized, wise, knowledgeable about procedures, politically shrewd, and able to turn out the ever-present report in forty-eight hours.

Groups make shameful demands of their leaders, sometimes; yet if they did not, most groups wouldn't get anything done. Some*one* ultimately has to be in charge, to execute the group's *leadership functions*—handling procedural aspects of group operation, seeing that ideas are explored fully and fairly, and taking care that the feelings and contributions of everyone in the group are brought out. In this short review of leading meetings and of leadership functions, we will discuss a leader's job as it falls into three phases: *pre-meeting preparation, running the meeting,* and *post-meeting evaluation.* By examining the responsibilities in these three phases, perhaps we can help demystify the leader's jobs and necessary skills.

Phase I: Pre-Meeting Preparation

As a leader, your principal job throughout all three phases is to operate as a *facilitator.* While leadership in general is diffused among all members of a group (because all are responsible for helping produce a quality end-result), nevertheless "the" leader has special duties. This is especially true in Phase I, pre-meeting preparation. Group members are counting on you to do what you can to make the actual discussion, committee, team, session, or meeting function smoothly. Although your tasks will vary with the precise goal and the degree of formality of the group, they may include some of the following:

Announcing the Time and Place. You probably will be responsible for getting information about the meeting to interested parties. This may include contacting the group members (one hopes you got telephone numbers on a sign-up sheet earlier), making sure the room or facility is open and available, letting the press know of the meeting if it's open to the public. It's a little task, but skipping it can produce disastrous results.

Assembling Background Material. You may also have to get some general materials ready for the meeting. In a book club, the thoughtful leader looks up information on the author or on the issue being discussed, to orient the group. The business team leader digs through old files, to find out how the firm last approached this question and to unearth pertinent cost-benefit statistics, sales histories, or whatever. For an in-class symposium, the leader may assign specific tasks to the other members—sources to cover, kinds of articles to read, topics on which to be prepared. If these sorts of backgrounding activities are carried out carefully, you'll save the group a lot of frustration and wheel-spinning during the actual discussion.

Constructing an Agenda. Even if the topics for the upcoming meeting were announced in the previous meeting, a group usually needs more guidance. That guidance often takes the form of an *agenda,* a structured list of topics, questions, resolutions, and the like. Agendas vary, obviously, in detail and length; their completeness depends on the specialization of the group and the expertise of its members.

Final Check of Arrangements. Just before the meeting is to begin, you as leader may have to check on the facilities one last time. Are the seating arrangements conducive to discussion? If there are microphones, are they working? Are the refreshments prepared?

Make sure your meeting isn't problematic because you have overlooked the "little" details people expect leaders to care for.

Phase II: Running the Meeting

With careful preplanning, you should have little trouble actually running the meeting. Your primary jobs are to keep the discussion progressing toward its goal and to serve the participants in whatever ways you can. To carry out these two jobs, you probably will use some of the following communication techniques in each stage of the meeting.

Beginning the Meeting.   Of course, you will have to start the meeting. This may involve nothing more complicated than a "Can I have your attention, please? It's time we begin." In other settings, you may have responsibilities for opening remarks, a short speech orienting the group to the meeting's purpose, the procedures you will follow, and the like. Prepare opening remarks carefully, so that you will not embarrass yourself, not forget anything, and *not* drone endlessly. You're a facilitator, not an orator. If this is a formal meeting of an organization, you may have to begin it in the usual parliamentary fashion:

1. Call to order
2. Review of the minutes of the previous meeting
3. Report from any committees or officers scheduled
4. Review of old business (considerations carrying over from the previous meeting)
5. New business (new resolutions and considerations)

Whatever the situation, begin the meeting crisply and clearly. Your group will thank you for your sense of organization and your concern that they have time to talk.

Leading the Discussion.   Once the discussion is launched, you ought to stay out of the substance of it as much as possible. Think of yourself as an interested troubleshooter. You're watching for confusion, omissions, conflict, procedural tangles, and the like. When you see any of these sorts of problems, only then do you move in. In most groups, you have several major responsibilities during the discussion:

    Bringing out reticent individuals.   Except in the most formal parliamentary groups, you ought to be on the lookout for nonparticipants, people who hang back because they are hesitant or because talkative souls are dominating the group. "What do you think, Harry?" is a simple but effective way to bring someone out. If that doesn't work, you may need to add a bit of encouragement: "Harry, you're the person here closest to our problems in Missouri. We really could use your thoughts." If you still get no response, move on, looking back at good old Harry periodically to see if he's ready to talk yet.

    Summarizing at key points.   Another essential job is that of objectively summarizing particular ideas, conflicts, analyses, and agenda items. A summary from a leader does several things for a group: *(a)* It shows them you are a fair leader, summarizing both sides of a dispute cleanly; *(b)* it gently reminds them to finish off a particular point and move on; *(c)* it catches up members whose minds have drifted off to other matters; and, *(d)* if well done, it can push a group to a decision. Don't be afraid to take notes to make summaries accurate and well structured.

Tying down the key facts, generalizations, and cause-effect relationships.   Even though you try to stay out of the discussion as much as possible, often you are needed to fill out the factual picture, to go after a particularly obvious causal relationship no one has mentioned, to intrude a valuative perspective needing consideration, and so forth. Because you don't want others to think you're running the meeting with a heavy hand, try to draw out the missing information, relationship, or value from the participants, if possible. Tact is all-important; if you're going to make a statement, you might even want to ask the group's permission: "Excuse me, but I was reading an article last week bearing on this point, and I wonder if it would be all right for me to. . . ." Otherwise, you can go to open calls for information: 'Has anyone come across material on . . . ?" Or you might refer to a previous discussion: "During last week's session, someone mentioned that. . . . Is that idea appropriate here?" A leader can always make a direct reference to a document members supposedly are familiar with: "So far, we've not said anything about Appendix B in the Jackson Report. Should its recommendations be considered now?" Try to leave the matter up to the group; you thus preserve your objectivity and impartiality.

Handling conflict.   All methods for handling conflict are applicable here: depersonalizing the conflict, using outside authorities to undercut positions, trying to get the participants in the melee to settle it themselves, and referring to the need for dispatch. A leader is in a tricky position when it comes to conflict. On the one hand, a leader realizes that conflict can be creative and can lead to group-generated agreements. Conflict is absolutely necessary for testing ideas and exploring positions, feelings, and proposals. On the other hand, if it becomes dominant and personalized, conflict can destroy a group. The skillful leader watches—watches to see if it's getting too bloody; watches noncombatants to see if they are getting bored, scared, or frustrated; and watches the clock. Then the leader moves in gingerly, with something like: "O.K., you two certainly have demonstrated how complex and touchy this issue is. We really, however, must keep progressing, so how about the rest of you? Now that Jack and June have explored this idea fully, what do you think? Does anyone else have an opinion on it?" If you can succeed in getting the rest of the group to pick up on the controversy— and, hopefully, resolve it—your job is done. Go to harsher measures only if the combatants won't quit. Try to slow down the dominating individuals and more equitably spread the communicative load. Reprimand if necessary, but only in the name of the group itself.

Terminating the discussion.   It is the leader's job to terminate the discussion. You must find a way of ending it positively. Your greatest ally in all this, of course, is the clock: "Excuse me, but even though I'm finding this discussion fascinating and enlightening, we've got to quit in five minutes. Any last word or two before we break?" Beyond actually stopping the proceedings, the articulate leader moves to a summary: a summary of what's been discussed and decided, what remains open, and what is left to be treated in another session. A round of thanks (naming names, even) never hurts. A clear wrap-up sets important notions in members' minds, getting them ready for further consideration or discussion at another time.

Leading the actual discussion, therefore, really doesn't involve too many tricks or strategies of communication. As long as you are a careful listener, one sensitive to the intellectual and emotional processes which are developing, you can handle it easily. Keep your head working and your heart dispassionate, being warm but firm.

Phase III: Post-Meeting Responsibilities

Too many leaders forget their post-meeting responsibilities. Some of these duties are courtesies (thank-you notes to the parliamentarian, for example); others are economic (paying bills if hall rental and catering were involved). Other important details have to do with the ongoing life of the group or organization (minutes of the meeting, plans for the next meeting, refiling of materials used, reports to others in the organization, or evaluations to be passed on to your successor).

Because, as leader, you are in so many ways responsible for the social-emotional and substantive life of the organization, be sure you carry out such duties promptly. If people don't receive minutes of the meeting for a month or more, they'll think less of you and will have forgotten some of the salient features of the discussion you can only hint at in the minutes. Thank-you notes leave a good impression and probably prod the recipients to render good service the next time the group meets. If the news release you want to peddle as a result of the meeting doesn't get to the press the next day, your group's decisions, recommendations, or actions will be old news, and hardly fit to print. Even though you are tired, finish off your post-meeting duties quickly. It will pay off in what you get done and in how people think of you.

Being a leader, as you can see, is not a piece of cake. Leadership demands forethought, anticipation, organization, impartiality, sensitivity, and a truckload of good sense. By spacing your tasks, however, you can serve your club, organization, or group as an effective leader.

Group Discussion: Participation

Although most of this book deals with public speaking, it is important to include also an introduction to group communication as another important kind of multi-person public communicative activity. A group discussion is a shared, purposive communication transaction in which a small group of people exchanges and evaluates ideas and information in order to understand a subject or solve a problem.

As this definition suggests, there are two major kinds of discussion. In a *learning or study discussion,* participants seek to educate each other, to come to a fuller understanding of some subject or problems. A number of persons interested in art, computer programming, or religious study, for example, may gather monthly to share thoughts and expertise. In an *action or decision-making group,* participants are attempting to reach an agreement on what the group as a whole should believe or do, or are seeking ways of implementing a decision already made. In such discussions, conflicting facts and values are examined, differences of opinion are evaluated, and proposed courses of action are explored for their feasibility or practicality, in an effort to arrive at a consensus. For example, a neighborhood block association may gather periodically to decide on projects to undertake; a city council will decide what to do with its federal revenue-sharing funds; a subcommittee in a business may be asked to recommend useful ways to expand markets.

You will probably spend much personal and work-related time in group discussions. Your communicative tasks in those groups will be complicated by the fact that, as a participant, you are focusing in three directions at once: on yourself, on others in the group, and on the group's task.

Focus on self.   Because you are you and not someone else, you must focus on your own needs, desires, attitudes, knowledge, opinions, hopes, and fears. You participate in group discussions because, reasonably, you expect some sort of gain. That gain can be emotional, as you become accepted by others. That gain can be reinforcing, as you use others to add authority to ideas or positions you want to defend publicly. That gain can include time or money, as your group shares the burden of a task and helps you implement a project quickly.

Focus on others.   In a group, however, you cannot be completely self-absorbed. Other members also have their biases, priorities, and experiences. If they get turned off, if they drop out, or if they strike out because of feelings of injustice or intolerance, a group can be reduced to shambles and lose its reasons for existence. As a participant, you are partially responsible for *group maintenance*—for building a supportive social-emotional atmosphere in which everyone feels comfortable even in times of conflict, in which mutual respect is a norm or expectation, in which there is interdependence and honest openness to others.

Focus on the task.   In addition to everyone's feelings, the group purpose must be kept in mind. You've joined a group to accomplish something—to learn something, to solve a problem, to launch a plan or campaign. If you do not keep that task in mind, you're liable to run down blind alleys and around irrelevant issues, to spend more time talking about next week's fishing trip than the job to be done.

Participating in a group can be tricky business, therefore, because you're looking in these three directions at once. If you lose sight of yourself, you're a mere pawn. If you forget about "them," you're a tyrant. And if you ignore the task, you're probably going to have to attend yet another meeting. In essence, as a discussant, you must engage in a mental juggling act, keeping track of your self, of others, and of the group's progress toward its goal. How can you do all that and remain sane?

Knowing and Revealing Your Self in Discussions

Selfishly, let's begin with you. You have both rights and responsibilities as you consider your own head and heart. The following suggestions include both head and heart:

Preparing.   Obviously, you must enter a discussion prepared to participate. This may mean reading the month's assignment in a book club, or scanning recommended articles and reports for a business meeting, or working out a "telephone tree" for an action group about to launch a public campaign. Getting intellectually ready for a discussion guarantees two things: First, it will ensure that you are able to offer positive contributions, and hence uphold your end of the bargain that constitutes "groupness." And second, it protects you from glib but shallow sales pitches, silly proposals, ignorant allies, and overpowering opponents.

Getting Background on Others.   You ought to have information not only on the topic, but also on the other participants. This may not be a problem in a group which has a history, but it certainly can be in newly-formed work teams and committees. The more you know about others, the better able you'll be to separate the crud from the cream, to anticipate the sources and strengths of your opposition, to know how to object without hurting someone's feelings, to guess at how tenacious various individuals will be. You'll know whom to trust, and how far. Ask around.

Introducing Ideas.   As a discussion is proceeding, you must calculate how and when to introduce your ideas, opinions, and feelings. That's the only way you can be true to your self. Several tactics for introducing ideas have proven successful:

    Hitchhiking.   In this tactic, you link up your idea with an idea that someone else has stated. It seems perfectly natural to say, "Carl said that we needed to consider the impact of this proposal on our clerical staff, and I agree. As a matter of fact, I've done some thinking about this problem, and. . . ." In this way, you build on someone else's notions, and probably gain an ally.

    Summary.   "So far, we've isolated three causes for declining school enrollments. And, I think they're accurate. But, I wonder if there isn't a fourth reason. . . ." In this tactic, you give everyone who has contributed to the discussion a psychological stroke, and then seek to move the discussion into new territory—yours.

    Shift in viewpoint.   Consider: "We've looked at the problem of child abuse from the perspectives of the child and of the abusing parent. What about those teachers, doctors, social workers, and other professionals who suspect they've seen a case. What's their role in all this?" This sort of introductory statement, once more, recognizes the ideas and feelings of others while it allows you—with the group's blessing—to intrude your own position.

    Disagreement.   You might say, "Now, Jean, I certainly can understand why you think no more parking ramps should be built downtown, but I think you've examined only two of the factors involved. Before we reach a decision on the issue, I think we must look at two additional factors. . . ." In this way, you express your disagreement softly. You leave Jean with the feeling you're accepting her analysis and integrity, and yet you give yourself an entering wedge. In all these tactics, take care that your remarks actually fit with what has been going on.

Listening to and Evaluating Others.   To protect yourself in a discussion, you must be a rapt and careful listener. You must be able to see through the swarm of words from an eloquent advocate. You must be sure you don't have mistaken impressions, for the consequences of misunderstanding can be great, both interpersonally and intellectually. To protect yourself and to understand the full implications of what others say, consider the following listening techniques:

Questioning.   Don't be afraid to ask polite questions of others: "I didn't follow that; could you repeat it?" "Can you translate that for me?" "I'm curious—where did you read that?" If you phrase the question in terms of your own needs, you won't seem to be suggesting that the other person is unclear or incorrect. Questioning in this way is relatively nonthreatening.

Rephrasing.   To check on your own listening abilities, and to make sure you know what position you're disagreeing with, try rephrasing another person's ideas: "Let's see if I followed you. First you said that . . . and then you noted that . . . , right?" Putting someone else's ideas into your own words protects you and can save the group time, especially if others also need the "translation."

Recording.   Of course, take notes. If, say, you're in a decision-making group and the discussion becomes protracted, by the time you arrive at a solution stage people may well have forgotten all the problems to be solved. Keeping track throughout the discussion will save embarrassment and make your own contributions useful later on.

Reacting to Disagreement and Criticism.   Not only must you carefully evaluate the ideas of others, but you should be mentally ready to react to their analyses of you. Your first impulse, of course, is to protect your own ego and feelings. Time and again, it may seem that others misunderstand you, imply that you're not too smart, and pick on you. And you want to fight back. Unless, for some reason, you simply want to destroy the group and its task, resist that temptation to become a gamester or a fighter. Be the debater, and focus on the disagreement rather than the personalized attack. This goal can be accomplished in several ways:

Interpreting.   "Now, let's see if I can figure out what part of my analysis you're having trouble with." By focusing on the substance of the disagreement, you're telling the group that you want to ignore personal innuendos and keep the group as a whole on track.

Turning the other cheek.   In all humility, you could say: "I'm sorry what I said bothered you so much, Fred. Let's see if we can resolve this issue." Poor Fred looks pretty bad after this response, and you can come out more highly credible.

Confronting the attacker.   Especially if another person seems to be disrupting and attacking everyone, you (and the rest) may have to confront that person directly: "Now, Janet, you're really feeling your oats this morning, blasting out in all sorts of directions. Is something wrong? Are we irritating you? Is something that we're doing or saying stirring you up? What can we do to make you more comfortable and to get on with the task at hand?" In thus confronting a particularly nasty person, you are extending the group's good wishes and sympathy, and, hopefully, you are returning the common focus to the job to be accomplished. And, with all three of these techniques, you are protecting your self, which is essential to your own sense of well-being.

Taking Care of Others in Discussions

Your second focal point is the other members of the group. Without that focus, you won't be doing your part to keep them happy and productive. A supportive social-emotional atmosphere, even in times of disagreement, is a must. There are many ways to build a supportive atmosphere.

Stroking.   It never hurts to give psychological "strokes" to other group members. It costs you little (unless your pride and ego get in the way), and it keeps everyone working and playing together. "That's a great idea!" "Thanks for the suggestion. It makes me see this question in a different light." "That's beautiful, Ralph." Such personal reactions to others show mutual trust and support.

Criticizing Constructively.   It doesn't hurt, either, to do a little stroking even while you're disagreeing with someone. There are ways to fight ("That's the dumbest thing I've ever heard!"); and then there are ways to criticize constructively. These can involve *(a)* bringing in additional authorities to erode the other person's position; *(b)* politely cataloguing facts which have been ignored; *(c)* introducing alternative statements of value ("You look at this as a political question, but I wonder if it's not more a matter of human rights"); and *(d)* calling for a discussion of the implications of an idea ("I think your plan sounds decent, but do you think it will alleviate the first problem we mentioned?"). The important point, as you communicate your criticisms, is to go as far as you can in depersonalizing the disagreement. If possible, keep the focus on *authorities* (who do the attacking instead of you); on the *facts* (which we would love to think speak for themselves); on *value* positions; and on the hard-headed *implications*.

Accepting Correction.   Not only must you be able to disagree positively with someone else's misrepresentation or misunderstanding of you, but you'll do the group a lot of good if you can gracefully accept others' positions and ideas as correctives to your own. It is tempting to be the gamester, and to fight back inch by inch. But if you see the basic logic of someone's analysis, or if you note that group opinion is running counter to your own, you'll have to surrender—or leave. You can get into a huff or a blue funk, or you can retreat with the aplomb of Robert E. Lee of Appomattox. Your ego cries out, "You fools! One day you'll see my wisdom!" But your sense of commitment to others demands, "OK, I'm still having a little problem with all this, but if the rest of you think we should try, then I'll certainly go along." Or, "I didn't realize some of those implications of my proposal, Paul. Thanks for pointing them out. Are there other proposals that won't have those bad effects?" Eating a little crow certainly leads to occasional indigestion, but sometimes it's better to cave in a bit than to be beaten to death. In this way, you'll live to fight another day.

Being Patient.   Patience is perhaps the essential quality in your focus on other group members. You're often forced to be an extraordinarily saintly, patient person while discussing. Just as you think you yourself have carved out a piece of truth and wisdom, so does everyone else. Work hard at allowing them—even forcing them—to show you the error of your ways. Ask them to repeat, to go further, to extend. Keep them talking in the hope that their contributions will be given full consideration. What they say may even be good! Especially with somewhat hesitant or reticent people, you often must gently prod them along, even if you know your own ideas will triumph. Patience is a small price for ultimate victory; it might actually produce a good suggestion or two; and it certainly will promote a positive social-emotional climate. Sure, it can be inefficient at times, but that's something you occasionally have to tolerate in groups.

Achieving the Group's Goals in Discussions

Finally, you must focus on the goal or task of the group. We often think, perhaps wistfully, that it's the leader's job to keep a discussion moving forward. Of course, it is. But leaders often need help, occasionally miss important points here and there, sometimes get flustered, and perhaps let the group get bogged down in an overextended discussion of some issue. While there is usually a person designated ''leader,'' leadership must be shared by all participants from time to time. Even if you don't have the word *boss* emblazoned on your forehead, you still have some responsibilities for moving the group ahead. A few of these responsibilities we already have suggested. Others are strictly procedural matters to which you should be attending.

Knowing the Agenda.   An *agenda* is an agreed-upon list of tasks to be accomplished or questions to be answered in a particular session. Know it. Know when it is appropriate to bring up a matter you're interested in. If necessary, as the group is about to begin, ask the others whether or not some idea you want to talk about is appropriate to the agenda. If it doesn't appear to be, ask if it can be inserted somewhere. Knowing the agenda, in other words, allows you (and the rest) to keep the discussion orderly and progressive, and tells you something about timing your remarks.

Asking Procedural Questions.   Never be afraid to ask questions about what's happening in a discussion: ''Are we still on point three, or have we moved to point four?'' ''Is there some way we can resolve this question and move ahead?'' ''Can we consider the feasibility of Art's proposal before we move on to Brenda's?'' Such questions can seem inordinately naive, and, if asked with a sneer in your voice, could reflect badly on the leader. Yet, sometimes naive questions are absolutely necessary.

Summarizing.   Seldom can a single leader carry out all of the summarizing that most groups need. Indeed, as you may have noticed, summary is a theme of this section— summarizing your own position, summarizing those of others, and, here, summarizing so that the group can keep progressing. A good summary allows you to check bases, to see what's been agreed to and what remains to be done. Summaries form the intellectual junctures in a discussion. They can be simple: ''Now, as I heard you two, Jack said this and this, and Bob said that and that, right?'' Or they can be elaborate attempts to trace through the whole of a discussion so that members have it clearly in mind before you adjourn.

Arbitrating.   Another important leadership function which should not fall solely on the leader's shoulders is that of arbitrating disputes. Being the peacemaker is sometimes risky business, for both parties may go for your throat. Yet if a discussion is going to be mutually supportive and satisfying, and if it's going to get its job done, then each person occasionally will have to help it get over intellectual and emotional rough spots. Sometimes you can arbitrate by offering a *compromise:* "O.K., is it possible for us to accept a part of Proposal A and a part of Proposal B, and forge those parts into a new Proposal C? It might go this way. . . ." At other times, you're going to have to call for *clarification:* "Now, Bill, you think Ron's idea is defective because of this. And you, Ron, seem to be saying that Bill has missed the point about the riverfront land, right?" By pointing out the idea in conflict rather than the personalities in conflict, you perhaps can deflate it. You may occasionally have to offer a *gentle reprimand:* "Whoa! If you two don't quit beating each other to death, we'll never get done in an hour! Let's see if we can get to the nub of the matter here." By thus holding out the standards of efficiency and expediency, you may succeed in getting two people to clarify, to remember the rest of the group, and to charge ahead.

Participating in a discussion can be a tremendously rewarding and efficient way of making your own ideas and feelings public, of learning new information and perspectives, of making key decisions at work or at home, and of implementing plans or proposals. You will achieve maximum satisfaction and gain, however, only if you constantly keep in focus yourself, others, and the task. Monitor all three focal points steadily. You must have some degree of trust (or even suspicion); you must do your part in bringing out the best in others; you must remember that discussion is an interdependent activity with both social-emotional and intellectual components; and you must abide by faith in a quasi-democratic outlook on life.

Humor and Public Speaking

In Chapter 18, while discussing the speech to entertain, we briefly discussed humor and its general uses in society. We suggested that humor could be used to *(1)* deflect an audience's antipathy toward a speaker, *(2)* make people in the audience feel more like a group than they did before hearing the speech, and *(3)* offer in palatable or biting form a critique of one's society. We noted that a speech to entertain generally had one of those uses of humor as its specific purpose.

More can and should be said, however, about particular uses of humor in other types of speeches. That is, in almost every speaking situation you may need to use humor in one or more parts of a speech. Following are some of the ways humor can be used in different portions of speeches.

Using Humor in Speech Introductions

Speakers ought to consider using humor in introductions to their speeches if *(1)* they themselves are tense and can tell relevant stories well enough to relax, or *(2)* the audience is stiff, bored, or hostile, and hence in need of some kind of jolt from the lectern. That is, a good story or joke is therapeutic for many of us, and, because beginning communication transactions often are traumatic for both speaker and listener, such therapy often will significantly improve the rest of the communicative exchange. Make sure that the story or joke is *relevant, in good taste,* and *well-told.* That is, don't just tell a story for the sake of telling a story; an audience sees through that technique right away. And don't tell a dirty joke, because even if you offend only one listener, others in the audience likely will recognize the offense, feel embarrassed themselves, and take their embarrassment out on you. Finally, don't tell jokes if your timing is bad, if you tend to forget the punch line, if you can't handle the dialect, and so on. A badly told joke is worse than no joke at all.

Consider the following speech introduction: "I came home the other night to find my eight-year-old ready with a joke. 'Daddy,' he said, 'what's green and red and goes a hundred miles an hour?' 'I don't know,' I said wearily. 'What?' 'A frog in a blender!' he shouted triumphantly. That time of the evening, the story merely turned me green. Upon reflection, however, it has caused me to think about the ways in which modern technology—right down to the blender on the kitchen counter—has invaded our thinking, our values, yes, even our humor. And today, I want to. . . ."

In this introduction you'll not find a rib-rattling funny story; as a matter of fact, most audience members probably would simply smile rather than laugh. That's all right, because the story still can do its job; it still can relax you and the audience. As a matter of fact, if you expect an audience to react with full hilarity to a joke and then it doesn't, you're liable to be more tense than you were before you started the story. Remember that you're a public speaker *using humor for your purposes,* not a comic.

Using Humor in Midspeech

You also may want to use humor in the middle segments of speeches to *(1)* lighten a section which is comparatively dense or heavy, *(2)* serve as a memorable illustration of an important point, or *(3)* improve certain aspects of your credibility. More specifically, humor gives:

- *contrast.* After an audience is hit with a lot of statistics or a pile of philosophical abstractions, a little humor not only provides some important psychological contrast, thereby improving listeners' abilities to attend to your speech (see Chapter 2); it also lifts their spirits and rallies their minds, making them more willing to stay with you for the rest of the speech.
- *illustration.* Most people can remember a joke more easily than an abstract discussion of something. Even concrete details are more memorable, for many people, if they are offered humorously. (See the examples from Henry Grady's speech in Chapter 18.)
- *credibility.* One important dimension of credibility is dynamism—the audience's perception of the speaker as an alive, vital human being. A speaker's dynamism ratings—and hence overall credibility—improve when humor is used.

Once again, we are not advising you to work long, involved comic monologues, or even full-blown funny stories into the middle of a speech. Simply the way you *phrase ideas* can add the contrast, make the illustration memorable, and give a little push to your credibility. Review the speech by Dick Cavett in Chapter 18 for examples.

Using Humor in Speech Conclusions

Good speakers may also end a speech on a humorous note. Humor can be used in speech conclusions to *(1)* make the separation of speaker and audience a pleasant event, *(2)* drive home the main point one last time, or *(3)* leave the audience with a sense of finality as the speech concludes.

1. *Separation*. It may seem odd, but think about it: When you're listening to good speakers, you often want their speeches to continue; when listening to people you greatly admire, you want to stay in their presence. Even good speakers and admirable lecturers, however, must quit talking sooner or later. To make their separation from the audience as painless as possible, such speakers often employ light humor to make the audience smile or laugh even as they leave the rostrum.

2. *Emphasis*. A good story likewise can emphasize the main point of the whole speech; nearly every cleric who's been trained to preach has been taught this type of concluding strategy.

3. *Finality*. The speaker who says, "And so, everything I've been saying can be summed up in the story about the ten-year-old who . . . . ," is overtly signalling an audience that the speech is about to end, that the audience should prepare themselves to ask questions or applaud or leave. Why should you offer such signals to listeners? All of us can think of occasions when we weren't sure when a speech was to end, when there was an awkward little moment when the speaker thought, "Can I go now?" and listeners thought, "Well, is it over or is she just thinking of the next words?" Signalling the end can reduce some of the awkwardness that otherwise might accompany the end of a good talk.

Overall, therefore, while humor certainly is very important to speeches to entertain, it likewise can be a part of any speech on almost any occasion. Only make sure that you use humor appropriately, that you use it to make some point rather than merely to get a cheap laugh, and that you train yourself to tell stories well—naturally, completely, and pointedly. Humor can bond speaker and listener together in a positive relationship, and hence is a tool important to any speaker's collection of skills.

Model for Organizing and Evaluating Arguments

Arguments are not simply random collections of reasons and claims. As we emphasized in Chapter 16, the relationship between the claim and the reasons offered for accepting the claim must strike the audience as appropriate. For instance, would you expect an audience to accept the claim "Wendy's hamburgers are the best" if the only reason offered is "Clara Peller says so"? They would have to believe that Clara, the "Where's the Beef?" lady, is an expert whose opinion is worthy of consideration. The link between reason and claim is only one facet of organizing an argument. Writing in 1958, the British philosopher Stephen Toulmin proposed that arguments be diagrammed in a visually clear pattern that would help ensure that all elements—implicit and explicit—were recognized. The following elements, and the visual model which illustrates the relationships between and among them, will aid you in analyzing and critiquing your and others' arguments.

1. *Claim*. Put simply, what are you proposing for audience consideration? This can be, as we suggested in Chapter 16, a claim of fact, value, or policy.

2. *Data*. What materials, in the form of illustrative parallels, expert opinion, statistical information, research studies, and the like, can you advance to support the claim?

3. *Warrant*. What is the relationship between the parallel case, statistical data, or expert opinion and the claim? On what kind of assumption or inferential pattern does its acceptance as support for the claim depend? Materials do not function as evidence or support for no reason; facts do not speak for themselves. What makes an audience believe in the strength of the reasons as support lies in the following kinds of assumptions that warrant acceptance of the link between data and claim:

   a. An expert knows what he or she is talking about;
   b. Past economic, social, or political practices are reliable predictors of future occurrences;
   c. Inferential patterns (for example, cause, sign) suggest the linkage is rational.

   We know, for instance, that the credibility of an expert is a major determinant in gaining acceptance of the opinions being offered. In the development of the argument, this factor operates as an implicit *warrant* connecting the opinion to the claim. In matters involving economics, we know that the regularity of certain marketplace functions such as supply and demand exert a powerful influence on events. Hence, when we claim that the prices of finished products will rise as a result of the increases in the cost of raw materials, we are tacitly assuming the normal operation of the marketplace. Likewise, the value of using parallel cases as support for your position rests on the regularity of an inferential pattern; when two cases are parallel, similar results can be expected.

4. *Backing*. Does the audience accept the relationship between the data and the claim as given? If not, what further data would be helpful in supporting the warrant? When the warrant linking a reason and claim is accepted by the audience, explicit development of this facet of the argument is unnecessary. Thus, if the audience accepts the opinion of a local university scientist, an extended development of her credentials would be a waste of time. If an audience already understands the logical pattern of an analogy and believes that the substance of the argument being presented is analogous, spending time to support the analogous nature of the relationship would be pointless.

   But when a relationship between the reason and the claim is not automatically accepted, you will have to provide additional support focused on the warrant rather than the original claim. Thus, in supporting an argument against the nuclear freeze with testimony from a politician, you might need to establish his expertise to increase the likelihood of audience acceptance. If the audience is not familiar with economic patterns, an argument which depends on such familiarity will not get very far. Thus, part of your argument will have to develop backing for the warrant.

5. *Reservations.* Can significant counterarguments be raised? In most cases, arguments on the opposite side are not only readily available, but may even be as strong as your own reasons. Anticipating reservations in advance will help you strengthen your own argument. In general, these can be thought of as "unless"-clauses in your argument.

6. *Qualifiers.* How certain is the claim? Note that we do not ask how certain *you* are; you may be absolutely sure of something for which you cannot offer verifiable support. How much can one bank on the claim that you are putting forward as an acceptable basis for belief or action? How certain are you that a nuclear freeze is a worthless idea? Are you *sure* that the "build-down" proposal is any more workable? Qualifiers such as *probably, presumably, virtually certain,* and *may* should be incorporated into the claim to reflect the strength of the argument.

These six elements operate as a general framework for the construction and analysis of an argument. The interrelationships between and among the elements can best be displayed through a visual diagram. The numbers in the diagram correspond to the elements discussed above.

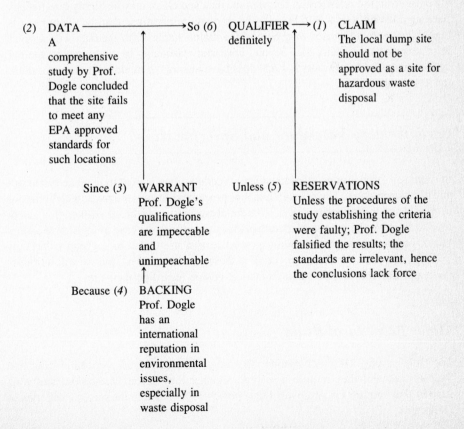

(2) DATA ——————→ So (6) QUALIFIER ——→ (1) CLAIM

A comprehensive study by Prof. Dogle concluded that the site fails to meet any EPA approved standards for such locations

definitely

The local dump site should not be approved as a site for hazardous waste disposal

Since (3) WARRANT   Unless (5) RESERVATIONS

Prof. Dogle's qualifications are impeccable and unimpeachable

Unless the procedures of the study establishing the criteria were faulty; Prof. Dogle falsified the results; the standards are irrelevant, hence the conclusions lack force

Because (4) BACKING

Prof. Dogle has an international reputation in environmental issues, especially in waste disposal

The model, as diagrammed on page 415, has three principal uses in organizing your arguments. First, by setting forth the arguments' components in the manner indicated, you will be able to capture visually the relationships between and among the components. How, for example, are the data you present linked to the claim? What sort of warrants (assumptions, precedents, rules of inference) are you employing to ensure that the audience sees the connection between the data and the claim?

Second, once you have written a brief description of the data and have identified the warrant on which its relationship to the claim rests, you can more clearly determine whether you wish to offer the claim as definite, or as only probable, likely, or possible. You also will be reminded to reflect on the audience's grasp of the warrant. Is it a generally accepted relationship—will it be in this case?

Finally, by thinking through the possible reservations that others will have to your argument, you will be in a better position to shore up weaknesses in advance and, where necessary, to build a stronger base from which to respond to issues that might undermine rather than directly refute your case. As you react to possible reservations, avoid the temptation to build into your case answers to every possible counterargument. Your case will become cumbersome, and there is nothing to be gained by answering reservations that your opponents haven't even thought of yet.

The model also is helpful to listeners in analyzing the strength of arguments. The elements help sharpen your ability to question an argument. The data may be misleading or in error; the relationship between the data and claim may be highly questionable (lacking a strong warrant); there may be so many reservations that the claim must be highly qualified; advocates may be pushing claims harder than the data will warrant. Recognizing that a claim goes beyond what can reasonably be supported by the evidence and available warrants is made possible by using the model as a means of thinking about arguments.

Parliamentary Procedure and Speechmaking

In small and large groups, parliamentary procedure often is used to regulate discussion and decision making. The primary intent of procedural rules is to ensure that discussion is orderly and that minority voices have the opportunity to be heard. Although it can be used to frustrate the wishes of members (as is sometimes the case in legislative assemblies), on the whole parliamentary procedure is a useful aid to a group's decision-making processes. We cannot cover all of these procedural rules, but we will introduce the major devices and offer some practical advice regarding their use.

Major Procedural Rules

The table on pages 420–21 outlines the most often employed procedural rules and indicates whether they require a second, whether they permit discussion, and what support they require for approval. First, however, let's define the major categories of motions.

The *main motion* is the proposal brought before the group. It may be introduced very simply: "I move that. . . ." The content of the main motion depends on what you want the group to act on (for example, "I move that we hold the fund-raising event on October 5"; "I move that we authorize the president and the treasurer to review existing needs and purchase equipment as needed to get us ready for the new year"; "I move that this group go on record as opposing the nuclear freeze movement"). The motion may simply express the sentiment of the group and require very little discussion prior to a formal vote. Or the motion may be highly controversial, and may engage group members in impassioned debate for an hour or more over the proposal's merits. Whether simple or momentous, the motion may be accepted in one group, and cause great consternation in another. When motions are controversial, the use of *subsidiary, incidental,* and *privileged motions* becomes important.

Subsidiary motions are those which have a direct bearing on the main motion. They seek to alter the content of the motion, to change the time of discussion, or to place the motion before a subgroup for further study. The motion to postpone indefinitely has the effect of killing future discussion of the proposal. Perhaps the most confusing of the subsidiary motions is that which seeks "to amend." If an amendment is offered and seconded, the discussion must focus on the merits of the proposed change in the main motion. Once discussion has concluded, the *amendment* is passed or negated. In either case, the discussion now must revert to the main motion, either as originally presented (the amendment failed) or as altered (the amendment passed). Once discussion is concluded (assuming no new amendments are offered), the vote is taken on the main motion as presented or altered. As long as you work backward from any amendment to the main motion, voting at each step, you will avoid controversy and confusion. When discussion seems to lag or becomes highly repetitious, the *previous-question motion* serves to end discussion. Voting on the previous question also causes confusion, as some may think they are voting on the main motion. All the previous-question motion does is seek agreement to stop discussion. In some groups, moving the previous question can be handled informally. Once it has been moved, the chair can ask if there are any objections to ceasing discussion. Hearing none, the chair can move immediately to a vote on the main motion. This saves time by avoiding a separate vote to close debate when the result is clearly favorable. The amendment, previous question, and the remainder of the subsidiary motions can be raised at any time—they take precedence over the main motion and over each other. The following sequence could occur:

1. Main motion is presented and seconded, discussion ensues.
2. The main motion is amended, seconded, and discussion continues.
3. A member seeks to limit discussion to ten minutes—this is seconded but is not open to discussion.
4. Another member moves to amend the limit-discussion motion by striking ten minutes and inserting twenty minutes. This is seconded and discussion begins until someone reminds the group that the amendment is not debatable because the motion to which it is applied in this case is not open to discussion.
5. The chair reminds everyone that the motion before the group is the amendment to limit discussion to twenty minutes instead of ten. The group votes on the amendment; it fails.
6. The chair announces that the motion to limit discussion to ten minutes is now before

the group and is not open to discussion. The chair calls for a vote; the motion passes.

7. Eight minutes of discussion ensue, during which the previous question is called. The chair asks if there is any objection; hearing none, she bypasses a formal vote on the previous question and reminds everyone that the vote is on the *amendment* to the main motion. The amendment passes.

8. The chair reminds everyone that discussion is now open on the main motion as amended. A member moves to refer the motion as amended to a committee. This is seconded and discussion ensues on the move to a committee. The chair reminds the group that the discussion limit has passed and asks if everyone is ready to vote on the referral-to-committee motion. Hearing no objection, the chair calls for a vote; the motion fails.

9. The chair restates the motion as amended and once again asks if the group is ready to vote. Hearing no comment, the chair asks if all are ready to vote. The chair restates the main motion as amended and the vote is taken. The motion passes.

Although ordinary discussion may not be so contorted, this sequence does suggest the confusion that group members can create for themselves if they do not have a clear sense of the rules of procedure (and a chair that seeks to make each step clear).

Incidental motions also affect the progress of a main motion. They are important in reserving rights for individuals who are attempting to influence the flow of events. The motion to *suspend the rules* allows a person to introduce a proposal out of its normal order; the *point of order* motion can come at any time during a discussion and allows a member to remind a group that it is not following accepted rules of procedure (for example, in point 4 of the above illustration, the discussion of an amendment to the limit-discussion motion could be questioned by rising to a point of order). If the chair did not know the rules and said "It's O.K., let's continue discussion," a member would have the right to appeal the decision of the chair. Check the accompanying table and note the problem that has been created: Is the appeal debatable? When in doubt, discuss. After all, the purpose is not to alienate members, but to regulate the discussion. The motion to *divide a question* is useful when the main motion contains more than one main idea. It also can be used when you sense that one part of a motion may pass and a second portion may fail. By moving to divide, you may save part of the proposal.

Privileged motions also help regulate the process. There is little to be gained by a *call for the orders of the day* if everyone but you is satisfied with the events of the meeting. If, on the other hand, the group appears restless and is wandering around several topics, it may be well to issue this form of reminder. The *question of privilege* protects an individual's right to hear what is going on or to understand what action is being voted on. The motions to *recess* and to *adjourn* are not intended to frustrate a group's desire to resolve whatever problem is before it. If there is a great deal of tension, it may be wise to request a recess in order to allow tempers to cool; likewise, if tensions persist, it might be useful to suggest an adjournment to a specific time. The unclassified motions provide a means to bring a topic that has been tabled at a previous meeting before the group, or to alter action that has been taken *(to reconsider, to rescind)*. Take special note of the restrictions on the use of these latter motions (see Table, notes 13 and 14).

Speaking in Parliamentary Groups

If you are in a meeting that is governed by parliamentary rules, there are several things you can do to increase your effectiveness:

1. *Know the appropriate rules yourself.* Do not depend on a good chair to keep you informed regarding the process. The more knowledgeable you are, the less confused you will become as the process of using parliamentary rules unfolds. Also, you will be able to counteract efforts to use the rules to create an unfair advantage for one or more persons.

2. *Listen carefully.* Stay on top of what is going on. If the chair does not keep the group on track by constantly reminding members what is pending, you may need to take on that responsibility. Hopefully, you and others will be kept informed regarding what is on the floor by a conscientious leader.

3. *Ask questions.* If you are not sure about the procedures or become lost in the parliamentary thicket, do not hesitate to raise a question of personal privilege. Be specific in asking the chair or the parliamentarian (if there is one appointed) what is on the floor or what motions are appropriate under the circumstances.

4. *Speak to the motion.* Limit your remarks to the specific motion on the floor. Do not discuss the entire main motion if an amendment is pending; instead, comment directly on the merits of the amendment.

5. *Avoid unnecessary parliamentary gymnastics.* If the members of a group yield to the temptation to play with the rules, parliamentary procedure becomes counterproductive. The rational process of decision making is undermined by such game-playing. Refrain from piling one motion on top of another, cluttering the floor (and the minds of members) with amendments to amendments. Also guard against raising petty points of order. Parliamentary procedure is instituted to ensure equal, fair, controlled participation by all members. It serves to provide a systematic means of the introduction and disposal of complex ideas. Unnecessary "gymnastics" will impede rather than foster group decision making.

A comprehensive guide to parliamentary procedure, adopted by many groups in their by-laws, is *Robert's Rules of Order*. Consult this or other guides to answer questions that go beyond the material presented in this review.

Reducing Communication Apprehension: Systematic Solutions

Research studies have estimated that as much as 20 percent of the college population may experience *communication apprehension,* defined as *"an individual's level of fear or anxiety associated with either real or anticipated communication with another person or persons."*[1] The consequences of a high level of communication apprehension

Parliamentary Procedure for Handling Motions

Classification of motions	Types of motions and their purposes	Order of handling	Must be seconded	Can be discussed	Can be amended	Vote required [1]	Can be reconsidered
Main motion	(To present a proposal to the assembly)	Cannot be made while any other motion is pending	Yes	Yes	Yes	Majority	Yes
Subsidiary motions [2]	To postpone indefinitely (to kill a motion)	Has precedence over above motion	Yes	Yes	No	Majority	Affirmative vote only
	To amend (to modify a motion)	Has precedence over above motions	Yes	When motion is debatable	Yes	Majority	Yes
	To refer (a motion) to committee	Has precedence over above motions	Yes	Yes	Yes	Majority	Until committee takes up subject
	To postpone (discussion of a motion) to a certain time	Has precedence over above motions	Yes	Yes	Yes	Majority	Yes
	To limit discussion (of a motion)	Has precedence over above motions	Yes	No	Yes	Two-thirds	Yes
	Previous question (to take a vote on the pending motion)	Has precedence over above motions	Yes	No	No	Two-thirds	No
	To table (to lay a motion aside until later)	Has precedence over above motions	Yes	No	No	Majority	No
Incidental motions [3]	To suspend the rules (to change the order of business temporarily)	Has precedence over a pending motion when its purpose relates to the motion	Yes	No	No	Two-thirds	No
	To close nominations [4]	[4]	Yes	No	Yes	Two-thirds	No
	To request leave to withdraw or modify a motion [5]	Has precedence over motion to which it pertains and other motions applied to it	No	No	No	Majority [5]	Negative vote only
	To rise to a point of order (to enforce the rules) [6]	Has precedence over pending motion out of which it arises	No	No	No	Chair decides [7]	No
	To appeal from the decision of the chair (to reverse chair's ruling) [6]	Is in order only when made immediately after chair announces ruling	Yes	When ruling was on debatable motion	No	Majority [1]	Yes
	To divide the question (to consider a motion by parts)	Has precedence over motion to which it pertains and motion to postpone indefinitely	[8]	No	Yes	Majority [8]	No

						Two-thirds	Negative vote only
Privileged motions	To object to consideration of a question	In order only when a main motion is first introduced	No	No	No	Chair decides	No
	To divide the assembly (to take a standing vote)	Has precedence after question has been put	No	No	No	No vote required	No
	To call for the orders of the day (to keep meeting to order of business) [6, 9]	Has precedence over above motions	No	No	No	Chair decides [7]	No
	To raise a question of privilege (to point out noise, etc.) [6]	Has precedence over above motions	No	No	No	Majority	No
	To recess [10]	Has precedence over above motions	Yes	No [10]	Yes	Majority	No
	To adjourn [11]	Has precedence over above motions	Yes	No [11]	No [11]	Majority	No
	To fix the time to which to adjourn (to set next meeting time) [12]	Has precedence over above motions	Yes	No [12]	Yes	Majority	Yes
Unclassified motions	To take from the table (to bring up tabled motion for consideration)	Cannot be made while another motion is pending	Yes	No	No	Majority	No
	To reconsider (to reverse vote on previously decided motion) [13]	Can be made while another motion is pending [13]	Yes	When motion to be reconsidered is debatable	No	Majority	No
	To rescind (to repeal decision on a motion) [14]	Cannot be made while another motion is pending	Yes	Yes	Yes	Majority or two-thirds [14]	Negative vote only

1. A tied vote is always lost except on an appeal from the decision of the chair. The vote is taken on the ruling, not the appeal, and a tie sustains the ruling.

2. Subsidiary motions are applied to a motion before the assembly for the purpose of disposing of it properly.

3. Incidental motions are incidental to the conduct of business. Most of them arise out of a pending motion and must be decided before the pending motion is decided.

4. The chair opens nominations with "Nominations are now in order." A member may move to close nominations, or the chair may declare nominations closed if there is no response to his/her inquiry, "Are there any further nominations?"

5. When the motion is before the assembly, the mover requests permission to withdraw or modify it, and if there is no objection from anyone, the chair announces that the motion is withdrawn or modified. If anyone objects, the chair puts the request to a vote.

6. A member may interrupt a speaker to rise to a point of order or of appeal, to call for orders of the day, or to raise a question of privilege.

7. Chair's ruling stands unless appealed and reversed.

8. If propositions or resolutions relate to independent subjects, they must be divided on the request of a single member. The request to divide the question may be made when another member has the floor. If they relate to the same subject but each part can stand alone, they may be divided only on a regular motion and vote.

9. The regular order of business may be changed by a motion to suspend the rules.

10. The motion to recess is not privileged if made at a time when no other motion is pending. When not privileged, it can be discussed. When privileged, it cannot be discussed, but can be amended as to length of recess.

11. The motion to adjourn is not privileged if qualified or if adoption would dissolve the assembly. When not privileged, it can be discussed and amended.

12. The motion to fix the time to which to adjourn is not privileged if no other motion is pending or if the assembly has scheduled another meeting on the same or following day. When not privileged, it can be discussed.

13. A motion to reconsider may be made only by one who voted on the prevailing side. It must be made during the meeting at which the vote to be reconsidered was taken, or on the succeeding day of the same session. If reconsideration is moved while another motion is pending, discussion on it is delayed until discussion is completed on the pending motion; then it has precedence over all new motions of equal rank.

14. It is impossible to rescind any action that has been taken as a result of a motion, but the unexecuted part may be rescinded. Adoption of the motion to rescind requires only a majority vote when notice is given at a previous meeting; it requires a two-thirds vote when no notice is given and the motion to rescind is voted on immediately.

include lowered self-esteem, lowered academic achievement, and, in general, negative effects on a person's relationships with other people.[2] This personality trait affects all areas of a person's communicative efforts, from calling on the telephone, to asking a question in a class or meeting, to presenting a public speech.

Communication apprehension is distinguished from the experience of *stage fright,* which involves specific situations in which a person is orally presenting material in a public setting (for instance, a play, speech, or panel presentation). Stage fright is a normal experience; it may or may not be accompanied by high communication apprehension. Thus, a person who has no major problems interacting with others in most situations can feel nervous when called on to present ideas in public.

Systematic solutions to reducing communication apprehension have focused on the phenomenon as a trait, rather than as a state. Thus, reducing the nervousness felt in presenting a public speech has been only one goal of treatment programs. Nevertheless, the treatments suggested for trait communication apprehension have relevance for the more specific situation speakers face. In this unit, we will focus on three major treatment approaches, and suggest ways in which they might be adapted to the reduction of your own stage fright.[3] As such, the advice will supplement that offered in Chapters 1 and 3.

Systematic Desensitization

Systematic desensitization is a treatment program which assumes that you *do* have the ability to accomplish a specific task. Your fear is so great, however, that it impedes your successful exercise of the behavior. For example, assume that you are afraid of height, and, as an actor, must walk the catwalks of the theatre. Walking, as a behavior, is not the problem. The fear of height causes you to become nauseated when on the catwalk, and thus is potentially harmful. Persons trained in systematic desensitization would establish an ascending series of events that would provoke increasing amounts of your fear. They would ask you to imagine each aversive situation while in a relaxed state. Once you are able to accept a low-level fear-producing situation, you would be asked to imagine a slightly higher-level situation. This would continue until you were able to imagine yourself on the catwalk and remain relaxed.

Cognitive Restructuring

As in the case of systematic desensitization, a treatment approach via cognitive restructuring assumes that you have the necessary behaviors, but are unable to enact them due to your anxiety. This approach further assumes that your fear is a result of a misperception of the event, and that you lack sufficient reinforcement to overcome your misperception. In the program, a trained counselor would seek to correct your perception of the event. In particular, the consultant would seek to change your mostly negative "self-talk" regarding the situation. You probably are your own worst critic; your presentation is not as bad as you tell yourself that it is. In cognitive restructuring, you would be counseled to see the event in more realistic, and less personally negating, terms.

Skills Training

Unlike the other programs, this approach assumes that your anxiety is due primarily to a lack of skilled behavior. Thus, if you are taught specific skills, you will be able to react more competently and comfortably in a situation. A trained instructor would utilize a variety of teaching strategies (coaching, modeling, rehearsal, goal-setting, actual performance) to help you acquire specific behaviors. Skills training can be employed to instill more assertive behavior, to learn how to say "no," or to respond effectively in clearly defined interpersonal or public situations. Specialized programs have been created as part of college interpersonal and public communication courses (separate sections, workshops, or labs) to help students reduce their apprehension. Typically, these programs have focused on those experiencing a high level of trait apprehension.[4]

Reducing Stage Fright

Systematic desensitization is a program which requires expert assistance. Thus, the advice offered below will not include this approach as one you could undertake on your own or with the assistance of an untrained person. We might assume that both cognitive restructuring and skills training would be beneficial aids. That is, you can work on your perception of the event—is it as terrible as you think? Are you really as poor a speaker as you think? By talking with a public speaking instructor, or simply by asking friends who observe your performance, you may get a clearer picture of your strengths and weaknesses. Being willing to let go of your own perceptions and to accept the critique of others is essential to the restructuring of your perspective on the situation.

Second, we might assume that your skills can be refined and improved. By taking this route, your self-confidence may grow and you will find it easier to control your anxiety. There are several things you can consider, either on your own or with an instructor's assistance.

1. *Audio- or videotape*. If the necessary equipment is available, you can practice your presentation and play it back on an audio or video recorder. A careful critique of your performance with or without assistance (if your own attitude is generally negative, self-appraisal may simply reinforce a negative image) will suggest areas for improvement.
2. *Role playing*. You or an instructor can create role-playing situations which simulate the behaviors that you need to refine. If these are realistic, they will help you feel more comfortable when you face an actual public-speaking situation.
3. *Rehearsal*. Practice your presentation before the live event, and ask friends or an instructor to critique your performance.

4. *Goal setting*. This can be a formal procedure worked out with an instructor, on your own informal assessment of what you want to work on.[5] Define a goal and then a set of specific behaviors that you want to accomplish in meeting that goal. For example, your goal might be expressed: "I want to be more articulate in the next presentation." A specific behavior would be: "I want to reduce the use of words such as *like* and *you know* to no more than two in the entire performance."

REFERENCE NOTES

[1]James C. McCroskey, "Oral Communication Apprehension: A Summary of Recent Theory and Research," *Human Communication Research,* 4 (1977): 78.

[2]McCroskey, pp. 78–96; Susan R. Glaser, "Oral Communication Apprehension and Avoidance: The Current Status of Treatment Research," *Communication Education,* 30 (1981): 321–41.

[3]Glaser's essay is used as the basis for this review.

[4]For additional information on treatment programs, see Jan Hoffman and Jo Sprague, "A Survey of Reticence and Communication Apprehension Treatment Programs at U.S. Colleges and Universities," *Communication Education,* 31 (1982): 185–93; Karen A. Foss, "Communication Apprehension: Resources for the Instructor," *Communication Education,* 31 (1982): 195–203.

[5]Gerald M. Phillips, "Rhetoritherapy vs. the Medical Model: Dealing with Reticence," *Communication Education,* 26 (1977): 34–43.

Responses to Questions and Objections

In most meetings (and at other times as well), listeners are given a chance to ask questions of speakers. Panelists frequently direct questions to each other; professors ask students to clarify points made in classroom reports; clubs' treasurers often are asked to justify particular expenditures; political candidates normally must field objections to positions they have taken.

Sometimes, questions require only a short response—some factual material, a "yes" or "no," a reference to an authoritative source. These sorts of questions need not concern us. But at other times, questions from listeners can require a good deal more. Specifically: *(1)* Some questions call for *elaboration and explanation*. For example, after an oral report, you might be asked to elaborate on statistical information you presented, or called upon to explain how a financial situation arose. *(2)* Other questions call for *justification and defense*. In open hearings, school boards seeking to cut expenditures justify their selection of school buildings to be closed. At city council meetings, the city manager often has to defend ways council policies are being implemented. In these two situations, a "speech" is called for in response to questions and objections.

Techniques for Responding to Questions

Questions calling for elaboration and explanation are, in many ways, equivalent to requests for an informative speech. Think about them as you would any situation wherein you are offering listeners ideas and information in response to their needs and interests. This means:

Give a "whole" speech.   Your response should include an introduction, a body, and a conclusion. Even though you may be offering an impromptu speech (see Chapter 3), you nonetheless are expected to structure ideas and information clearly and rationally. A typical pattern for an elaborative remark might look like this:

1. Introduction—a rephrasing of the question to clarify it for the other audience members; an indication of why the question is a good one; a forecast of the steps you will take in answering it.
2. Body—first point, often a brief historical review; second point, the information or explanation called for.
3. Conclusions—a very brief summary (unless the answer was extraordinarily long); a direct reference to the person asking the question, to see if further elaboration or explanation is needed.

Directly address the question as it has been asked.   Nothing is more frustrating to a questioner than an answer which misses the point or which drifts off into territory irrelevant to the query. Suppose, after you have advocated a "pass-fail" grading system for all colleges, you are questioned about how graduate schools can evaluate potential candidates for advanced degrees. The questioner is calling for information and an explanation. If, in response, you launch a tirade against the unfairness of letter grades or the cowardice of professors who refuse to give failing grades, you probably will not satisfy the questioner. Better would be an explanation of all the other factors—letters of recommendation, standardized tests, number of advanced courses taken—in addition to grade point averages that graduate schools can employ when evaluating candidates. If you are unsure what the point of the question is, do not hesitate to ask before you attempt an answer.

Be succinct.   While you certainly do not want to give a terse "yes" or "no" in response to a question calling for detail, neither should you talk for eight minutes when two minutes will suffice. If you really think a long, complex answer is called for, you can say, "To understand why we should institute a summer orientation program at this school, you should know more about recruitment, student fears, problems with placement testing, and so on. I can go into these topics if you would like, but for now, in response to the particular question I was asked, I would say that. . . ." In this way, you are able to offer a short answer, yet are leaving the door open for additional questions from listeners wishing more information.

Be courteous.   During question periods, you may be amazed that one person asks a question you know you answered in your oral report, and another person asks for information so basic you realize your whole presentation probably went over his or her head. In such situations, it is easy to become flippant or overly patronizing. Avoid these temptations. Do not embarrass a questioner by pointing out you have already answered that query, and do not treat listeners like children. If you really think it would be a waste of the audience's time for you to review fundamental details, simply say that the group does not have time to discuss them, but that you are willing to talk with individuals after the meeting to go over that ground.

Techniques for Responding to Objections

A full, potentially satisfying response to an objection is composed of two verbal-intellectual activities. *Rebuttal* is an answer to an objection or counterargument, and *reestablishment* is a process of rebuilding the ideas originally attacked.

Suppose, for example, that at an office meeting you propose your division institute a "management-by-objectives" system of employee evaluation. With this approach the supervisor and employee together plan goals for a specified period of time; so, you argue, it tends to increase productivity, it makes employees feel they are in part determining their own future, and it makes company expectations more concrete. During a question period, another person might object to management-by-objectives, saying that such systems are mere busywork, that supervisors are not really interested in involving underlings in work decisions, and that job frustration rather than job satisfaction is the more likely result.

You then return to the lectern, *rebutting* those objections with the results of studies at other companies much like your own (reasoning from parallel case); those studies indicate that paperwork is not drastically increased, that supervisors like to have concrete commitments on paper from employees, and that employee satisfaction must increase because job turnover rates usually go down (reasoning from sign). Furthermore, you *reestablish* your original arguments by reporting on the results of interviews with selected employees in your own company, almost all of whom think the system would be a good one. This extended illustration employs most of the principal communicative techniques used by successful respondents, as we discussed them in Chapter 16.

Team Presentations: Panels and Symposiums

When a group is too large to engage in effective roundtable discussion, when its members are not well enough informed to make such discussion profitable, or when subgroups in the larger collectivity represent distinct viewpoints on important issues, a *panel* of individuals—from three to five, usually—may be selected to discuss the topic for the benefit of others, who then become an audience. Members of a panel are chosen either because they are particularly well informed on the subject or because they represent divergent views on the issue.

Another type of audience-oriented discussion is the *symposium*. In this format, several persons—again, usually from three to five—present short speeches, each focusing

TYPES OF GROUP PRESENTATIONS

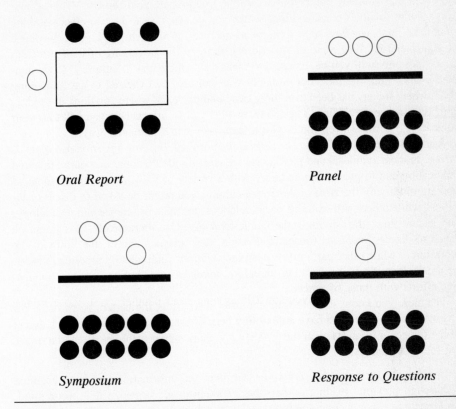

Oral Report

Panel

Symposium

Response to Questions

on a different facet of the subject or offering a different solution to the problem under consideration. Usually, the short presentations are followed by periods of discussion among the symposiasts and question-and-answer sessions with the onlooking audience. The symposium is especially valuable when recognized experts with well-defined points of view or areas of competence are available as speakers, and thus is the discussion procedure commonly employed at large conferences and conventions.

When you are asked to participate in a communication event with these types of formats, remember that the techniques you employ do not vary substantially from those used for other types of speeches. Bear in mind, however, that you are participating as a member of a group which is centering its remarks, information, and opinions upon a specific topic or problem. You, therefore, have an obligation to function as part of a team, to coordinate your communicative behaviors with the efforts of others in order to give your audience a full range of viewpoints and options. Thus, you must sacrifice part of your individual freedom and latitude for the greater good of all. With this important caution in mind, we can discuss techniques useful in preparing for and participating in group and conference presentations.

Preparation for Panels and Conferences

Because in panels and conferences you are one of a team of communicators, it is important that you take others into account as you prepare your remarks. This taking-into-account involves considerations which you do not have to face in other speaking situations. First, *you have to fit your comments into a general theme*. If, say, the theme of your panel is "The State of American Culture at the Beginning of Its Third Century," not only will you be expected to mention "American," "culture," "two hundred years," and the like, but probably you will also be expected to say something about where society has been over those two hundred years, where you think it is today, and how you see it evolving. The theme, in other words, affects how you will treat your subject, and perhaps even forces you to approach it in a particular way.

Also, *remember that you may be responsible for covering only a portion of a topic or theme*. In most symposia and panels, the speakers divide the topic into parts, to avoid duplication and to provide an audience with a variety of viewpoints. For example, if you are discussing the state of American culture, you might be asked to discuss education, while others will examine social relations, the state of science and technology, and leisure time, thus dividing the theme *topically*. Or, alternatively, you might be asked to discuss *problems* (depersonalization, the "plastic" world, the limits of the work force) while other participants examine *solutions* (individual, corporate, ethical, political). Part of your preparation, therefore, involves coordinating your communicative efforts with those of others.

The more you know about the subject under discussion, the better. To be ready for any eventuality, you must have a flexibility born of broad knowledge. For each aspect of the subject or implication of the problem you think may possibly be discussed, make the following analysis:

1. *Review the facts you already know*. Go over the information you have acquired through previous reading or personal experience and organize it in your mind. Prepare as if you were going to present a speech on every phase of the matter. You will then be better qualified to discuss any part of it.
2. *Bring your knowledge up to date*. Find out if recent changes have affected the situation. Fit the newly acquired information into what you already know.
3. *Determine a tentative point of view on each of the important issues*. Make up your mind what your attitude will be. Do you think that Hemingway was a greater writer than Faulkner? If so, exactly how and why? What three or four steps might be taken to attract new members into your club? On what medical or health-related grounds should cigarette-smoking be declared illegal? Stake out a tentative position on each question or issue that is likely to come before the group, and have clearly in mind the facts and reasons that support your view. Be ready to state and substantiate the opinion at whatever point in the discussion seems most appropriate, but also be willing to change your mind if information or points of view provided by others show you to be wrong.
4. *To the best of your ability, anticipate the effect of your ideas or proposals on the other members of the group or the organization of which the group is a part*. For instance, what you propose may possibly cause someone to lose money or to retract a promise that has been made. Forethought concerning such eventualities will

enable you to understand opposition to your view if it arises and to make a valid and intelligent adjustment. The more thoroughly you organize your facts and relate them to the subject and to the people involved, the more effective your contributions to the discussion will be.

Participating in Panels and Conferences

Your style and vocal tone will, of course, vary according to the nature and purpose of the discussion as a whole, the degree of formality that is being observed, and your frame of mind as you approach the task. In general, however, *speak in a direct, friendly, conversational style.* As the interaction proceeds, differences of opinion are likely to arise, tensions may increase, and some conflict may surface. You will need, therefore, to be sensitive to these changes and to make necessary adjustments in the way you voice your ideas and reactions.

Present your point of view clearly, succinctly, and fairly.   Participation in a panel or conference should always be guided by one underlying aim: to help the group think objectively and creatively in analyzing the subject or solving the problem at hand. To this end, you should organize your contributions not in the way best calculated to win other people to your point of view, but rather in the fashion that will best stimulate them to think for themselves. Therefore, instead of stating your conclusion first and then supplying the arguments in favor of it, let your contribution recount how and why you came to think as you do. Begin by stating the nature of the problem as you see it; outline the various hypotheses or solutions that occurred to you as you were thinking about it; tell why you rejected certain solutions; and only after all this, state your own opinion and explain the reasons that support it. In this way, you give other members of the group a chance to check the accuracy and completeness of your thinking on the matter and to point out any deficiencies or fallacies that may not have occurred to you. At the same time, you will also be making your contribution in the most objective and rational manner possible.

Maintain attitudes of sincerity, open-mindedness, and objectivity.   Above all, remember that a serious discussion is not a showplace for prima donnas or an arena for verbal combatants. When you have something to say, say it modestly and sincerely, and always maintain an open, objective attitude. Accept criticism with dignity and treat disagreement with an open mind. Your primary purpose is not to get your own view accepted, but to work out with the other members of the group the best possible choice or decision that all of you together can devise, and as a team to present a variety of viewpoints to the audience.

Working Bibliography: Additional Readings

The bibliography which follows is not meant to be comprehensive, but rather suggestive. Additional books and articles can be found in the reference notes which follow most units of this Resource Book.

Other Public Speaking Textbooks

Bryant, Donald C., Karl Wallace, and Michael C. McGee. *Oral Communication: A Short Course in Speaking*. 5th ed. Englewood Cliffs, NJ: Prentice-Hall, Inc., 1982.

Gronbeck, Bruce E. *The Articulate Person: A Guide to Everyday Public Speaking*. 2nd ed. Glenview, IL: Scott, Foresman and Company, 1983.

Hart, Roderick, Gustav Friedrich, and Barry Brummett. *Public Communication*. 2nd ed. New York: Harper & Row, 1984.

Jeffrey, Robert, and Owen Peterson. *Speech*. 2nd ed. New York: Harper and Row, 1984.

Logue, Cal M., et al. *Speaking: Back to Fundamentals*. 3rd ed. Boston: Allyn and Bacon, 1982.

Lucas, Stephen. *The Art of Public Speaking*. Westminster, MD: Random House, 1983.

Minnick, Wayne C. *Public Speaking*. 2nd ed. Palo Alto, CA: Houghton Mifflin, 1983.

Osborn, Michael. *Speaking in Public*. Palo Alto, CA: Houghton Mifflin, 1982.

Patton, Bobby R., Kim Giffin, and Wil A. Linkugel. *Responsible Public Speaking*. Glenview, IL: Scott, Foresman and Company, 1983.

Thrash, Artie, and John I. Sisco. *The Basic Skills of Public Speaking*. Minneapolis, MN: Burgess Publishing Co., 1984.

Verderber, Rudolph F. *The Challenge of Effective Speaking*. 6th ed. Belmont, CA: Wadsworth Publishing Co., 1985.

Walter, Otis M., and Robert L. Scott. *Thinking and Speaking*. 5th ed. New York: Macmillan, 1984.

White, Eugene E. *Basic Public Speaking*. New York: Macmillan, 1984.

Supplementary Reading for the Chapters

Addington, David W. "The Relationship of Selected Vocal Characteristics to Personality Perception." *Speech Monographs*, 35 (November 1968): 492–503.

Andrews, James R. *The Practice of Rhetorical Criticism*. New York: Macmillan Publishing Co., 1983.

Arnold, Carroll C., and John Waite Bowers, eds. *Handbook of Rhetorical and Communication Theory*. Boston: Allyn and Bacon, 1984.

Becker, Samuel L., and Leah V. Ekdom. "That Forgotten Basic Skill: Oral Communication." *Association for Communication Administration Bulletin*, #33 (August 1980).

Bem, Daryl. *Beliefs, Attitudes, and Human Affairs*. Belmont, CA: Brooks/Cole Publishing Co., 1980.

Bettinghaus, Erwin P. *Persuasive Communication*. 3rd ed. New York: Holt, Rinehart & Winston, 1980.

Bitzer, Lloyd. "The Rhetorical Situation." *Philosophy & Rhetoric*, 1 (January 1968): 1–14.

Bormann, Ernest G. *Communication Theory*. New York: Holt, Rinehart & Winston, 1980.

Burgoon, Judee K., and Thomas Saine. *The Unspoken Dialogue: An Introduction to Nonverbal Communication*. Dallas: Houghton Mifflin Co., 1978.

DeVito, Joseph A., Jill Giattino, and T. D. Schon. *Articulation and Voice: Effective Communication*. Indianapolis: The Bobbs-Merrill Co., Inc., 1975.

Einhorn, Lois J., Patricia Hayes Bradley, and John E. Baird, Jr. *Effective Employment Interviewing: Unlocking Human Potential*. Glenview, IL: Scott, Foresman and Company, 1982.

Harper, Nancy L., and John Waite Bowers. "Communication and Your Career." In Douglas Ehninger, Bruce E. Gronbeck, and Alan Monroe, *Principles of Speech Communication*. 9th brief ed. Glenview, IL: Scott, Foresman and Company, 1984.

Harte, Thomas. "The Effects of Evidence in Persuasive Communication." *Central States Speech Journal,* 27 (Spring 1976): 42–46.

Knapp, Mark L. *Essentials of Nonverbal Communication.* New York: Holt, Rinehart & Winston, 1980.

Littlejohn, Stephen W. "A Bibliography of Studies Related to Variables of Source Credibility." *Bibliographical Annual in Speech Communication: 1971.* Ed. Ned A. Shearer. New York: Speech Communication Association, 1972, pp. 1–40.

Malandro, Loretta A., and Larry Barker. *Nonverbal Communication.* Reading, MA: Addison-Wesley, 1983.

Ong, Walter J., S. J. *Orality and Literacy: The Technologizing of the Word.* New Accents Series. New York: Methuen, 1982.

Osborn, Michael. *Orientations to Rhetorical Style.* Procomm Series. Chicago: Science Research Associates, 1976.

Rieke, Richard D., and Malcolm O. Sillars. *Argumentation and Decision Making Processes.* 2nd ed. Glenview, IL: Scott, Foresman and Company, 1984.

Salomon, Gavriel. *Interaction of Media, Cognition, and Learning.* San Francisco: Jossey-Bass, Inc., 1979.

Satterthwaite, Les. *Graphics: Skills, Media and Materials.* 4th ed. Dubuque: Kendall/Hunt, 1980.

Severin, Werner J., and James W. Tankard, Jr. *Communication Theories: Origins Methods Uses.* Humanistic Studies in the Arts. New York: Hastings House, 1979.

Shimanoff, Susan B. *Communication Rules: Theory and Research.* Sage Library of Social Research, No. 97. Beverly Hills: Sage Pub. Inc., 1980.

Simons, Herbert W. *Persuasion: Understanding, Practice, and Analysis.* Reading, MA: Addison-Wesley, 1976.

Smith, Mary John. *Persuasion and Human Action: A Review and Critique of Social Influence Theories.* Belmont, CA: Wadsworth Pub. Co., 1982.

Steil, Lyman K., Larry L. Barker, and Kittie W. Watson. *Effective Listening.* Reading, MA: Addison-Wesley, 1983.

Stewart, Charles S., and William B. Cash, Jr. *Interviewing: Principles and Practices.* 4th ed. Dubuque: Wm. C. Brown, Publishers, 1985.

Toulmin, Stephen, Richard Rieke, and Allan Janik. *An Introduction to Reasoning.* 2nd ed. New York: Macmillan Pub. Co., 1984.

Vernon, Magdalen D. "Perception, Attention, and Consciousness." *Foundations of Communication Theory.* Ed. Kenneth K. Sereno and C. David Mortensen. New York: Harper & Row, 1970, pp. 137–151.

Wilcox, Roger P. "Characteristics and Organization of the Technical Report." *Communicating Through Behavior.* Ed. William E. Arnold and Robert O. Hirsch. St. Paul: West Publishing Co., 1977, pp. 201–206.

Wolfgang, Aaron, ed. *Nonverbal Behavior: Perspectives, Applications, Intercultural Insights.* New York: C. J. Hogrefe, Inc., 1984.

Wolvin, Andrew D., and Carolyn G. Coakley. *Listening.* Dubuque: Wm. C. Brown, 1982.

Zimbardo, Philip G., Ebbe B. Ebbesen, and Christina Maslach. *Influencing Attitudes and Changing Behavior.* 2nd ed. Reading, MA: Addison-Wesley, 1977.

Photo credits:

INDEX

A

Abstract representations, as visual aids, 250–56

Accuracy, need for, 223

Action step, of motivated sequence, 164

Activity, as factor of attention, 44

Actuative speeches
defined, 338
motivated sequence for, 350–53
see also Persuasive speeches

Advisory reports, 291

Affect displays, 277

Age, of audience, 82

Agenda, for group discussions, 402, 410

Aims, of speaker, 74–75

Ambiguity, fallacy of, 321

Amendments, in parliamentary procedure, 417

Analogical definition, 233

Analogy, as supporting material, 127–28

Analysis of speeches, 378–89. *See also* Criticism; Evaluation

Anderson, Floyd D., 379

Anecdotes, as speech introductions, 193–94

Animate objects, as visual aids, 248

Anticipating, as listener skill, 31

Appeal, as speech conclusion, 197–98

Appeal to ignorance, 320

Appeal to popular opinion, 321

Appreciative listening, 24

Apprehension, 48

Appropriateness, 12
of language, 225
and selecting a subject, 64

Archetypal metaphors, 383

Argumentation, 309–31
anticipating counterarguments, 325
constructing your case, 322–25
fallacies in, 320–22
and kinds of evidence, 314–16
organizing and evaluating, 413–16
and reasoning, 316–18

rebuilding your case, 325–28
as social process, 309, 310–12
structuring, 322–28
tests for reasoning, 318–19
types of claims in, 312–14

Aristotle, 228, 388

Arousal, and gestures, 278

Articulation, control of, 397–98

Atmosphere, and speaking style, 227–28. *See also* Setting

Attention, 43–47
capturing and holding, 32
factors of, 43–47
holding, 47
and speech beginnings, 188

Attention step, of motivated sequence, 158

Attitudes, of audience, 10, 27, 75, 86–88
and audience segmentation, 96–97
changing, 336–37
predispositions, 341
toward purpose, 87
toward speaker, 86
toward subject, 86–87

Attitudes, of speaker, 7–8, 29, 34

Audience, 5
attitudes of, 86–88
factors of, and attention, 47
interest and setting purpose, 94
motives of, 105–106, 295–96
and narrowing a topic, 64
and organization of speeches, 173–74
satisfying demands of, 188
and selecting introductions and conclusions, 188, 201–202
and selecting a subject, 63–64
speakers' attitude toward, 7
and visual aids, 260–61
and wording titles, 73

Audience analysis, 10, 41, 50, 81–89
demographic, 81, 82–83
goal of, 81
and motivational appeals, 114–16
psychological, 84–89
using in preparation, 92–102

Audience segmentation, 95–98
Audience targeting, 93–95
Auditory imagery, 236
Aural channel, 10
Authoritarian personalities, 342
Authorities
  citing for credibility, 8
  listener analysis of, 28–29
  quoting, and persuasion, 343
Axiom, reasoning from, 318
  tests for, 319

B

Bar graphs, 252
Begging the question, 321
Beginnings (of speeches), 186–95
  clarifying scope of speech, 189
  creating good will, 188–89
  gaining attention, 188
  questions about, 186–88
  satisfying demands, 188
  stating qualifications, 188
  see also Introductions
Beliefs, of audience, 84–85
  and audience segmentation, 96–97
  changing, 336
Bilaterality, social convention of, 310
Biographies, 139
Bitzer, Lloyd, 384
Body language. See Nonverbal communication
Boomerang effect, 341
Breathing, and voice practice, 395–96

C

Causal organization, 178, 180
Causal relations, reasoning from, 317
  tests for, 319
Cause-effect relationships, in group discussions, 404

Central ideas, 71–73
Chalkboard drawings, as visual aids, 250–51
Challenge, as speech conclusion, 197–98
Channels, of communication, 10–11
Charts, as visual aids, 254, 259
Chronological organization, 175–76
Claims, defined, 71
Claims of fact, 313
Claims of policy, 313–14
Claims of value, 313
Clarity, need for, in informative speeches, 290, 293–94
Cognitive complexity, and persuasive speeches, 340
Cognitive restructuring, 422–23
Coherence, 224–25
  need for, in informative speeches, 294
Communication, defined, 4
Communication apprehension, 419, 422–24
Communication rules, 13, 89
Communicative situation, 11–12
Comparison. See Analogy
Competency, 12, 14
  and persuasive speeches, 343
Comprehension
  listening for, 25
  and visual aids, 247
Conclusions (of speeches), 195–202
  additional inducement, 200
  challenge or appeal, 197–98
  considerations in, 195–97
  to group discussions, 404–405
  humor in, 413
  illustration, 199–200
  to oral reports, 302
  and outlines, 217–18
  personal intention or endorsement, 200
  quotations, 199
  selecting, 200–202
  to speeches of demonstration or instruction, 301
  to speeches of denotation, 298–99

to speeches of explanation, 303
summary, 199
Concrete representations, as visual aids, 249–50
Condensation, and gestures, 278
Condensation symbols, 382
Conferences, 426–29. *See also* Group discussions
Confidence, 48–52
  communicating, 50–52
  developing, 48–50
  see also Nonverbal communication; Voice
Conflict
  as factor of attention, 46
  handling, in group discussions, 404
Content, 8–9
Context, and communication models, 391
Contextual definition, 233
Contrast, for humor, 412
Conventional gestures, 278
Credibility, 8, 28
  and eye contact, 277
  and humor, 412
  and persuasive speeches, 343–44
Critical listening, 25
Critical perspective, 382
Criticism (of speeches), 378–89
  defined, 378
  essentials of, 384–86
  organization of, 386–87
  vs. speech evaluation, 379–84
Criticism, in group discussions, 409
Cueing, and audience attention, 47
Cultural background, of audience, 83
Culture, and communication models, 391–92
Customs, 91

D

Data bases, 139–40
Dedication speeches, 360
Definitions, 231–33

Delivery, 43–52
  and attention, 43–47
  and confidence, 48–52
Demonstrations, 289–90
  structuring, 299–301
Denotation, speeches of, 289
  structuring, 299–301
Descriptive gestures, 278
Dewey, John, 152, 153
Dialects, 269–70
Dictionaries, definitions from, 231–32
Disagreements
  arbitrating, 410–11
  handling, in group discussions, 407, 408
  see also Conflict
Discriminative listening, 24
Discussions. *See* Group discussions
Diversity (of audience), and attention, 47
Documents, 139
Dogmatic personalities, 342
"Drive to complete," 152

E

Education, of audience, 82
Either-or logic, 321
Emphasis, and voice, 271–72
Employment interviews, 399–401
Encyclopedias, 138–39
Endings (of speeches). *See* Conclusions
Endorsement, as speech conclusion, 200
Entertaining speeches, 68–69, 368–74
  and motivated sequence, 167–68
  satisfaction step in, 160–61
Enunciation, 269
Ethics, and public speaking, 393–95
Etymological definition, 232
Eulogies, 362
Evaluation, for argumentation, 413–16
Evidence, in argumentation, 314–16
Examples, defining by, 232–33
Examples, reasoning from, 316–17
  tests for, 318
Exemplar definition, 232–33

Expectations, 27, 28, 89
  about subject, 87
  setting realistic, 85
Explanations, 292–93
  as form of supporting material, 124–27
  structuring, 302–303
Extemporaneous speeches, 266–67
Eye contact, 277, 280
  and confidence, 51

F

Facial expressions, 277
Facts
  claims of, 313
  vs. opinions, 84
Facts on File, 136
Factual illustrations, 129–30
Factual reports, 291
Fairness doctrine, 310
Fallacies, 320–22
False division, fallacy of, 320
Familiarity, as factor of attention, 45
Farewell speeches, 360
Feedback, 5, 10
  and communication models, 390–91
  interpreting, 33
  see also Audience
Figurative analogies, 127
Films, as visual aids, 250, 260
"Fixed beliefs," 84–85
Flow charts, as visual aids, 254
Forecasting
  and holding attention, 47
  in speech introductions, 195
Friesen, Wallace V., 277
Full-content outlines, 208
Full-sentence outlines, 208, 213–15

G

Gender, of audience, 82
Generalization, reasoning from, 318
  tests for, 319

Generalizations, in group discussions, 404
Genetic definition, 232
Genetic fallacy, 320
Gestures, 277–79. *See also* Nonverbal communication
Gibson, Eleanor, 47
Good will speeches, 365–68
Graphs, 251–54
Greeting, as speech introduction, 190–91
Group discussions, 401–411
  leading, 401–405
  participation in, 405–411
Group membership, of audience, 83
Gustatory imagery, 236–37

H

Hall, Edward T., 275
Hasty generalizations, 320
Humor, 411–13
  as factor of attention, 46
  in speaking style, 227–28
Hypothetical illustration, 128–29

I

Illustrations
  as form of supporting material, 128–30
  for humor, 412
  as speech conclusion, 199–200
  as speech introduction, 194
Imagery, 234–39
Impromptu speeches, 265
Inanimate objects, as visual aids, 248–49
Incremental change, and persuasive speeches, 341
Indicators, 278
Inducement, as speech conclusion, 200
Inflection, 398–99
Informative speeches, 67–68, 288–306
  applying motivated sequence to, 165–67
  demonstrations and instructions, 289–90, 299–301

essential features of, 293–96
explanations, 292–93, 302–303
oral reports, 290–92, 301–302
satisfaction step in, 160
speeches of denotation, 289, 296–99
structure of, 296–303
Instructions, as informative speeches, 289–90
structuring, 299–301
Integrity, 14
Intensity, of language, 239–40
Interactive process, listening as, 20
Interviews, 140–45
purpose of, 140
skills for successful, 144
structuring, 141–42
types of questions for, 142–44
see also Employment interviews
Introduction, speeches of, 357–59
Introductions (to speeches), 189–95
anecdotes as, 193–94
combining methods in, 195
humor in, 411–12
illustrations as, 194
to oral reports, 301
and outlines, 217–18
personal reference or greeting as, 190–91
quotations as, 192–93
reference to subject or problem in, 189–90
reference to occasion in, 190
rhetorical question as, 191–92
selecting, 200–202
to speeches of demonstration or instruction, 299
to speeches of denotation, 296
to speeches of explanation, 302–303
startling statements as, 192
Is-faults, fallacy of, 321

J
Journals, 138

K
Key facts, in group discussions, 404
Key-word outlines, 208
Kinesthetic imagery, 237–38
King, Andrew A., 381
Knowledge
importance of, 14–15, 27
of listener, 9–10
and selecting subjects, 63
of speaker, 6–7

L
Language
and accuracy, 223
and appropriateness, 225
and coherence, 224–25
intensity, 239–40
metaphor, 240–42
personal- *vs.* material-centered, 228–29
propositional *vs.* narrative, 230–31
selecting appropriate styles of, 225–31
serious *vs.* humorous, 227–28
and simplicity, 223–24
strategies, 231–39
written *vs.* oral, 226–27
Lattitude of change, and persuasive speeches, 341–42
Leathers, Dale G., 274
Letters, 144–45
Line graphs, 252
Listeners, 9–10
analysis of message by, 29–30
analysis of self by, 26–27
analysis of speaker by, 28–29
characteristics of, 22–24
and organization of a speech, 151–53
responsibilities of, 26–30
and selecting subjects and purposes, 75
sensitivity to needs of, 16
see also Audience
Listening
appreciative, 24
behavior, 20–26

for comprehension, 25
critical, 25
discriminative, 24
in group discussions, 407–408
and hearing, 20–22
as interactive process, 20
and listener characteristics, 22–24
passive *vs.* active, 22
purpose of, 24–26
as physiological process, 20–21
as psychological process, 21
skills, 10
in speech classrooms, 34–36
therapeutic, 24–25
Lists, as part of organization, 179–80
Literal analogies, 127–28
Logic, need for in outlining, 207
Logical proof, as organizational pattern, 180–81
Loudness, of voice, 268–69. *See also* Pitch, Resonance

M

Magazines, 138
Magnitudes, 131–32
Manuscript speeches, 265
Maslow, Abraham, 106, 109, 118
Meaning-centered model, 390
Measell, James S., 381–82
Mehrabian, Albert, 277
Memorial service speeches, 362
Memorized speeches, 265
Memory, and visual aids, 247
Message, 8–9
listener analysis of, 29–30
Message-centered models, 389
Metaphors, 240–42
archetypal, 382
Models, as visual aids, 255–56, 259
Models of communication, 388–93
Monroe, Alan, 153
Monroe's Motivated Sequence. *See* Motivated sequence

Mood, creating, in speech endings, 197
Motions, in parliamentary procedures, 416–17, 420–21
Motivated sequence, 151, 153–71
action step, 164
and actuative speeches, 350–53
applying, 164–71
attention step, 158
examples of, 155–58
five steps of, 153–55
and good will speeches, 367–68
need step, 159–60
normal order in, 161, 162
parallel order in, 161, 162
and psychological change speeches, 348–50
and reinforcement speeches, 344–48
satisfaction step, 160–63
structure and development of, 158–64
and traditional patterns of organization, 173–81
visualization step, 163–64
Motivation, 105–106
in persuasive speeches, 334
in informative speeches, 295–96
Motivational appeals, 106–113
defined, 107
strategic choice of, 116–19
types and examples of, 108–113
using with audience analysis, 114–16
Motive needs, 105–106
classification of, 106
Movement, when speaking, 276–77, 280

N

Name-calling, fallacy of, 322
Narrative form, 230–31
Narrative sequence, 175–76
Needs
Maslow's hierarchy of, 106
for structure, 151–52
see also Motive needs
Need step, of motivated sequence, 159–60

Negative definition, 232
Negative judgments, 270
Nervousness, 48–50
Newspapers, 136, 138
New York Times, 136, 137
Nomination, speeches of, 364–65
Nonqualification, fallacy of, 321
Nonverbal communication, 274–83
  choices about, 279–83
  and confidence, 51
  facial expression, 277
  gestures, 277–79, 280
  movement and stance, 276–77
  proxemics, 275–76, 280
Normal order, of satisfaction step in motivated sequence, 161–62
Novelty, as factor of attention, 45–46

O

Objections, techniques for responding to, 426
Occasion
  analysis of, 89–92, 98–102
  reference to, in introductions, 190
  satisfying demands of, in speech beginnings, 188
  and selecting subject and purpose, 75
  and visual aids, 260–61
Olfactory imagery, 237
Operational definition, 233
Opinions, *vs.* facts, 84
Oral language, *vs.* written language, 226–27
Oral reports, 290–92
  structuring, 301–302
Oral skills, 16–17
Organic imagery, 238–39
Organization, 9, 173–83
  for argumentation, 413–16
  arranging subpoints, 179–81
  causal patterns, 178
  chronological patterns, 175–76
  of criticism, 386–87

importance of, for credibility, 8
and the listener, 151–53
listener analysis of, 28–29
and motivated sequence, 173
narrative sequence, 176
selecting a pattern for, 181–83
spatial patterns, 177
for speeches of good will, 367–68
for speeches of introduction, 358–59
for speeches of tribute, 363–64
temporal sequence, 175–76
topical patterns, 178–79
see also Motivated sequence; Outlines; Preparation; Structure
Outlines, 9, 205–218
  and conclusions, 217–18
  and introductions, 217–18
  normal order *vs.* parallel order, 161–62
  phrase, 209–210
  requirements of, 205–207
  rough draft of, 212–13
  sentence, 208
  speaking, 215–16
  for speech preparation, 42
  steps in preparing, 208–209, 210, 210–13
  and technical plot, 213
  types of, 208, 209–210

P

Panels, 426–29
Paralinguistic medium, 10
Parallel case, reasoning from, 317
  tests for, 318–19
Parallel development, in motivated sequence, 161–62
Parallel order, in outlines, 161–62
Parliamentary procedure, 89–90, 416–19
  for group discussions, 403
Participation, in panels and conferences, 429
Parts of a whole, as organizational pattern, 179

Pauses, need for, 272
Personal Speech Journals, 18
Persuasion
as purpose, 69
and visual aids, 247
Persuasive definition, 322
Persuasive speeches, 333–53
and actuation, 338
applying motivated sequence in, 169–71
and credibility, 343–44
essential features of, 339–44
and incremental change, 341–42
and psychological change, 334–38
and psychological states, 339–41
and reinforcement, 334
and saliency, 343
satisfaction step in, 161
structuring, 344–53
Petitio principii, 321
Phonation, control of, 396
Photographs, as visual aids, 249
Phrase outlines, 209–210
Physical conditions, 91
Physical setting, 11
Physiology, of listening, 20–21
Pictorialization, and gestures, 278
Pictorial graphs, 254
Pie graphs, 253
Pitch, 270–71
Polarization, 381
Policy, claims of, 313–14
Post hoc, ergo propter hoc, 321
Posture, 276–77
Preparation
for group discussions, 402, 406–407
importance of, 31–32
for leading group discussions, 401–403
for panels and conferences, 428–29
see also Outlines; Speech preparation
Presentation, method of, 264–67
Pronunciation, 269–70
Propositional form, 230–31
Proxemics, 275–76, 280

Proximity, as factor of attention, 45
Psychological change speeches, motivated sequence for, 348–50
Psychological states, and persuasive speeches, 339–41
Psychology of listening, 21
Public speaking, 4–6
elements of, 6–12
and ethics, 393–95
as part of personal survival, 5–6
as a public service, 4–5
Purpose
and analyzing the speech occasion, 90–91
audience attitude toward, 87
and central ideas, 71–73
determining, 40, 66–74
to entertain, 68–69
general, 66–69
to inform, 67–68
and interviewing, 140
of listener, 9, 27
of listening, 24–26
and outlining, 210–211
to persuade, 69
setting realistic, 93–95
and social context, 12
of speaker, 7
specific, 69–70, 93–94
and speeches of introduction, 358
and speeches to entertain, 369
for tribute speeches, 362–63
and wording the title, 73–74

Q

Qualifications, and speech beginnings, 188
Questionnaires, 144–45
Questions
for interviews, 142–44
techniques for responding to, 425–26

Quotations, books of, 139
 as speech conclusions, 199
 as speech introductions, 192–93

R

Rader, Nancy, 47
Rationality, as social convention, 310–11
Raum, Richard D., 281–82
Rate (of speaking), control of, 269, 270, 398–99
Reality, as factor of attention, 45
Rebuttals, 326–27
Reference groups, and persuasive speeches, 340–41
Reinforcement speeches, 112, 334
 motivated sequence for, 344–48
Reiteration, 234
Relating, as listening skill, 31
Rephrasing, 234
Reportive definition, 231
Reports, 139
Resonance, control of, 397
Resource materials
 biographies, 139
 collections of quotations, 139
 data bases, 139–40
 documents and reports, 139
 integrating, 146–48
 interviews, 140–45
 journals, 138
 letters and questionnaires, 144–45
 magazines, 138
 newspapers, 136, 138
 nonprint sources, 140
 special interest books, 138
 using, 145–46
Restatement, 233–34
 as form of supporting material, 135–36
Reviewing, as listening skill, 31

Rhetorical question, as speech introduction, 191–92
Rhetorical sensitivity, 16
Rhetorical situation, 384
Robert's Rules of Order, 90, 312, 420
Rules of argumentation, 312

S

Saliency, and persuasive speeches, 343
Satisfaction step, of motivated sequence, 160–63
Schramm, Wilbur, 390
Segments, 132
Self-analysis, as listener responsibility, 26–27
Self-concept, of speaker, 7
Self-confidence, 17
Self-control, 17
Self-experience, importance of, for credibility, 8
Self-focus, in group discussions, 406–408
Self-risk, social convention of, 310
Sentence outlines. *See* Full-sentence outlines
Sequential fallacy, 321
Serial presentation, 290
Setting, 11
 and selecting introductions and conclusions, 202
Similarity, and audience attention, 47
Simplicity, 223–24
 of visual aids, 259
Sign, reasoning from, 317
 tests for, 319
Sincerity
 and credibility, 8
 and persuasive speeches, 343
Slides, as visual aids, 249–50, 260
Social context, 12

Social conventions, and argumentation, 309, 310

Spatial organization, 177

Speaker, 6–8
audience attitude toward, 86
attitudes of, 7–8
capturing and holding attention, 32
credibility of, 8
knowledge of, 6–7
listener analysis of, 28–29
and preparation, 31–32
and presentation, 32–34
purpose of, 6
responsibilities of, 31–34
self-concept of, 7

Speaker-centered model, 388

Speaking situation, listener analysis of, 27

Speaking styles
and language, 222–25
person- vs. material-centered, 228–29
propositional vs. narrative, 230–31
selecting appropriate, 225–31
serious vs. humorous, 227–28
written vs. oral language, 226–27
see also Language

Specific instance, as form of supporting material, 130

Speeches of introduction, 357–59

Speeches of nomination, 364–65

Speeches of tribute, 359–64

Speeches to actuate
and motivated sequence, 168–69
see also Persuasive speeches

Speeches to create good will, 365–68

Speeches to entertain, 368–74. See also Entertaining speeches

Speeches to inform. See Informative speeches

Speeches to persuade. See Persuasive speeches

Speech evaluation, vs. speech criticism, 379

Speech Evaluation Form, 34, 35–36

Speechmaking process, model of, 12–14

Speech occasion, and selecting subjects and purposes, 75

Speech preparation, 38–43
analyzing the audience, 41
analyzing the occasion, 41
arranging materials, 42
determining the central idea, 40–41
determining the purpose, 40
gathering materials, 41–42
phases of, 38–39
practicing aloud, 43
selecting and narrowing a subject, 39–40
see also Audience analysis; Motivational appeals; Preparation; Supporting materials

Stage fright, 422, 424

State apprehension, 48

Statistics, as form of supporting material, 130–33

Stipulative definition, 232

"Straw man" approach, 46

Stress, in voice, 271–72

Stroking, in group discussions, 409

Structure
of argumentation, 322–28
of explanations, 302–303
human need for, 151–52
of informative speeches, 296–303
of instructions, 299–301
of interviews, 141–42
of the message, importance of, 9
of motivated sequence, 158–64
of persuasive speeches, 344–53
of speeches of denotation, 299–301
see also Outlining

Subjects (of speeches)
audience attitude toward, 86–87
and aims of speaker, 74–75
and determining a purpose, 66–74
narrowing, 39–40, 64–66
and outlines, 210–11
selecting, 39–40, 62–64, 74–76

Summary, as speech conclusion, 199
Supporting materials, 123–46
    analogy or comparison, 127–28
    explanation, 124–27
    illustration, 128–30
    restatement, 135–36
    specific instance, 130
    sources for, 136–46
    statistics, 130–33
    testimony, 133–35
    see also Resource materials
Suspense, as factor of attention, 46
Symbols, in outlines, 207
Symposiums, 426–29
Systematic desensitization, 422

T

Tables, as visual aids, 254
Tactual imagery, 237
Technical plot, and outlines, 213
Temporal sequence, 175–76
Testimony, as form of supporting material, 133–35
Therapeutic listening, 24
Time limits, and narrowing a topic, 64, 75–76
Titles, wording, 73–74
Topical organization, 178–79
Topics. See Subjects (of speeches)
Trait apprehension, 48
Transactional model, 12–14
Transitions, and holding attention, 47
Trends, 132–33
Tribute, speeches of, 359–64

V

Value, claims of, 313
Values (personal), 88–89
    and audience segmentation, 97–98
    changing, 337
Variable beliefs, 84–85
Variety, of pitch and rate of voice, 270

Verbal channel, 10
Vertical File Index, 139
Videotapes, as visual aids, 250, 260
Visual aids, 10, 246–61, 280
    abstract representations as, 250–56, 258
    actual objects as, 247–49
    functions of, 247
    with oral reports, 292
    for reality, 45
    selecting and using, 256–61
    symbolic representations as, 249–56
    types of, 247–56
Visual bonding, 277
Visual channel, 10
Visual imagery, 235–36
Visualization step, in motivated sequence, 163–64
Vital matters, to gain attention, 46–47
Voice, 267–74
    and articulation, 397–98
    and breath control, 395–96
    emotional quality of, 272–73
    enunciation, 269
    improvement, 395–99
    intelligibility, 267–68
    loudness of, 268–69
    and phonation, 396
    practicing control of, 273–74
    pronunciation, 269–70
    and rate, pause, and inflection, 398–99
    rate of speech, 269, 270
    and resonance, 397
    and stress, 271–72
    variety, 270

W

Written language, vs. oral language, 226–27

Y

Year books, 138–39

Some suggestions for Using the

Checklist and Index for Evaluation and Improvement of Student Speeches

which appears on the Endsheet following this page

This chart identifies many of the factors contributing to effective public speech communication. It may be used by both instructors and students in evaluating speech plans and manuscripts and also when reacting to speeches as they are being delivered. By using a plus (+) or minus (−) sign together with symbols keyed to specific items in the Checklist, the instructor may readily indicate point-by-point reactions to a speech or a speech outline. For example, a *plus* sign before SUBJ./9 indicates that the speaker has narrowed the speech subject satisfactorily; a *minus* sign placed before the code ADAPT./27 suggests that further attention should be given to using the factors of attention, etc. Students will find the Checklist especially helpful when preparing oral and written assignments or reviewing for examinations. The parenthetical reference to specific pages in the textbook makes it possible to find relevant textual explanations quickly and easily.